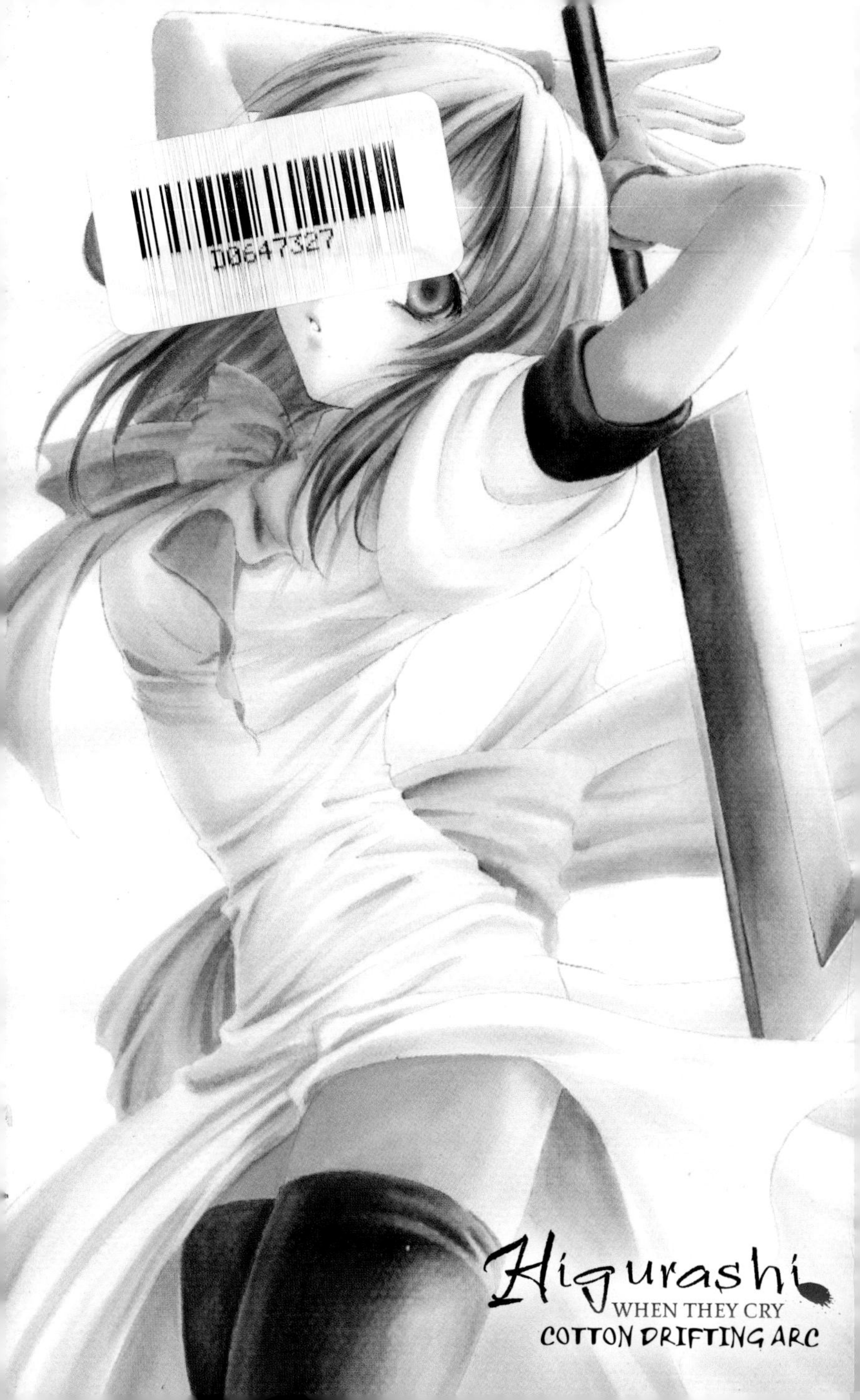
Higurashi
WHEN THEY CRY
COTTON DRIFTING ARC

Higurashi WHEN THEY CRY

COTTON DRIFTING ARC

2

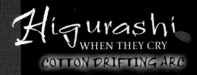

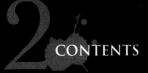

CONTENTS

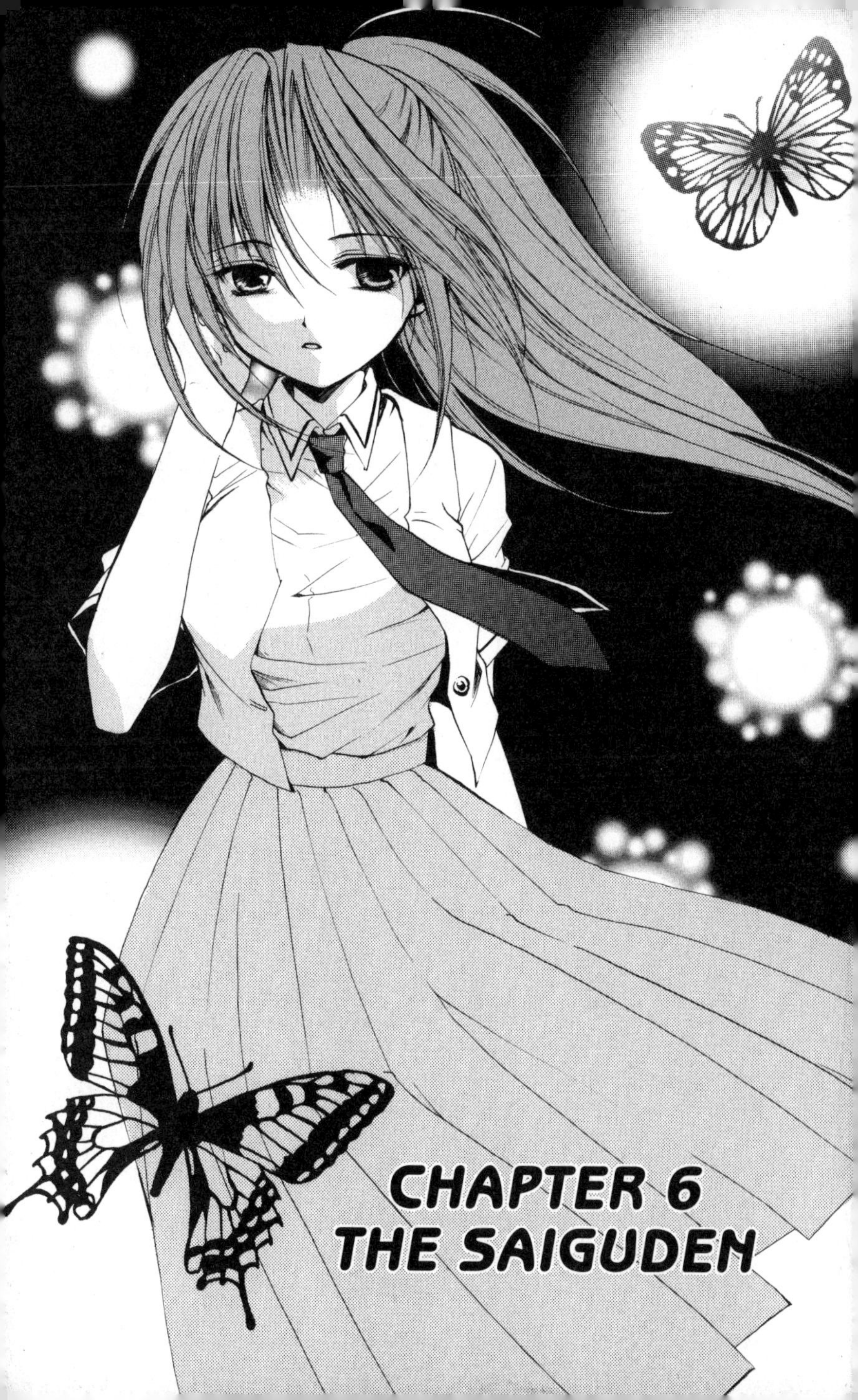
CHAPTER 6
THE SAIGUDEN

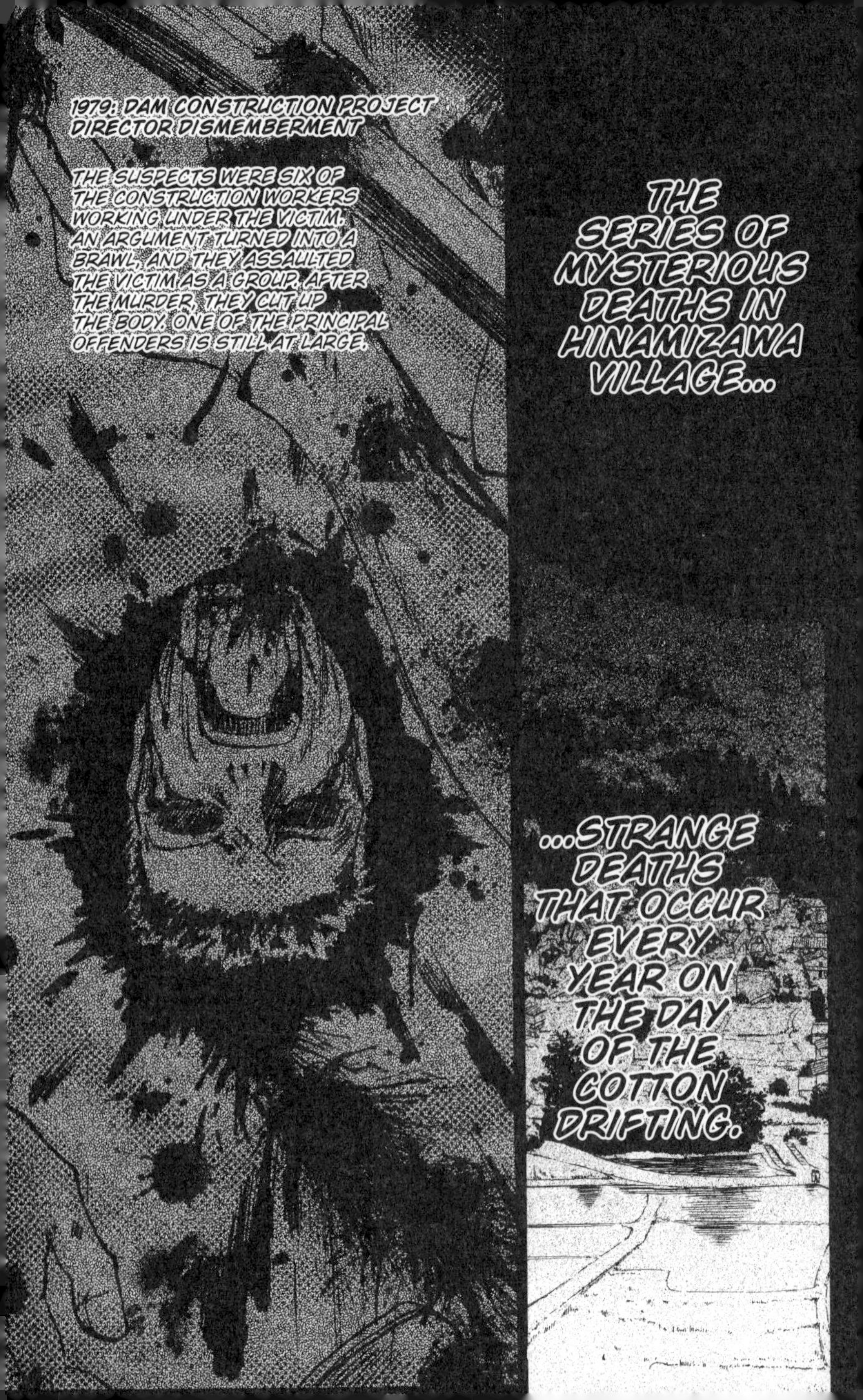
THE SERIES OF MYSTERIOUS DEATHS IN HINAMIZAWA VILLAGE...
...STRANGE DEATHS THAT OCCUR EVERY YEAR ON THE DAY OF THE COTTON DRIFTING.
1979: DAM CONSTRUCTION PROJECT DIRECTOR DISMEMBERMENT
THE SUSPECTS WERE SIX OF THE CONSTRUCTION WORKERS WORKING UNDER THE VICTIM. AN ARGUMENT TURNED INTO A BRAWL, AND THEY ASSAULTED THE VICTIM AS A GROUP. AFTER THE MURDER, THEY CUT UP THE BODY. ONE OF THE PRINCIPAL OFFENDERS IS STILL AT LARGE.

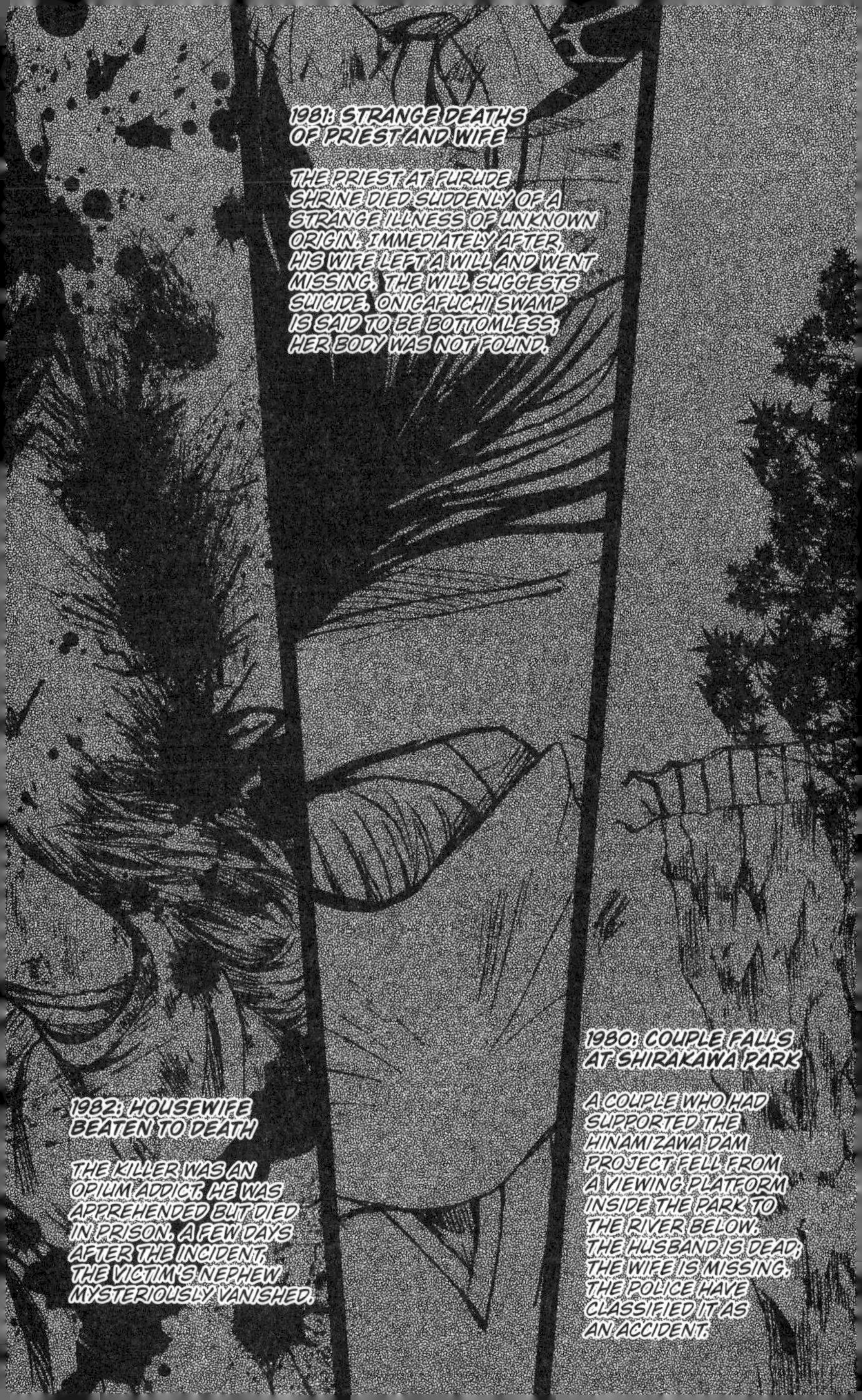
1980: COUPLE FALLS AT SHIRAKAWA PARK
A COUPLE WHO HAD SUPPORTED THE HINAMIZAWA DAM PROJECT FELL FROM A VIEWING PLATFORM INSIDE THE PARK TO THE RIVER BELOW. THE HUSBAND IS DEAD; THE WIFE IS MISSING. THE POLICE HAVE CLASSIFIED IT AS AN ACCIDENT.
1981: STRANGE DEATHS OF PRIEST AND WIFE
THE PRIEST AT FURUDE SHRINE DIED SUDDENLY OF A STRANGE ILLNESS OF UNKNOWN ORIGIN. IMMEDIATELY AFTER, HIS WIFE LEFT A WILL AND WENT MISSING. THE WILL SUGGESTS SUICIDE. ONIGAFUCHI SWAMP IS SAID TO BE BOTTOMLESS; HER BODY WAS NOT FOUND.
1982: HOUSEWIFE BEATEN TO DEATH
THE KILLER WAS AN OPIUM ADDICT. HE WAS APPREHENDED BUT DIED IN PRISON. A FEW DAYS AFTER THE INCIDENT, THE VICTIM'S NEPHEW MYSTERIOUSLY VANISHED.

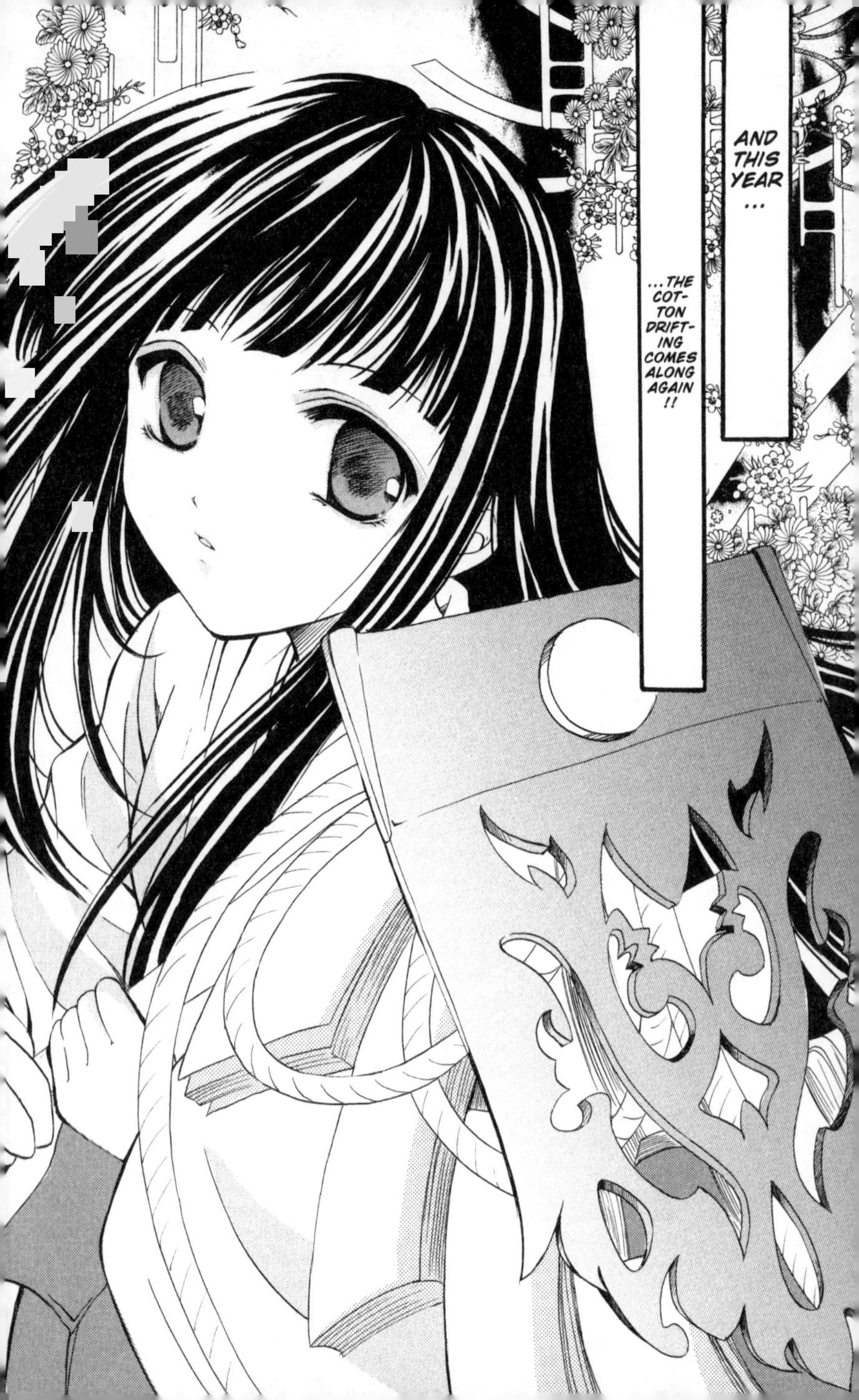
AND THIS YEAR ...
...THE COT-TON DRIFT-ING COMES ALONG AGAIN !!

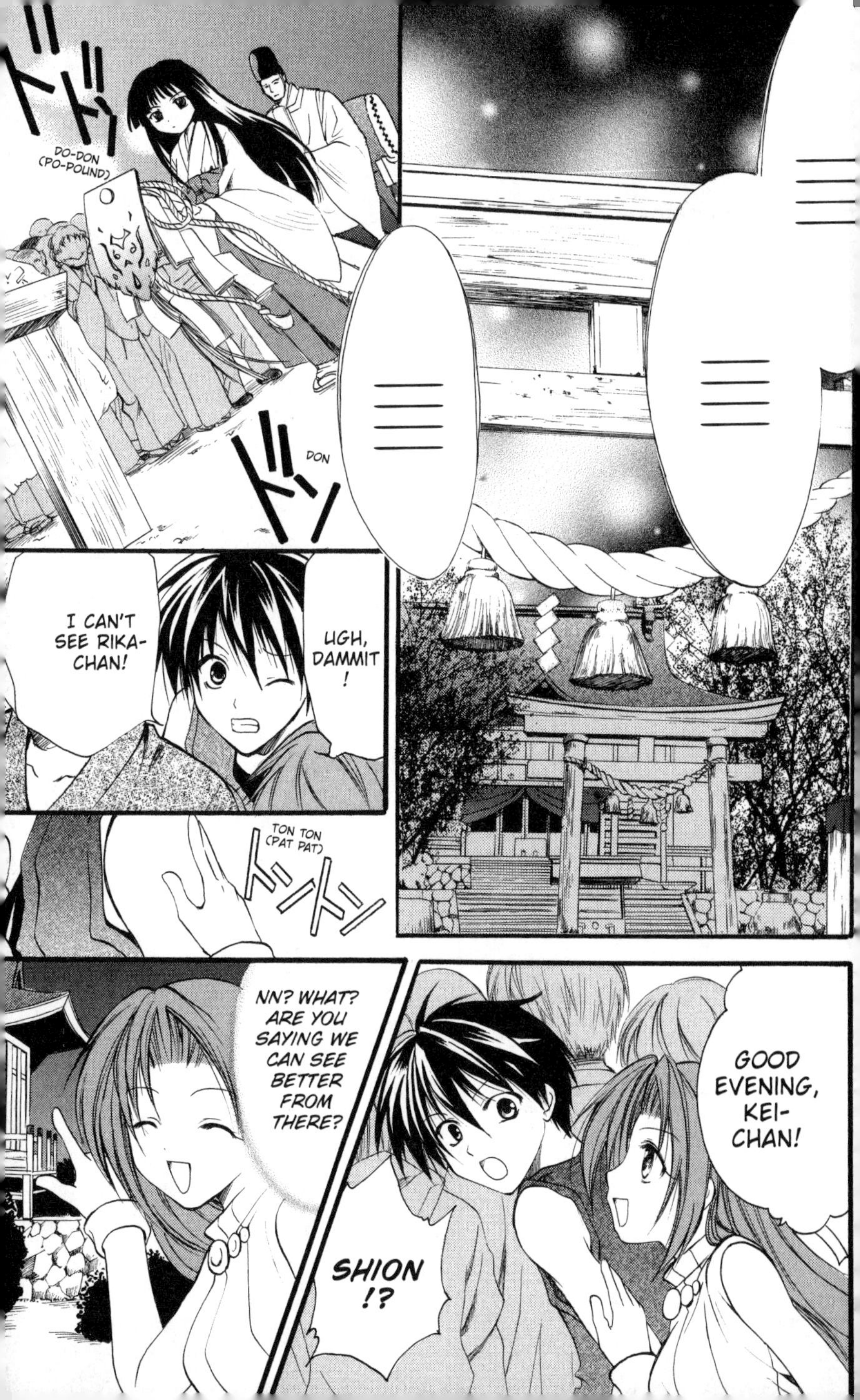
DO-DON (PO-POUND)
DON
UGH, DAMMIT!
I CAN'T SEE RIKA-CHAN!
TON TON (PAT PAT)
GOOD EVENING, KEI-CHAN!
SHION!?
NN? WHAT? ARE YOU SAYING WE CAN SEE BETTER FROM THERE?

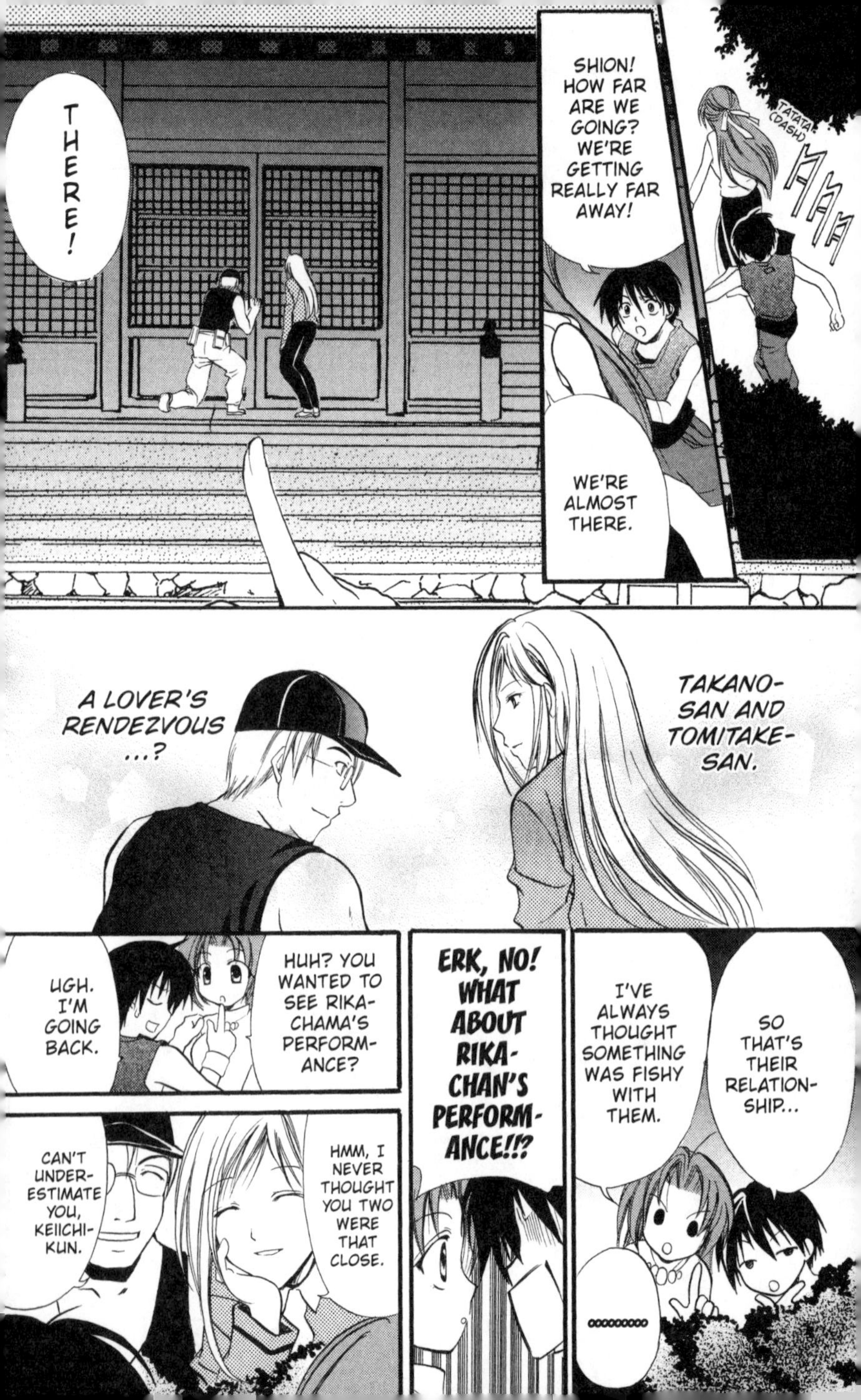
SHION! HOW FAR ARE WE GOING? WE'RE GETTING REALLY FAR AWAY!
TATATA (DASH)
WE'RE ALMOST THERE.
THERE!
TAKANO-SAN AND TOMITAKE-SAN.
A LOVER'S RENDEZVOUS ...?
SO THAT'S THEIR RELATIONSHIP...
I'VE ALWAYS THOUGHT SOMETHING WAS FISHY WITH THEM.
....
ERK, NO! WHAT ABOUT RIKA-CHAN'S PERFORMANCE!!?
HUH? YOU WANTED TO SEE RIKA-CHAMA'S PERFORMANCE?
UGH. I'M GOING BACK.
HMM, I NEVER THOUGHT YOU TWO WERE THAT CLOSE.
CAN'T UNDERESTIMATE YOU, KEIICHI-KUN.

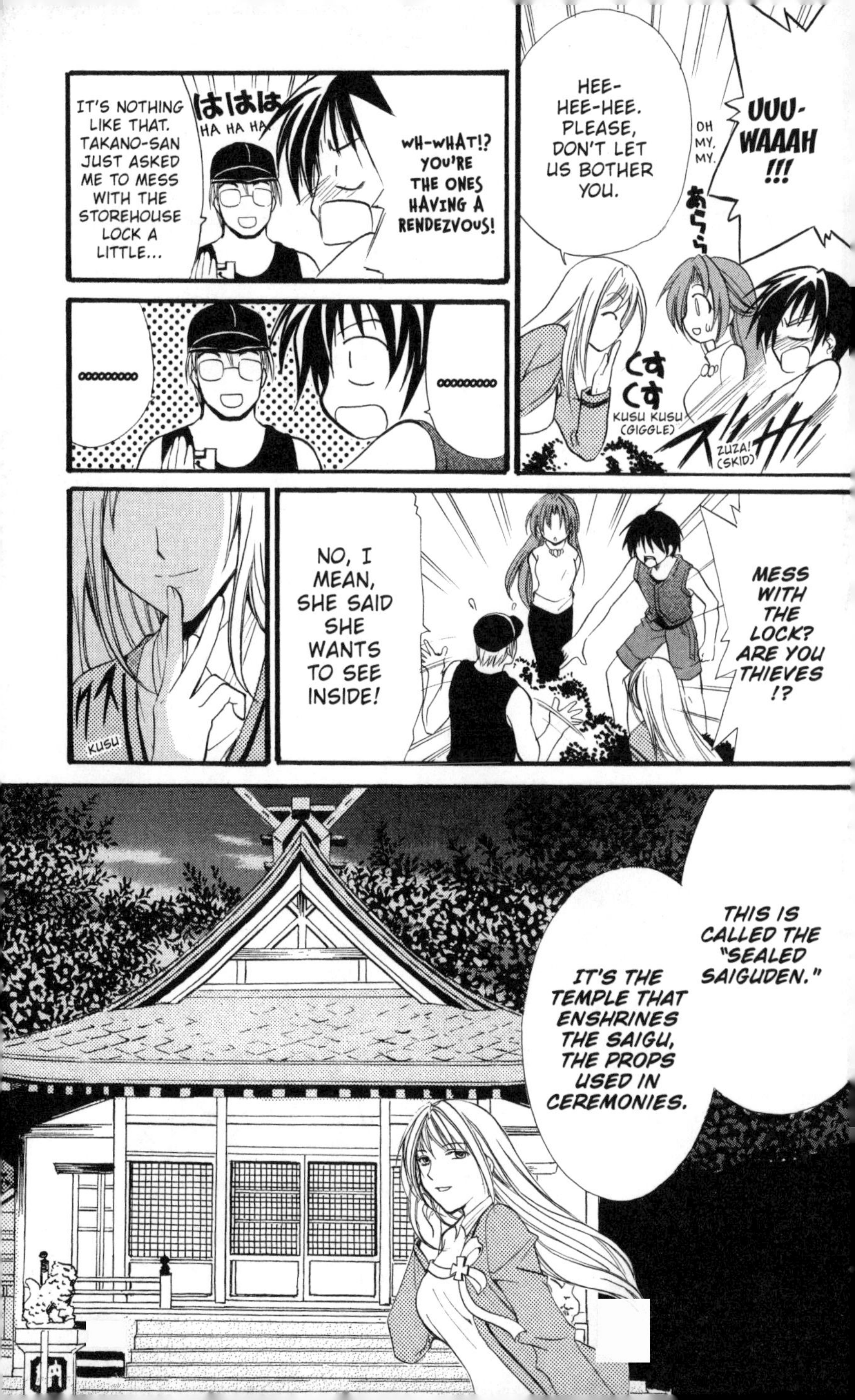
UUU-WAAAH!!!
OH MY, MY.
あらら
HEE-HEE-HEE. PLEASE, DON'T LET US BOTHER YOU.
くすくす
KUSU KUSU (GIGGLE)
ZUZA! (SKID)
WH-WHAT!? YOU'RE THE ONES HAVING A RENDEZVOUS!
ははは
HA HA HA
IT'S NOTHING LIKE THAT. TAKANO-SAN JUST ASKED ME TO MESS WITH THE STOREHOUSE LOCK A LITTLE...
ooooooooo
ooooooooo
MESS WITH THE LOCK? ARE YOU THIEVES!?
NO, I MEAN, SHE SAID SHE WANTS TO SEE INSIDE!
KUSU
THIS IS CALLED THE "SEALED SAIGUDEN."
IT'S THE TEMPLE THAT ENSHRINES THE SAIGU, THE PROPS USED IN CEREMONIES.

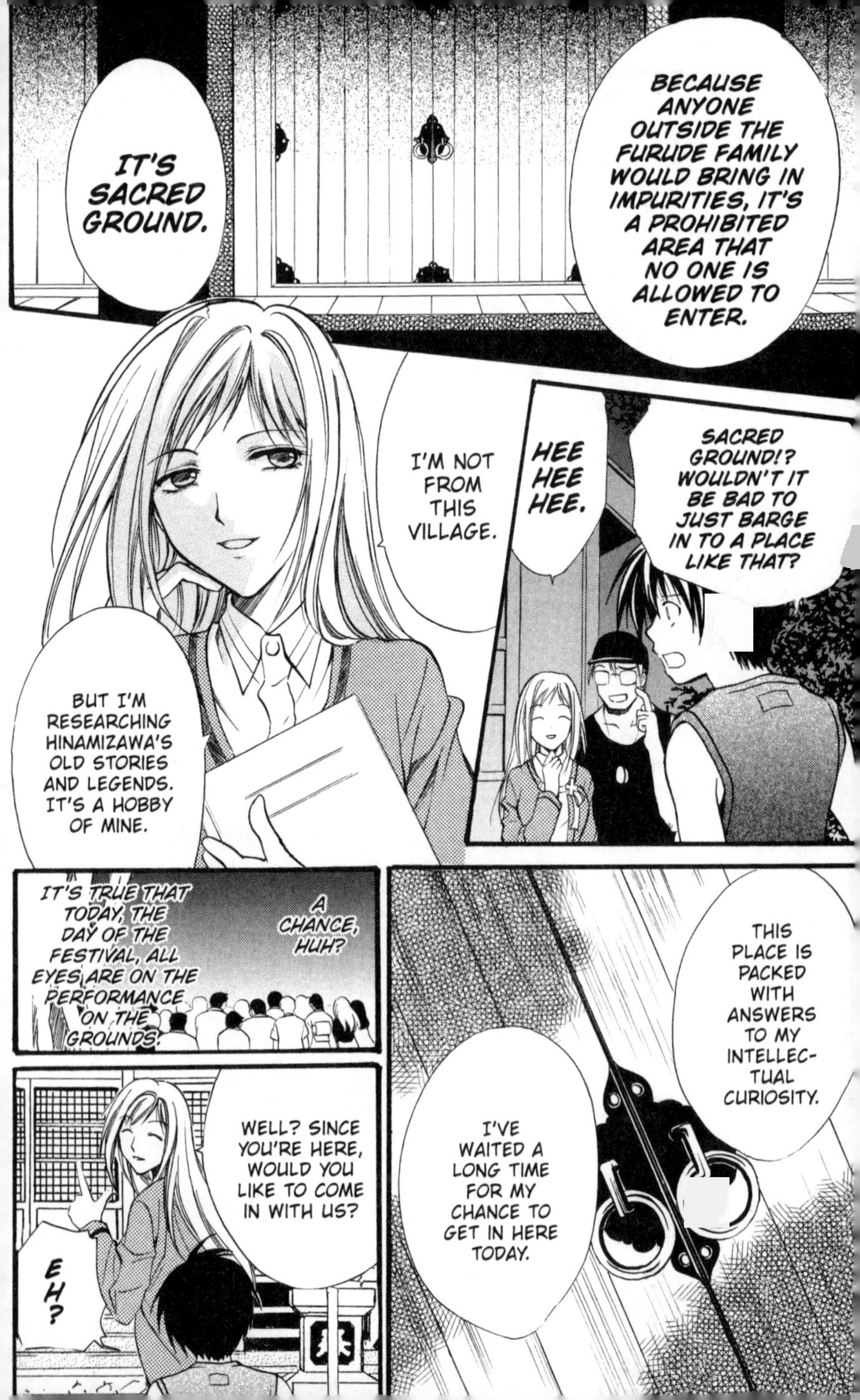
BECAUSE ANYONE OUTSIDE THE FURUDE FAMILY WOULD BRING IN IMPURITIES, IT'S A PROHIBITED AREA THAT NO ONE IS ALLOWED TO ENTER.
IT'S SACRED GROUND.
SACRED GROUND!? WOULDN'T IT BE BAD TO JUST BARGE IN TO A PLACE LIKE THAT?
HEE HEE HEE.
I'M NOT FROM THIS VILLAGE.
BUT I'M RESEARCHING HINAMIZAWA'S OLD STORIES AND LEGENDS. IT'S A HOBBY OF MINE.
THIS PLACE IS PACKED WITH ANSWERS TO MY INTELLEC-TUAL CURIOSITY.
I'VE WAITED A LONG TIME FOR MY CHANCE TO GET IN HERE TODAY.
A CHANCE, HUH?
IT'S TRUE THAT TODAY, THE DAY OF THE FESTIVAL, ALL EYES ARE ON THE PERFORMANCE ON THE GROUNDS.
WELL? SINCE YOU'RE HERE, WOULD YOU LIKE TO COME IN WITH US?
EH?

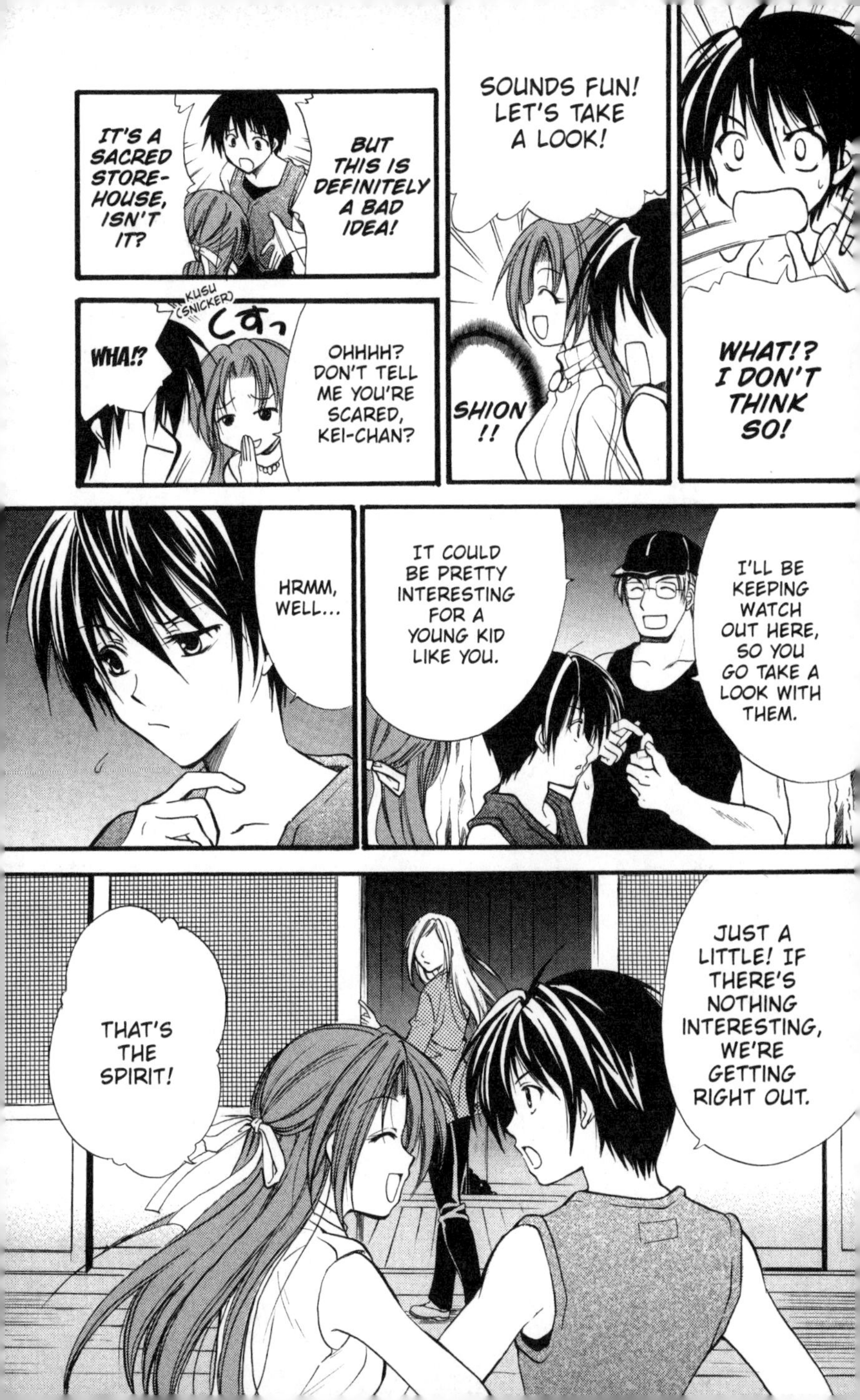
WHAT!? I DON'T THINK SO!
SOUNDS FUN! LET'S TAKE A LOOK!
SHION!!
BUT THIS IS DEFINITELY A BAD IDEA!
IT'S A SACRED STOREHOUSE, ISN'T IT?
OHHHH? DON'T TELL ME YOU'RE SCARED, KEI-CHAN?
くすっ
KUSU (SNICKER)
WHA!?
I'LL BE KEEPING WATCH OUT HERE, SO YOU GO TAKE A LOOK WITH THEM.
IT COULD BE PRETTY INTERESTING FOR A YOUNG KID LIKE YOU.
HRMM, WELL...
JUST A LITTLE! IF THERE'S NOTHING INTERESTING, WE'RE GETTING RIGHT OUT.
THAT'S THE SPIRIT!

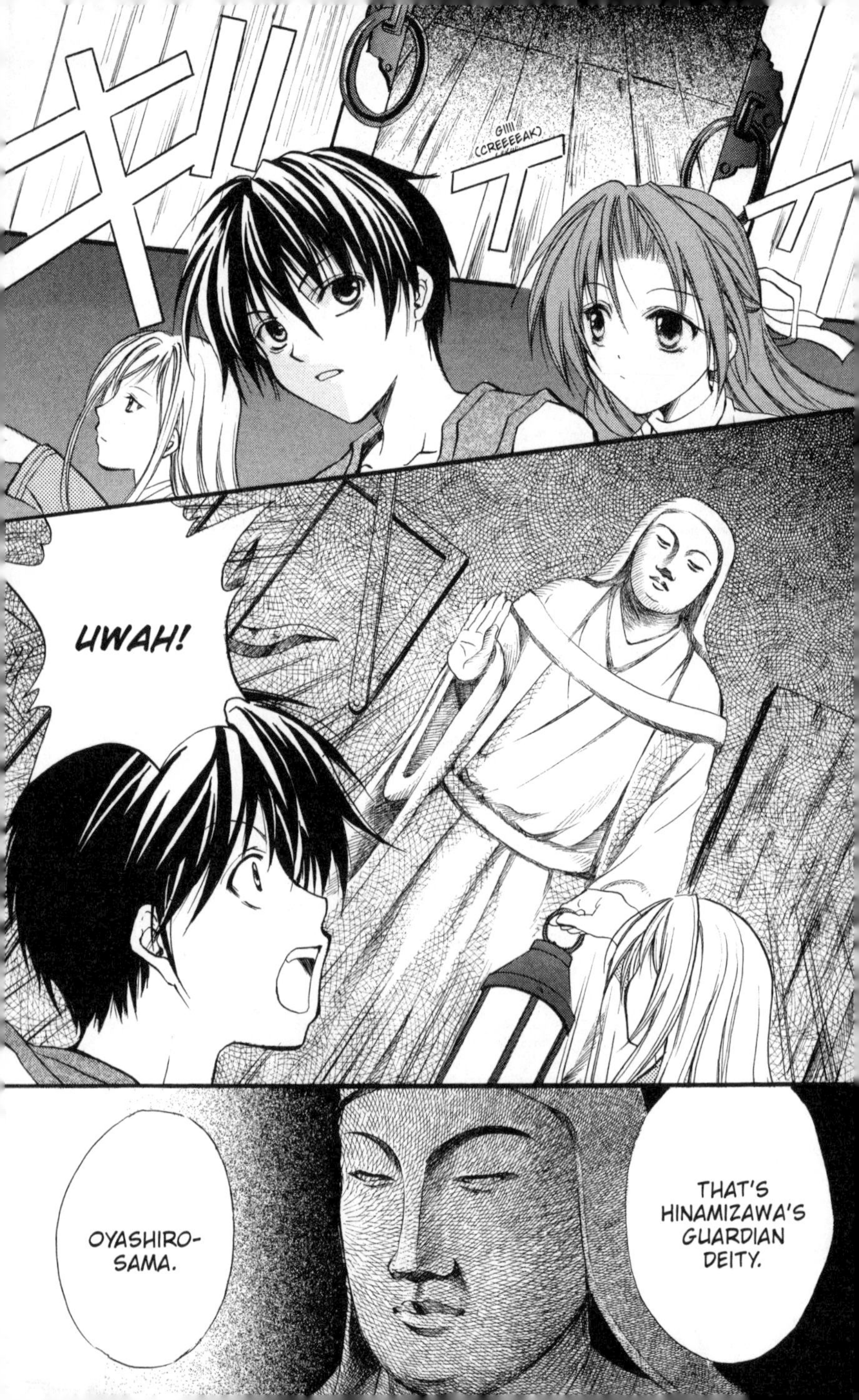
GIIII
(CREEEEAK)
UWAH!
THAT'S HINAMIZAWA'S GUARDIAN DEITY.
OYASHIRO-SAMA.

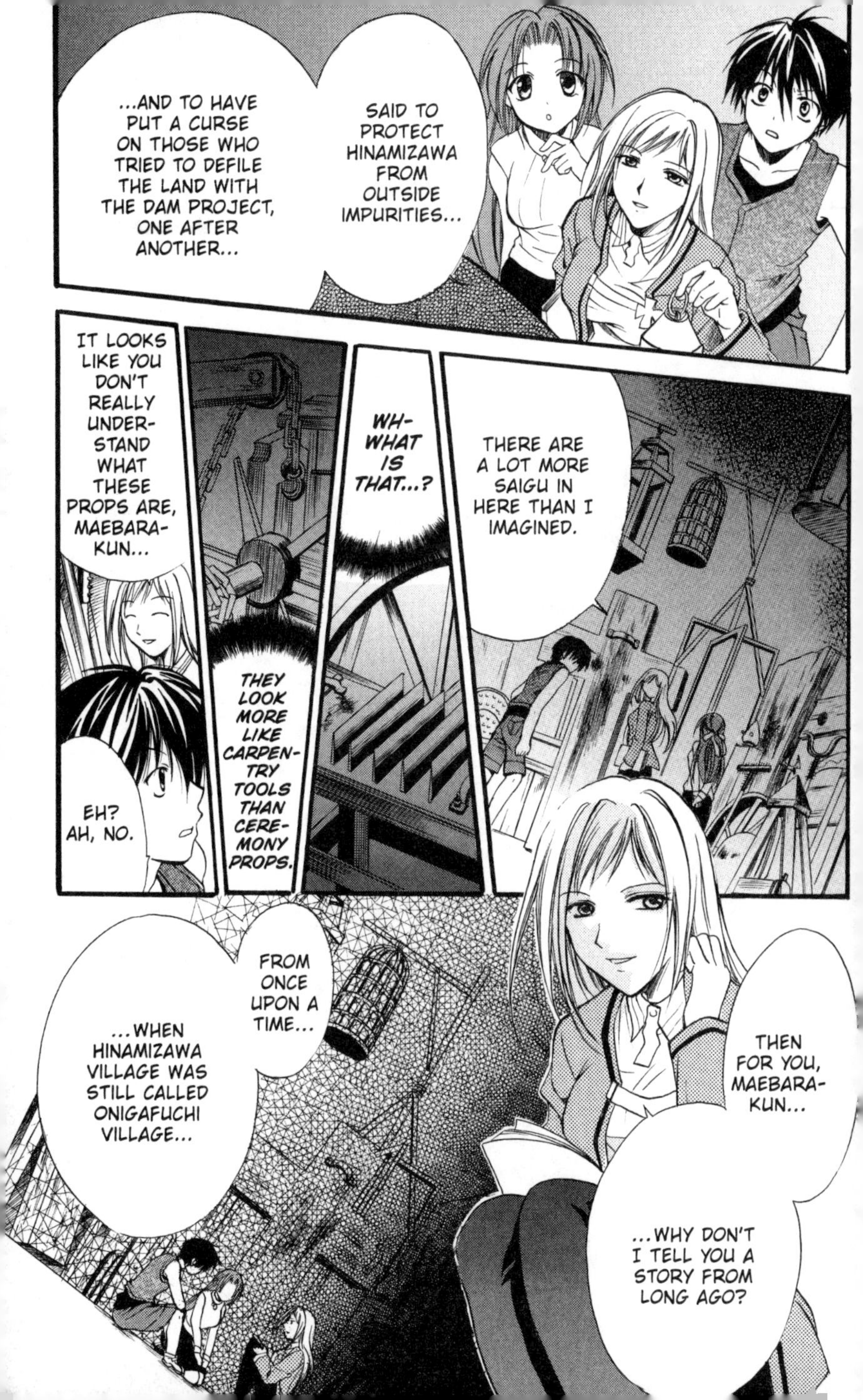
SAID TO PROTECT HINAMIZAWA FROM OUTSIDE IMPURITIES...
...AND TO HAVE PUT A CURSE ON THOSE WHO TRIED TO DEFILE THE LAND WITH THE DAM PROJECT, ONE AFTER ANOTHER...
THERE ARE A LOT MORE SAIGU IN HERE THAN I IMAGINED.
WH-WHAT IS THAT...?
THEY LOOK MORE LIKE CARPENTRY TOOLS THAN CEREMONY PROPS.
IT LOOKS LIKE YOU DON'T REALLY UNDERSTAND WHAT THESE PROPS ARE, MAEBARA-KUN...
EH? AH, NO.
THEN FOR YOU, MAEBARA-KUN...
...WHY DON'T I TELL YOU A STORY FROM LONG AGO?
FROM ONCE UPON A TIME...
...WHEN HINAMIZAWA VILLAGE WAS STILL CALLED ONIGAFUCHI VILLAGE...

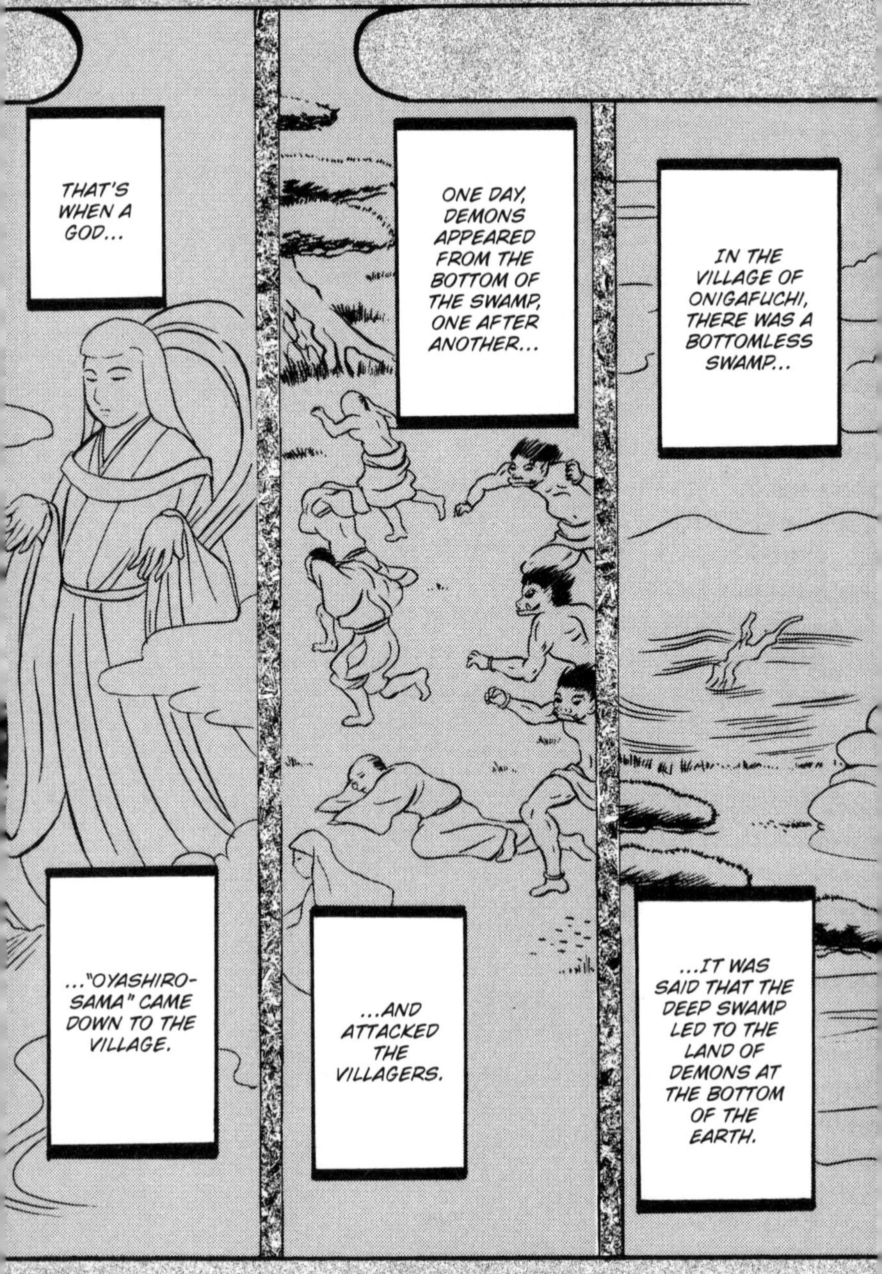
IN THE VILLAGE OF ONIGAFUCHI, THERE WAS A BOTTOMLESS SWAMP...
...IT WAS SAID THAT THE DEEP SWAMP LED TO THE LAND OF DEMONS AT THE BOTTOM OF THE EARTH.
ONE DAY, DEMONS APPEARED FROM THE BOTTOM OF THE SWAMP, ONE AFTER ANOTHER...
...AND ATTACKED THE VILLAGERS.
THAT'S WHEN A GOD...
..."OYASHIRO-SAMA" CAME DOWN TO THE VILLAGE.

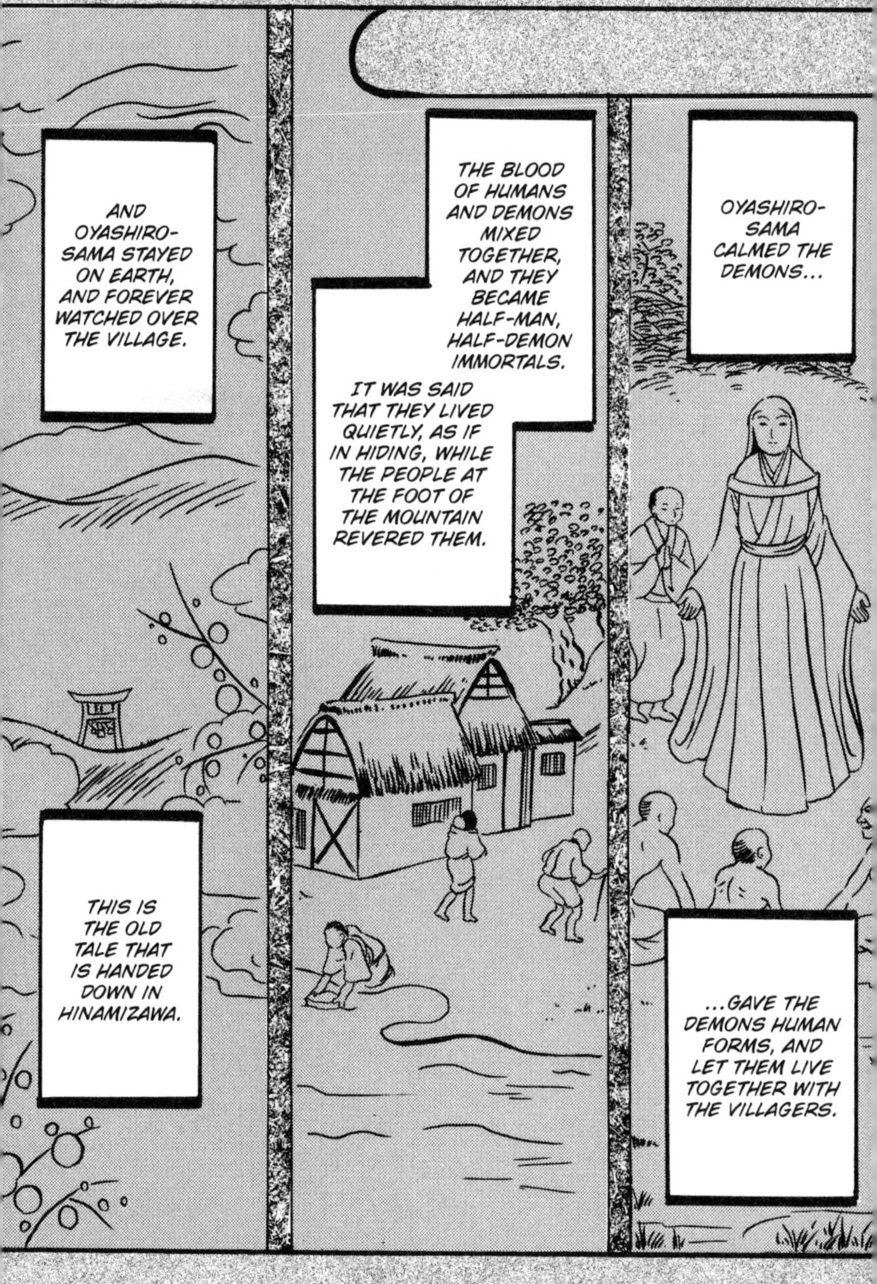
OYASHIRO-SAMA CALMED THE DEMONS...
...GAVE THE DEMONS HUMAN FORMS, AND LET THEM LIVE TOGETHER WITH THE VILLAGERS.
THE BLOOD OF HUMANS AND DEMONS MIXED TOGETHER, AND THEY BECAME HALF-MAN, HALF-DEMON IMMORTALS.
IT WAS SAID THAT THEY LIVED QUIETLY, AS IF IN HIDING, WHILE THE PEOPLE AT THE FOOT OF THE MOUNTAIN REVERED THEM.
AND OYASHIRO-SAMA STAYED ON EARTH, AND FOREVER WATCHED OVER THE VILLAGE.
THIS IS THE OLD TALE THAT IS HANDED DOWN IN HINAMIZAWA.

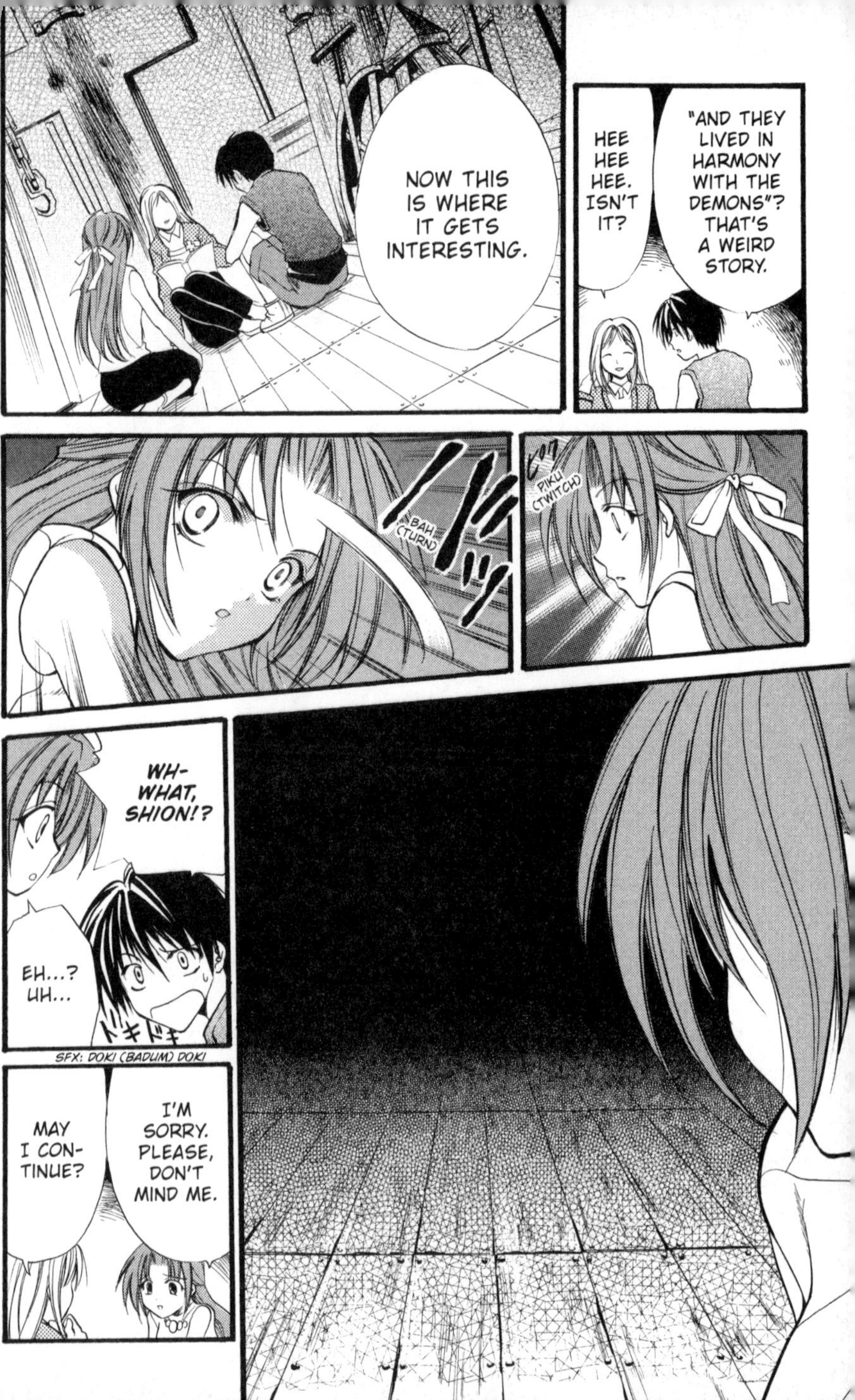
"AND THEY LIVED IN HARMONY WITH THE DEMONS"? THAT'S A WEIRD STORY.
HEE HEE HEE. ISN'T IT?
NOW THIS IS WHERE IT GETS INTERESTING.
PIKU (TWITCH)
BAH (TURN)
WH- WHAT, SHION!?
EH...? UH...
SFX: DOKI (BADUM) DOKI
I'M SORRY. PLEASE, DON'T MIND ME.
MAY I CONTINUE?

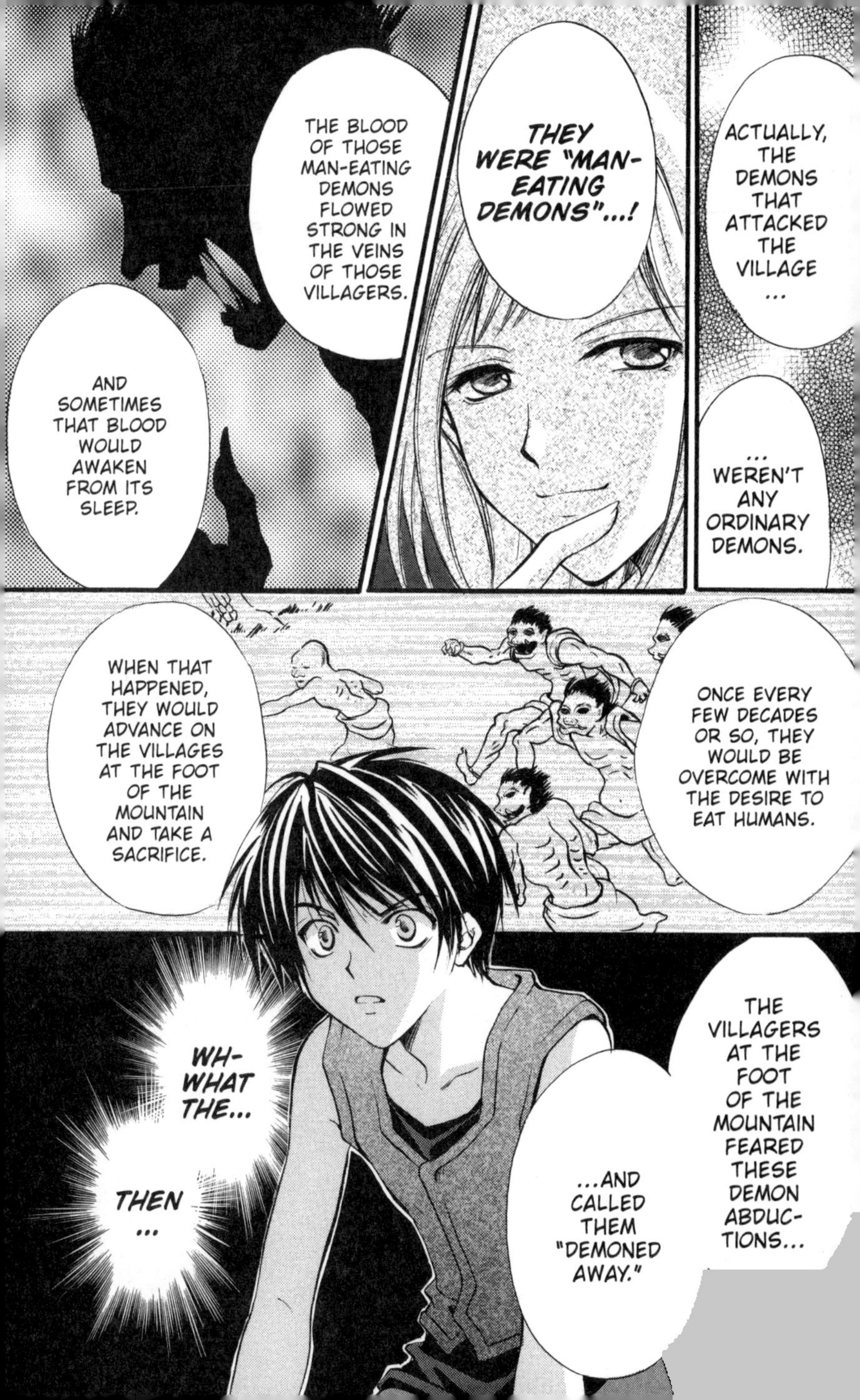
ACTUALLY, THE DEMONS THAT ATTACKED THE VILLAGE ...
... WEREN'T ANY ORDINARY DEMONS.
THEY WERE "MAN-EATING DEMONS"...!
THE BLOOD OF THOSE MAN-EATING DEMONS FLOWED STRONG IN THE VEINS OF THOSE VILLAGERS.
AND SOMETIMES THAT BLOOD WOULD AWAKEN FROM ITS SLEEP.
ONCE EVERY FEW DECADES OR SO, THEY WOULD BE OVERCOME WITH THE DESIRE TO EAT HUMANS.
WHEN THAT HAPPENED, THEY WOULD ADVANCE ON THE VILLAGES AT THE FOOT OF THE MOUNTAIN AND TAKE A SACRIFICE.
THE VILLAGERS AT THE FOOT OF THE MOUNTAIN FEARED THESE DEMON ABDUC-TIONS...
...AND CALLED THEM "DEMONED AWAY."
WH-WHAT THE...
THEN ...

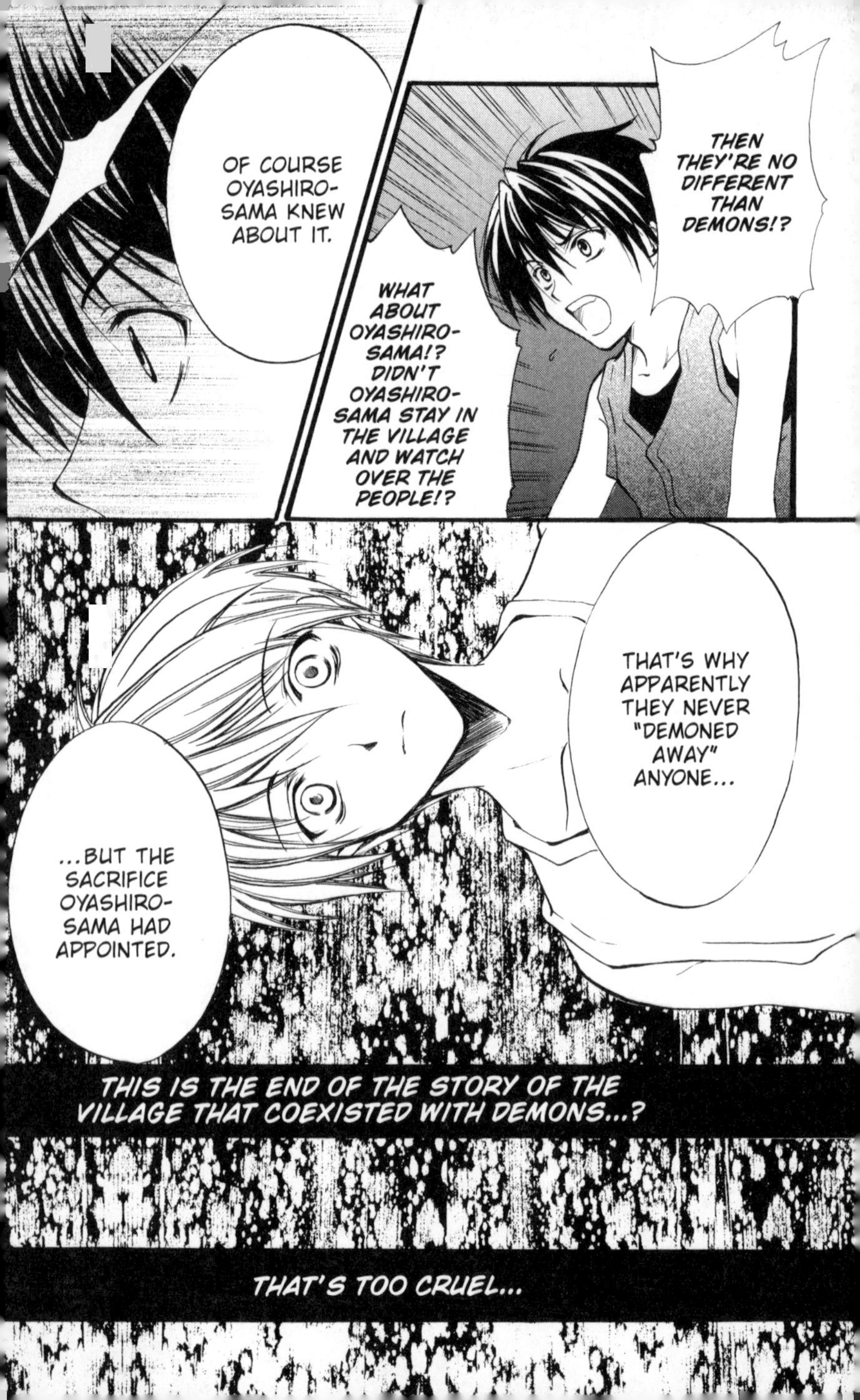
THEN THEY'RE NO DIFFERENT THAN DEMONS!?
WHAT ABOUT OYASHIRO-SAMA!? DIDN'T OYASHIRO-SAMA STAY IN THE VILLAGE AND WATCH OVER THE PEOPLE!?
OF COURSE OYASHIRO-SAMA KNEW ABOUT IT.
THAT'S WHY APPARENTLY THEY NEVER "DEMONED AWAY" ANYONE...
...BUT THE SACRIFICE OYASHIRO-SAMA HAD APPOINTED.
THIS IS THE END OF THE STORY OF THE VILLAGE THAT COEXISTED WITH DEMONS...?
THAT'S TOO CRUEL...

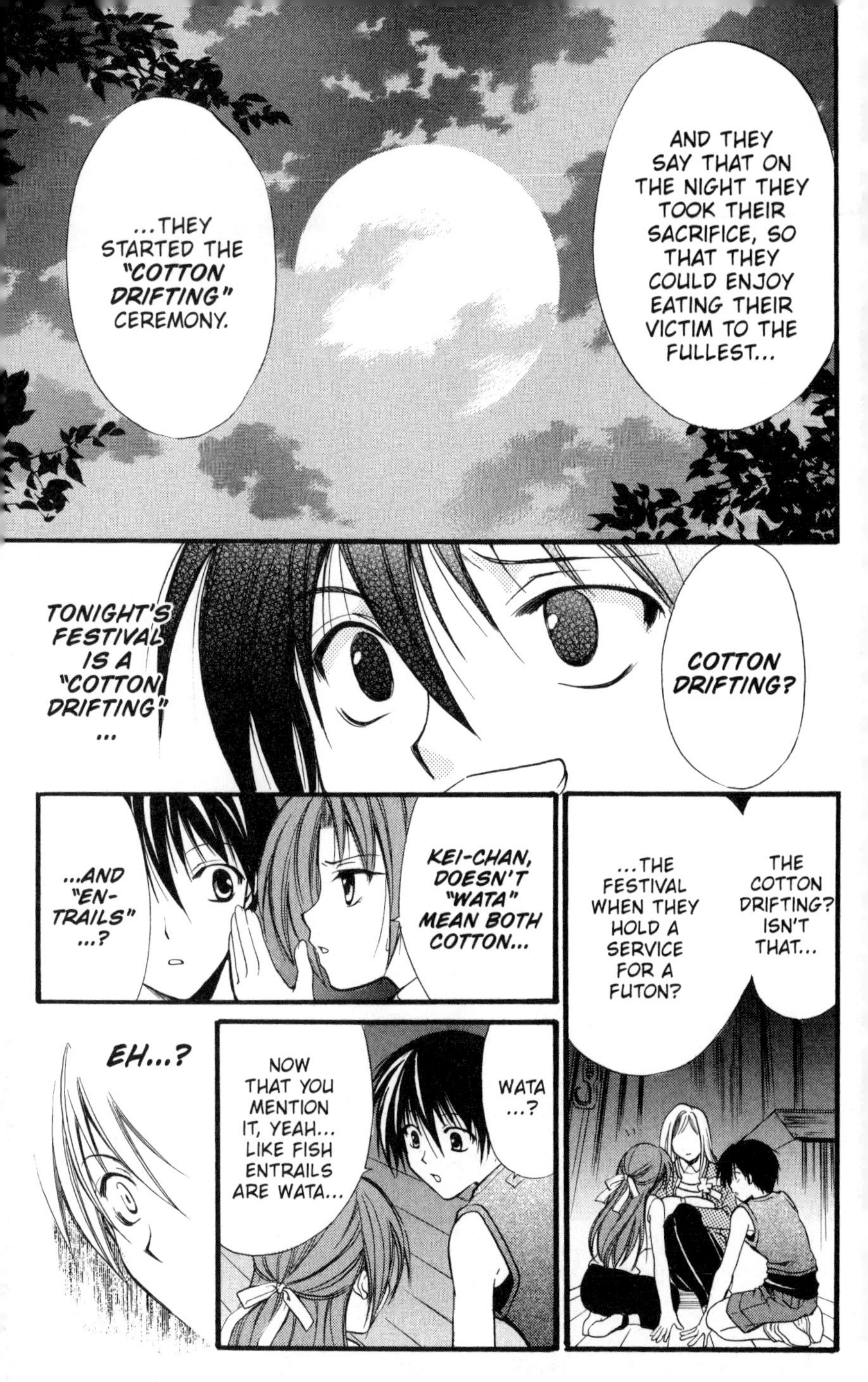
AND THEY SAY THAT ON THE NIGHT THEY TOOK THEIR SACRIFICE, SO THAT THEY COULD ENJOY EATING THEIR VICTIM TO THE FULLEST...
...THEY STARTED THE "COTTON DRIFTING" CEREMONY.
COTTON DRIFTING?
TONIGHT'S FESTIVAL IS A "COTTON DRIFTING" ...
THE COTTON DRIFTING? ISN'T THAT...
...THE FESTIVAL WHEN THEY HOLD A SERVICE FOR A FUTON?
KEI-CHAN, DOESN'T "WATA" MEAN BOTH COTTON...
...AND "EN-TRAILS" ...?
WATA ...?
NOW THAT YOU MENTION IT, YEAH... LIKE FISH ENTRAILS ARE WATA...
EH...?

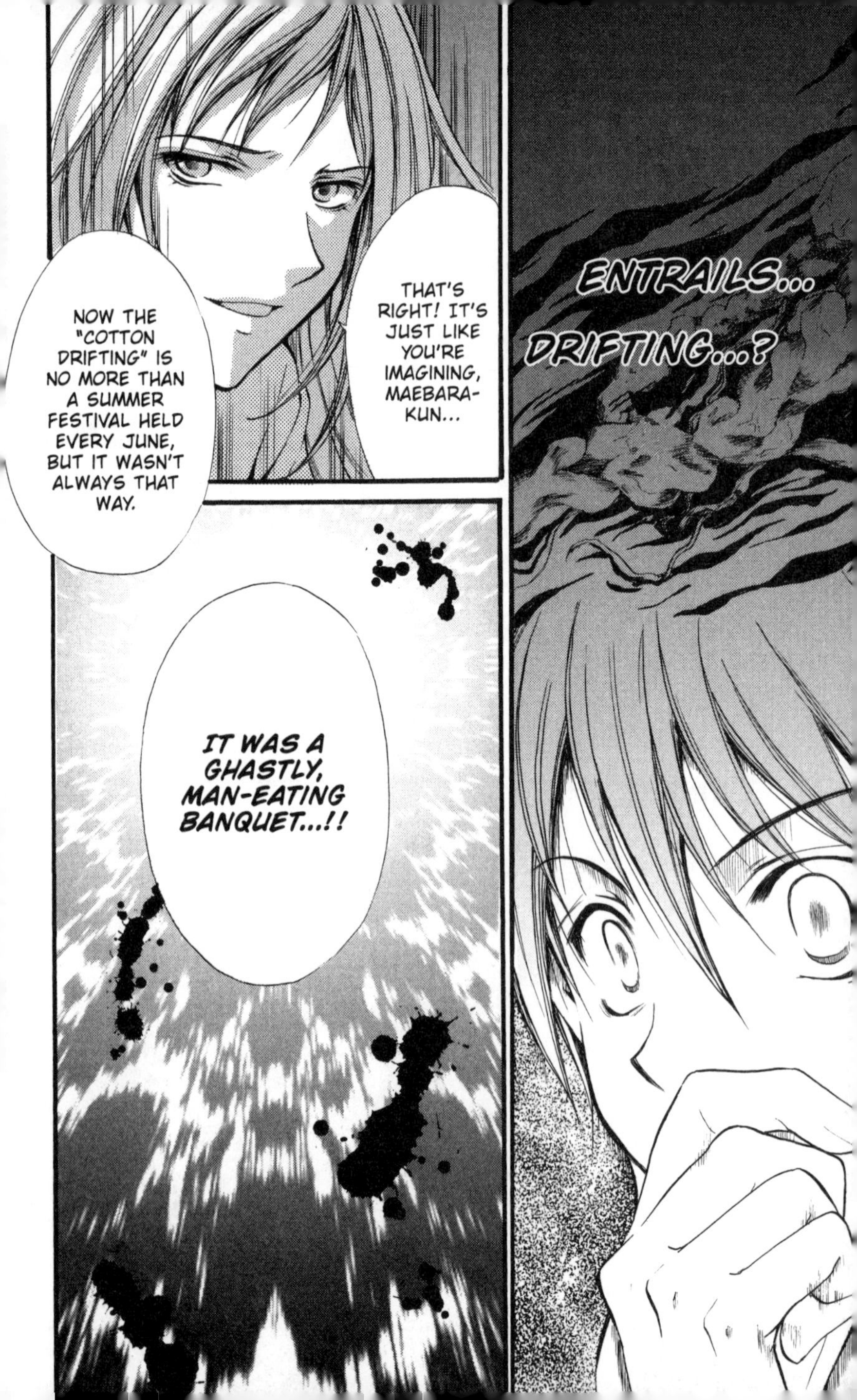
ENTRAILS...
DRIFTING...?
THAT'S RIGHT! IT'S JUST LIKE YOU'RE IMAGINING, MAEBARA-KUN...
NOW THE "COTTON DRIFTING" IS NO MORE THAN A SUMMER FESTIVAL HELD EVERY JUNE, BUT IT WASN'T ALWAYS THAT WAY.
IT WAS A GHASTLY, MAN-EATING BANQUET...!!

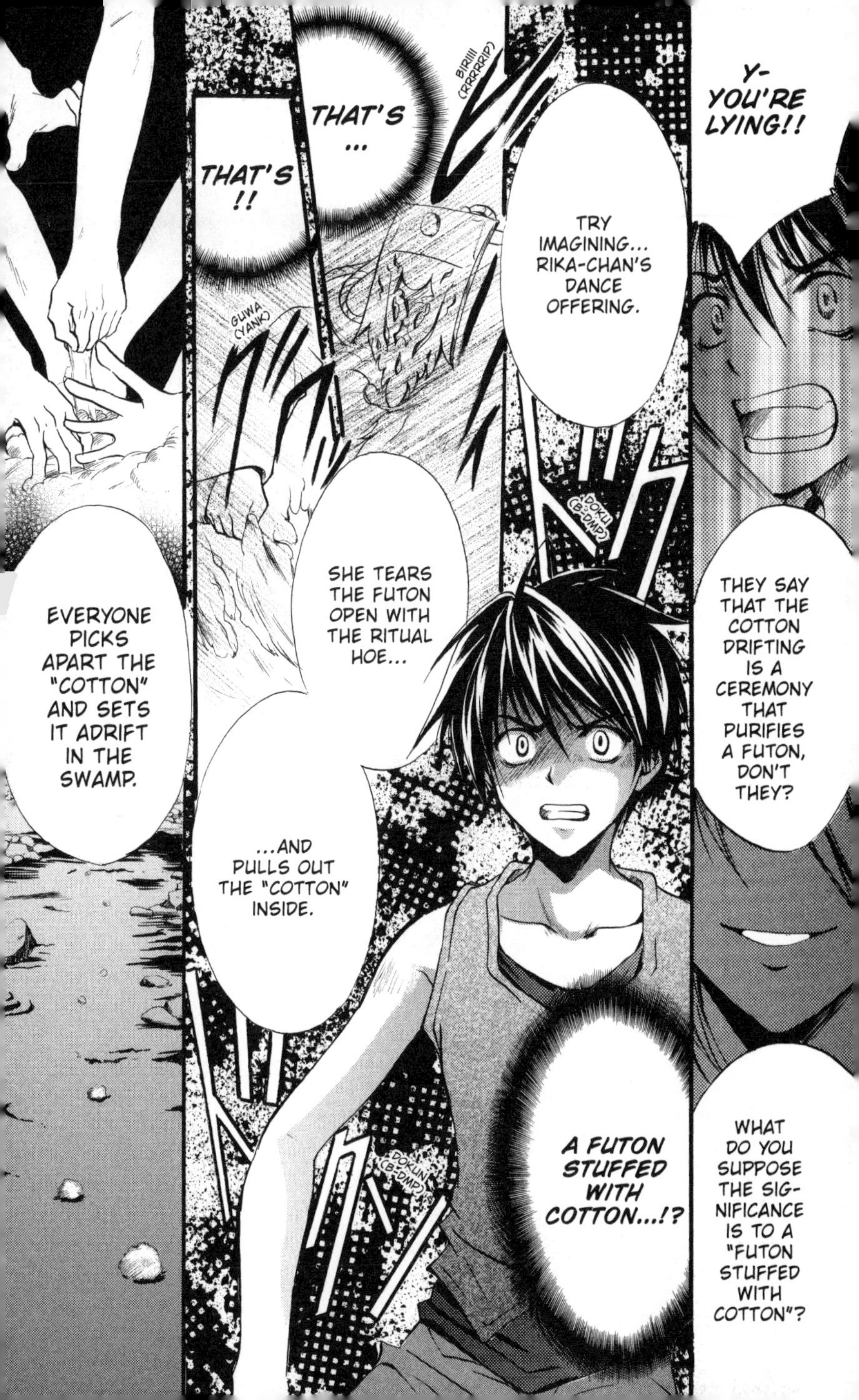
Y- YOU'RE LYING!!
THEY SAY THAT THE COTTON DRIFTING IS A CEREMONY THAT PURIFIES A FUTON, DON'T THEY?
WHAT DO YOU SUPPOSE THE SIG-NIFICANCE IS TO A "FUTON STUFFED WITH COTTON"?
DOKUN (B-DMP)
A FUTON STUFFED WITH COTTON...!?
DOKU (B-DMP)
TRY IMAGINING... RIKA-CHAN'S DANCE OFFERING.
BIRIIII (RRRRRIP)
SHE TEARS THE FUTON OPEN WITH THE RITUAL HOE...
GUWA (YANK)
...AND PULLS OUT THE "COTTON" INSIDE.
EVERYONE PICKS APART THE "COTTON" AND SETS IT ADRIFT IN THE SWAMP.
THAT'S ...
THAT'S !!

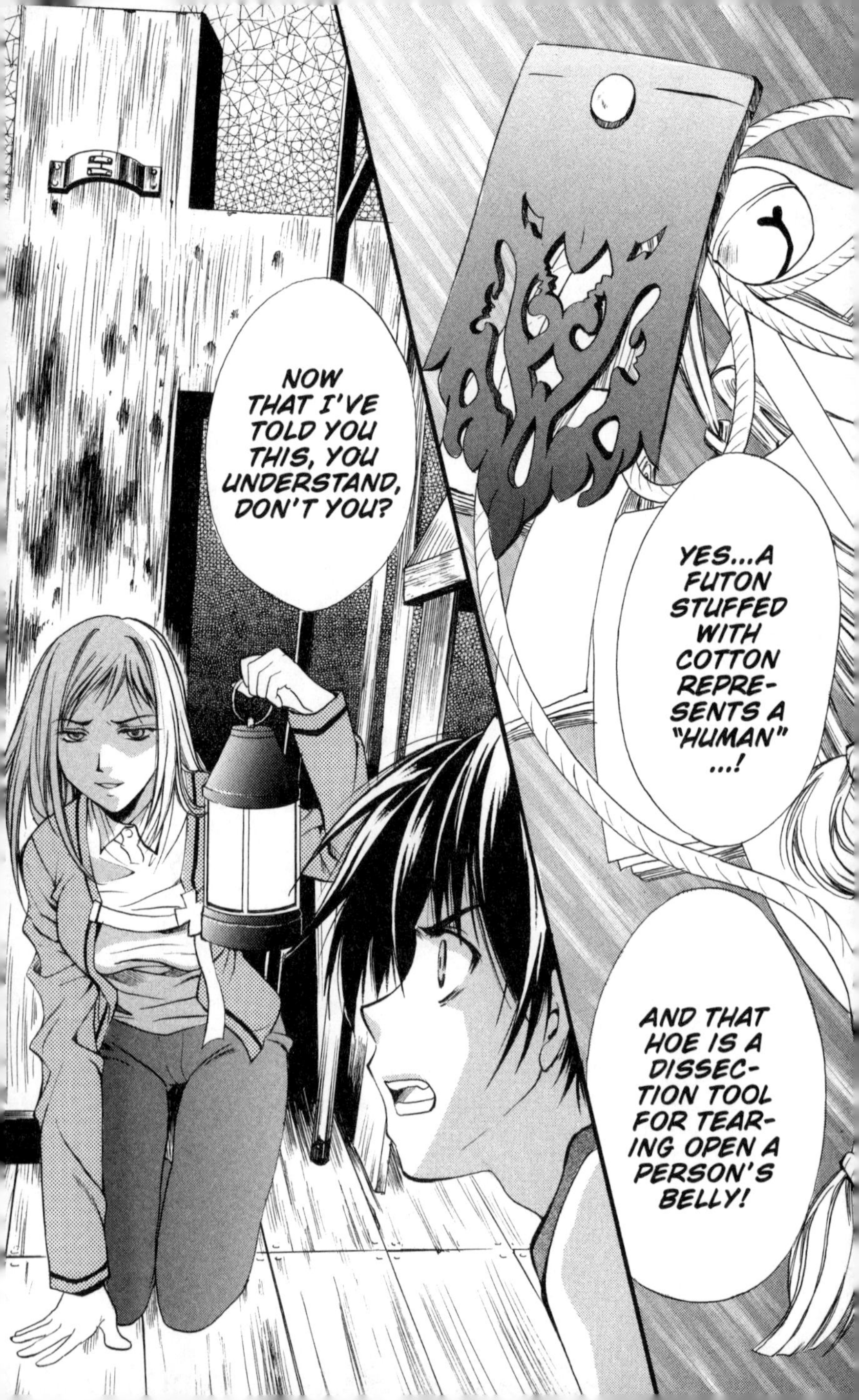
NOW THAT I'VE TOLD YOU THIS, YOU UNDERSTAND, DON'T YOU?
YES...A FUTON STUFFED WITH COTTON REPRE-SENTS A "HUMAN" ...!
AND THAT HOE IS A DISSEC-TION TOOL FOR TEAR-ING OPEN A PERSON'S BELLY!

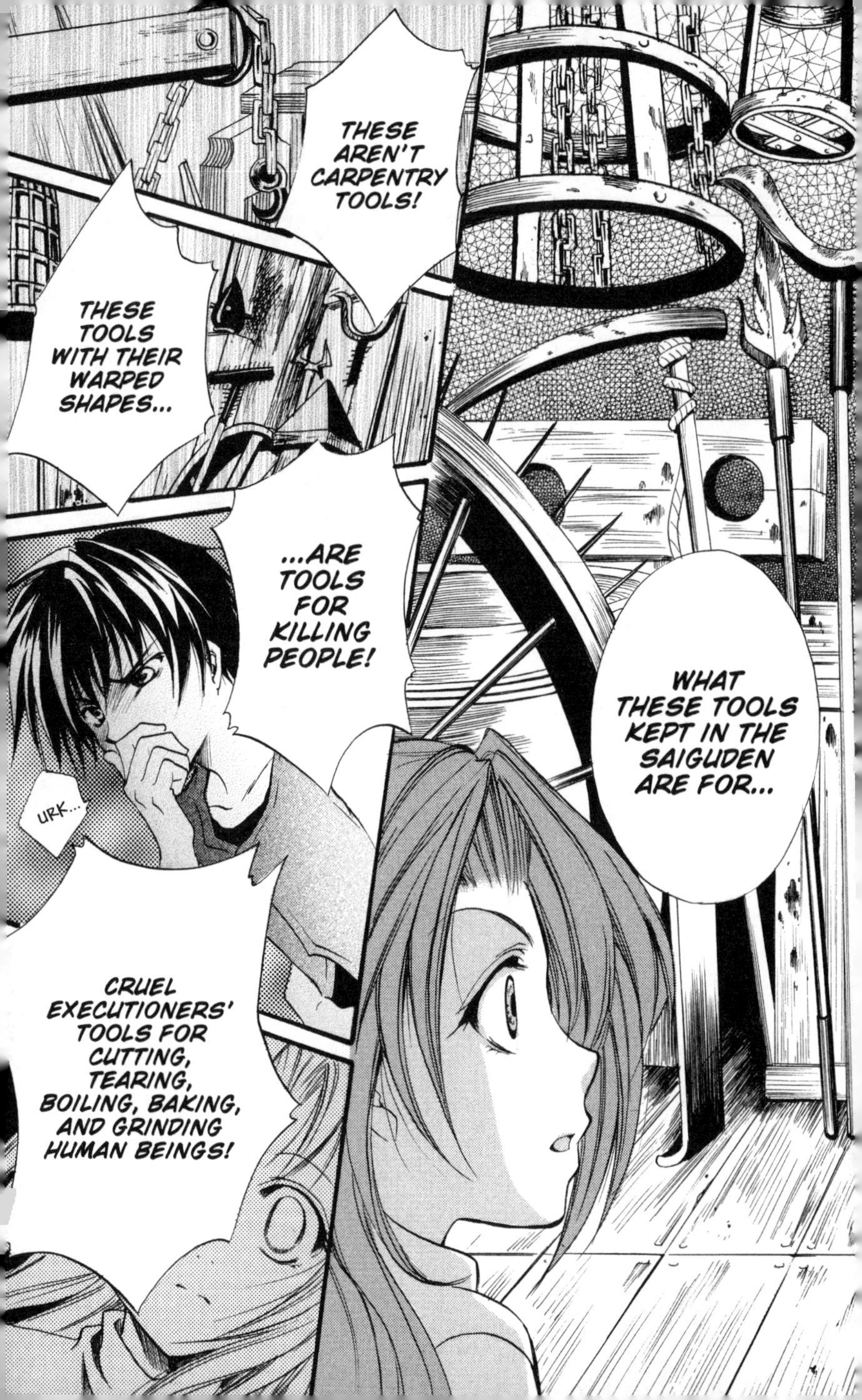
THESE AREN'T CARPENTRY TOOLS!
THESE TOOLS WITH THEIR WARPED SHAPES...
...ARE TOOLS FOR KILLING PEOPLE!
URK...
WHAT THESE TOOLS KEPT IN THE SAIGUDEN ARE FOR...
CRUEL EXECUTIONERS' TOOLS FOR CUTTING, TEARING, BOILING, BAKING, AND GRINDING HUMAN BEINGS!

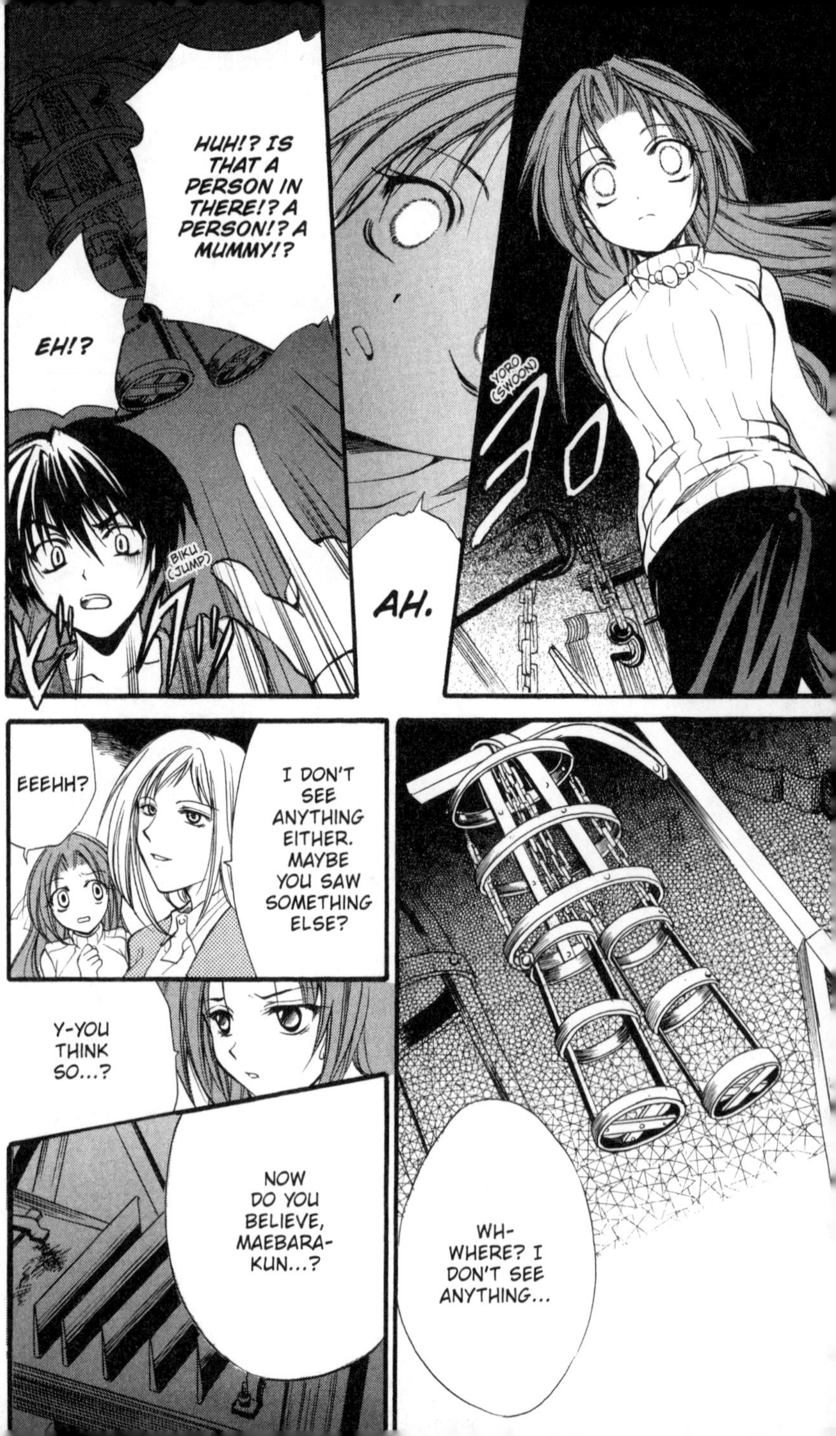
YORO (SWOON)
AH.
HUH!? IS THAT A PERSON IN THERE!? A PERSON!? A MUMMY!?
EH!?
BIKU (JUMP)
WH- WHERE? I DON'T SEE ANYTHING...
I DON'T SEE ANYTHING EITHER. MAYBE YOU SAW SOMETHING ELSE?
EEEHH?
Y-YOU THINK SO...?
NOW DO YOU BELIEVE, MAEBARA-KUN...?

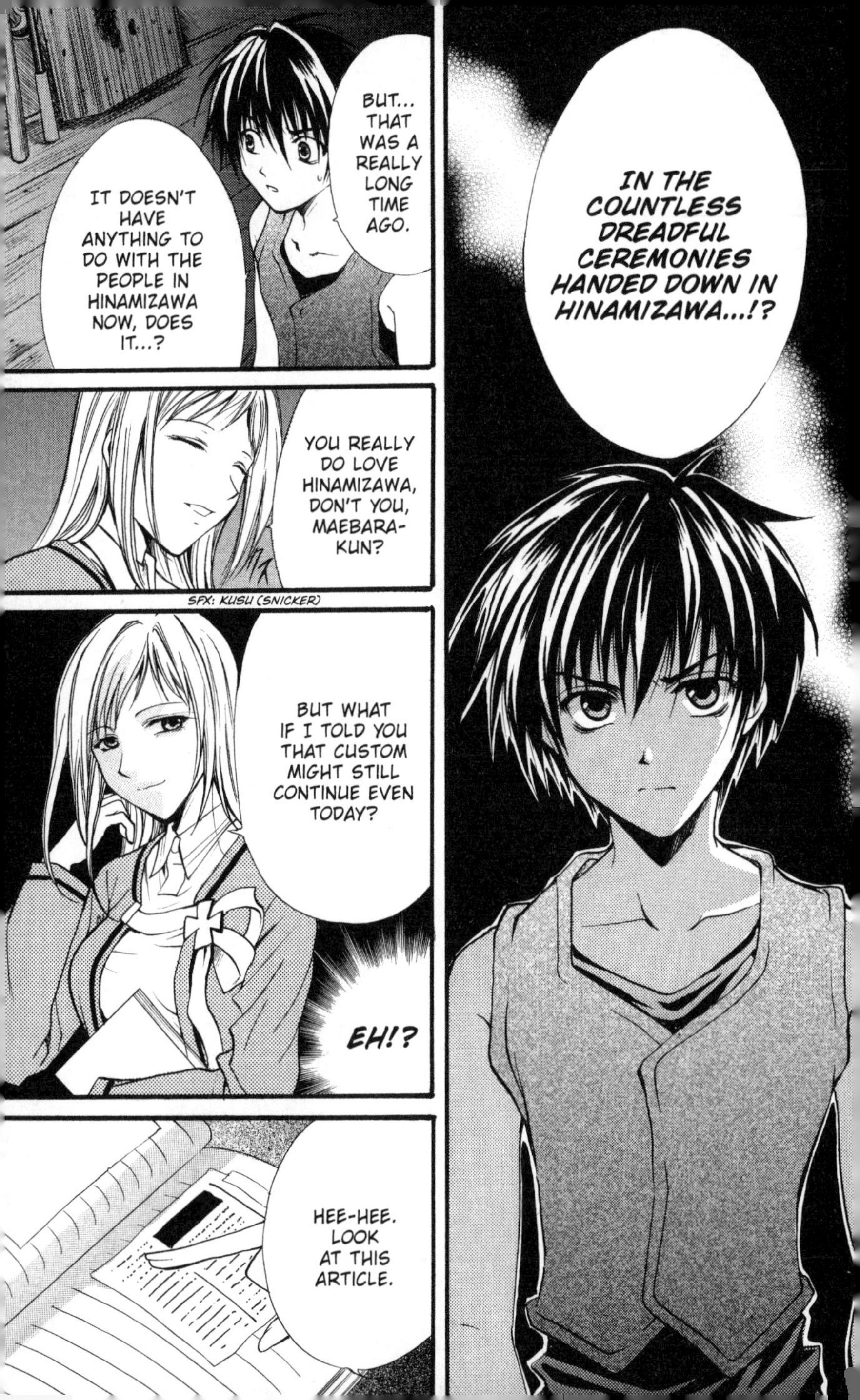
IN THE COUNTLESS DREADFUL CEREMONIES HANDED DOWN IN HINAMIZAWA...!?
BUT... THAT WAS A REALLY LONG TIME AGO.
IT DOESN'T HAVE ANYTHING TO DO WITH THE PEOPLE IN HINAMIZAWA NOW, DOES IT...?
YOU REALLY DO LOVE HINAMIZAWA, DON'T YOU, MAEBARA-KUN?
SFX: KUSU (SNICKER)
BUT WHAT IF I TOLD YOU THAT CUSTOM MIGHT STILL CONTINUE EVEN TODAY?
EH!?
HEE-HEE. LOOK AT THIS ARTICLE.

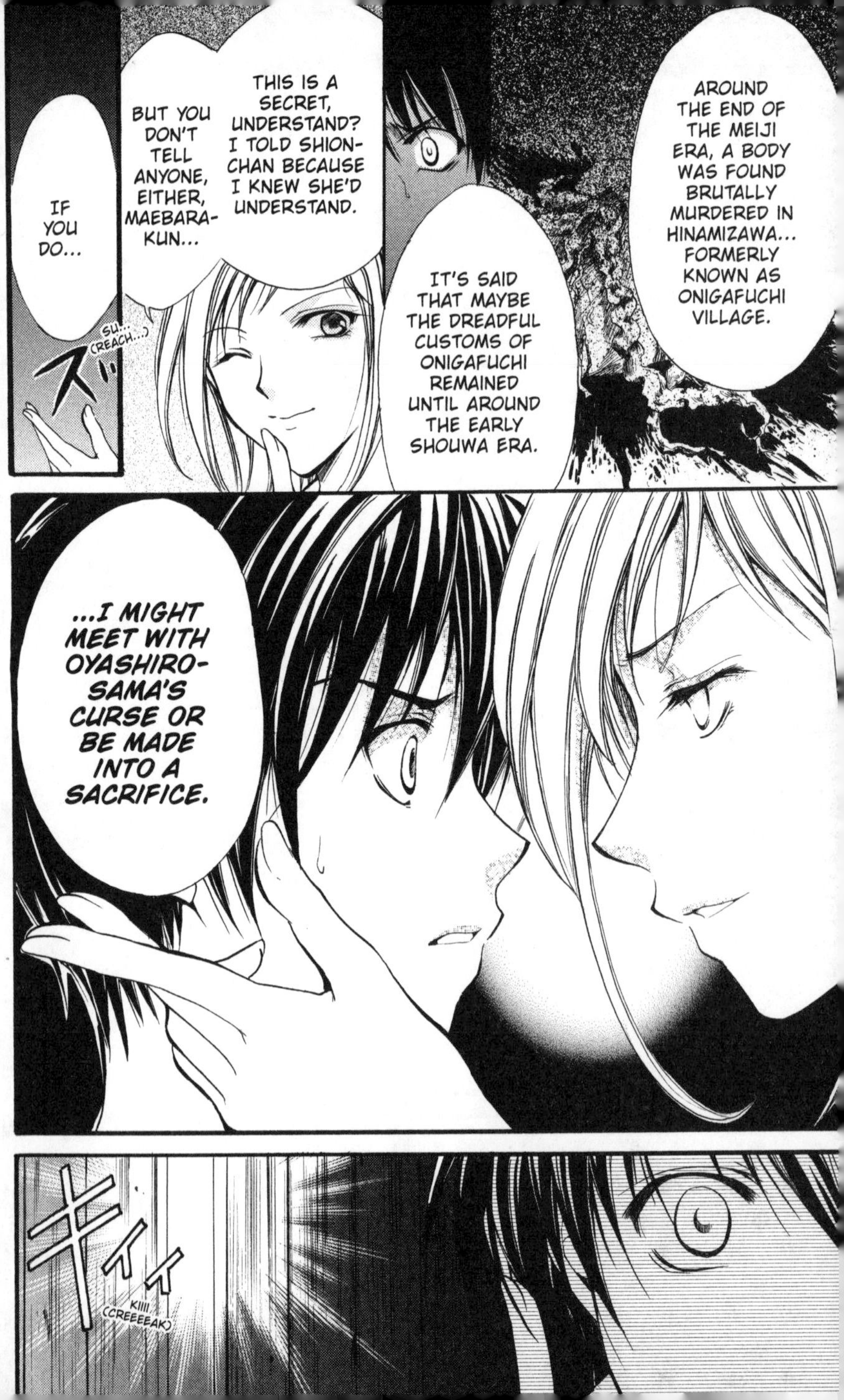
AROUND THE END OF THE MEIJI ERA, A BODY WAS FOUND BRUTALLY MURDERED IN HINAMIZAWA... FORMERLY KNOWN AS ONIGAFUCHI VILLAGE.
IT'S SAID THAT MAYBE THE DREADFUL CUSTOMS OF ONIGAFUCHI REMAINED UNTIL AROUND THE EARLY SHOUWA ERA.
THIS IS A SECRET, UNDERSTAND? I TOLD SHION-CHAN BECAUSE I KNEW SHE'D UNDERSTAND.
BUT YOU DON'T TELL ANYONE, EITHER, MAEBARA-KUN...
IF YOU DO...
SU... (REACH...)
...I MIGHT MEET WITH OYASHIRO-SAMA'S CURSE OR BE MADE INTO A SACRIFICE.
KIIII (CREEEEAK)

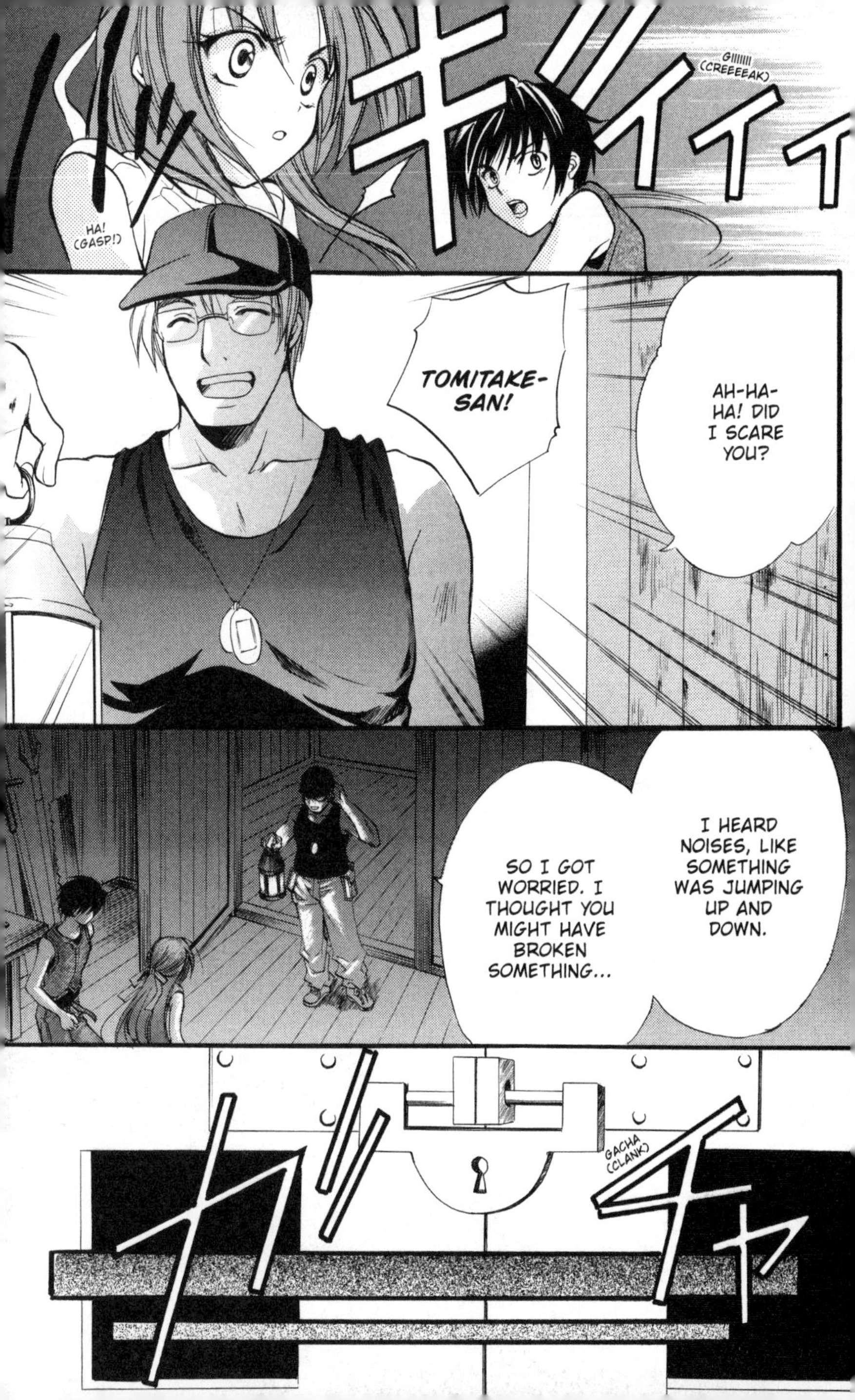
GIIIIII (CREEEEAK)
HA! (GASP!)
AH-HA-HA! DID I SCARE YOU?
TOMITAKE-SAN!
I HEARD NOISES, LIKE SOMETHING WAS JUMPING UP AND DOWN.
SO I GOT WORRIED. I THOUGHT YOU MIGHT HAVE BROKEN SOMETHING...
GACHA (CLANK)

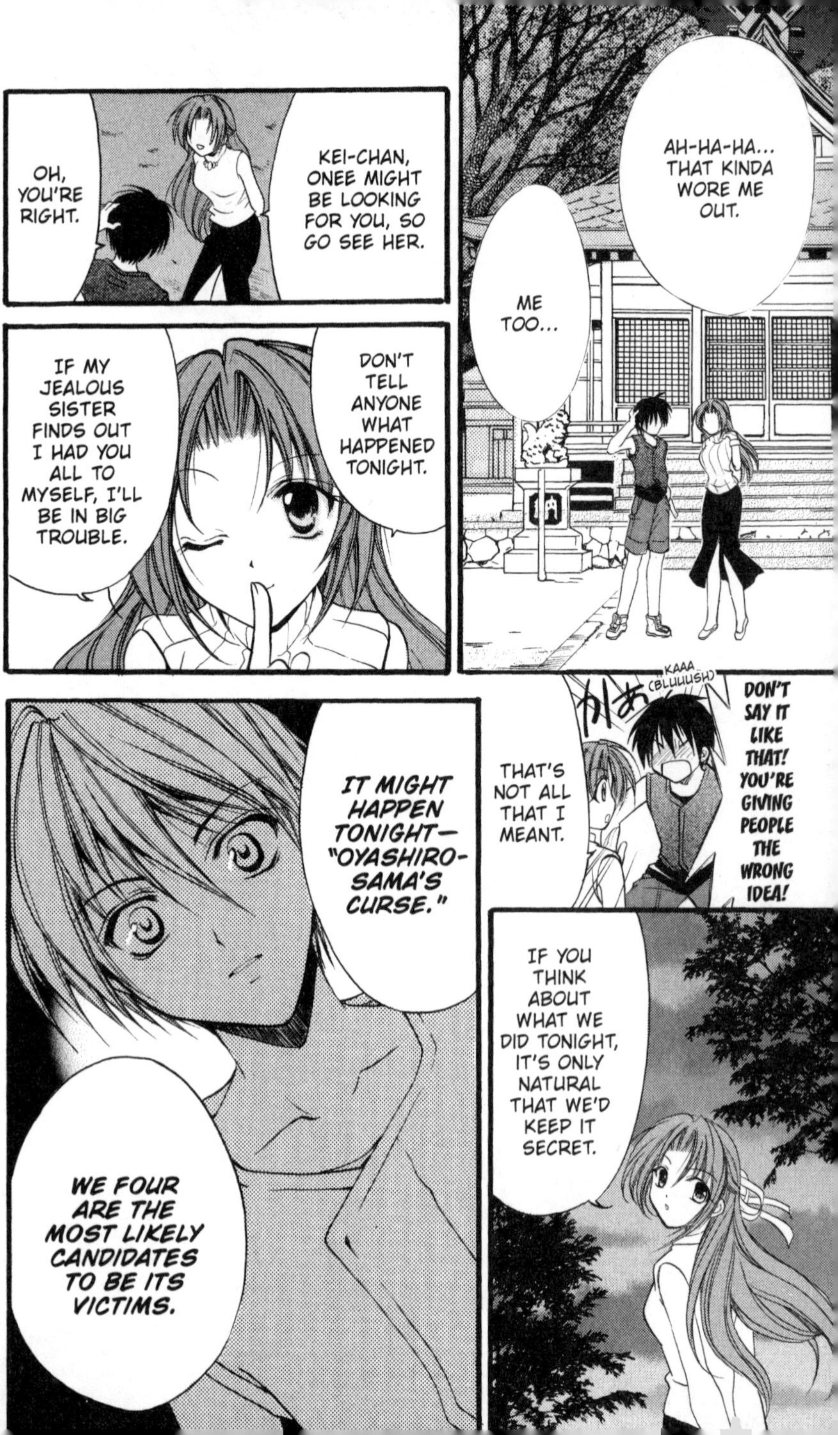
AH-HA-HA... THAT KINDA WORE ME OUT.
ME TOO...
KEI-CHAN, ONEE MIGHT BE LOOKING FOR YOU, SO GO SEE HER.
OH, YOU'RE RIGHT.
DON'T TELL ANYONE WHAT HAPPENED TONIGHT.
IF MY JEALOUS SISTER FINDS OUT I HAD YOU ALL TO MYSELF, I'LL BE IN BIG TROUBLE.
かあ
KAAA (BLUUUSH)
DON'T SAY IT LIKE THAT! YOU'RE GIVING PEOPLE THE WRONG IDEA!
THAT'S NOT ALL THAT I MEANT.
IF YOU THINK ABOUT WHAT WE DID TONIGHT, IT'S ONLY NATURAL THAT WE'D KEEP IT SECRET.
IT MIGHT HAPPEN TONIGHT—"OYASHIRO-SAMA'S CURSE."
WE FOUR ARE THE MOST LIKELY CANDIDATES TO BE ITS VICTIMS.

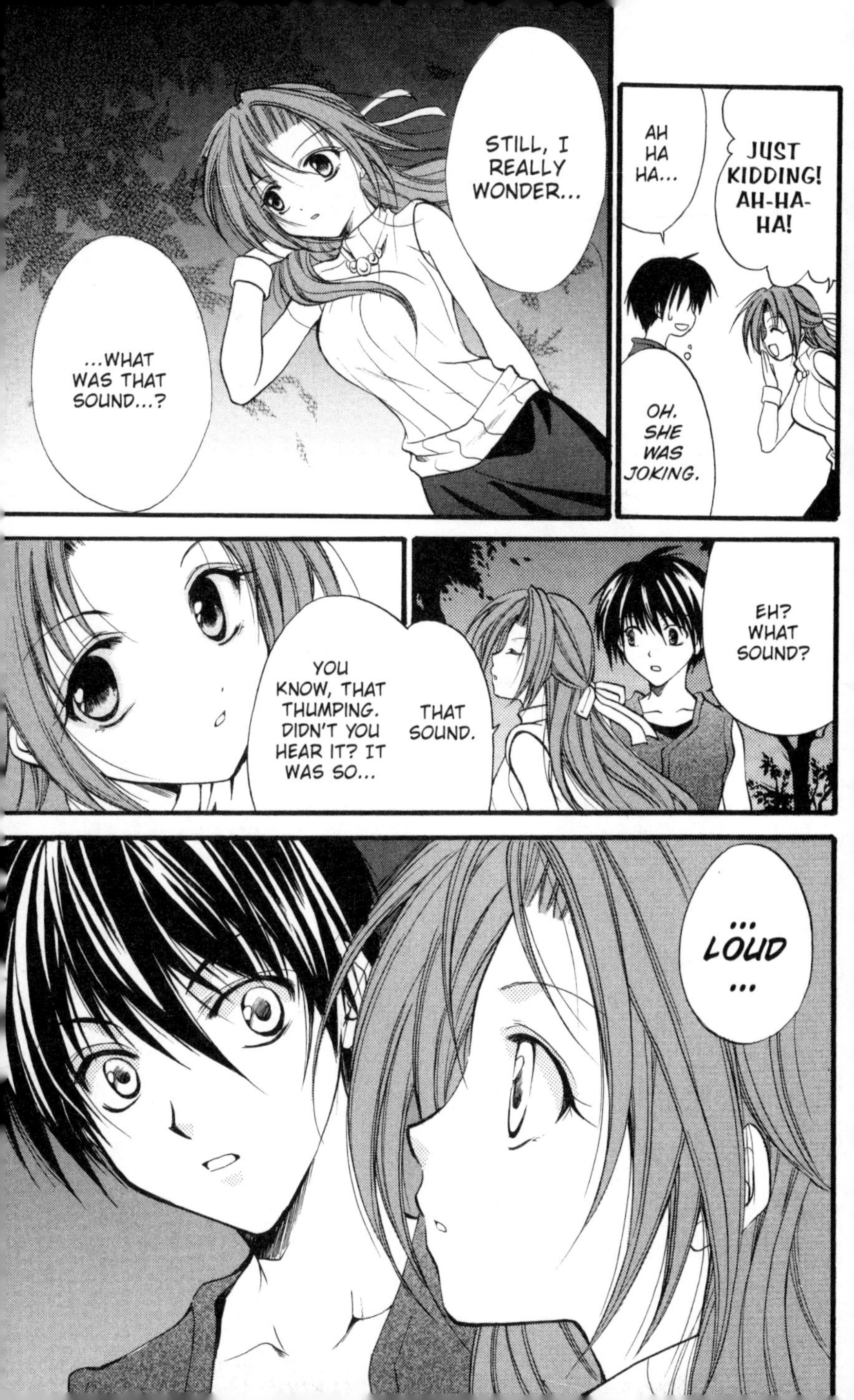
JUST KIDDING! AH-HA-HA!
AH HA HA...
OH. SHE WAS JOKING.
STILL, I REALLY WONDER...
...WHAT WAS THAT SOUND...?
EH? WHAT SOUND?
THAT SOUND.
YOU KNOW, THAT THUMPING. DIDN'T YOU HEAR IT? IT WAS SO...
... LOUD ...

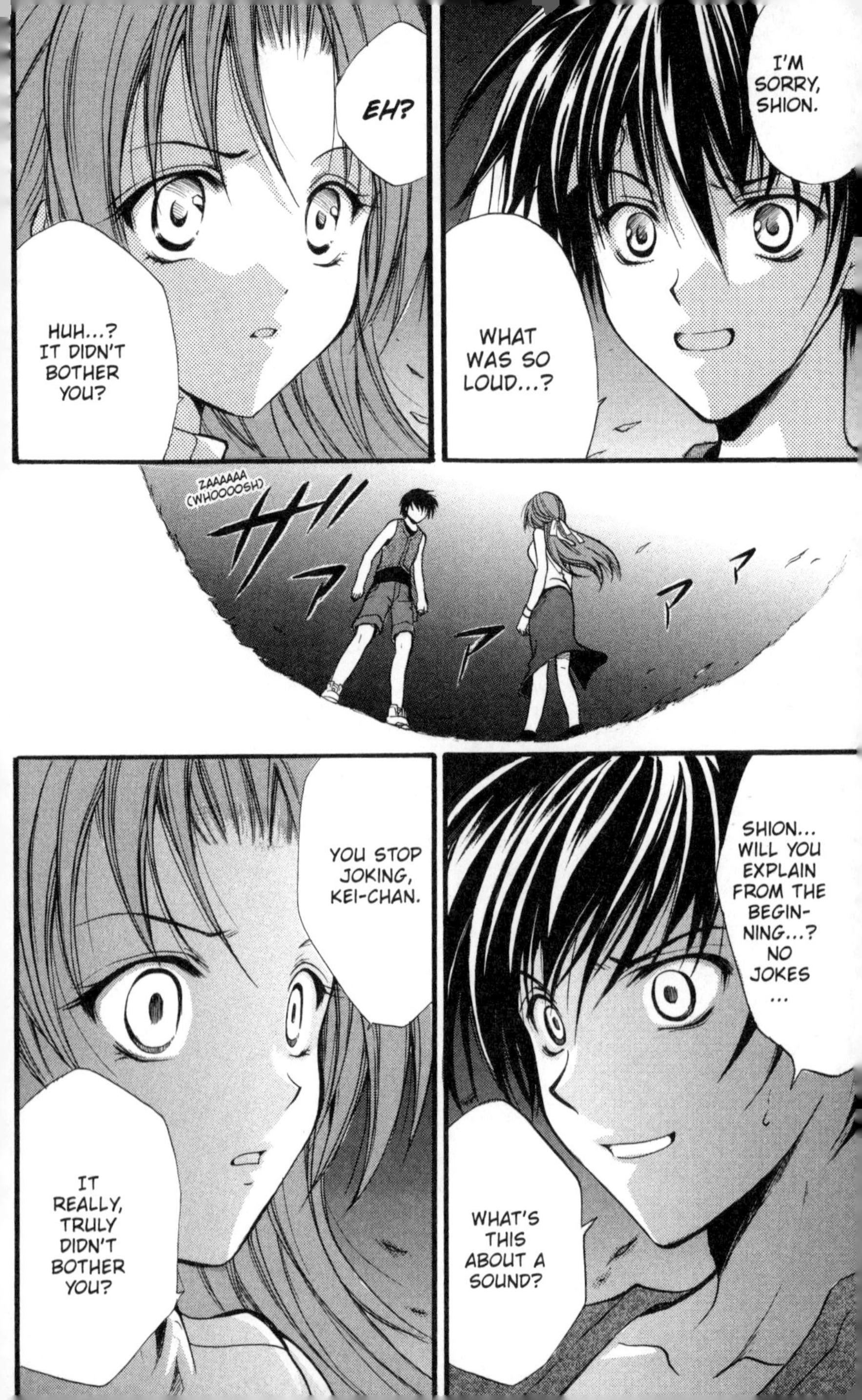
I'M SORRY, SHION.
WHAT WAS SO LOUD...?
EH?
HUH...? IT DIDN'T BOTHER YOU?
ZAAAAAA (WHOOOOSH)
SHION... WILL YOU EXPLAIN FROM THE BEGIN-NING...? NO JOKES ...
WHAT'S THIS ABOUT A SOUND?
YOU STOP JOKING, KEI-CHAN.
IT REALLY, TRULY DIDN'T BOTHER YOU?

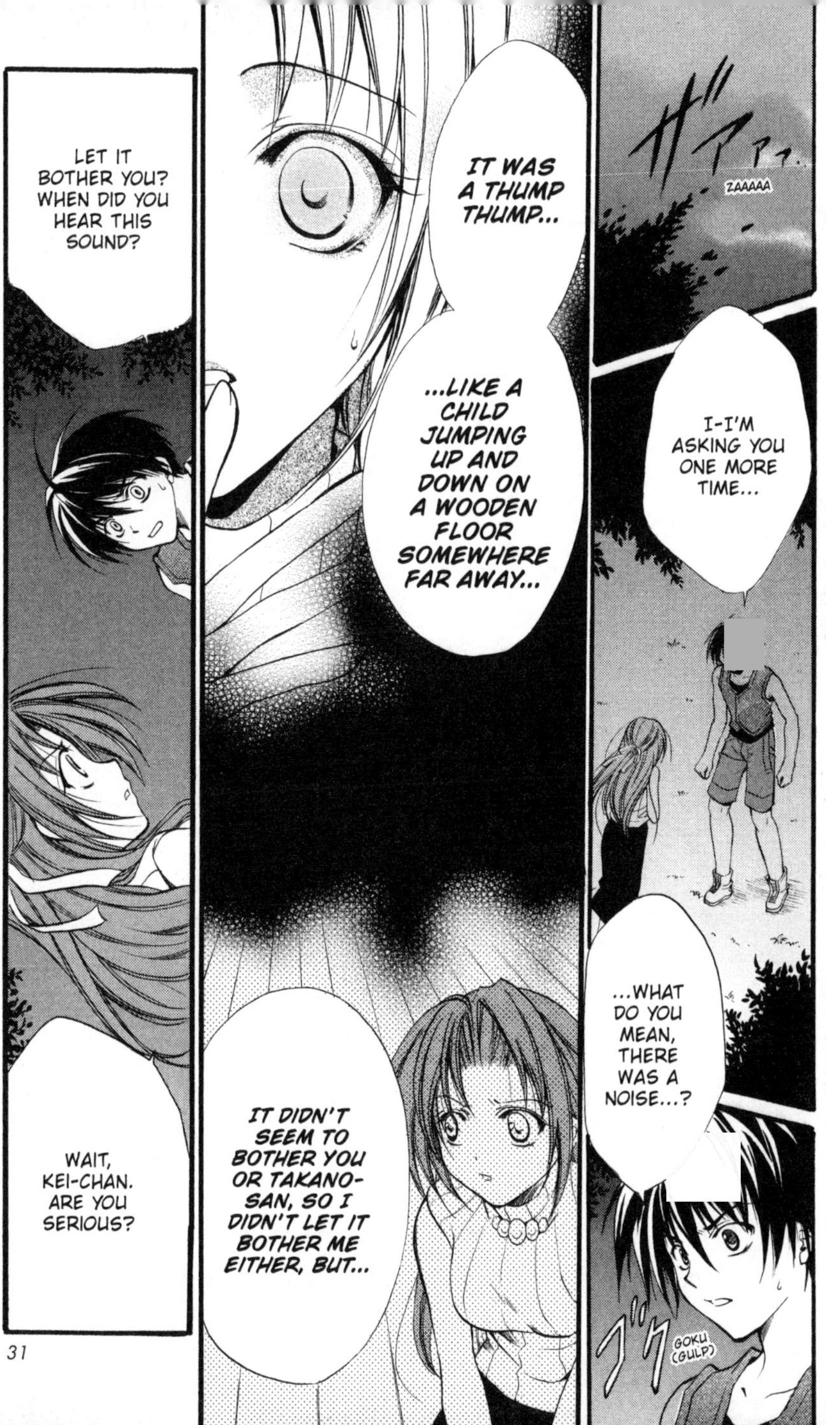
ZAAAAA
I-I'M ASKING YOU ONE MORE TIME...
...WHAT DO YOU MEAN, THERE WAS A NOISE...?
GOKU (GULP)
IT WAS A THUMP THUMP...
...LIKE A CHILD JUMPING UP AND DOWN ON A WOODEN FLOOR SOMEWHERE FAR AWAY...
IT DIDN'T SEEM TO BOTHER YOU OR TAKANO-SAN, SO I DIDN'T LET IT BOTHER ME EITHER, BUT...
LET IT BOTHER YOU? WHEN DID YOU HEAR THIS SOUND?
WAIT, KEI-CHAN. ARE YOU SERIOUS?

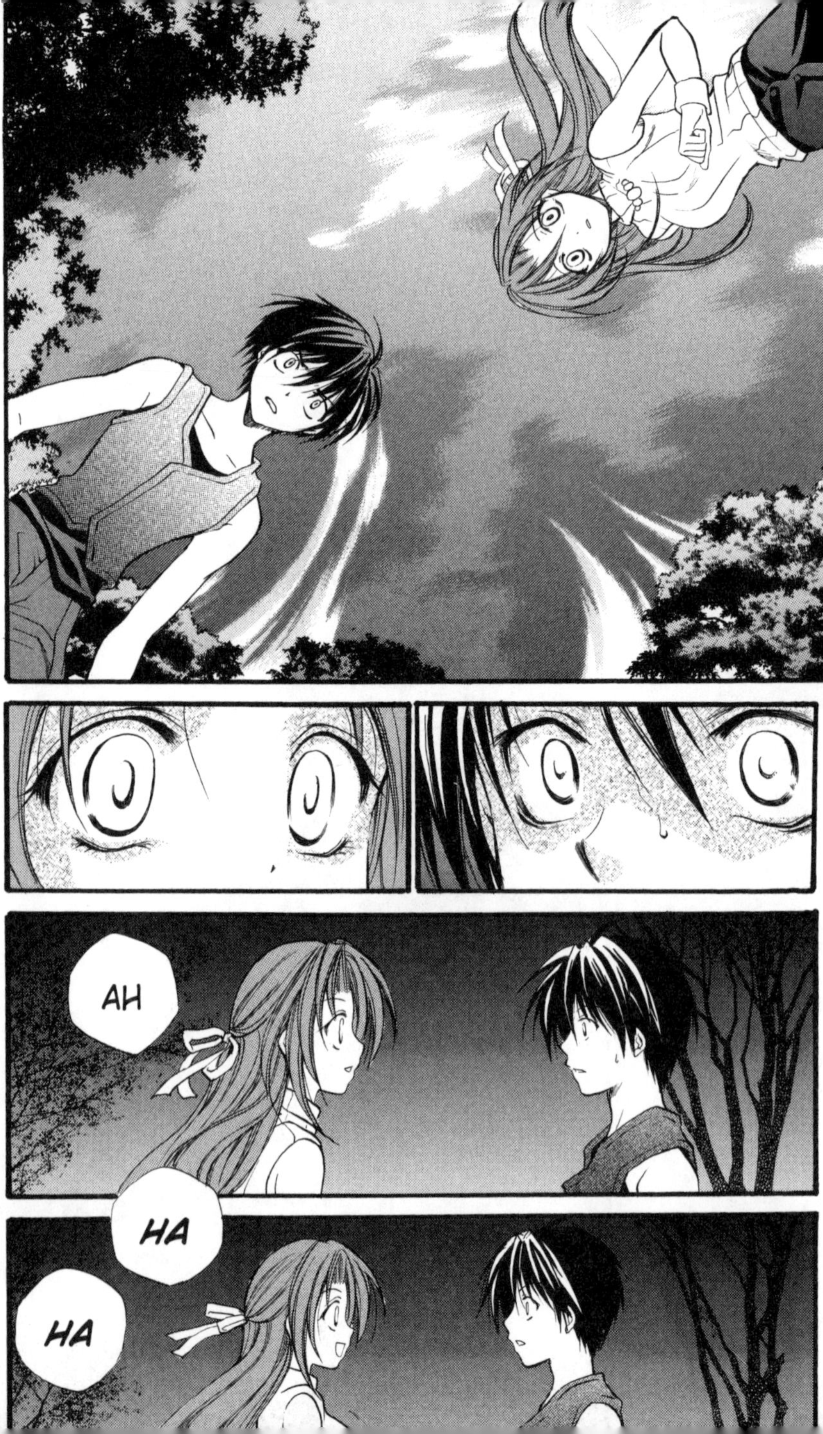
AH
HA
HA

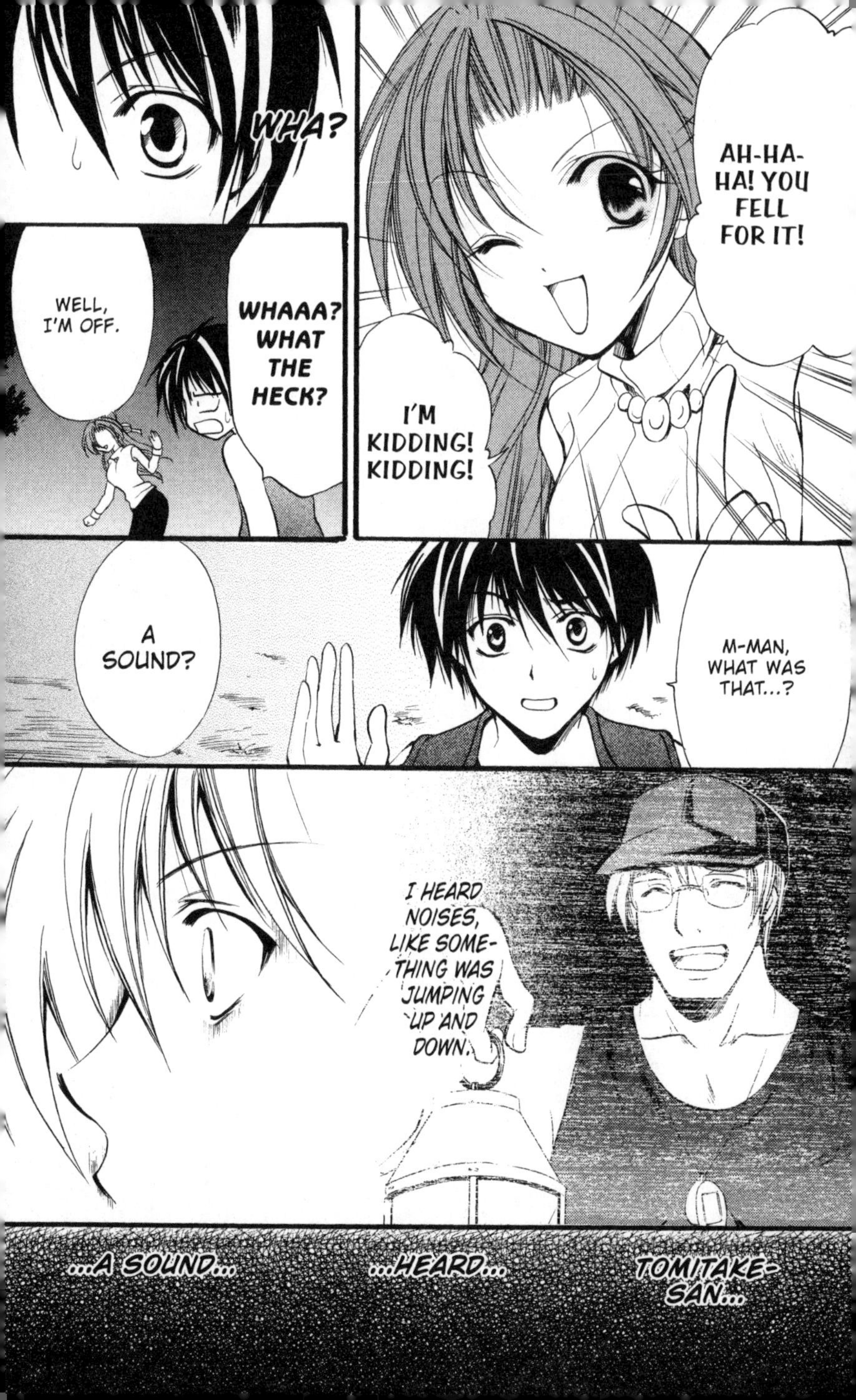
AH-HA-HA! YOU FELL FOR IT!
I'M KIDDING! KIDDING!
WHA?
WHAAA? WHAT THE HECK?
WELL, I'M OFF.
M-MAN, WHAT WAS THAT...?
A SOUND?
I HEARD NOISES, LIKE SOME-THING WAS JUMPING UP AND DOWN.
TOMITAKE-SAN...
...HEARD...
...A SOUND...

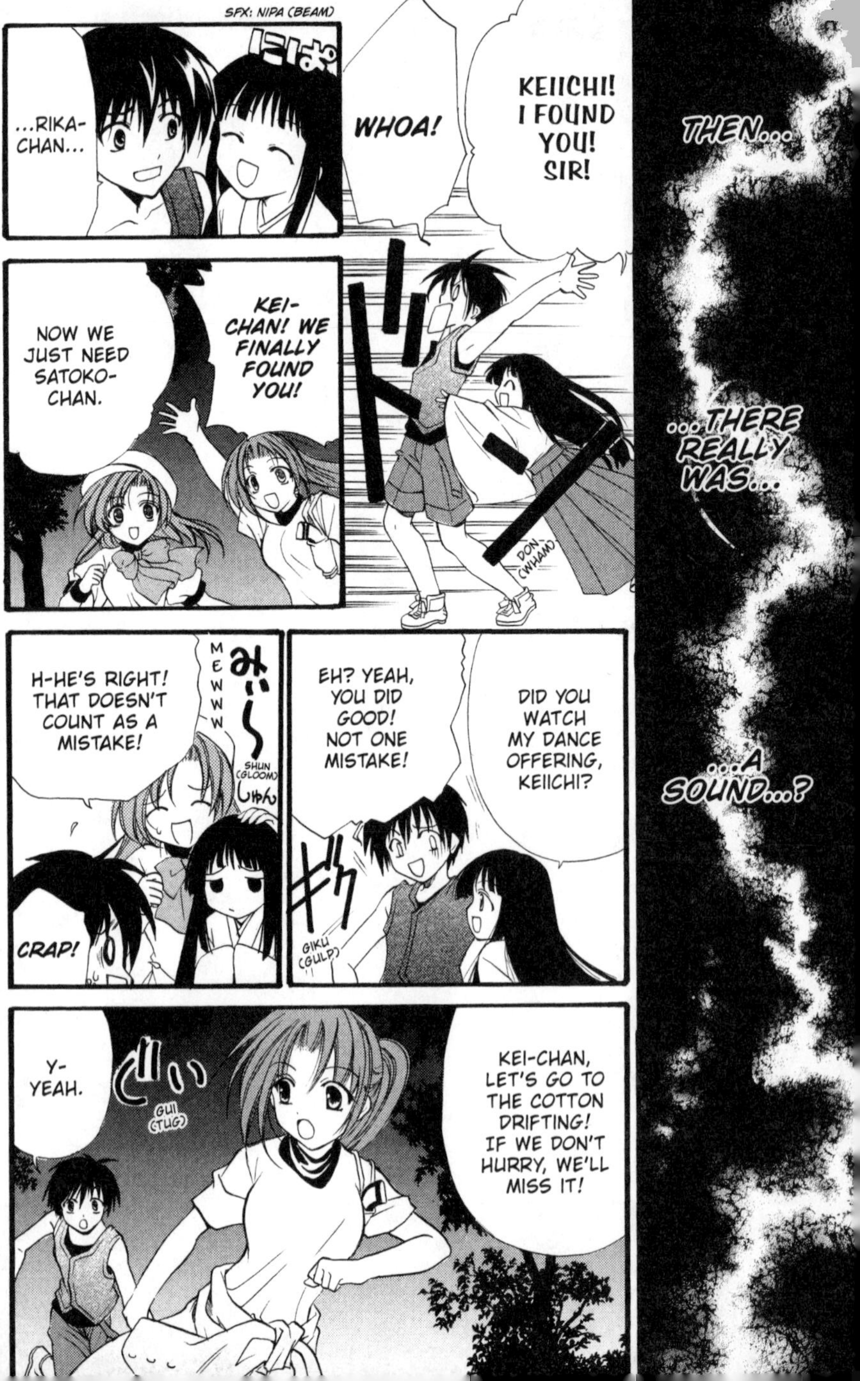
THEN...
...THERE REALLY WAS...
...A SOUND...?
KEIICHI! I FOUND YOU! SIR!
WHOA!
DON (WHAM)
SFX: NIPA (BEAM)
...RIKA-CHAN...
KEI-CHAN! WE FINALLY FOUND YOU!
NOW WE JUST NEED SATOKO-CHAN.
DID YOU WATCH MY DANCE OFFERING, KEIICHI?
EH? YEAH, YOU DID GOOD! NOT ONE MISTAKE!
GIKU (GULP)
MEWWW
SHUN (GLOOM)
H-HE'S RIGHT! THAT DOESN'T COUNT AS A MISTAKE!
CRAP!
KEI-CHAN, LET'S GO TO THE COTTON DRIFTING! IF WE DON'T HURRY, WE'LL MISS IT!
GUI (TUG)
Y-YEAH.

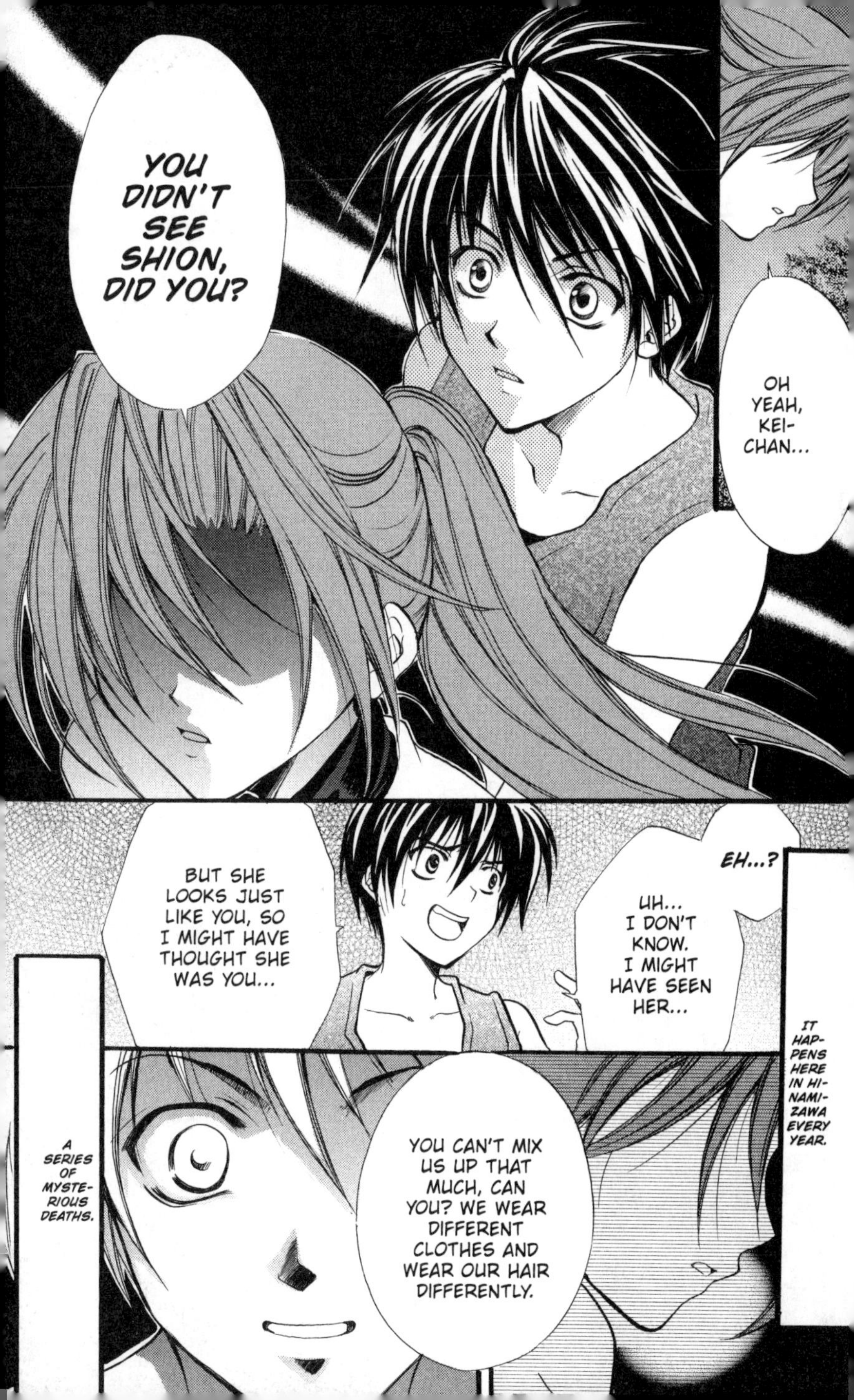
OH YEAH, KEI-CHAN...
YOU DIDN'T SEE SHION, DID YOU?
EH...?
UH... I DON'T KNOW. I MIGHT HAVE SEEN HER...
BUT SHE LOOKS JUST LIKE YOU, SO I MIGHT HAVE THOUGHT SHE WAS YOU...
IT HAPPENS HERE IN HINAMIZAWA EVERY YEAR.
YOU CAN'T MIX US UP THAT MUCH, CAN YOU? WE WEAR DIFFERENT CLOTHES AND WEAR OUR HAIR DIFFERENTLY.
A SERIES OF MYSTERIOUS DEATHS.

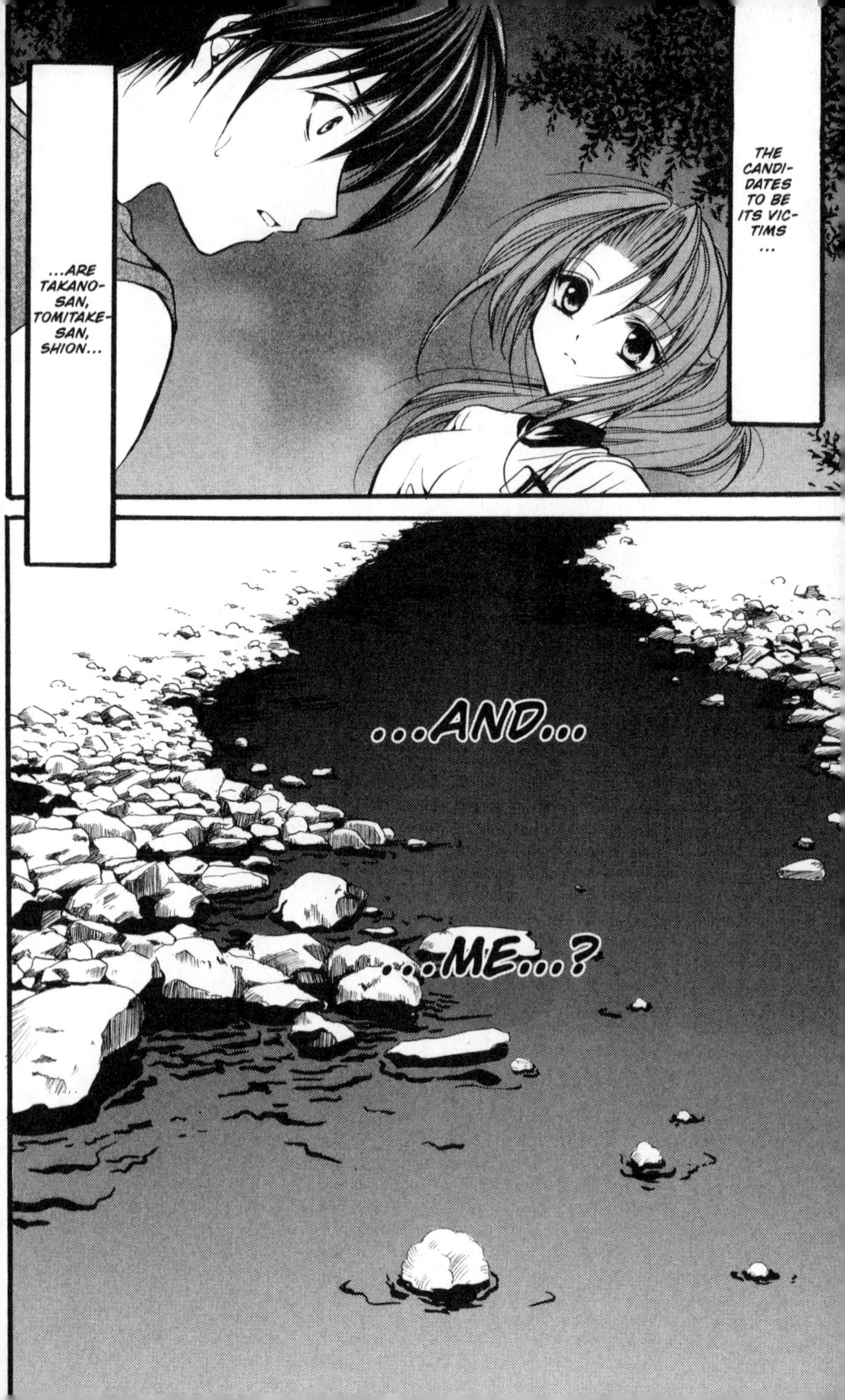
THE CANDIDATES TO BE ITS VICTIMS...
...ARE TAKANO-SAN, TOMITAKE-SAN, SHION...
...AND...
...ME...?

CHAPTER 7
THE FIFTH YEAR'S CURSE

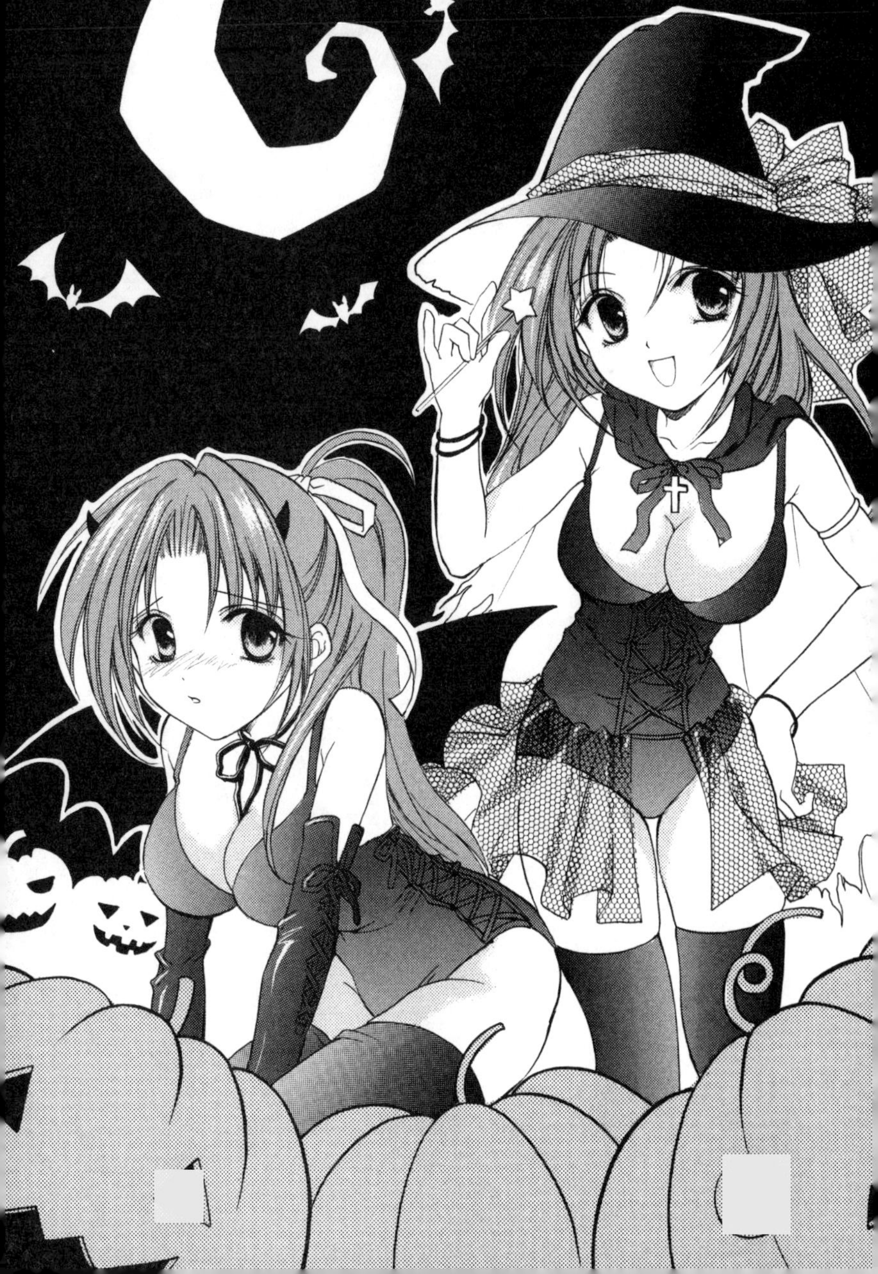

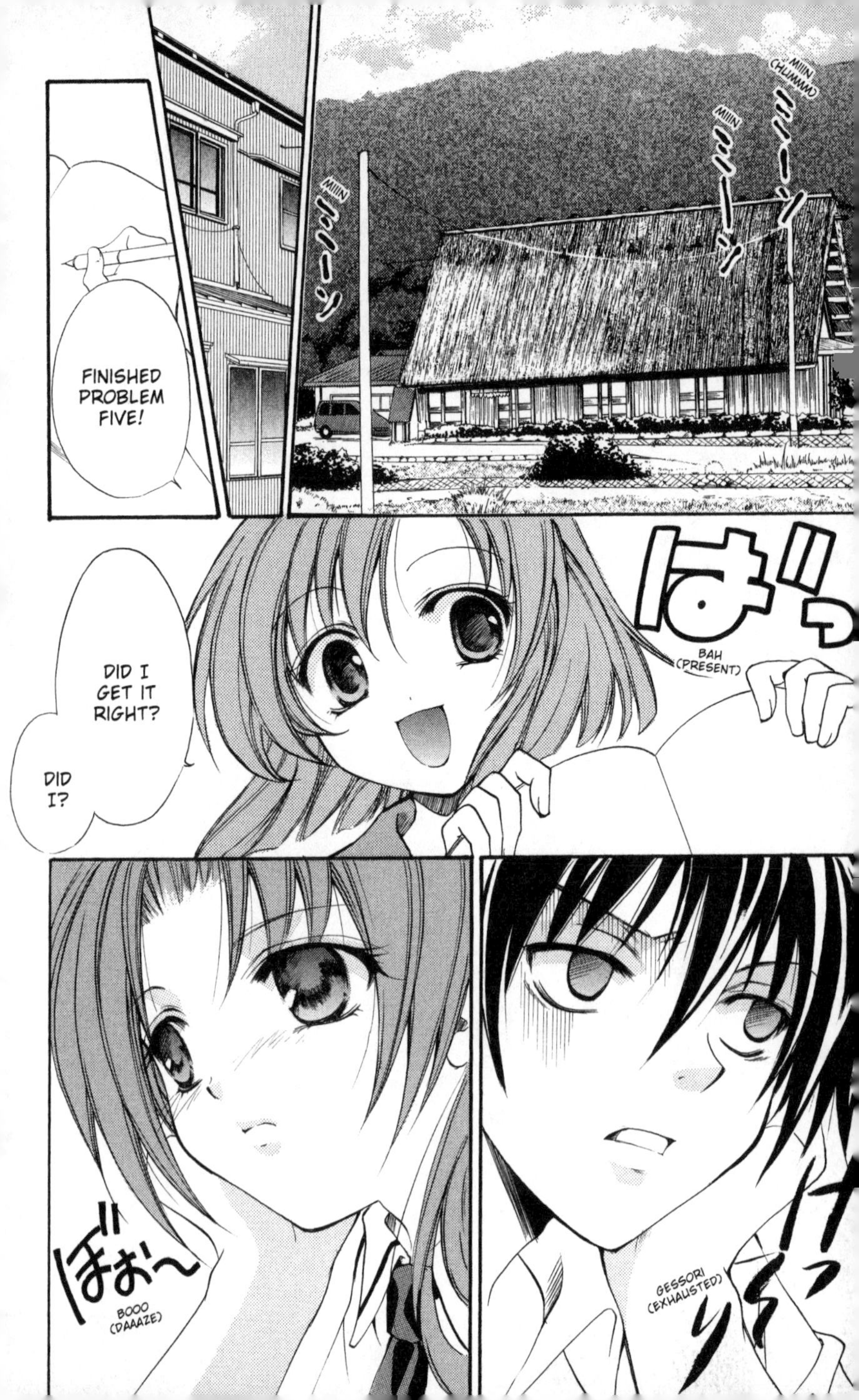
MIIN (HUMMM)
MIIN
MIIN
FINISHED PROBLEM FIVE!
BAH (PRESENT)
DID I GET IT RIGHT?
DID I?
GESSORI (EXHAUSTED)
BOOO (DAAAZE)

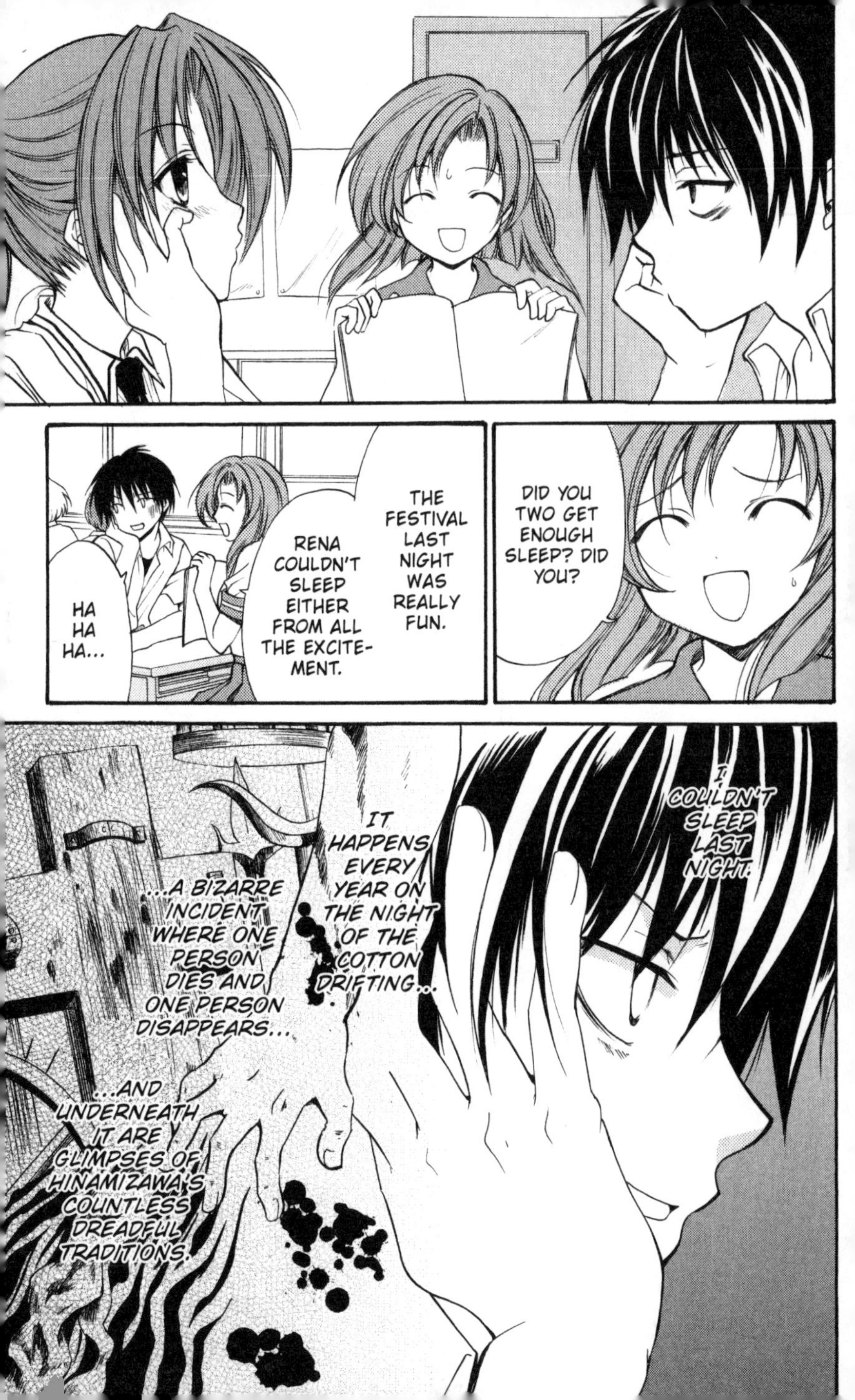
DID YOU TWO GET ENOUGH SLEEP? DID YOU?
THE FESTIVAL LAST NIGHT WAS REALLY FUN.
RENA COULDN'T SLEEP EITHER FROM ALL THE EXCITEMENT.
HA HA HA...
I COULDN'T SLEEP LAST NIGHT.
IT HAPPENS EVERY YEAR ON THE NIGHT OF THE COTTON DRIFTING...
...A BIZARRE INCIDENT WHERE ONE PERSON DIES AND ONE PERSON DISAPPEARS...
...AND UNDERNEATH IT ARE GLIMPSES OF HINAMIZAWA'S COUNTLESS DREADFUL TRADITIONS.

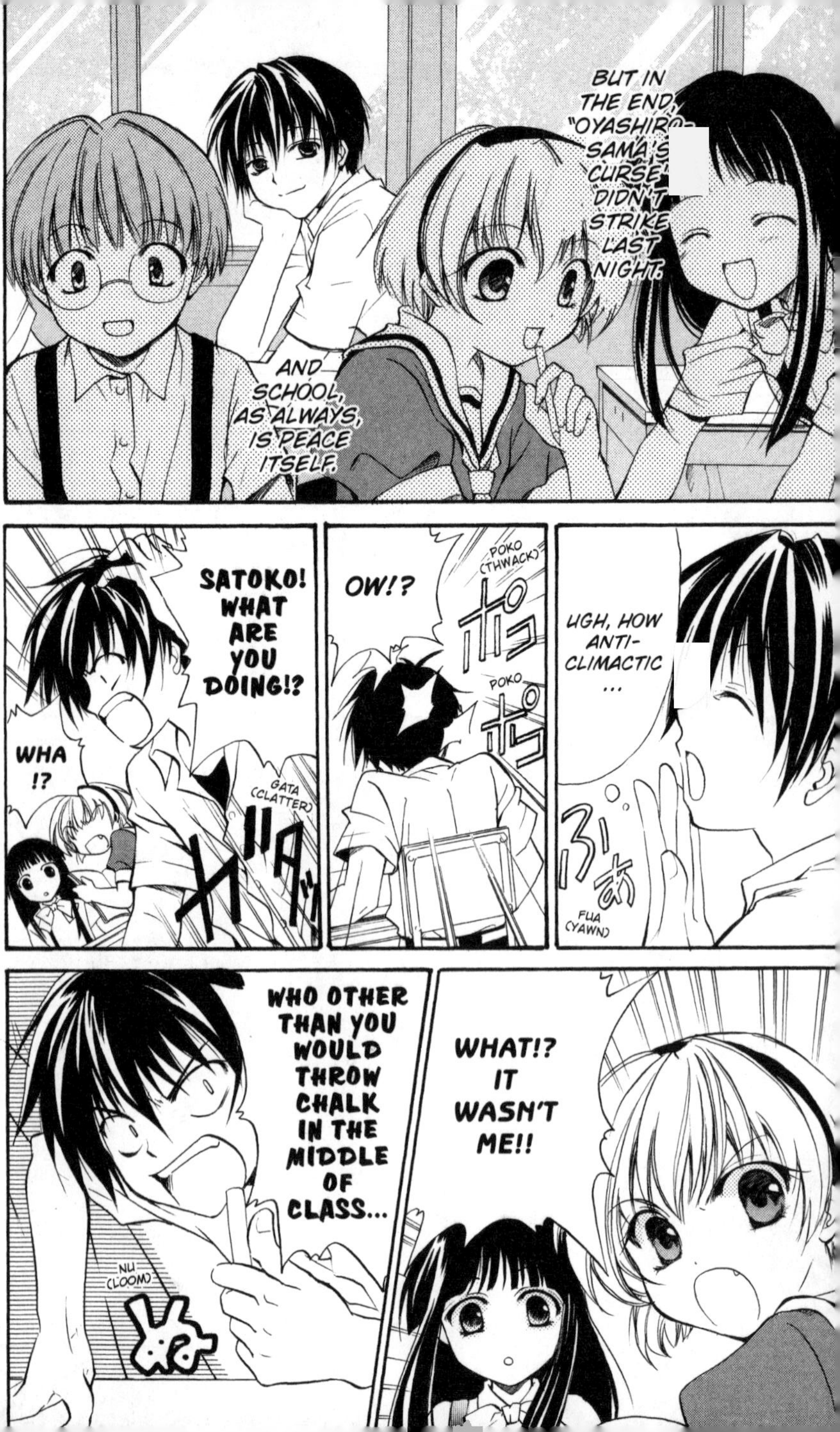
BUT IN THE END, "OYASHIRO-SAMA'S CURSE" DIDN'T STRIKE LAST NIGHT.
AND SCHOOL, AS ALWAYS, IS PEACE ITSELF.
UGH, HOW ANTI-CLIMACTIC ...
FUA (YAWN)
OW!?
POKO (THWACK)
POKO
SATOKO! WHAT ARE YOU DOING!?
WHA !?
GATA (CLATTER)
WHAT!? IT WASN'T ME!!
WHO OTHER THAN YOU WOULD THROW CHALK IN THE MIDDLE OF CLASS...
NU (LOOM)

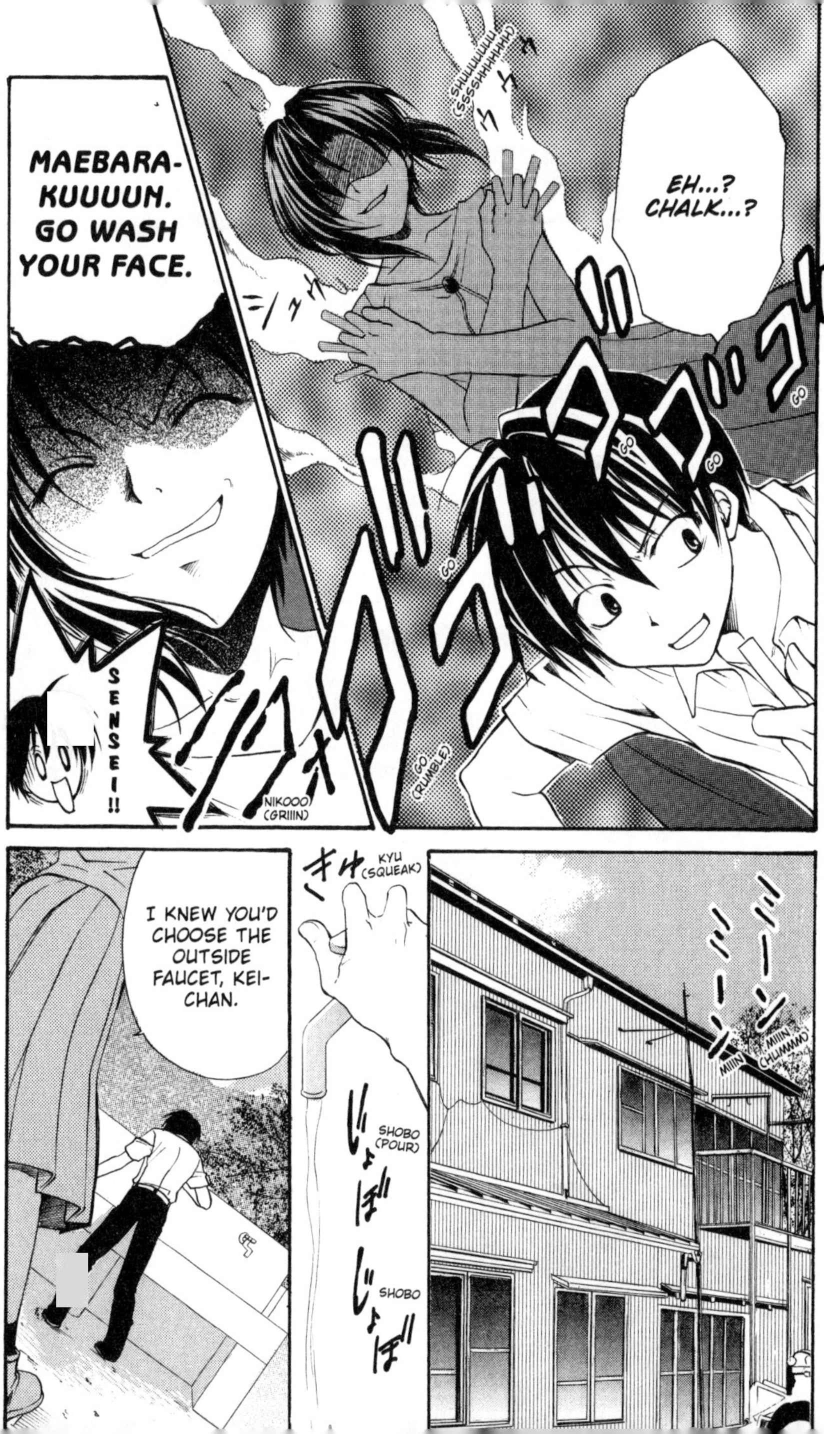
SHUUUUUUUU (SSSSHHHHHHH)
EH...? CHALK...?
GO
GO
GO
GO (RUMBLE)
MAEBARA-KUUUUN. GO WASH YOUR FACE.
NIKOOO (GRIIIN)
SENSEI!!
MIIN
MIIN (HUMMMM)
KYU (SQUEAK)
SHOBO (POUR)
SHOBO
I KNEW YOU'D CHOOSE THE OUTSIDE FAUCET, KEI-CHAN.

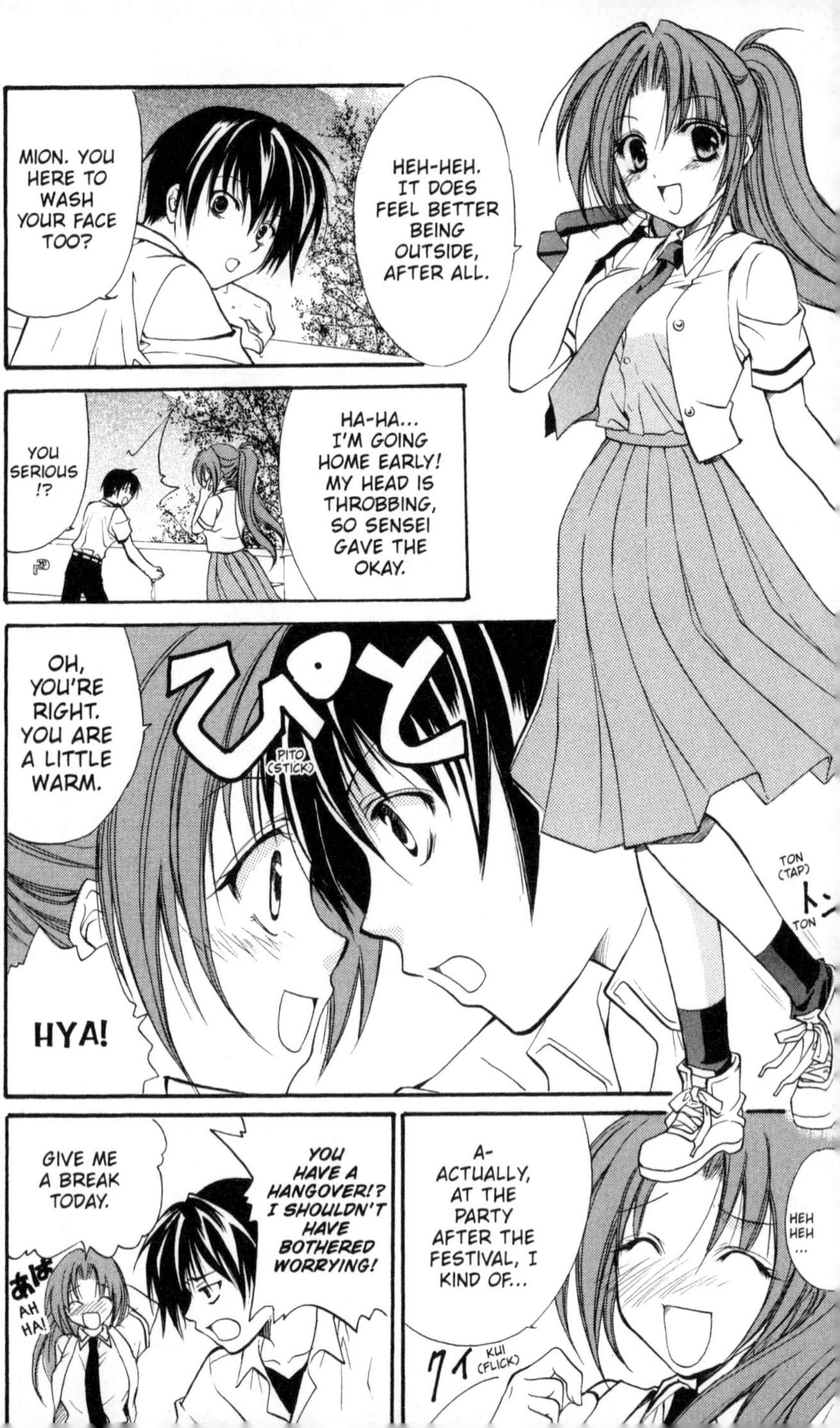
TON (TAP)
トン
TON
MION. YOU HERE TO WASH YOUR FACE TOO?
HEH-HEH. IT DOES FEEL BETTER BEING OUTSIDE, AFTER ALL.
HA-HA... I'M GOING HOME EARLY! MY HEAD IS THROBBING, SO SENSEI GAVE THE OKAY.
YOU SERIOUS !?
ぴと
PITO (STICK)
OH, YOU'RE RIGHT. YOU ARE A LITTLE WARM.
HYA!
HEH HEH ...
A-ACTUALLY, AT THE PARTY AFTER THE FESTIVAL, I KIND OF...
クイ
KUI (FLICK)
YOU HAVE A HANGOVER!? I SHOULDN'T HAVE BOTHERED WORRYING!
GIVE ME A BREAK TODAY.
あは
AH HA!

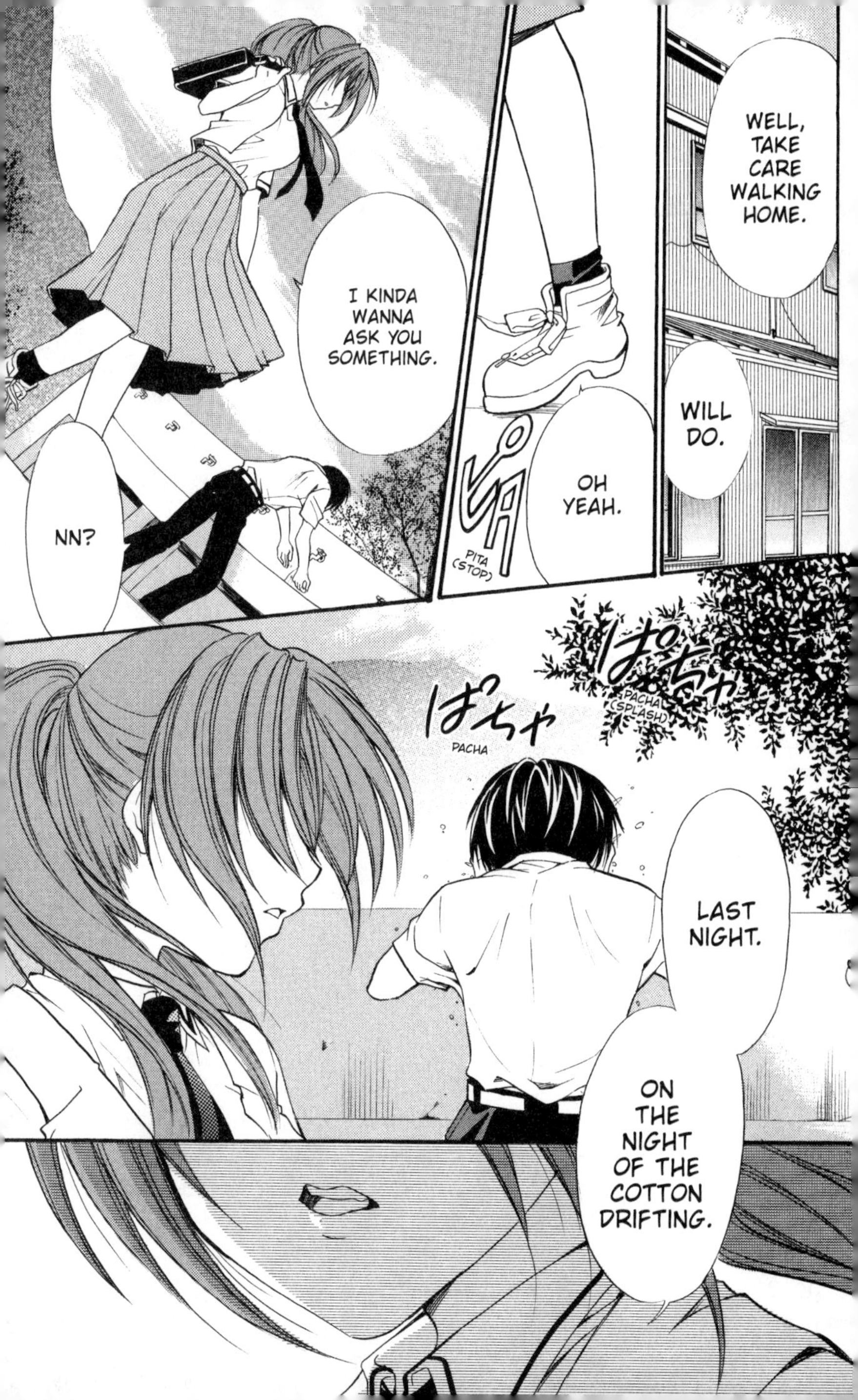
WELL, TAKE CARE WALKING HOME.
WILL DO.
PITA (STOP)
OH YEAH.
I KINDA WANNA ASK YOU SOMETHING.
NN?
ぱちゃ
PACHA (SPLASH)
ぱちゃ
PACHA
LAST NIGHT.
ON THE NIGHT OF THE COTTON DRIFTING.

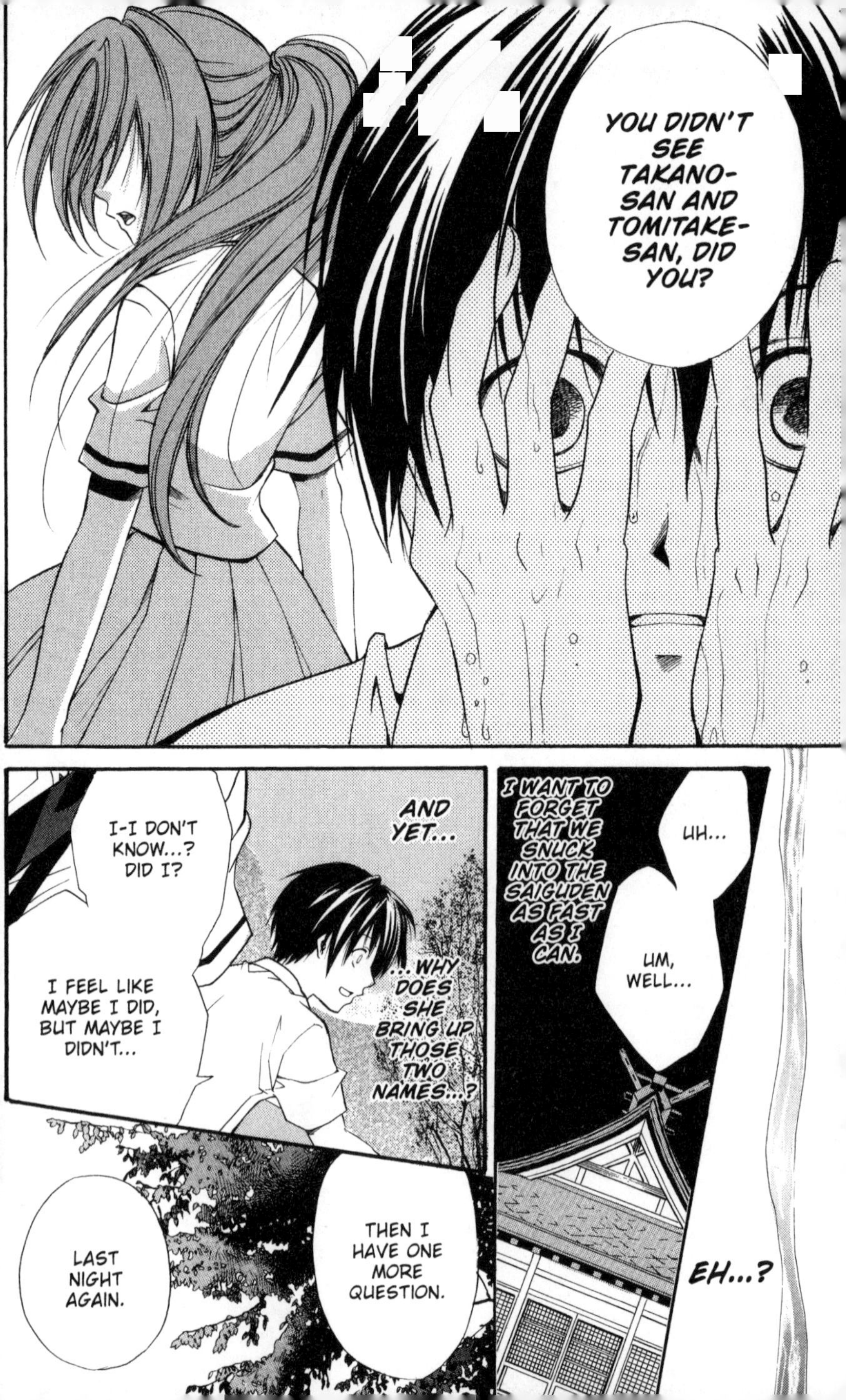
YOU DIDN'T SEE TAKANO-SAN AND TOMITAKE-SAN, DID YOU?
UH...
I WANT TO FORGET THAT WE SNUCK INTO THE SAIGUDEN AS FAST AS I CAN.
UM, WELL...
EH...?
AND YET...
I-I DON'T KNOW...? DID I?
...WHY DOES SHE BRING UP THOSE TWO NAMES...?
I FEEL LIKE MAYBE I DID, BUT MAYBE I DIDN'T...
THEN I HAVE ONE MORE QUESTION.
LAST NIGHT AGAIN.

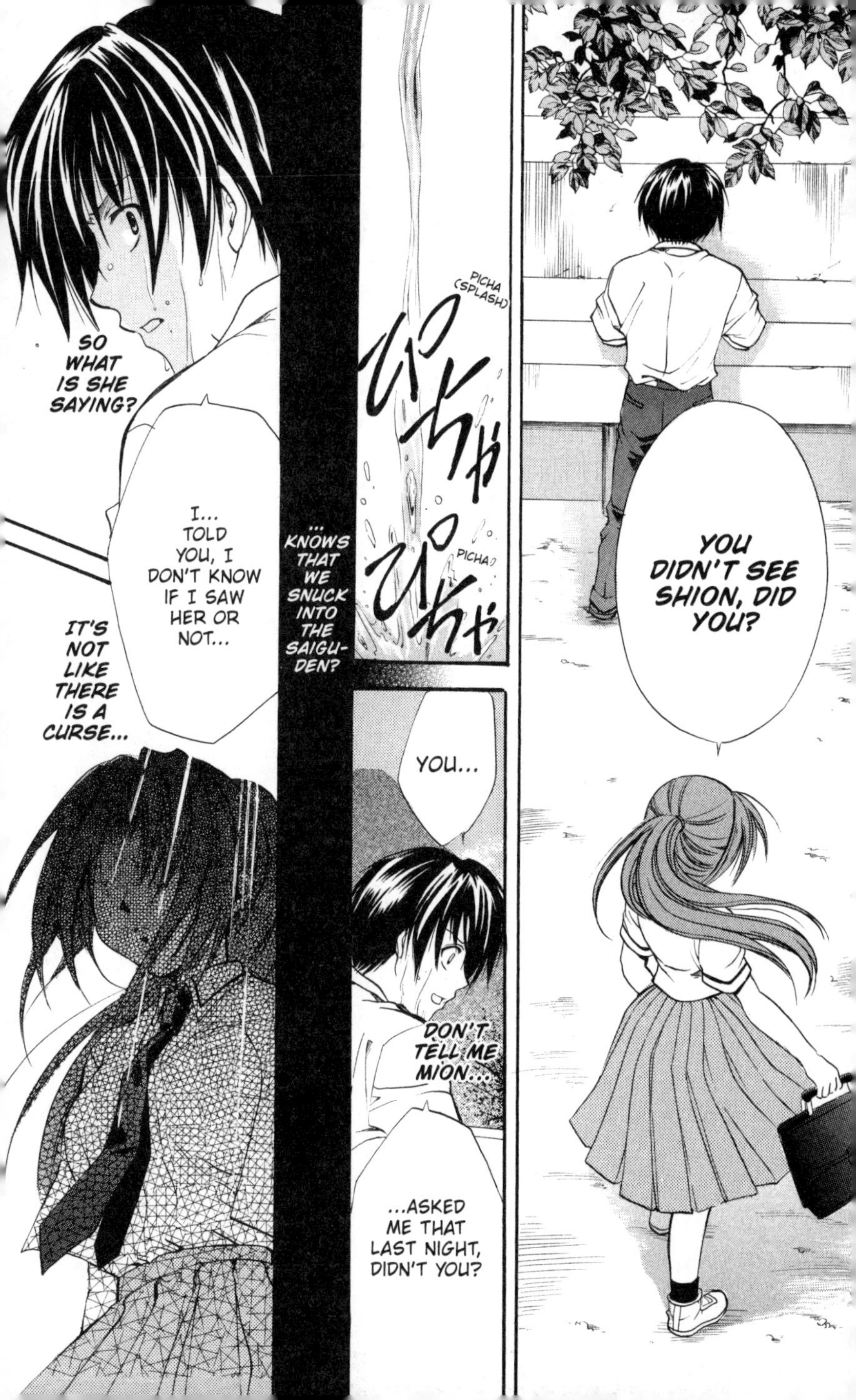
YOU DIDN'T SEE SHION, DID YOU?
PICHA (SPLASH)
PICHA
YOU...
DON'T TELL ME MION...
...KNOWS THAT WE SNUCK INTO THE SAIGUDEN?
...ASKED ME THAT LAST NIGHT, DIDN'T YOU?
SO WHAT IS SHE SAYING?
I... TOLD YOU, I DON'T KNOW IF I SAW HER OR NOT...
IT'S NOT LIKE THERE IS A CURSE...

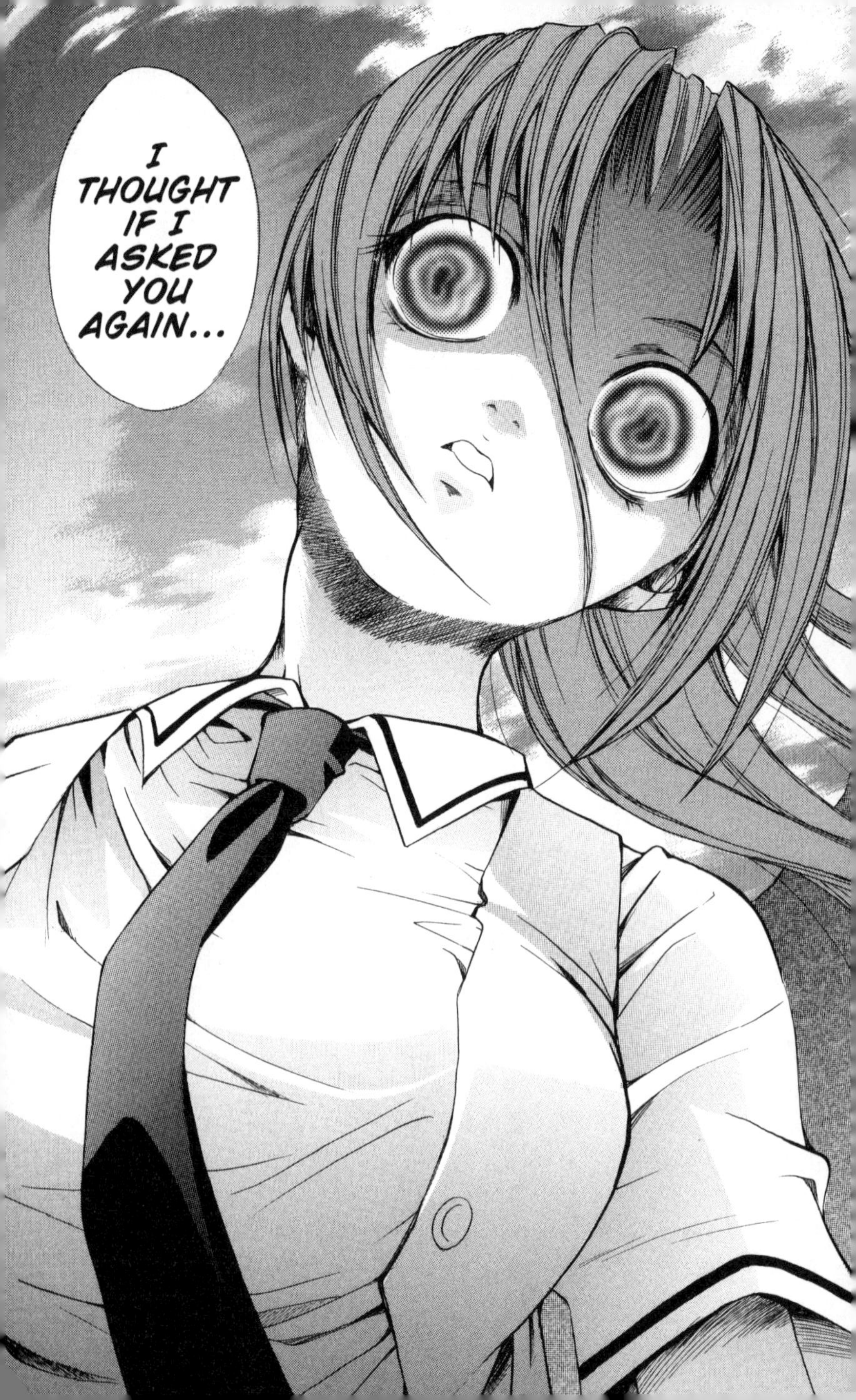
I THOUGHT IF I ASKED YOU AGAIN...

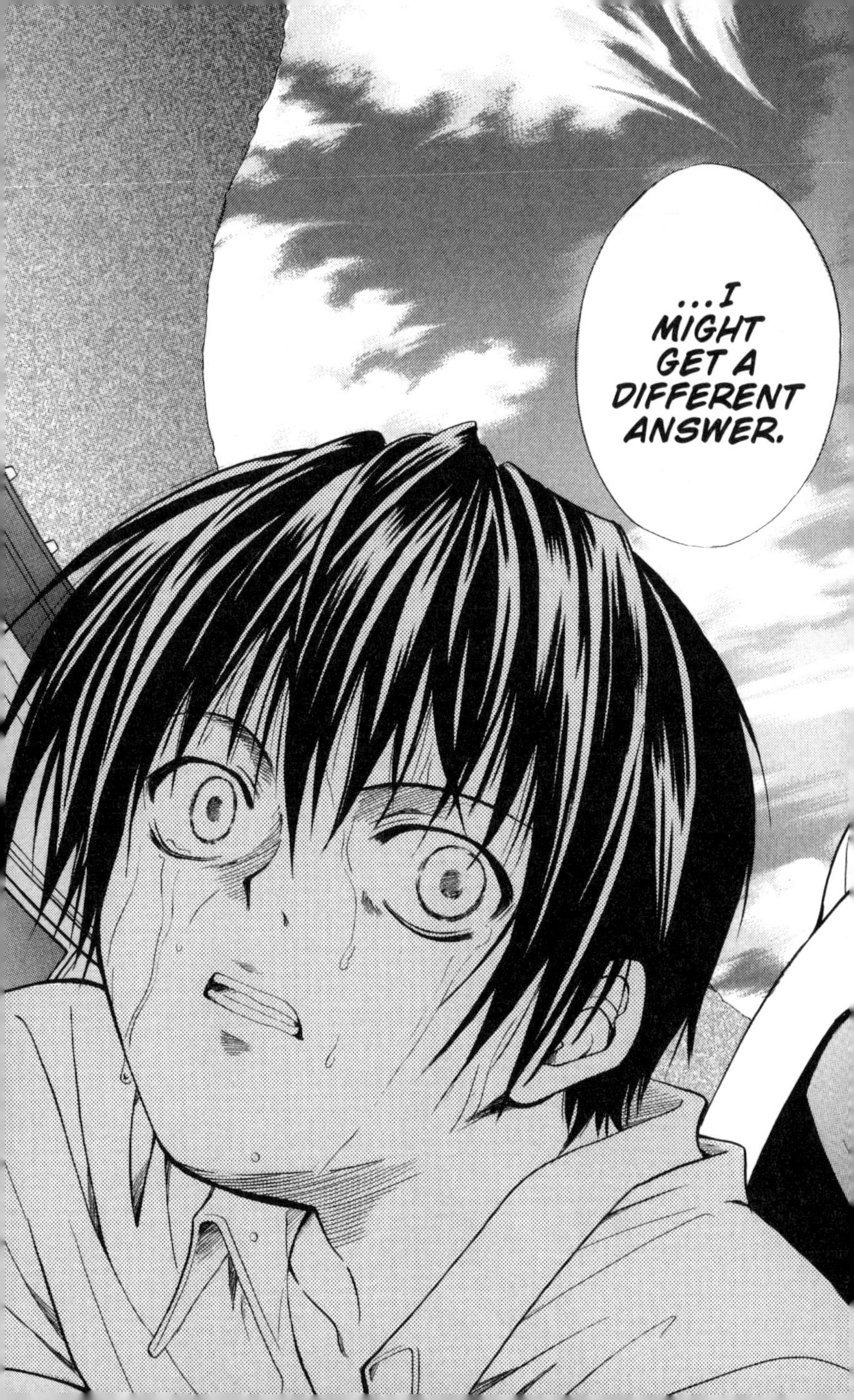
...I MIGHT GET A DIFFERENT ANSWER.

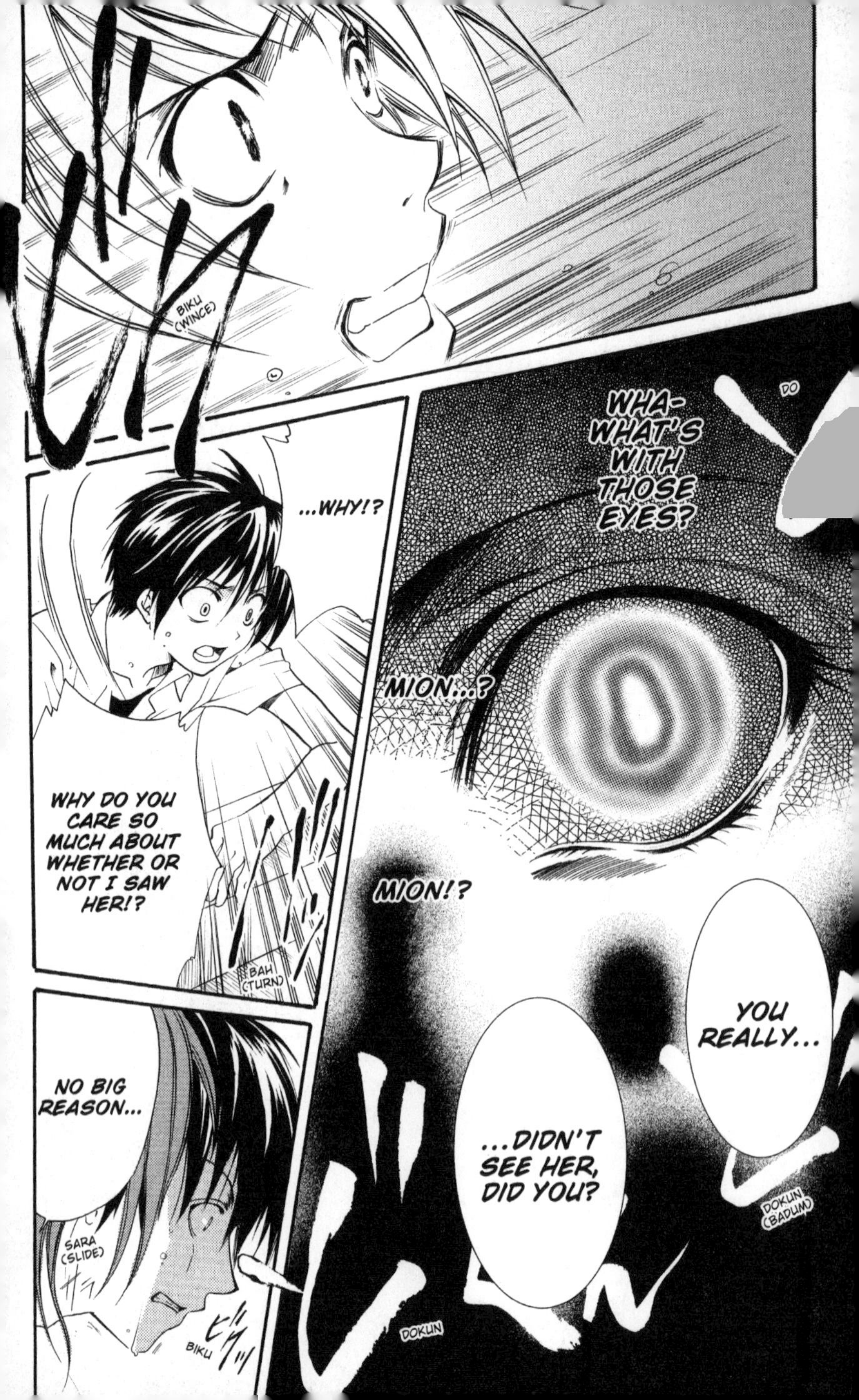
BIKU (WINCE)
DO
WHA-WHAT'S WITH THOSE EYES?
MION...?
MION!?
YOU REALLY...
...DIDN'T SEE HER, DID YOU?
DOKUN (BADUM)
DOKUN
...WHY!?
WHY DO YOU CARE SO MUCH ABOUT WHETHER OR NOT I SAW HER!?
BAH (TURN)
NO BIG REASON...
SARA (SLIDE)
BIKU

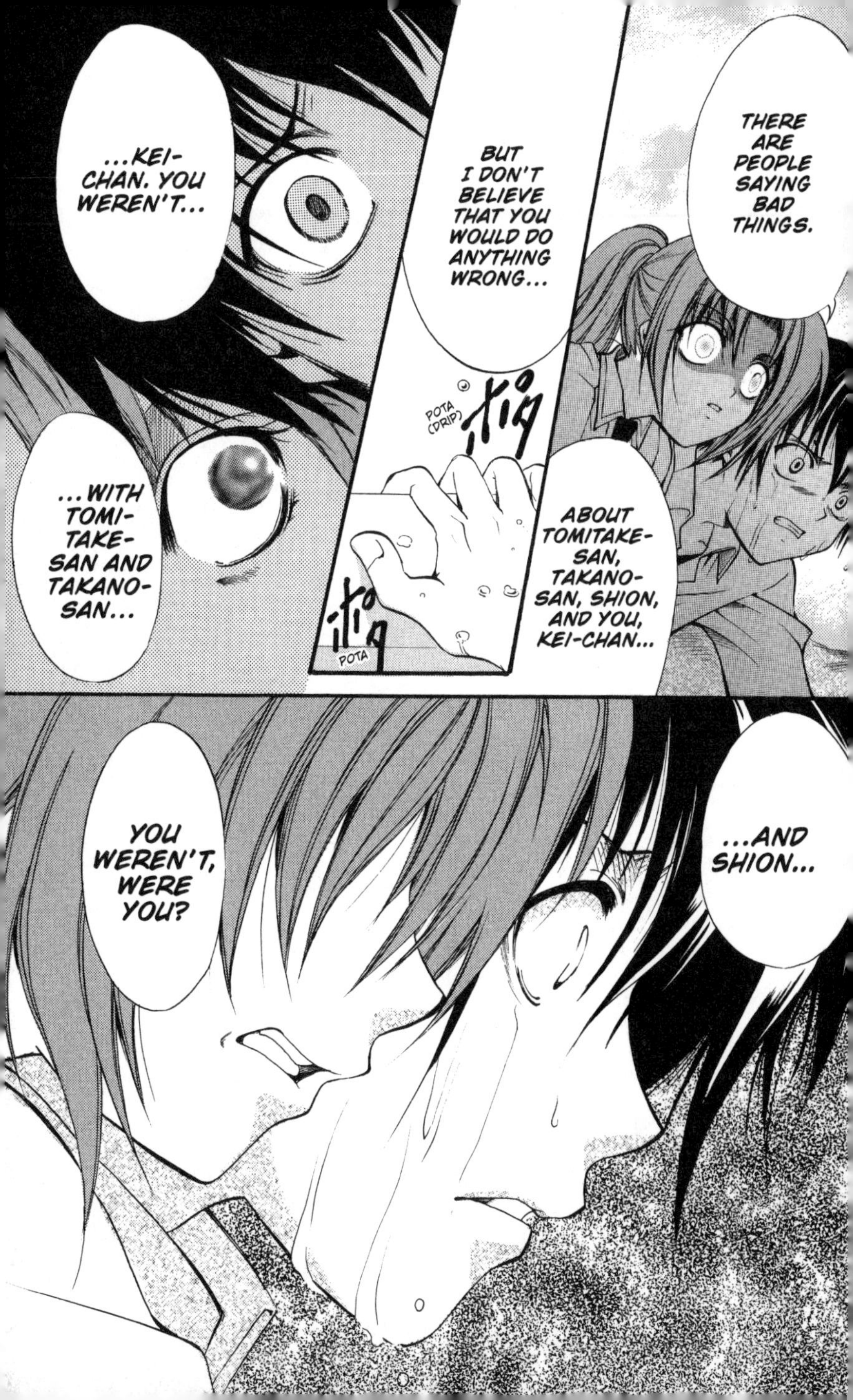
THERE ARE PEOPLE SAYING BAD THINGS.
ABOUT TOMITAKE-SAN, TAKANO-SAN, SHION, AND YOU, KEI-CHAN...
BUT I DON'T BELIEVE THAT YOU WOULD DO ANYTHING WRONG...
POTA (DRIP)
POTA
...KEI-CHAN. YOU WEREN'T...
...WITH TOMI-TAKE-SAN AND TAKANO-SAN...
...AND SHION...
YOU WEREN'T, WERE YOU?

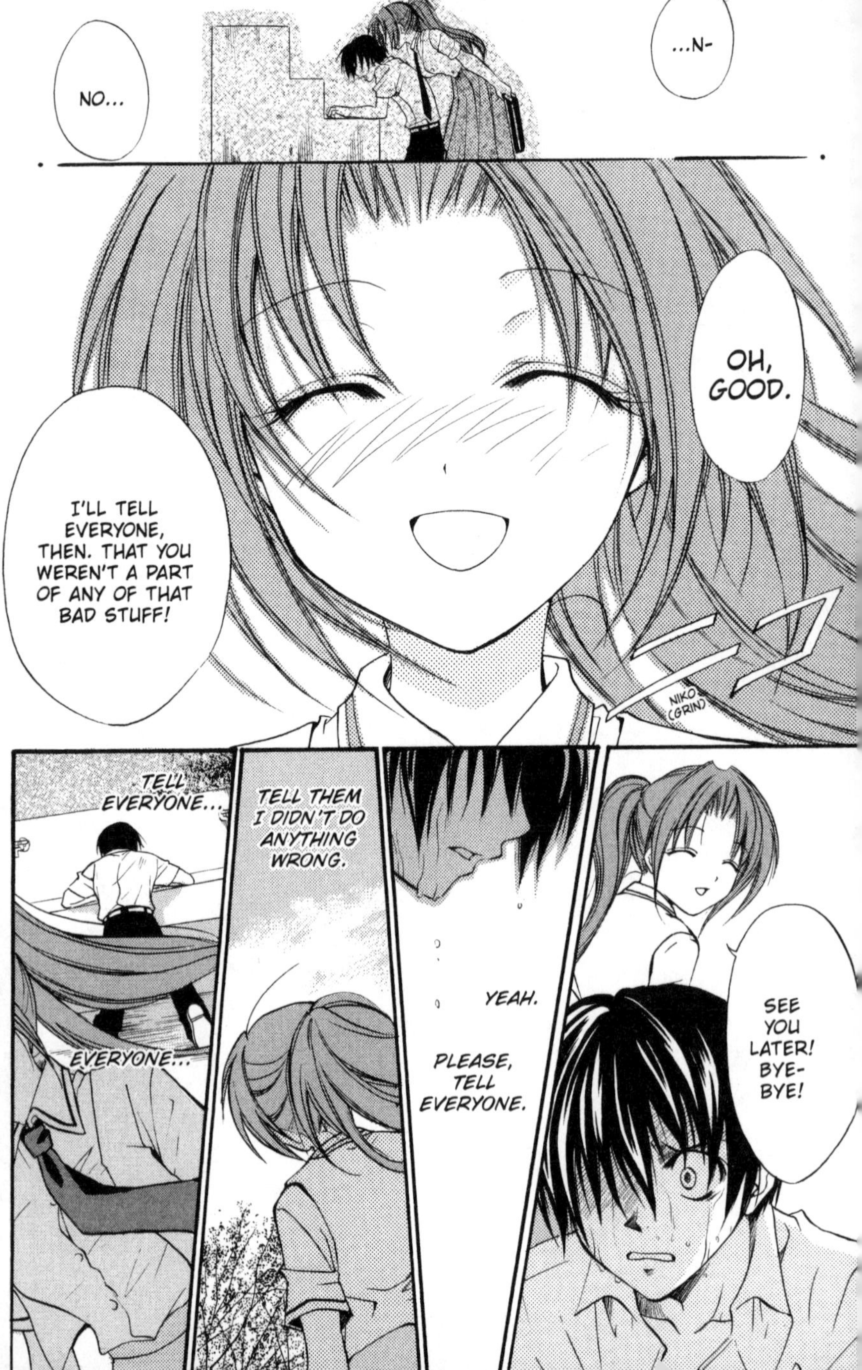
...N-
NO...
OH, GOOD.
I'LL TELL EVERYONE, THEN. THAT YOU WEREN'T A PART OF ANY OF THAT BAD STUFF!
NIKO (GRIN)
SEE YOU LATER! BYE-BYE!
YEAH.
PLEASE, TELL EVERYONE.
TELL THEM I DIDN'T DO ANYTHING WRONG.
TELL EVERYONE...
EVERYONE...

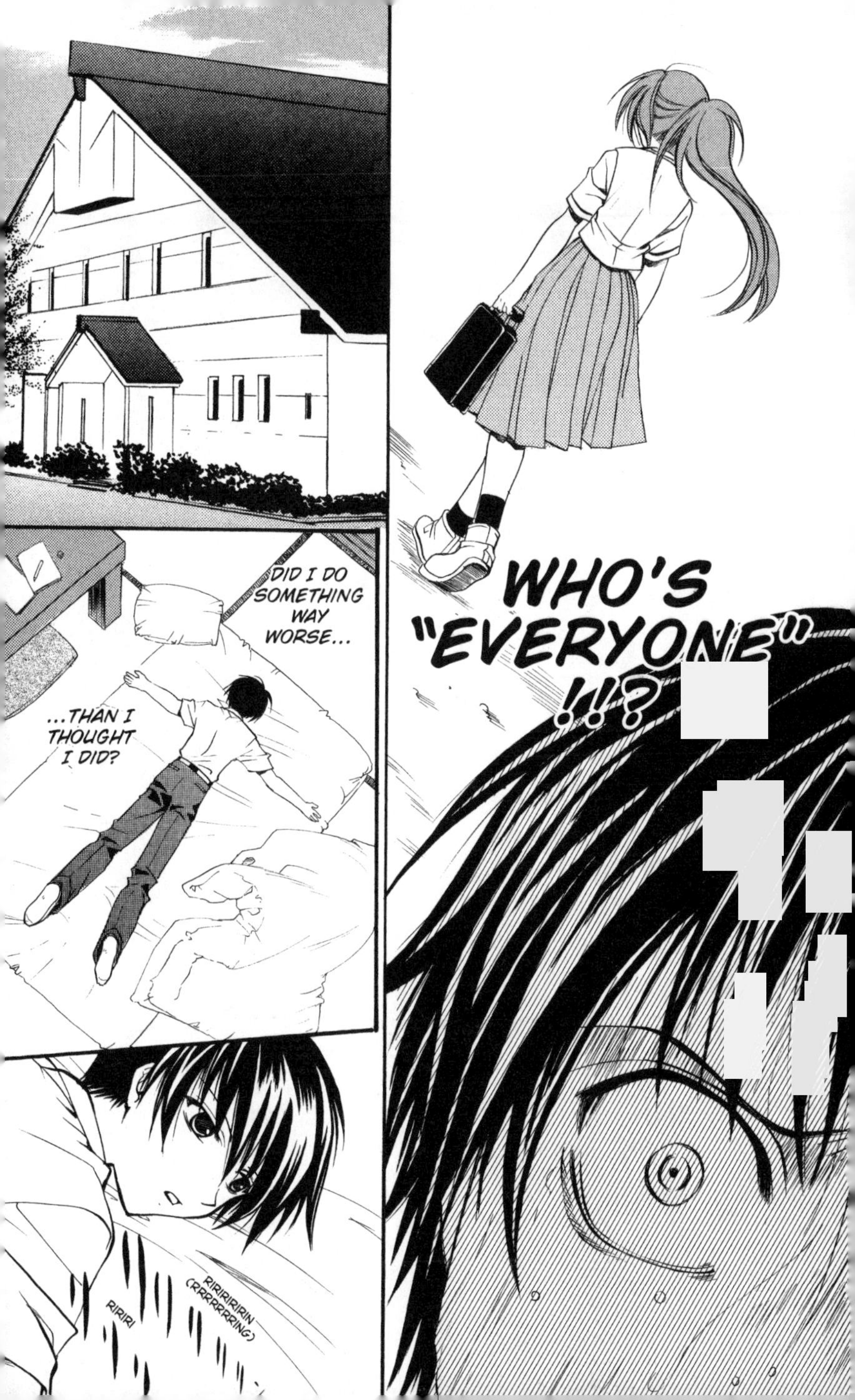
WHO'S "EVERYONE"!!?
DID I DO SOMETHING WAY WORSE...
...THAN I THOUGHT I DID?
RIRIRIRIRIN (RRRRRRRING)
RIRIRI

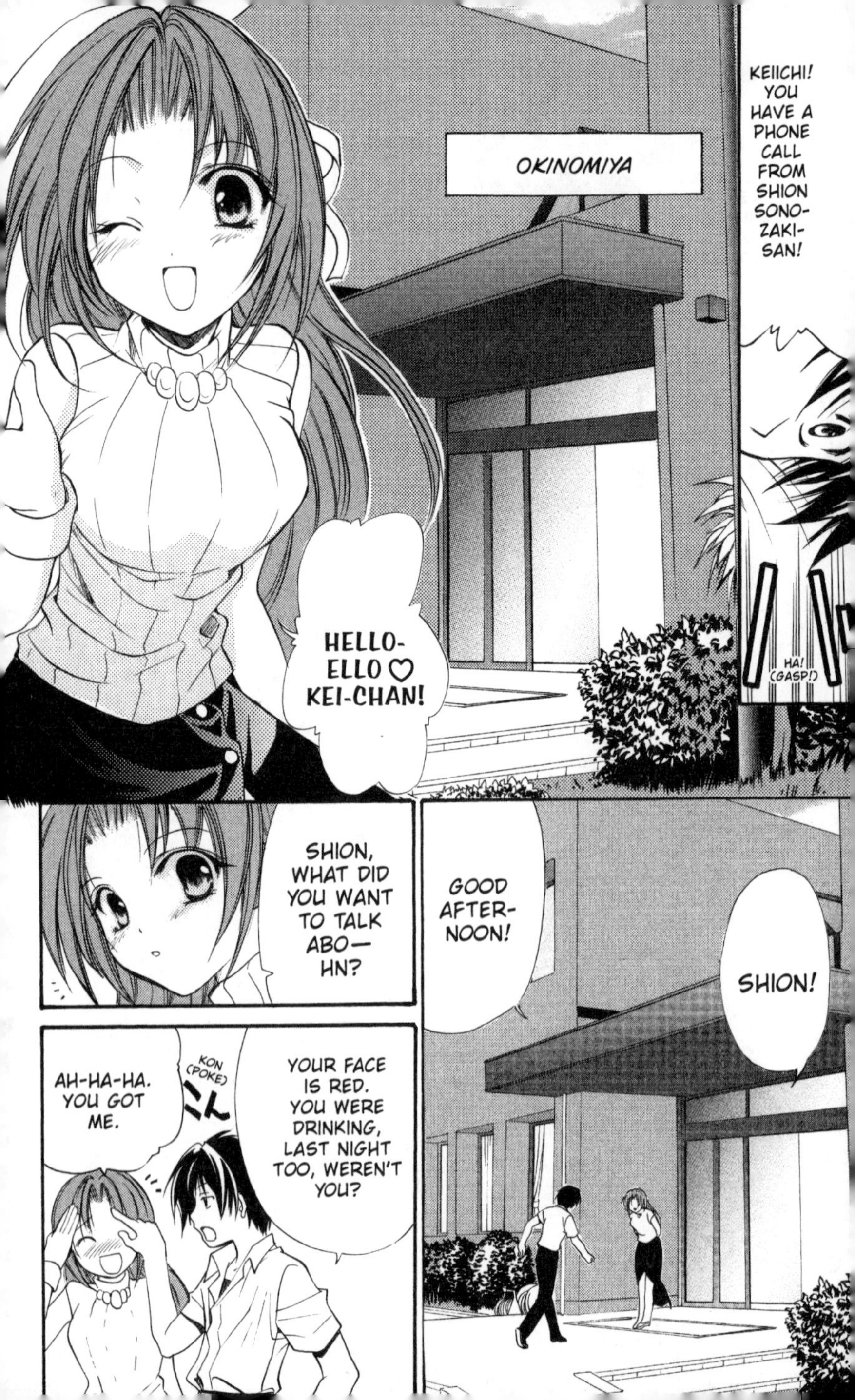
KEIICHI! YOU HAVE A PHONE CALL FROM SHION SONOZAKI-SAN!
HA! (GASP!)
OKINOMIYA
HELLO-ELLO ♡ KEI-CHAN!
SHION!
GOOD AFTERNOON!
SHION, WHAT DID YOU WANT TO TALK ABO—HN?
YOUR FACE IS RED. YOU WERE DRINKING, LAST NIGHT TOO, WEREN'T YOU?
KON (POKE)
こん
AH-HA-HA. YOU GOT ME.

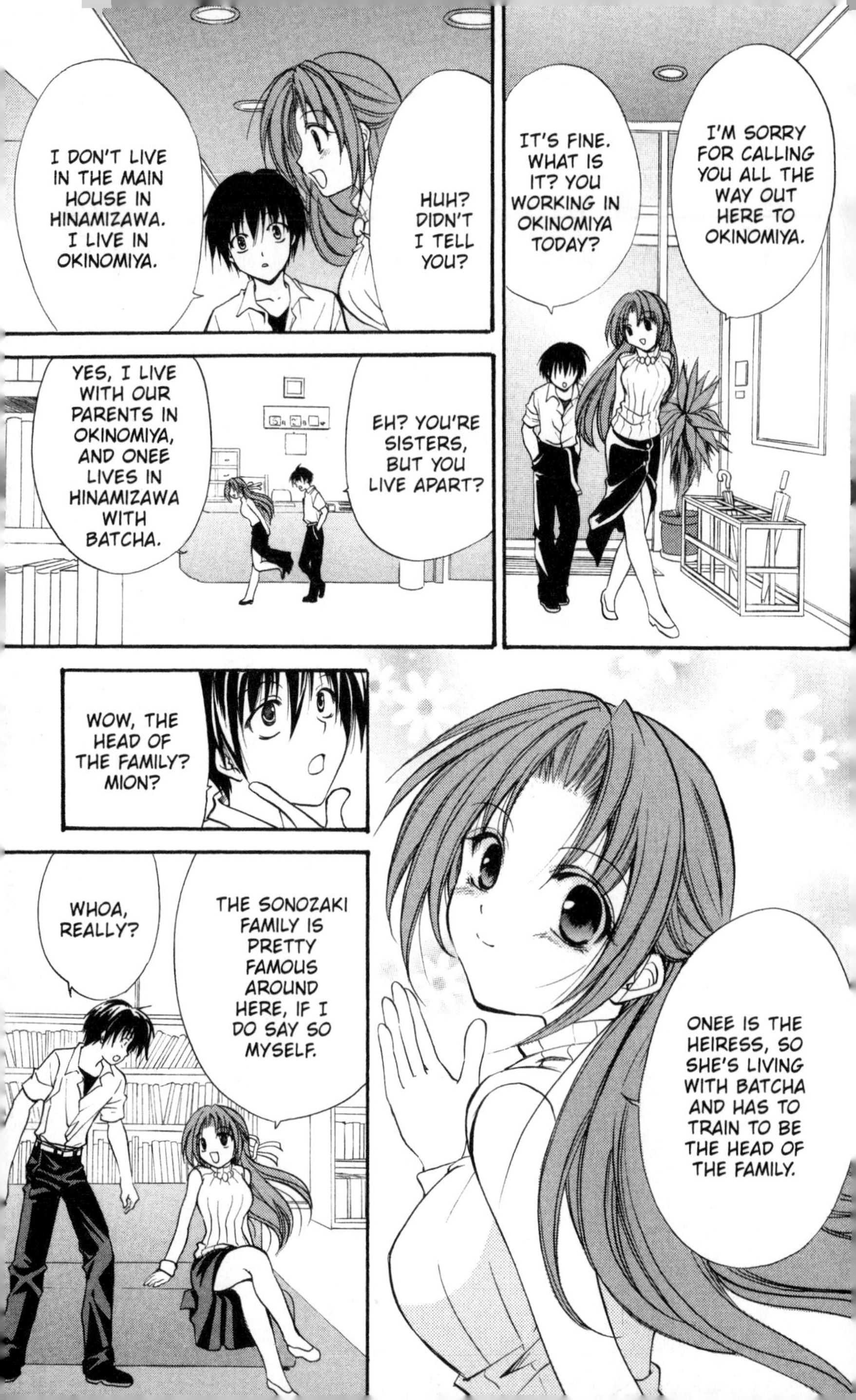
I'M SORRY FOR CALLING YOU ALL THE WAY OUT HERE TO OKINOMIYA.
IT'S FINE. WHAT IS IT? YOU WORKING IN OKINOMIYA TODAY?
HUH? DIDN'T I TELL YOU?
I DON'T LIVE IN THE MAIN HOUSE IN HINAMIZAWA. I LIVE IN OKINOMIYA.
EH? YOU'RE SISTERS, BUT YOU LIVE APART?
YES, I LIVE WITH OUR PARENTS IN OKINOMIYA, AND ONEE LIVES IN HINAMIZAWA WITH BATCHA.
ONEE IS THE HEIRESS, SO SHE'S LIVING WITH BATCHA AND HAS TO TRAIN TO BE THE HEAD OF THE FAMILY.
WOW, THE HEAD OF THE FAMILY? MION?
THE SONOZAKI FAMILY IS PRETTY FAMOUS AROUND HERE, IF I DO SAY SO MYSELF.
WHOA, REALLY?

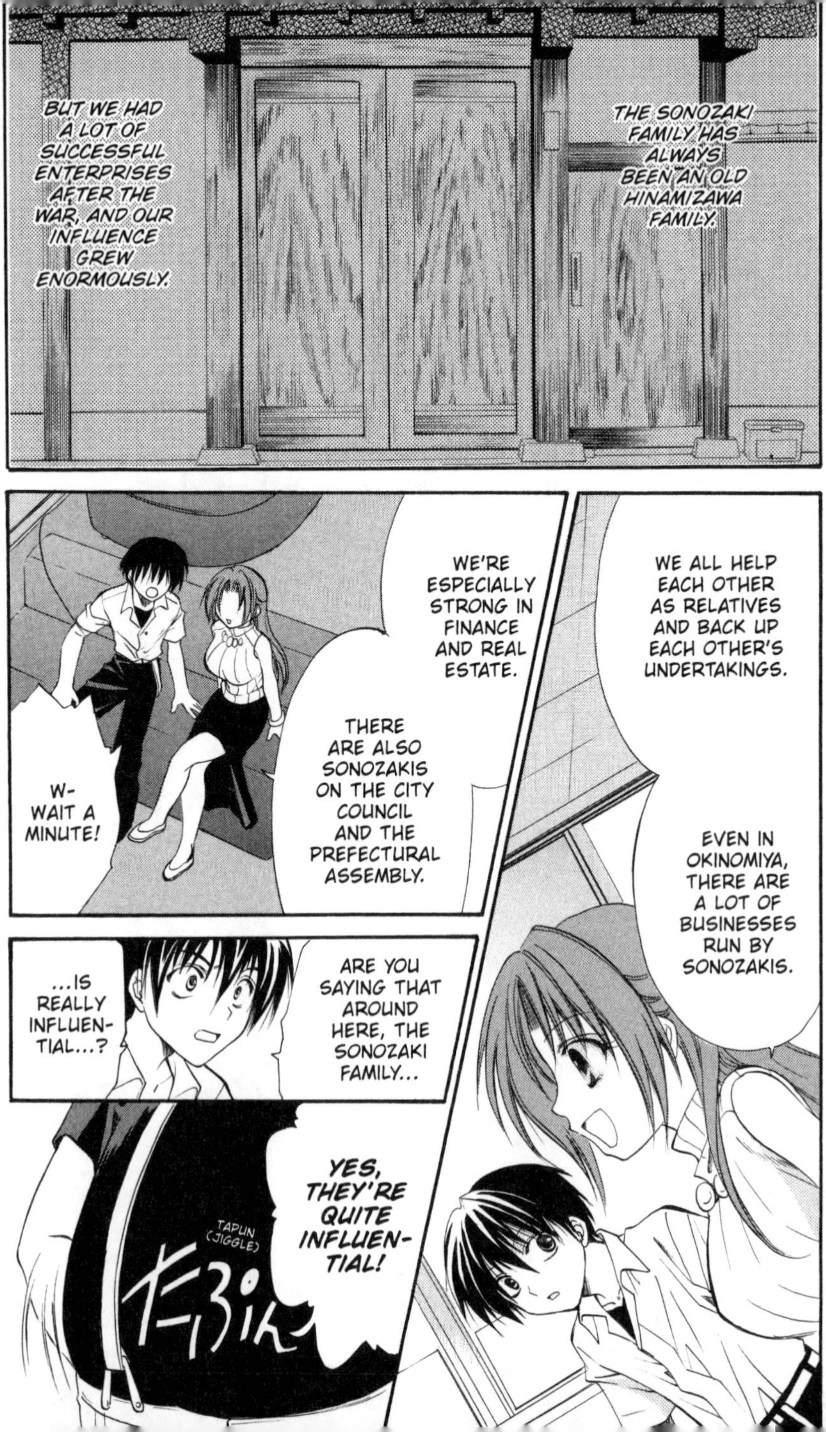
THE SONOZAKI FAMILY HAS ALWAYS BEEN AN OLD HINAMIZAWA FAMILY.
BUT WE HAD A LOT OF SUCCESSFUL ENTERPRISES AFTER THE WAR, AND OUR INFLUENCE GREW ENORMOUSLY.
WE ALL HELP EACH OTHER AS RELATIVES AND BACK UP EACH OTHER'S UNDERTAKINGS.
EVEN IN OKINOMIYA, THERE ARE A LOT OF BUSINESSES RUN BY SONOZAKIS.
WE'RE ESPECIALLY STRONG IN FINANCE AND REAL ESTATE.
THERE ARE ALSO SONOZAKIS ON THE CITY COUNCIL AND THE PREFECTURAL ASSEMBLY.
W-WAIT A MINUTE!
ARE YOU SAYING THAT AROUND HERE, THE SONOZAKI FAMILY...
...IS REALLY INFLUENTIAL...?
YES, THEY'RE QUITE INFLUENTIAL!
TAPUN (JIGGLE)

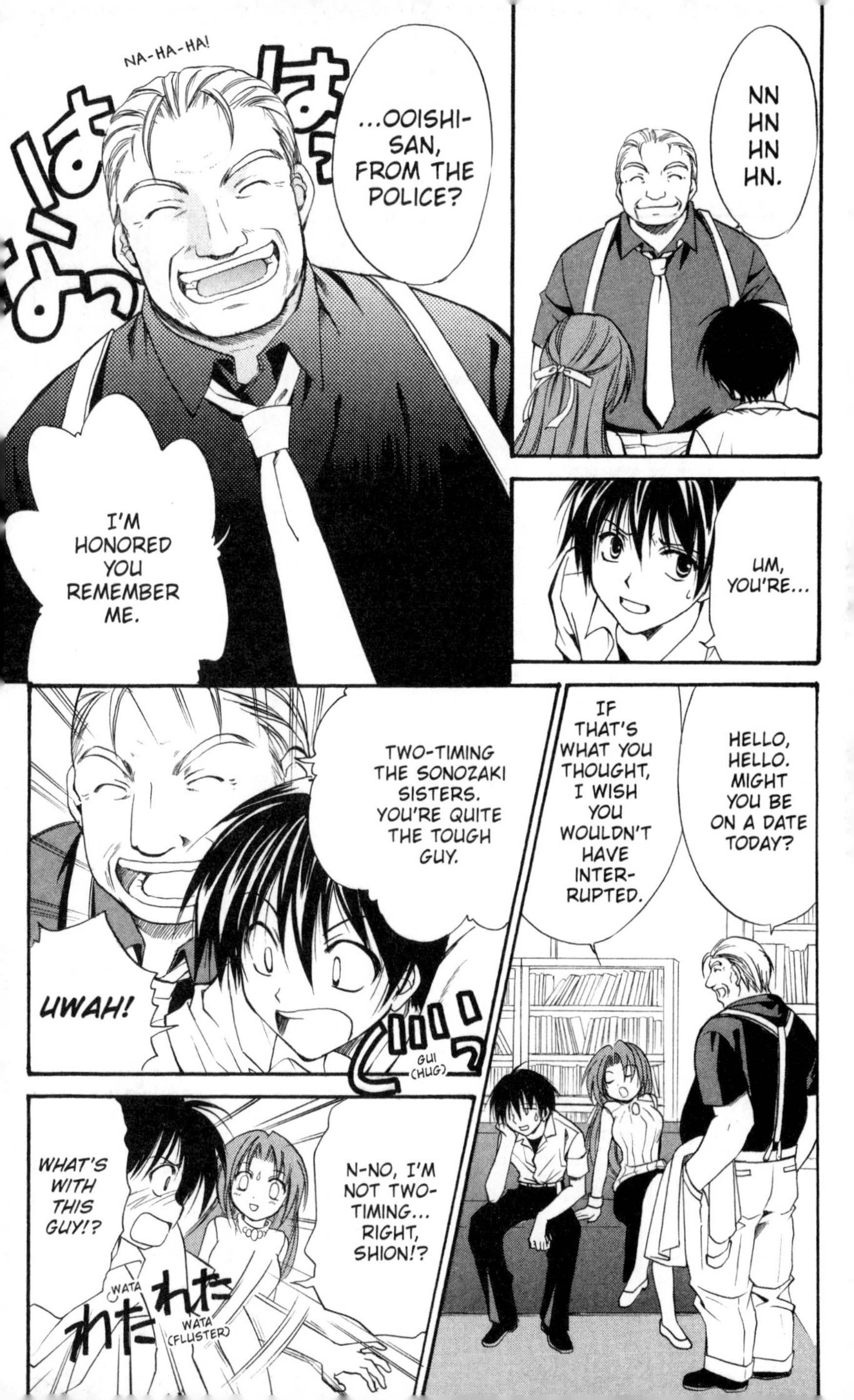
NN HN HN HN.
UM, YOU'RE...
...OOISHI-SAN, FROM THE POLICE?
NA-HA-HA!
I'M HONORED YOU REMEMBER ME.
HELLO, HELLO. MIGHT YOU BE ON A DATE TODAY?
IF THAT'S WHAT YOU THOUGHT, I WISH YOU WOULDN'T HAVE INTER-RUPTED.
TWO-TIMING THE SONOZAKI SISTERS. YOU'RE QUITE THE TOUGH GUY.
UWAH!
GUI (HUG)
N-NO, I'M NOT TWO-TIMING... RIGHT, SHION!?
WHAT'S WITH THIS GUY!?
WATA WATA (FLUSTER)

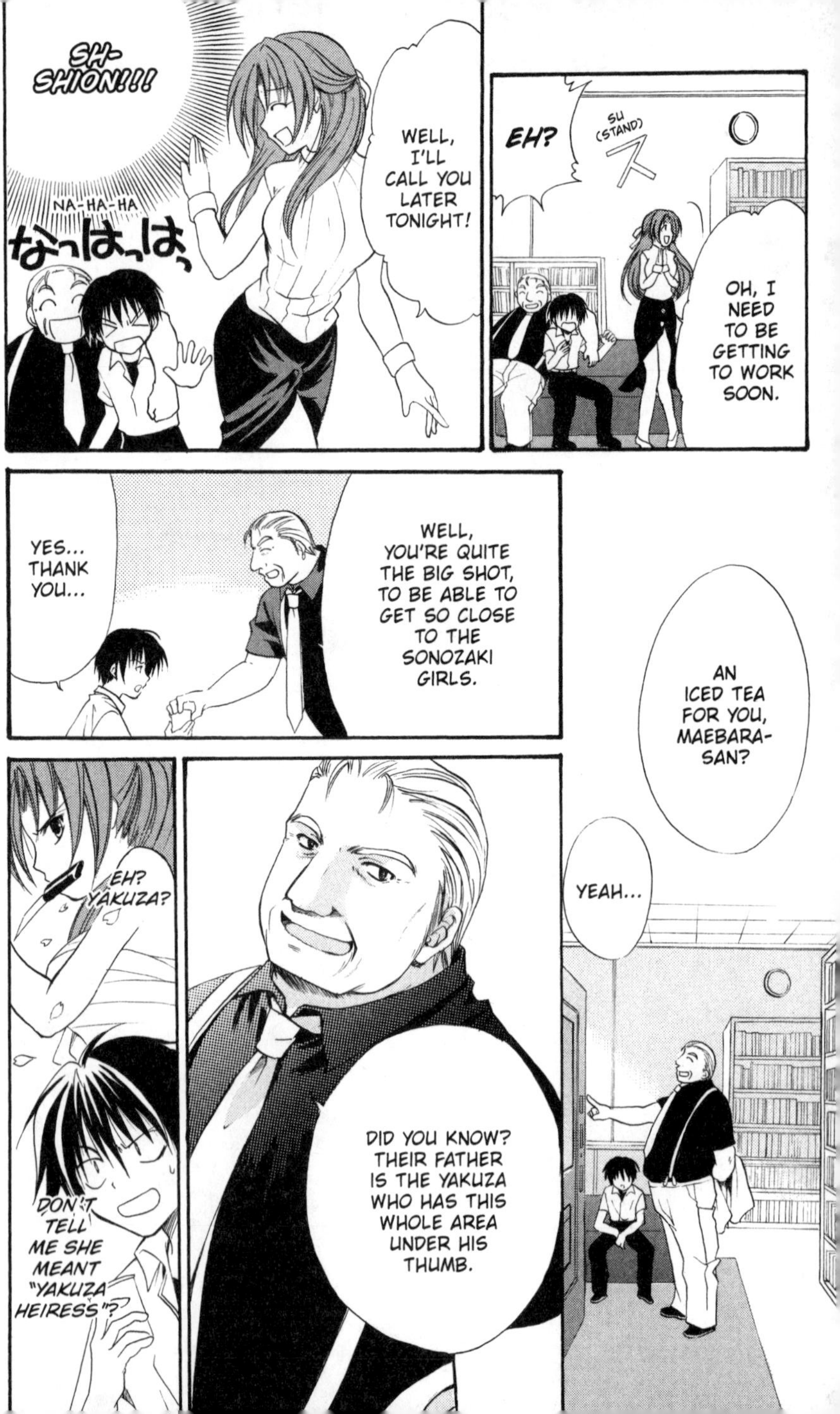

SU (STAND)
ス
OH, I NEED TO BE GETTING TO WORK SOON.
EH?
WELL, I'LL CALL YOU LATER TONIGHT!
SH-SHION!!!
NA-HA-HA
なっはっは、
WELL, YOU'RE QUITE THE BIG SHOT, TO BE ABLE TO GET SO CLOSE TO THE SONOZAKI GIRLS.
YES... THANK YOU...
AN ICED TEA FOR YOU, MAEBARA-SAN?
YEAH...
DID YOU KNOW? THEIR FATHER IS THE YAKUZA WHO HAS THIS WHOLE AREA UNDER HIS THUMB.
EH? YAKUZA?
DON'T TELL ME SHE MEANT "YAKUZA HEIRESS"?

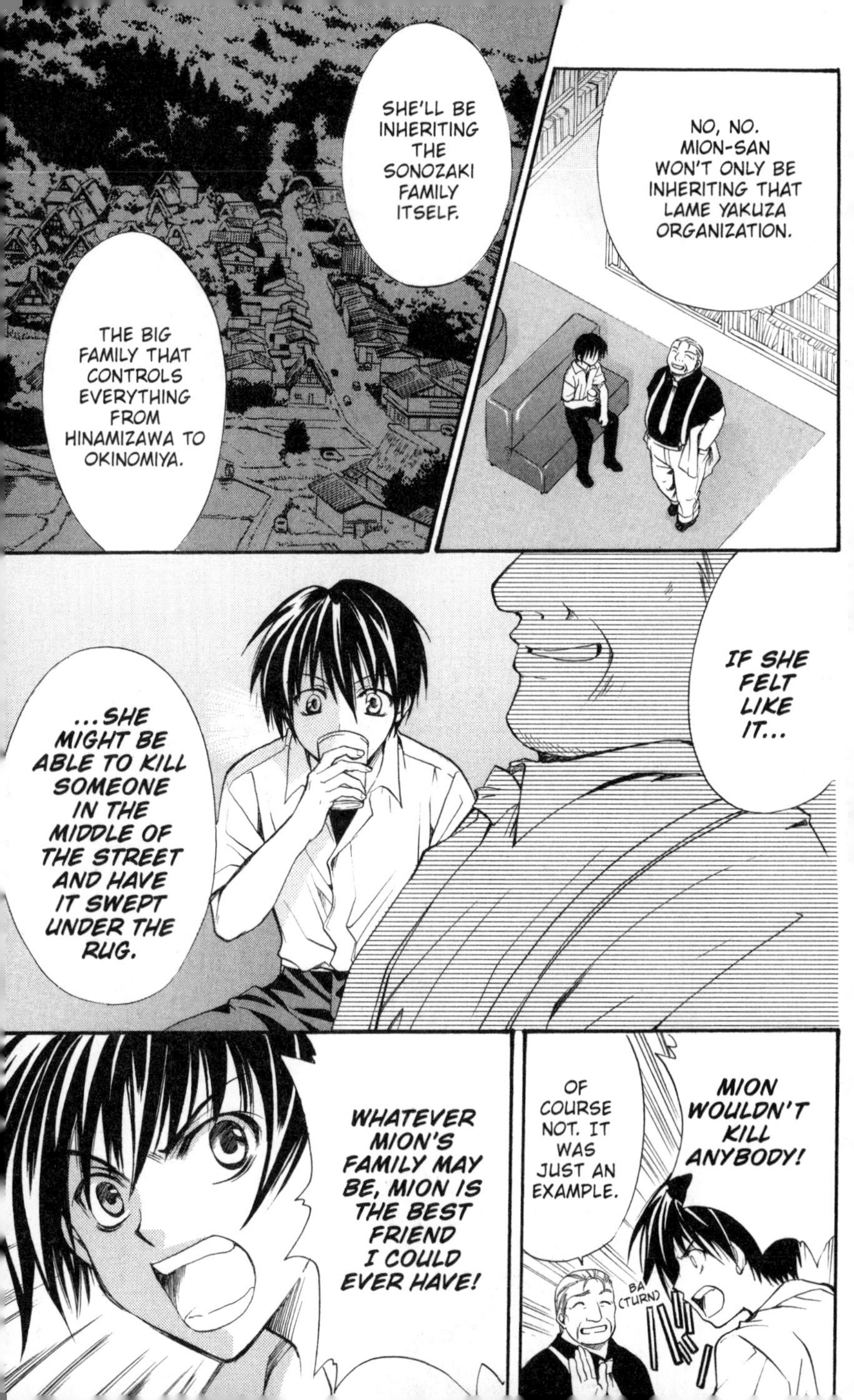
NO, NO. MION-SAN WON'T ONLY BE INHERITING THAT LAME YAKUZA ORGANIZATION.
SHE'LL BE INHERITING THE SONOZAKI FAMILY ITSELF.
THE BIG FAMILY THAT CONTROLS EVERYTHING FROM HINAMIZAWA TO OKINOMIYA.
IF SHE FELT LIKE IT...
...SHE MIGHT BE ABLE TO KILL SOMEONE IN THE MIDDLE OF THE STREET AND HAVE IT SWEPT UNDER THE RUG.
MION WOULDN'T KILL ANYBODY!
BA (TURN)
OF COURSE NOT. IT WAS JUST AN EXAMPLE.
WHATEVER MION'S FAMILY MAY BE, MION IS THE BEST FRIEND I COULD EVER HAVE!

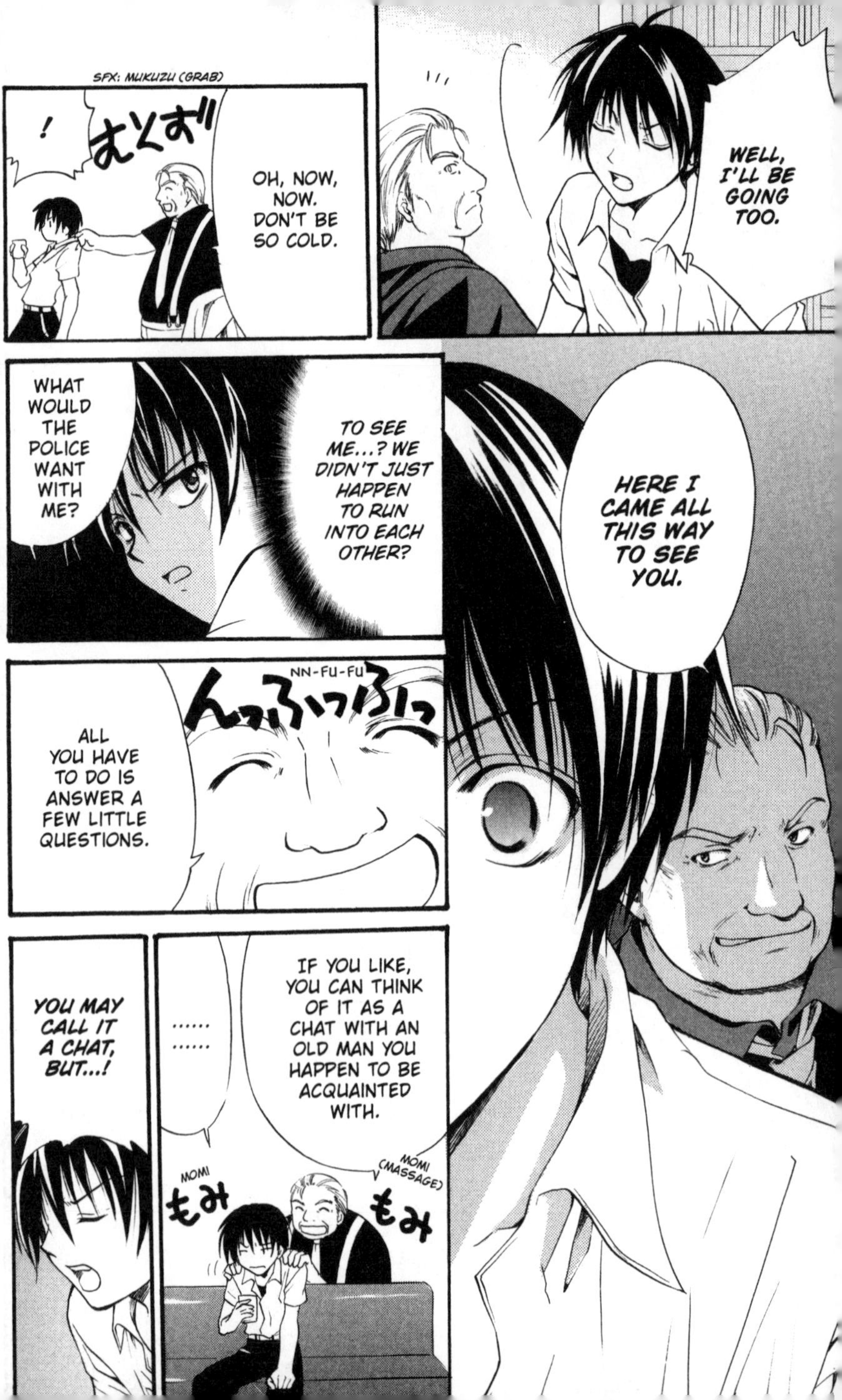
WELL, I'LL BE GOING TOO.
SFX: MUKUZU (GRAB)
!
むくず
OH, NOW, NOW. DON'T BE SO COLD.
HERE I CAME ALL THIS WAY TO SEE YOU.
TO SEE ME...? WE DIDN'T JUST HAPPEN TO RUN INTO EACH OTHER?
WHAT WOULD THE POLICE WANT WITH ME?
NN-FU-FU
んっふっふっ
ALL YOU HAVE TO DO IS ANSWER A FEW LITTLE QUESTIONS.
IF YOU LIKE, YOU CAN THINK OF IT AS A CHAT WITH AN OLD MAN YOU HAPPEN TO BE ACQUAINTED WITH.
MOMI (MASSAGE)
もみ
MOMI
もみ
......
......
YOU MAY CALL IT A CHAT, BUT...!

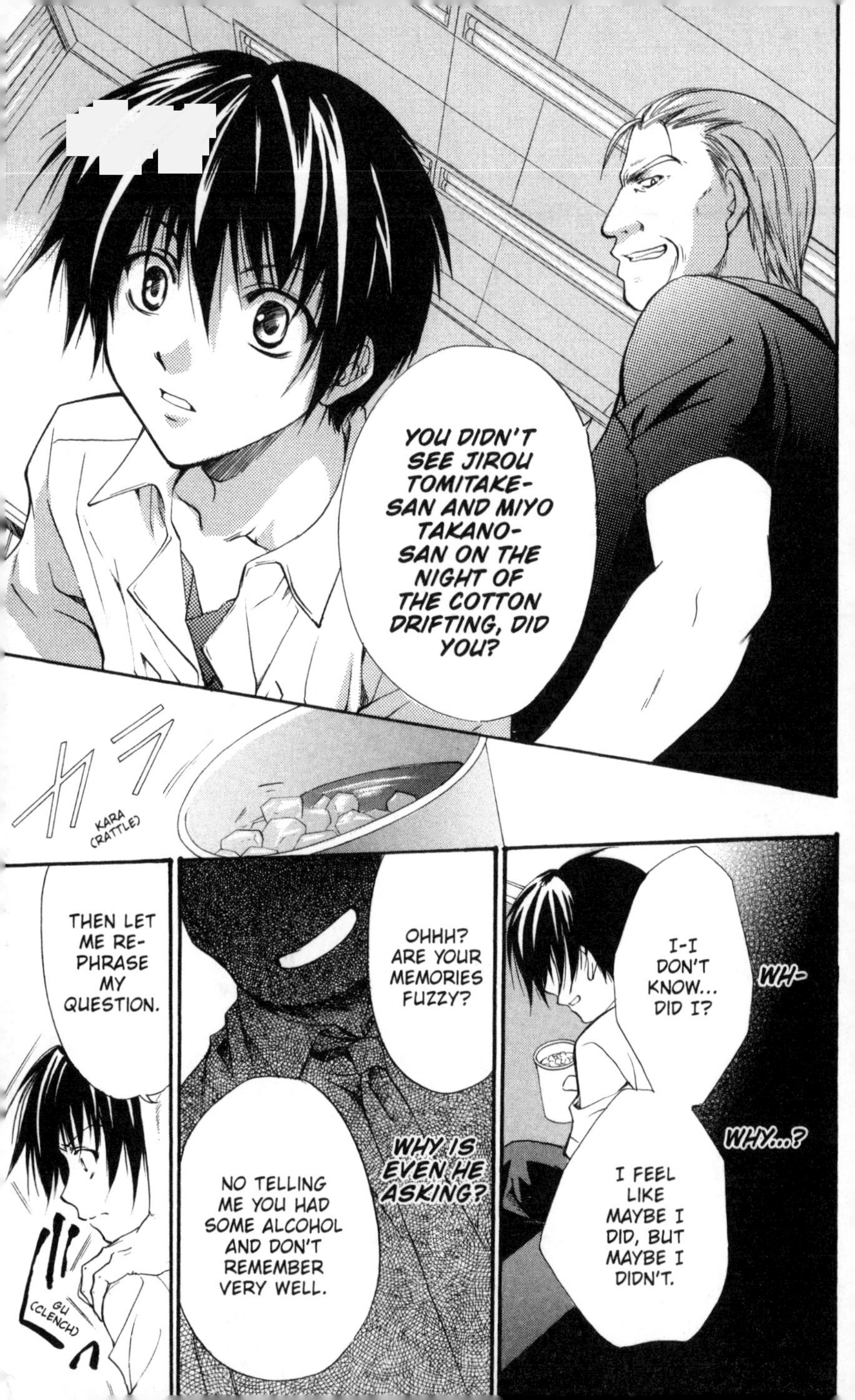
YOU DIDN'T SEE JIROU TOMITAKE-SAN AND MIYO TAKANO-SAN ON THE NIGHT OF THE COTTON DRIFTING, DID YOU?
KARA (RATTLE)
WH-
I-I DON'T KNOW... DID I?
WHY...?
I FEEL LIKE MAYBE I DID, BUT MAYBE I DIDN'T.
OHHH? ARE YOUR MEMORIES FUZZY?
WHY IS EVEN HE ASKING?
NO TELLING ME YOU HAD SOME ALCOHOL AND DON'T REMEMBER VERY WELL.
THEN LET ME RE-PHRASE MY QUESTION.
GU (CLENCH)

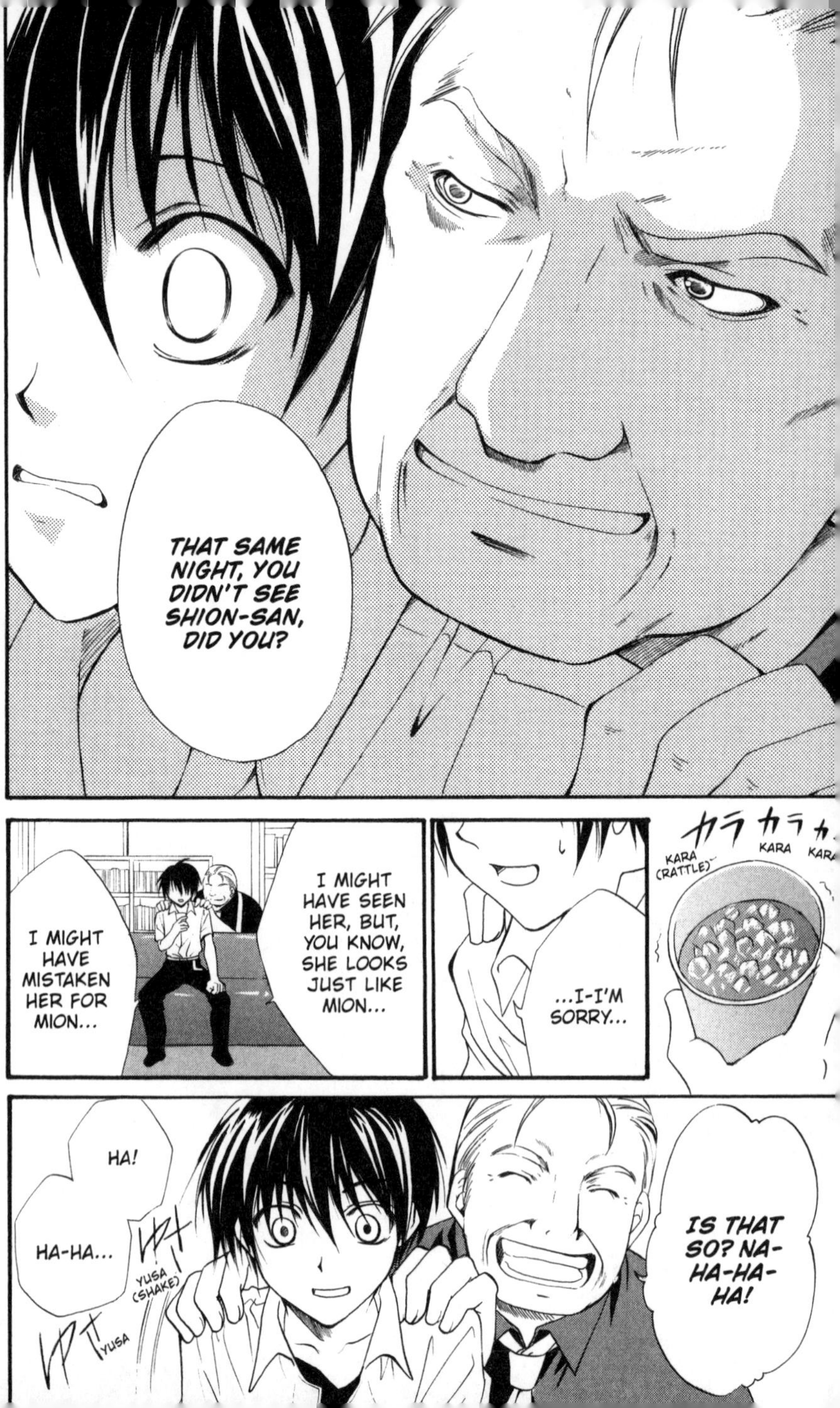
THAT SAME NIGHT, YOU DIDN'T SEE SHION-SAN, DID YOU?
KARA (RATTLE)
KARA
KARA
...I-I'M SORRY...
I MIGHT HAVE SEEN HER, BUT, YOU KNOW, SHE LOOKS JUST LIKE MION...
I MIGHT HAVE MISTAKEN HER FOR MION...
IS THAT SO? NA-HA-HA-HA!
HA!
HA-HA...
YUSA (SHAKE)
YUSA

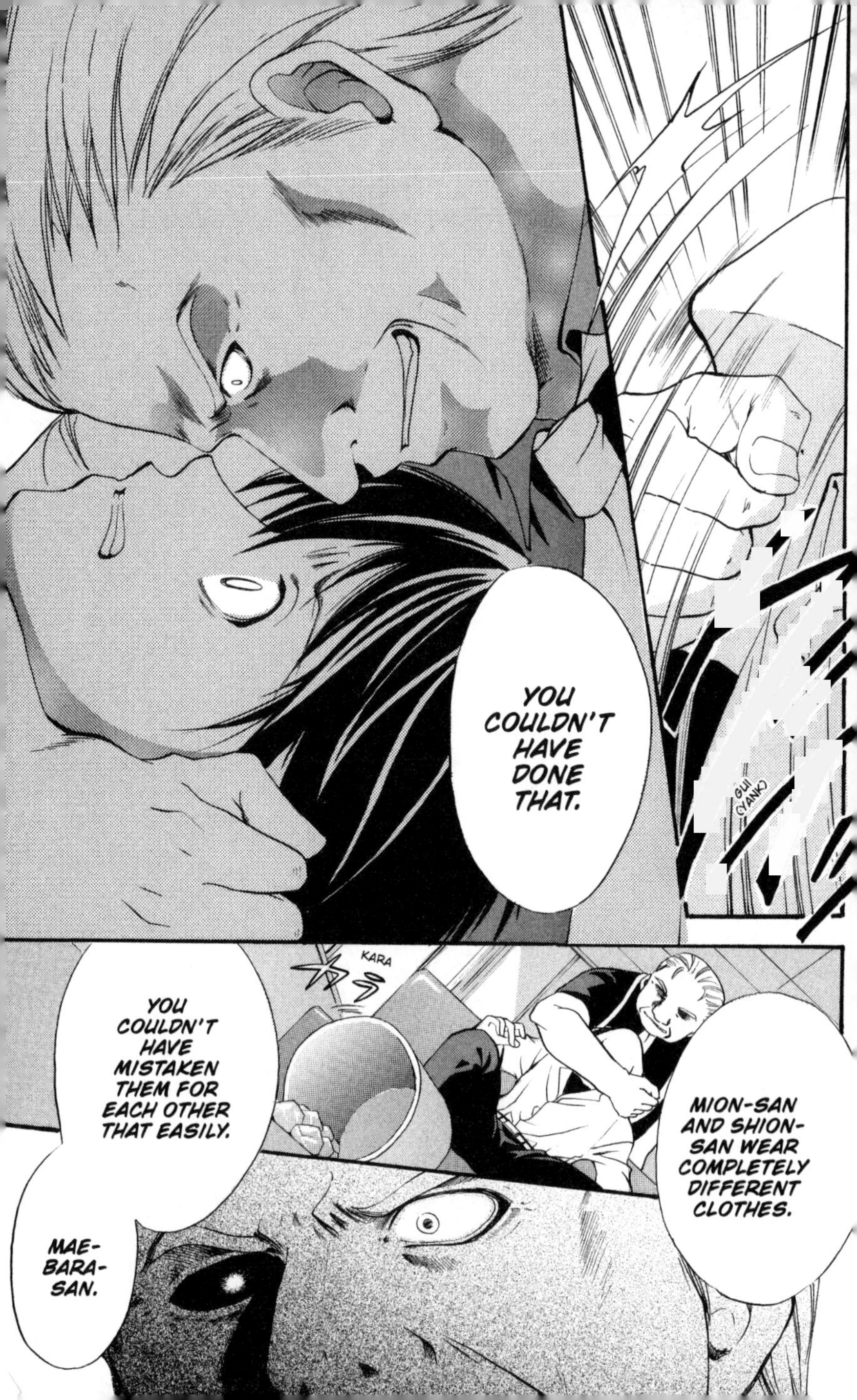
GUI (YANK)
YOU COULDN'T HAVE DONE THAT.
KARA
MION-SAN AND SHION-SAN WEAR COMPLETELY DIFFERENT CLOTHES.
YOU COULDN'T HAVE MISTAKEN THEM FOR EACH OTHER THAT EASILY.
MAE-BARA-SAN.

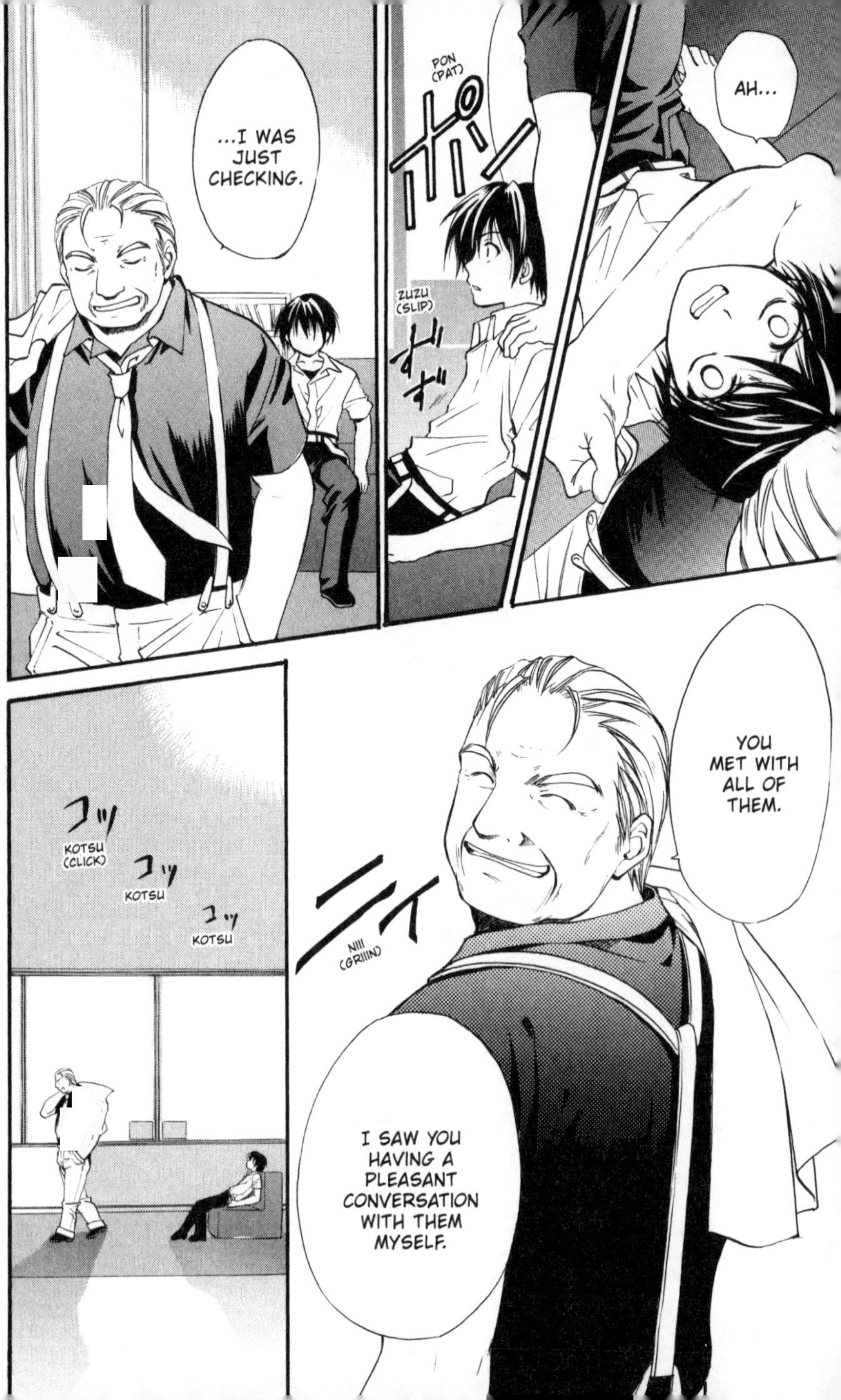
AH...
PON (PAT)
ZUZU (SLIP)
...I WAS JUST CHECKING.
YOU MET WITH ALL OF THEM.
NIII (GRIIIN)
I SAW YOU HAVING A PLEASANT CONVERSATION WITH THEM MYSELF.
KOTSU (CLICK)
KOTSU
KOTSU

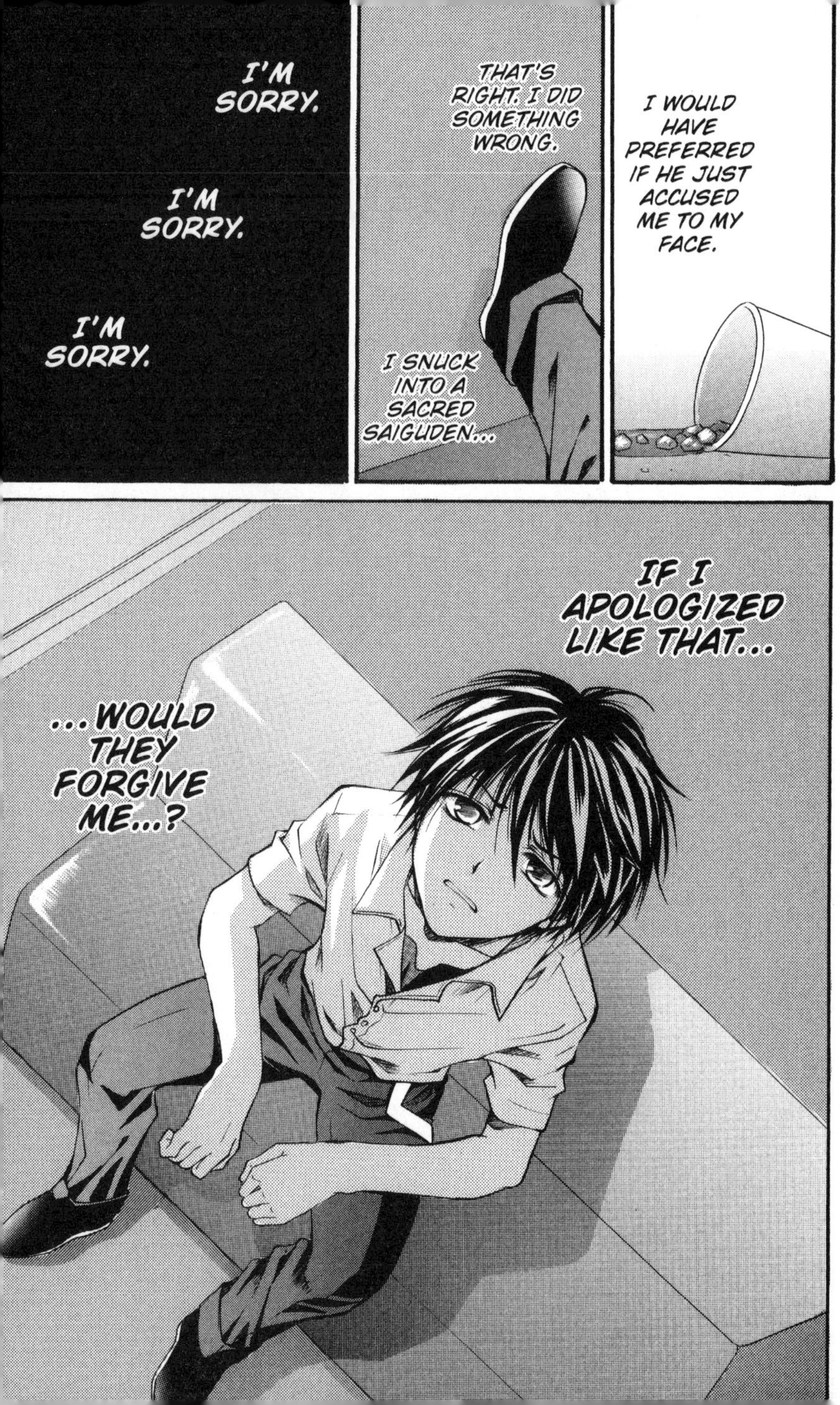
I WOULD HAVE PREFERRED IF HE JUST ACCUSED ME TO MY FACE.
THAT'S RIGHT. I DID SOMETHING WRONG.
I SNUCK INTO A SACRED SAIGUDEN...
I'M SORRY.
I'M SORRY.
I'M SORRY.
IF I APOLOGIZED LIKE THAT...
...WOULD THEY FORGIVE ME...?

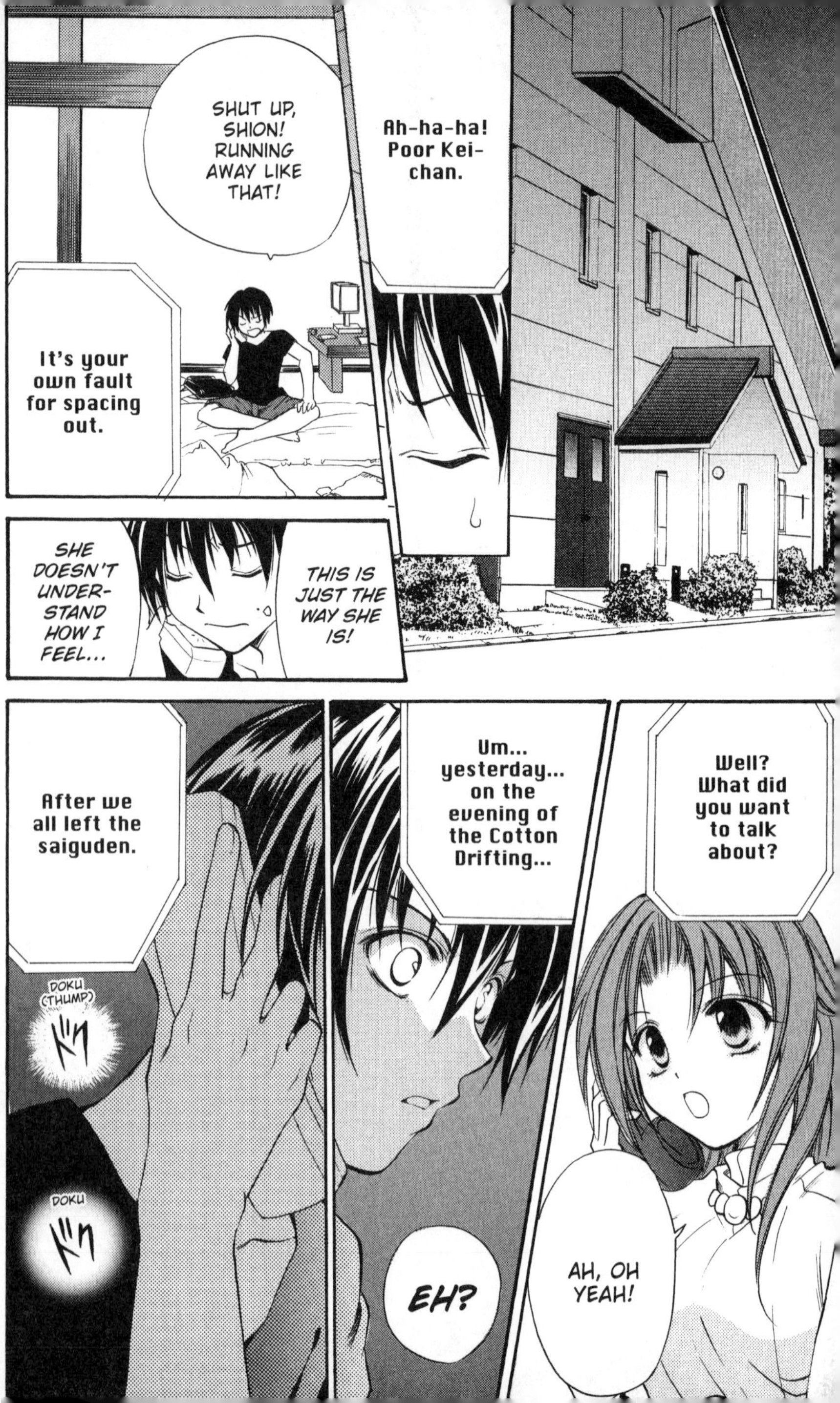
Ah-ha-ha! Poor Kei-chan.
SHUT UP, SHION! RUNNING AWAY LIKE THAT!
It's your own fault for spacing out.
THIS IS JUST THE WAY SHE IS!
SHE DOESN'T UNDERSTAND HOW I FEEL...
Well? What did you want to talk about?
AH, OH YEAH!
Um... yesterday... on the evening of the Cotton Drifting...
EH?
After we all left the saiguden.
DOKU (THUMP)
ドク
DOKU
ドク

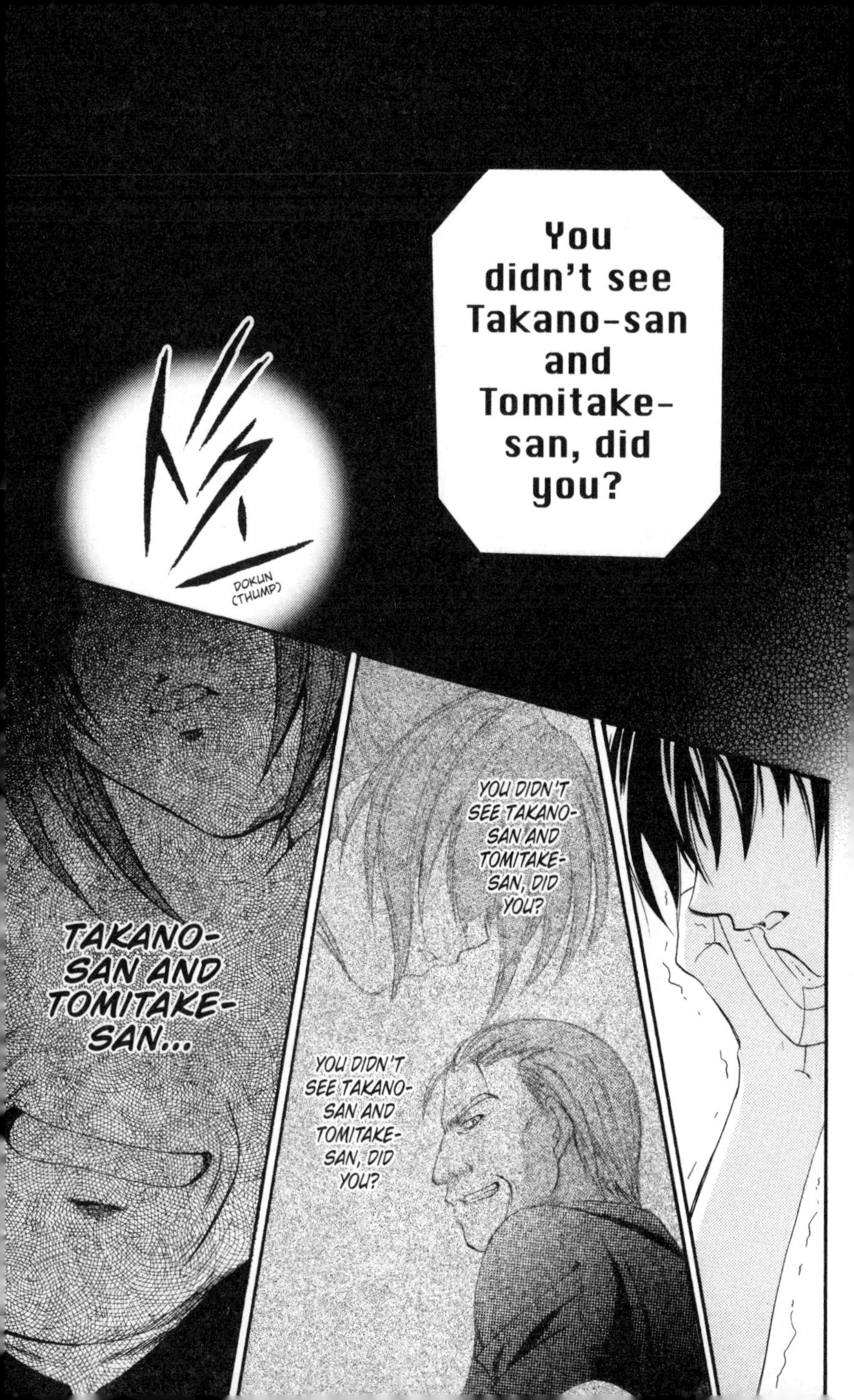
You didn't see Takano-san and Tomitake-san, did you?
DOKUN (THUMP)
YOU DIDN'T SEE TAKANO-SAN AND TOMITAKE-SAN, DID YOU?
YOU DIDN'T SEE TAKANO-SAN AND TOMITAKE-SAN, DID YOU?
TAKANO-SAN AND TOMITAKE-SAN...

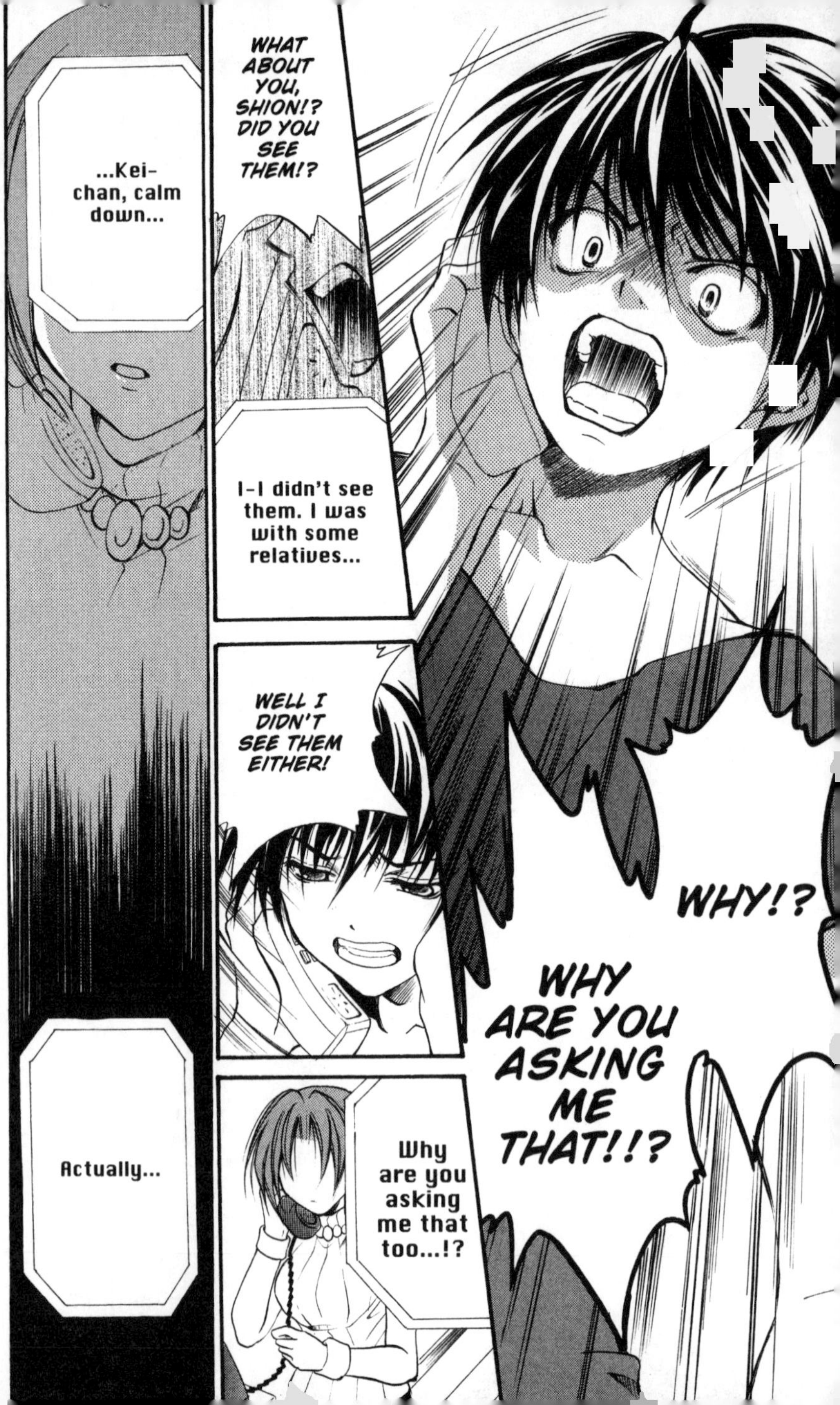
WHAT ABOUT YOU, SHION!? DID YOU SEE THEM!?
I-I didn't see them. I was with some relatives...
WELL I DIDN'T SEE THEM EITHER!
Why are you asking me that too...!?
WHY!?
WHY ARE YOU ASKING ME THAT!!?
...Kei-chan, calm down...
Actually...

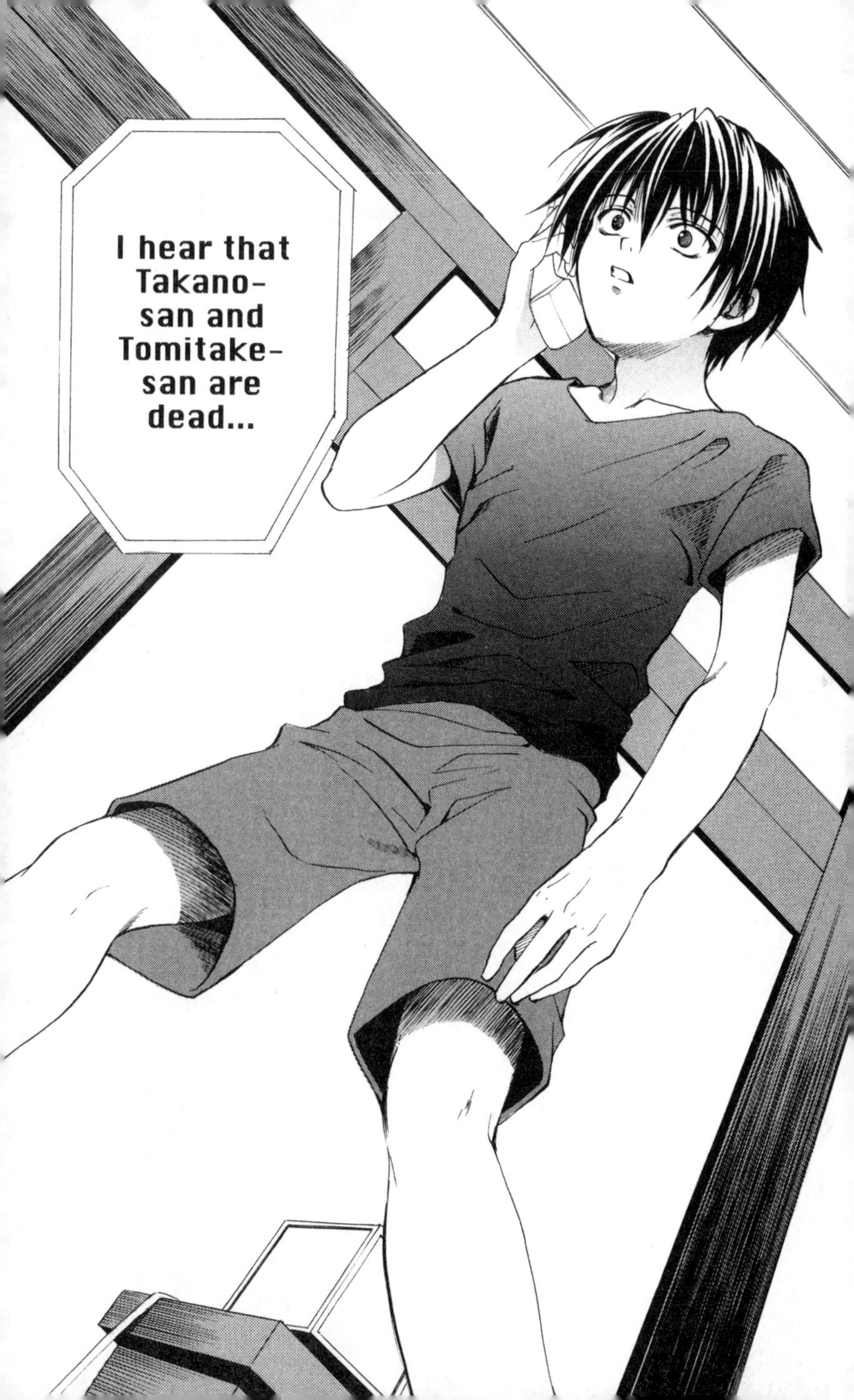
I hear that Takano-san and Tomitake-san are dead...

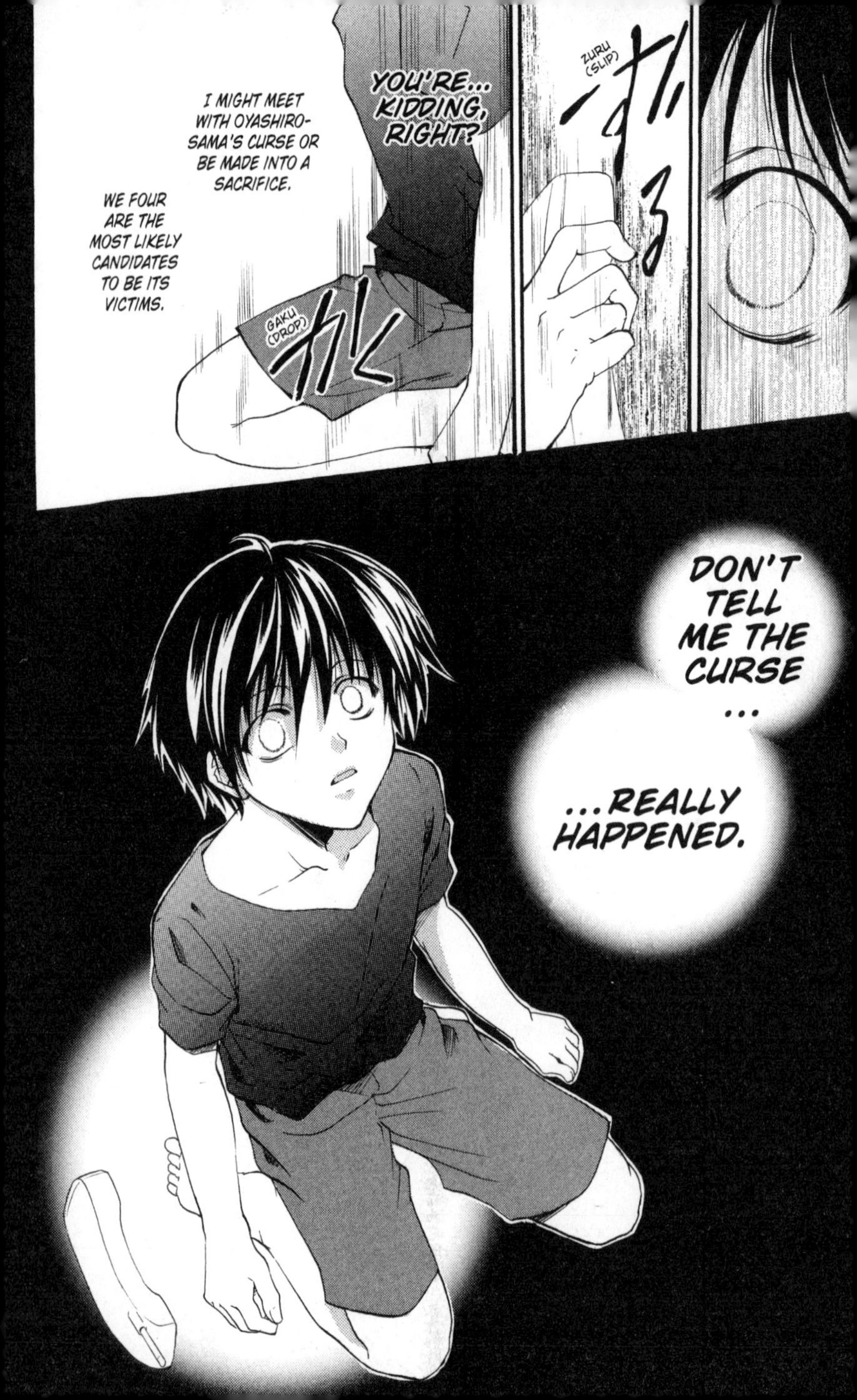
ZURU (SLIP)
YOU'RE... KIDDING, RIGHT?
I MIGHT MEET WITH OYASHIRO-SAMA'S CURSE OR BE MADE INTO A SACRIFICE.
WE FOUR ARE THE MOST LIKELY CANDIDATES TO BE ITS VICTIMS.
GAKU (DROP)
DON'T TELL ME THE CURSE ...
...REALLY HAPPENED.

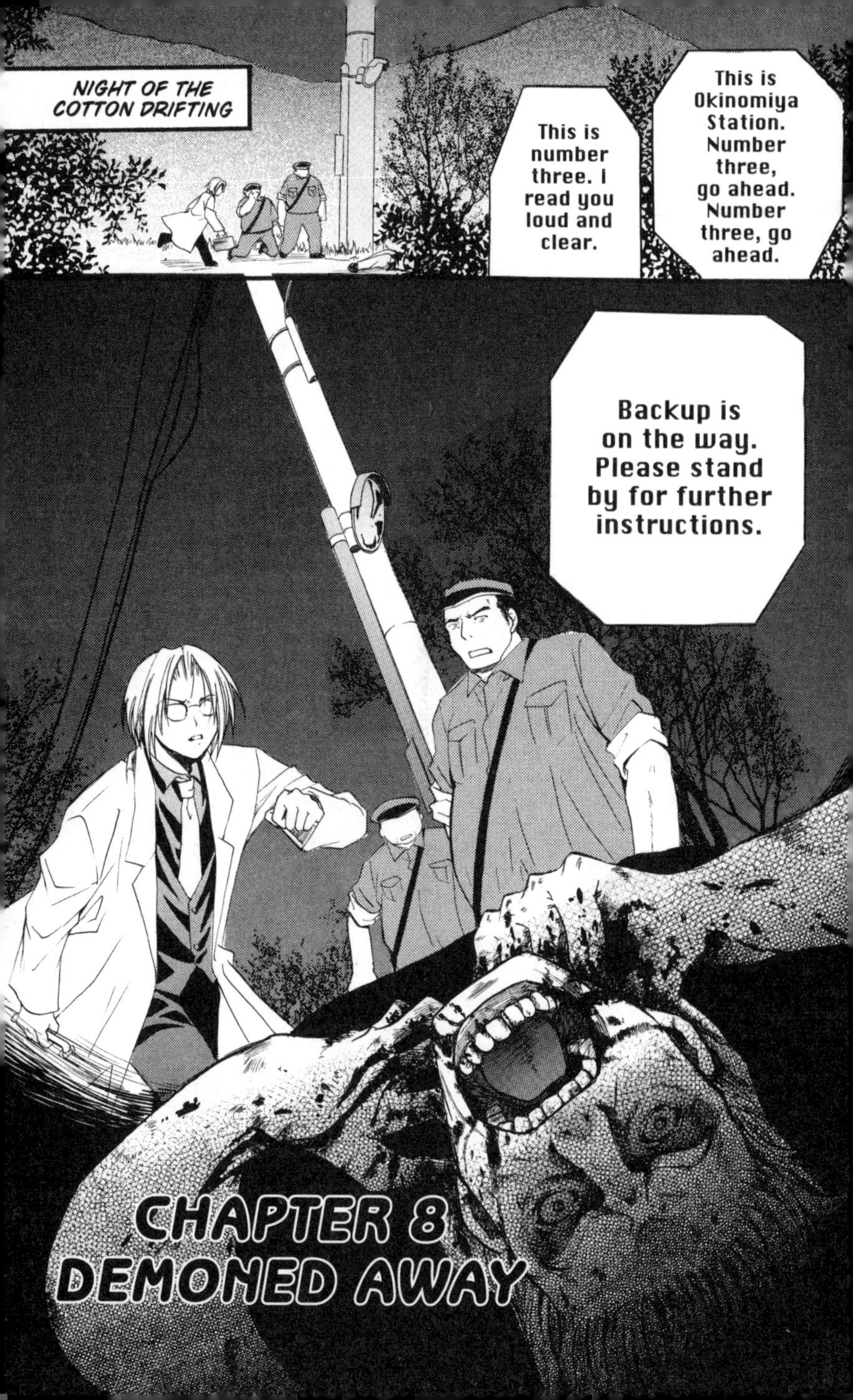
This is Okinomiya Station. Number three, go ahead. Number three, go ahead.
This is number three. I read you loud and clear.
NIGHT OF THE COTTON DRIFTING
Backup is on the way. Please stand by for further instructions.
CHAPTER 8
DEMONED AWAY

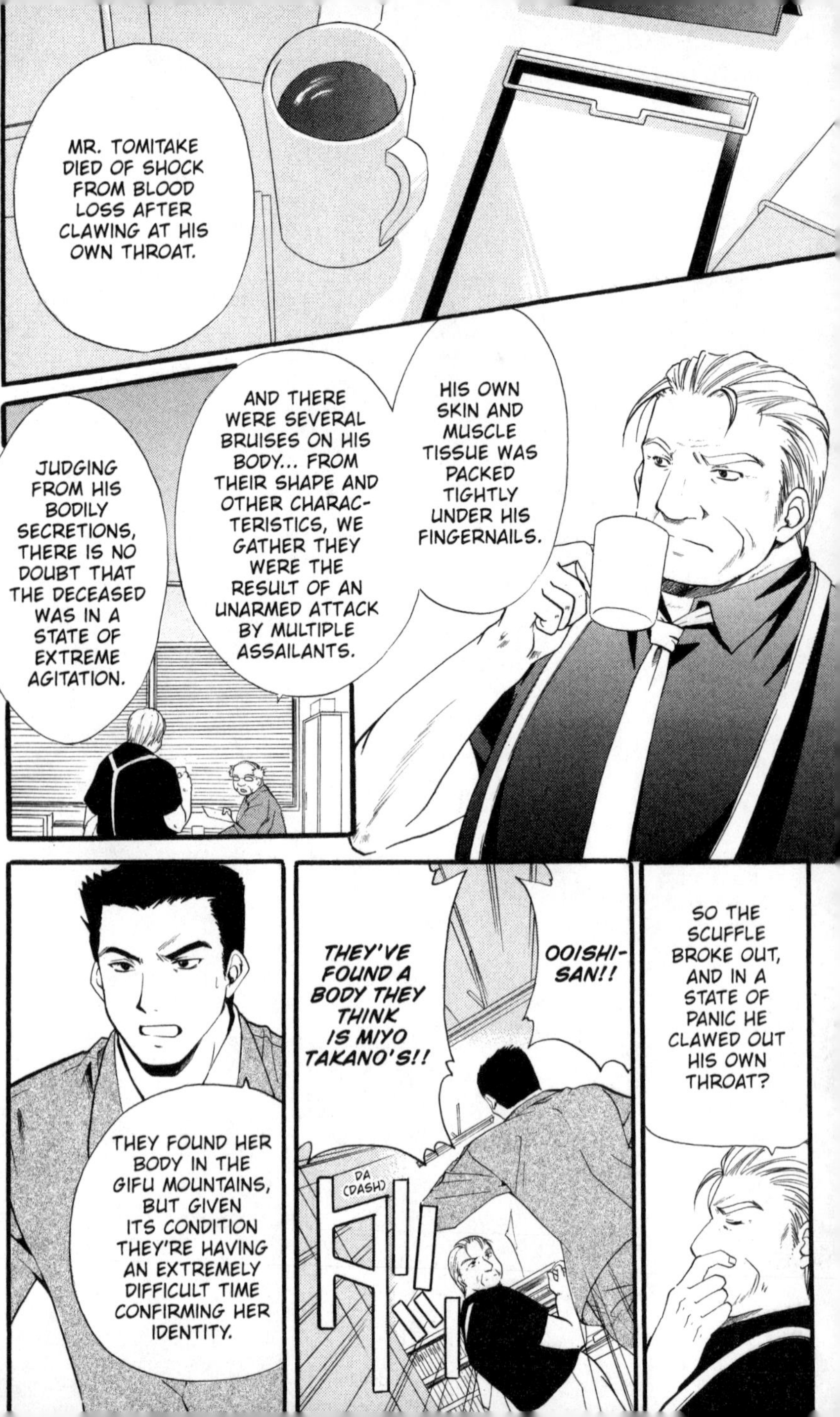
MR. TOMITAKE DIED OF SHOCK FROM BLOOD LOSS AFTER CLAWING AT HIS OWN THROAT.
HIS OWN SKIN AND MUSCLE TISSUE WAS PACKED TIGHTLY UNDER HIS FINGERNAILS.
AND THERE WERE SEVERAL BRUISES ON HIS BODY... FROM THEIR SHAPE AND OTHER CHARAC-TERISTICS, WE GATHER THEY WERE THE RESULT OF AN UNARMED ATTACK BY MULTIPLE ASSAILANTS.
JUDGING FROM HIS BODILY SECRETIONS, THERE IS NO DOUBT THAT THE DECEASED WAS IN A STATE OF EXTREME AGITATION.
SO THE SCUFFLE BROKE OUT, AND IN A STATE OF PANIC HE CLAWED OUT HIS OWN THROAT?
OOISHI-SAN!!
THEY'VE FOUND A BODY THEY THINK IS MIYO TAKANO'S!!
DA (DASH)
THEY FOUND HER BODY IN THE GIFU MOUNTAINS, BUT GIVEN ITS CONDITION THEY'RE HAVING AN EXTREMELY DIFFICULT TIME CONFIRMING HER IDENTITY.

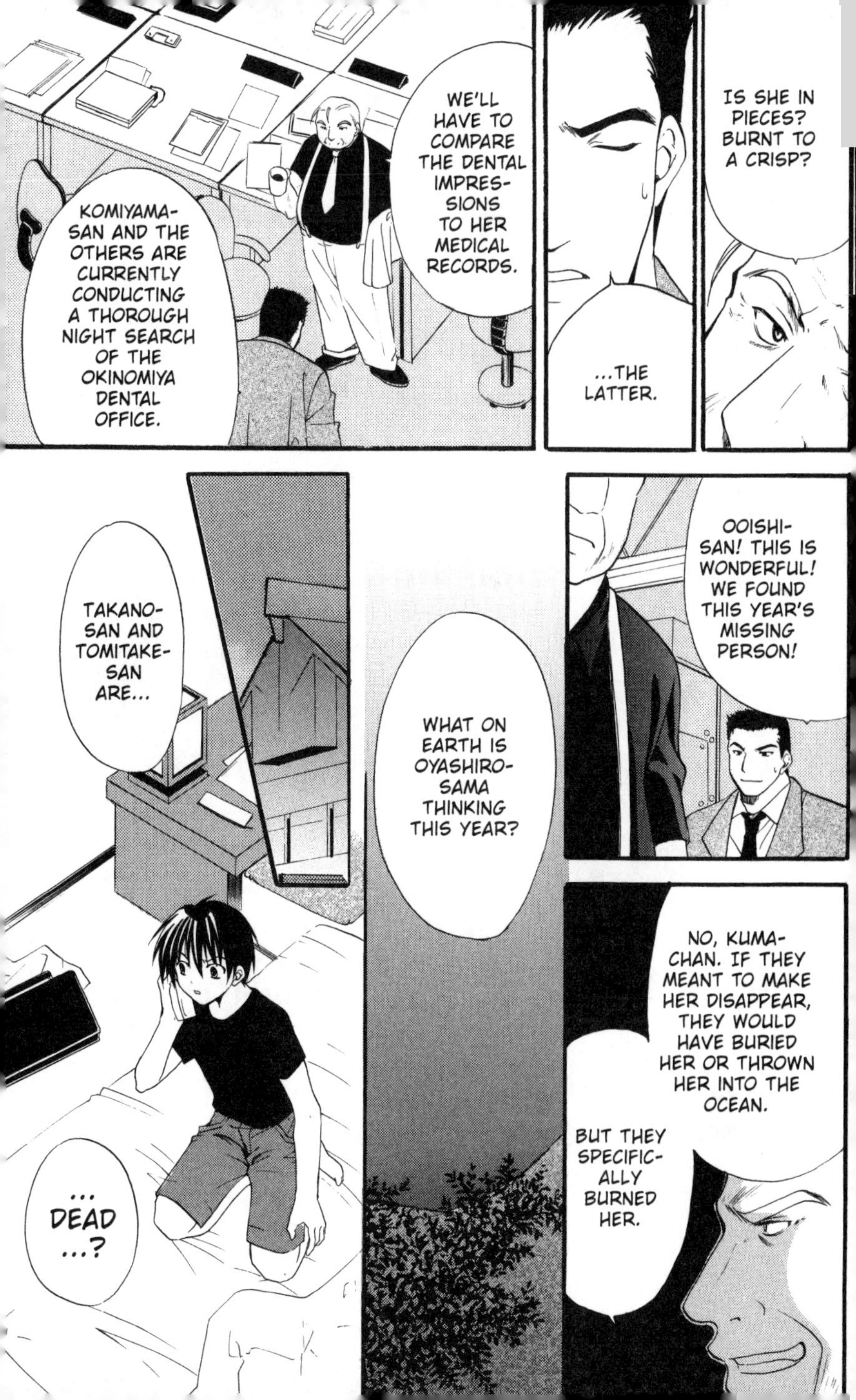
IS SHE IN PIECES? BURNT TO A CRISP?
...THE LATTER.
WE'LL HAVE TO COMPARE THE DENTAL IMPRES-SIONS TO HER MEDICAL RECORDS.
KOMIYAMA-SAN AND THE OTHERS ARE CURRENTLY CONDUCTING A THOROUGH NIGHT SEARCH OF THE OKINOMIYA DENTAL OFFICE.
OOISHI-SAN! THIS IS WONDERFUL! WE FOUND THIS YEAR'S MISSING PERSON!
NO, KUMA-CHAN. IF THEY MEANT TO MAKE HER DISAPPEAR, THEY WOULD HAVE BURIED HER OR THROWN HER INTO THE OCEAN.
BUT THEY SPECIFIC-ALLY BURNED HER.
WHAT ON EARTH IS OYASHIRO-SAMA THINKING THIS YEAR?
TAKANO-SAN AND TOMITAKE-SAN ARE...
...DEAD...?

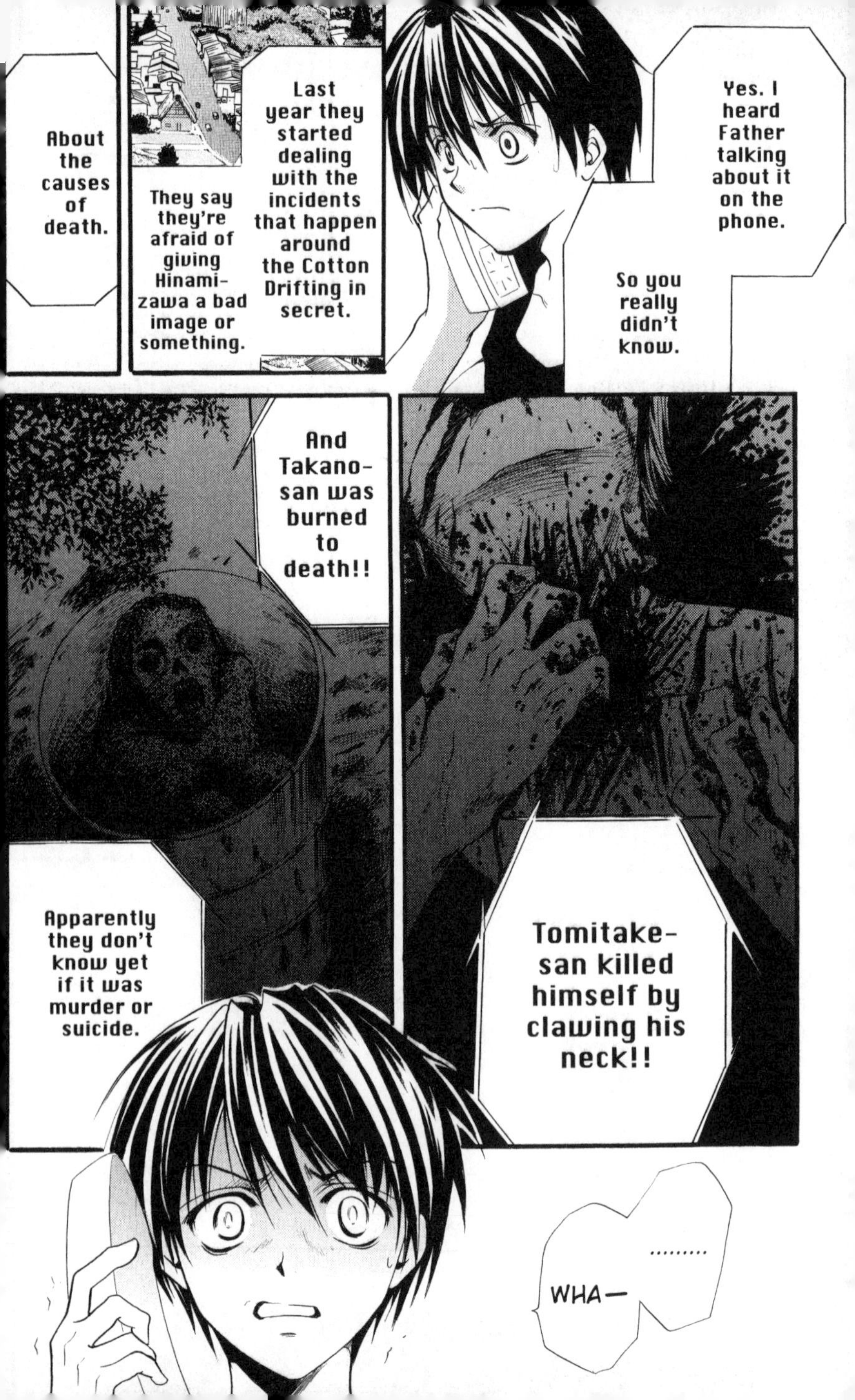
Yes. I heard Father talking about it on the phone.
So you really didn't know.
Last year they started dealing with the incidents that happen around the Cotton Drifting in secret.
They say they're afraid of giving Hinamizawa a bad image or something.
About the causes of death.
Tomitake-san killed himself by clawing his neck!!
And Takano-san was burned to death!!
Apparently they don't know yet if it was murder or suicide.
....
WHA—

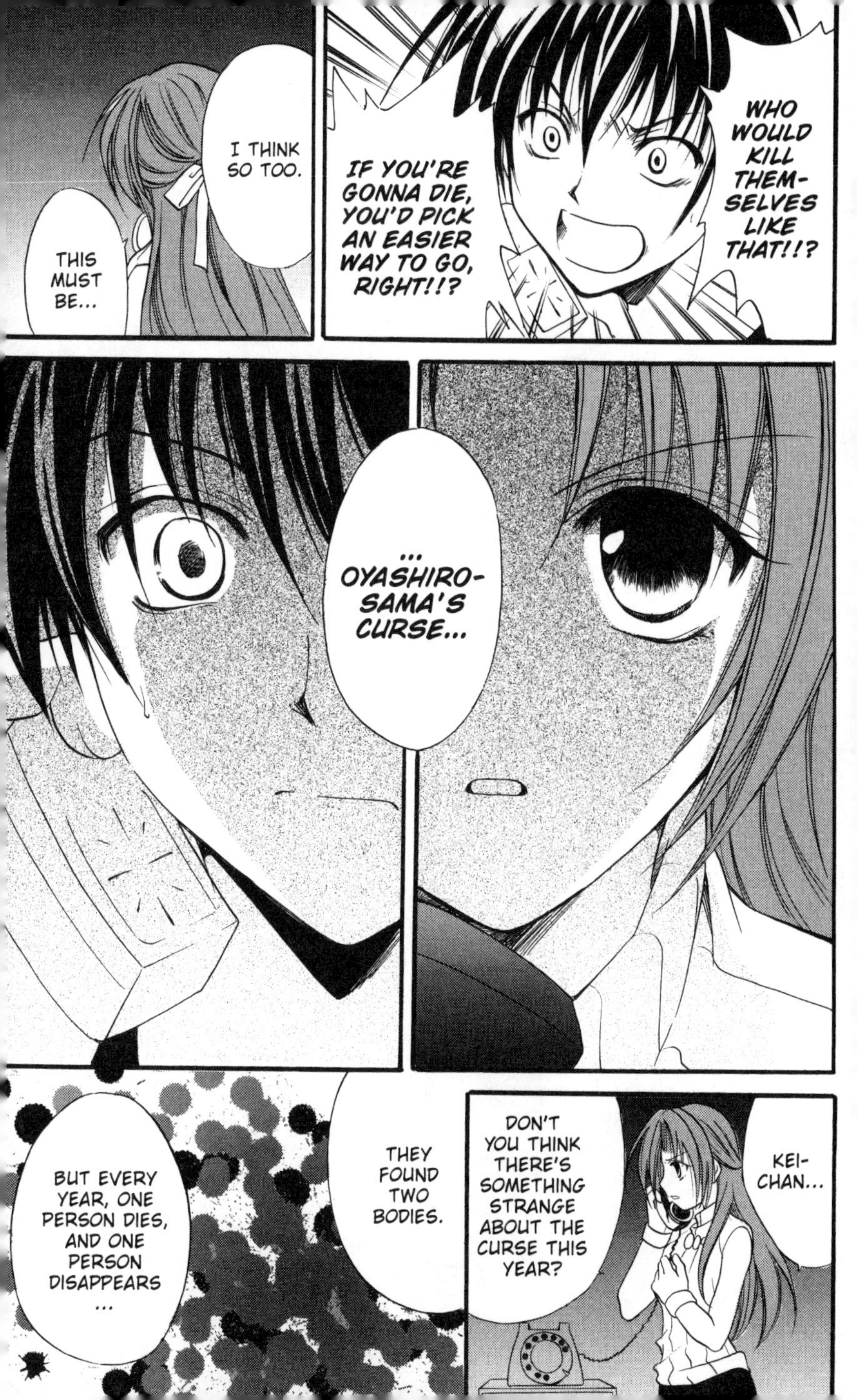
WHO WOULD KILL THEM-SELVES LIKE THAT!!?
IF YOU'RE GONNA DIE, YOU'D PICK AN EASIER WAY TO GO, RIGHT!!?
I THINK SO TOO.
THIS MUST BE...
... OYASHIRO-SAMA'S CURSE...
KEI-CHAN...
DON'T YOU THINK THERE'S SOMETHING STRANGE ABOUT THE CURSE THIS YEAR?
THEY FOUND TWO BODIES.
BUT EVERY YEAR, ONE PERSON DIES, AND ONE PERSON DISAPPEARS...

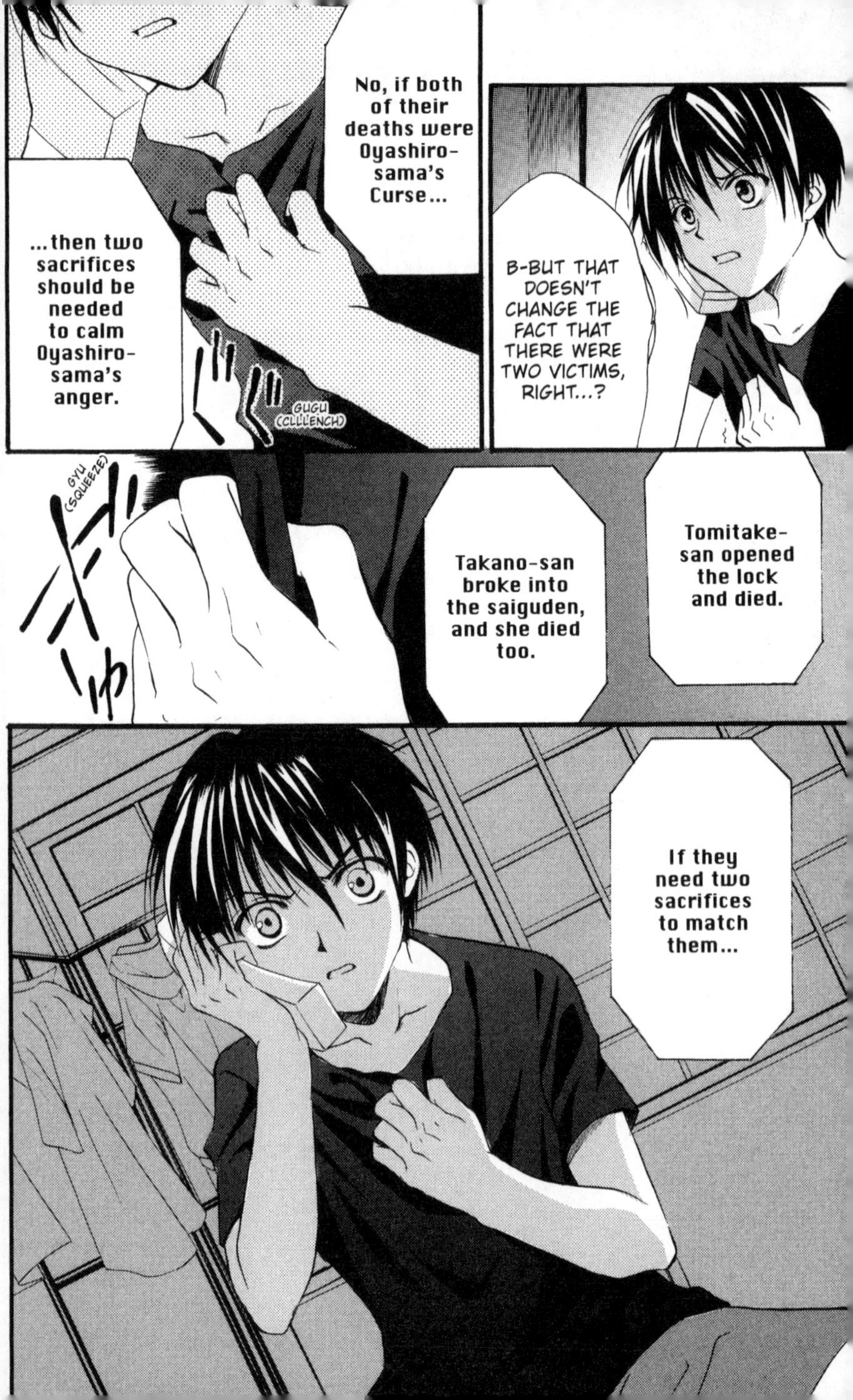
B-BUT THAT DOESN'T CHANGE THE FACT THAT THERE WERE TWO VICTIMS, RIGHT...?
No, if both of their deaths were Oyashiro-sama's Curse...
...then two sacrifices should be needed to calm Oyashiro-sama's anger.
GUGU (CLLLLENCH)
Tomitake-san opened the lock and died.
Takano-san broke into the saiguden, and she died too.
GYU (SQUEEZE)
If they need two sacrifices to match them...

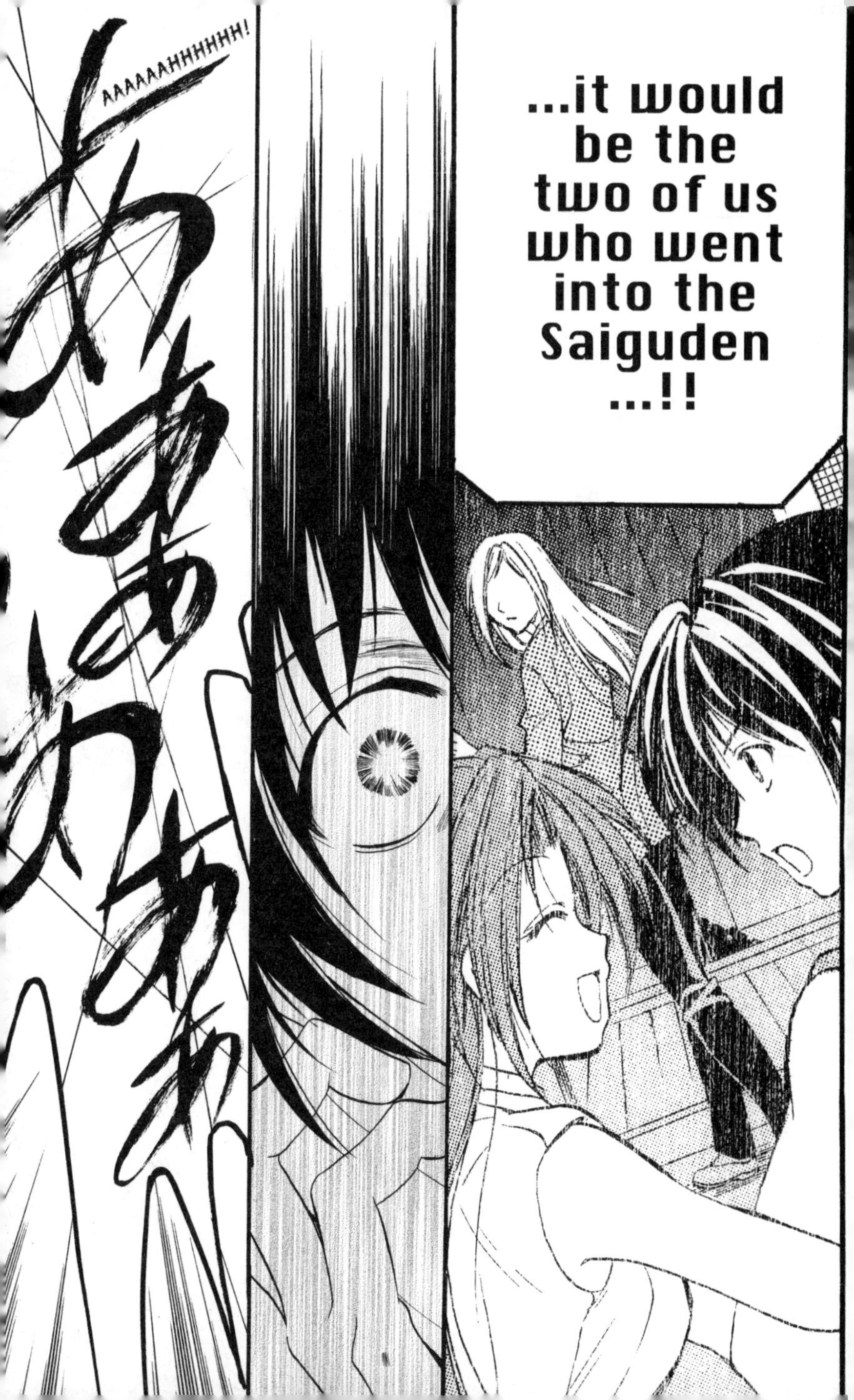
...it would be the two of us who went into the Saiguden ...!!
AAAAAAHHHHHHH!

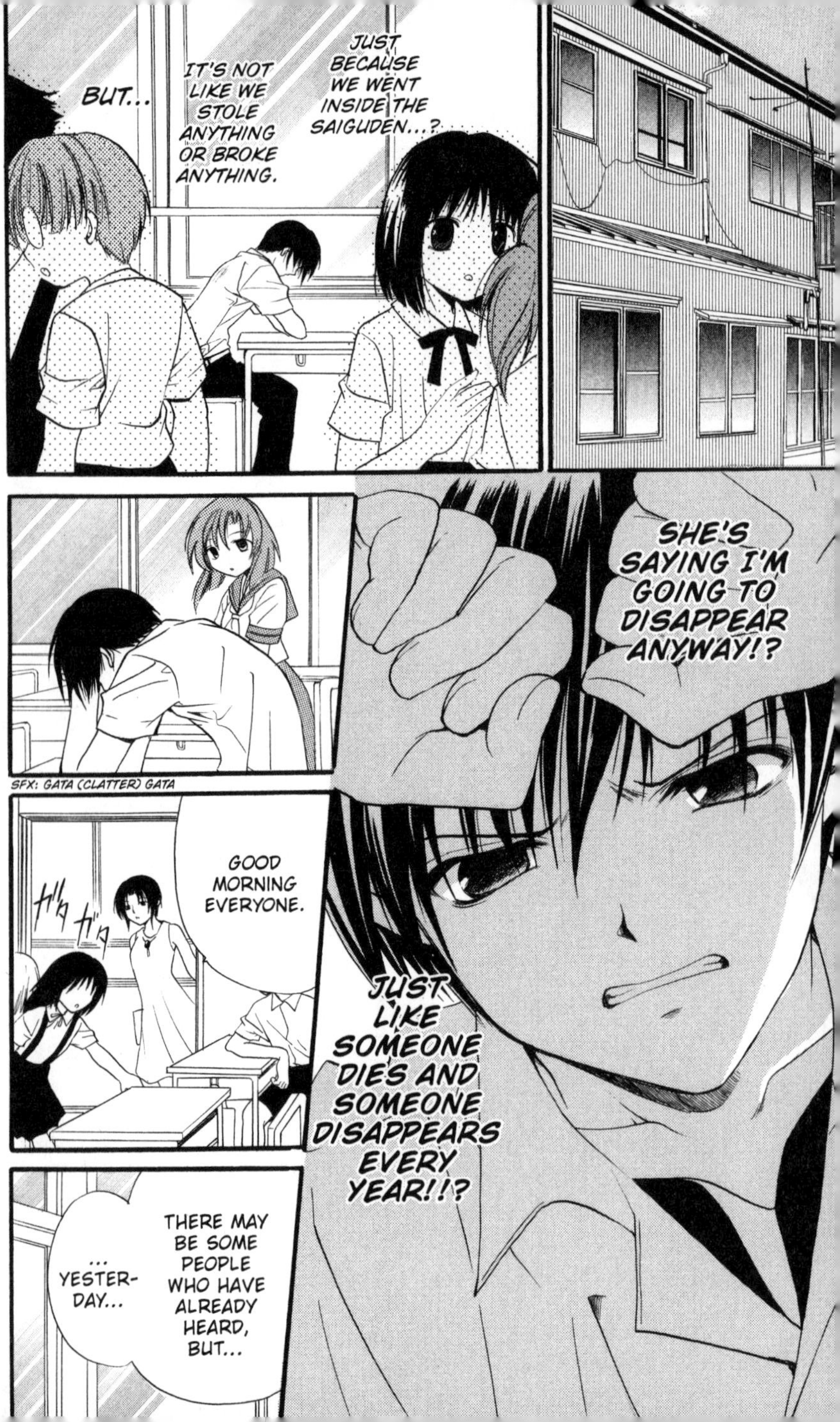
JUST BECAUSE WE WENT INSIDE THE SAIGUDEN...?
IT'S NOT LIKE WE STOLE ANYTHING OR BROKE ANYTHING.
BUT...
SHE'S SAYING I'M GOING TO DISAPPEAR ANYWAY!?
JUST LIKE SOMEONE DIES AND SOMEONE DISAPPEARS EVERY YEAR!!?
SFX: GATA (CLATTER) GATA
GOOD MORNING EVERYONE.
ガタ ガタ
THERE MAY BE SOME PEOPLE WHO HAVE ALREADY HEARD, BUT...
...YESTER-DAY...

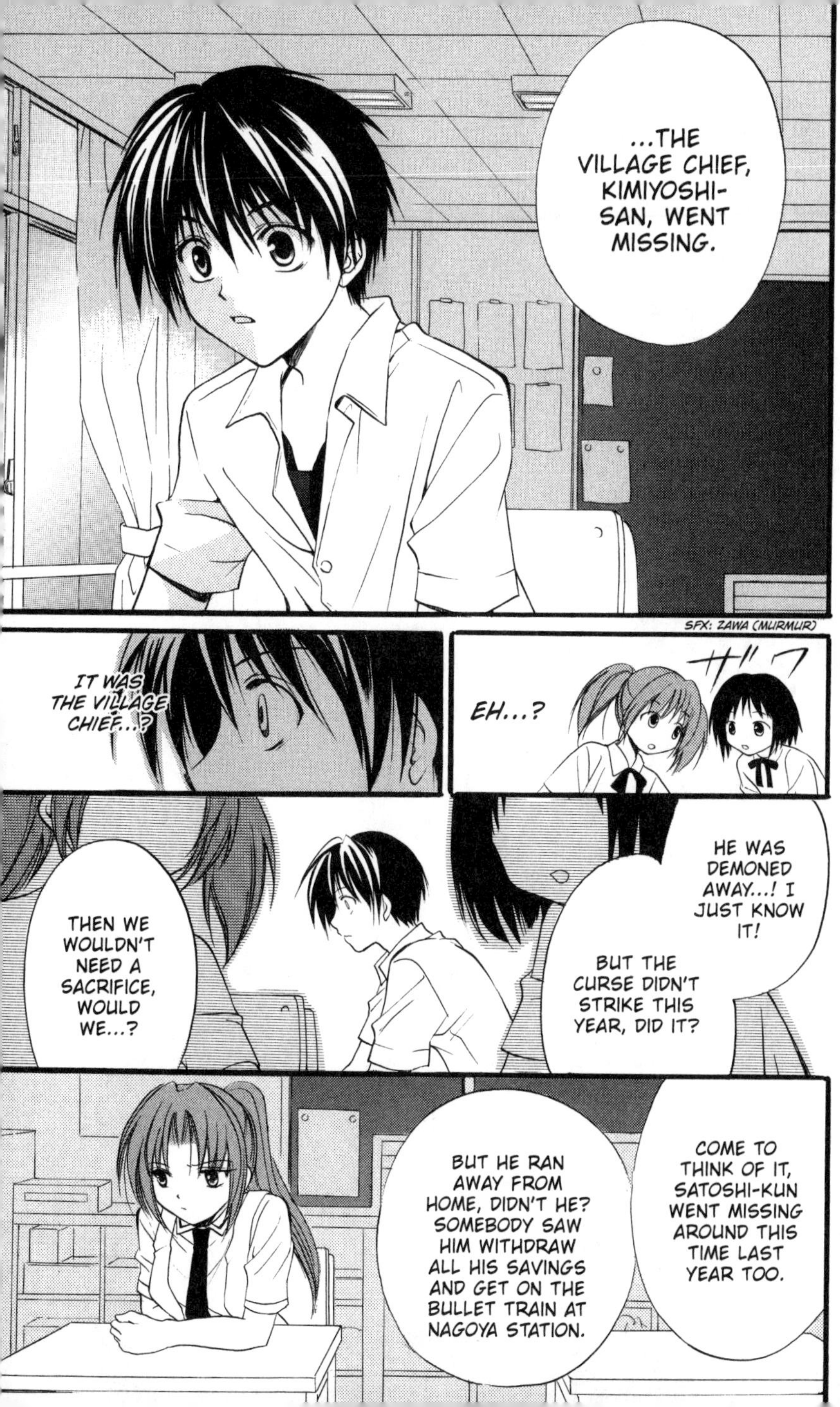
...THE VILLAGE CHIEF, KIMIYOSHI-SAN, WENT MISSING.
SFX: ZAWA (MURMUR)
ザワ
EH...?
IT WAS THE VILLAGE CHIEF...?
HE WAS DEMONED AWAY...! I JUST KNOW IT!
BUT THE CURSE DIDN'T STRIKE THIS YEAR, DID IT?
THEN WE WOULDN'T NEED A SACRIFICE, WOULD WE...?
COME TO THINK OF IT, SATOSHI-KUN WENT MISSING AROUND THIS TIME LAST YEAR TOO.
BUT HE RAN AWAY FROM HOME, DIDN'T HE? SOMEBODY SAW HIM WITHDRAW ALL HIS SAVINGS AND GET ON THE BULLET TRAIN AT NAGOYA STATION.

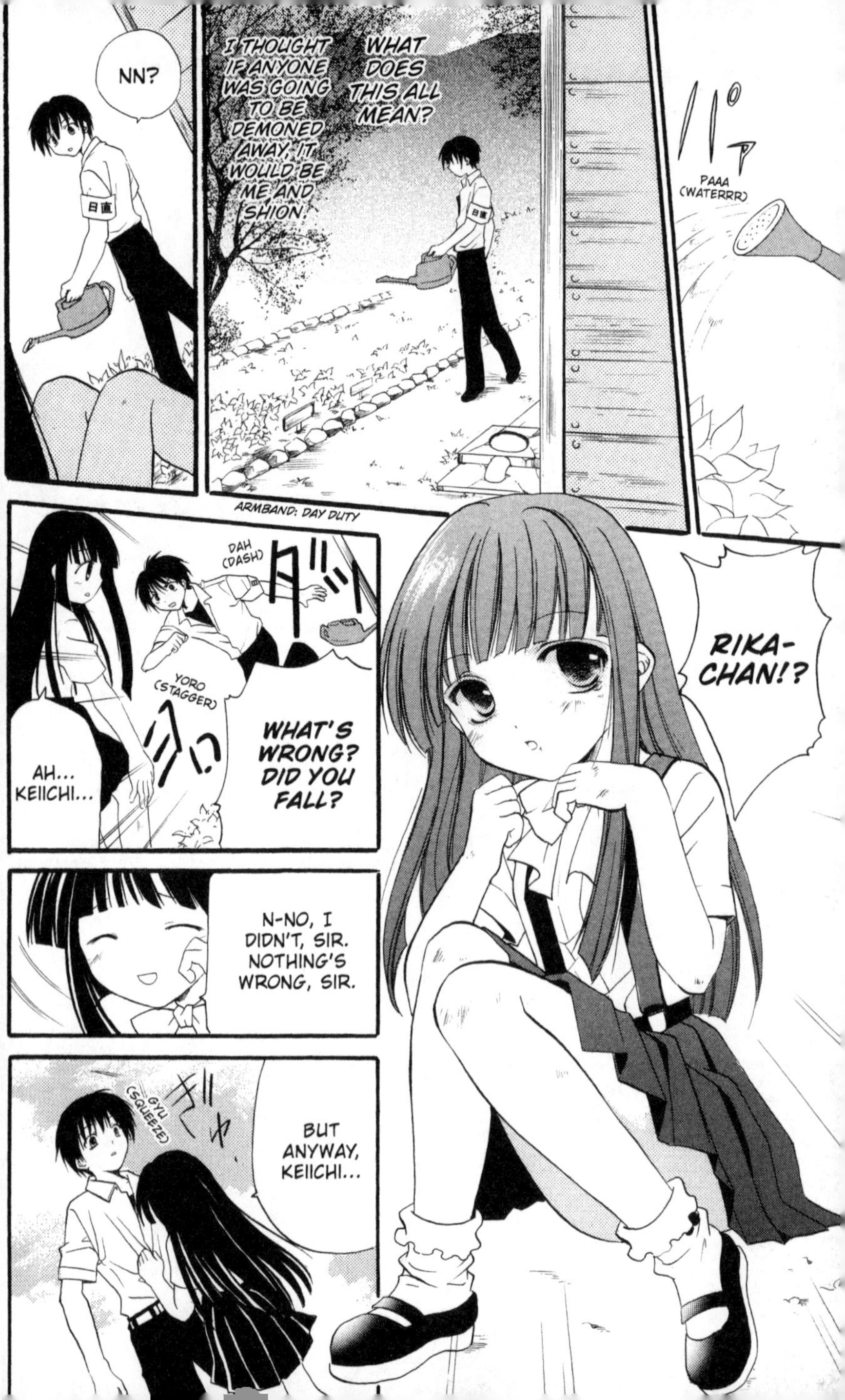

PAAA (WATERRR)
WHAT DOES THIS ALL MEAN?
I THOUGHT IF ANYONE WAS GOING TO BE DEMONED AWAY, IT WOULD BE ME AND SHION.
NN?
ARMBAND: DAY DUTY
RIKA-CHAN!?
DAH (DASH)
WHAT'S WRONG? DID YOU FALL?
YORO (STAGGER)
AH... KEIICHI...
N-NO, I DIDN'T, SIR. NOTHING'S WRONG, SIR.
BUT ANYWAY, KEIICHI...
GYU (SQUEEZE)

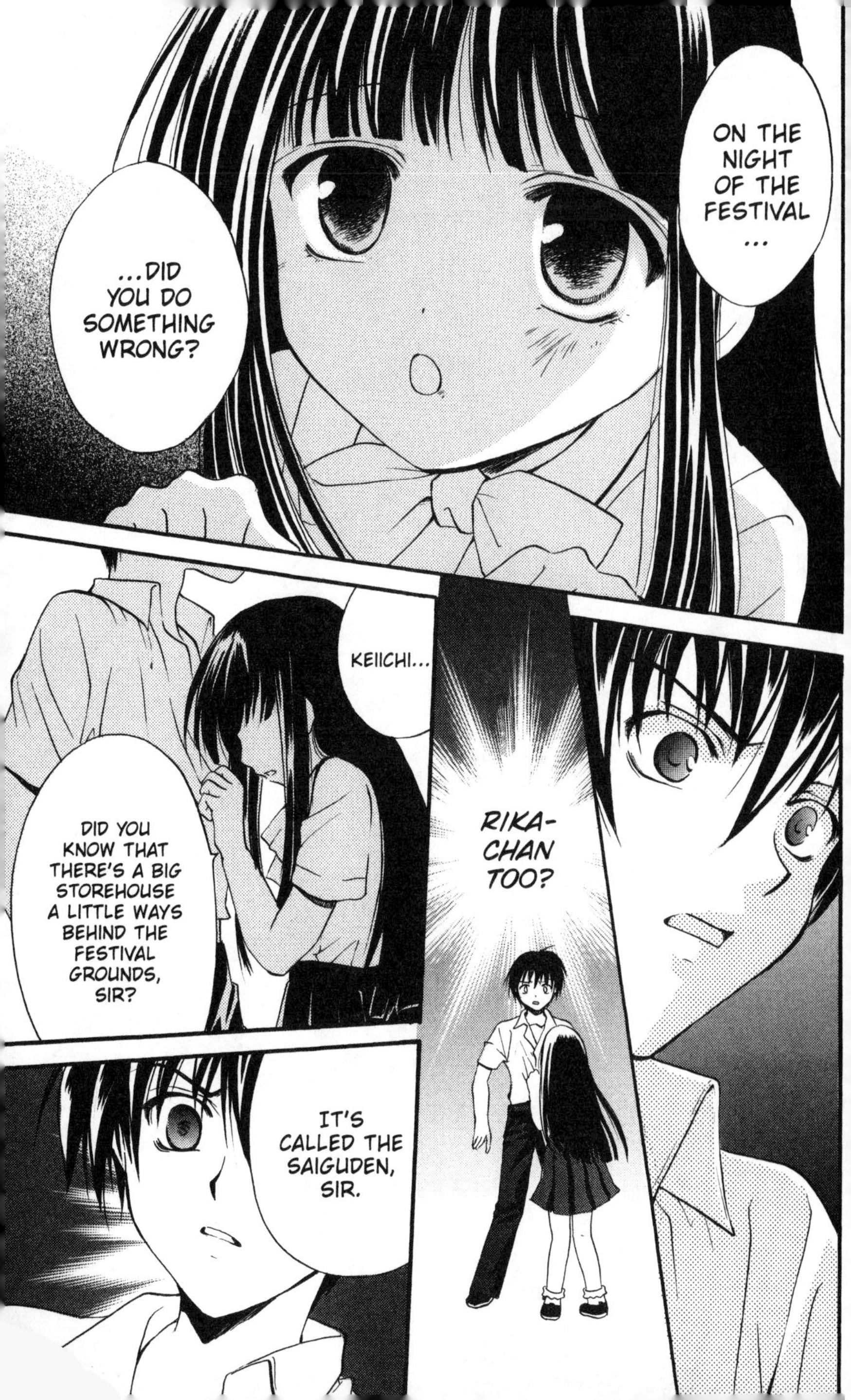
ON THE NIGHT OF THE FESTIVAL...
...DID YOU DO SOMETHING WRONG?
RIKA-CHAN TOO?
KEIICHI...
DID YOU KNOW THAT THERE'S A BIG STOREHOUSE A LITTLE WAYS BEHIND THE FESTIVAL GROUNDS, SIR?
IT'S CALLED THE SAIGUDEN, SIR.

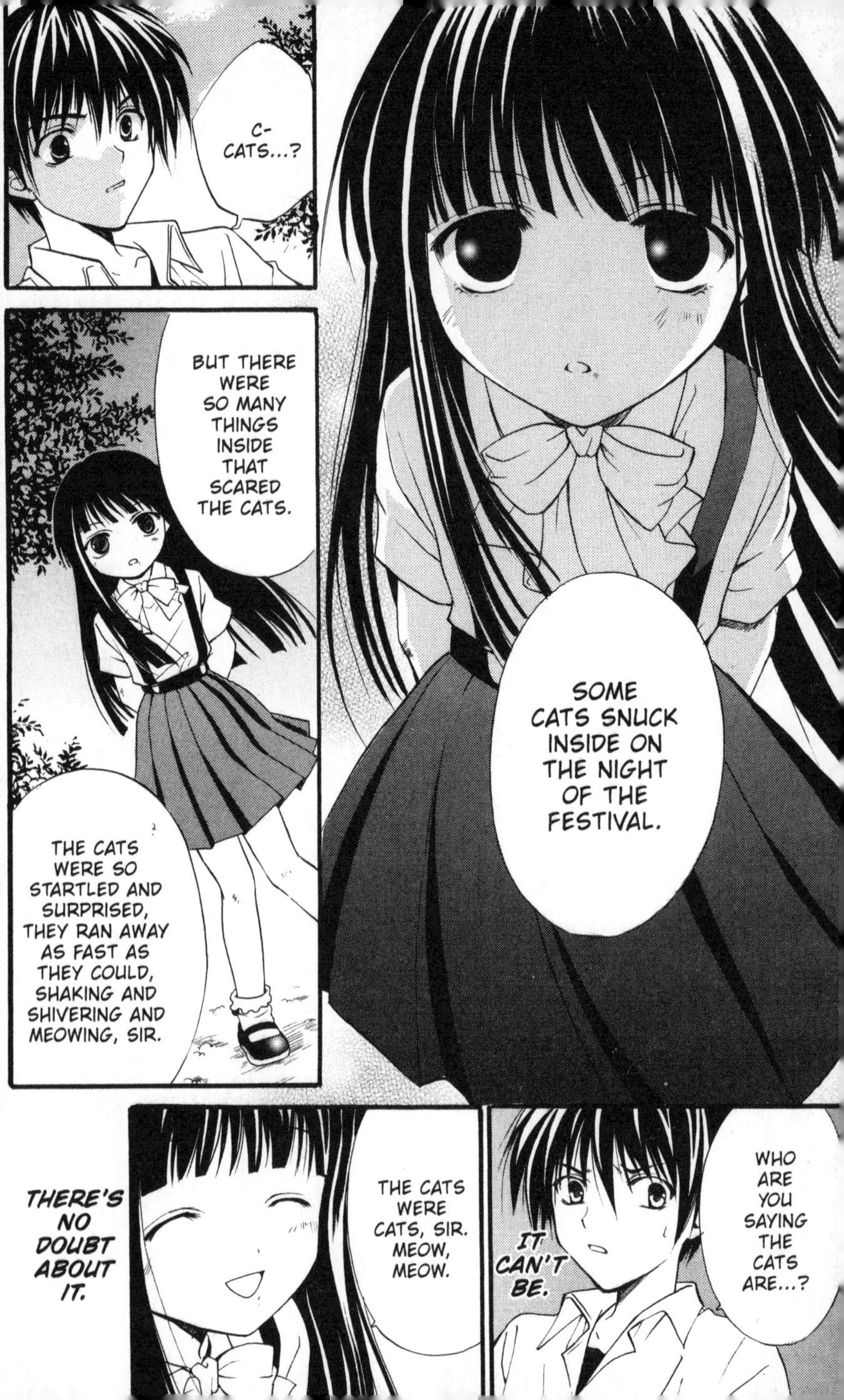
SOME CATS SNUCK INSIDE ON THE NIGHT OF THE FESTIVAL.
C-CATS...?
BUT THERE WERE SO MANY THINGS INSIDE THAT SCARED THE CATS.
THE CATS WERE SO STARTLED AND SURPRISED, THEY RAN AWAY AS FAST AS THEY COULD, SHAKING AND SHIVERING AND MEOWING, SIR.
WHO ARE YOU SAYING THE CATS ARE...?
IT CAN'T BE.
THE CATS WERE CATS, SIR. MEOW, MEOW.
THERE'S NO DOUBT ABOUT IT.

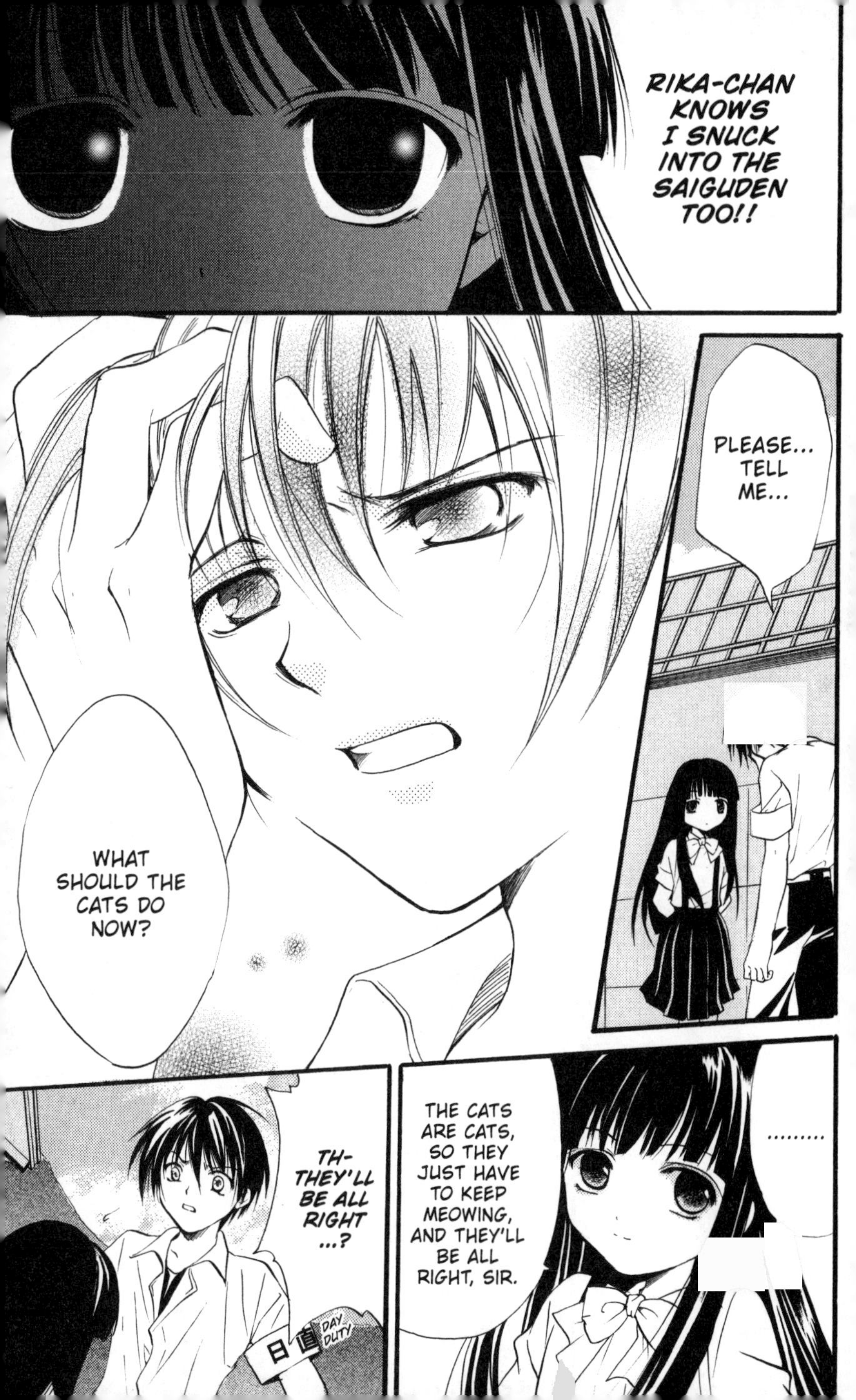
RIKA-CHAN KNOWS I SNUCK INTO THE SAIGUDEN TOO!!
PLEASE... TELL ME...
WHAT SHOULD THE CATS DO NOW?
....
THE CATS ARE CATS, SO THEY JUST HAVE TO KEEP MEOWING, AND THEY'LL BE ALL RIGHT, SIR.
TH-THEY'LL BE ALL RIGHT ...?
日直
DAY DUTY

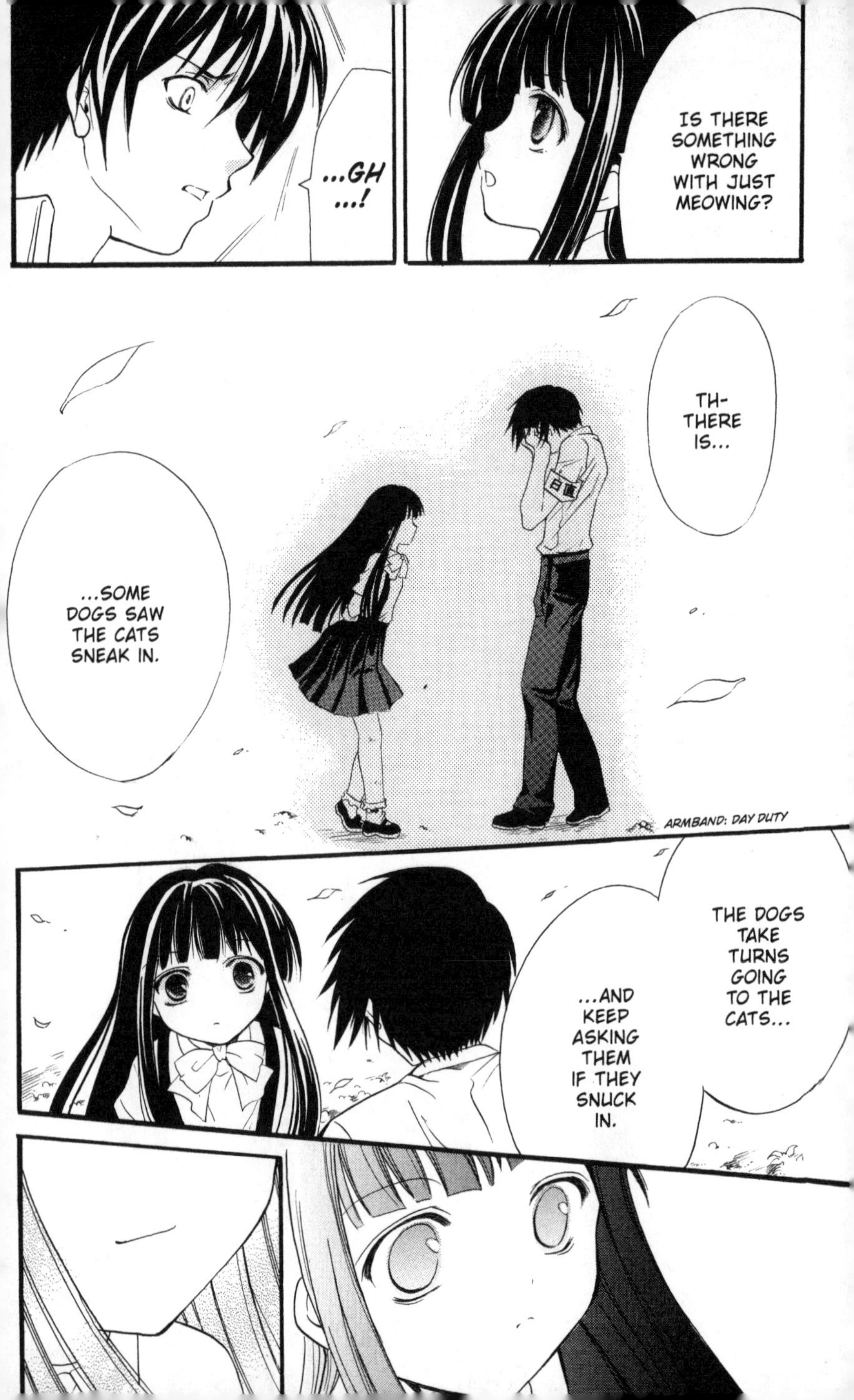
IS THERE SOMETHING WRONG WITH JUST MEOWING?
...GH ...!
TH- THERE IS...
...SOME DOGS SAW THE CATS SNEAK IN.
ARMBAND: DAY DUTY
THE DOGS TAKE TURNS GOING TO THE CATS...
...AND KEEP ASKING THEM IF THEY SNUCK IN.

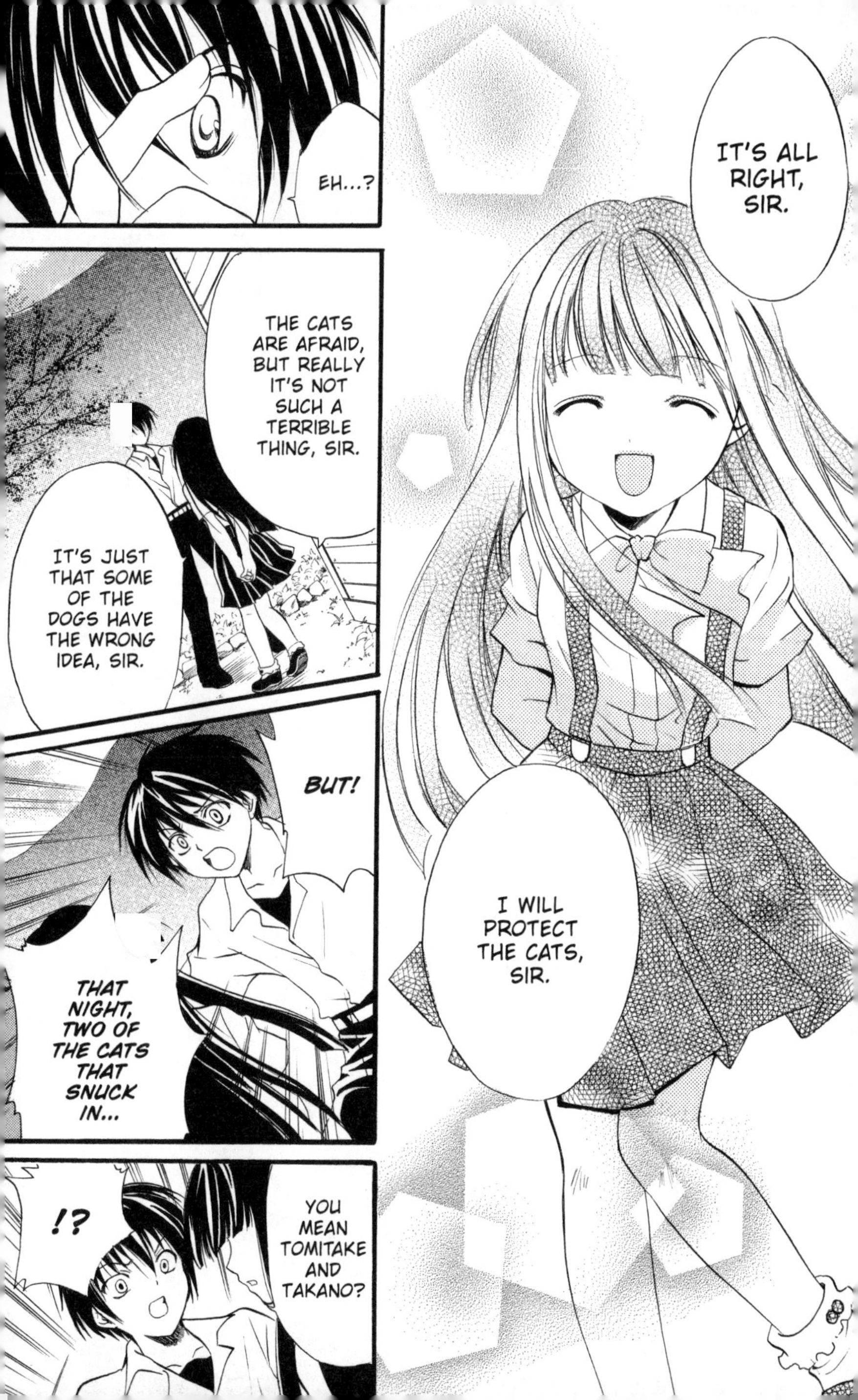
IT'S ALL RIGHT, SIR.
I WILL PROTECT THE CATS, SIR.
EH...?
THE CATS ARE AFRAID, BUT REALLY IT'S NOT SUCH A TERRIBLE THING, SIR.
IT'S JUST THAT SOME OF THE DOGS HAVE THE WRONG IDEA, SIR.
BUT!
THAT NIGHT, TWO OF THE CATS THAT SNUCK IN...
YOU MEAN TOMITAKE AND TAKANO?
!?

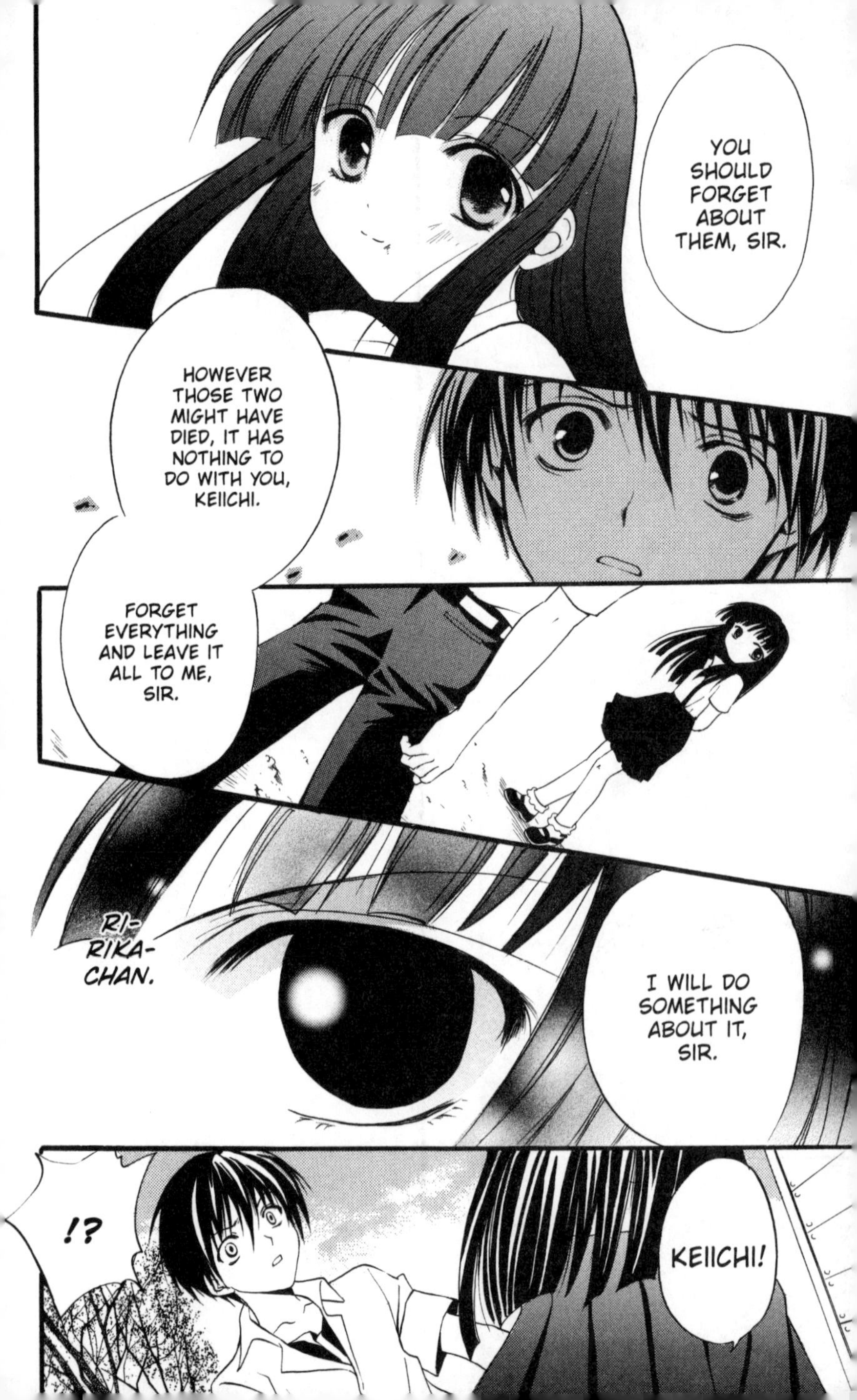
YOU SHOULD FORGET ABOUT THEM, SIR.
HOWEVER THOSE TWO MIGHT HAVE DIED, IT HAS NOTHING TO DO WITH YOU, KEIICHI.
FORGET EVERYTHING AND LEAVE IT ALL TO ME, SIR.
I WILL DO SOMETHING ABOUT IT, SIR.
RI-RIKA-CHAN.
KEIICHI!
!?

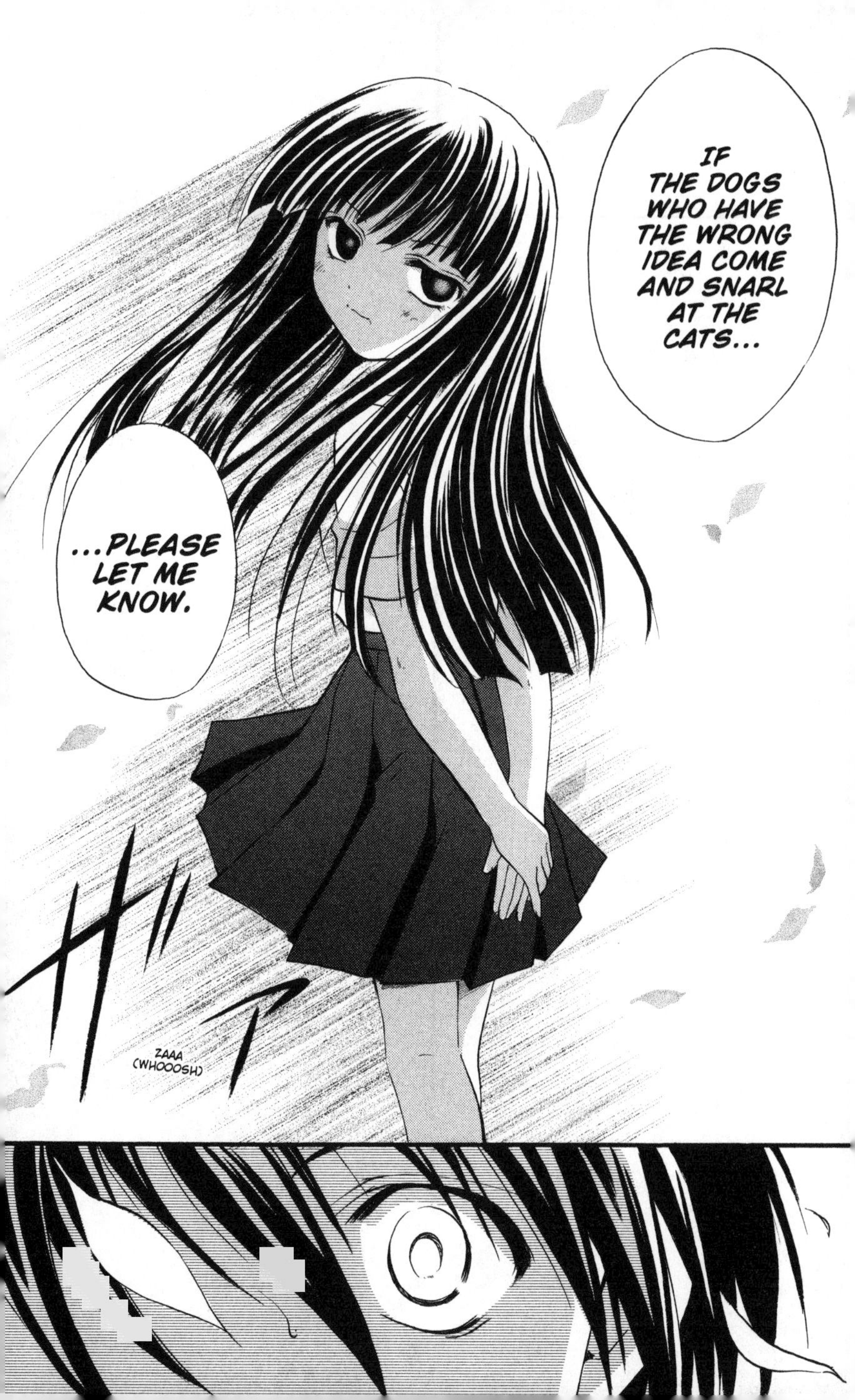
IF THE DOGS WHO HAVE THE WRONG IDEA COME AND SNARL AT THE CATS...
...PLEASE LET ME KNOW.
ZAAA (WHOOOSH)

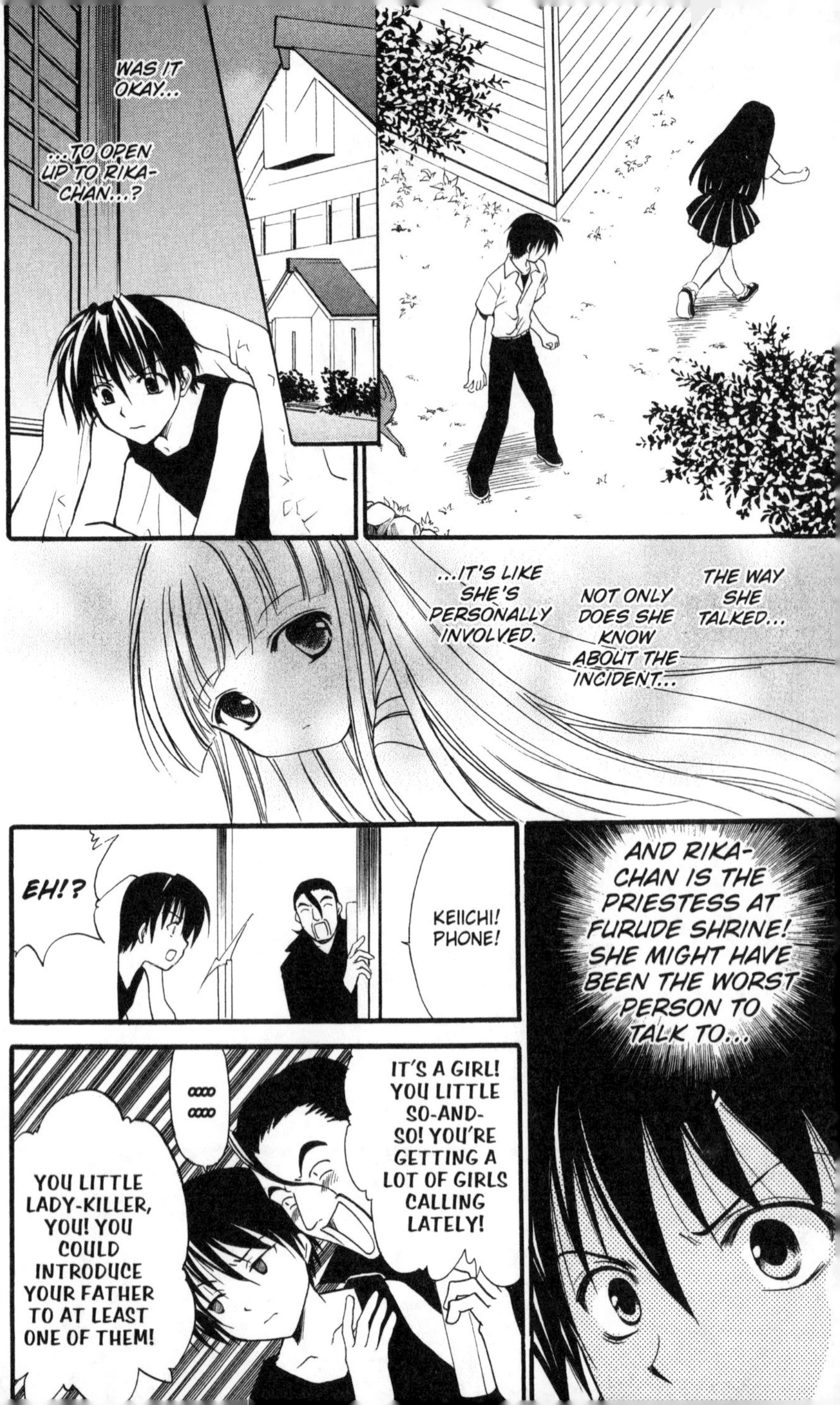
WAS IT OKAY...
...TO OPEN UP TO RIKA-CHAN...?
THE WAY SHE TALKED...
NOT ONLY DOES SHE KNOW ABOUT THE INCIDENT...
...IT'S LIKE SHE'S PERSONALLY INVOLVED.
AND RIKA-CHAN IS THE PRIESTESS AT FURUDE SHRINE! SHE MIGHT HAVE BEEN THE WORST PERSON TO TALK TO...
KEIICHI! PHONE!
EH!?
IT'S A GIRL! YOU LITTLE SO-AND-SO! YOU'RE GETTING A LOT OF GIRLS CALLING LATELY!
YOU LITTLE LADY-KILLER, YOU! YOU COULD INTRODUCE YOUR FATHER TO AT LEAST ONE OF THEM!

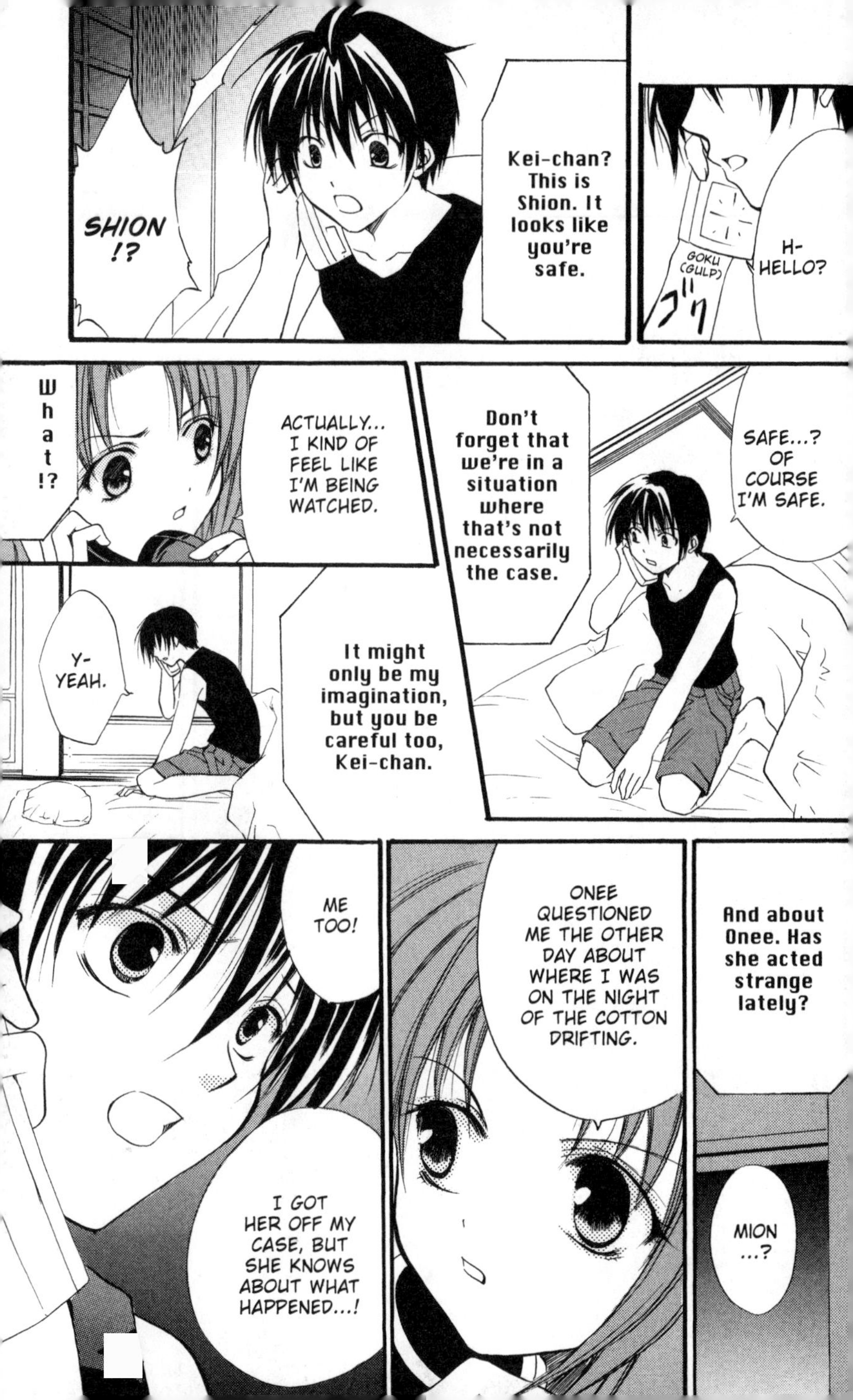
H-HELLO?
GOKU (GULP)
ゴク
Kei-chan? This is Shion. It looks like you're safe.
SHION !?
SAFE...? OF COURSE I'M SAFE.
Don't forget that we're in a situation where that's not necessarily the case.
ACTUALLY... I KIND OF FEEL LIKE I'M BEING WATCHED.
What !?
It might only be my imagination, but you be careful too, Kei-chan.
Y-YEAH.
And about Onee. Has she acted strange lately?
MION ...?
ONEE QUESTIONED ME THE OTHER DAY ABOUT WHERE I WAS ON THE NIGHT OF THE COTTON DRIFTING.
ME TOO!
I GOT HER OFF MY CASE, BUT SHE KNOWS ABOUT WHAT HAPPENED...!

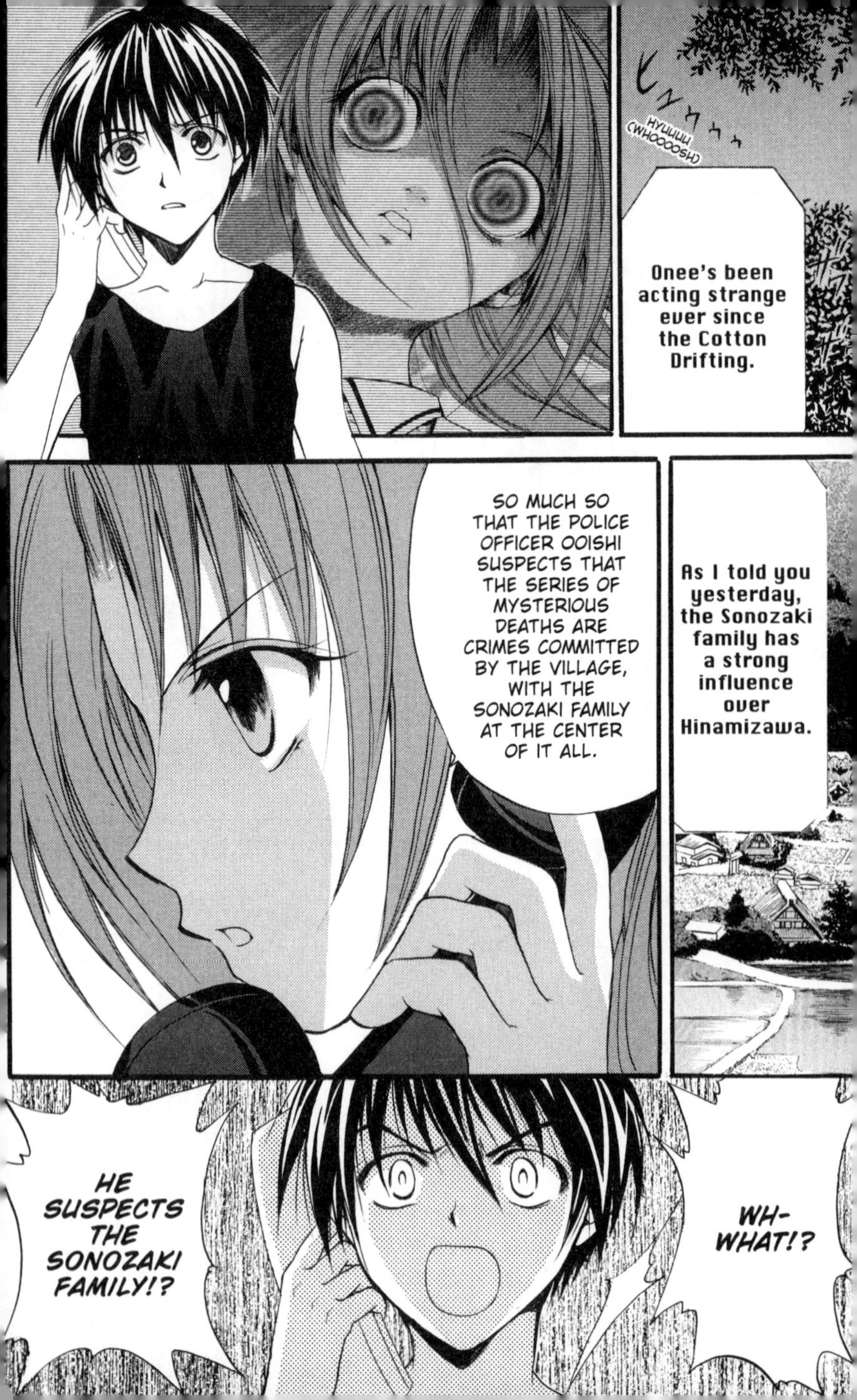
HYUUUU (WHOOOOSH)
Onee's been acting strange ever since the Cotton Drifting.
As I told you yesterday, the Sonozaki family has a strong influence over Hinamizawa.
SO MUCH SO THAT THE POLICE OFFICER OOISHI SUSPECTS THAT THE SERIES OF MYSTERIOUS DEATHS ARE CRIMES COMMITTED BY THE VILLAGE, WITH THE SONOZAKI FAMILY AT THE CENTER OF IT ALL.
WH-WHAT!?
HE SUSPECTS THE SONOZAKI FAMILY!?

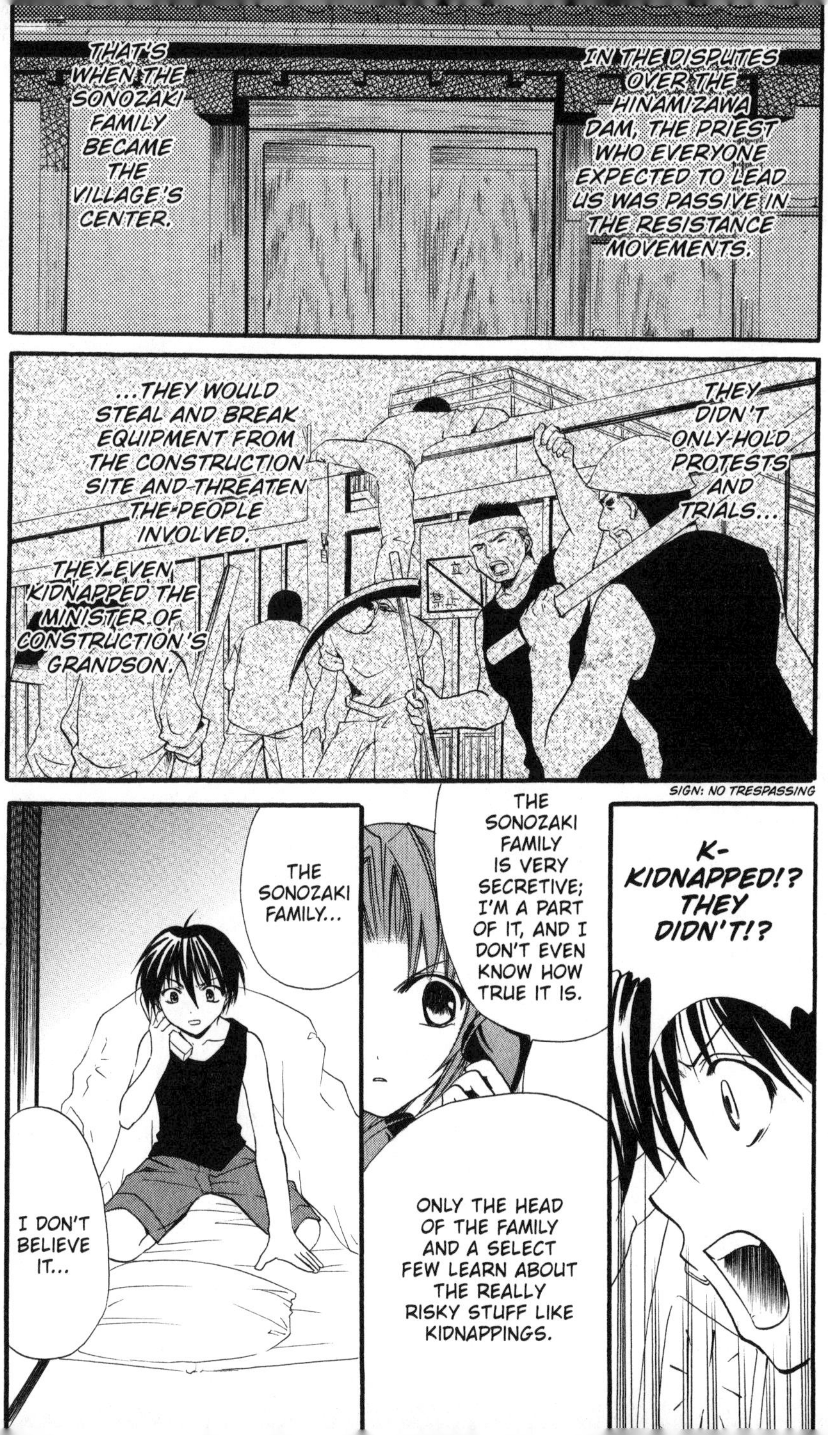
IN THE DISPUTES OVER THE HINAMIZAWA DAM, THE PRIEST WHO EVERYONE EXPECTED TO LEAD US WAS PASSIVE IN THE RESISTANCE MOVEMENTS.
THAT'S WHEN THE SONOZAKI FAMILY BECAME THE VILLAGE'S CENTER.
THEY DIDN'T ONLY HOLD PROTESTS AND TRIALS...
...THEY WOULD STEAL AND BREAK EQUIPMENT FROM THE CONSTRUCTION SITE AND THREATEN THE PEOPLE INVOLVED.
THEY EVEN KIDNAPPED THE MINISTER OF CONSTRUCTION'S GRANDSON.
SIGN: NO TRESPASSING
K-KIDNAPPED!? THEY DIDN'T!?
THE SONOZAKI FAMILY IS VERY SECRETIVE; I'M A PART OF IT, AND I DON'T EVEN KNOW HOW TRUE IT IS.
ONLY THE HEAD OF THE FAMILY AND A SELECT FEW LEARN ABOUT THE REALLY RISKY STUFF LIKE KIDNAPPINGS.
THE SONOZAKI FAMILY...
I DON'T BELIEVE IT...

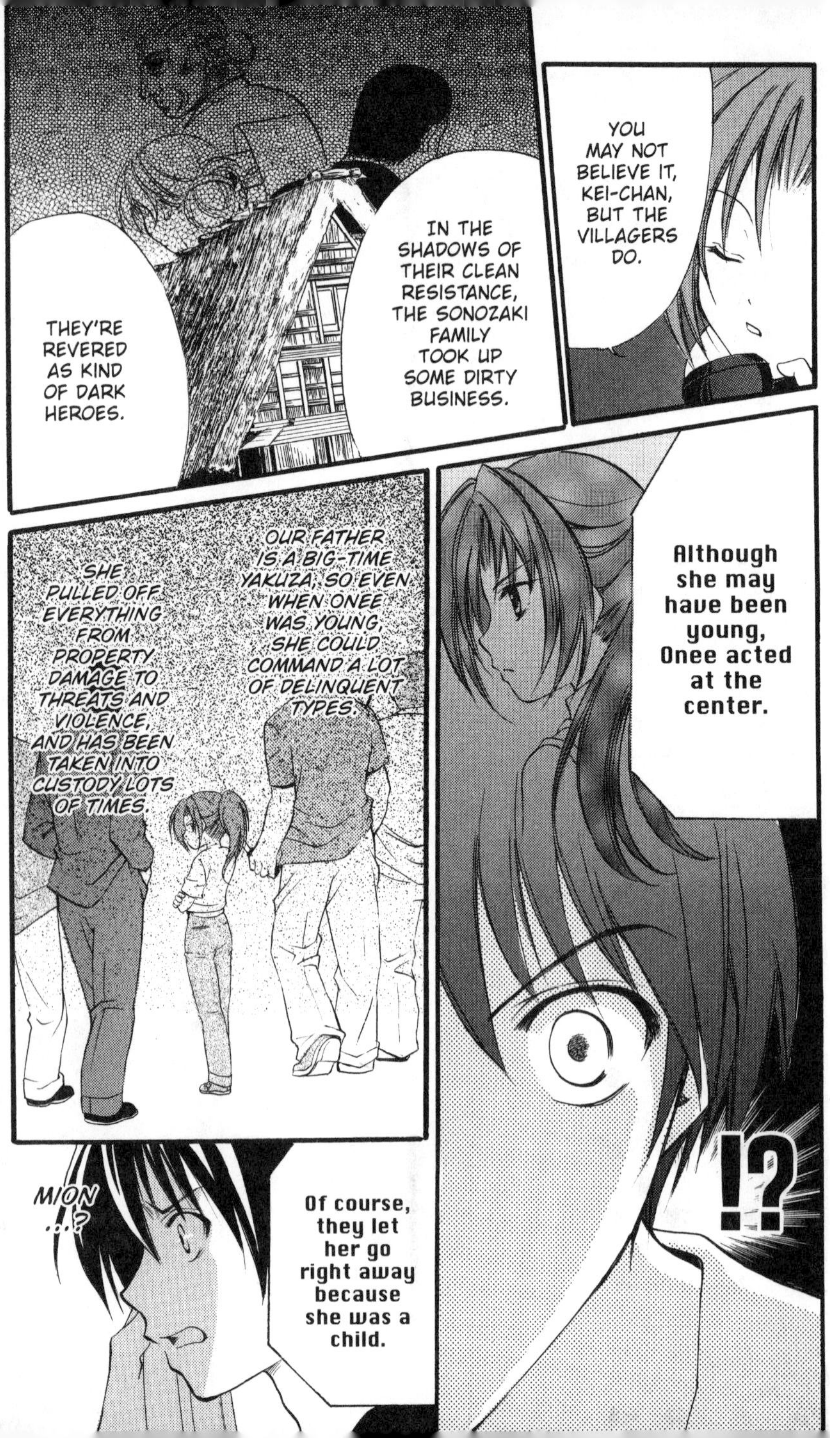
YOU MAY NOT BELIEVE IT, KEI-CHAN, BUT THE VILLAGERS DO.
IN THE SHADOWS OF THEIR CLEAN RESISTANCE, THE SONOZAKI FAMILY TOOK UP SOME DIRTY BUSINESS.
THEY'RE REVERED AS KIND OF DARK HEROES.
Although she may have been young, Onee acted at the center.
!?
OUR FATHER IS A BIG-TIME YAKUZA, SO EVEN WHEN ONEE WAS YOUNG, SHE COULD COMMAND A LOT OF DELINQUENT TYPES.
SHE PULLED OFF EVERYTHING FROM PROPERTY DAMAGE TO THREATS AND VIOLENCE, AND HAS BEEN TAKEN INTO CUSTODY LOTS OF TIMES.
Of course, they let her go right away because she was a child.
MION ...?

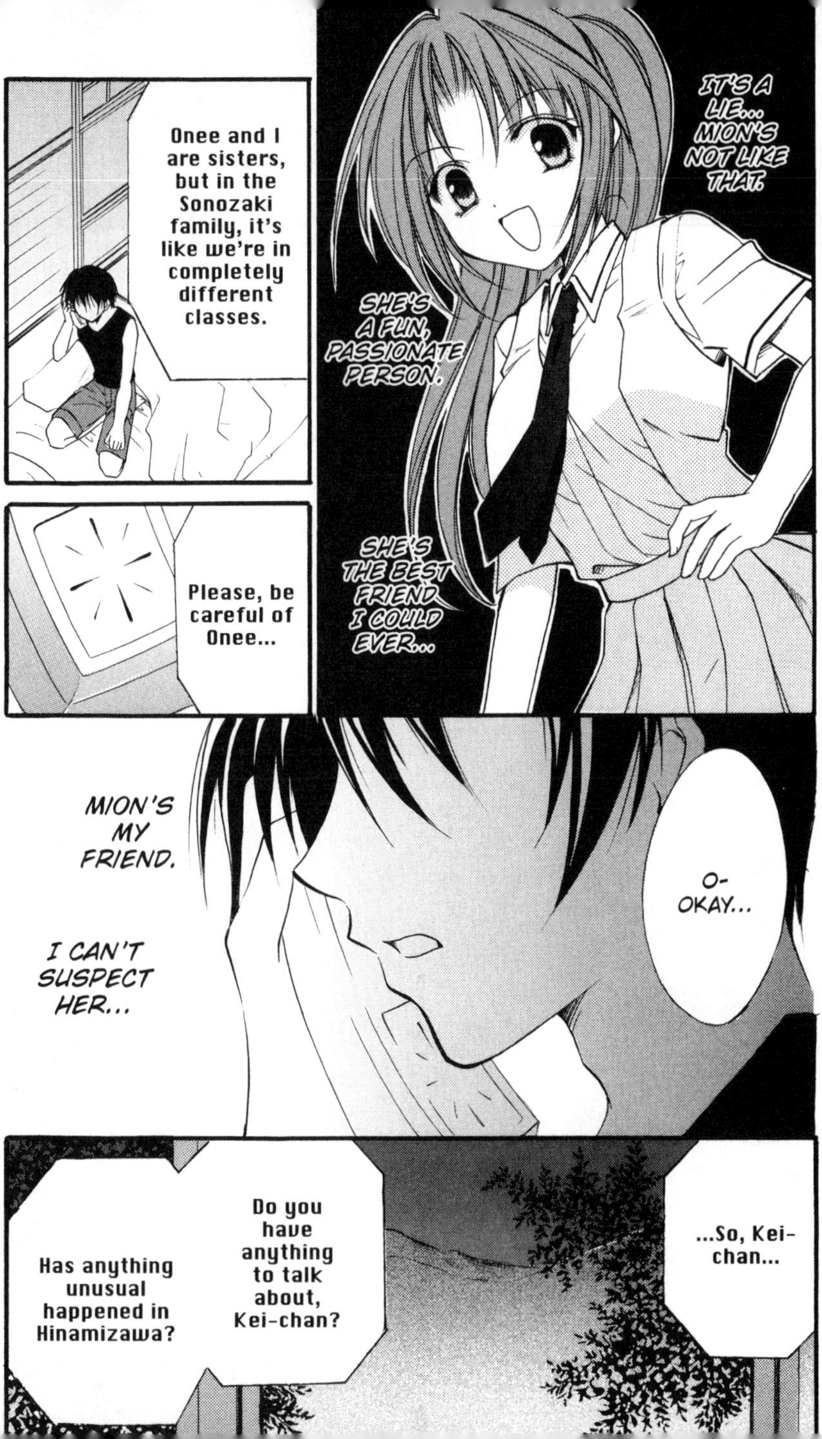
IT'S A LIE... MION'S NOT LIKE THAT.
SHE'S A FUN, PASSIONATE PERSON.
SHE'S THE BEST FRIEND I COULD EVER...
Onee and I are sisters, but in the Sonozaki family, it's like we're in completely different classes.
Please, be careful of Onee...
O-OKAY...
MION'S MY FRIEND.
I CAN'T SUSPECT HER...
...So, Kei-chan...
Do you have anything to talk about, Kei-chan?
Has anything unusual happened in Hinamizawa?

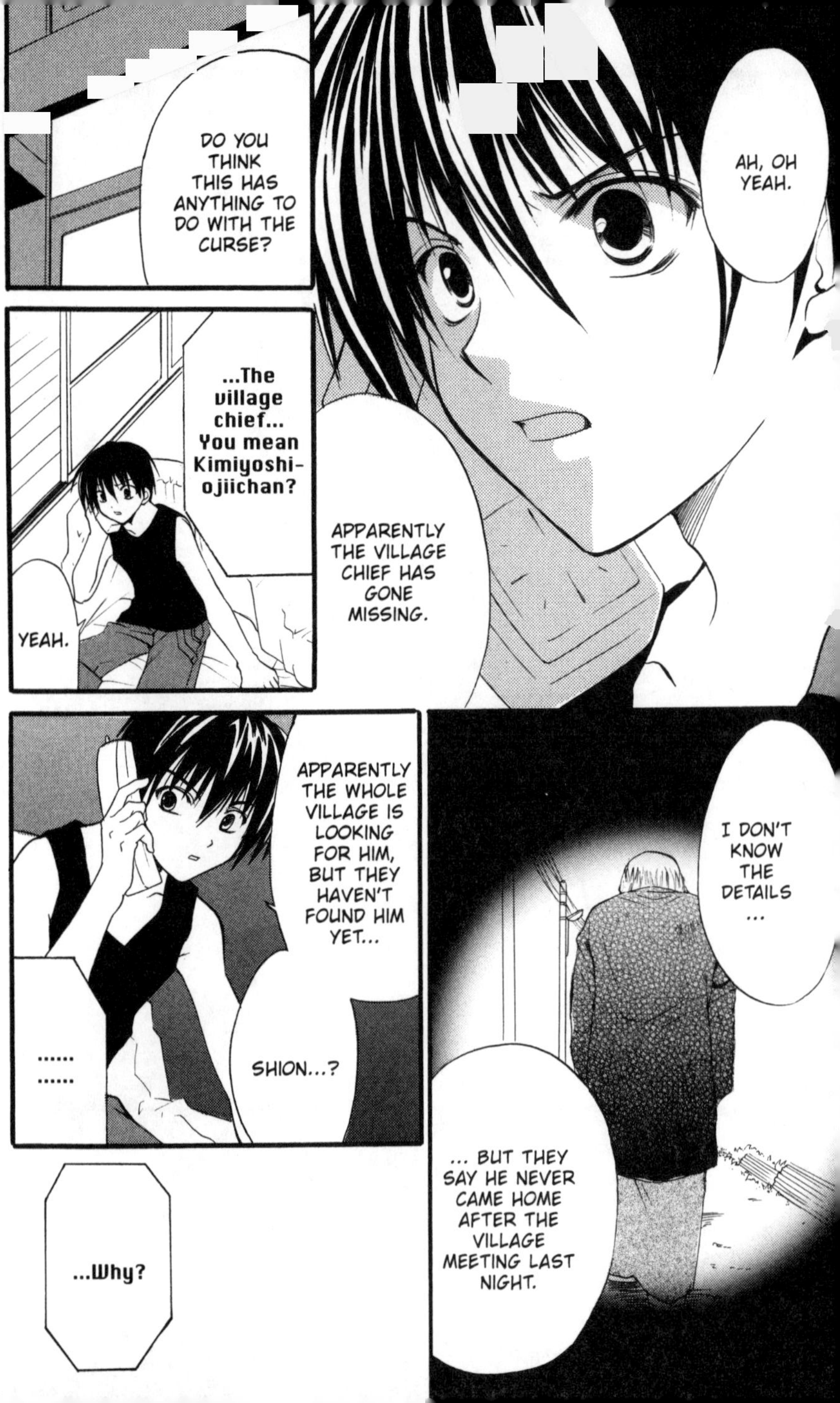
AH, OH YEAH.
APPARENTLY THE VILLAGE CHIEF HAS GONE MISSING.
DO YOU THINK THIS HAS ANYTHING TO DO WITH THE CURSE?
...The village chief... You mean Kimiyoshi-ojiichan?
YEAH.
I DON'T KNOW THE DETAILS...
... BUT THEY SAY HE NEVER CAME HOME AFTER THE VILLAGE MEETING LAST NIGHT.
APPARENTLY THE WHOLE VILLAGE IS LOOKING FOR HIM, BUT THEY HAVEN'T FOUND HIM YET...
SHION...?
....
...Why?

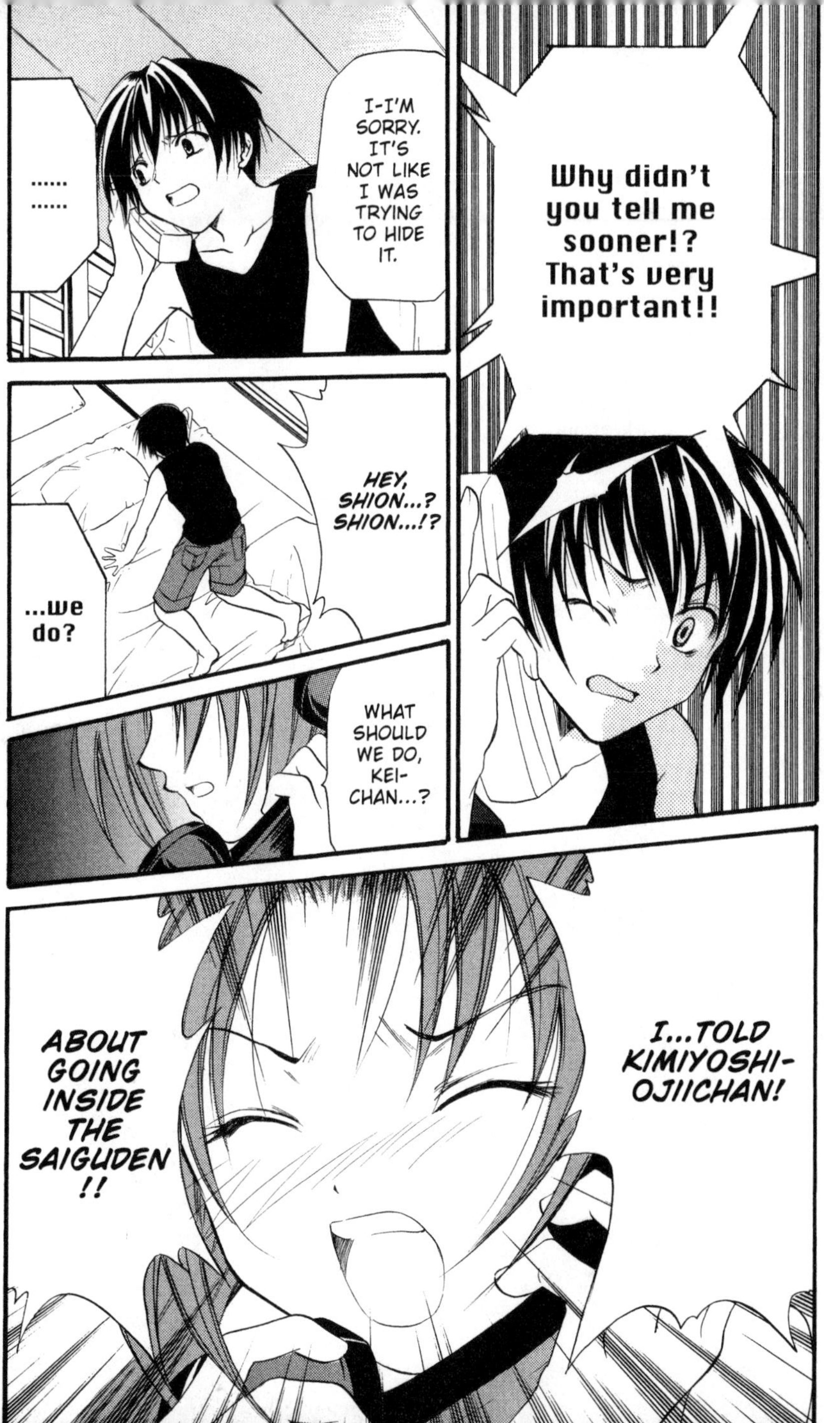

Why didn't you tell me sooner!? That's very important!!
I-I'M SORRY. IT'S NOT LIKE I WAS TRYING TO HIDE IT.
....
HEY, SHION...? SHION...!?
...we do?
WHAT SHOULD WE DO, KEI-CHAN...?
I...TOLD KIMIYOSHI-OJIICHAN!
ABOUT GOING INSIDE THE SAIGUDEN!!

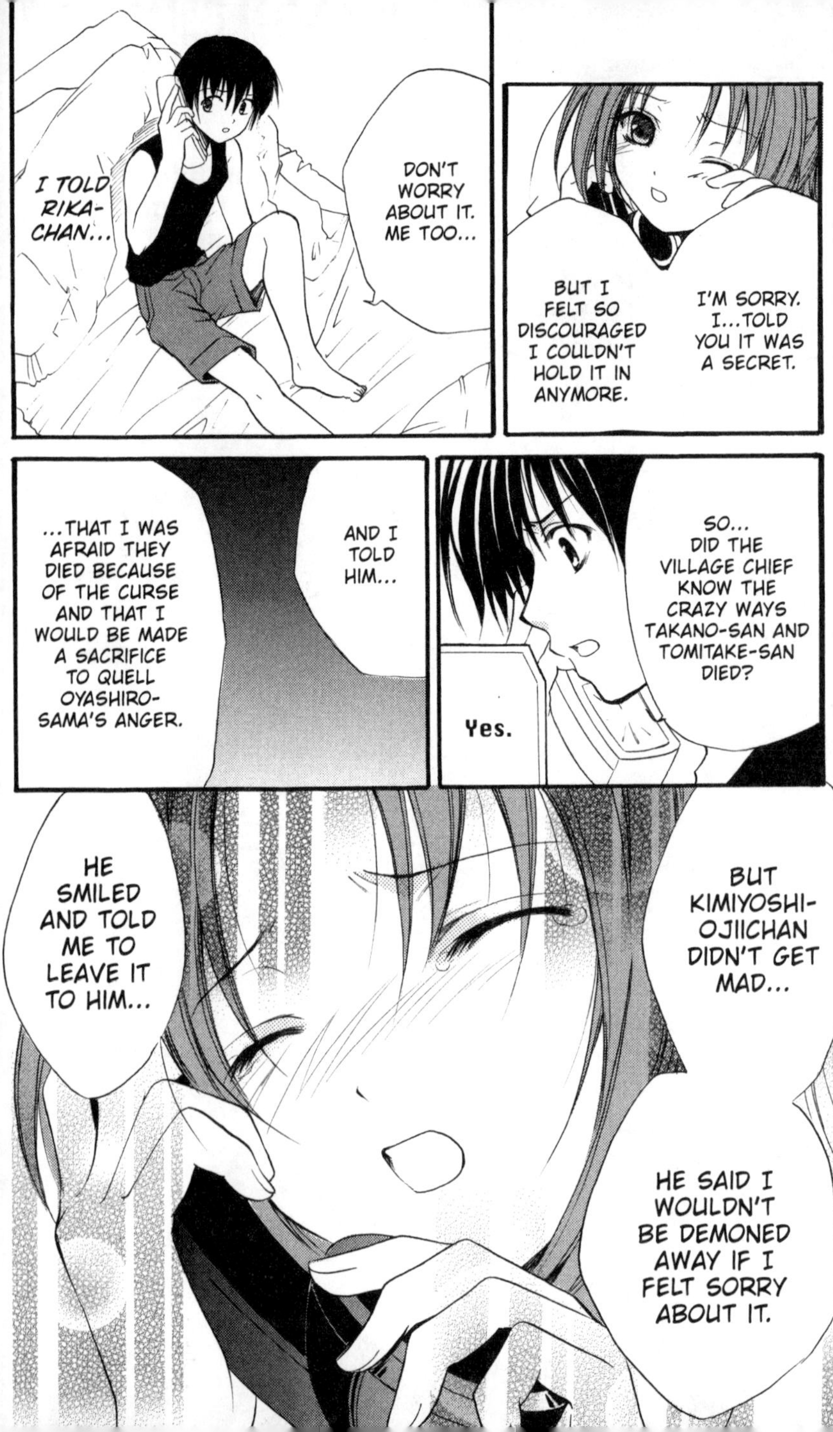
I'M SORRY. I...TOLD YOU IT WAS A SECRET.
BUT I FELT SO DISCOURAGED I COULDN'T HOLD IT IN ANYMORE.
DON'T WORRY ABOUT IT. ME TOO...
I TOLD RIKA-CHAN...
SO... DID THE VILLAGE CHIEF KNOW THE CRAZY WAYS TAKANO-SAN AND TOMITAKE-SAN DIED?
Yes.
AND I TOLD HIM...
...THAT I WAS AFRAID THEY DIED BECAUSE OF THE CURSE AND THAT I WOULD BE MADE A SACRIFICE TO QUELL OYASHIRO-SAMA'S ANGER.
BUT KIMIYOSHI-OJIICHAN DIDN'T GET MAD...
HE SMILED AND TOLD ME TO LEAVE IT TO HIM...
HE SAID I WOULDN'T BE DEMONED AWAY IF I FELT SORRY ABOUT IT.

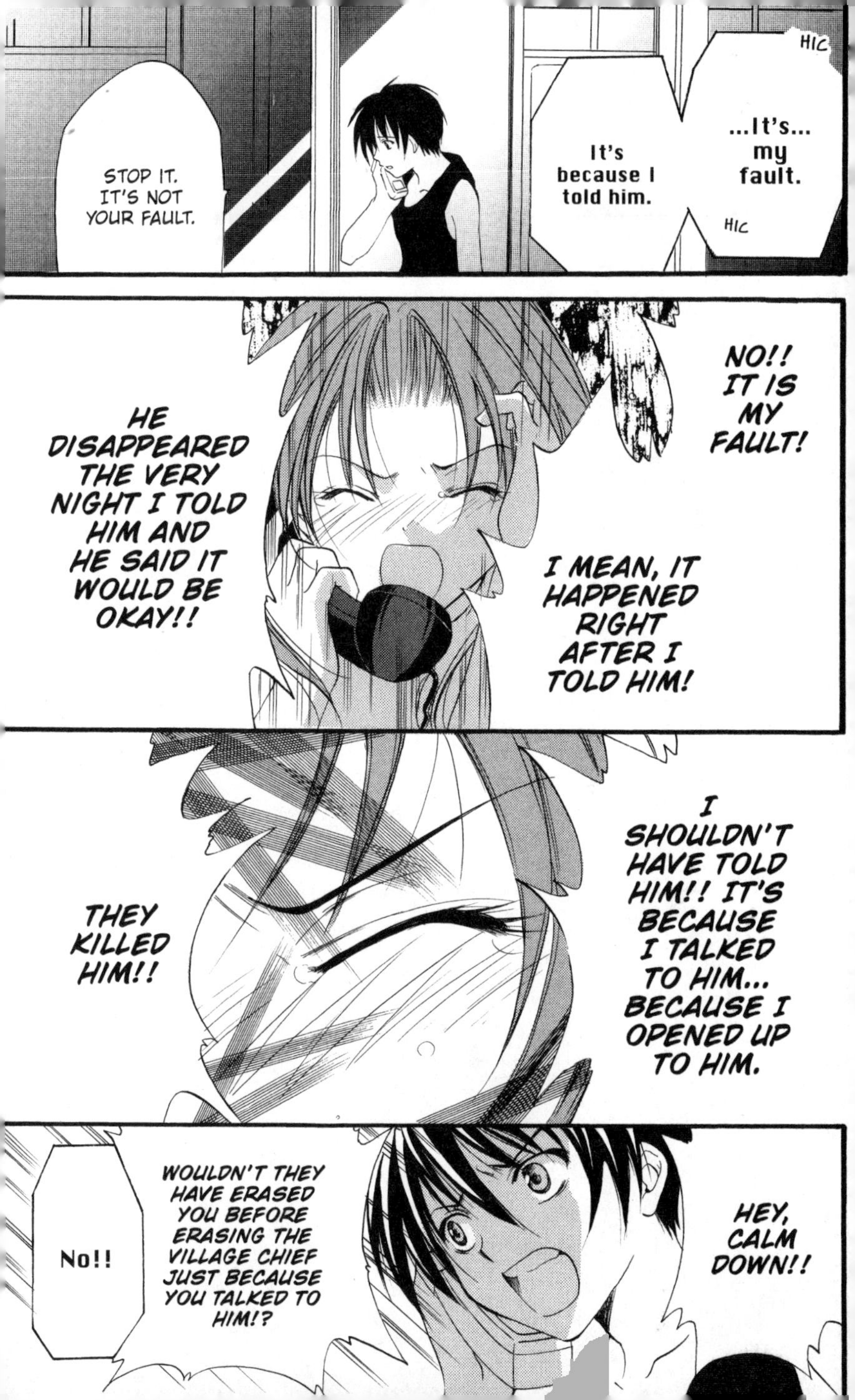
HIC
...It's... my fault.
HIC
It's because I told him.
STOP IT. IT'S NOT YOUR FAULT.
NO!! IT IS MY FAULT!
I MEAN, IT HAPPENED RIGHT AFTER I TOLD HIM!
HE DISAPPEARED THE VERY NIGHT I TOLD HIM AND HE SAID IT WOULD BE OKAY!!
I SHOULDN'T HAVE TOLD HIM!! IT'S BECAUSE I TALKED TO HIM... BECAUSE I OPENED UP TO HIM.
THEY KILLED HIM!!
HEY, CALM DOWN!!
WOULDN'T THEY HAVE ERASED YOU BEFORE ERASING THE VILLAGE CHIEF JUST BECAUSE YOU TALKED TO HIM!?
No!!

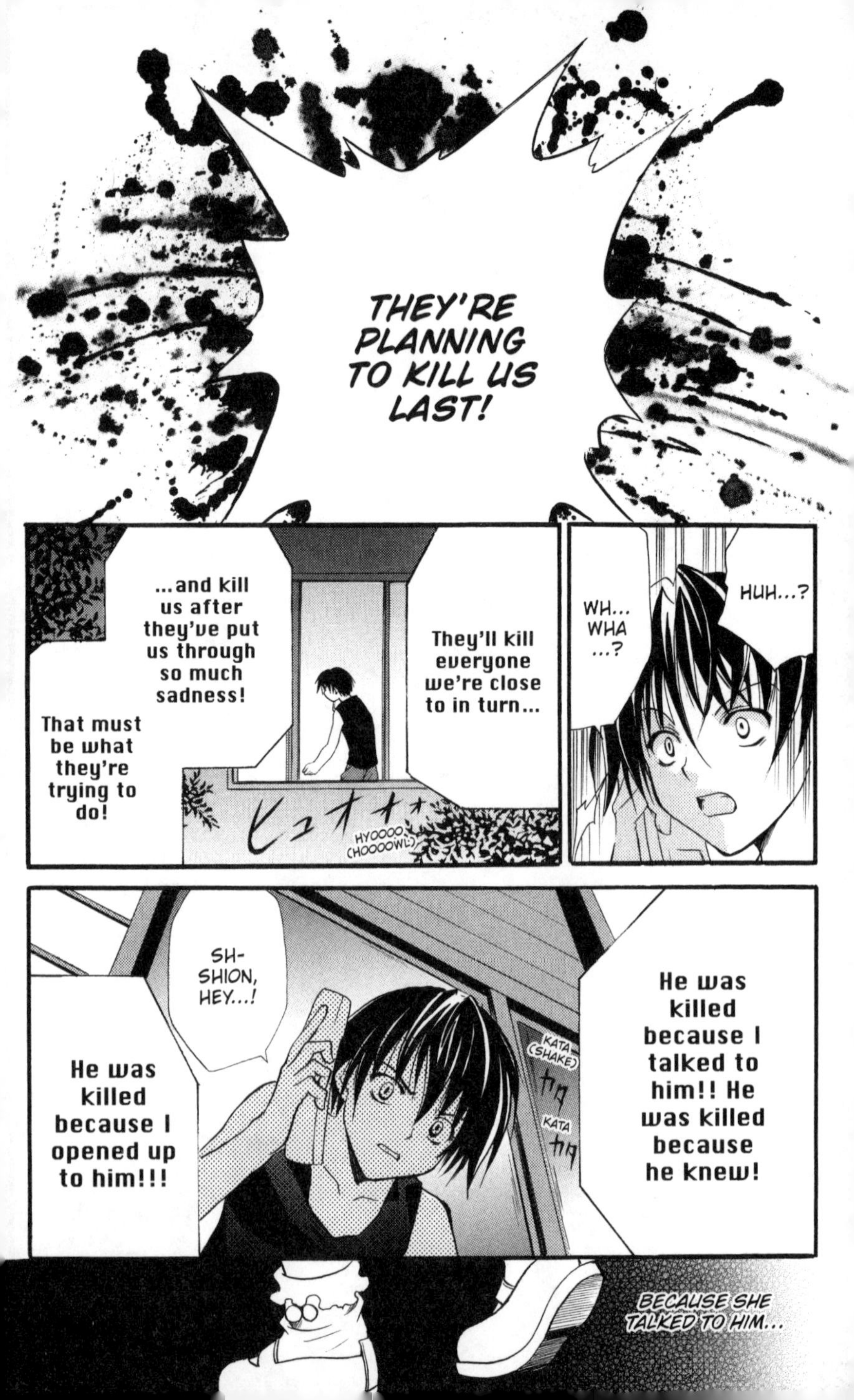
THEY'RE PLANNING TO KILL US LAST!
HUH...?
WH... WHA ...?
They'll kill everyone we're close to in turn...
...and kill us after they've put us through so much sadness!
That must be what they're trying to do!
HYOOOO (HOOOOWL)
He was killed because I talked to him!! He was killed because he knew!
KATA (SHAKE)
KATA
SH- SHION, HEY...!
He was killed because I opened up to him!!!
BECAUSE SHE TALKED TO HIM...

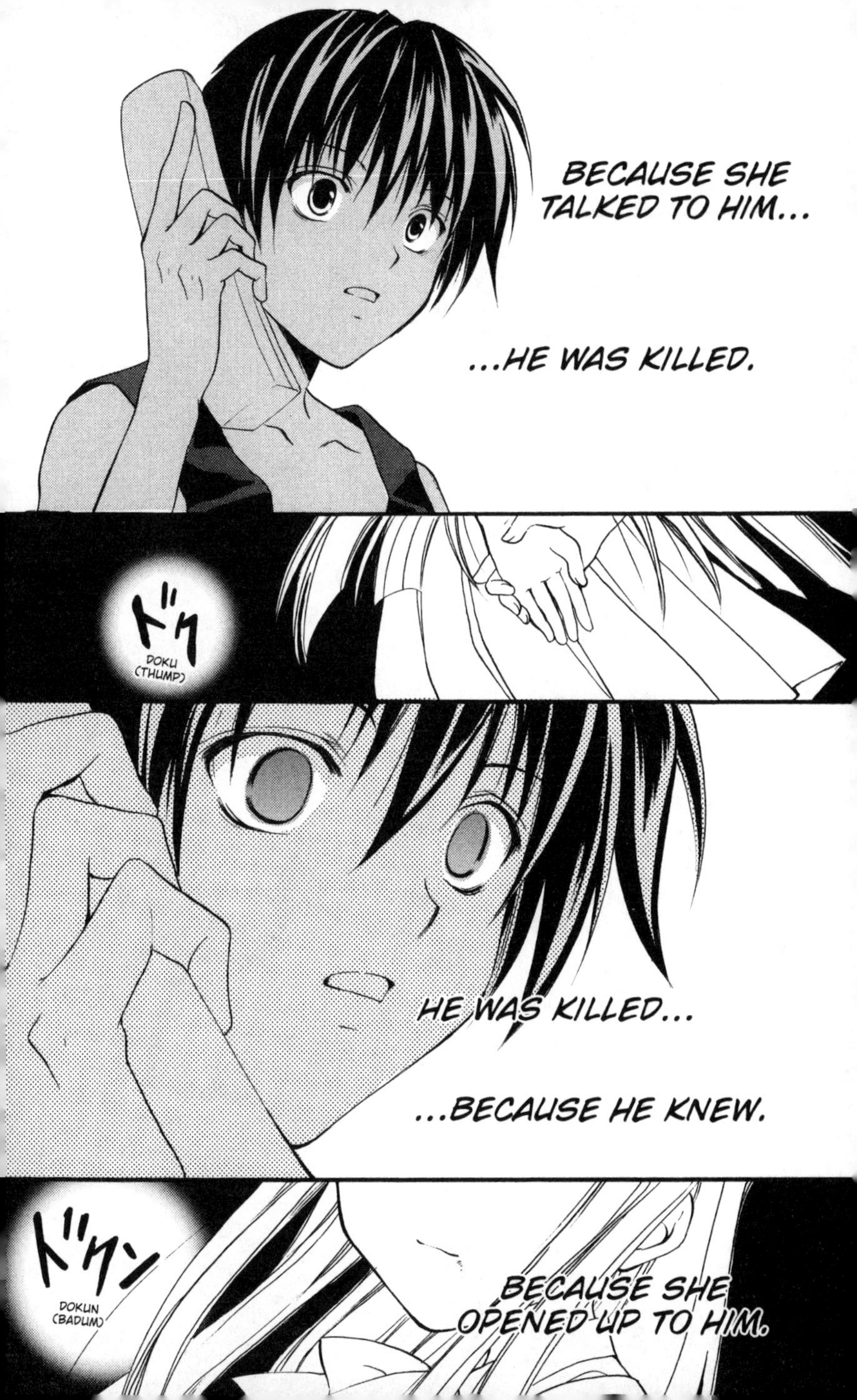
BECAUSE SHE TALKED TO HIM...
...HE WAS KILLED.
ドク
DOKU (THUMP)
HE WAS KILLED...
...BECAUSE HE KNEW.
ドクン
DOKUN (BADUM)
BECAUSE SHE OPENED UP TO HIM.

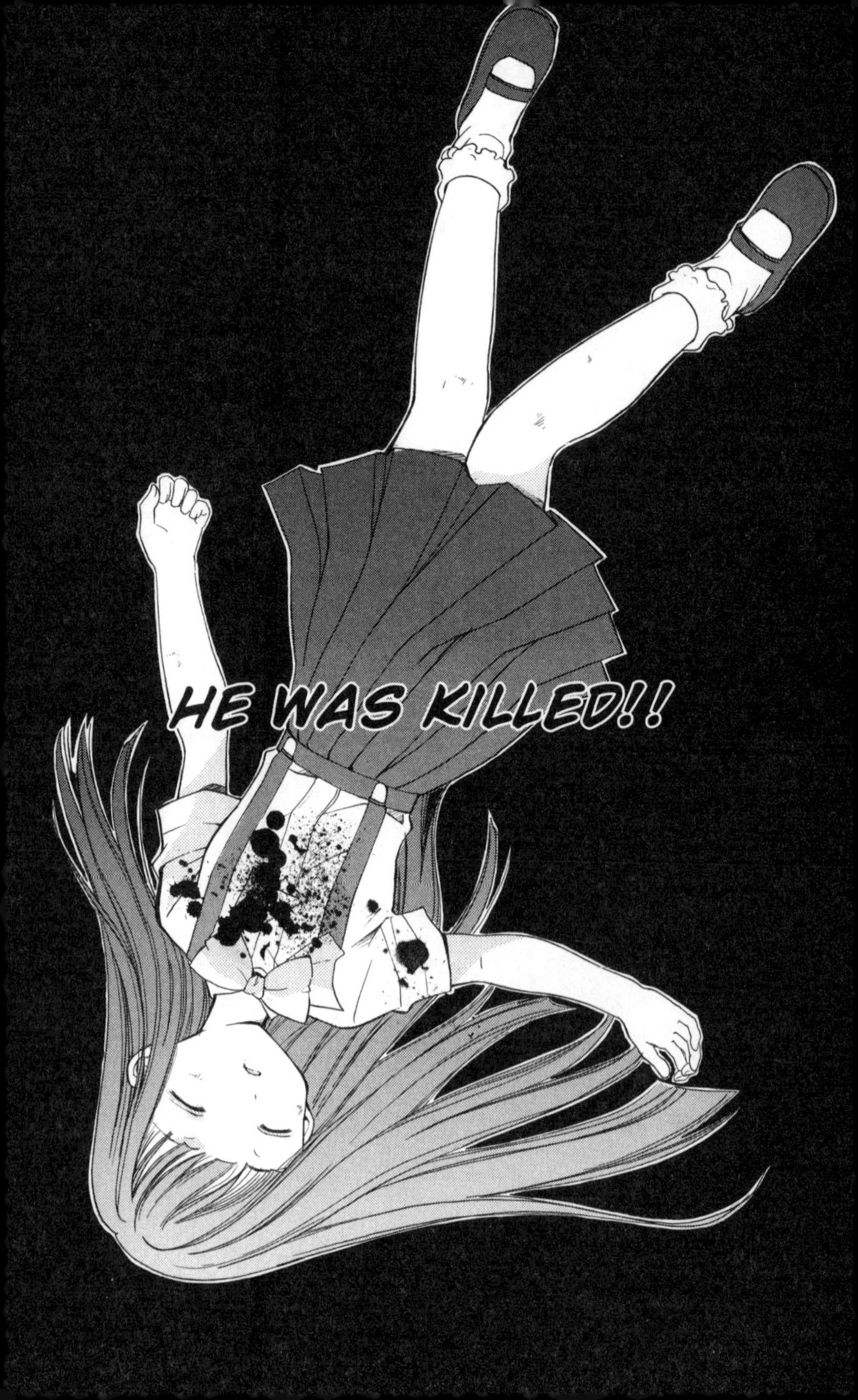
HE WAS KILLED!!

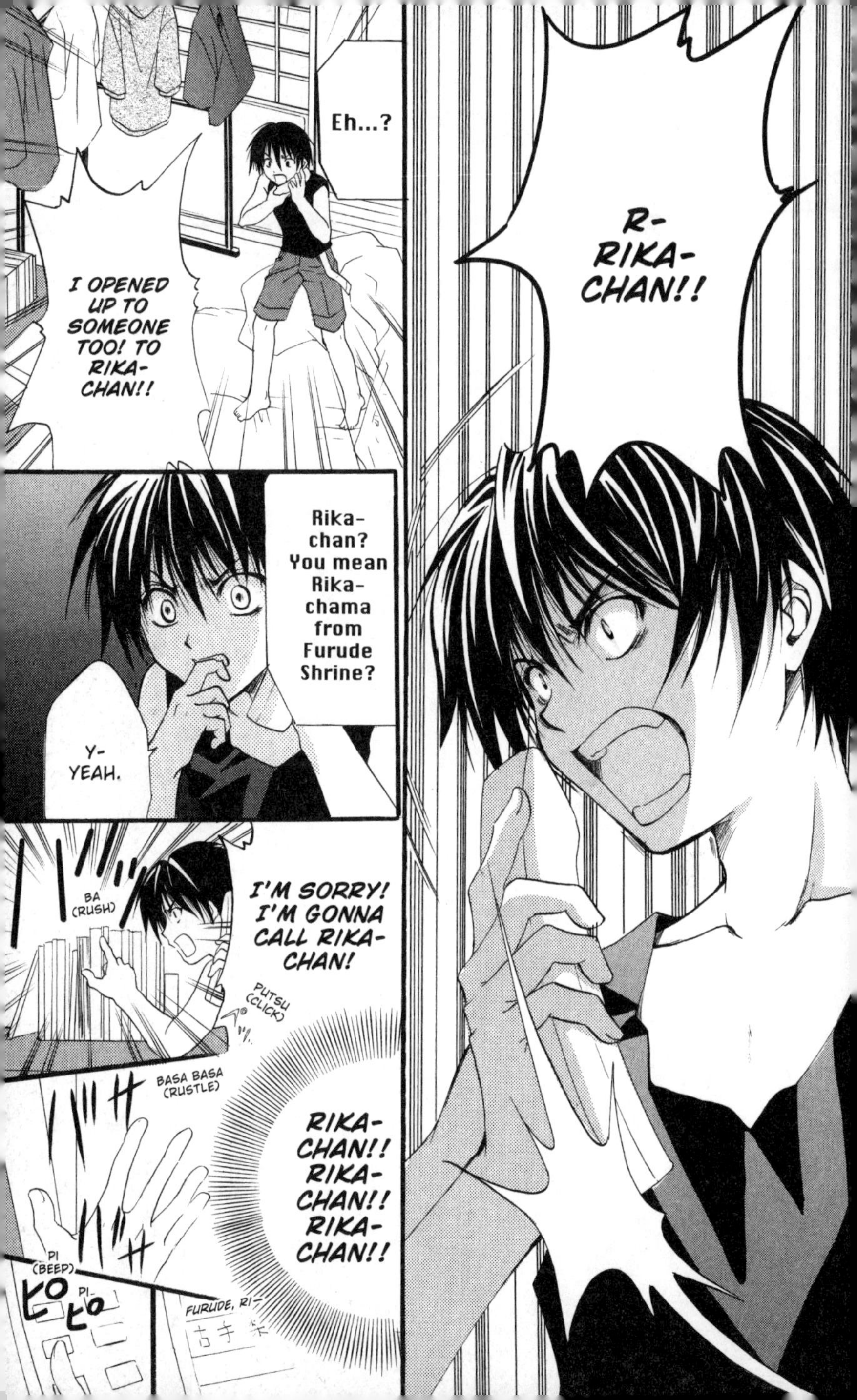
R-RIKA-CHAN!!
Eh...?
I OPENED UP TO SOMEONE TOO! TO RIKA-CHAN!!
Rika-chan? You mean Rika-chama from Furude Shrine?
Y-YEAH.
I'M SORRY! I'M GONNA CALL RIKA-CHAN!
BA (RUSH)
PUTSU (CLICK)
BASA BASA (RUSTLE)
RIKA-CHAN!! RIKA-CHAN!! RIKA-CHAN!!
PI (BEEP)
PI
FURUDE, RI—

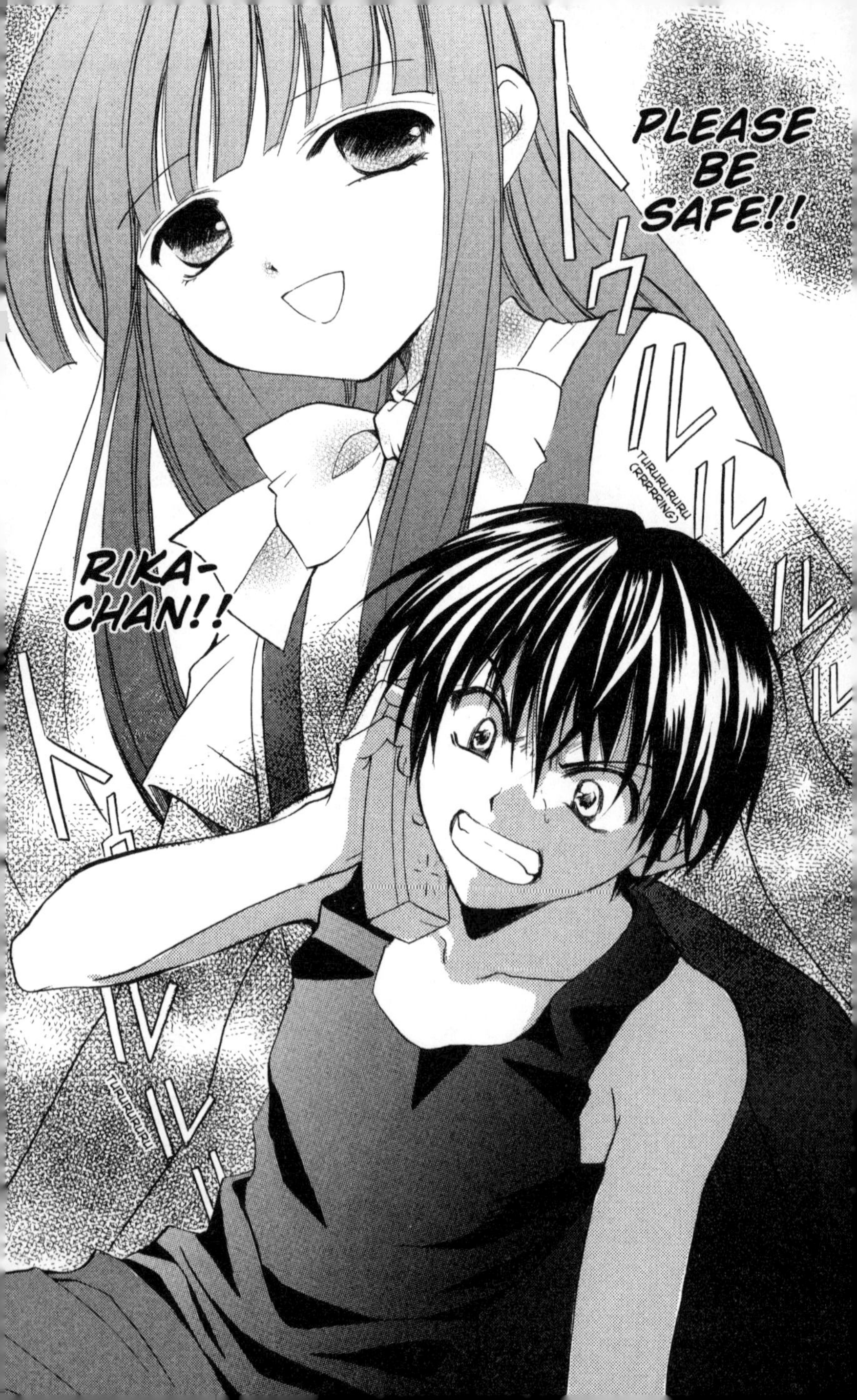
PLEASE BE SAFE!!
TURURURURU (RRRRRING)
RIKA-CHAN!!
TURURURURU

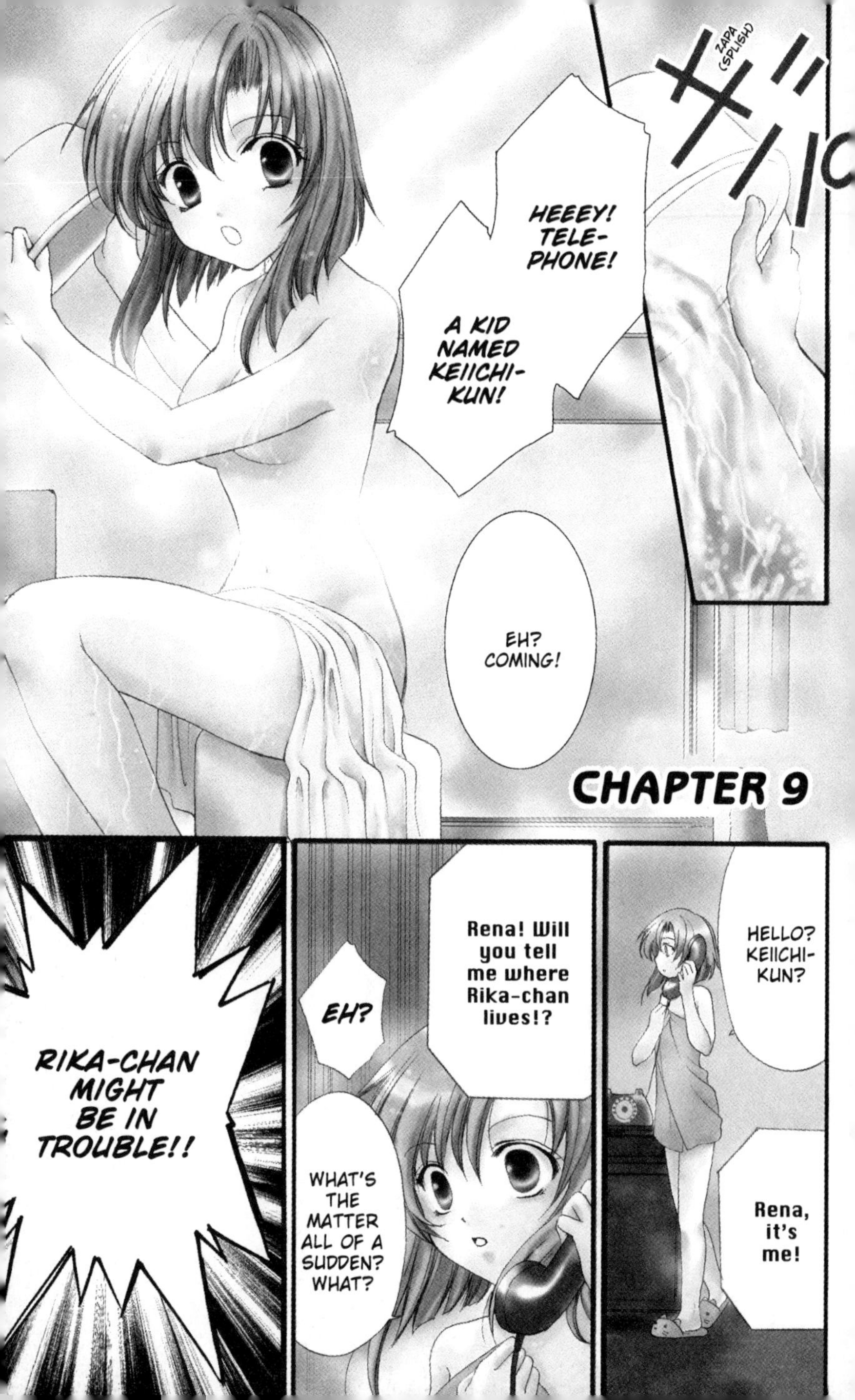
ZAPA (SPLISH)
HEEEY! TELE-PHONE!
A KID NAMED KEIICHI-KUN!
EH? COMING!
CHAPTER 9
HELLO? KEIICHI-KUN?
Rena, it's me!
Rena! Will you tell me where Rika-chan lives!?
EH?
WHAT'S THE MATTER ALL OF A SUDDEN? WHAT?
RIKA-CHAN MIGHT BE IN TROUBLE!!

CHAPTER 9
DISAPPEARANCE

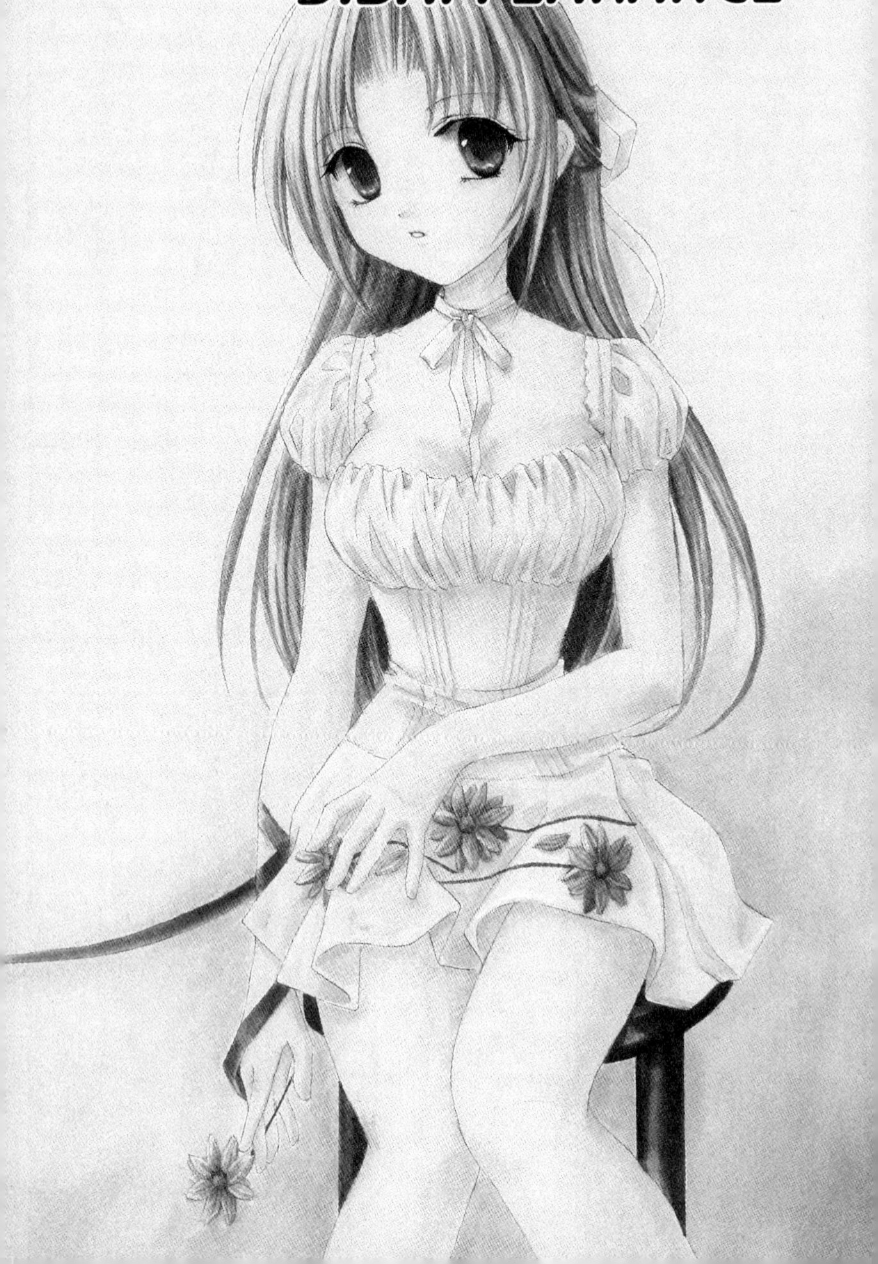

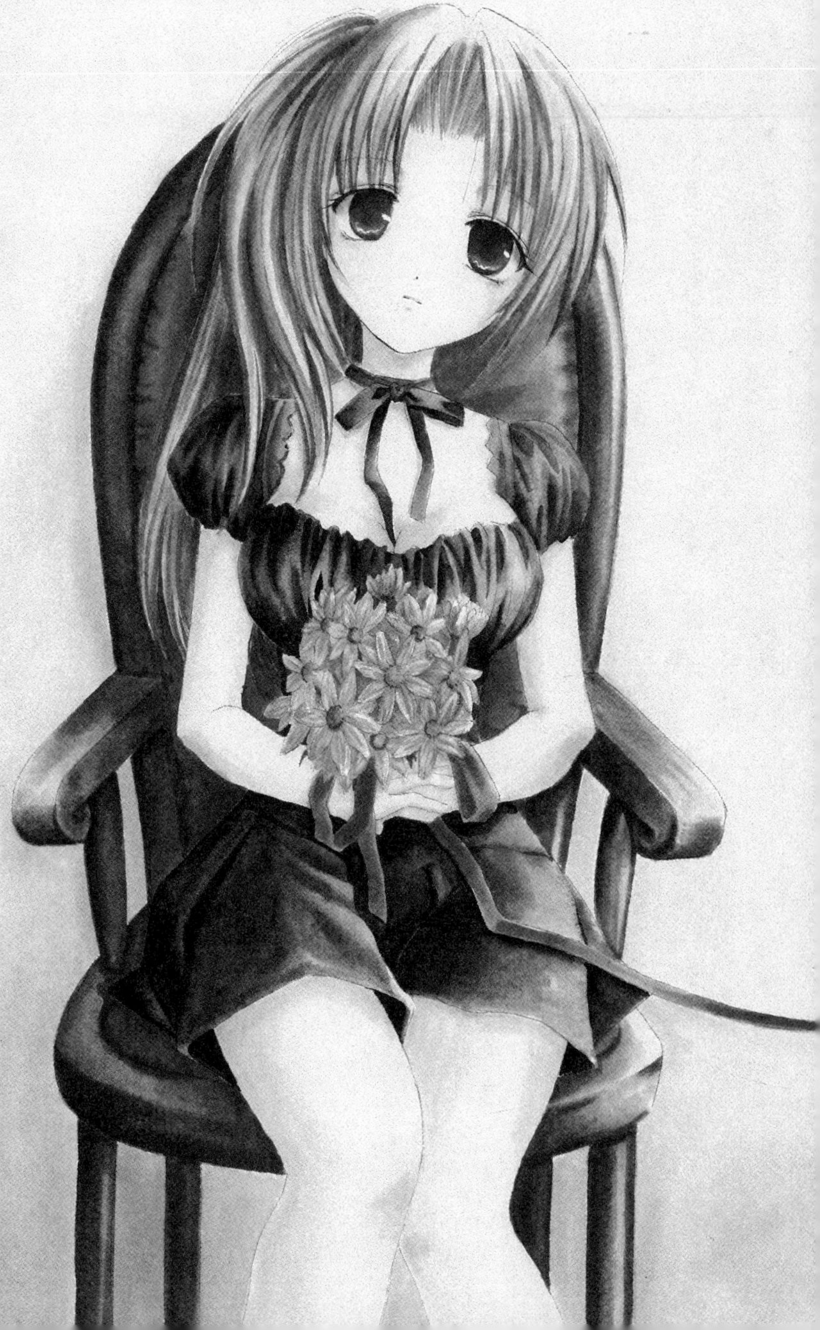

Higurashi
WHEN THEY CRY
COTTON DRIFTING ARC

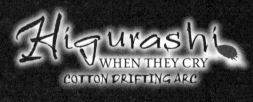

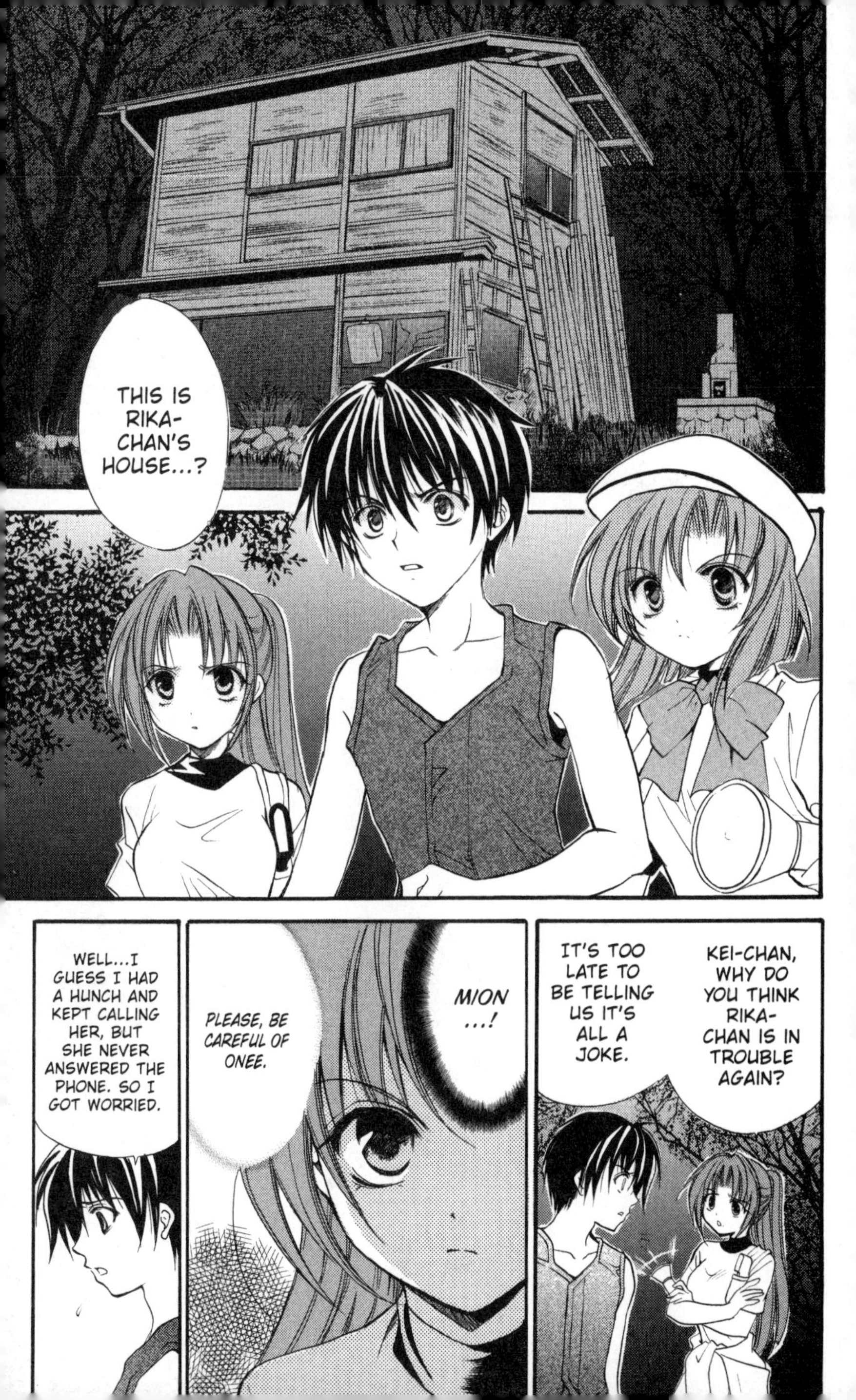
THIS IS RIKA-CHAN'S HOUSE...?
KEI-CHAN, WHY DO YOU THINK RIKA-CHAN IS IN TROUBLE AGAIN?
IT'S TOO LATE TO BE TELLING US IT'S ALL A JOKE.
MION ...!
PLEASE, BE CAREFUL OF ONEE.
WELL...I GUESS I HAD A HUNCH AND KEPT CALLING HER, BUT SHE NEVER ANSWERED THE PHONE. SO I GOT WORRIED.

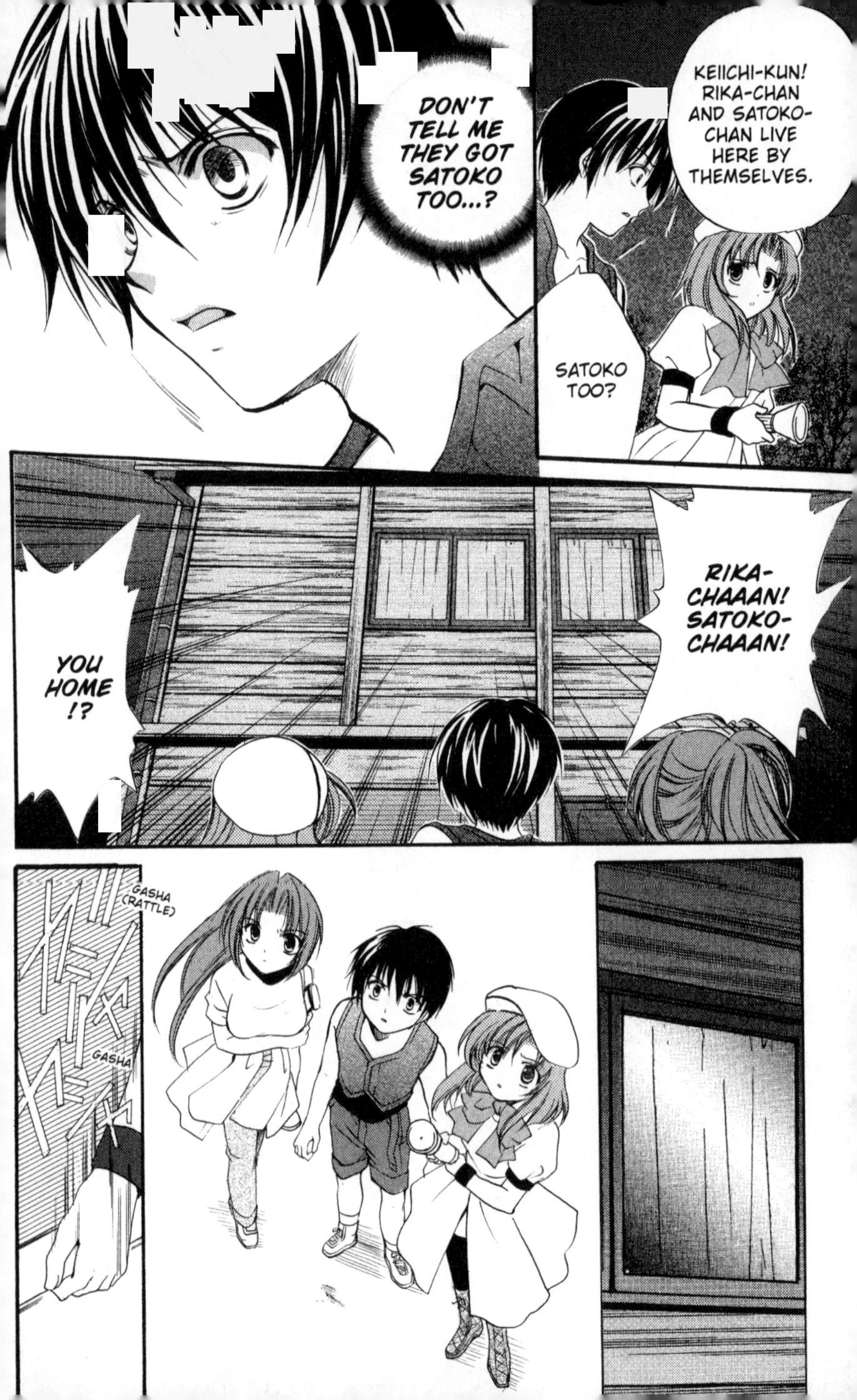
KEIICHI-KUN! RIKA-CHAN AND SATOKO-CHAN LIVE HERE BY THEMSELVES.
SATOKO TOO?
DON'T TELL ME THEY GOT SATOKO TOO...?
RIKA-CHAAAN! SATOKO-CHAAAN!
YOU HOME!?
GASHA (RATTLE)
GASHA

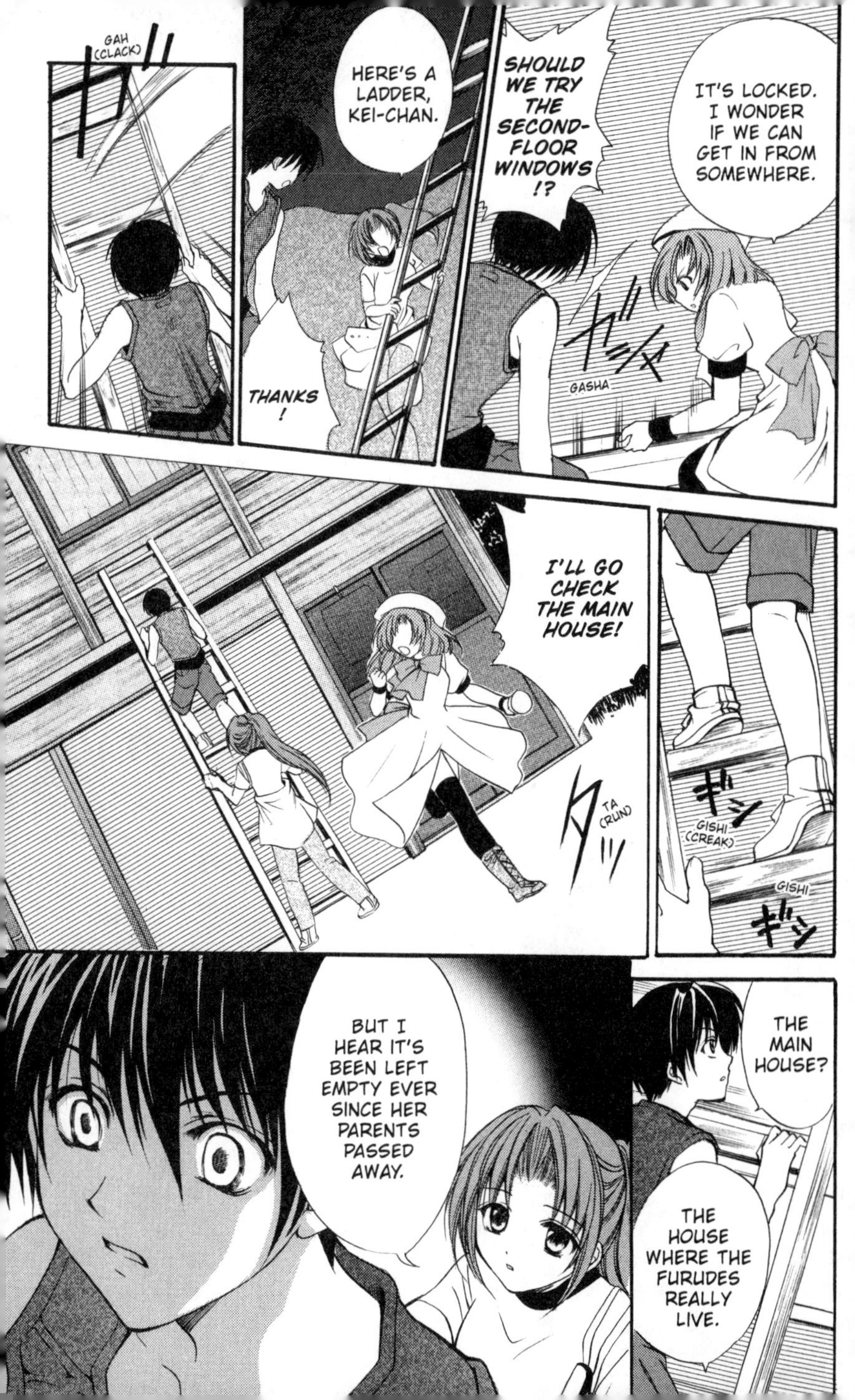
IT'S LOCKED. I WONDER IF WE CAN GET IN FROM SOMEWHERE.
GASHA
SHOULD WE TRY THE SECOND-FLOOR WINDOWS!?
HERE'S A LADDER, KEI-CHAN.
THANKS!
GAH (CLACK)
GISHI (CREAK)
GISHI
I'LL GO CHECK THE MAIN HOUSE!
TA (RUN)
THE MAIN HOUSE?
THE HOUSE WHERE THE FURUDES REALLY LIVE.
BUT I HEAR IT'S BEEN LEFT EMPTY EVER SINCE HER PARENTS PASSED AWAY.

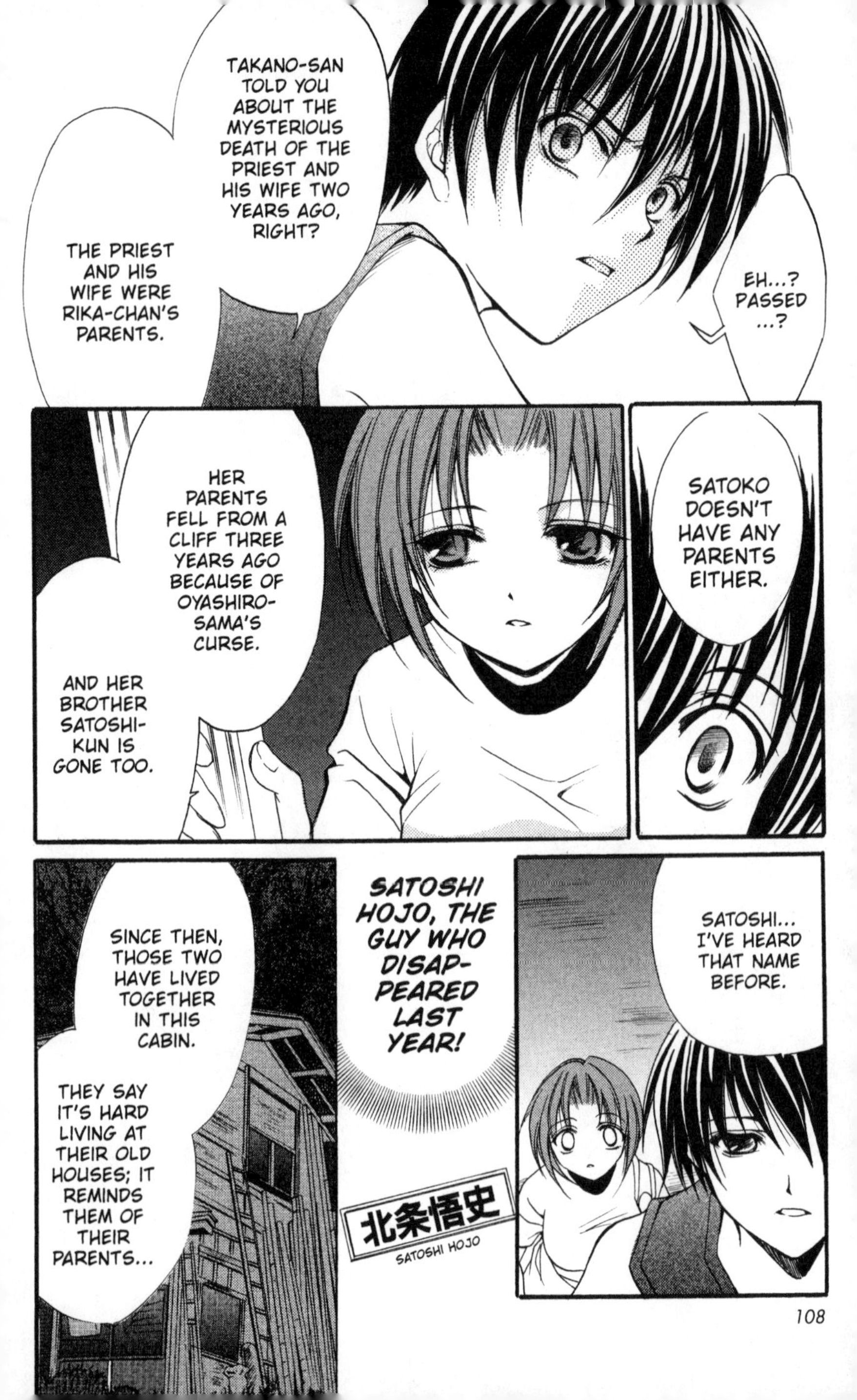
EH...? PASSED ...?
TAKANO-SAN TOLD YOU ABOUT THE MYSTERIOUS DEATH OF THE PRIEST AND HIS WIFE TWO YEARS AGO, RIGHT?
THE PRIEST AND HIS WIFE WERE RIKA-CHAN'S PARENTS.
SATOKO DOESN'T HAVE ANY PARENTS EITHER.
HER PARENTS FELL FROM A CLIFF THREE YEARS AGO BECAUSE OF OYASHIRO-SAMA'S CURSE.
AND HER BROTHER SATOSHI-KUN IS GONE TOO.
SATOSHI... I'VE HEARD THAT NAME BEFORE.
SATOSHI HOJO, THE GUY WHO DISAP-PEARED LAST YEAR!
北条悟史
SATOSHI HOJO
SINCE THEN, THOSE TWO HAVE LIVED TOGETHER IN THIS CABIN.
THEY SAY IT'S HARD LIVING AT THEIR OLD HOUSES; IT REMINDS THEM OF THEIR PARENTS...

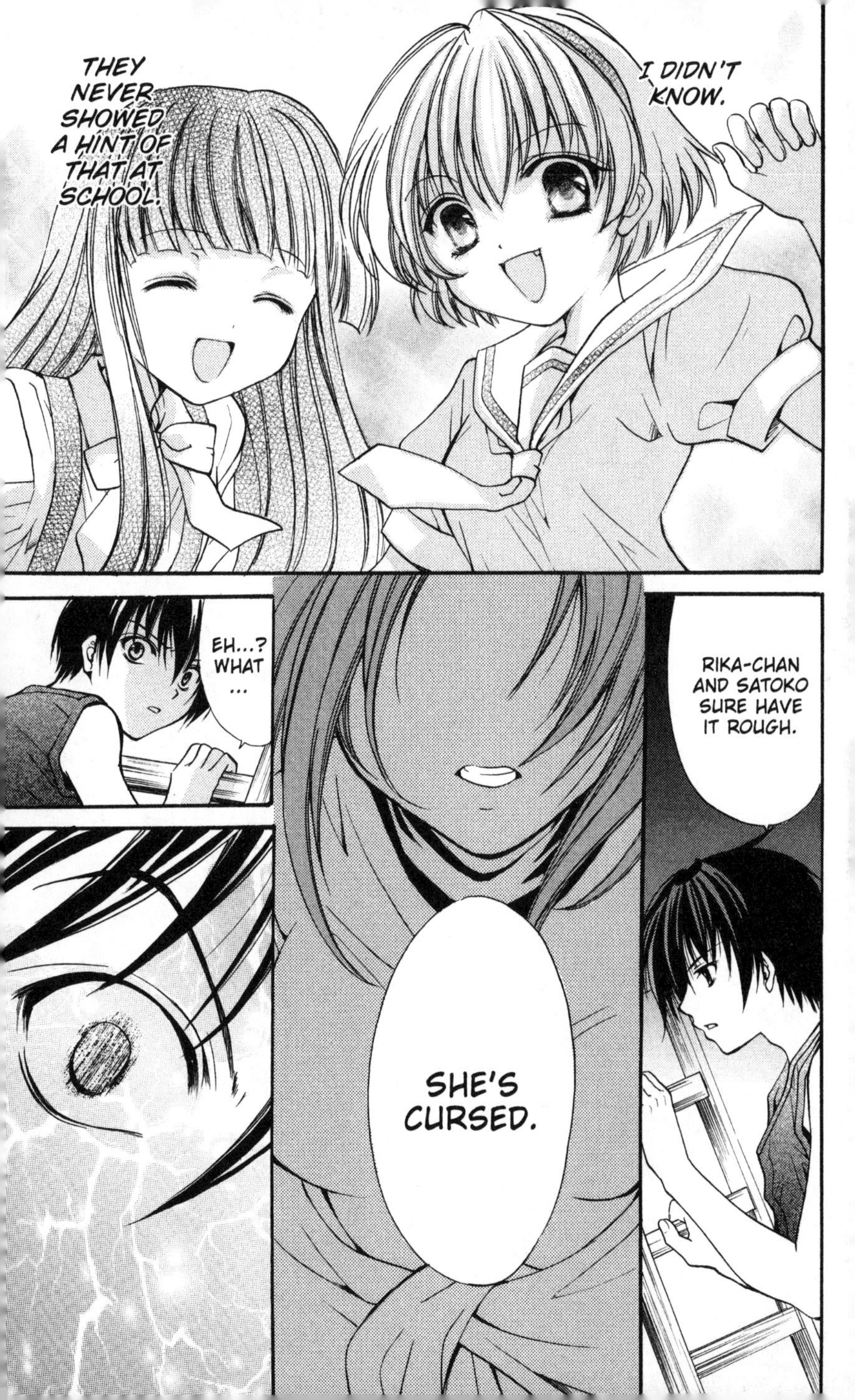

I DIDN'T KNOW.
THEY NEVER SHOWED A HINT OF THAT AT SCHOOL.
RIKA-CHAN AND SATOKO SURE HAVE IT ROUGH.
SHE'S CURSED.
EH...? WHAT ...

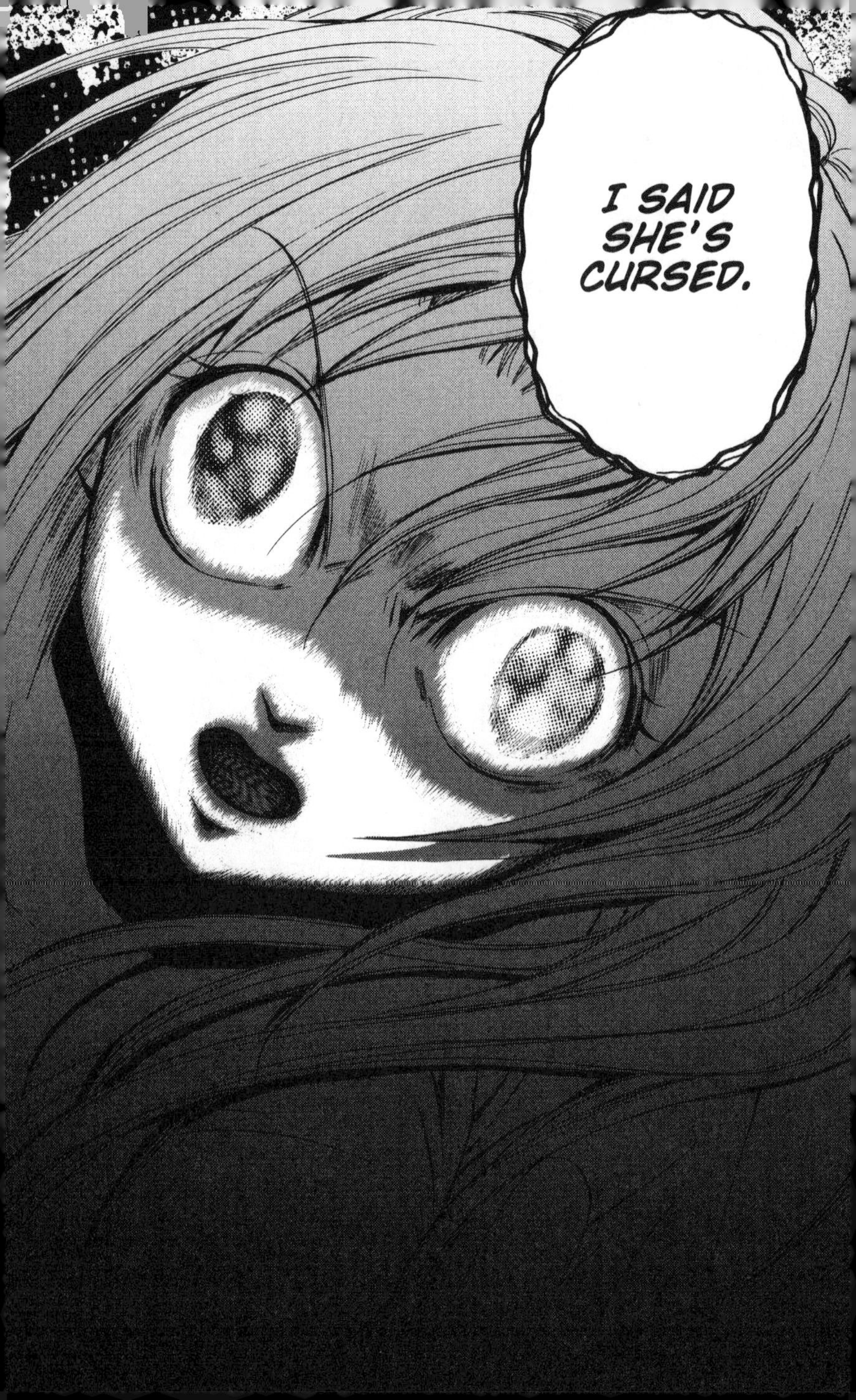
I SAID SHE'S CURSED.

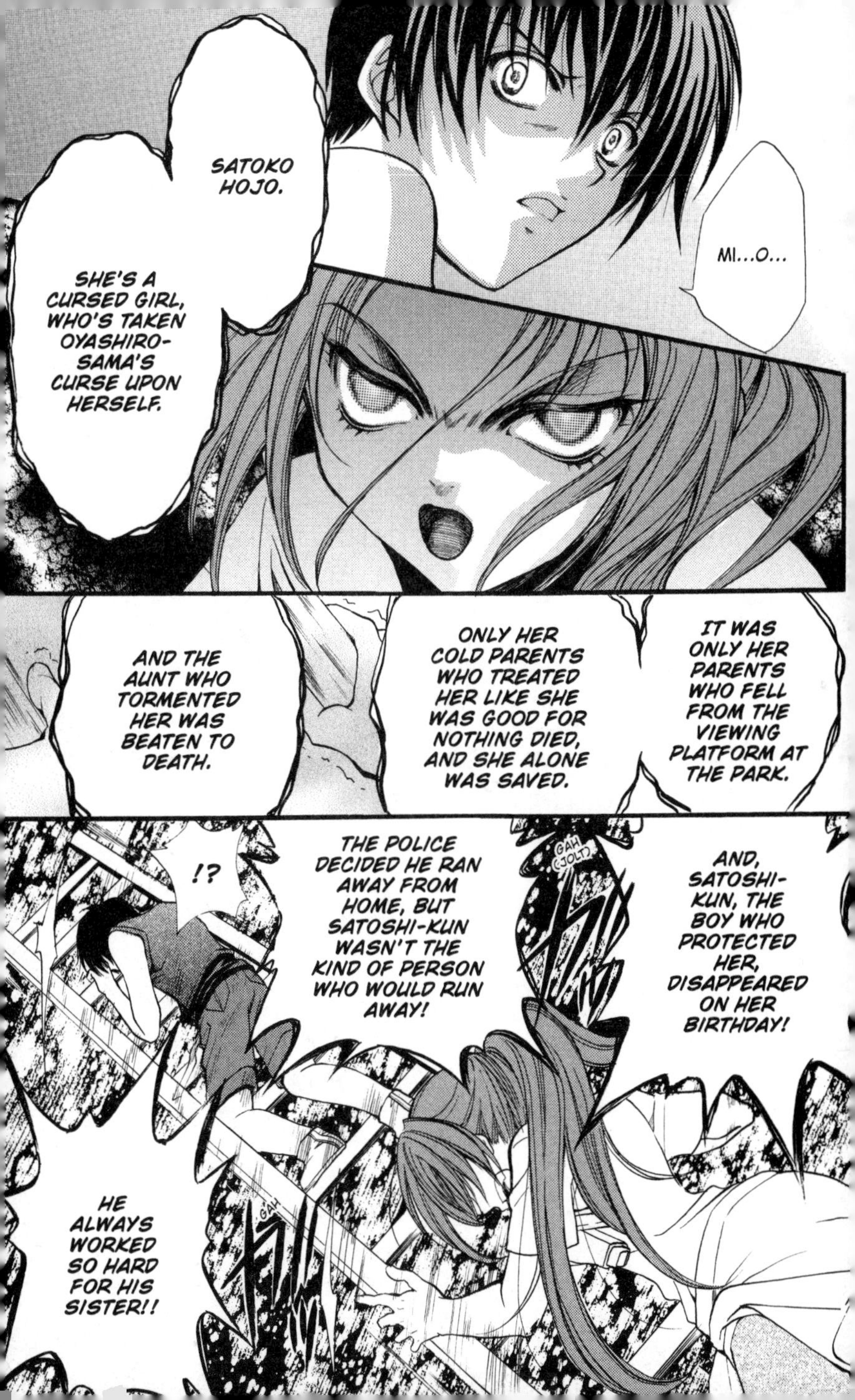
MI...O...
SATOKO HOJO.
SHE'S A CURSED GIRL, WHO'S TAKEN OYASHIRO-SAMA'S CURSE UPON HERSELF.
IT WAS ONLY HER PARENTS WHO FELL FROM THE VIEWING PLATFORM AT THE PARK.
ONLY HER COLD PARENTS WHO TREATED HER LIKE SHE WAS GOOD FOR NOTHING DIED, AND SHE ALONE WAS SAVED.
AND THE AUNT WHO TORMENTED HER WAS BEATEN TO DEATH.
GAH (JOLT)
AND, SATOSHI-KUN, THE BOY WHO PROTECTED HER, DISAPPEARED ON HER BIRTHDAY!
THE POLICE DECIDED HE RAN AWAY FROM HOME, BUT SATOSHI-KUN WASN'T THE KIND OF PERSON WHO WOULD RUN AWAY!
!?
GAH
HE ALWAYS WORKED SO HARD FOR HIS SISTER!!

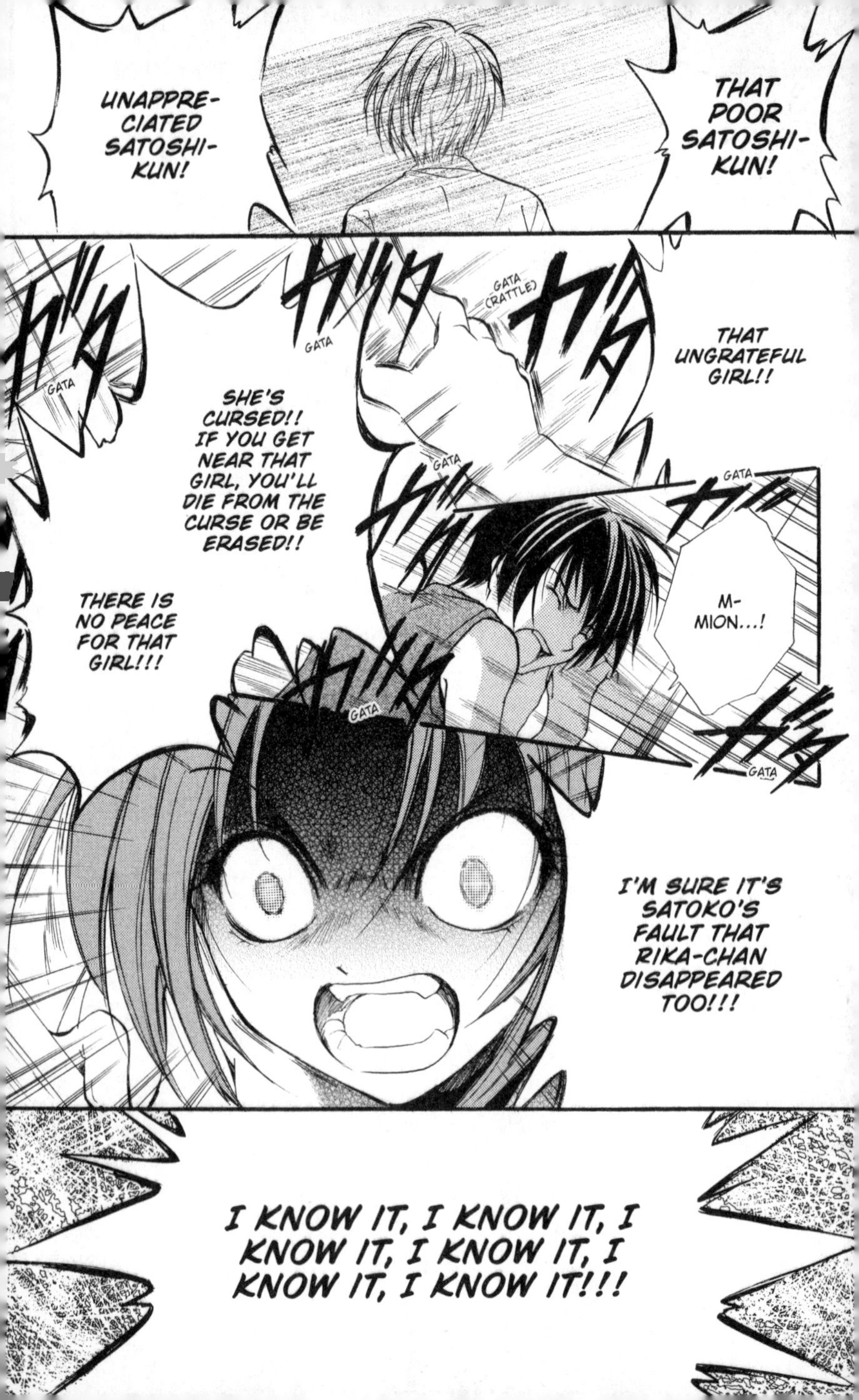
THAT POOR SATOSHI-KUN!
UNAPPRECIATED SATOSHI-KUN!
GATA (RATTLE)
GATA
GATA
THAT UNGRATEFUL GIRL!!
SHE'S CURSED!! IF YOU GET NEAR THAT GIRL, YOU'LL DIE FROM THE CURSE OR BE ERASED!!
THERE IS NO PEACE FOR THAT GIRL!!!
GATA
GATA
M-MION...!
GATA
GATA
I'M SURE IT'S SATOKO'S FAULT THAT RIKA-CHAN DISAPPEARED TOO!!!
I KNOW IT, I KNOW IT, I KNOW IT, I KNOW IT, I KNOW IT, I KNOW IT!!!

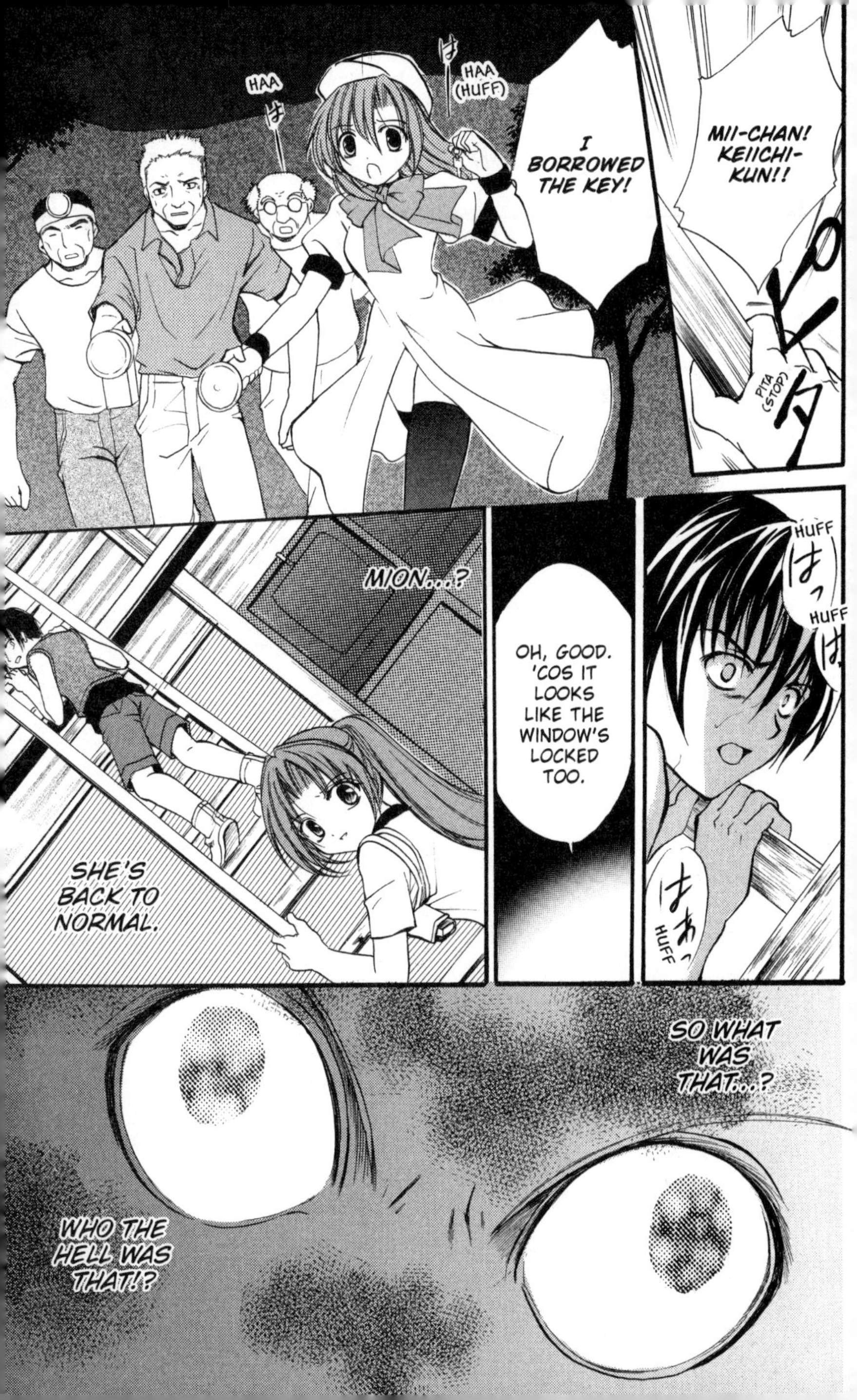
MII-CHAN! KEIICHI-KUN!!
ピタ
PITA (STOP)
I BORROWED THE KEY!
は
HAA (HUFF)
は
HAA
はっ
HUFF
は
HUFF
はあっ
HUFF
OH, GOOD. 'COS IT LOOKS LIKE THE WINDOW'S LOCKED TOO.
MION...?
SHE'S BACK TO NORMAL.
SO WHAT WAS THAT...?
WHO THE HELL WAS THAT!?

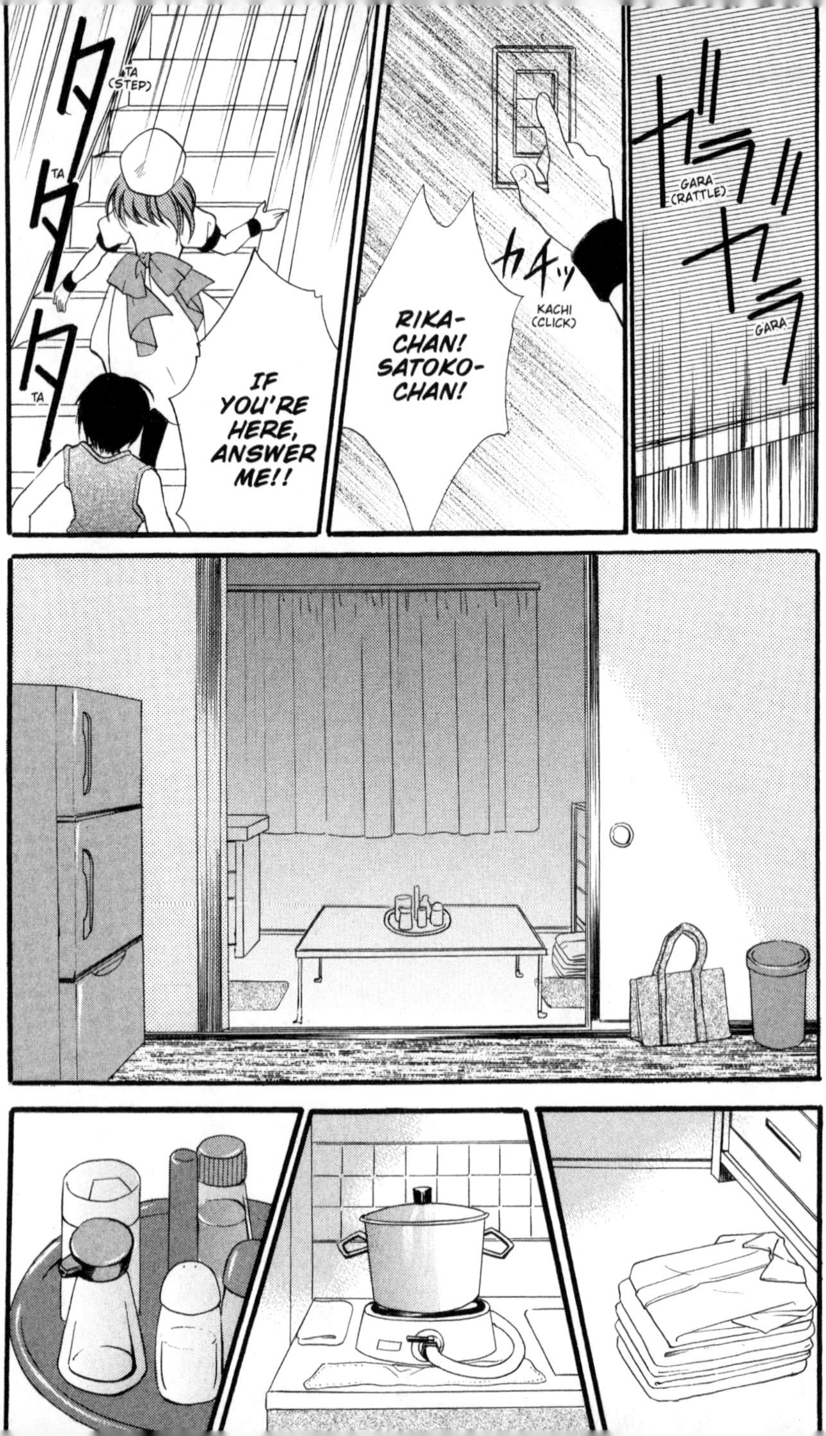
GARA (RATTLE)
GARA
カチッ
KACHI (CLICK)
RIKA-CHAN! SATOKO-CHAN!
タタタ
TA (STEP)
TA
TA
IF YOU'RE HERE, ANSWER ME!!

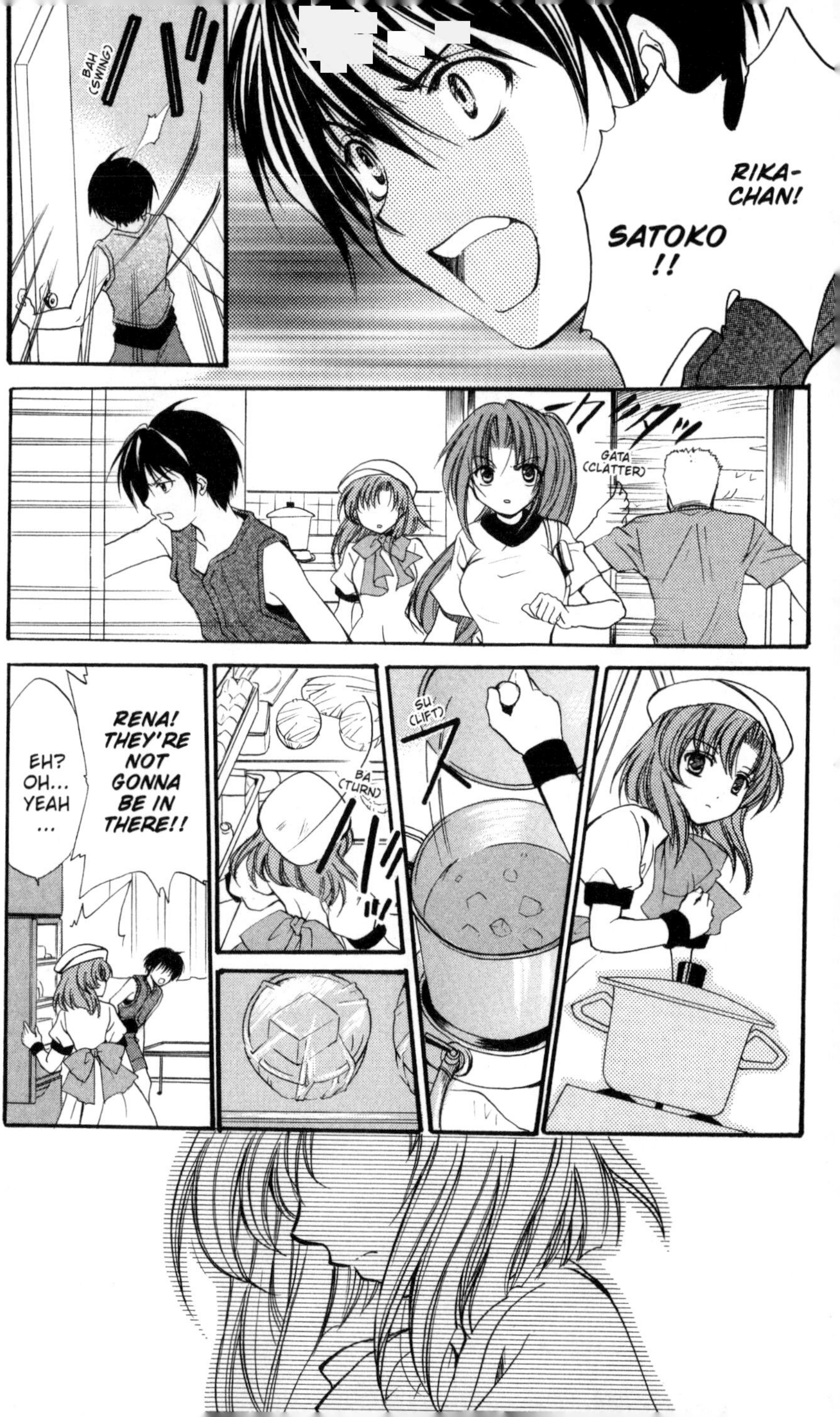
RIKA-CHAN!
SATOKO !!
BAH (SWING)
GATA (CLATTER)
SU (LIFT)
BA (TURN)
RENA! THEY'RE NOT GONNA BE IN THERE!!
EH? OH... YEAH ...

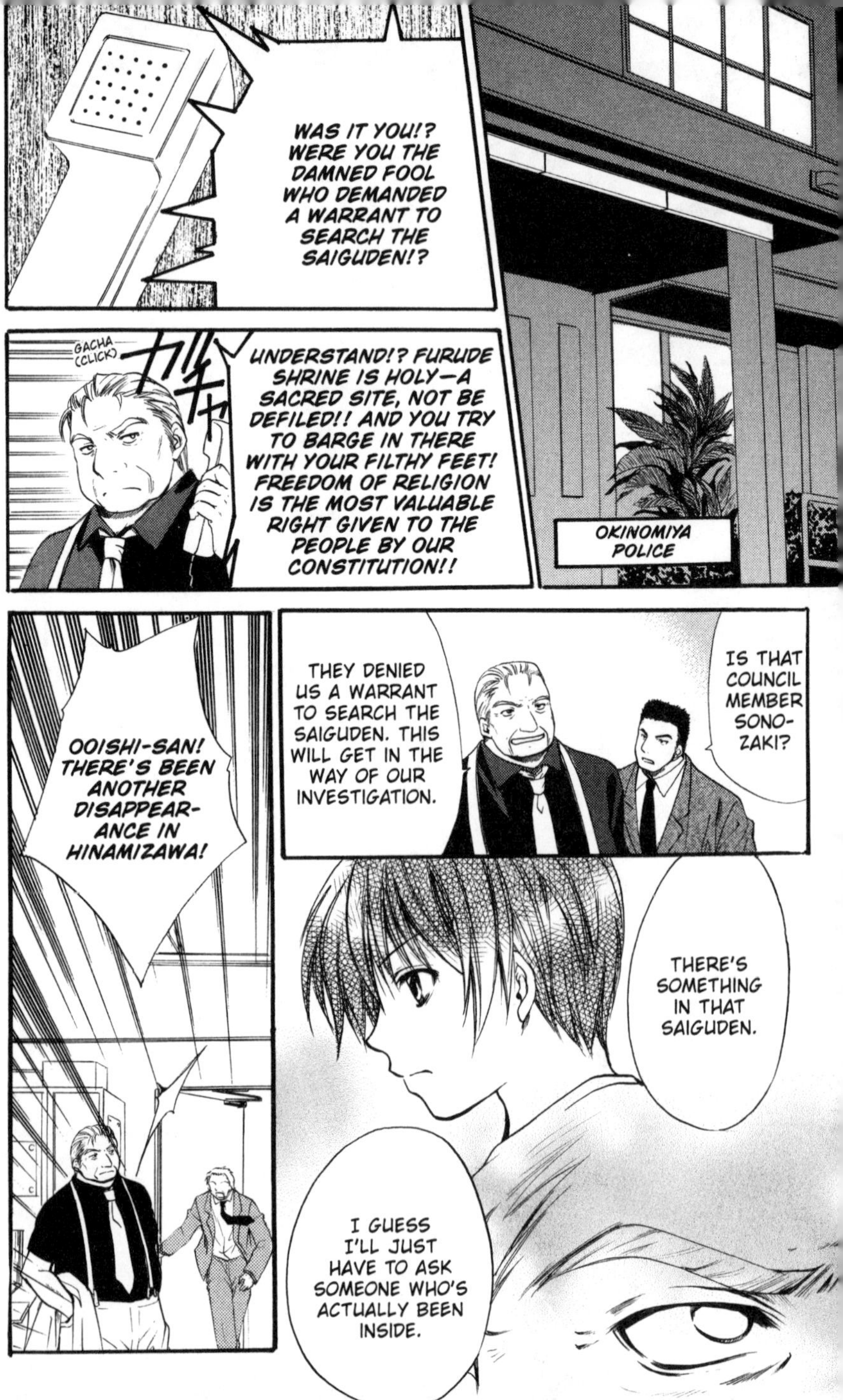
OKINOMIYA POLICE
WAS IT YOU!? WERE YOU THE DAMNED FOOL WHO DEMANDED A WARRANT TO SEARCH THE SAIGUDEN!?
GACHA (CLICK)
UNDERSTAND!? FURUDE SHRINE IS HOLY—A SACRED SITE, NOT BE DEFILED!! AND YOU TRY TO BARGE IN THERE WITH YOUR FILTHY FEET! FREEDOM OF RELIGION IS THE MOST VALUABLE RIGHT GIVEN TO THE PEOPLE BY OUR CONSTITUTION!!
IS THAT COUNCIL MEMBER SONO-ZAKI?
THEY DENIED US A WARRANT TO SEARCH THE SAIGUDEN. THIS WILL GET IN THE WAY OF OUR INVESTIGATION.
THERE'S SOMETHING IN THAT SAIGUDEN.
I GUESS I'LL JUST HAVE TO ASK SOMEONE WHO'S ACTUALLY BEEN INSIDE.
OOISHI-SAN! THERE'S BEEN ANOTHER DISAPPEAR-ANCE IN HINAMIZAWA!

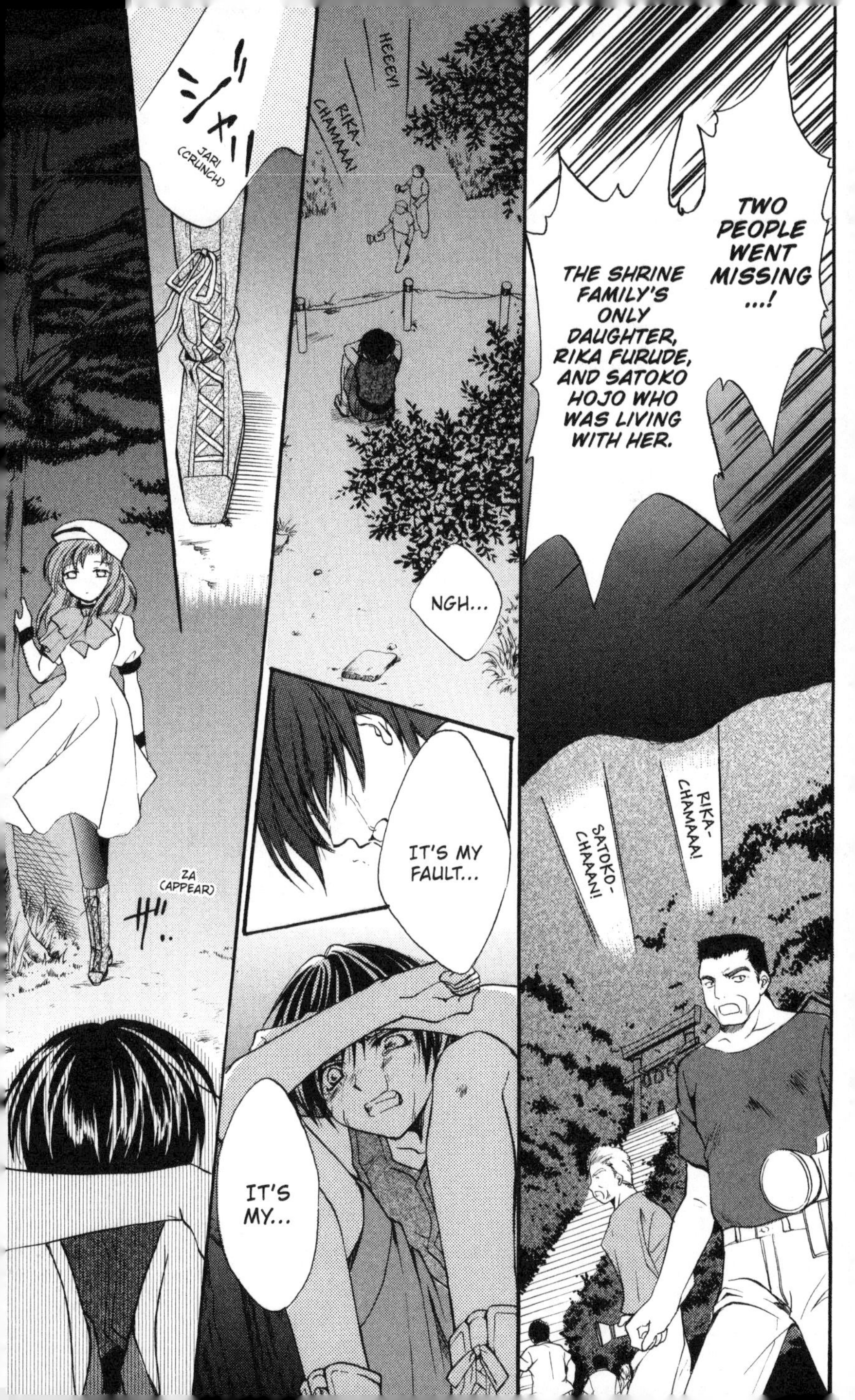
TWO PEOPLE WENT MISSING...!
THE SHRINE FAMILY'S ONLY DAUGHTER, RIKA FURUDE, AND SATOKO HOJO WHO WAS LIVING WITH HER.
RIKA-CHAMAAA!
SATOKO-CHAAAN!
HEEEY!
RIKA-CHAMAAA!
NGH...
IT'S MY FAULT...
IT'S MY...
JARI (CRUNCH)
ZA (APPEAR)

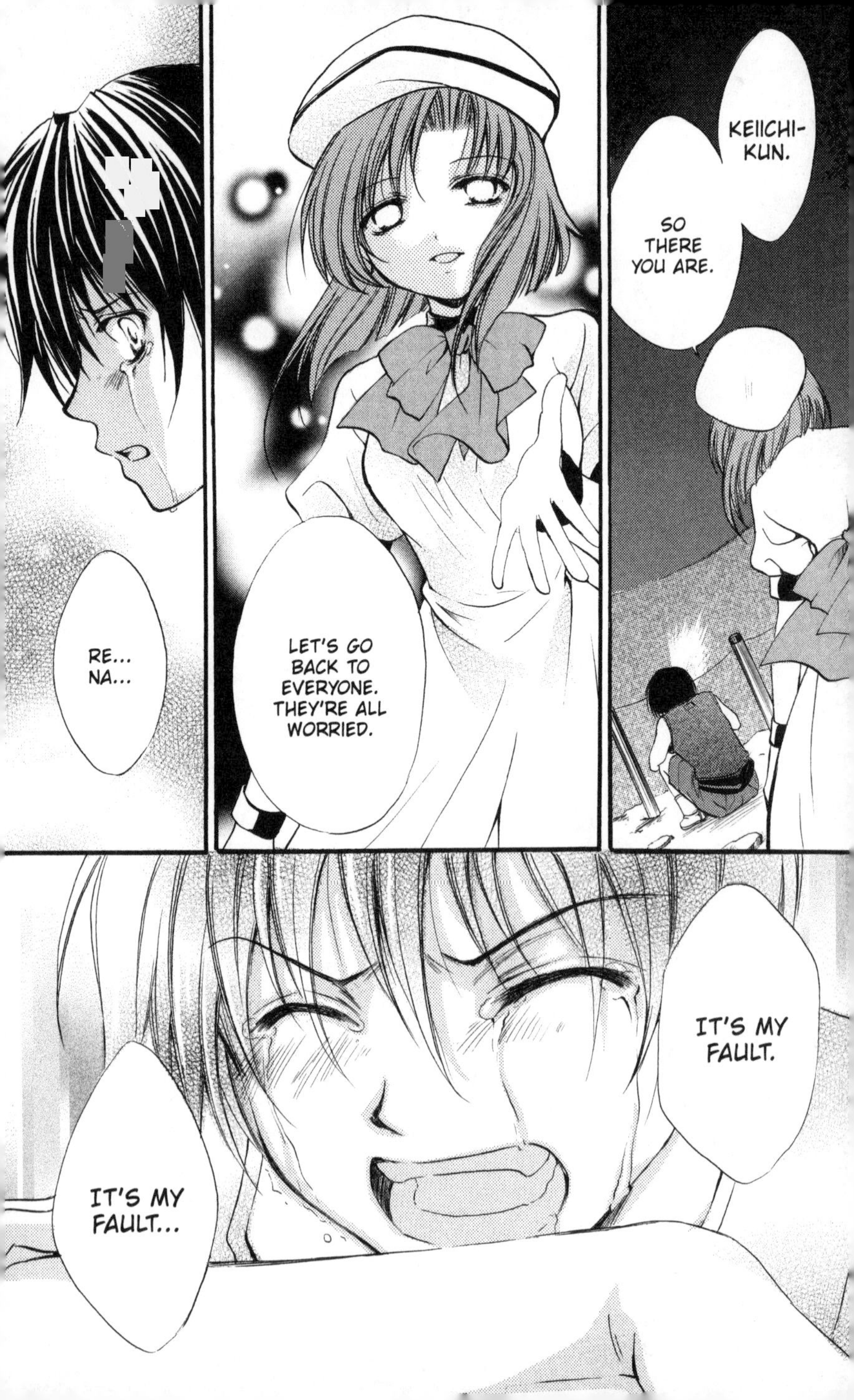
KEIICHI-KUN.
SO THERE YOU ARE.
LET'S GO BACK TO EVERYONE. THEY'RE ALL WORRIED.
RE... NA...
IT'S MY FAULT.
IT'S MY FAULT...

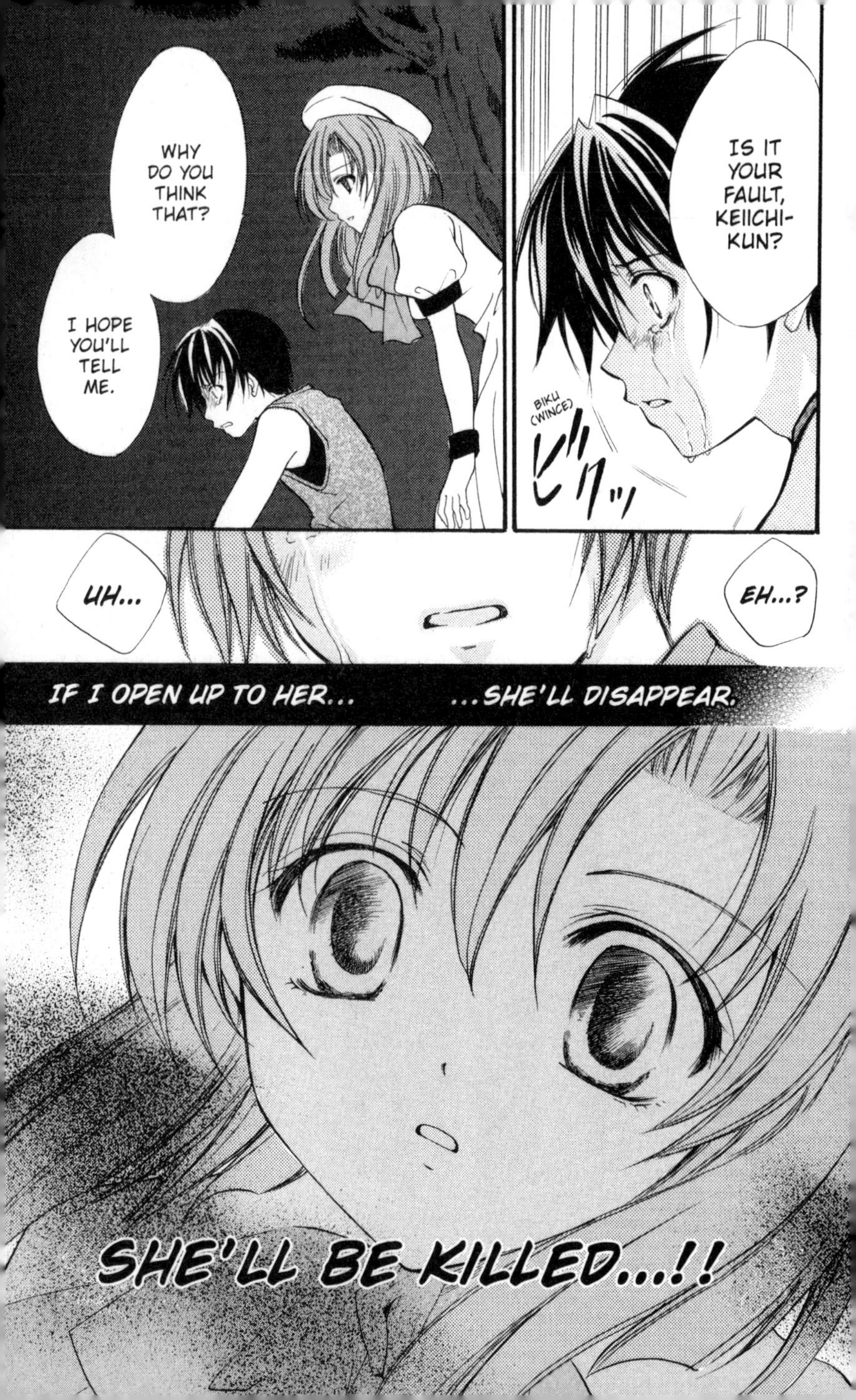
IS IT YOUR FAULT, KEIICHI-KUN?
BIKU (WINCE)
WHY DO YOU THINK THAT?
I HOPE YOU'LL TELL ME.
EH...?
UH...
IF I OPEN UP TO HER...
...SHE'LL DISAPPEAR.
SHE'LL BE KILLED...!!

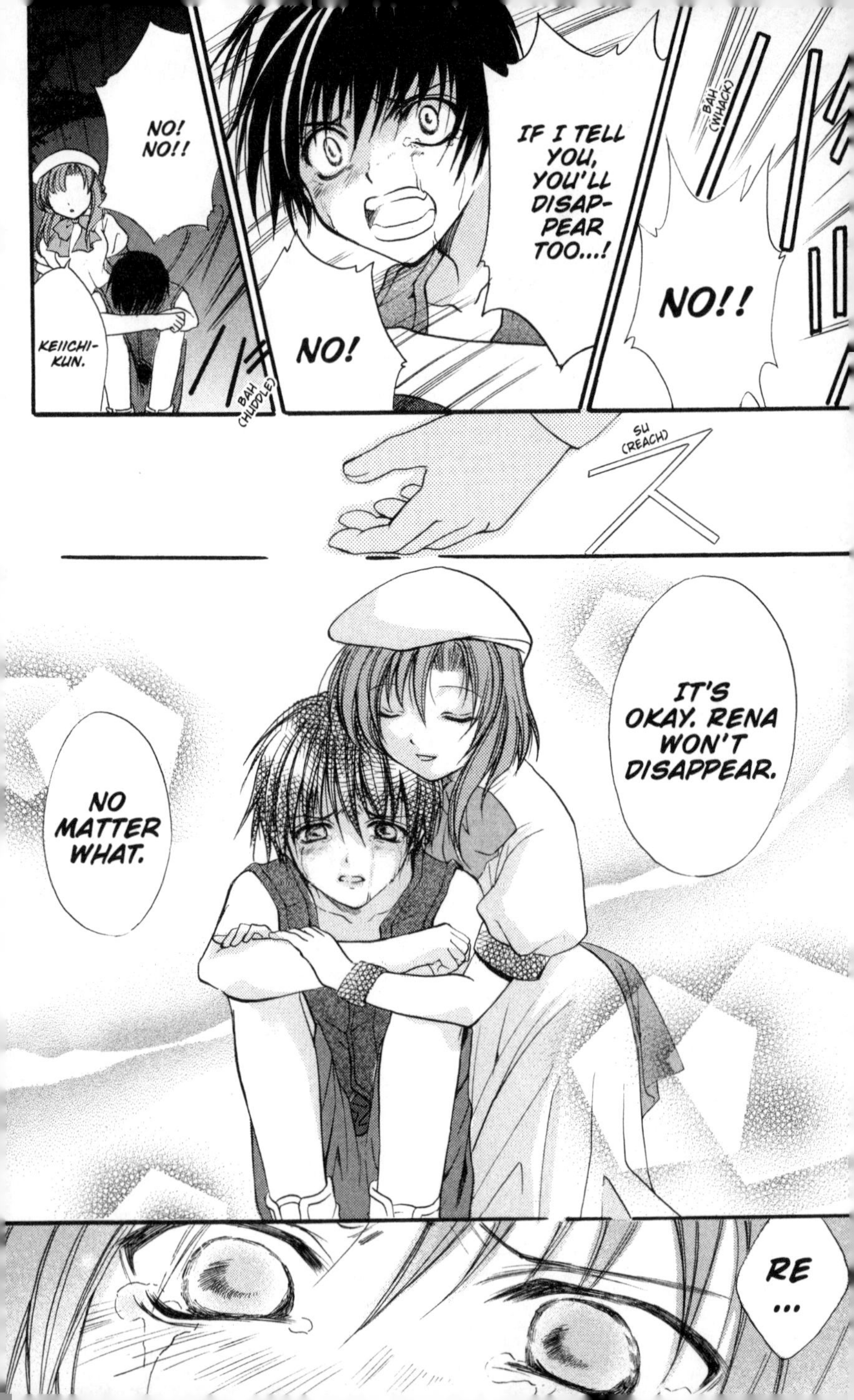
BAH- (WHACK)
NO!!
IF I TELL YOU, YOU'LL DISAP-PEAR TOO...!
NO!
NO! NO!!
KEIICHI-KUN.
BAH (HUDDLE)
SU (REACH)
IT'S OKAY. RENA WON'T DISAPPEAR.
NO MATTER WHAT.
RE ...

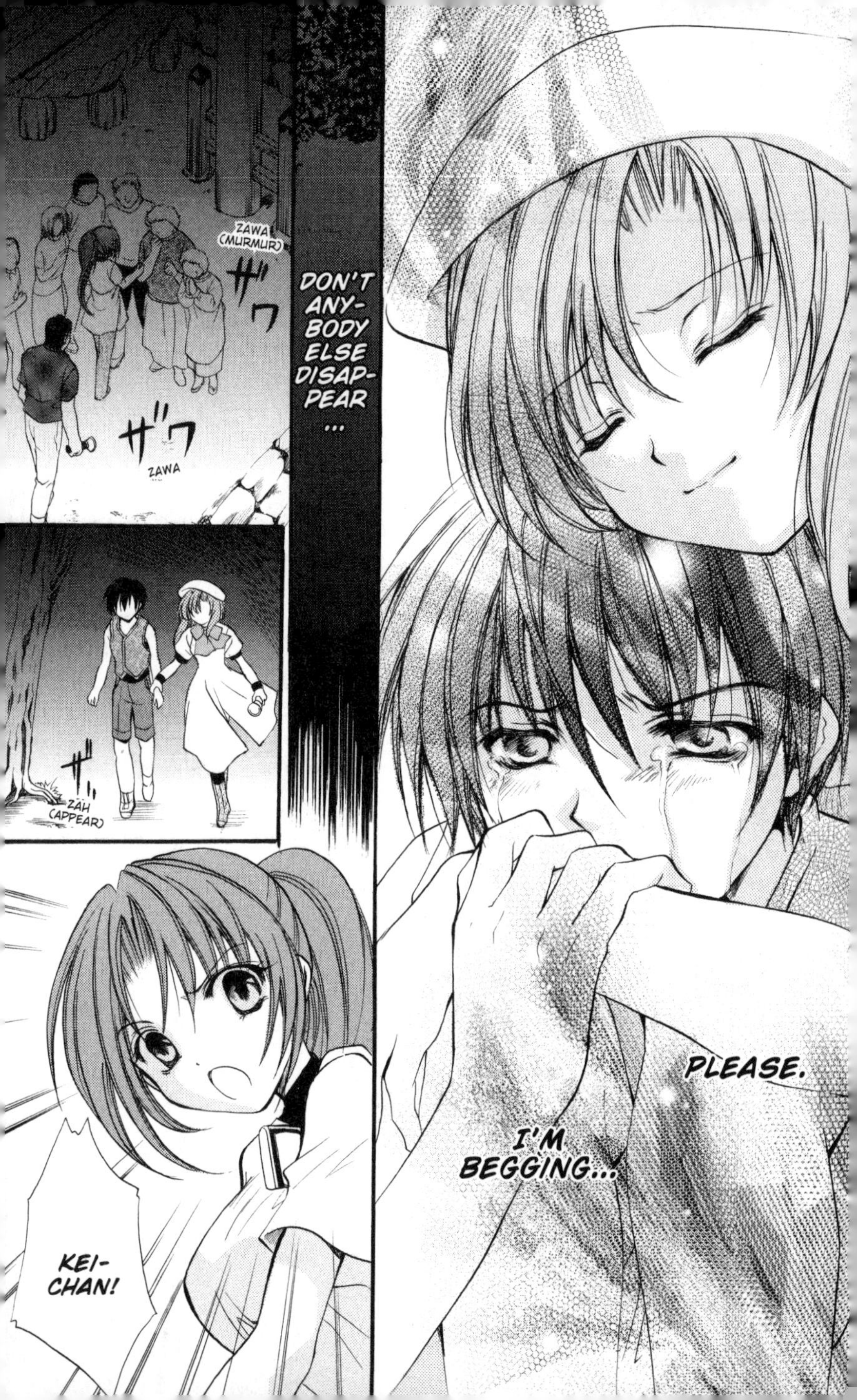
PLEASE.
I'M BEGGING...
DON'T ANYBODY ELSE DISAPPEAR...
ZAWA (MURMUR)
ザワ
ザワ
ZAWA
ZÄH (APPEAR)
KEI-CHAN!

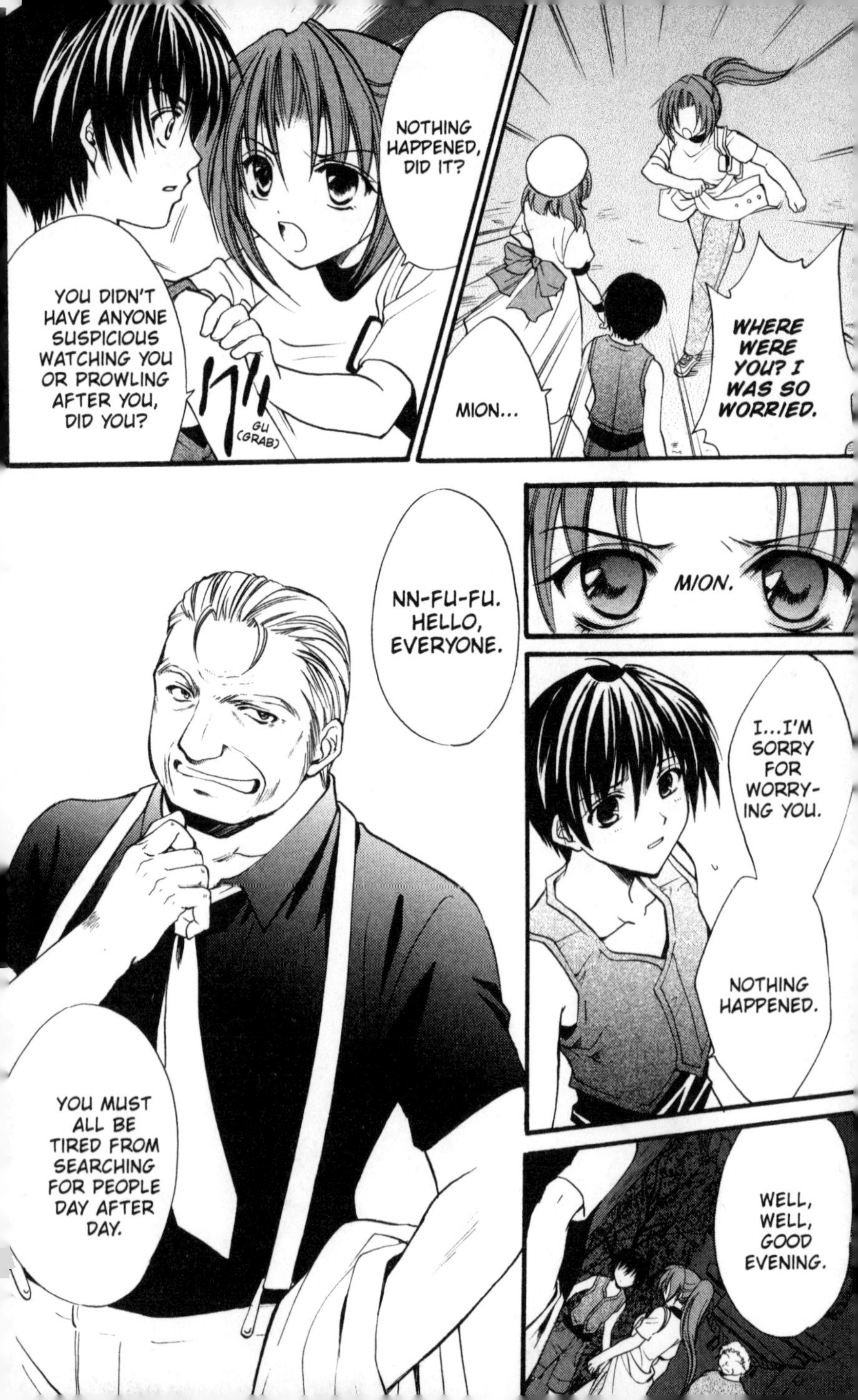
WHERE WERE YOU? I WAS SO WORRIED.
MION...
NOTHING HAPPENED, DID IT?
YOU DIDN'T HAVE ANYONE SUSPICIOUS WATCHING YOU OR PROWLING AFTER YOU, DID YOU?
GU (GRAB)
MION.
I...I'M SORRY FOR WORRYING YOU.
NOTHING HAPPENED.
WELL, WELL, GOOD EVENING.
NN-FU-FU. HELLO, EVERYONE.
YOU MUST ALL BE TIRED FROM SEARCHING FOR PEOPLE DAY AFTER DAY.

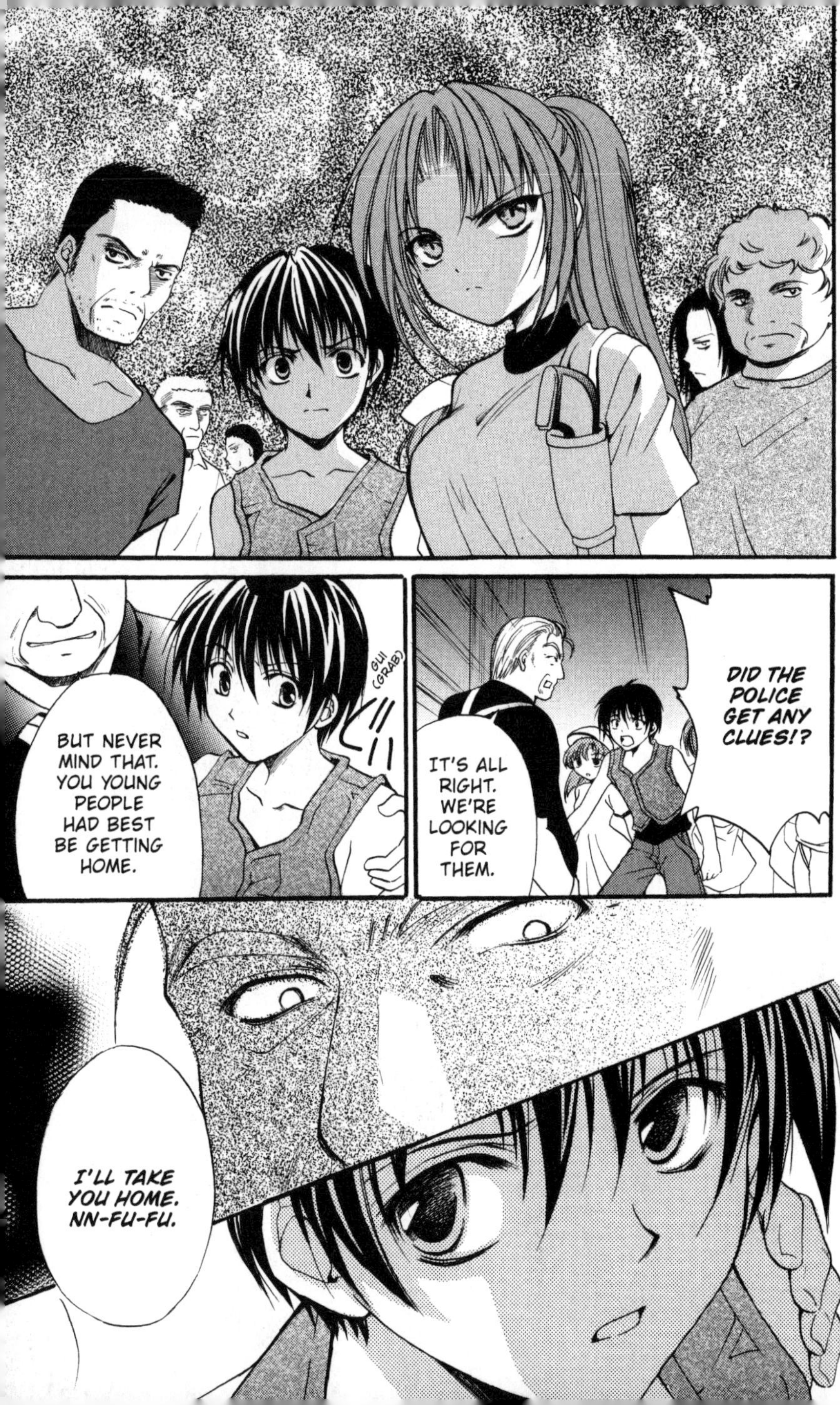
DID THE POLICE GET ANY CLUES!?
IT'S ALL RIGHT. WE'RE LOOKING FOR THEM.
GUI (GRAB)
BUT NEVER MIND THAT. YOU YOUNG PEOPLE HAD BEST BE GETTING HOME.
I'LL TAKE YOU HOME. NN-FU-FU.

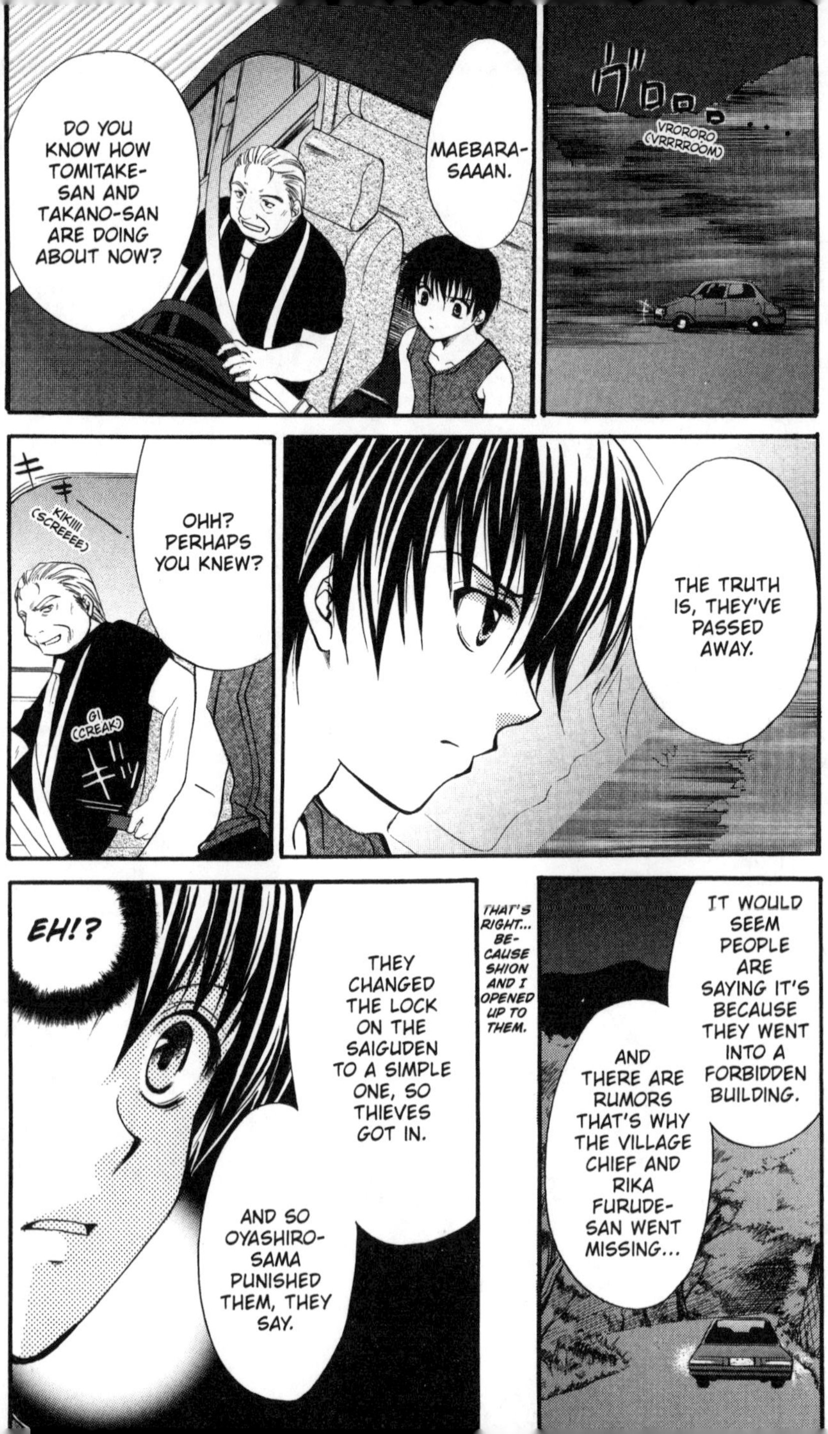
VROROROO (VRRRROOM)
MAEBARA-SAAAN.
DO YOU KNOW HOW TOMITAKE-SAN AND TAKANO-SAN ARE DOING ABOUT NOW?
THE TRUTH IS, THEY'VE PASSED AWAY.
KIKIIII (SCREEEE)
OHH? PERHAPS YOU KNEW?
GI (CREAK)
IT WOULD SEEM PEOPLE ARE SAYING IT'S BECAUSE THEY WENT INTO A FORBIDDEN BUILDING.
AND THERE ARE RUMORS THAT'S WHY THE VILLAGE CHIEF AND RIKA FURUDE-SAN WENT MISSING...
THAT'S RIGHT... BE-CAUSE SHION AND I OPENED UP TO THEM.
THEY CHANGED THE LOCK ON THE SAIGUDEN TO A SIMPLE ONE, SO THIEVES GOT IN.
EH!?
AND SO OYASHIRO-SAMA PUNISHED THEM, THEY SAY.

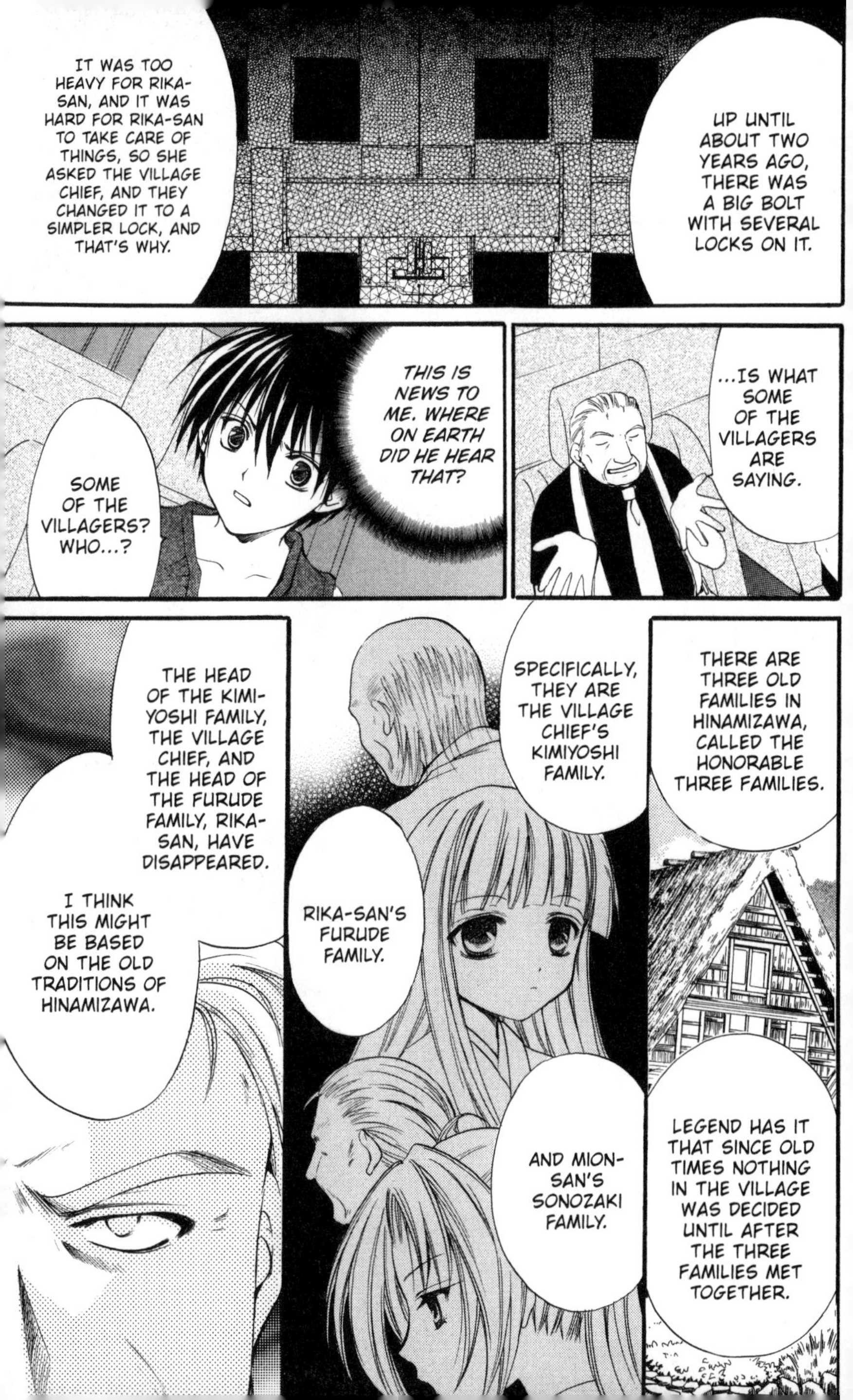
UP UNTIL ABOUT TWO YEARS AGO, THERE WAS A BIG BOLT WITH SEVERAL LOCKS ON IT.
IT WAS TOO HEAVY FOR RIKA-SAN, AND IT WAS HARD FOR RIKA-SAN TO TAKE CARE OF THINGS, SO SHE ASKED THE VILLAGE CHIEF, AND THEY CHANGED IT TO A SIMPLER LOCK, AND THAT'S WHY.
...IS WHAT SOME OF THE VILLAGERS ARE SAYING.
THIS IS NEWS TO ME. WHERE ON EARTH DID HE HEAR THAT?
SOME OF THE VILLAGERS? WHO...?
THERE ARE THREE OLD FAMILIES IN HINAMIZAWA, CALLED THE HONORABLE THREE FAMILIES.
LEGEND HAS IT THAT SINCE OLD TIMES NOTHING IN THE VILLAGE WAS DECIDED UNTIL AFTER THE THREE FAMILIES MET TOGETHER.
SPECIFICALLY, THEY ARE THE VILLAGE CHIEF'S KIMIYOSHI FAMILY.
RIKA-SAN'S FURUDE FAMILY.
AND MION-SAN'S SONOZAKI FAMILY.
THE HEAD OF THE KIMIYOSHI FAMILY, THE VILLAGE CHIEF, AND THE HEAD OF THE FURUDE FAMILY, RIKA-SAN, HAVE DISAPPEARED.
I THINK THIS MIGHT BE BASED ON THE OLD TRADITIONS OF HINAMIZAWA.

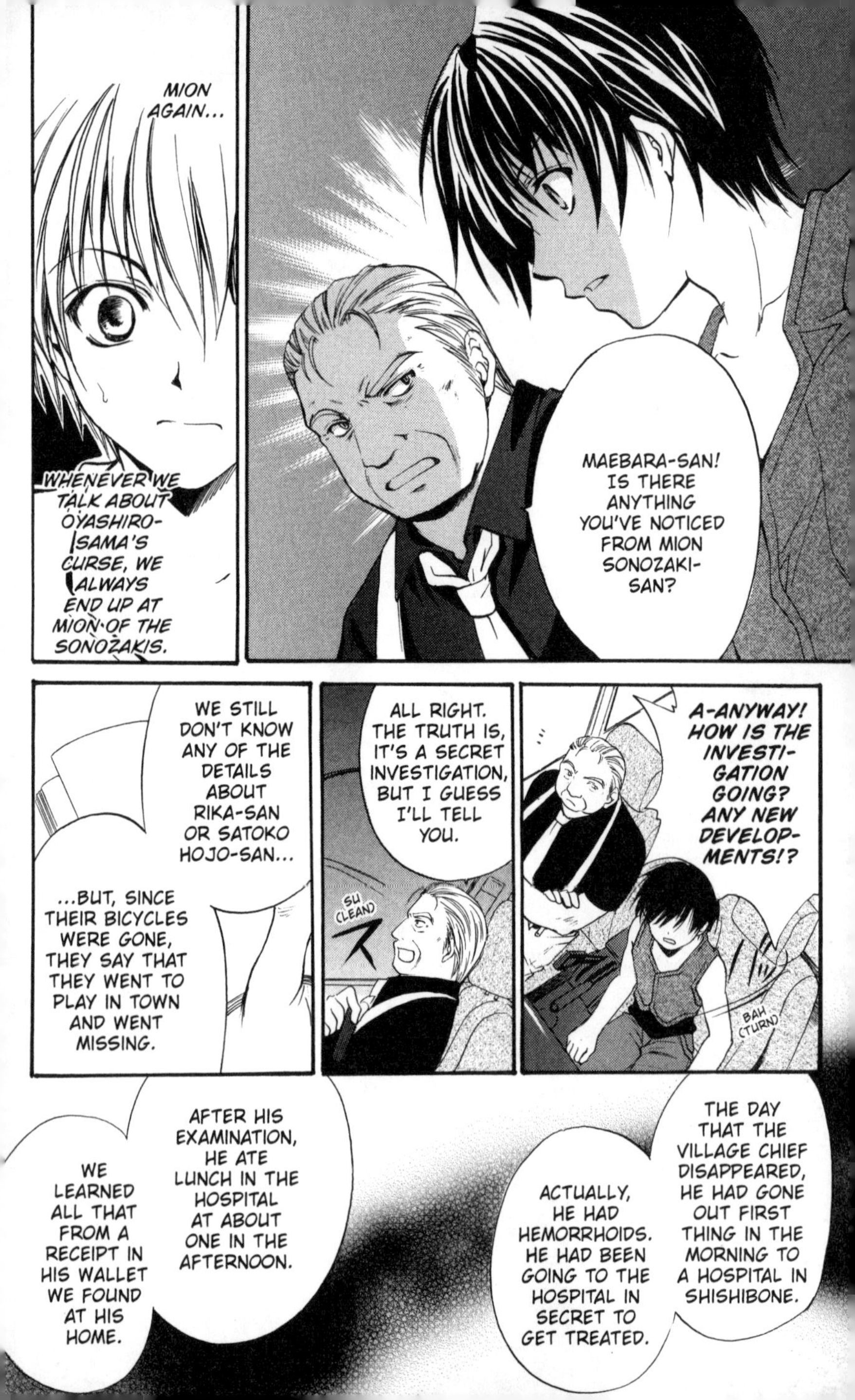
MAEBARA-SAN! IS THERE ANYTHING YOU'VE NOTICED FROM MION SONOZAKI-SAN?
MION AGAIN...
WHENEVER WE TALK ABOUT OYASHIRO-SAMA'S CURSE, WE ALWAYS END UP AT MION OF THE SONOZAKIS.
A-ANYWAY! HOW IS THE INVESTIGATION GOING? ANY NEW DEVELOPMENTS!?
...
BAH (TURN)
ALL RIGHT. THE TRUTH IS, IT'S A SECRET INVESTIGATION, BUT I GUESS I'LL TELL YOU.
SU (CLEAN)
WE STILL DON'T KNOW ANY OF THE DETAILS ABOUT RIKA-SAN OR SATOKO HOJO-SAN...
...BUT, SINCE THEIR BICYCLES WERE GONE, THEY SAY THAT THEY WENT TO PLAY IN TOWN AND WENT MISSING.
THE DAY THAT THE VILLAGE CHIEF DISAPPEARED, HE HAD GONE OUT FIRST THING IN THE MORNING TO A HOSPITAL IN SHISHIBONE.
ACTUALLY, HE HAD HEMORRHOIDS. HE HAD BEEN GOING TO THE HOSPITAL IN SECRET TO GET TREATED.
AFTER HIS EXAMINATION, HE ATE LUNCH IN THE HOSPITAL AT ABOUT ONE IN THE AFTERNOON.
WE LEARNED ALL THAT FROM A RECEIPT IN HIS WALLET WE FOUND AT HIS HOME.

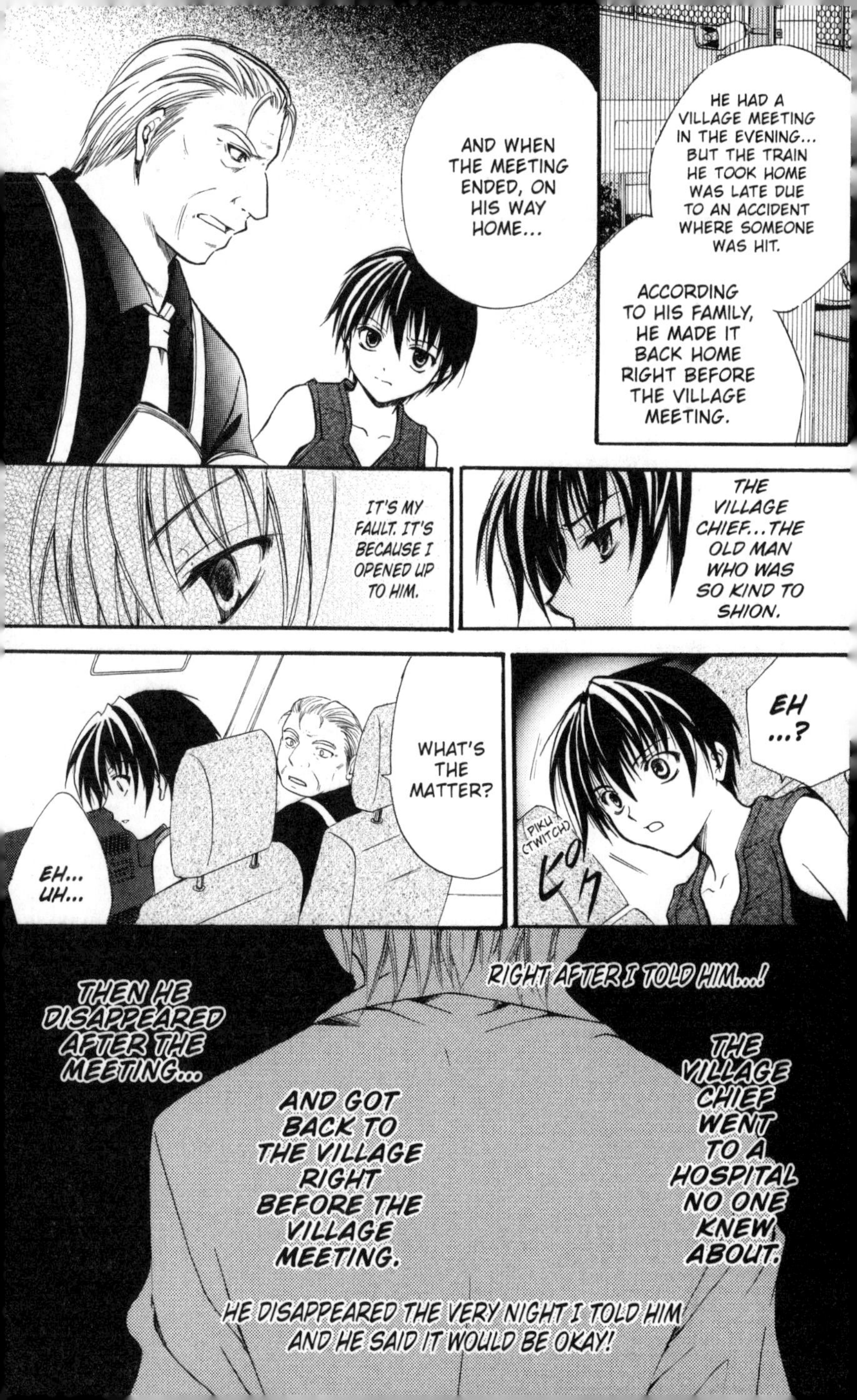
HE HAD A VILLAGE MEETING IN THE EVENING... BUT THE TRAIN HE TOOK HOME WAS LATE DUE TO AN ACCIDENT WHERE SOMEONE WAS HIT.
ACCORDING TO HIS FAMILY, HE MADE IT BACK HOME RIGHT BEFORE THE VILLAGE MEETING.
AND WHEN THE MEETING ENDED, ON HIS WAY HOME...
THE VILLAGE CHIEF...THE OLD MAN WHO WAS SO KIND TO SHION.
IT'S MY FAULT. IT'S BECAUSE I OPENED UP TO HIM.
EH ...?
PIKU (TWITCH)
WHAT'S THE MATTER?
EH... UH...
RIGHT AFTER I TOLD HIM...!
THE VILLAGE CHIEF WENT TO A HOSPITAL NO ONE KNEW ABOUT.
THEN HE DISAPPEARED AFTER THE MEETING...
AND GOT BACK TO THE VILLAGE RIGHT BEFORE THE VILLAGE MEETING.
HE DISAPPEARED THE VERY NIGHT I TOLD HIM AND HE SAID IT WOULD BE OKAY!

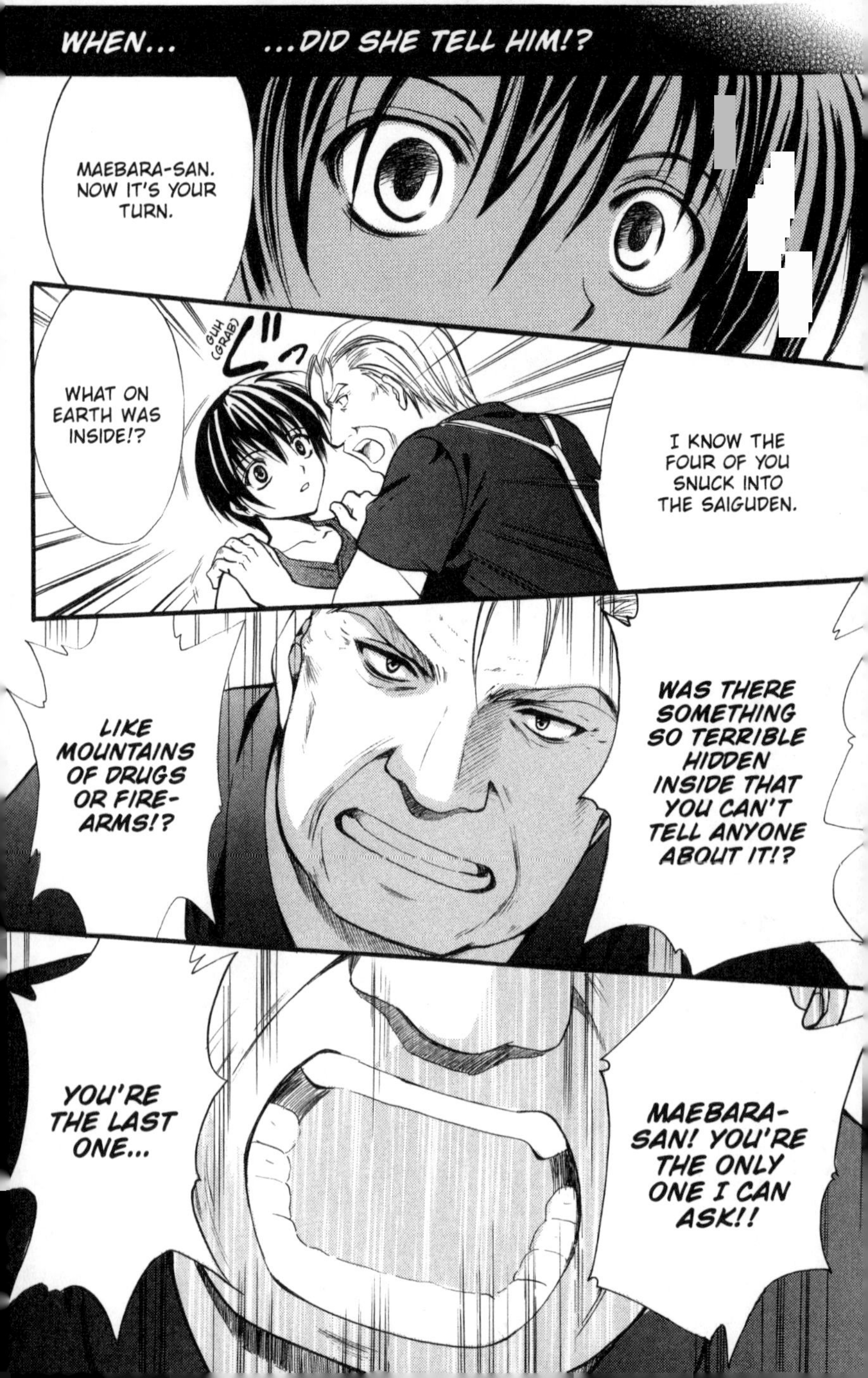
WHEN... ...DID SHE TELL HIM!?
MAEBARA-SAN. NOW IT'S YOUR TURN.
I KNOW THE FOUR OF YOU SNUCK INTO THE SAIGUDEN.
GUH (GRAB)
WHAT ON EARTH WAS INSIDE!?
WAS THERE SOMETHING SO TERRIBLE HIDDEN INSIDE THAT YOU CAN'T TELL ANYONE ABOUT IT!?
LIKE MOUNTAINS OF DRUGS OR FIRE-ARMS!?
MAEBARA-SAN! YOU'RE THE ONLY ONE I CAN ASK!!
YOU'RE THE LAST ONE...

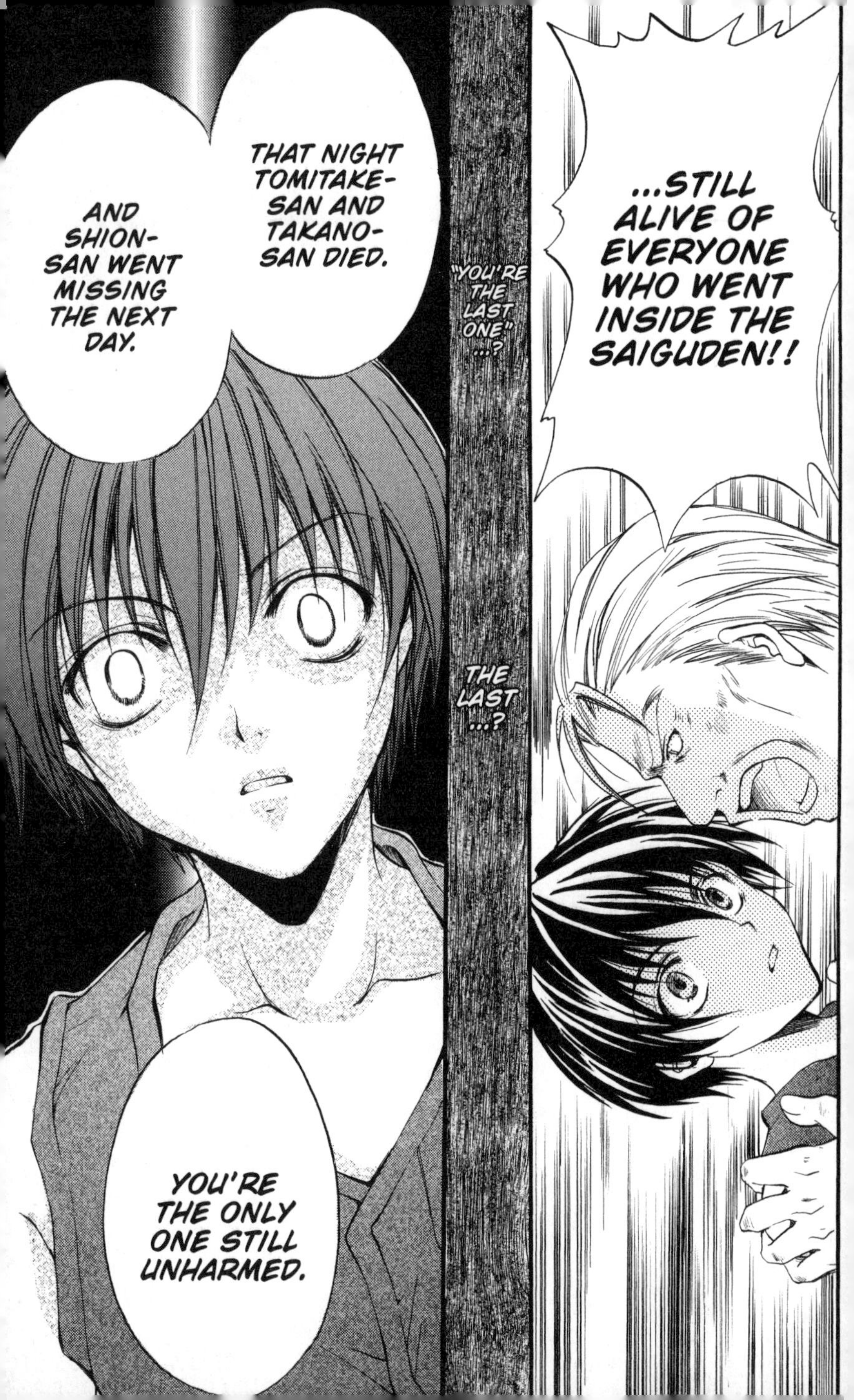
...STILL ALIVE OF EVERYONE WHO WENT INSIDE THE SAIGUDEN!!
"YOU'RE THE LAST ONE" ...?
THE LAST ...?
THAT NIGHT TOMITAKE-SAN AND TAKANO-SAN DIED.
AND SHION-SAN WENT MISSING THE NEXT DAY.
YOU'RE THE ONLY ONE STILL UNHARMED.

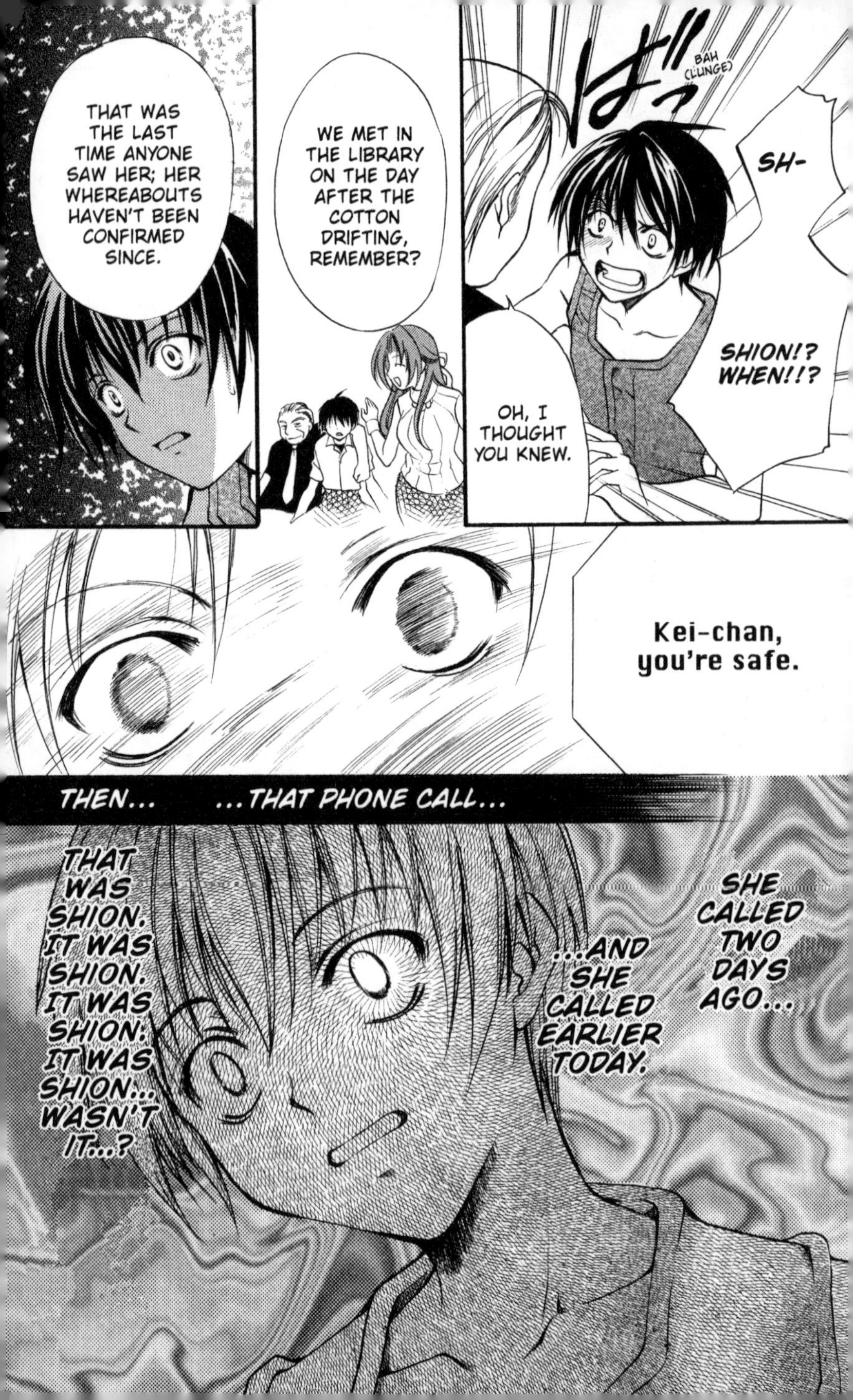
ばっ
BAH (LUNGE)
SH-
SHION!? WHEN!!?
OH, I THOUGHT YOU KNEW.
WE MET IN THE LIBRARY ON THE DAY AFTER THE COTTON DRIFTING, REMEMBER?
THAT WAS THE LAST TIME ANYONE SAW HER; HER WHEREABOUTS HAVEN'T BEEN CONFIRMED SINCE.
Kei-chan, you're safe.
THEN... ...THAT PHONE CALL...
SHE CALLED TWO DAYS AGO...
...AND SHE CALLED EARLIER TODAY.
THAT WAS SHION. IT WAS SHION. IT WAS SHION. IT WAS SHION... WASN'T IT...?

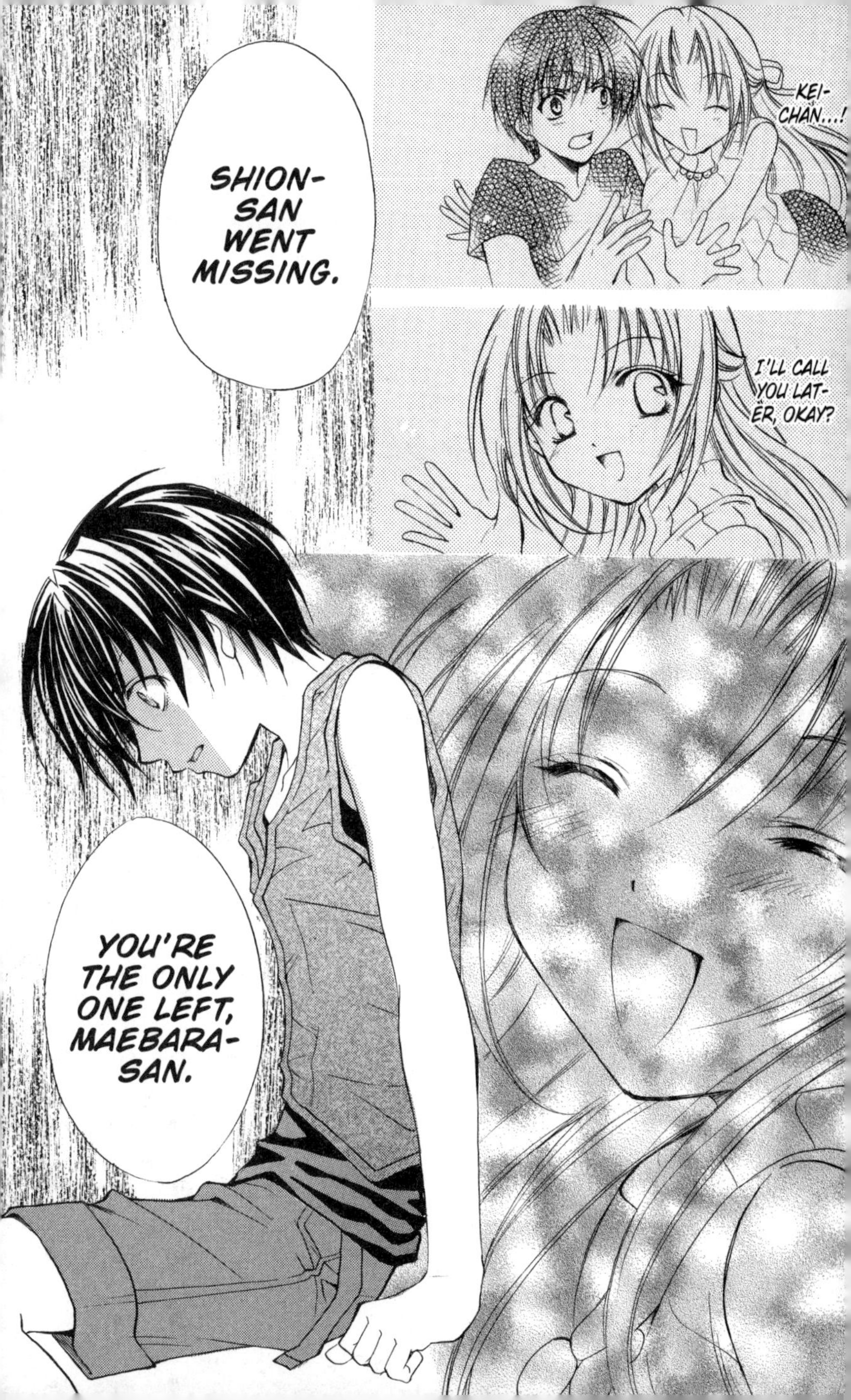
KEI-CHAN...!
I'LL CALL YOU LAT-ER, OKAY?
SHION-SAN WENT MISSING.
YOU'RE THE ONLY ONE LEFT, MAEBARA-SAN.

Higurashi
WHEN THEY CRY
COTTON DRIFTING ARC

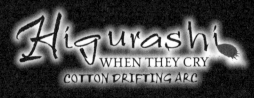

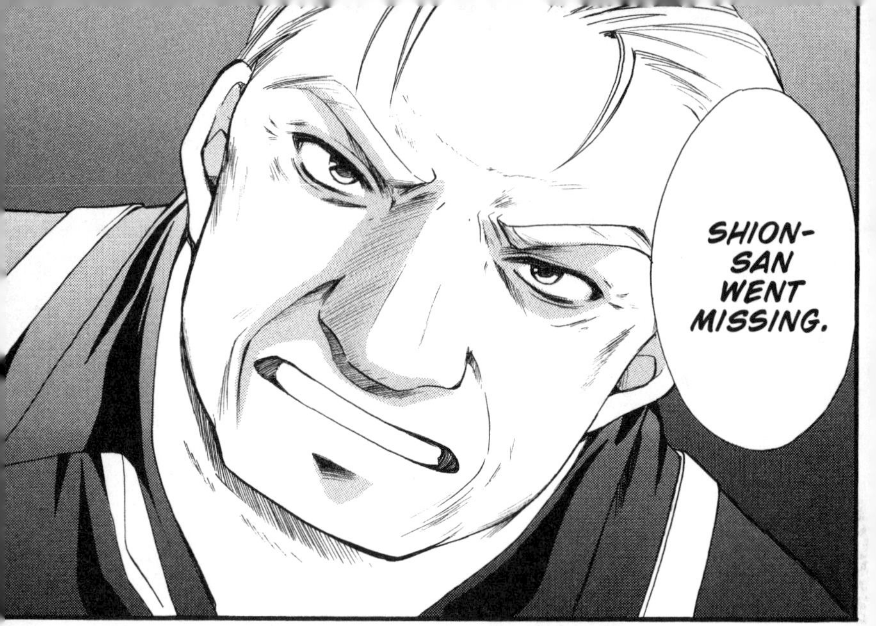
SHION-SAN WENT MISSING.

CHAPTER 10
PHONE CALL

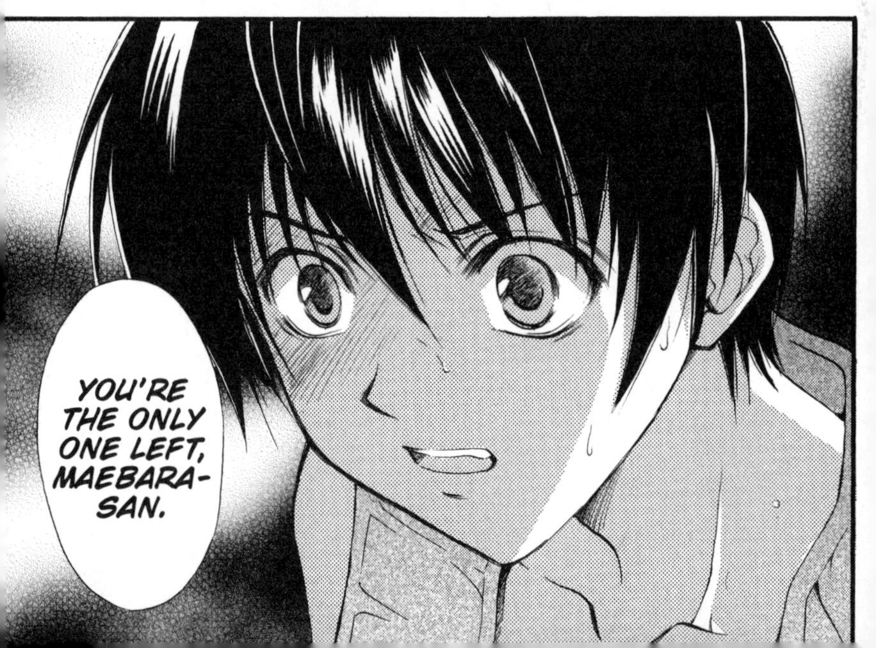
YOU'RE THE ONLY ONE LEFT, MAEBARA-SAN.

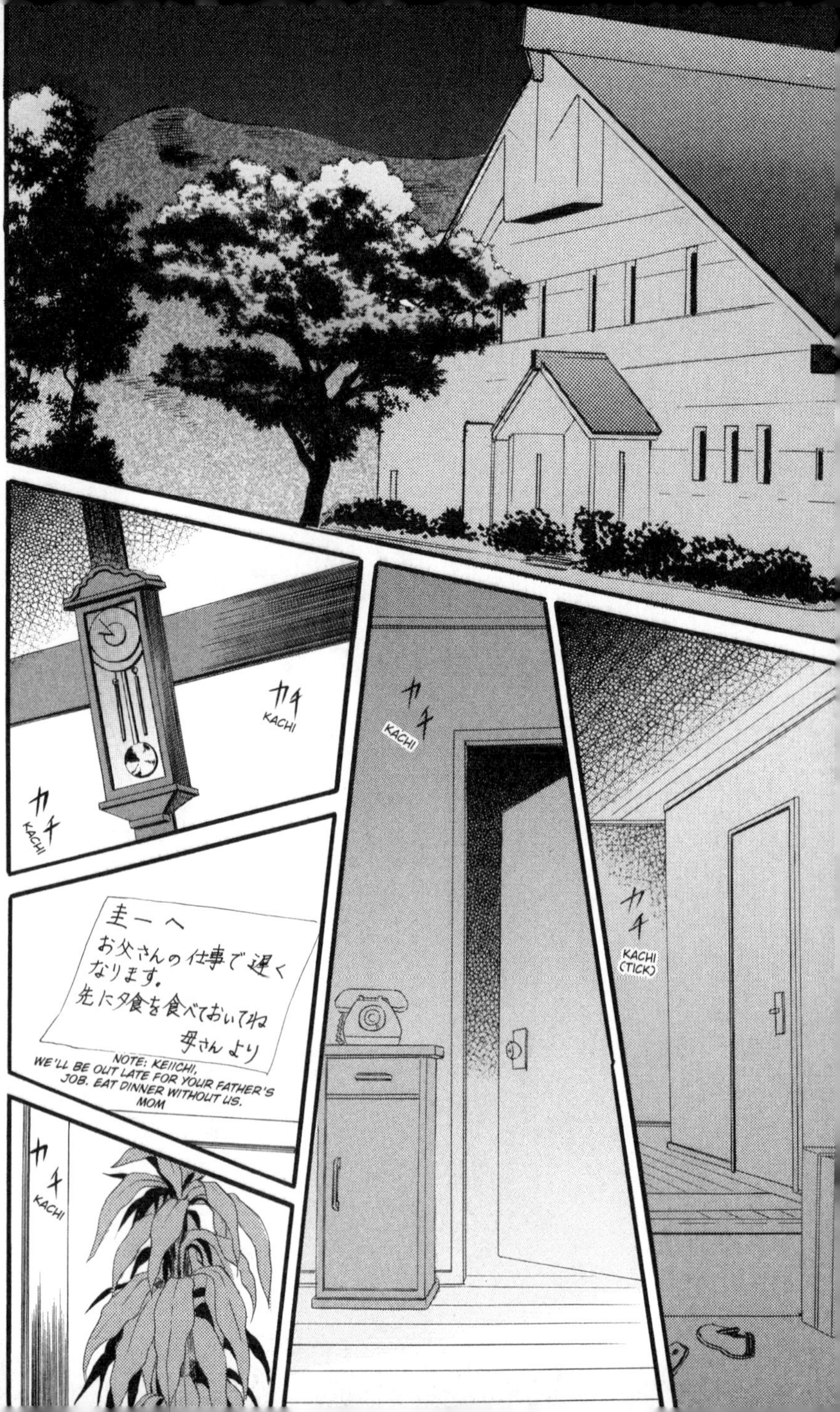
カチ
KACHI (TICK)
カチ
KACHI
カチ
KACHI
カチ
KACHI
圭一へ
お父さんの仕事で遅くなります。
先に夕食を食べておいてね
母さんより
NOTE: KEIICHI, WE'LL BE OUT LATE FOR YOUR FATHER'S JOB. EAT DINNER WITHOUT US. MOM
カチ
KACHI

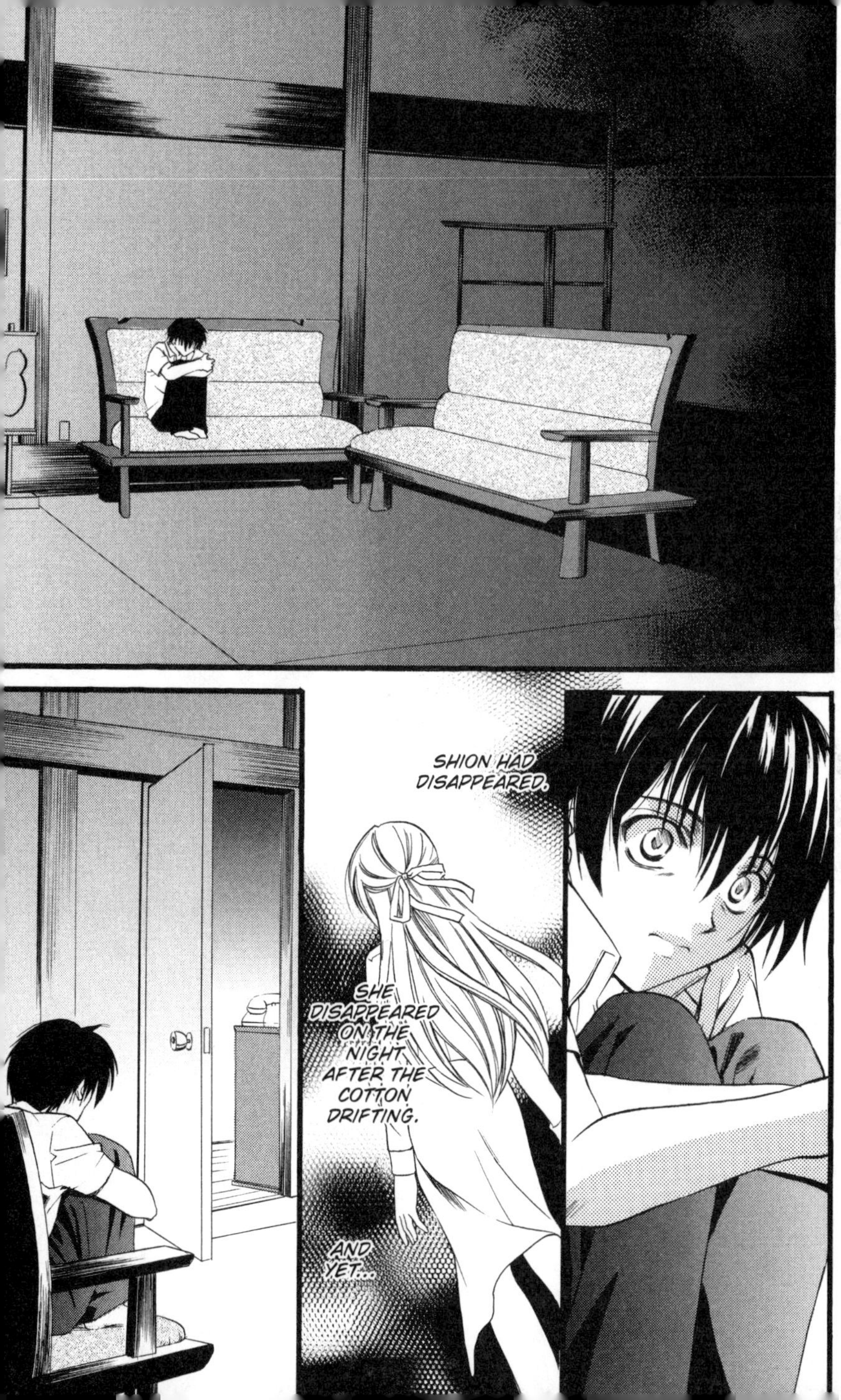
SHION HAD DISAPPEARED.
SHE DISAPPEARED ON THE NIGHT AFTER THE COTTON DRIFTING.
AND YET...

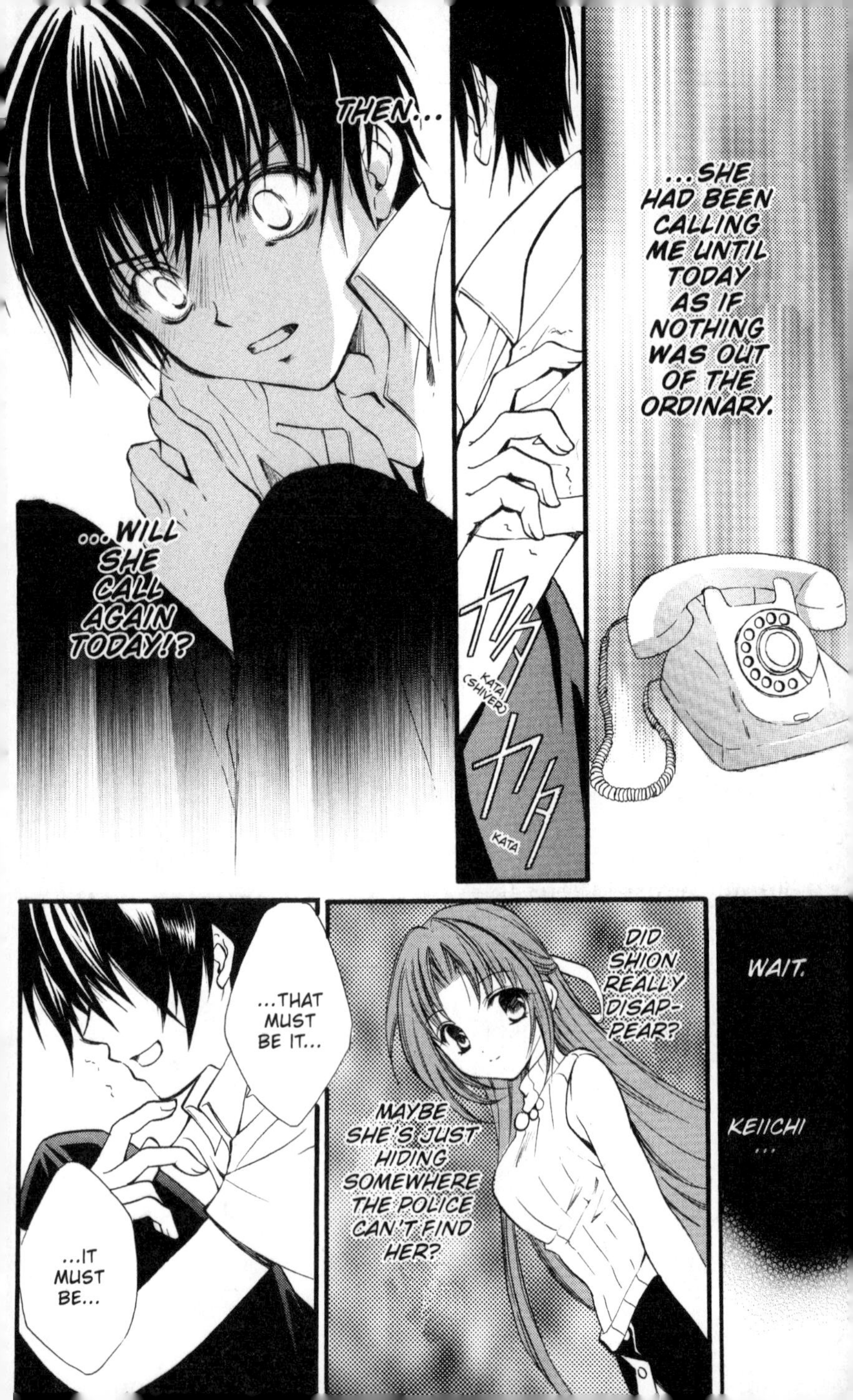
...SHE HAD BEEN CALLING ME UNTIL TODAY AS IF NOTHING WAS OUT OF THE ORDINARY.
KATA (SHIVER)
KATA
THEN...
...WILL SHE CALL AGAIN TODAY!?
WAIT.
KEIICHI ...
DID SHION REALLY DISAP-PEAR?
MAYBE SHE'S JUST HIDING SOMEWHERE THE POLICE CAN'T FIND HER?
...THAT MUST BE IT...
...IT MUST BE...

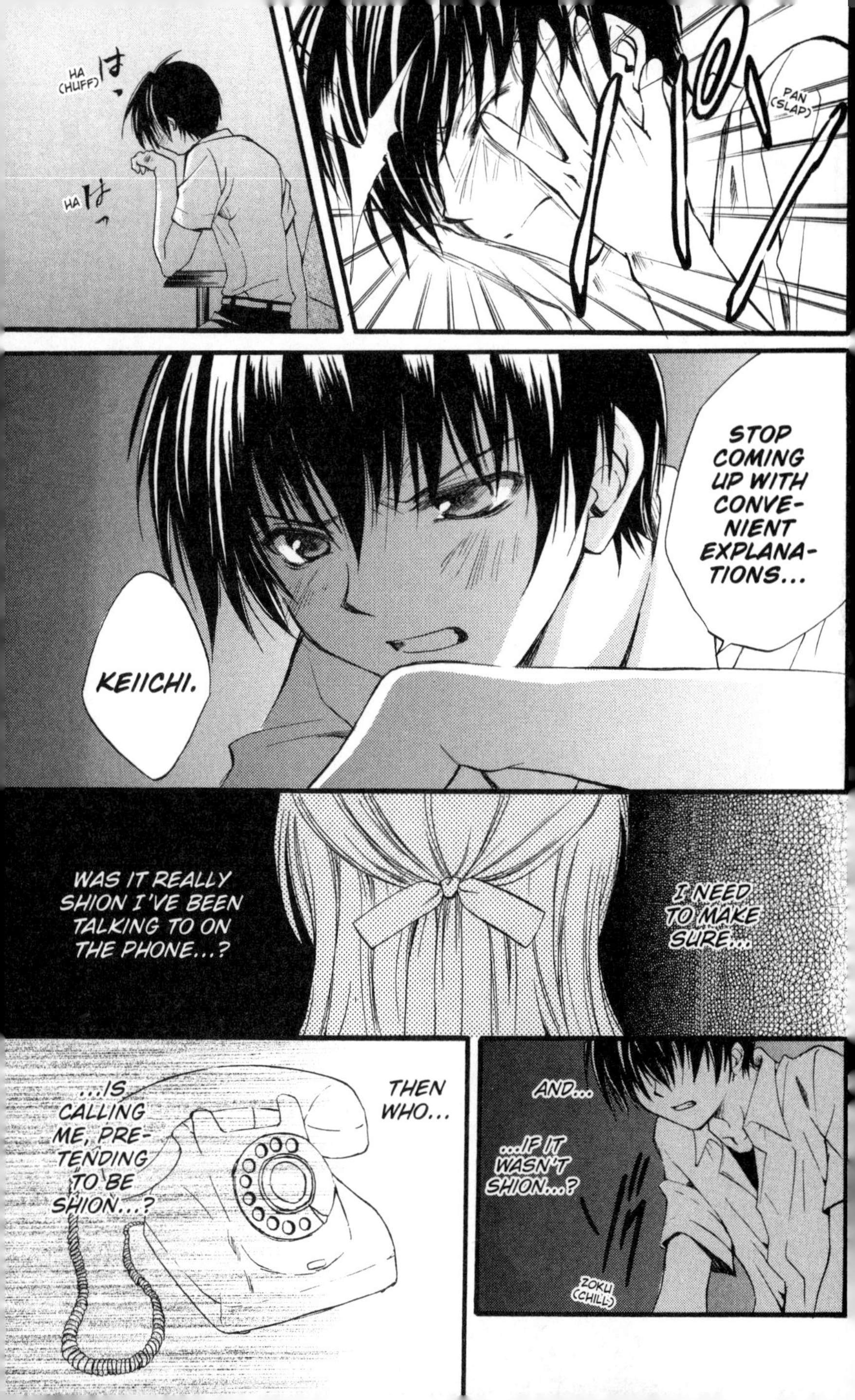
PAN (SLAP)
HA (HUFF)
はっ
HA
はっ
STOP COMING UP WITH CONVENIENT EXPLANATIONS...
KEIICHI.
I NEED TO MAKE SURE...
WAS IT REALLY SHION I'VE BEEN TALKING TO ON THE PHONE...?
AND...
...IF IT WASN'T SHION...?
ZOKU (CHILL)
THEN WHO...
...IS CALLING ME, PRETENDING TO BE SHION...?

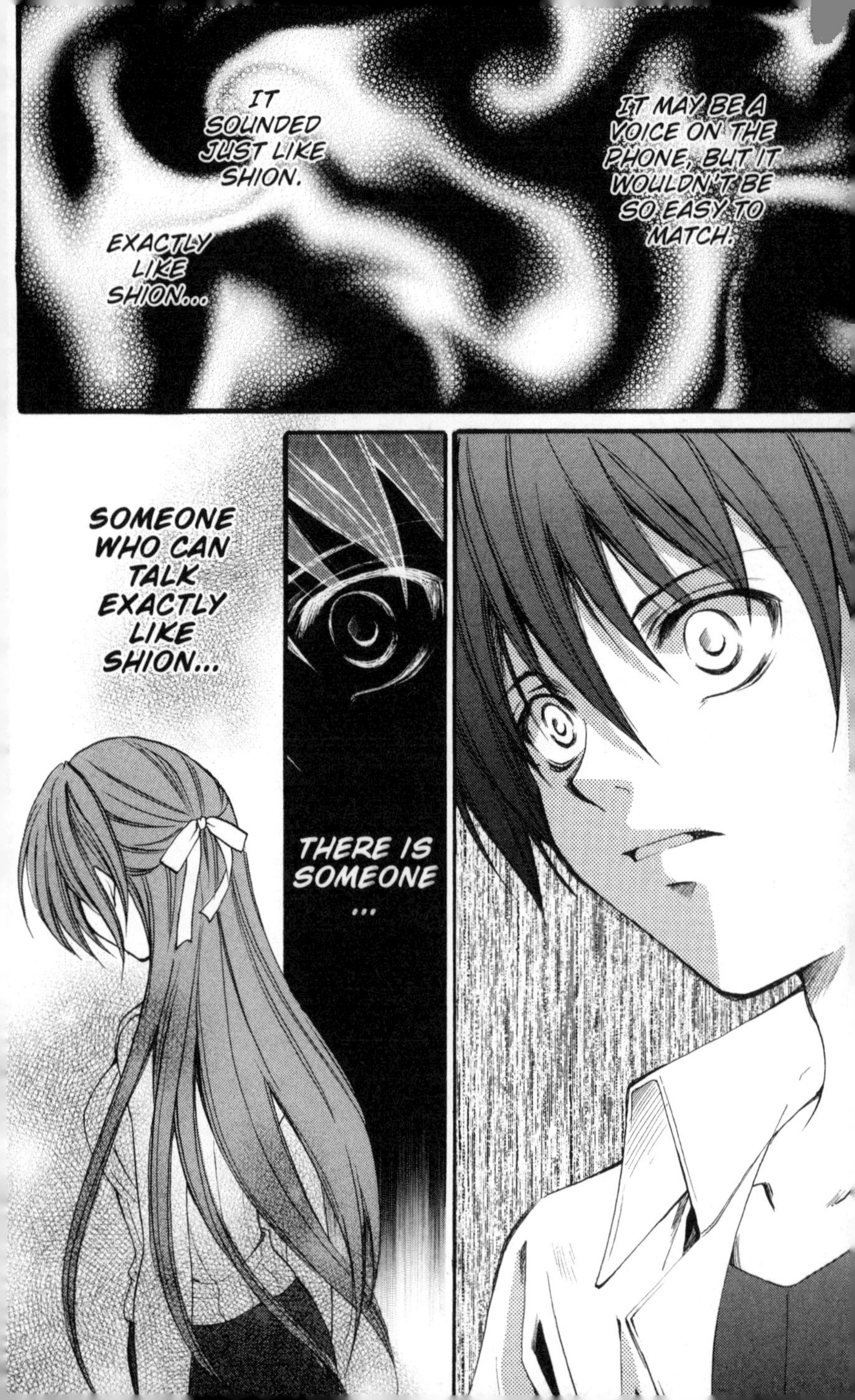
IT MAY BE A VOICE ON THE PHONE, BUT IT WOULDN'T BE SO EASY TO MATCH.
IT SOUNDED JUST LIKE SHION.
EXACTLY LIKE SHION...
THERE IS SOMEONE ...
SOMEONE WHO CAN TALK EXACTLY LIKE SHION...

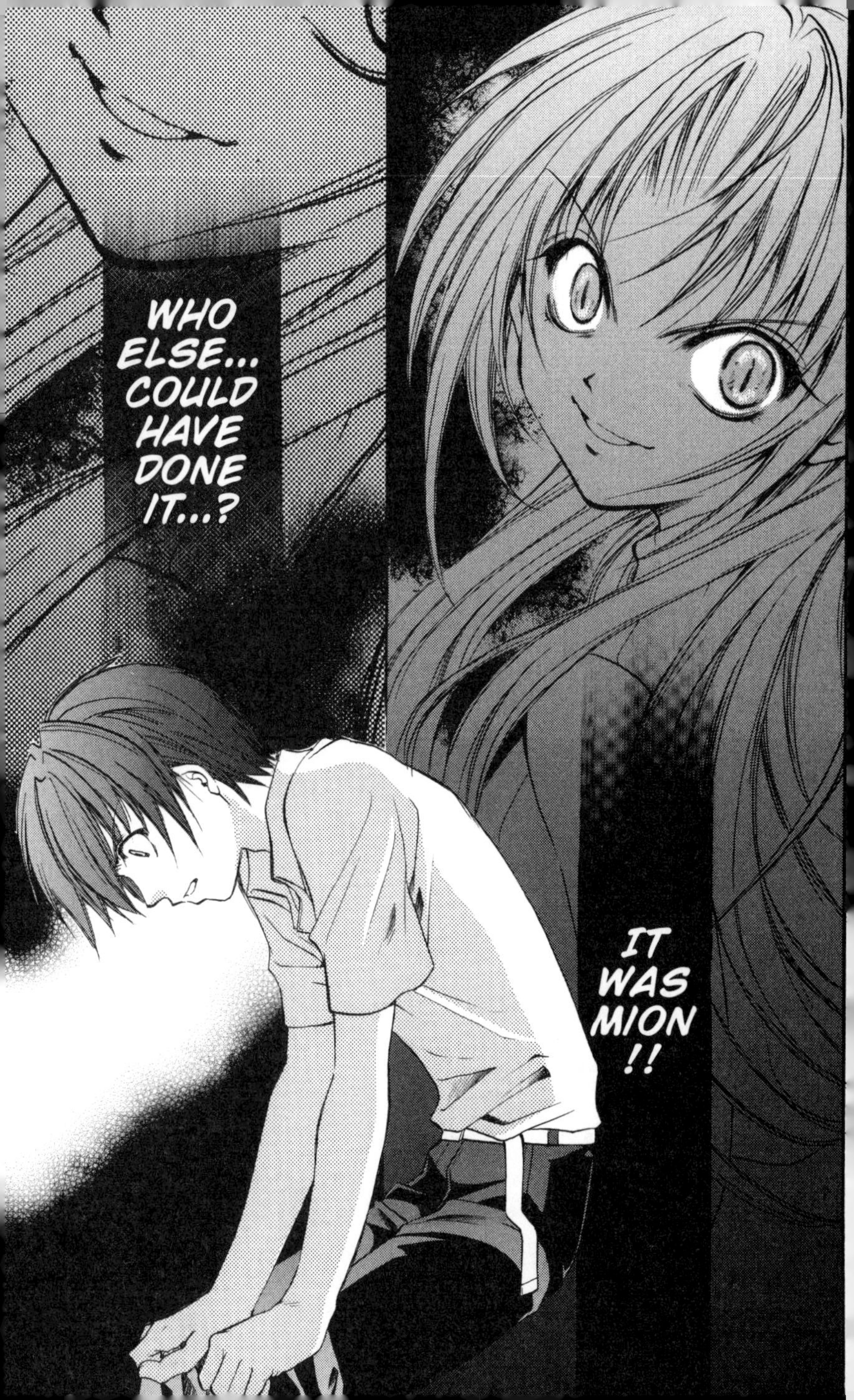
IT WAS MION !!
WHO ELSE... COULD HAVE DONE IT...?

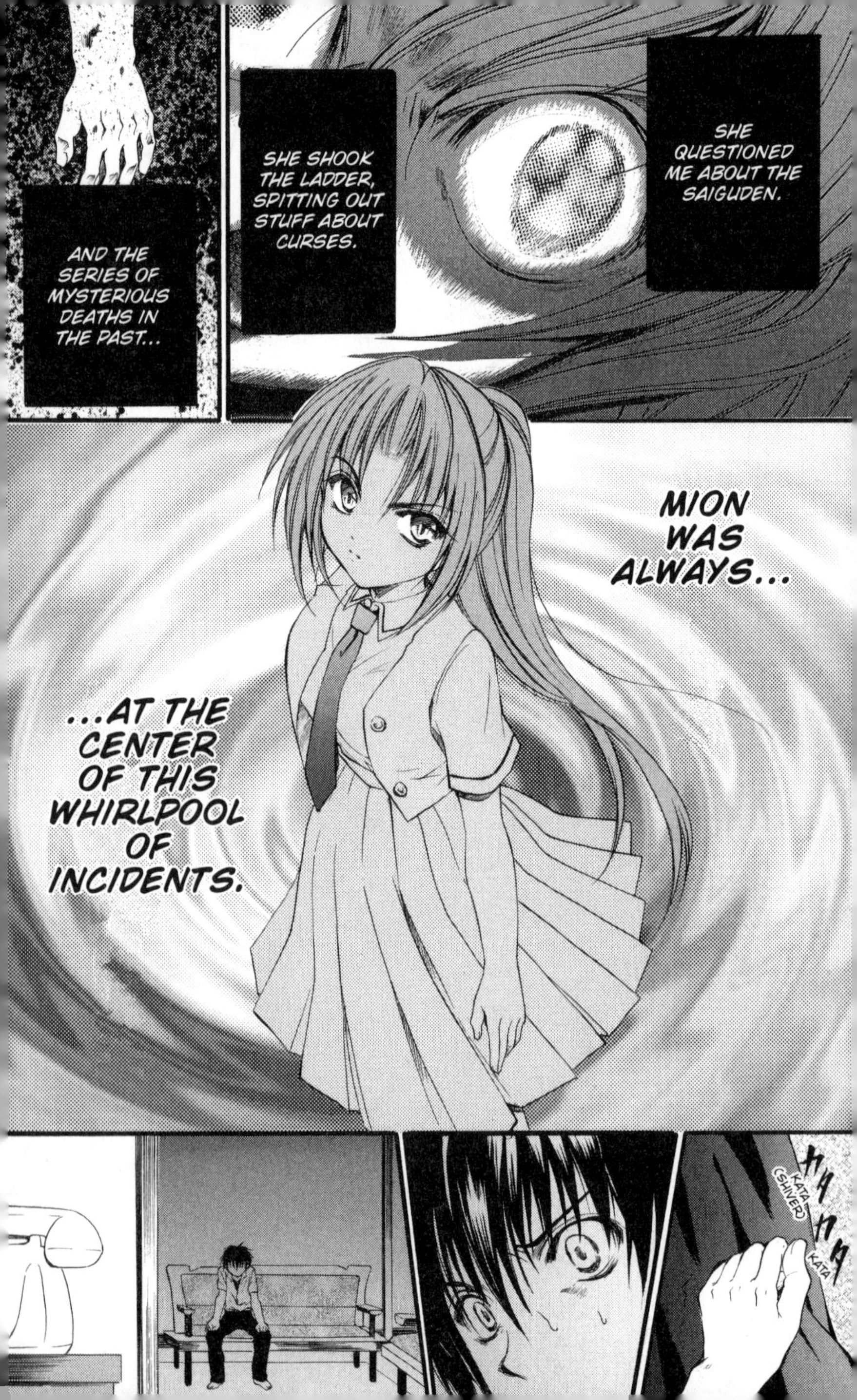
SHE QUESTIONED ME ABOUT THE SAIGUDEN.
SHE SHOOK THE LADDER, SPITTING OUT STUFF ABOUT CURSES.
AND THE SERIES OF MYSTERIOUS DEATHS IN THE PAST...
MION WAS ALWAYS...
...AT THE CENTER OF THIS WHIRLPOOL OF INCIDENTS.
KATA (SHIVER)
KATA

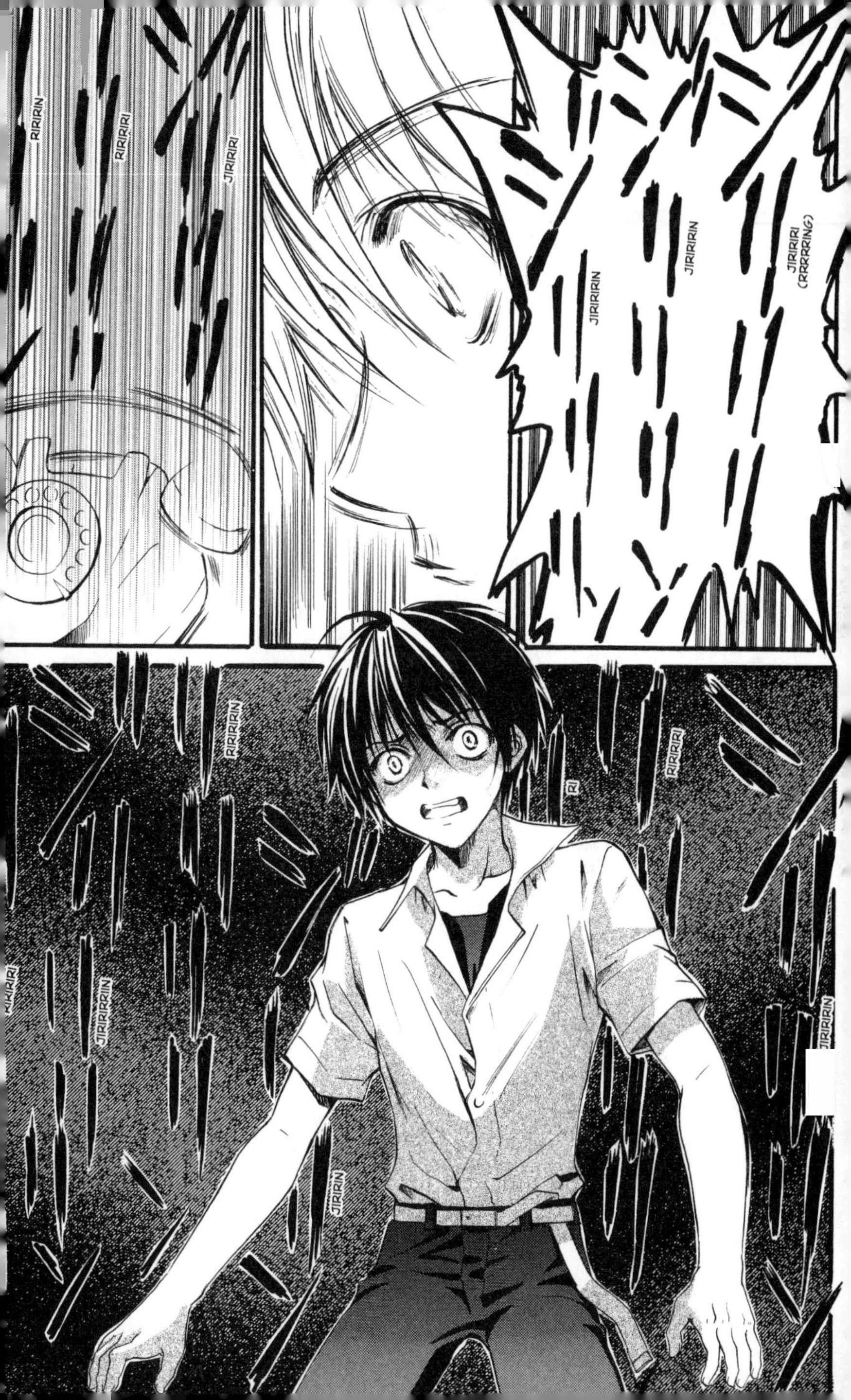

JIRIRIRI (RRRRRING)
JIRIRIRIN
JIRIRIRIN
JIRIRIRI
RIRIRIRI
RIRIRIN
JIRIRIRIN
RIRIRIRI
RI
RIRIRIRIN
JIRIRIRIN
RIRIRIRI
JIRIRIN

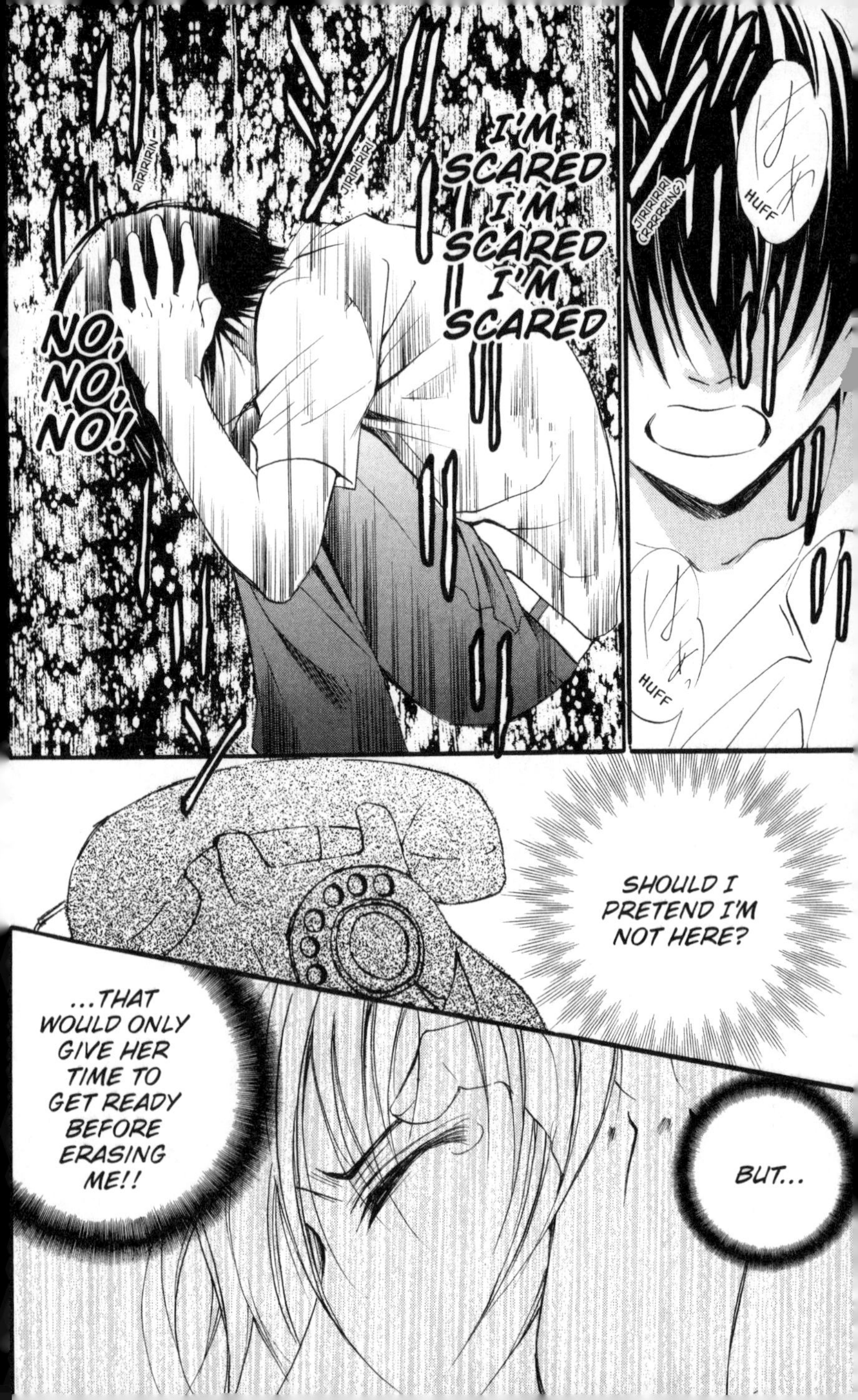
はぁ
HUFF
JIRIRIRIRI (RRRRRING)
はぁ
HUFF
JIRIRIRI
RIRIRIRIN
I'M SCARED I'M SCARED I'M SCARED
NO, NO, NO!
SHOULD I PRETEND I'M NOT HERE?
...THAT WOULD ONLY GIVE HER TIME TO GET READY BEFORE ERASING ME!!
BUT...

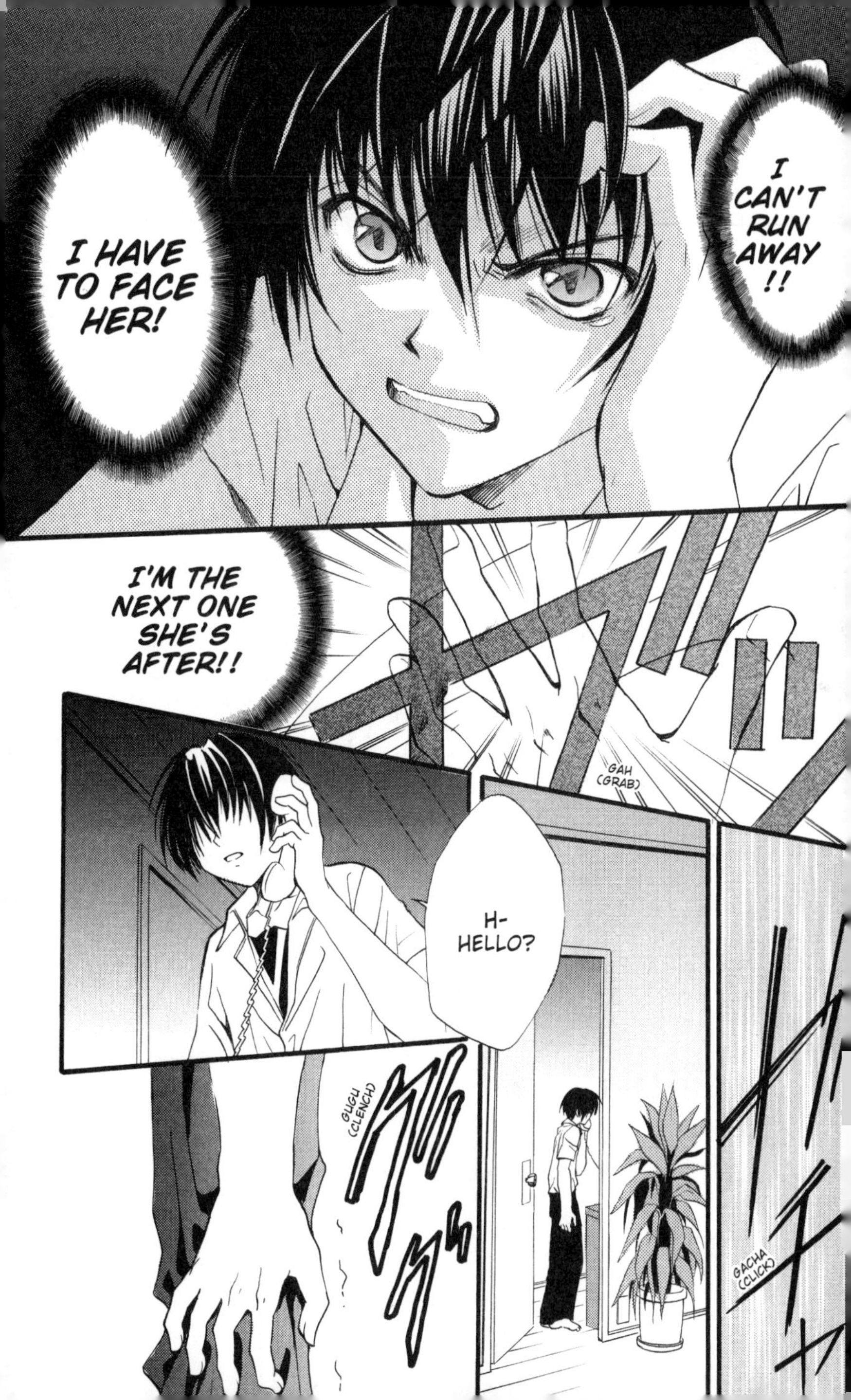
I CAN'T RUN AWAY!!
I HAVE TO FACE HER!
I'M THE NEXT ONE SHE'S AFTER!!
GAH (GRAB)
GACHA (CLICK)
H- HELLO?
GUGU (CLENCH)

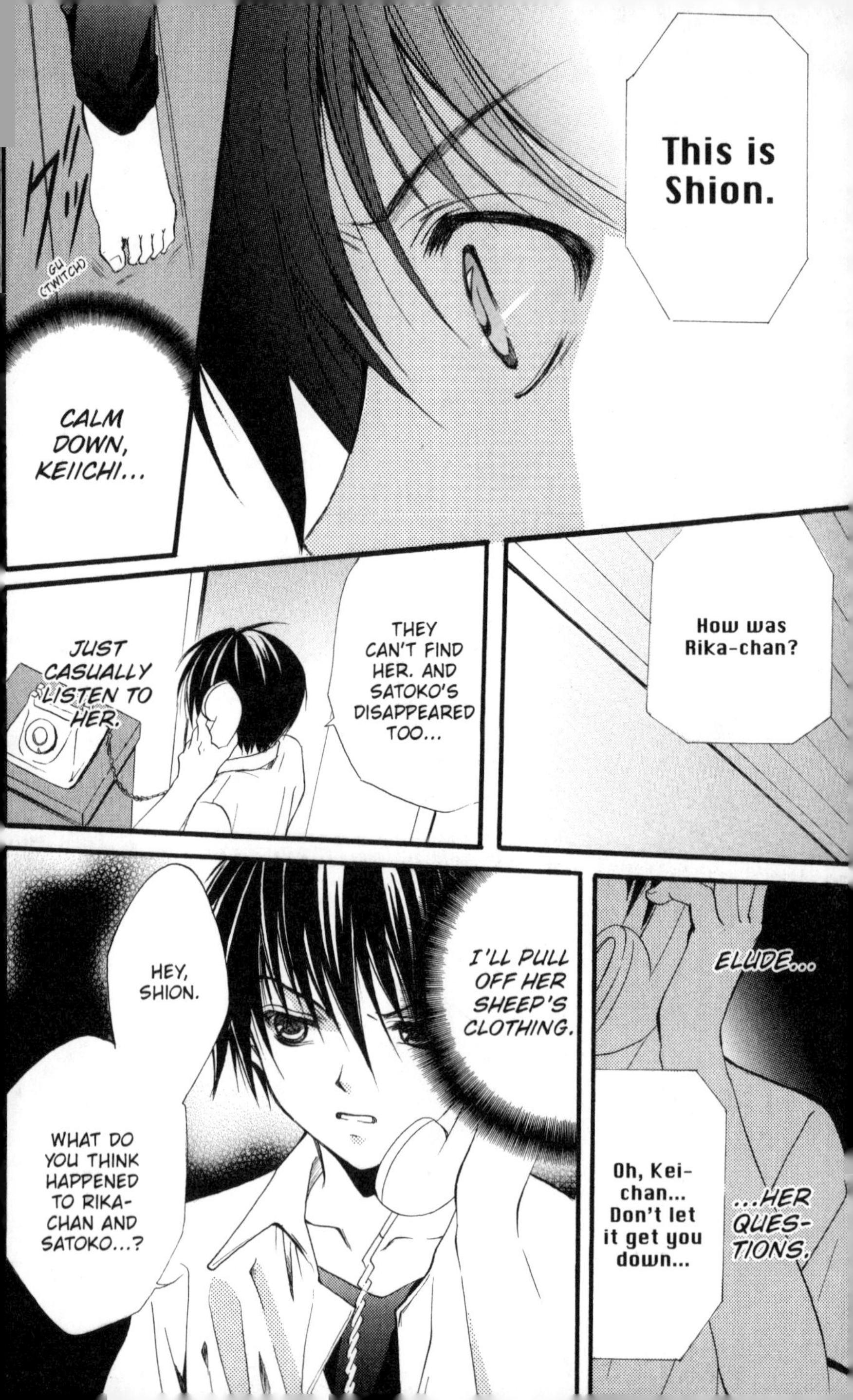
This is Shion.
GU (TWITCH)
CALM DOWN, KEIICHI...
How was Rika-chan?
THEY CAN'T FIND HER. AND SATOKO'S DISAPPEARED TOO...
JUST CASUALLY LISTEN TO HER.
ELUDE...
...HER QUESTIONS.
Oh, Kei-chan... Don't let it get you down...
I'LL PULL OFF HER SHEEP'S CLOTHING.
HEY, SHION.
WHAT DO YOU THINK HAPPENED TO RIKA-CHAN AND SATOKO...?

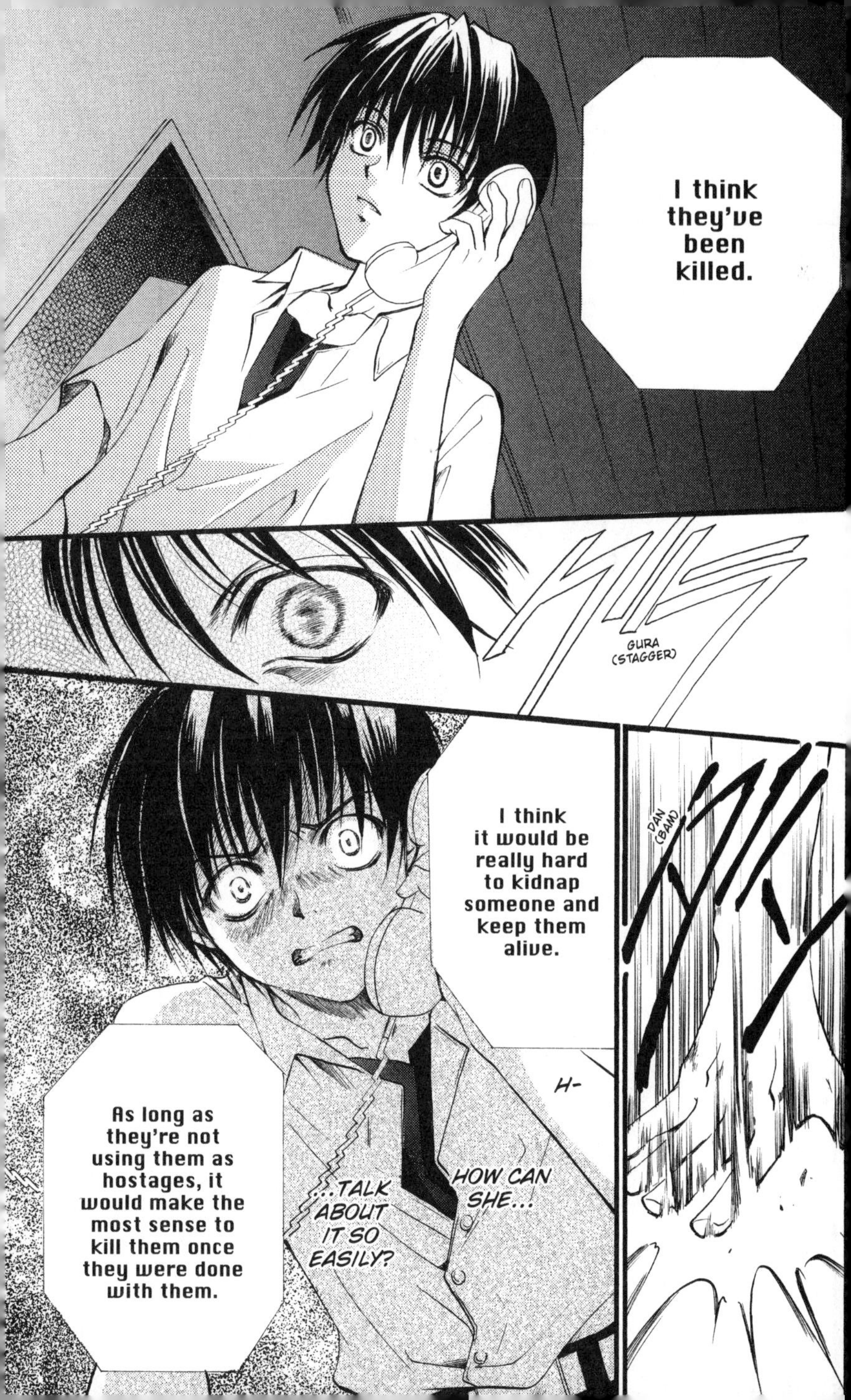
I think they've been killed.
GURA (STAGGER)
DAN (BAM)
I think it would be really hard to kidnap someone and keep them alive.
H-
HOW CAN SHE...
...TALK ABOUT IT SO EASILY?
As long as they're not using them as hostages, it would make the most sense to kill them once they were done with them.

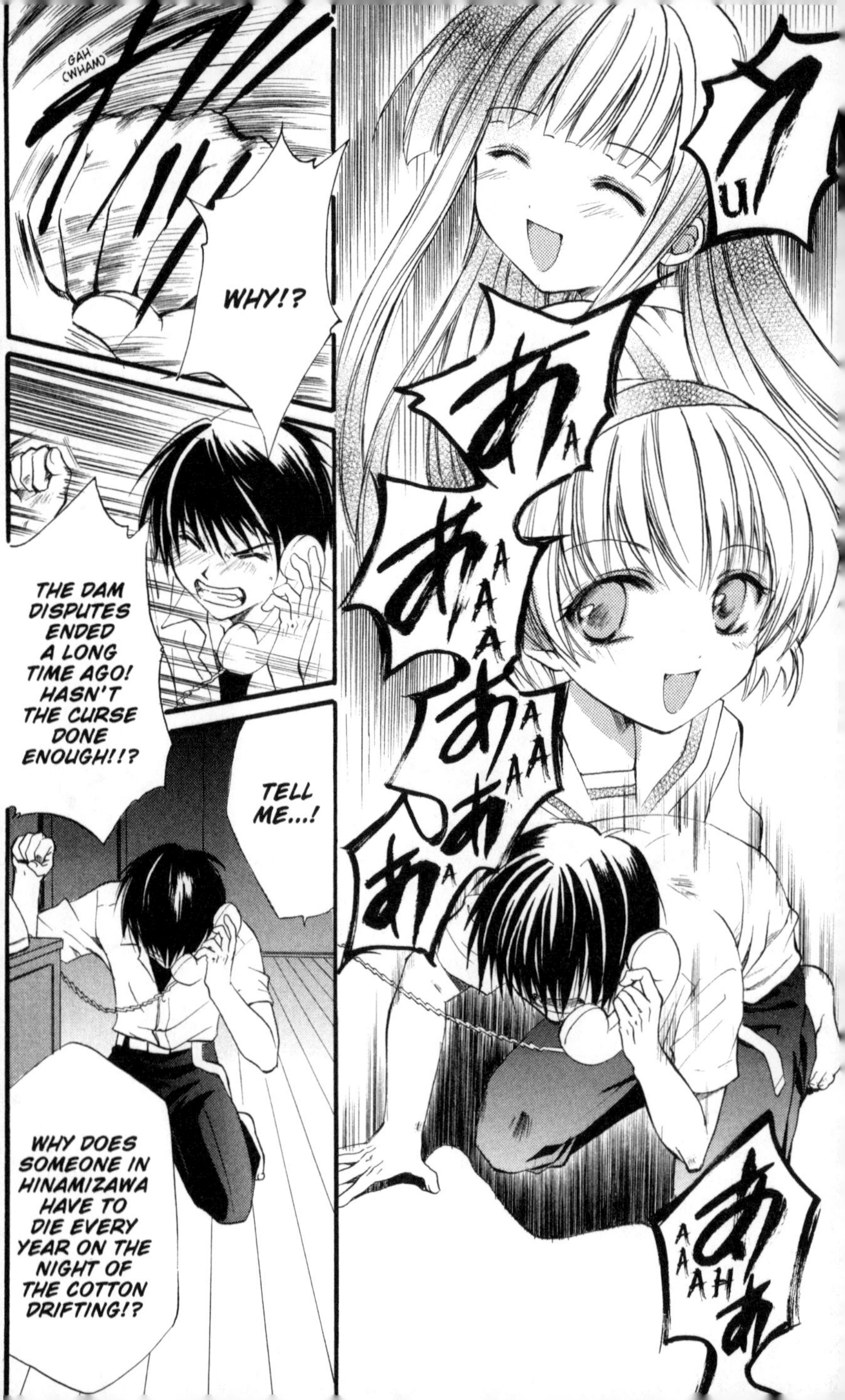
U
A A A A A A A A A A A
AAAH
GAH (WHAM)
WHY!?
THE DAM DISPUTES ENDED A LONG TIME AGO! HASN'T THE CURSE DONE ENOUGH!!?
TELL ME...!
WHY DOES SOMEONE IN HINAMIZAWA HAVE TO DIE EVERY YEAR ON THE NIGHT OF THE COTTON DRIFTING!?

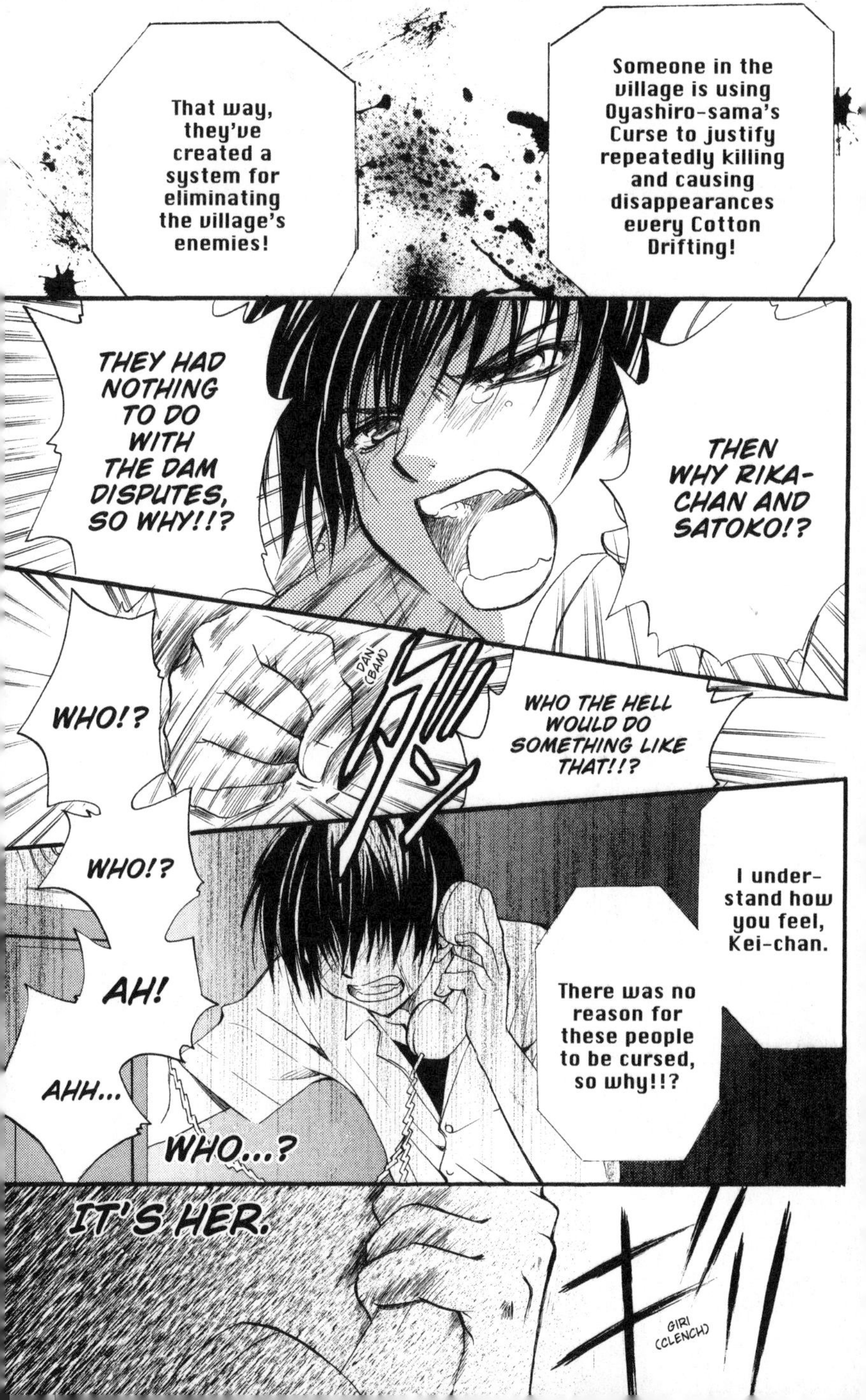
Someone in the village is using Oyashiro-sama's Curse to justify repeatedly killing and causing disappearances every Cotton Drifting!
That way, they've created a system for eliminating the village's enemies!
THEN WHY RIKA-CHAN AND SATOKO!?
THEY HAD NOTHING TO DO WITH THE DAM DISPUTES, SO WHY!!?
WHO THE HELL WOULD DO SOMETHING LIKE THAT!!?
DAN (BAM)
WHO!?
I under-stand how you feel, Kei-chan.
There was no reason for these people to be cursed, so why!!?
WHO!?
AH!
AHH...
WHO...?
GIRI (CLENCH)
IT'S HER.

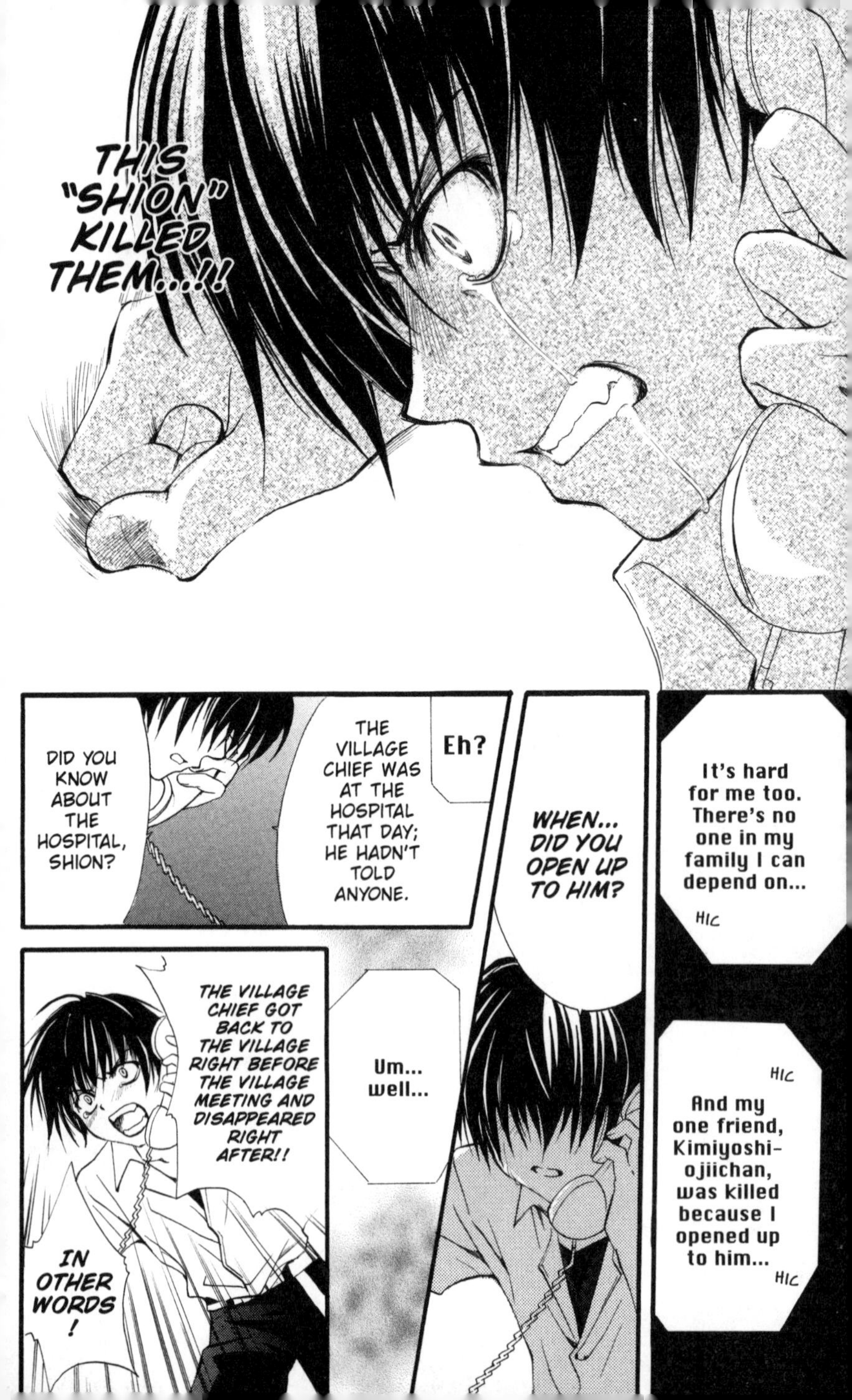
THIS "SHION" KILLED THEM...!!
It's hard for me too. There's no one in my family I can depend on...
HIC
HIC
And my one friend, Kimiyoshi-ojiichan, was killed because I opened up to him...
HIC
WHEN... DID YOU OPEN UP TO HIM?
Um... well...
Eh?
THE VILLAGE CHIEF WAS AT THE HOSPITAL THAT DAY; HE HADN'T TOLD ANYONE.
DID YOU KNOW ABOUT THE HOSPITAL, SHION?
THE VILLAGE CHIEF GOT BACK TO THE VILLAGE RIGHT BEFORE THE VILLAGE MEETING AND DISAPPEARED RIGHT AFTER!!
IN OTHER WORDS!

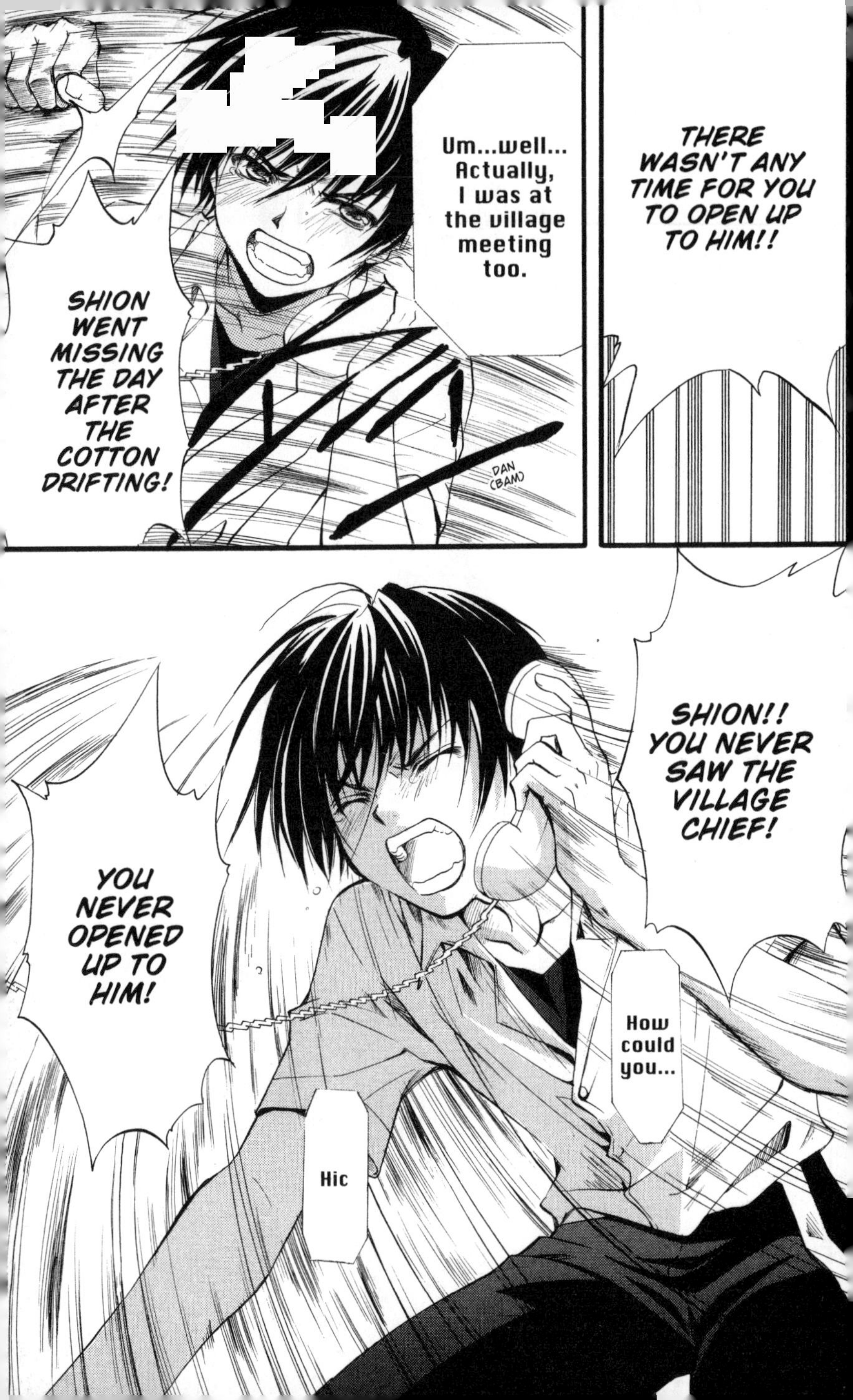
THERE WASN'T ANY TIME FOR YOU TO OPEN UP TO HIM!!
Um...well... Actually, I was at the village meeting too.
SHION WENT MISSING THE DAY AFTER THE COTTON DRIFTING!
DAN (BAM)
SHION!! YOU NEVER SAW THE VILLAGE CHIEF!
YOU NEVER OPENED UP TO HIM!
How could you...
Hic

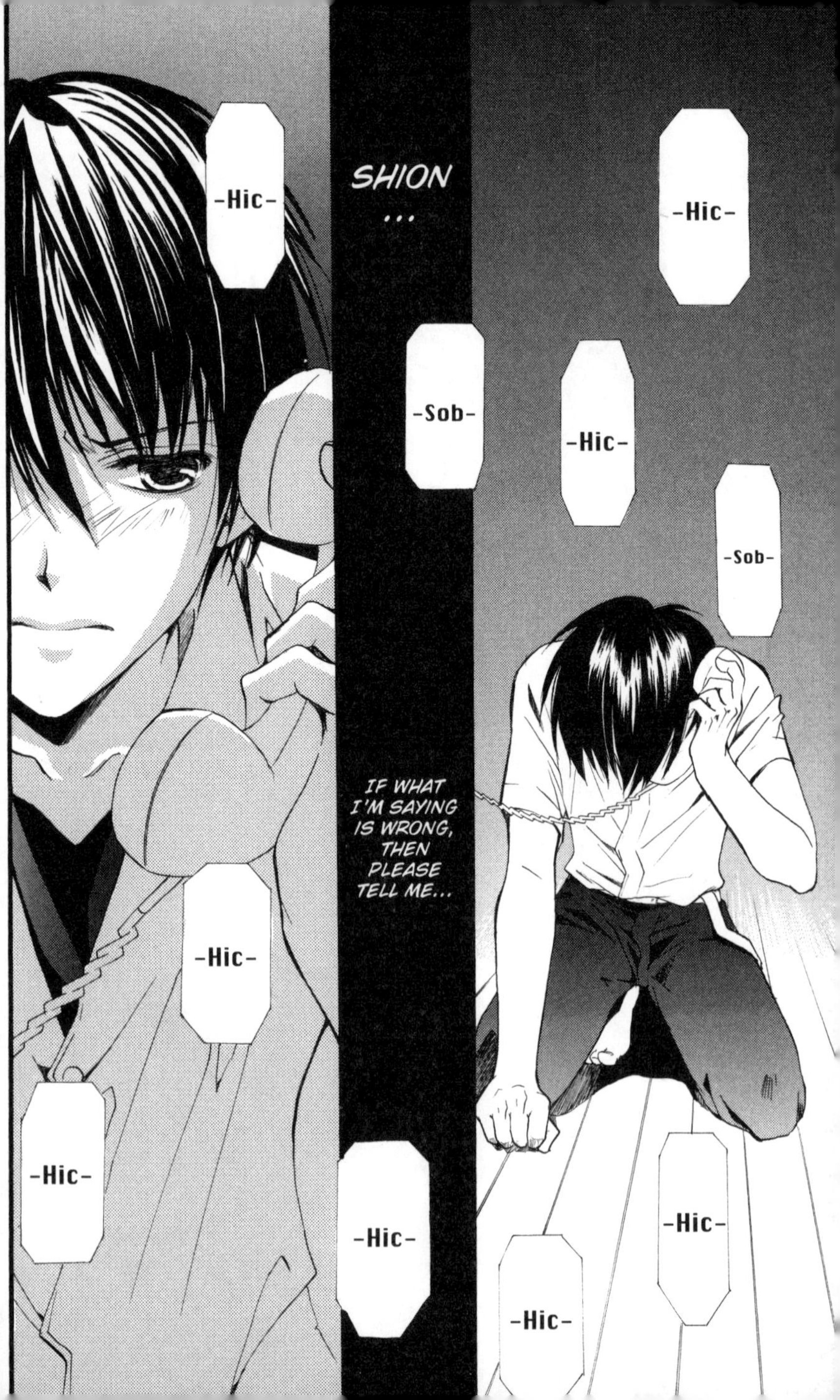
-Hic-
-Hic-
-Sob-
-Hic-
-Hic-
SHION ...
-Sob-
IF WHAT I'M SAYING IS WRONG, THEN PLEASE TELL ME...
-Hic-
-Hic-
-Hic-
-Hic-

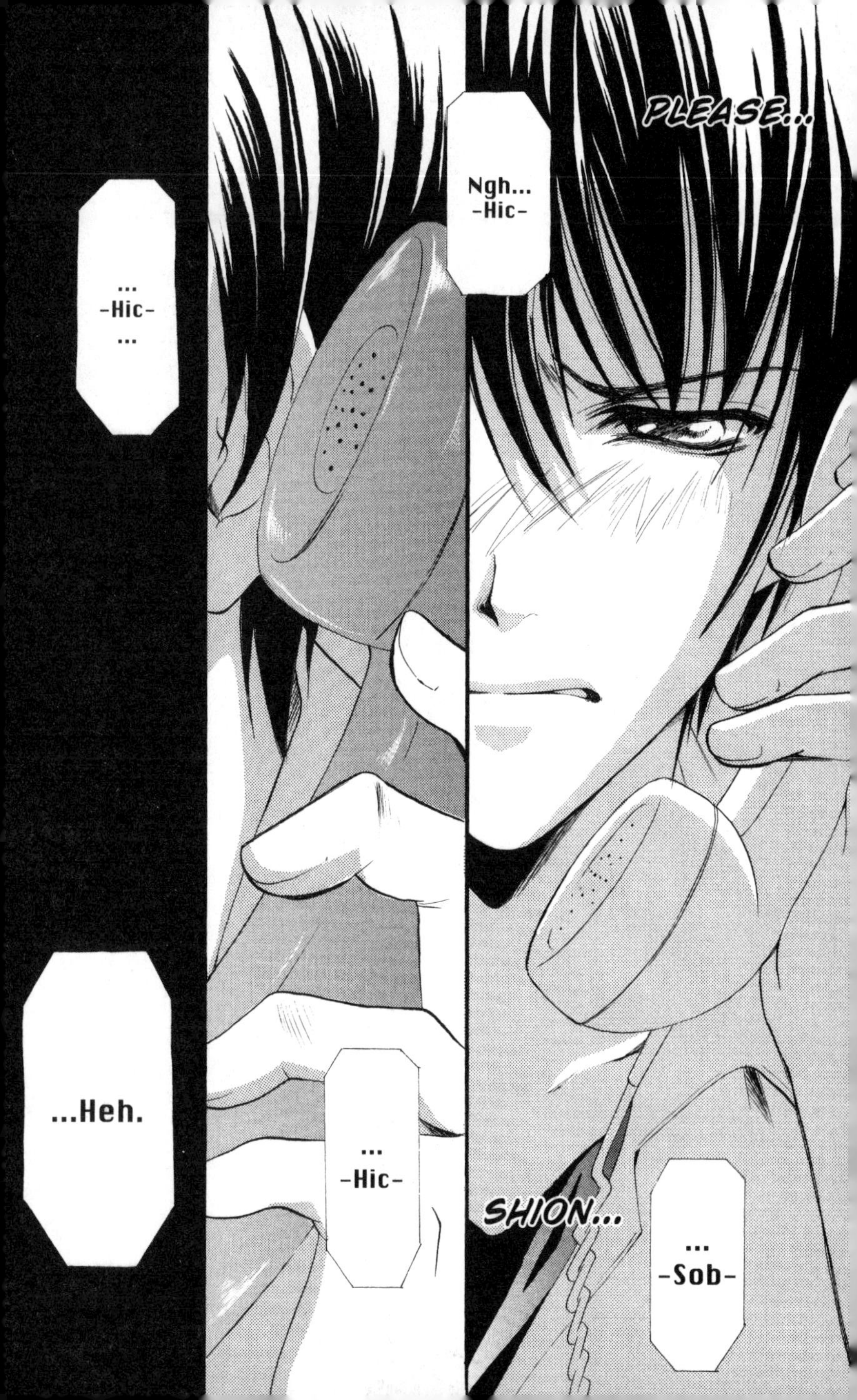
PLEASE...
Ngh... -Hic-
... -Sob-
SHION...
... -Hic-
... -Hic- ...
...Heh.

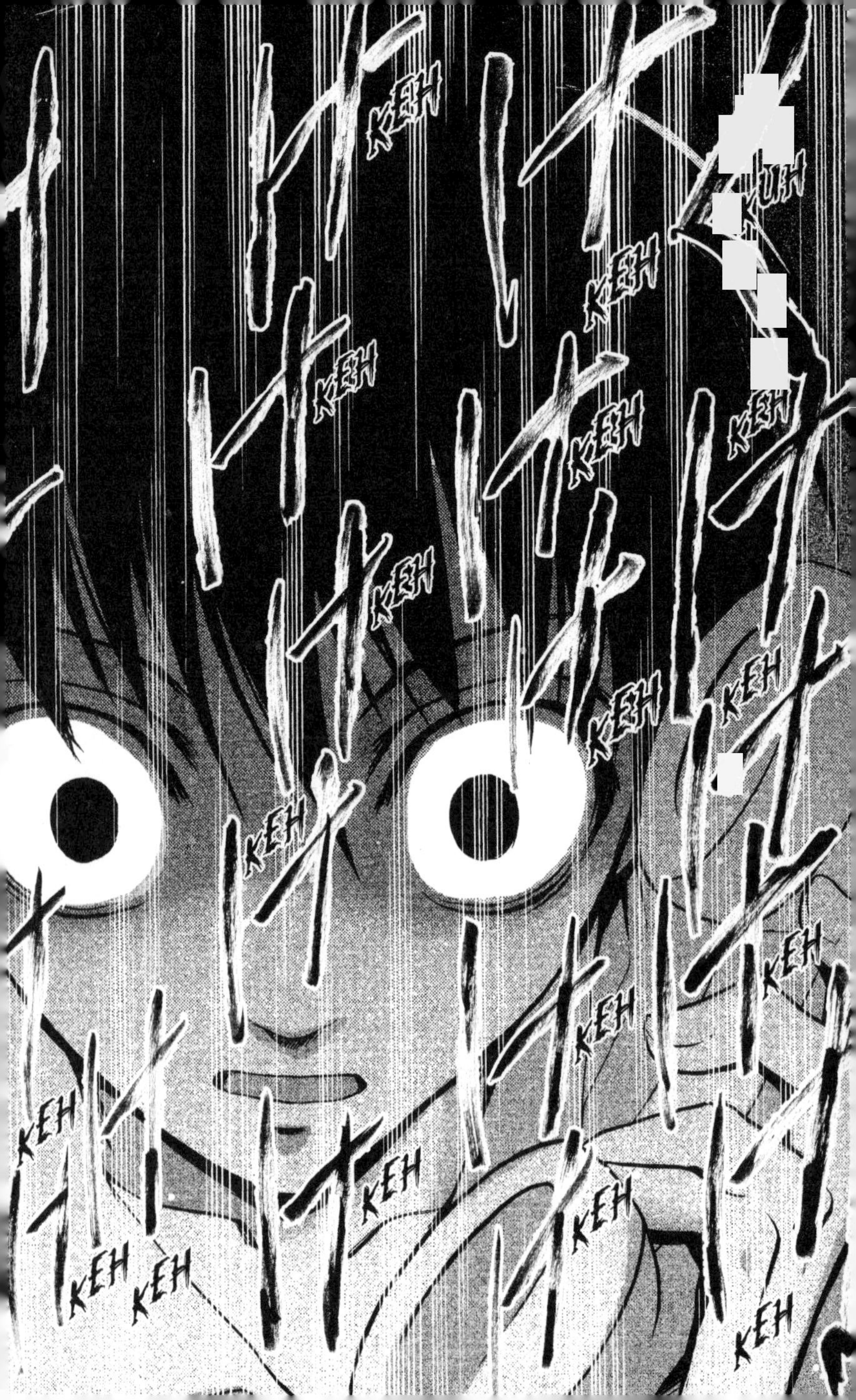
KUH
KEH
KEH
KEH
KEH
KEH
KEH
KEH
KEH
KEH
KEH
KEH
KEH
KEH
KEH
KEH
KEH
KEH
KEH

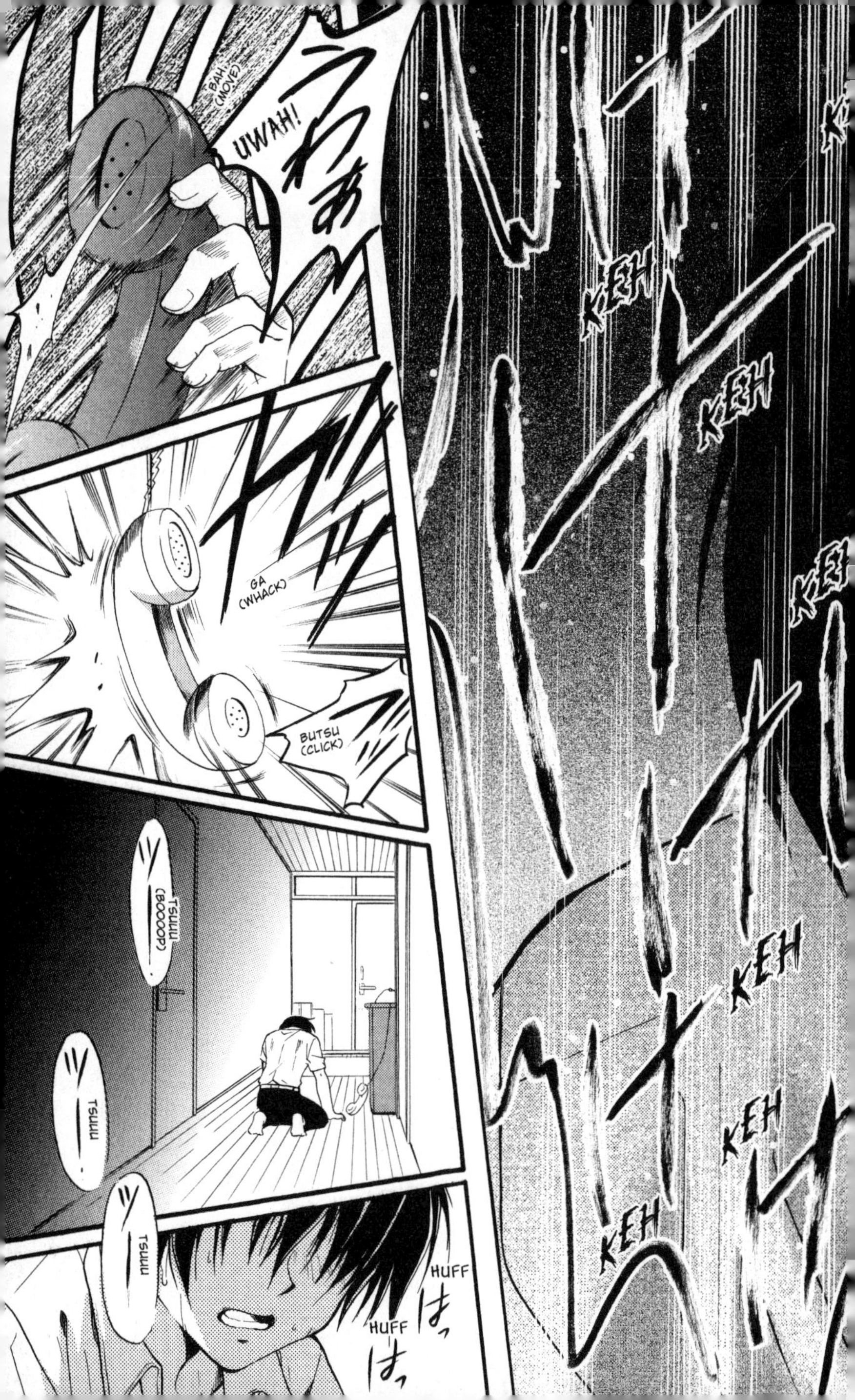
KEH
KEH
KEH
KEH
KEH
BAH (MOVE)
UWAH!
GA (WHACK)
BUTSU (CLICK)
TSUUU (BOOOOP)
TSUUU
TSUUU
HUFF
HUFF

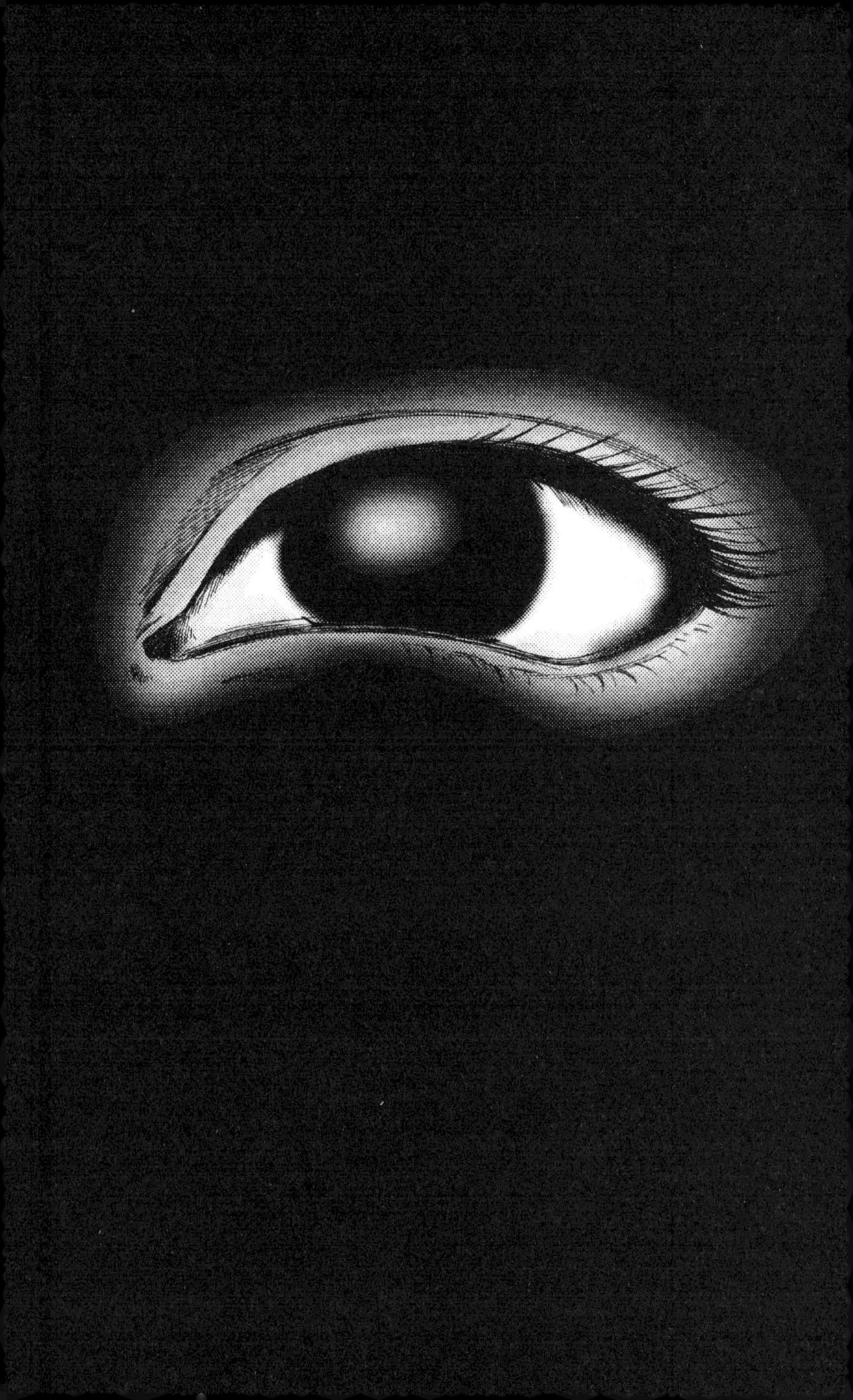

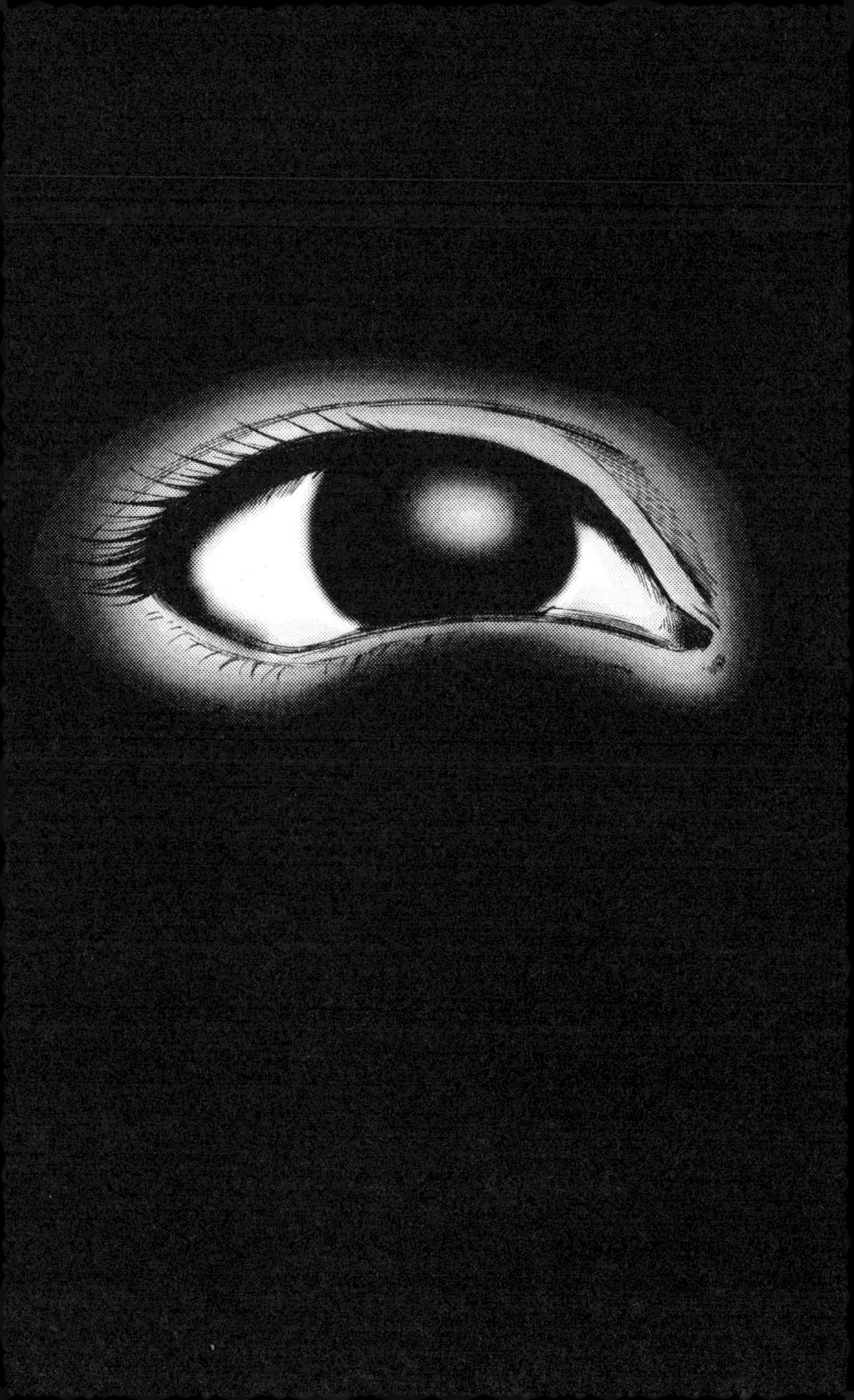

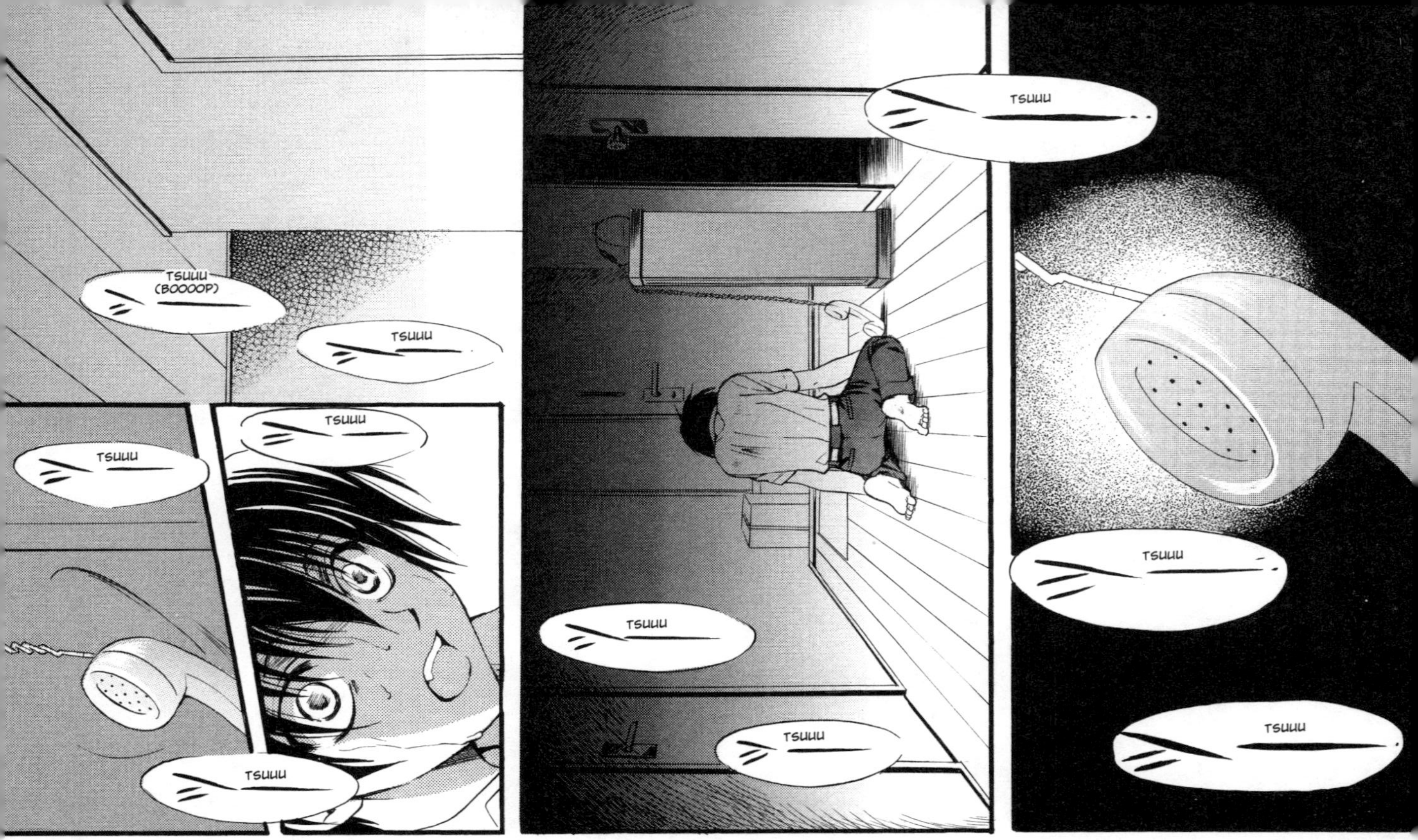
TSUUU
TSUUU
TSUUU
TSUUU
TSUUU
TSUUU (BOOOOP)
TSUUU
TSUUU
TSUUU
TSUUU

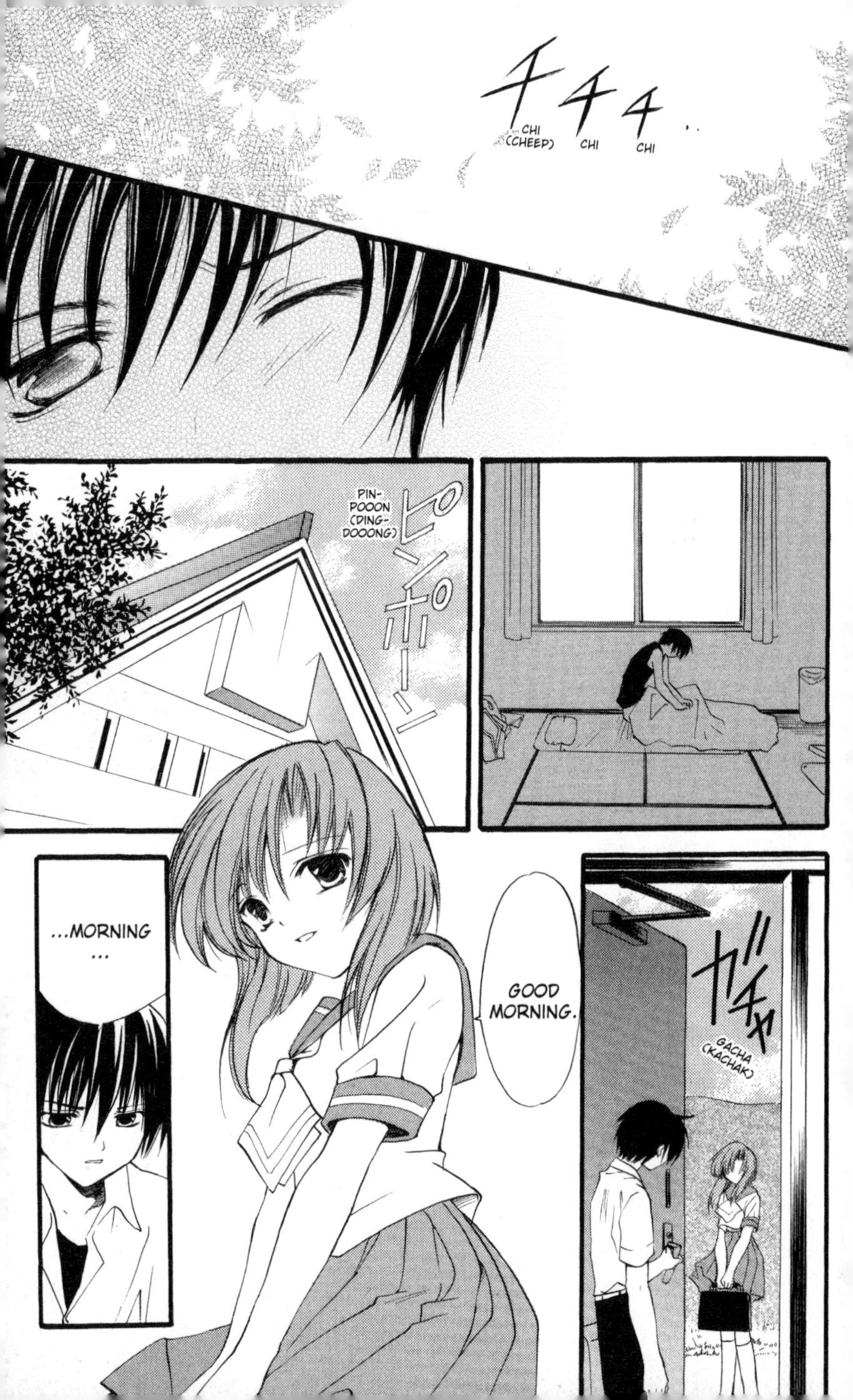
チチチ..
CHI (CHEEP) CHI CHI
ピンポーン
PIN-POOON (DING-DOOONG)
ガチャ
GACHA (KACHAK)
GOOD MORNING.
...MORNING ...

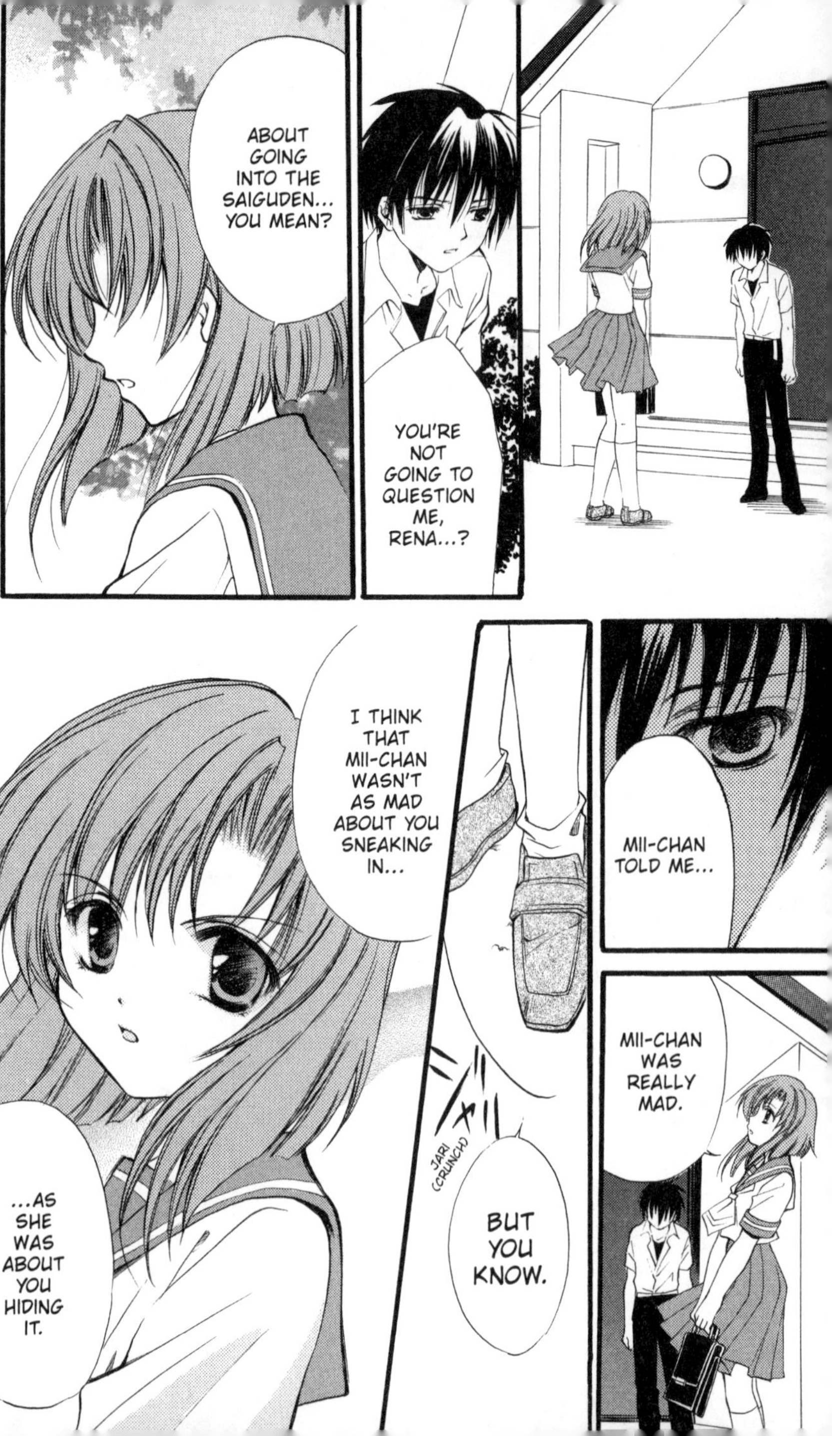
YOU'RE NOT GOING TO QUESTION ME, RENA...?
ABOUT GOING INTO THE SAIGUDEN... YOU MEAN?
MII-CHAN TOLD ME...
MII-CHAN WAS REALLY MAD.
JARI (CRUNCH)
BUT YOU KNOW.
I THINK THAT MII-CHAN WASN'T AS MAD ABOUT YOU SNEAKING IN...
...AS SHE WAS ABOUT YOU HIDING IT.

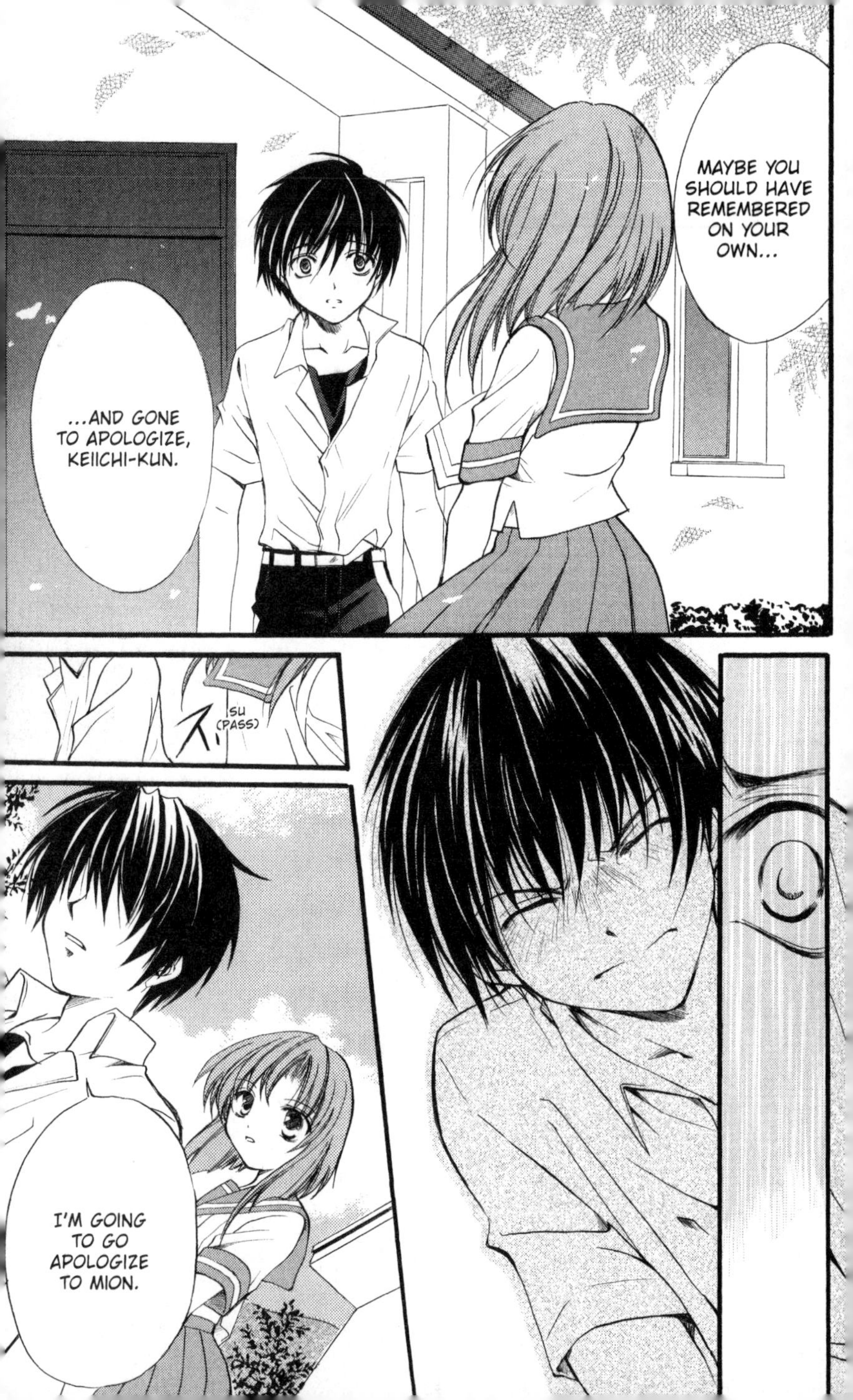
MAYBE YOU SHOULD HAVE REMEMBERED ON YOUR OWN...
...AND GONE TO APOLOGIZE, KEIICHI-KUN.
SU (PASS)
I'M GOING TO GO APOLOGIZE TO MION.

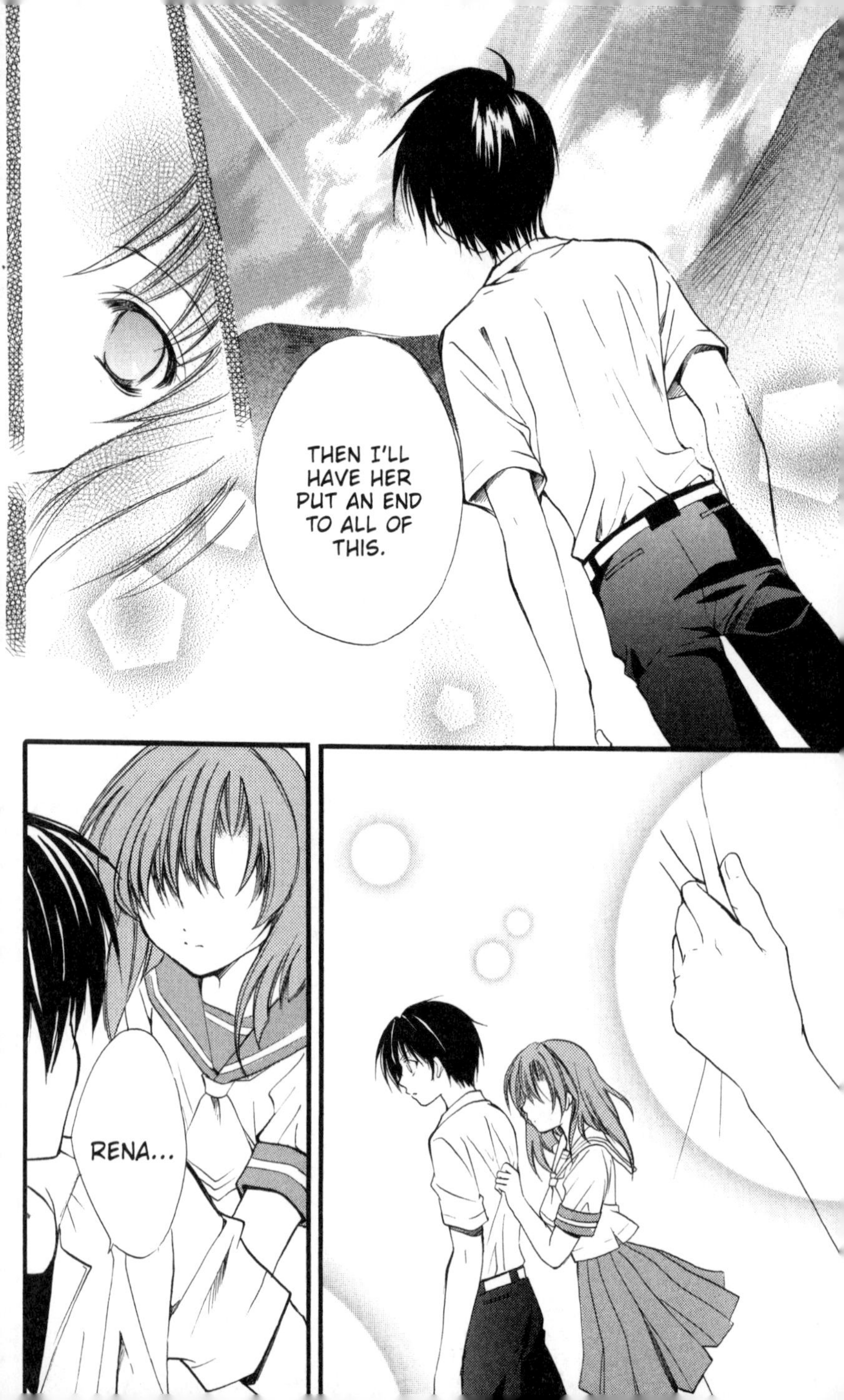
THEN I'LL HAVE HER PUT AN END TO ALL OF THIS.
RENA...

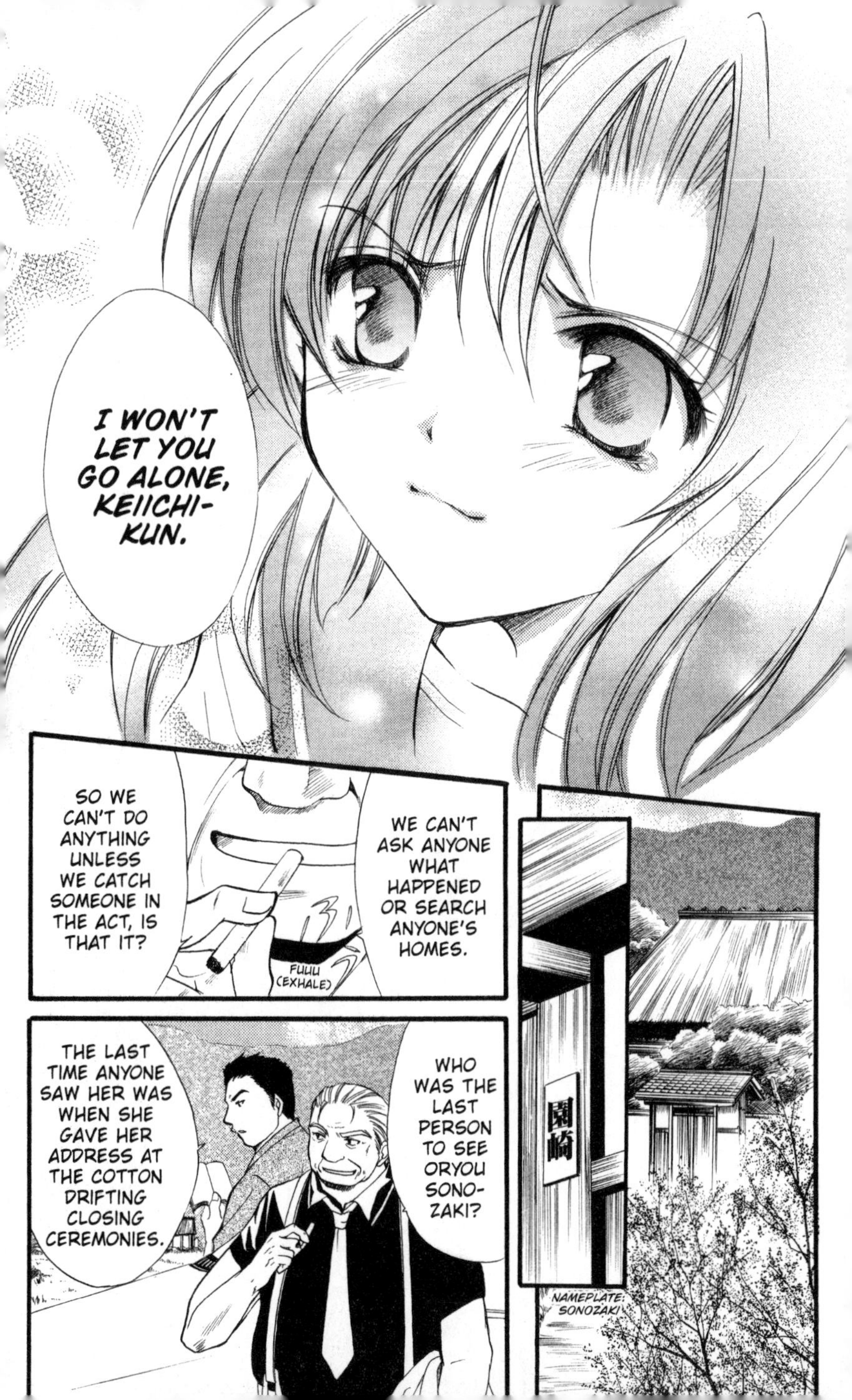
I WON'T LET YOU GO ALONE, KEIICHI-KUN.
NAMEPLATE: SONOZAKI
園崎
WE CAN'T ASK ANYONE WHAT HAPPENED OR SEARCH ANYONE'S HOMES.
FUUU (EXHALE)
SO WE CAN'T DO ANYTHING UNLESS WE CATCH SOMEONE IN THE ACT, IS THAT IT?
WHO WAS THE LAST PERSON TO SEE ORYOU SONOZAKI?
THE LAST TIME ANYONE SAW HER WAS WHEN SHE GAVE HER ADDRESS AT THE COTTON DRIFTING CLOSING CEREMONIES.

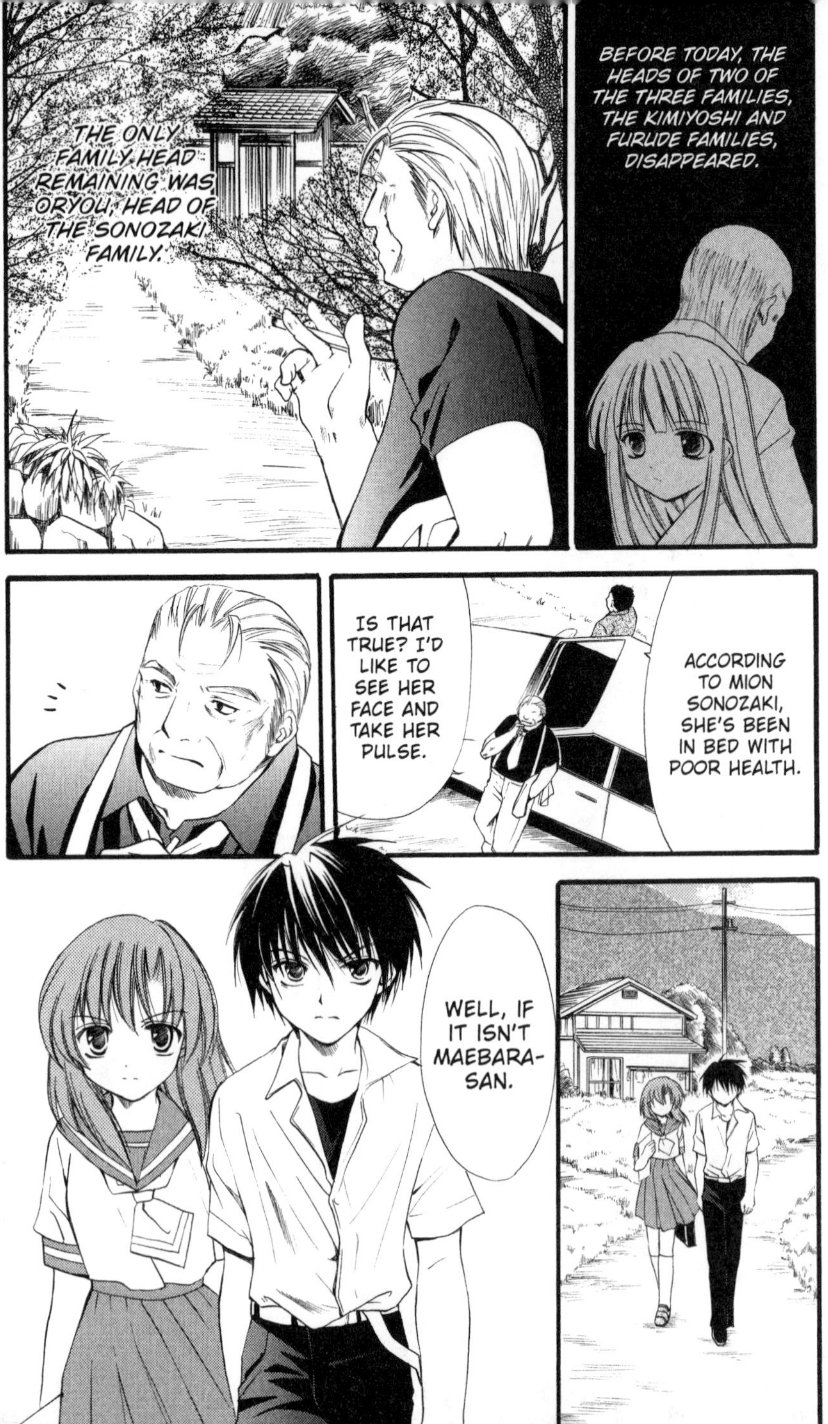
BEFORE TODAY, THE HEADS OF TWO OF THE THREE FAMILIES, THE KIMIYOSHI AND FURUDE FAMILIES, DISAPPEARED.
THE ONLY FAMILY HEAD REMAINING WAS ORYOU, HEAD OF THE SONOZAKI FAMILY.
ACCORDING TO MION SONOZAKI, SHE'S BEEN IN BED WITH POOR HEALTH.
IS THAT TRUE? I'D LIKE TO SEE HER FACE AND TAKE HER PULSE.
WELL, IF IT ISN'T MAEBARA-SAN.

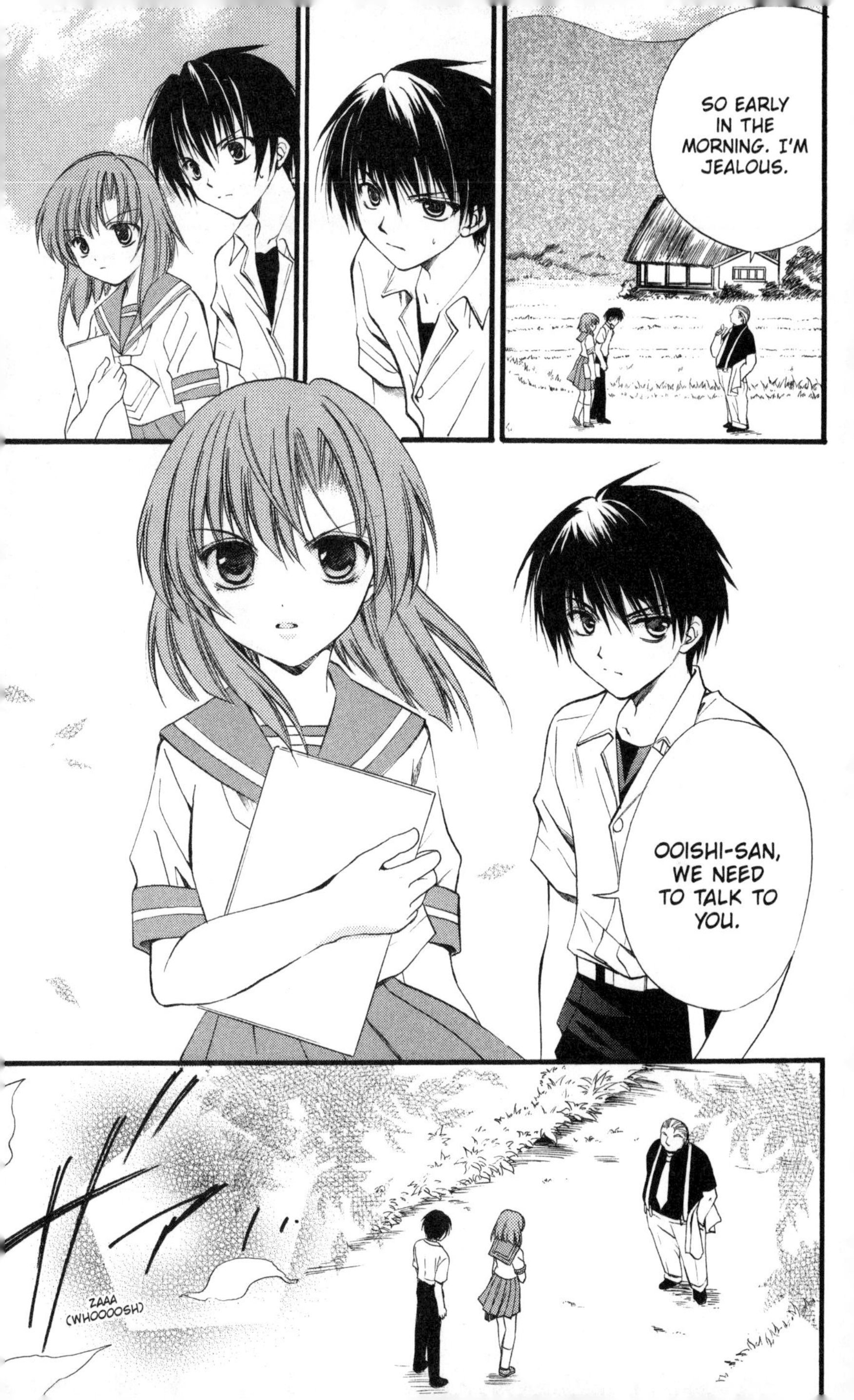
SO EARLY IN THE MORNING. I'M JEALOUS.
OOISHI-SAN, WE NEED TO TALK TO YOU.
ZAAA (WHOOOOSH)

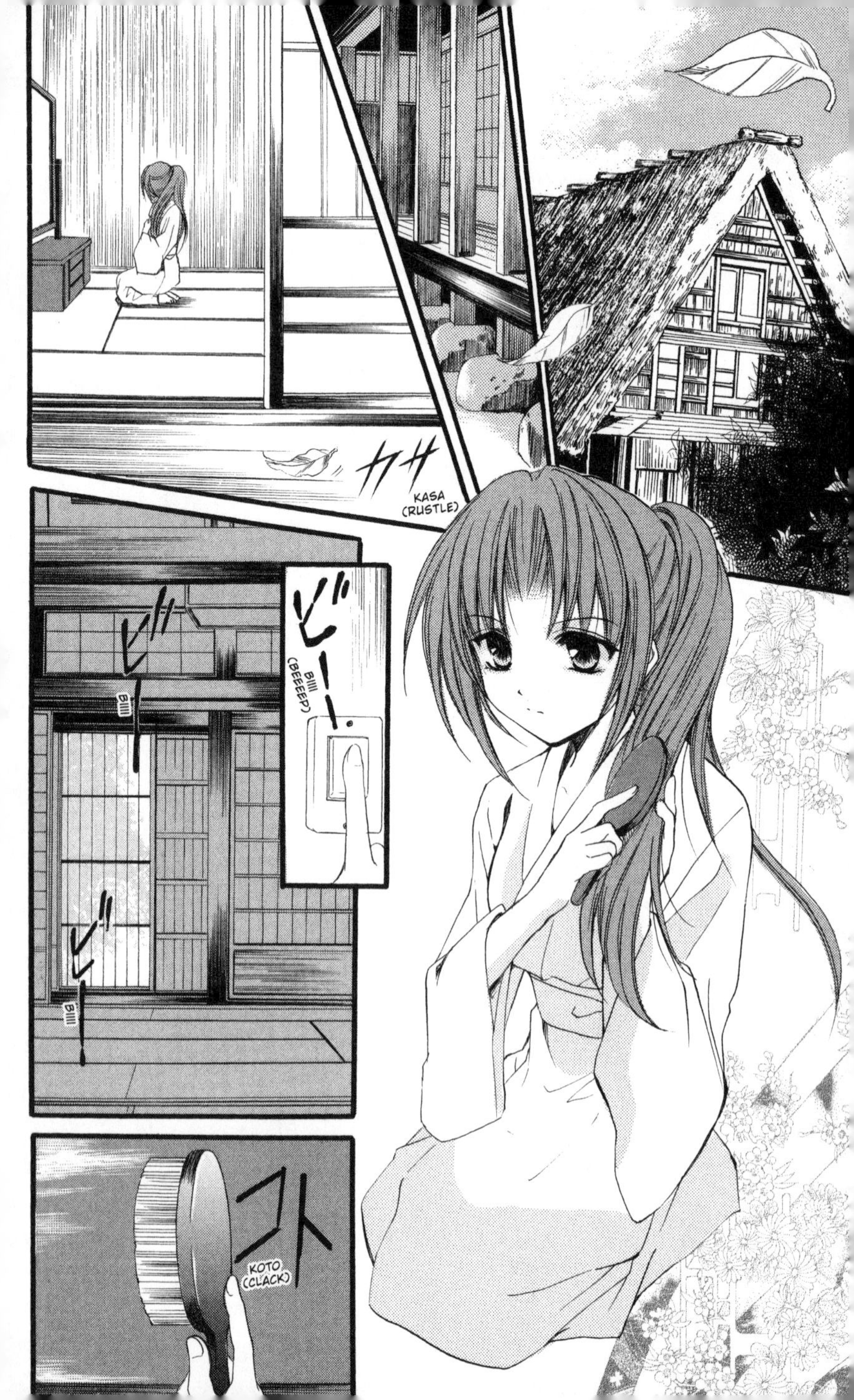

カサ
KASA (RUSTLE)
ビー
BIII (BEEEEP)
ビー
BIII
ビー
BIII
コト
KOTO (CLACK)

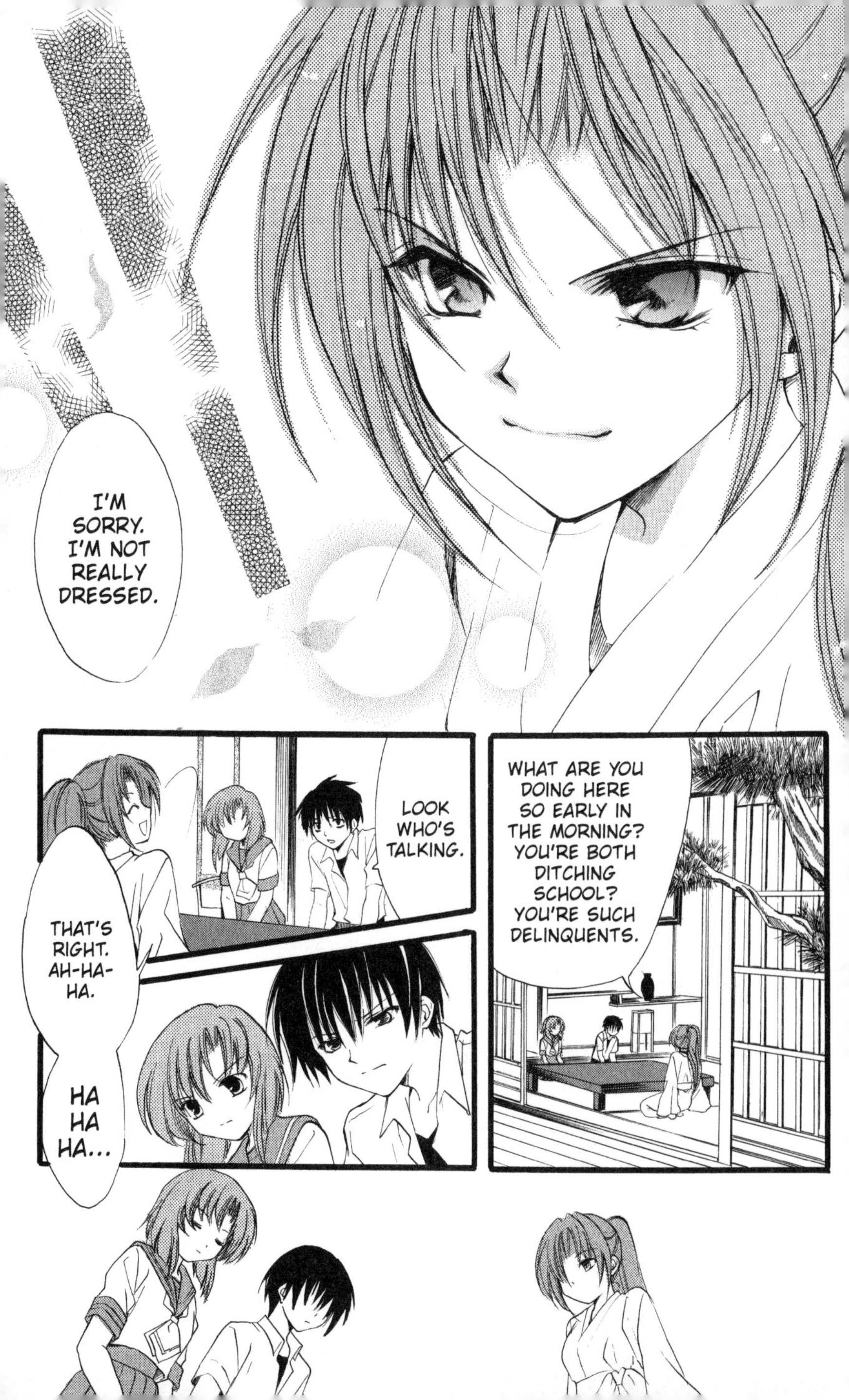
I'M SORRY. I'M NOT REALLY DRESSED.
WHAT ARE YOU DOING HERE SO EARLY IN THE MORNING? YOU'RE BOTH DITCHING SCHOOL? YOU'RE SUCH DELINQUENTS.
LOOK WHO'S TALKING.
THAT'S RIGHT. AH-HA-HA-HA.
HA HA HA...

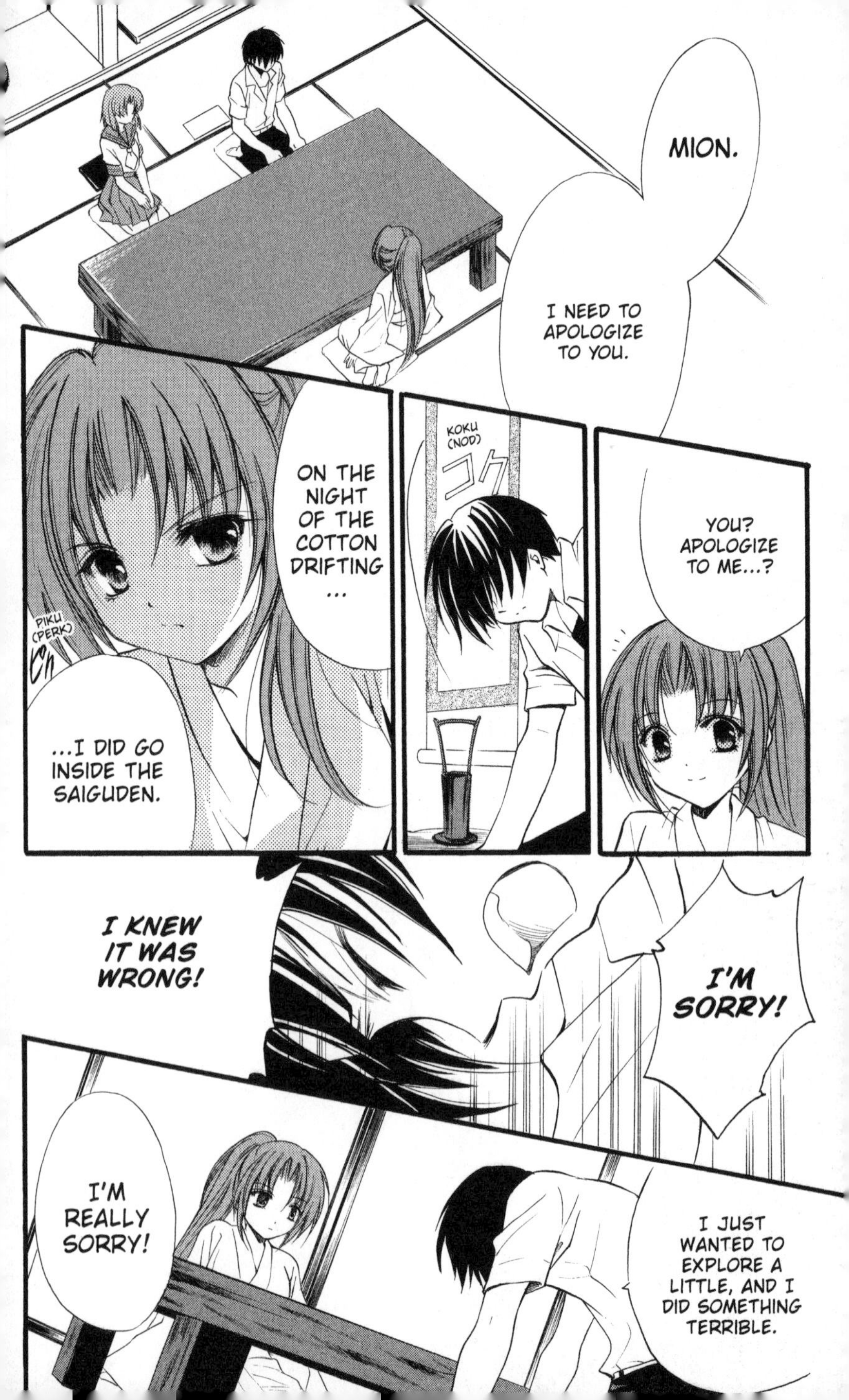
MION.
I NEED TO APOLOGIZE TO YOU.
YOU? APOLOGIZE TO ME...?
KOKU (NOD)
ON THE NIGHT OF THE COTTON DRIFTING ...
PIKU (PERK)
...I DID GO INSIDE THE SAIGUDEN.
I'M SORRY!
I KNEW IT WAS WRONG!
I JUST WANTED TO EXPLORE A LITTLE, AND I DID SOMETHING TERRIBLE.
I'M REALLY SORRY!

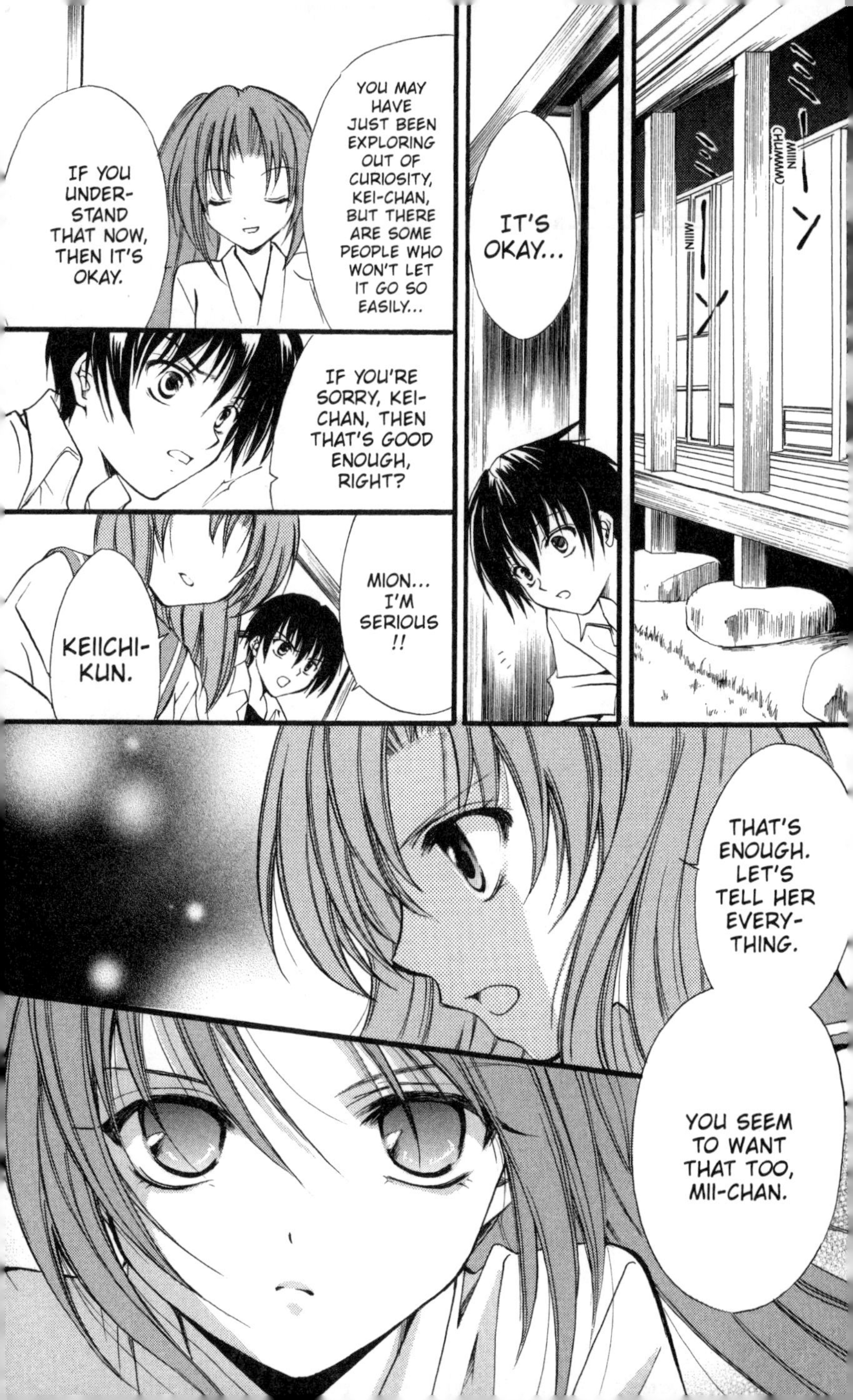
MIIIN (CHUMMM)
MIIIN
IT'S OKAY...
YOU MAY HAVE JUST BEEN EXPLORING OUT OF CURIOSITY, KEI-CHAN, BUT THERE ARE SOME PEOPLE WHO WON'T LET IT GO SO EASILY...
IF YOU UNDER-STAND THAT NOW, THEN IT'S OKAY.
IF YOU'RE SORRY, KEI-CHAN, THEN THAT'S GOOD ENOUGH, RIGHT?
MION... I'M SERIOUS !!
KEIICHI-KUN.
THAT'S ENOUGH. LET'S TELL HER EVERY-THING.
YOU SEEM TO WANT THAT TOO, MII-CHAN.

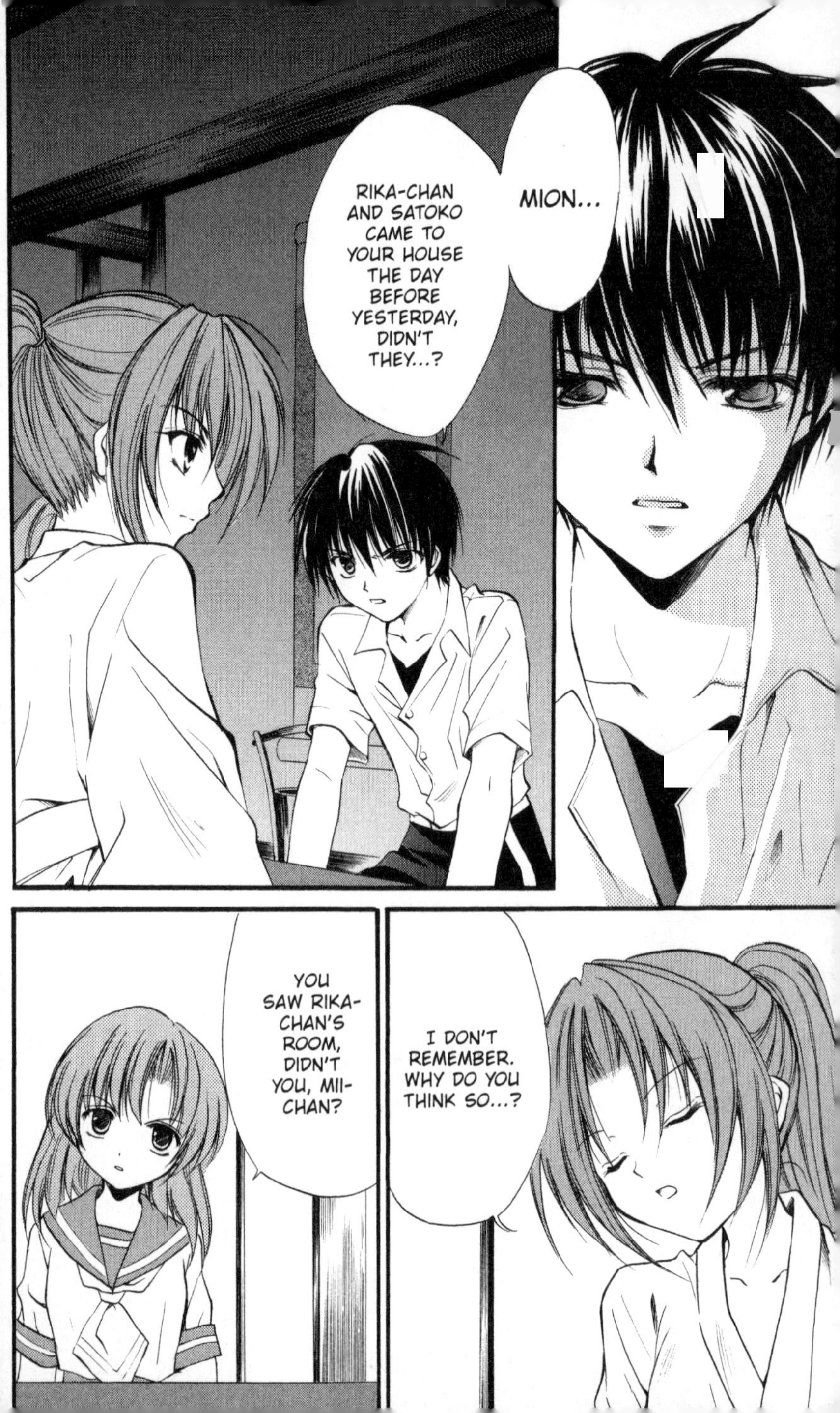
MION...
RIKA-CHAN AND SATOKO CAME TO YOUR HOUSE THE DAY BEFORE YESTERDAY, DIDN'T THEY...?
I DON'T REMEMBER. WHY DO YOU THINK SO...?
YOU SAW RIKA-CHAN'S ROOM, DIDN'T YOU, MII-CHAN?

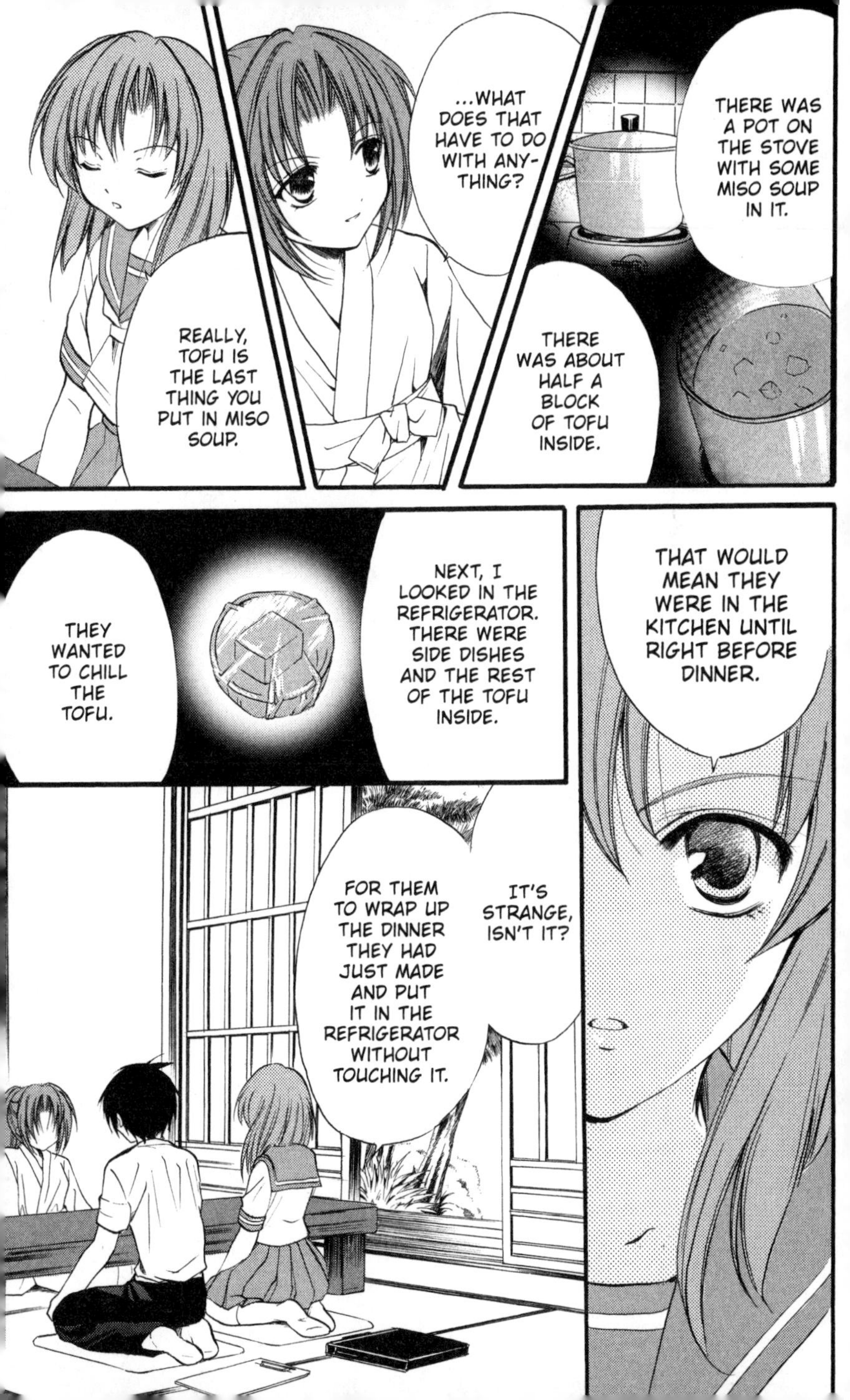
THERE WAS A POT ON THE STOVE WITH SOME MISO SOUP IN IT.
THERE WAS ABOUT HALF A BLOCK OF TOFU INSIDE.
...WHAT DOES THAT HAVE TO DO WITH ANY-THING?
REALLY, TOFU IS THE LAST THING YOU PUT IN MISO SOUP.
THAT WOULD MEAN THEY WERE IN THE KITCHEN UNTIL RIGHT BEFORE DINNER.
NEXT, I LOOKED IN THE REFRIGERATOR. THERE WERE SIDE DISHES AND THE REST OF THE TOFU INSIDE.
THEY WANTED TO CHILL THE TOFU.
IT'S STRANGE, ISN'T IT?
FOR THEM TO WRAP UP THE DINNER THEY HAD JUST MADE AND PUT IT IN THE REFRIGERATOR WITHOUT TOUCHING IT.

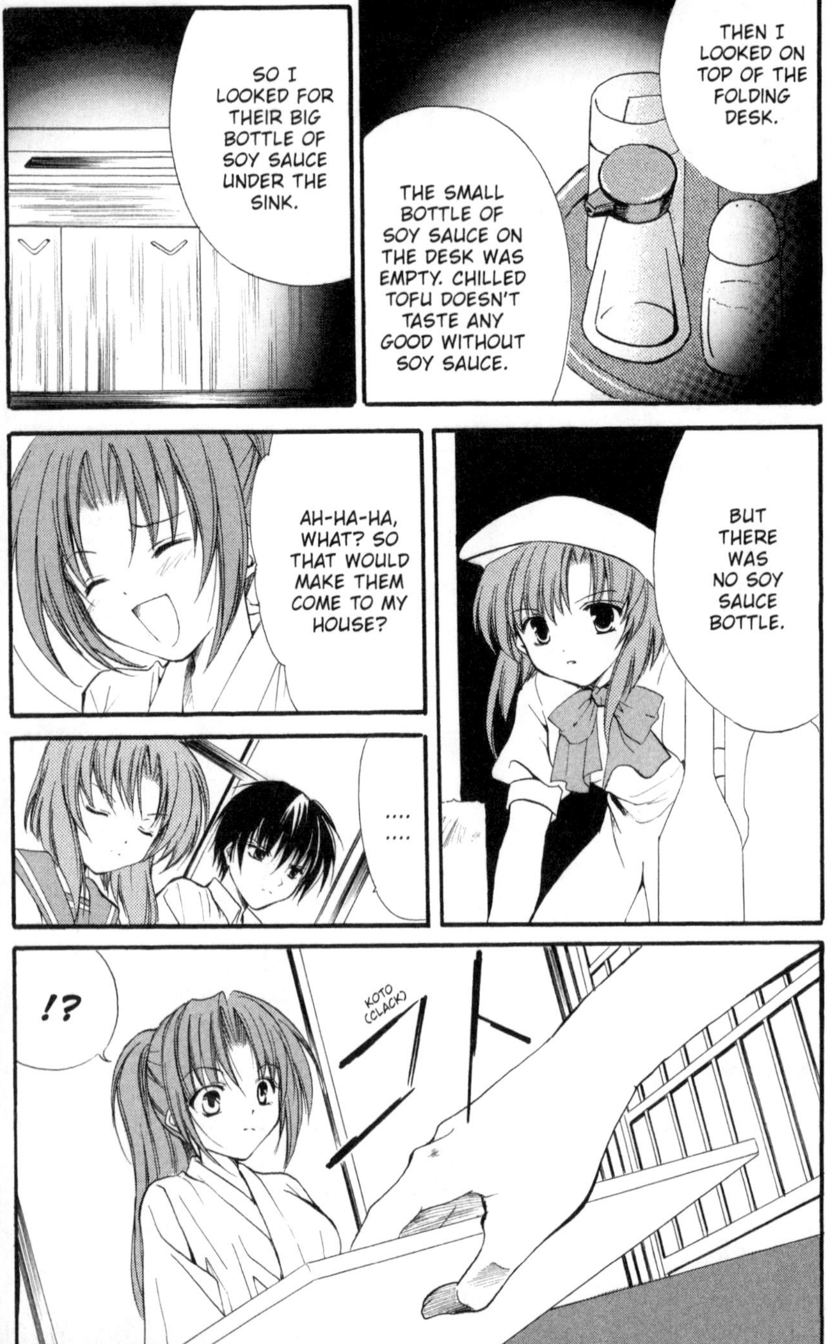
THEN I LOOKED ON TOP OF THE FOLDING DESK.
THE SMALL BOTTLE OF SOY SAUCE ON THE DESK WAS EMPTY. CHILLED TOFU DOESN'T TASTE ANY GOOD WITHOUT SOY SAUCE.
SO I LOOKED FOR THEIR BIG BOTTLE OF SOY SAUCE UNDER THE SINK.
BUT THERE WAS NO SOY SAUCE BOTTLE.
AH-HA-HA, WHAT? SO THAT WOULD MAKE THEM COME TO MY HOUSE?
....
KOTO (CLACK)
!?

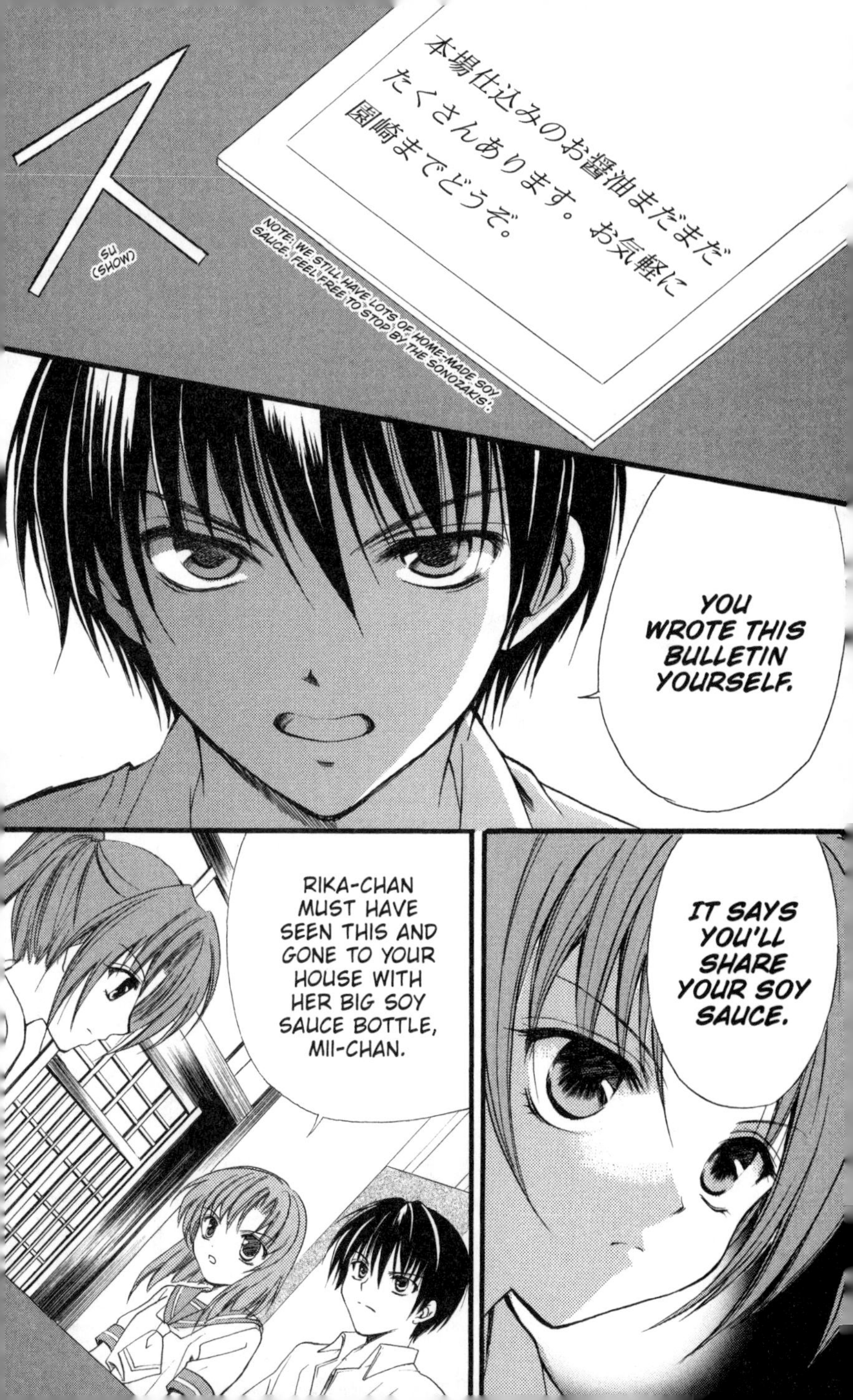
本場仕込みのお醤油まだまだ
たくさんあります。お気軽に
園崎までどうぞ。
NOTE: WE STILL HAVE LOTS OF HOME-MADE SOY SAUCE. FEEL FREE TO STOP BY THE SONOZAKIS'.
ス
SU (SHOW)
YOU WROTE THIS BULLETIN YOURSELF.
IT SAYS YOU'LL SHARE YOUR SOY SAUCE.
RIKA-CHAN MUST HAVE SEEN THIS AND GONE TO YOUR HOUSE WITH HER BIG SOY SAUCE BOTTLE, MII-CHAN.

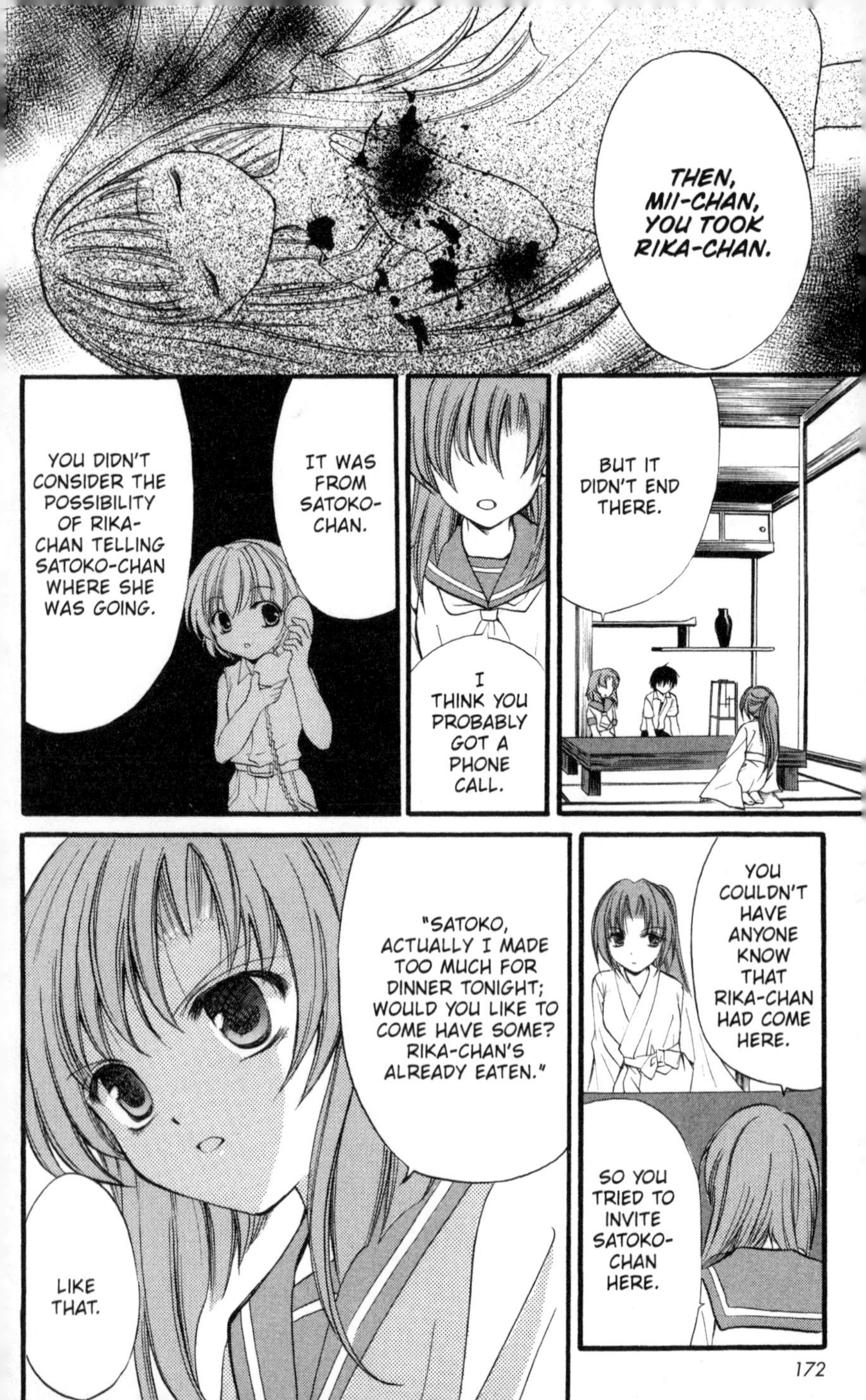
THEN, MII-CHAN, YOU TOOK RIKA-CHAN.
BUT IT DIDN'T END THERE.
I THINK YOU PROBABLY GOT A PHONE CALL.
IT WAS FROM SATOKO-CHAN.
YOU DIDN'T CONSIDER THE POSSIBILITY OF RIKA-CHAN TELLING SATOKO-CHAN WHERE SHE WAS GOING.
YOU COULDN'T HAVE ANYONE KNOW THAT RIKA-CHAN HAD COME HERE.
SO YOU TRIED TO INVITE SATOKO-CHAN HERE.
"SATOKO, ACTUALLY I MADE TOO MUCH FOR DINNER TONIGHT; WOULD YOU LIKE TO COME HAVE SOME? RIKA-CHAN'S ALREADY EATEN."
LIKE THAT.

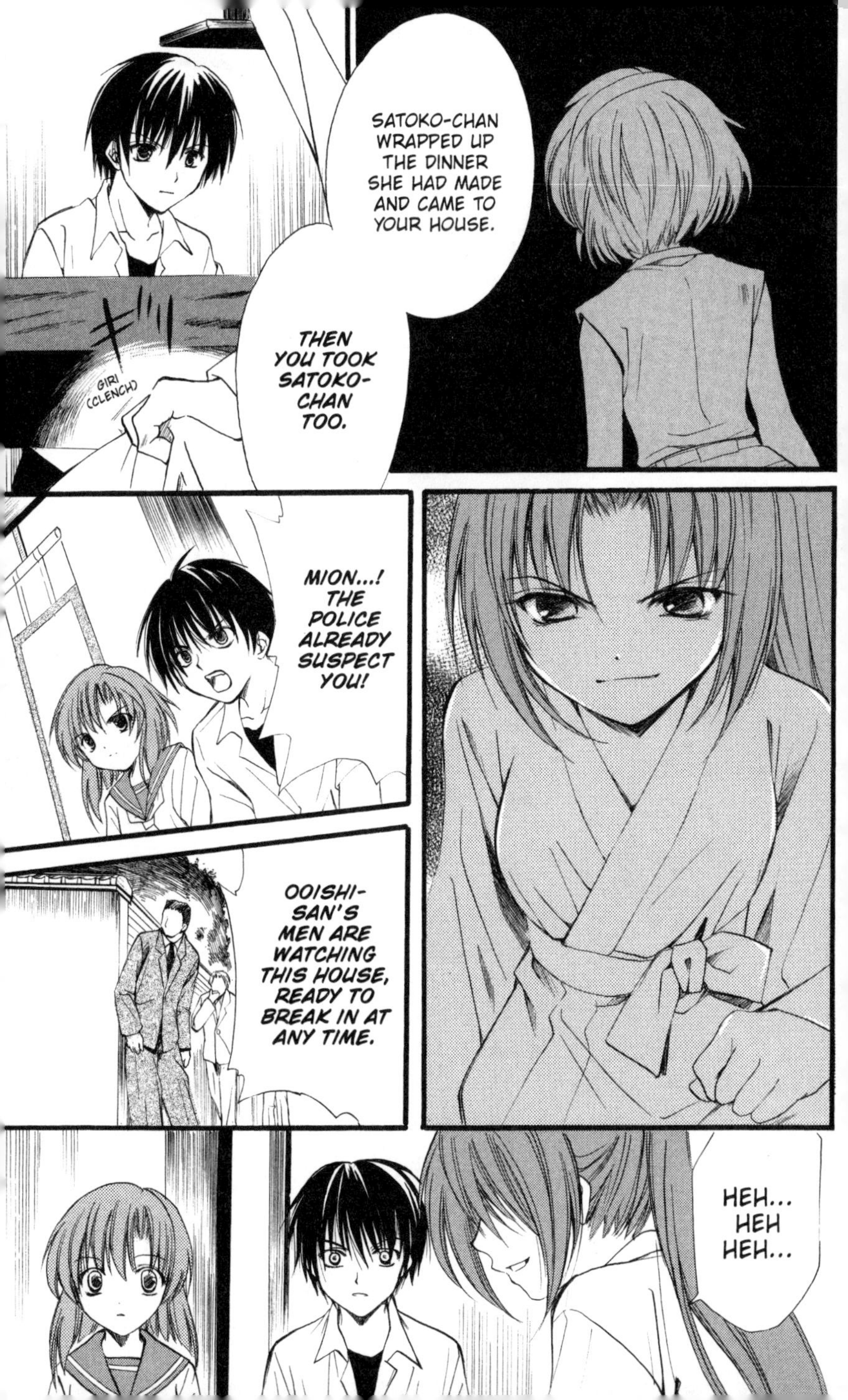
SATOKO-CHAN WRAPPED UP THE DINNER SHE HAD MADE AND CAME TO YOUR HOUSE.
THEN YOU TOOK SATOKO-CHAN TOO.
GIRI (CLENCH)
MION...! THE POLICE ALREADY SUSPECT YOU!
OOISHI-SAN'S MEN ARE WATCHING THIS HOUSE, READY TO BREAK IN AT ANY TIME.
HEH... HEH HEH...

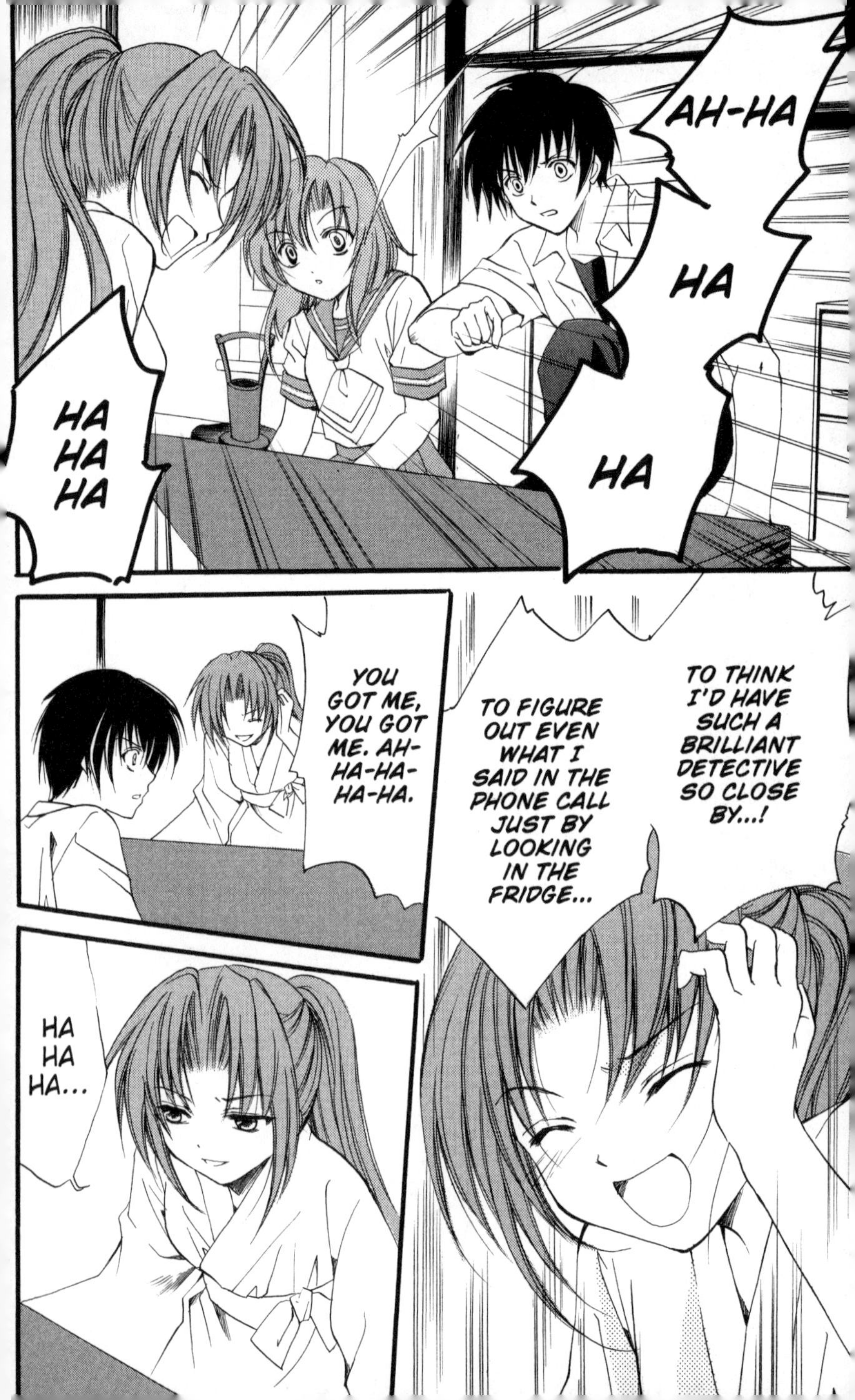
AH-HA
HA
HA
HA HA HA
TO THINK I'D HAVE SUCH A BRILLIANT DETECTIVE SO CLOSE BY...!
TO FIGURE OUT EVEN WHAT I SAID IN THE PHONE CALL JUST BY LOOKING IN THE FRIDGE...
YOU GOT ME, YOU GOT ME. AH-HA-HA-HA-HA.
HA HA HA...

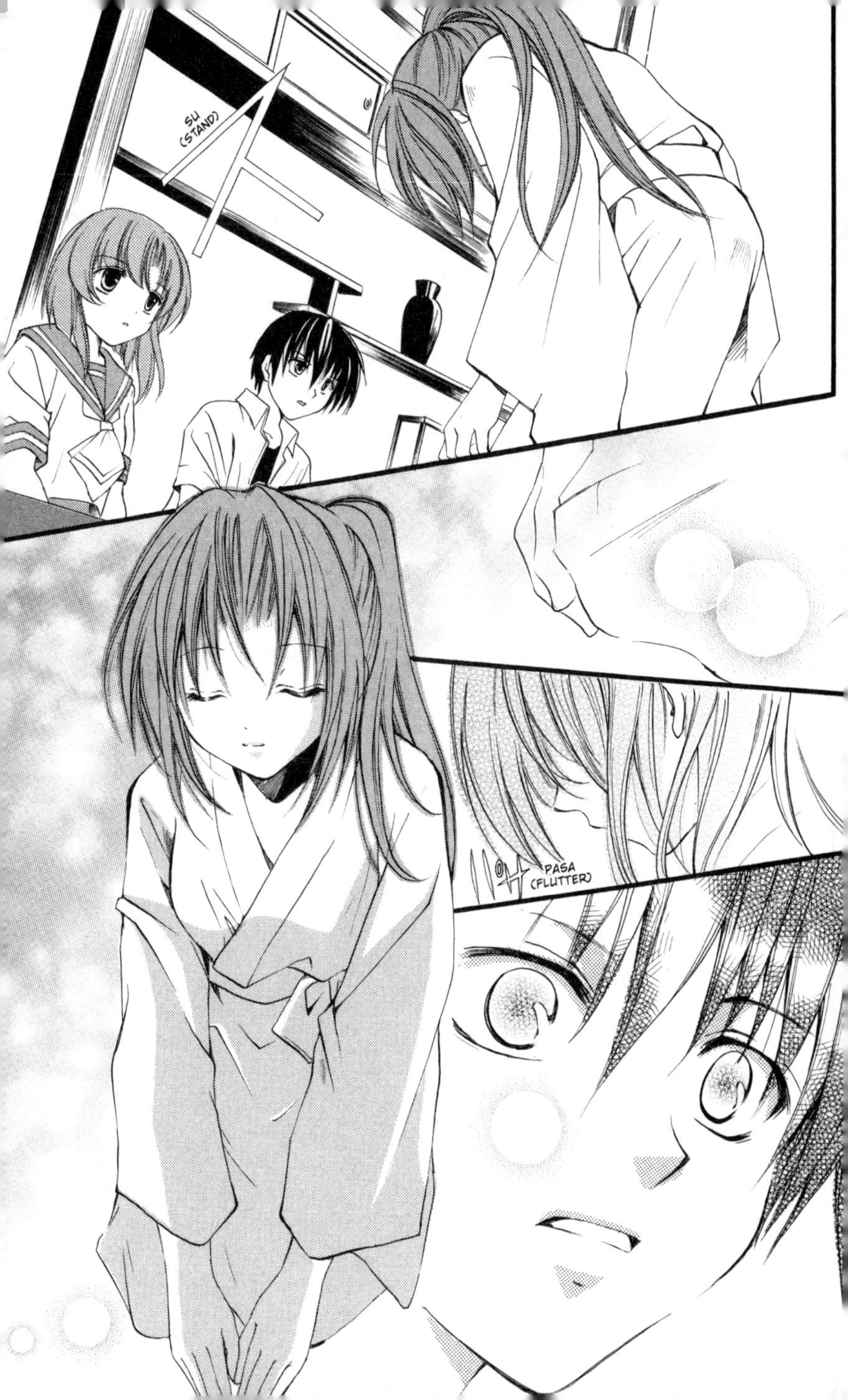
SU
(STAND)
PASA
(FLUTTER)

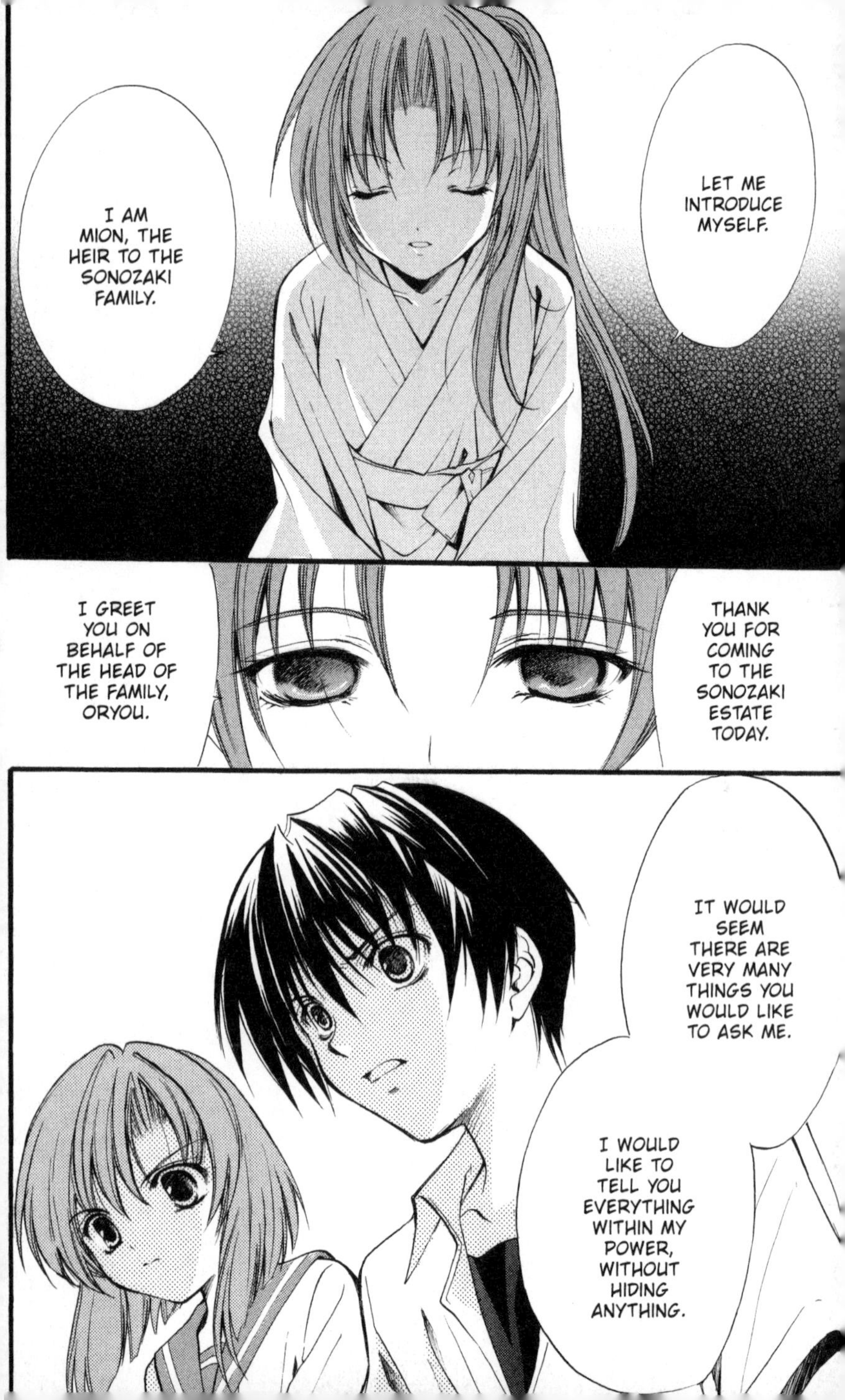
LET ME INTRODUCE MYSELF.
I AM MION, THE HEIR TO THE SONOZAKI FAMILY.
THANK YOU FOR COMING TO THE SONOZAKI ESTATE TODAY.
I GREET YOU ON BEHALF OF THE HEAD OF THE FAMILY, ORYOU.
IT WOULD SEEM THERE ARE VERY MANY THINGS YOU WOULD LIKE TO ASK ME.
I WOULD LIKE TO TELL YOU EVERYTHING WITHIN MY POWER, WITHOUT HIDING ANYTHING.

CHAPTER 11

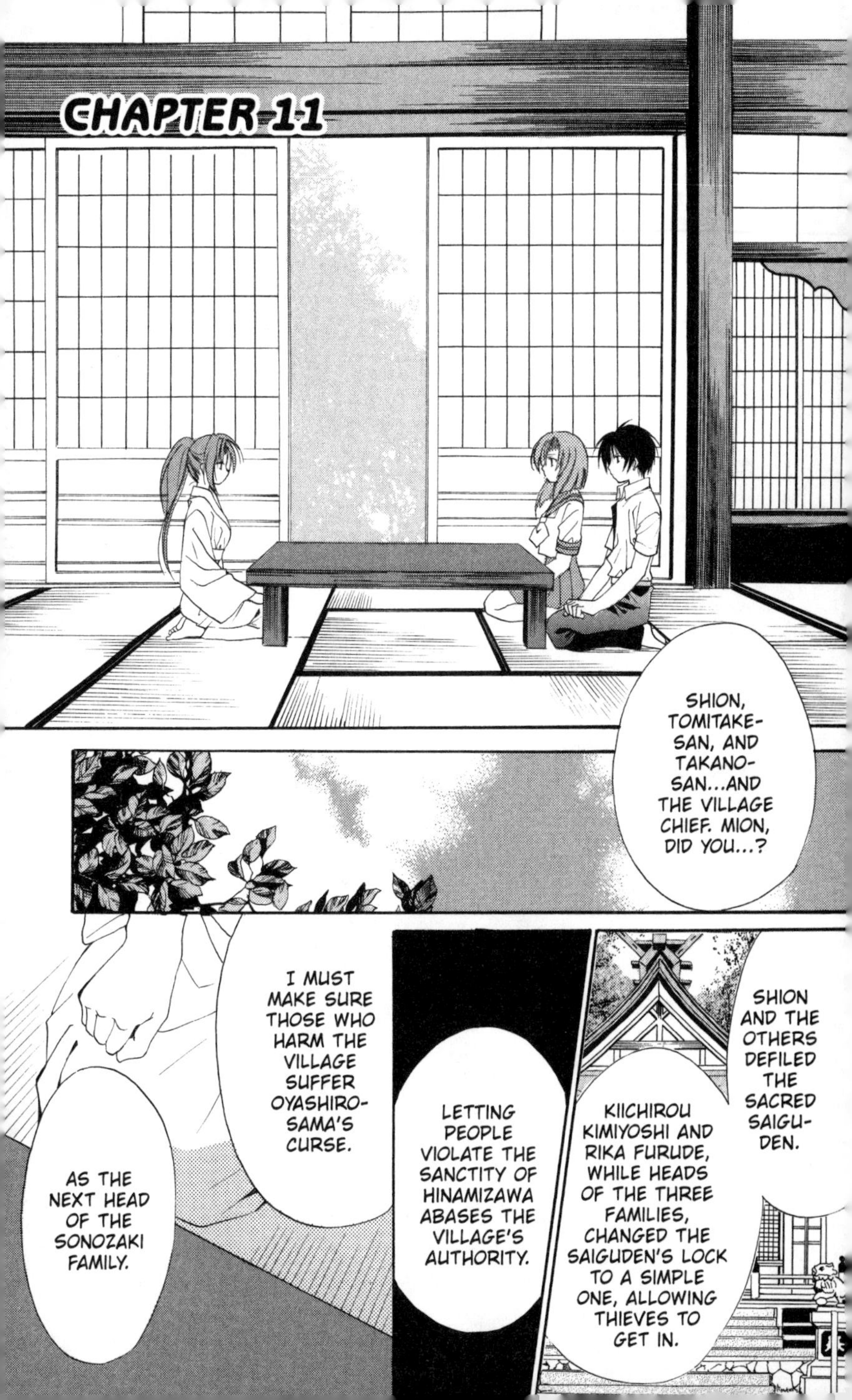
SHION, TOMITAKE-SAN, AND TAKANO-SAN...AND THE VILLAGE CHIEF. MION, DID YOU...?
SHION AND THE OTHERS DEFILED THE SACRED SAIGU-DEN.
KIICHIROU KIMIYOSHI AND RIKA FURUDE, WHILE HEADS OF THE THREE FAMILIES, CHANGED THE SAIGUDEN'S LOCK TO A SIMPLE ONE, ALLOWING THIEVES TO GET IN.
LETTING PEOPLE VIOLATE THE SANCTITY OF HINAMIZAWA ABASES THE VILLAGE'S AUTHORITY.
I MUST MAKE SURE THOSE WHO HARM THE VILLAGE SUFFER OYASHIRO-SAMA'S CURSE.
AS THE NEXT HEAD OF THE SONOZAKI FAMILY.

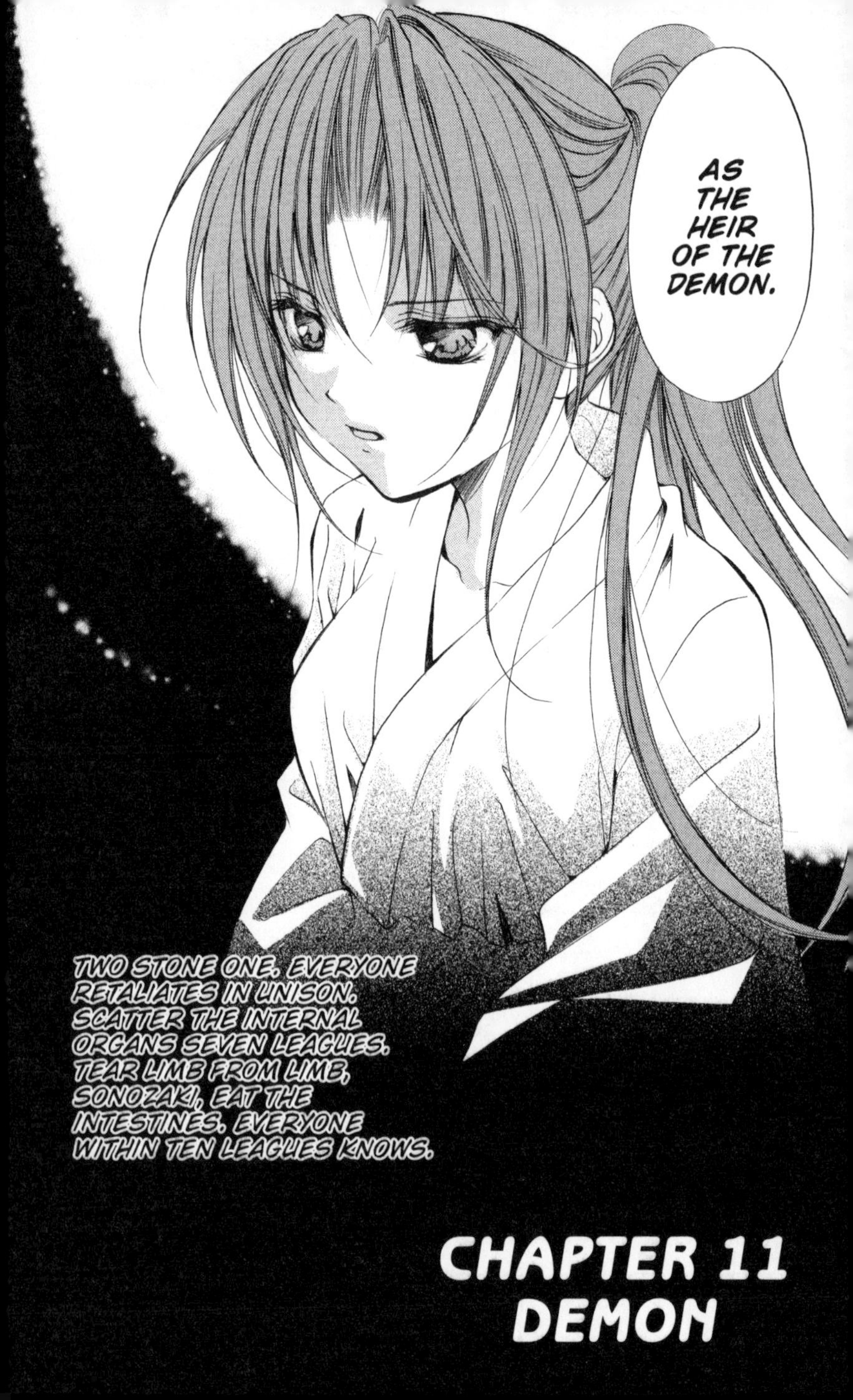
AS THE HEIR OF THE DEMON.
TWO STONE ONE. EVERYONE RETALIATES IN UNISON. SCATTER THE INTERNAL ORGANS SEVEN LEAGUES. TEAR LIMB FROM LIMB, SONOZAKI, EAT THE INTESTINES. EVERYONE WITHIN TEN LEAGUES KNOWS.

CHAPTER 11
DEMON

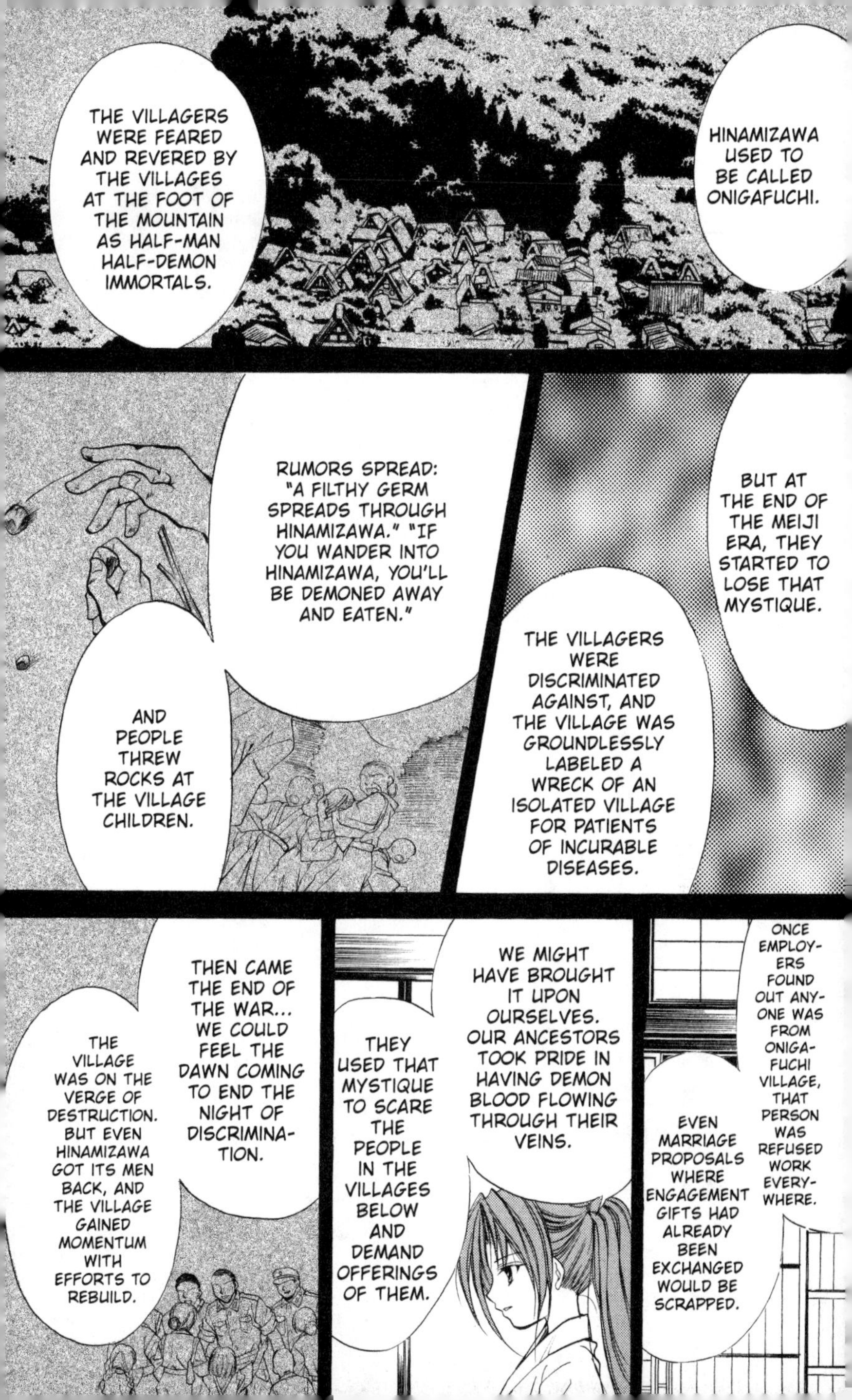
HINAMIZAWA USED TO BE CALLED ONIGAFUCHI.
THE VILLAGERS WERE FEARED AND REVERED BY THE VILLAGES AT THE FOOT OF THE MOUNTAIN AS HALF-MAN HALF-DEMON IMMORTALS.
BUT AT THE END OF THE MEIJI ERA, THEY STARTED TO LOSE THAT MYSTIQUE.
THE VILLAGERS WERE DISCRIMINATED AGAINST, AND THE VILLAGE WAS GROUNDLESSLY LABELED A WRECK OF AN ISOLATED VILLAGE FOR PATIENTS OF INCURABLE DISEASES.
RUMORS SPREAD: "A FILTHY GERM SPREADS THROUGH HINAMIZAWA." "IF YOU WANDER INTO HINAMIZAWA, YOU'LL BE DEMONED AWAY AND EATEN."
AND PEOPLE THREW ROCKS AT THE VILLAGE CHILDREN.
ONCE EMPLOYERS FOUND OUT ANYONE WAS FROM ONIGAFUCHI VILLAGE, THAT PERSON WAS REFUSED WORK EVERYWHERE.
EVEN MARRIAGE PROPOSALS WHERE ENGAGEMENT GIFTS HAD ALREADY BEEN EXCHANGED WOULD BE SCRAPPED.
WE MIGHT HAVE BROUGHT IT UPON OURSELVES. OUR ANCESTORS TOOK PRIDE IN HAVING DEMON BLOOD FLOWING THROUGH THEIR VEINS.
THEY USED THAT MYSTIQUE TO SCARE THE PEOPLE IN THE VILLAGES BELOW AND DEMAND OFFERINGS OF THEM.
THEN CAME THE END OF THE WAR... WE COULD FEEL THE DAWN COMING TO END THE NIGHT OF DISCRIMINATION.
THE VILLAGE WAS ON THE VERGE OF DESTRUCTION. BUT EVEN HINAMIZAWA GOT ITS MEN BACK, AND THE VILLAGE GAINED MOMENTUM WITH EFFORTS TO REBUILD.

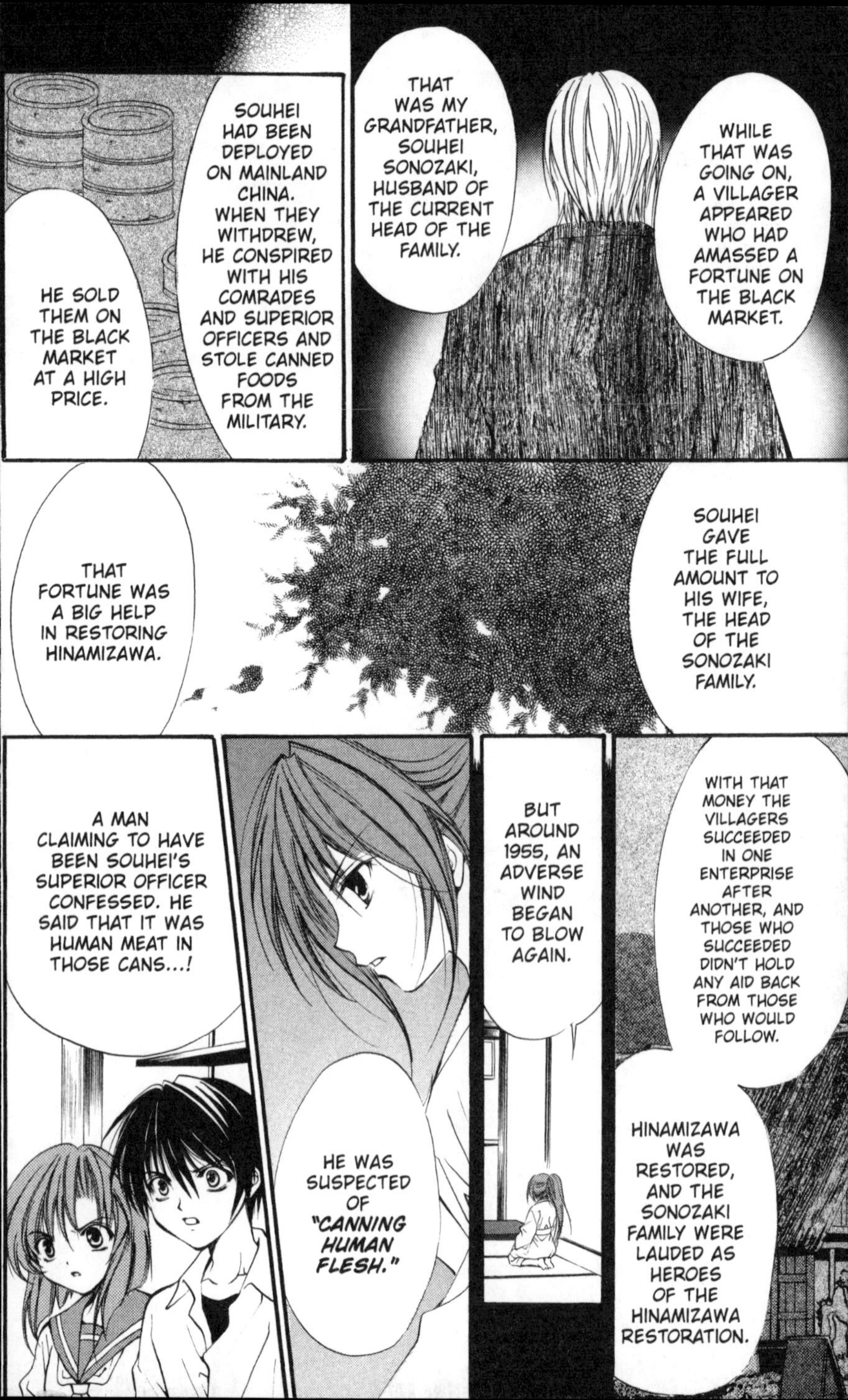
WHILE THAT WAS GOING ON, A VILLAGER APPEARED WHO HAD AMASSED A FORTUNE ON THE BLACK MARKET.
THAT WAS MY GRANDFATHER, SOUHEI SONOZAKI, HUSBAND OF THE CURRENT HEAD OF THE FAMILY.
SOUHEI HAD BEEN DEPLOYED ON MAINLAND CHINA. WHEN THEY WITHDREW, HE CONSPIRED WITH HIS COMRADES AND SUPERIOR OFFICERS AND STOLE CANNED FOODS FROM THE MILITARY.
HE SOLD THEM ON THE BLACK MARKET AT A HIGH PRICE.
SOUHEI GAVE THE FULL AMOUNT TO HIS WIFE, THE HEAD OF THE SONOZAKI FAMILY.
THAT FORTUNE WAS A BIG HELP IN RESTORING HINAMIZAWA.
WITH THAT MONEY THE VILLAGERS SUCCEEDED IN ONE ENTERPRISE AFTER ANOTHER, AND THOSE WHO SUCCEEDED DIDN'T HOLD ANY AID BACK FROM THOSE WHO WOULD FOLLOW.
HINAMIZAWA WAS RESTORED, AND THE SONOZAKI FAMILY WERE LAUDED AS HEROES OF THE HINAMIZAWA RESTORATION.
BUT AROUND 1955, AN ADVERSE WIND BEGAN TO BLOW AGAIN.
HE WAS SUSPECTED OF *"CANNING HUMAN FLESH."*
A MAN CLAIMING TO HAVE BEEN SOUHEI'S SUPERIOR OFFICER CONFESSED. HE SAID THAT IT WAS HUMAN MEAT IN THOSE CANS...!

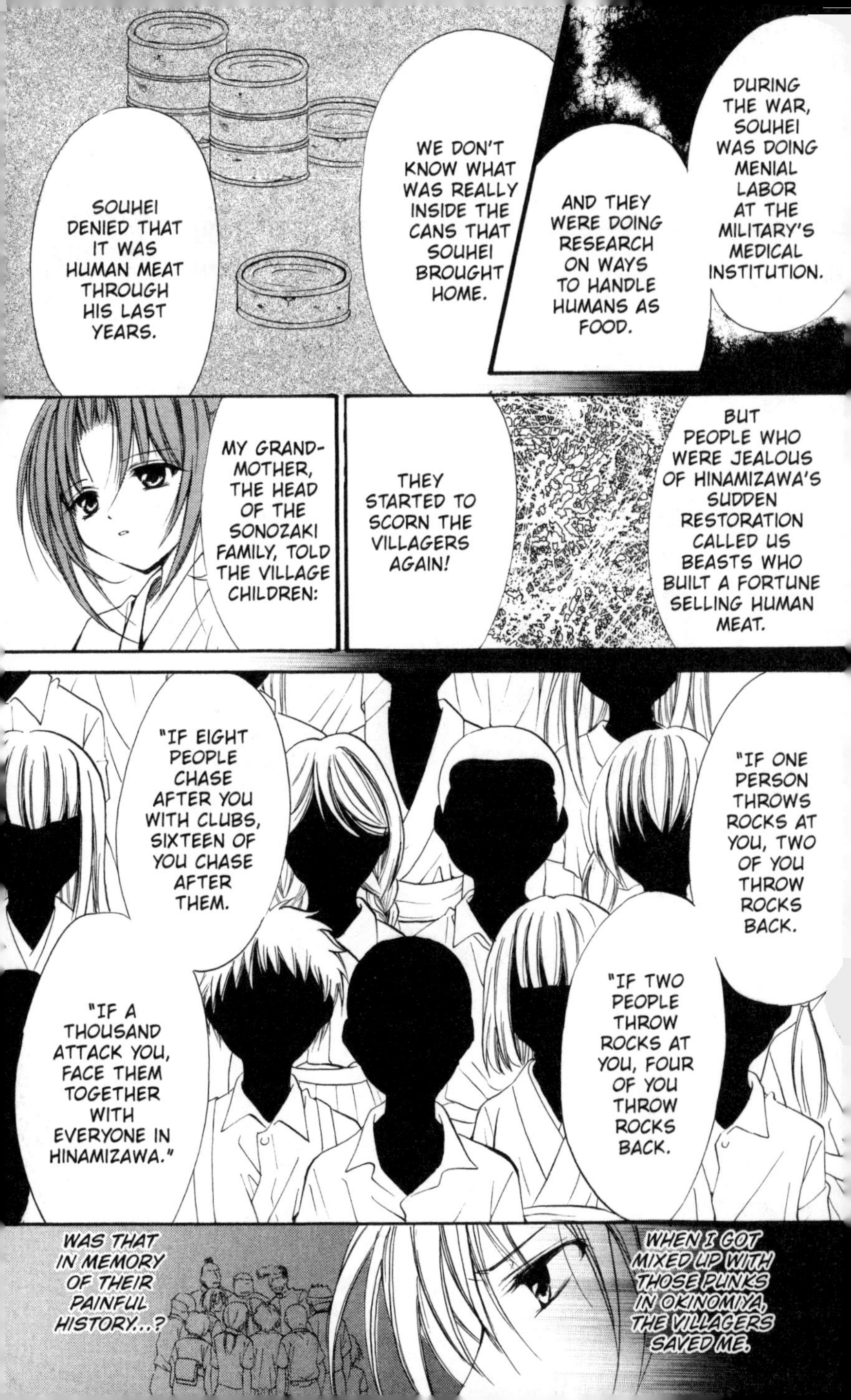
DURING THE WAR, SOUHEI WAS DOING MENIAL LABOR AT THE MILITARY'S MEDICAL INSTITUTION.
AND THEY WERE DOING RESEARCH ON WAYS TO HANDLE HUMANS AS FOOD.
WE DON'T KNOW WHAT WAS REALLY INSIDE THE CANS THAT SOUHEI BROUGHT HOME.
SOUHEI DENIED THAT IT WAS HUMAN MEAT THROUGH HIS LAST YEARS.
BUT PEOPLE WHO WERE JEALOUS OF HINAMIZAWA'S SUDDEN RESTORATION CALLED US BEASTS WHO BUILT A FORTUNE SELLING HUMAN MEAT.
THEY STARTED TO SCORN THE VILLAGERS AGAIN!
MY GRAND-MOTHER, THE HEAD OF THE SONOZAKI FAMILY, TOLD THE VILLAGE CHILDREN:
"IF ONE PERSON THROWS ROCKS AT YOU, TWO OF YOU THROW ROCKS BACK.
"IF TWO PEOPLE THROW ROCKS AT YOU, FOUR OF YOU THROW ROCKS BACK.
"IF EIGHT PEOPLE CHASE AFTER YOU WITH CLUBS, SIXTEEN OF YOU CHASE AFTER THEM.
"IF A THOUSAND ATTACK YOU, FACE THEM TOGETHER WITH EVERYONE IN HINAMIZAWA."
WHEN I GOT MIXED UP WITH THOSE PUNKS IN OKINOMIYA, THE VILLAGERS SAVED ME.
WAS THAT IN MEMORY OF THEIR PAINFUL HISTORY...?

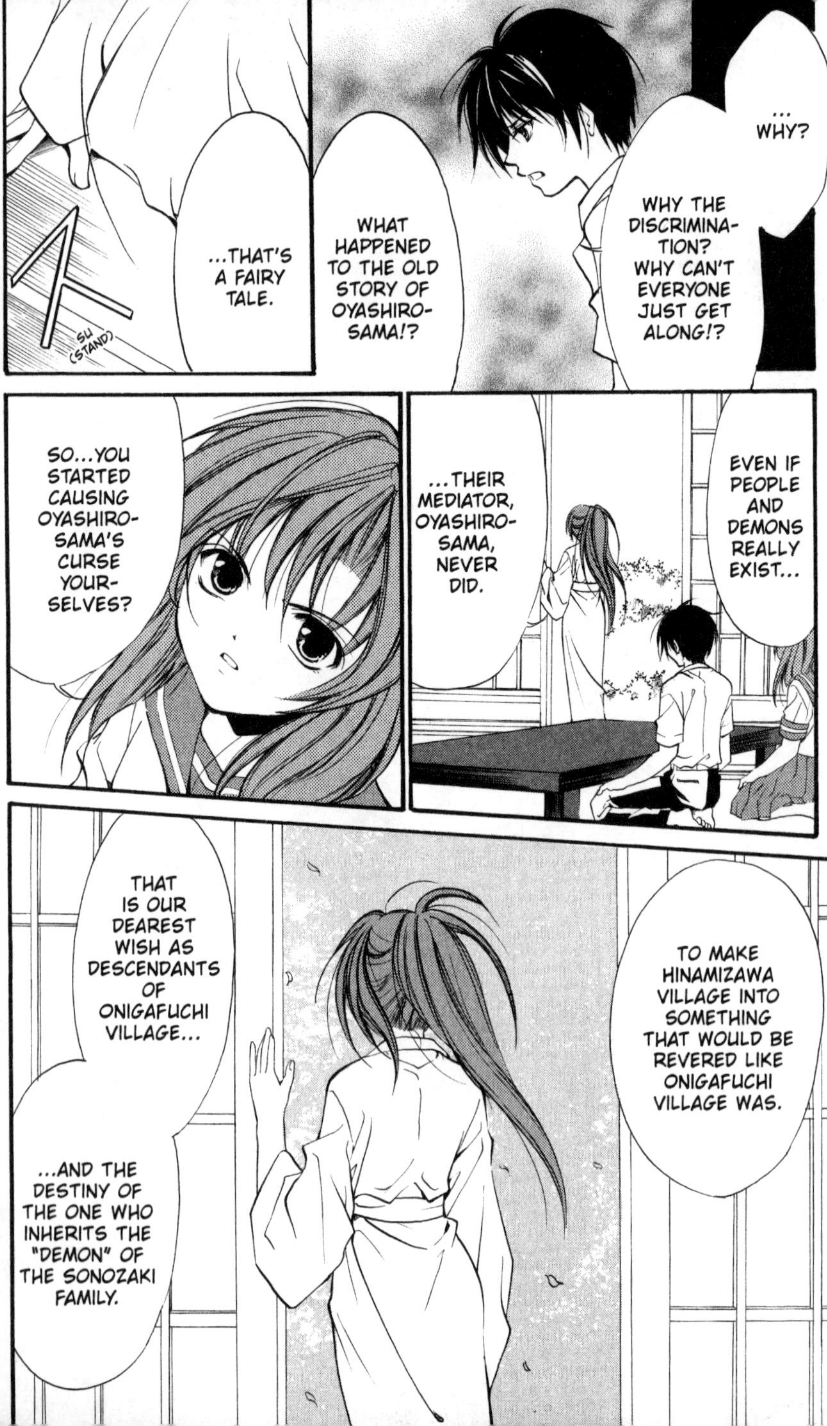
...WHY?
WHY THE DISCRIMINATION? WHY CAN'T EVERYONE JUST GET ALONG!?
WHAT HAPPENED TO THE OLD STORY OF OYASHIRO-SAMA!?
...THAT'S A FAIRY TALE.
SU (STAND)
EVEN IF PEOPLE AND DEMONS REALLY EXIST...
...THEIR MEDIATOR, OYASHIRO-SAMA, NEVER DID.
SO...YOU STARTED CAUSING OYASHIRO-SAMA'S CURSE YOURSELVES?
TO MAKE HINAMIZAWA VILLAGE INTO SOMETHING THAT WOULD BE REVERED LIKE ONIGAFUCHI VILLAGE WAS.
THAT IS OUR DEAREST WISH AS DESCENDANTS OF ONIGAFUCHI VILLAGE...
...AND THE DESTINY OF THE ONE WHO INHERITS THE "DEMON" OF THE SONOZAKI FAMILY.

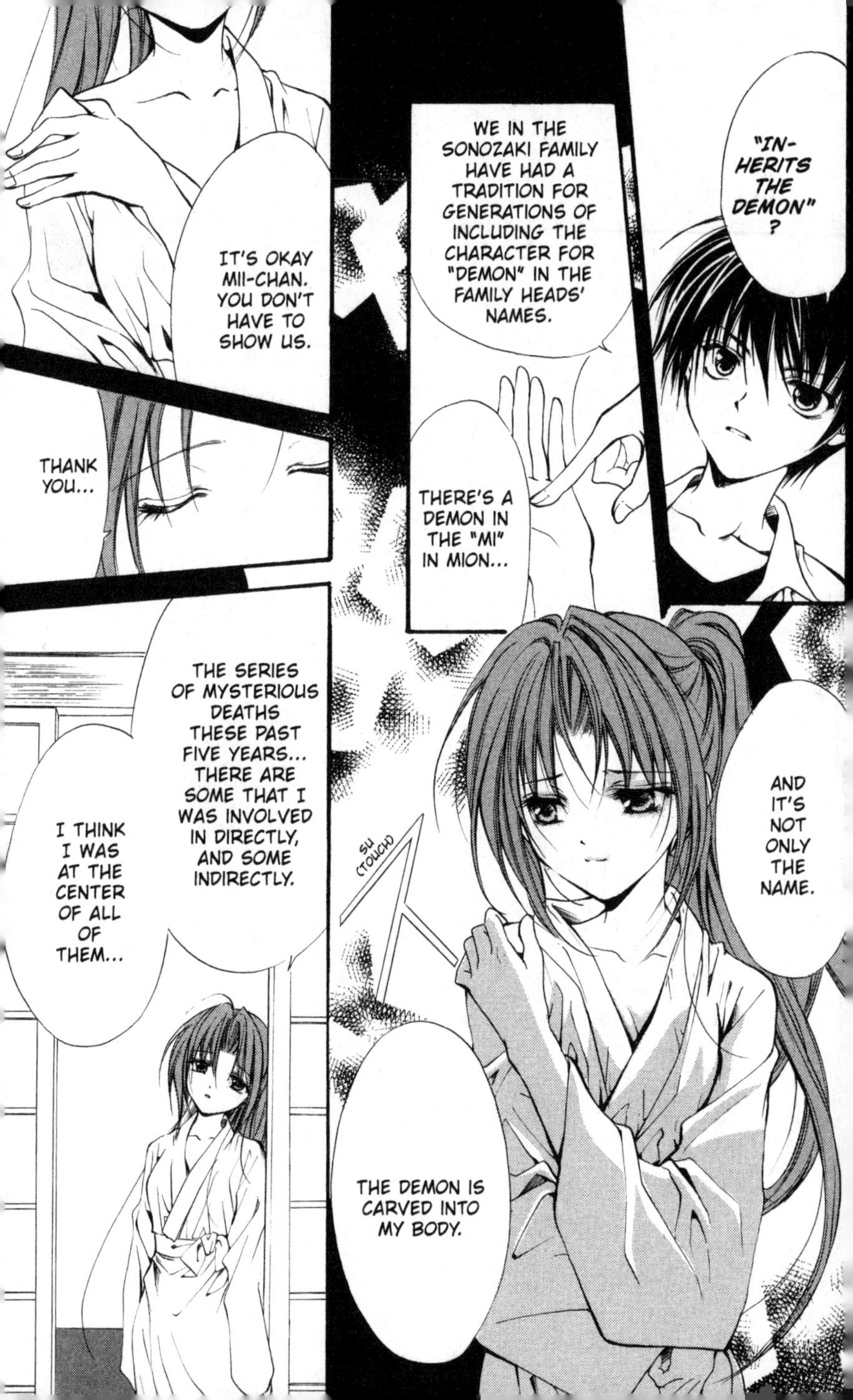

"IN-HERITS THE DEMON"?
WE IN THE SONOZAKI FAMILY HAVE HAD A TRADITION FOR GENERATIONS OF INCLUDING THE CHARACTER FOR "DEMON" IN THE FAMILY HEADS' NAMES.
THERE'S A DEMON IN THE "MI" IN MION...
AND IT'S NOT ONLY THE NAME.
SU (TOUCH)
THE DEMON IS CARVED INTO MY BODY.
IT'S OKAY MII-CHAN. YOU DON'T HAVE TO SHOW US.
THANK YOU...
THE SERIES OF MYSTERIOUS DEATHS THESE PAST FIVE YEARS... THERE ARE SOME THAT I WAS INVOLVED IN DIRECTLY, AND SOME INDIRECTLY.
I THINK I WAS AT THE CENTER OF ALL OF THEM...

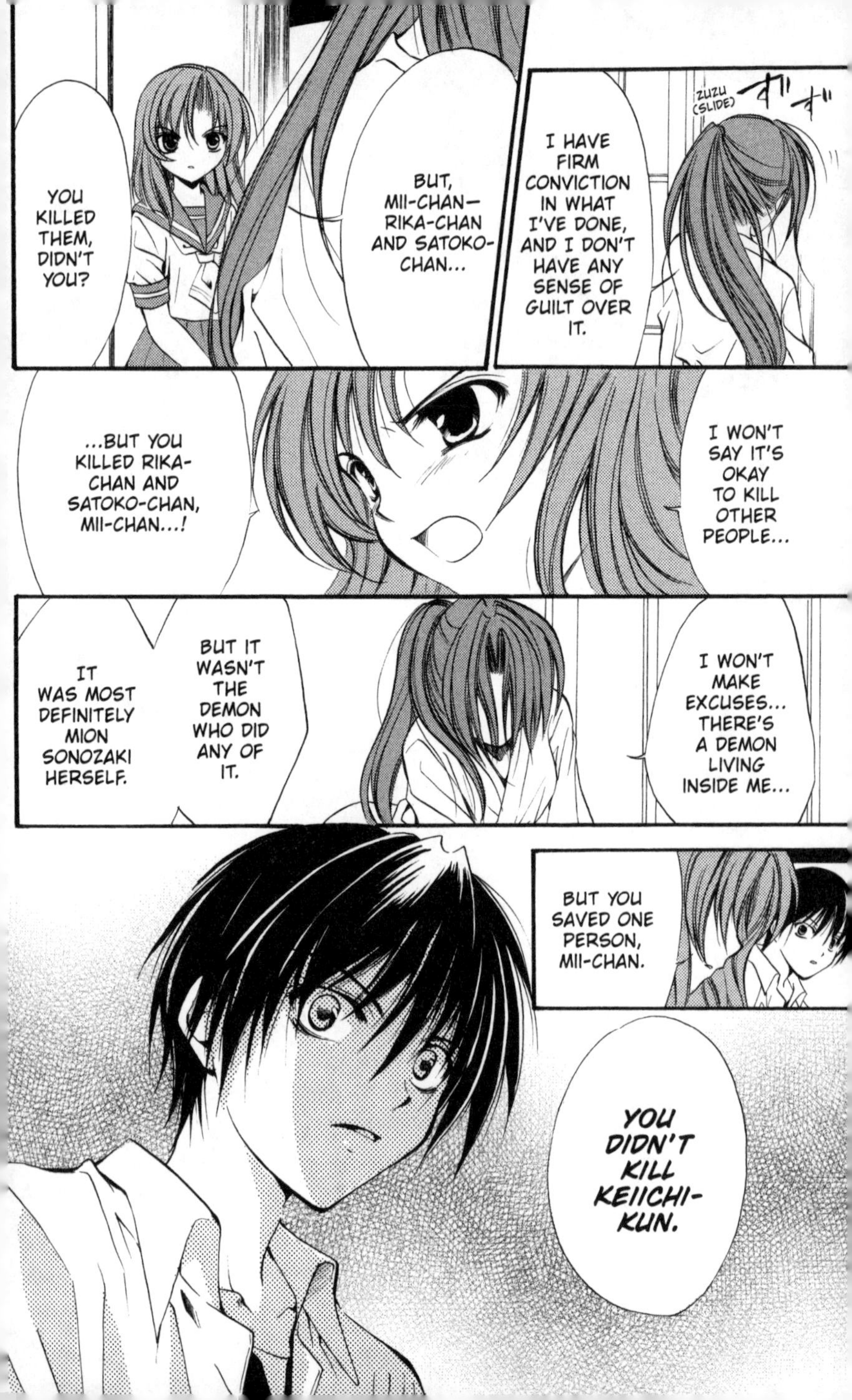
ずず
ZUZU (SLIDE)
I HAVE FIRM CONVICTION IN WHAT I'VE DONE, AND I DON'T HAVE ANY SENSE OF GUILT OVER IT.
BUT, MII-CHAN— RIKA-CHAN AND SATOKO-CHAN...
YOU KILLED THEM, DIDN'T YOU?
I WON'T SAY IT'S OKAY TO KILL OTHER PEOPLE...
...BUT YOU KILLED RIKA-CHAN AND SATOKO-CHAN, MII-CHAN...!
I WON'T MAKE EXCUSES... THERE'S A DEMON LIVING INSIDE ME...
BUT IT WASN'T THE DEMON WHO DID ANY OF IT.
IT WAS MOST DEFINITELY MION SONOZAKI HERSELF.
BUT YOU SAVED ONE PERSON, MII-CHAN.
YOU DIDN'T KILL KEIICHI-KUN.

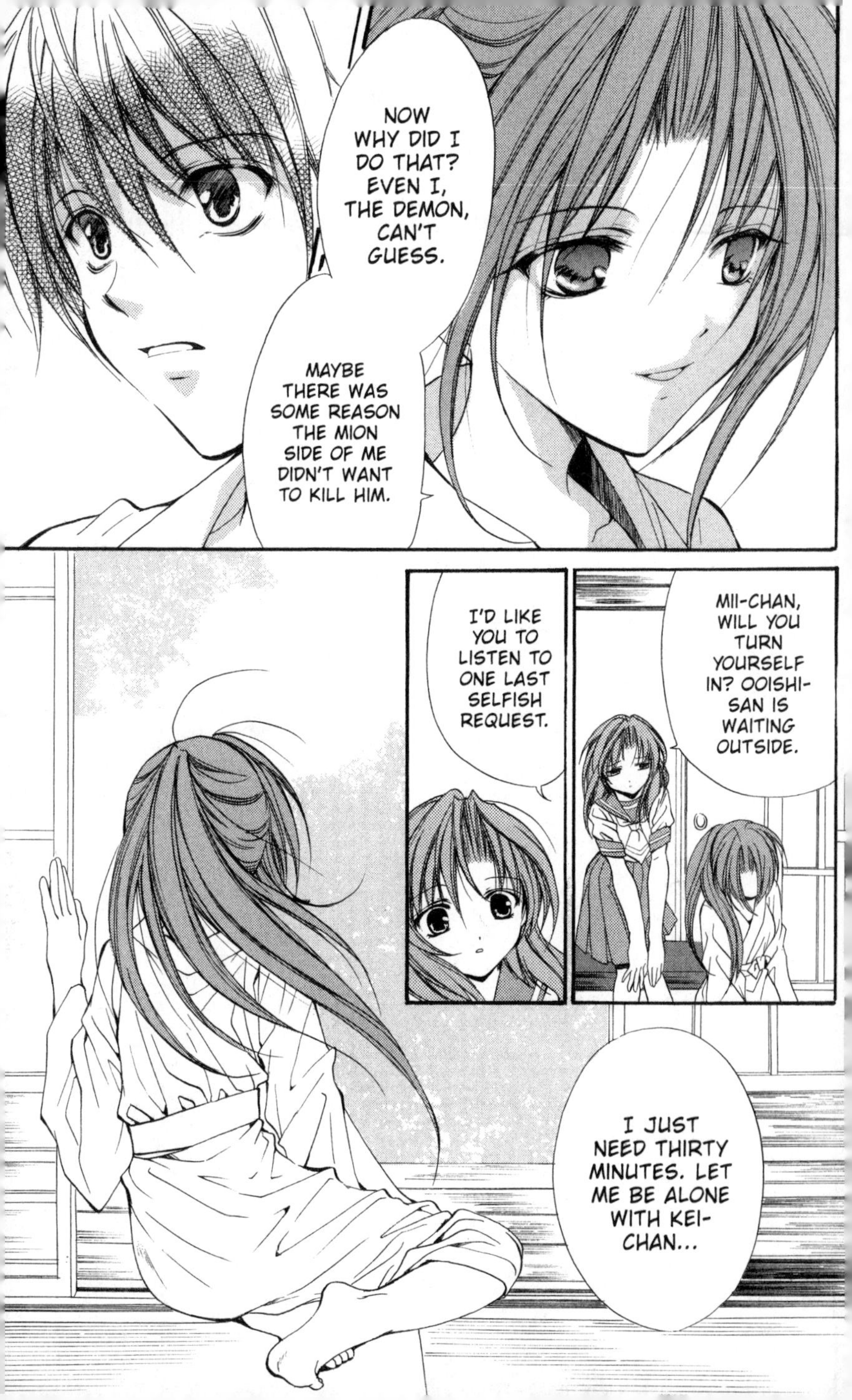
NOW WHY DID I DO THAT? EVEN I, THE DEMON, CAN'T GUESS.
MAYBE THERE WAS SOME REASON THE MION SIDE OF ME DIDN'T WANT TO KILL HIM.
MII-CHAN, WILL YOU TURN YOURSELF IN? OOISHI-SAN IS WAITING OUTSIDE.
I'D LIKE YOU TO LISTEN TO ONE LAST SELFISH REQUEST.
I JUST NEED THIRTY MINUTES. LET ME BE ALONE WITH KEI-CHAN...

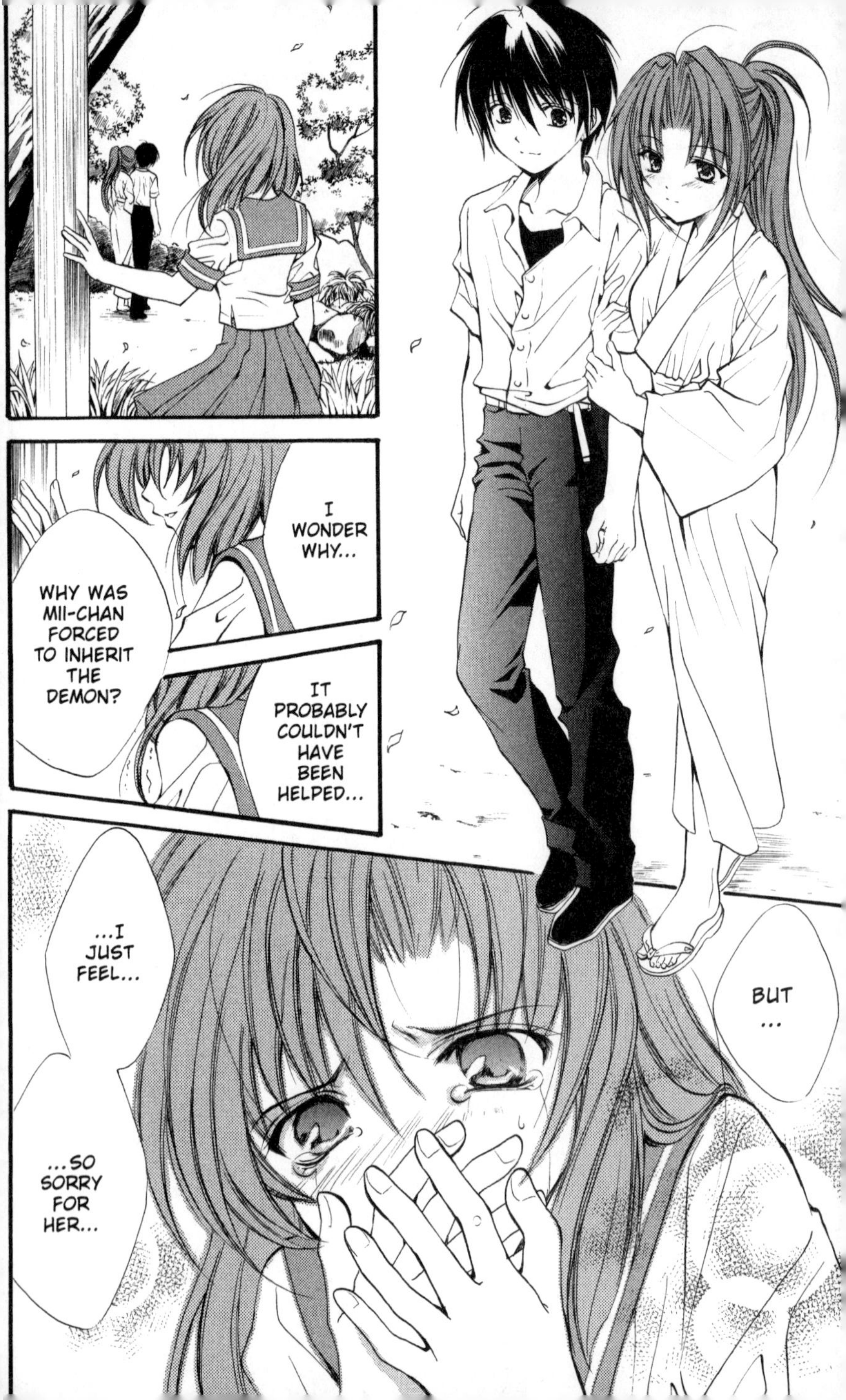
I WONDER WHY...
WHY WAS MII-CHAN FORCED TO INHERIT THE DEMON?
IT PROBABLY COULDN'T HAVE BEEN HELPED...
BUT ...
...I JUST FEEL...
...SO SORRY FOR HER...

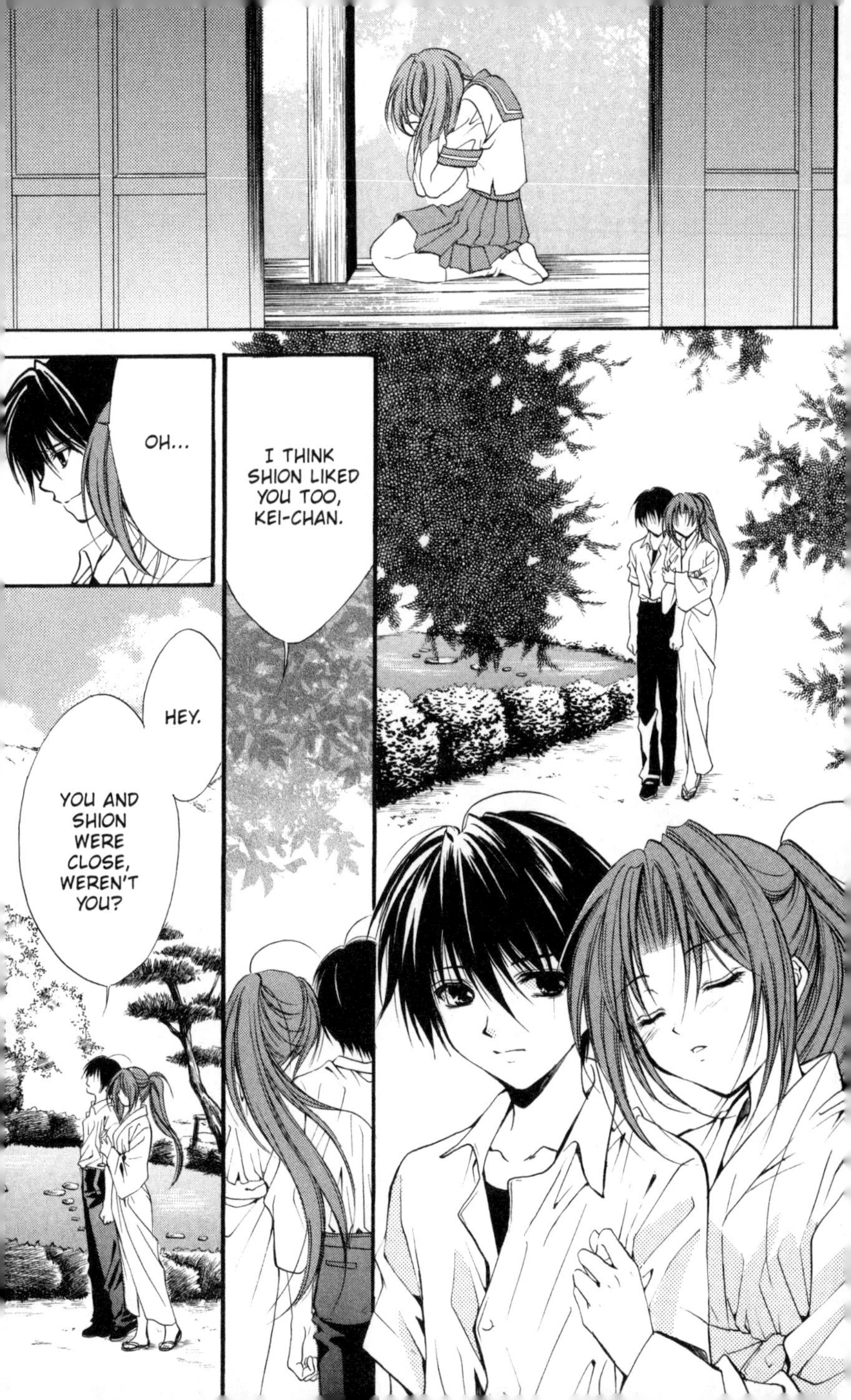
I THINK SHION LIKED YOU TOO, KEI-CHAN.
OH...
HEY.
YOU AND SHION WERE CLOSE, WEREN'T YOU?

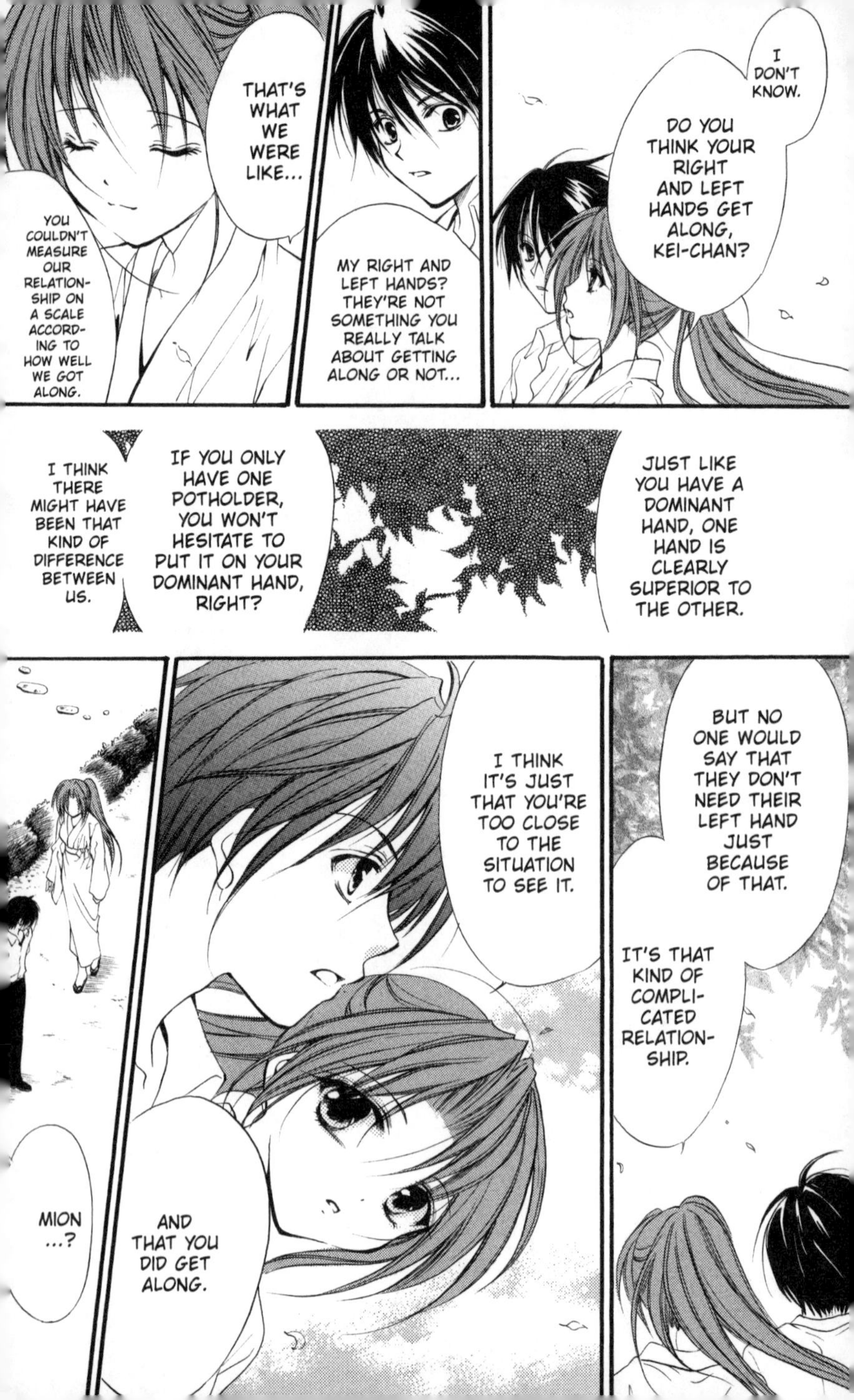
I DON'T KNOW.
DO YOU THINK YOUR RIGHT AND LEFT HANDS GET ALONG, KEI-CHAN?
MY RIGHT AND LEFT HANDS? THEY'RE NOT SOMETHING YOU REALLY TALK ABOUT GETTING ALONG OR NOT...
THAT'S WHAT WE WERE LIKE...
YOU COULDN'T MEASURE OUR RELATIONSHIP ON A SCALE ACCORDING TO HOW WELL WE GOT ALONG.
JUST LIKE YOU HAVE A DOMINANT HAND, ONE HAND IS CLEARLY SUPERIOR TO THE OTHER.
IF YOU ONLY HAVE ONE POTHOLDER, YOU WON'T HESITATE TO PUT IT ON YOUR DOMINANT HAND, RIGHT?
I THINK THERE MIGHT HAVE BEEN THAT KIND OF DIFFERENCE BETWEEN US.
BUT NO ONE WOULD SAY THAT THEY DON'T NEED THEIR LEFT HAND JUST BECAUSE OF THAT.
IT'S THAT KIND OF COMPLICATED RELATIONSHIP.
I THINK IT'S JUST THAT YOU'RE TOO CLOSE TO THE SITUATION TO SEE IT.
AND THAT YOU DID GET ALONG.
MION ...?

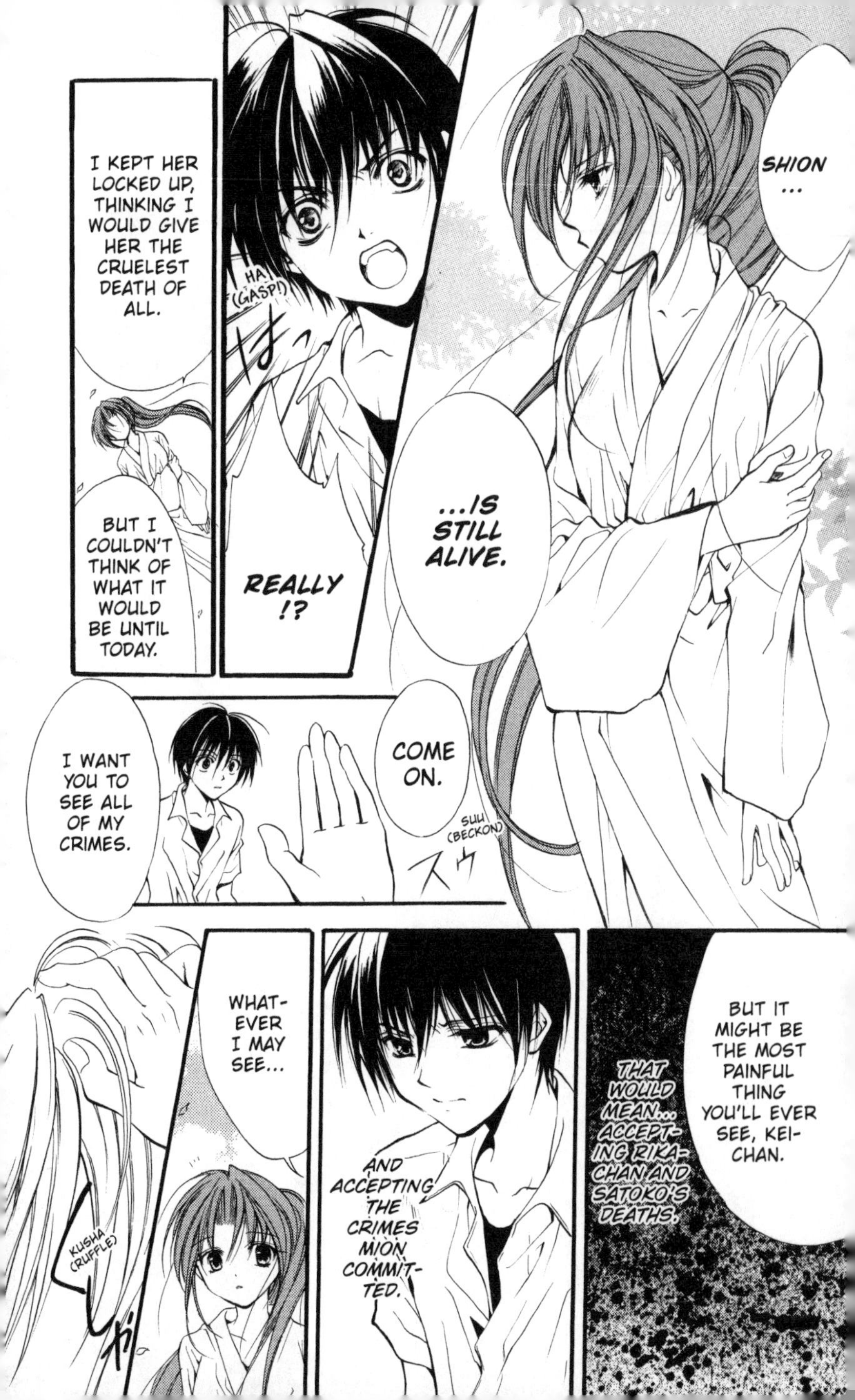
SHION ...
...IS STILL ALIVE.
HA (GASP!)
REALLY !?
I KEPT HER LOCKED UP, THINKING I WOULD GIVE HER THE CRUELEST DEATH OF ALL.
BUT I COULDN'T THINK OF WHAT IT WOULD BE UNTIL TODAY.
COME ON.
SUU (BECKON)
I WANT YOU TO SEE ALL OF MY CRIMES.
BUT IT MIGHT BE THE MOST PAINFUL THING YOU'LL EVER SEE, KEI-CHAN.
THAT WOULD MEAN... ACCEPTING RIKA-CHAN AND SATOKO'S DEATHS.
AND ACCEPTING THE CRIMES MION COMMIT-TED.
WHAT-EVER I MAY SEE...
KUSHA (RUFFLE)

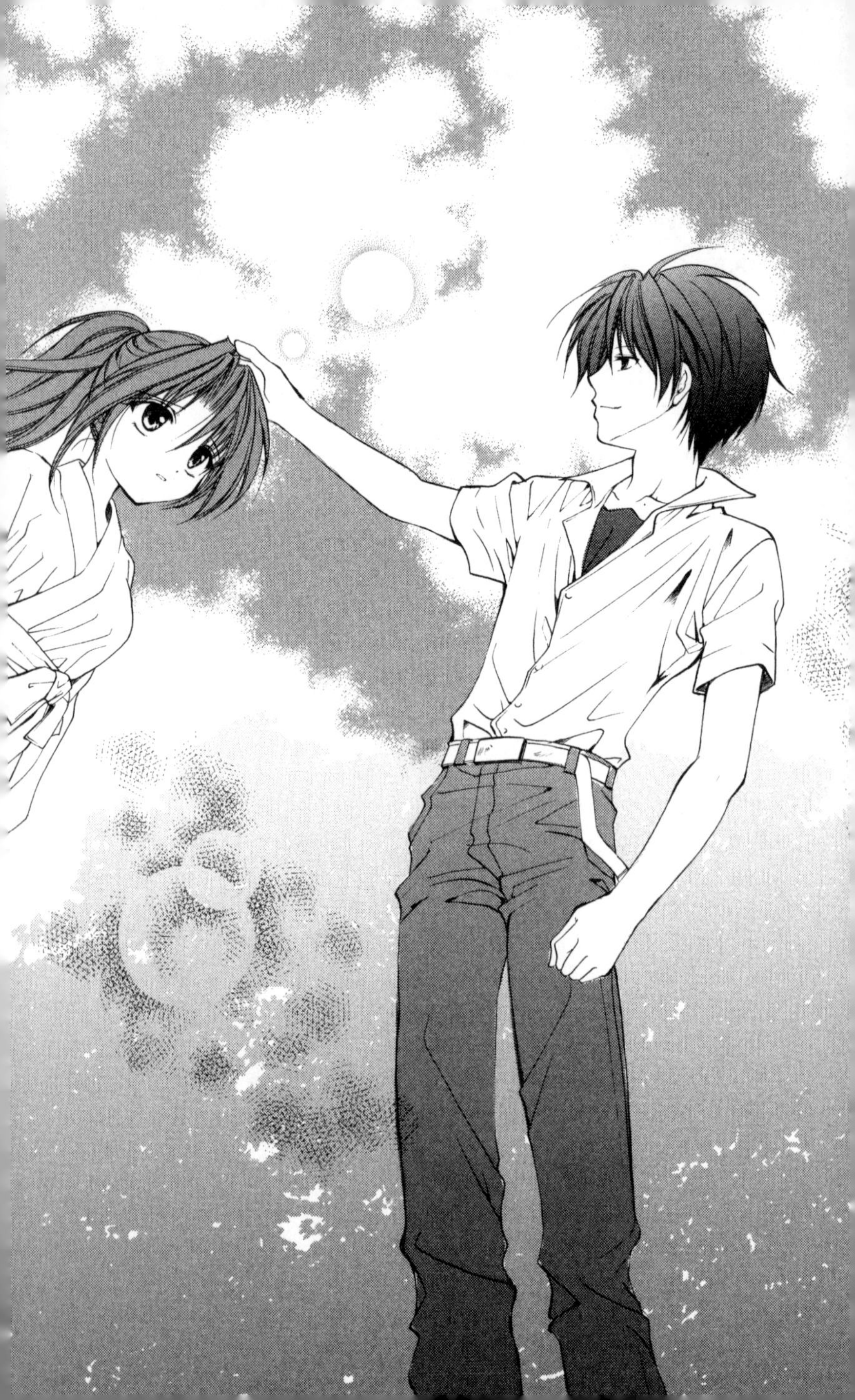

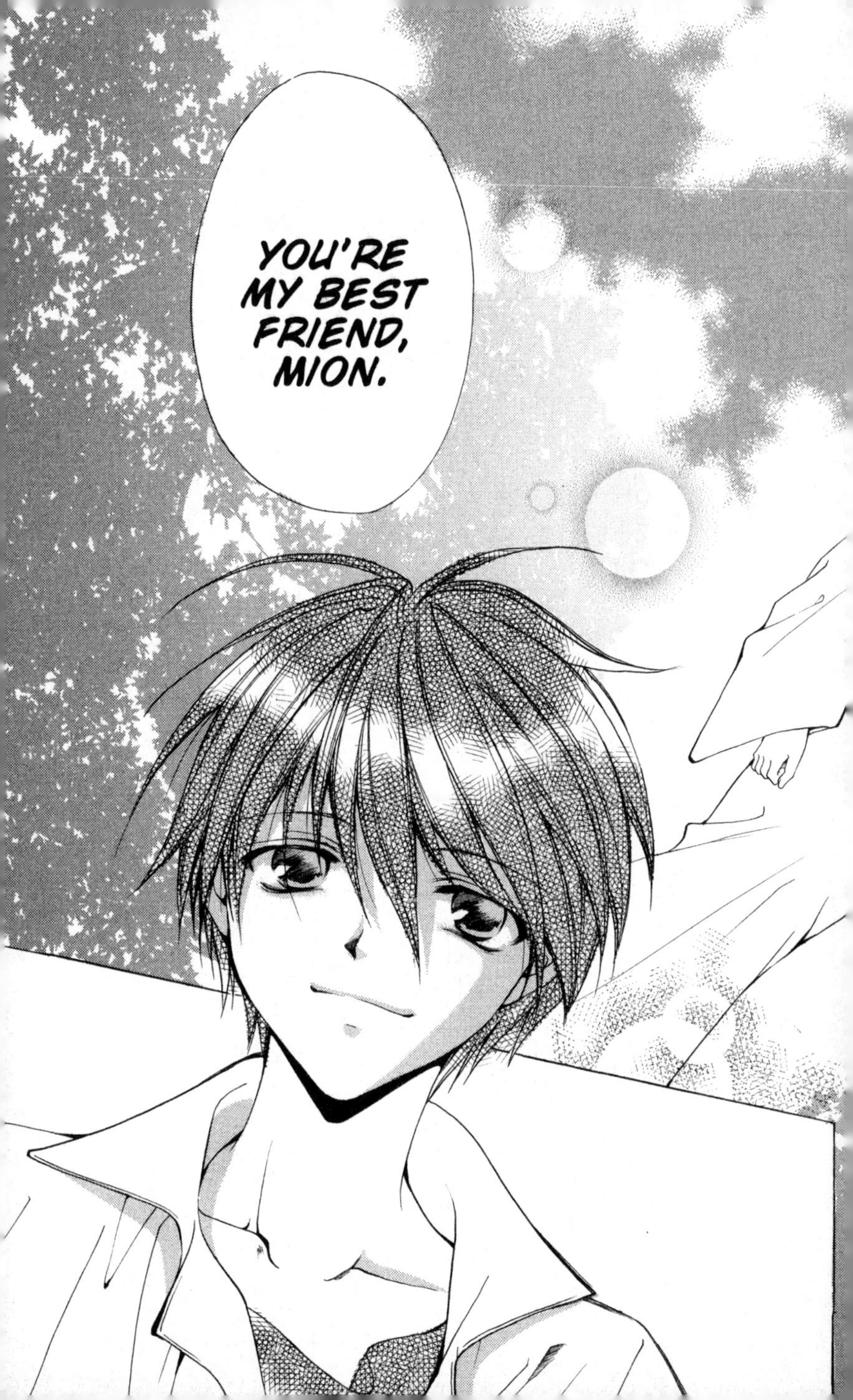
YOU'RE MY BEST FRIEND, MION.

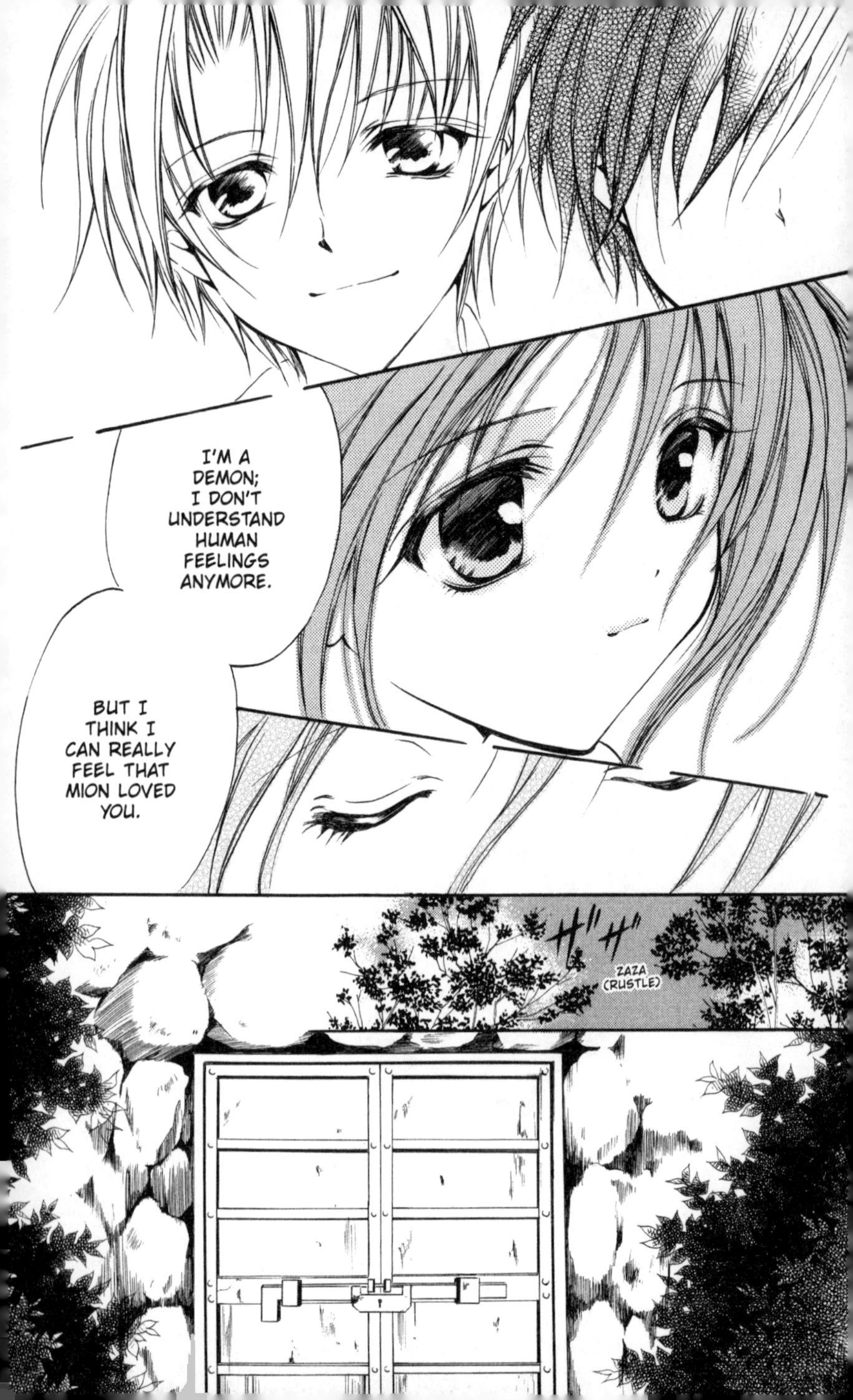
I'M A DEMON; I DON'T UNDERSTAND HUMAN FEELINGS ANYMORE.
BUT I THINK I CAN REALLY FEEL THAT MION LOVED YOU.
ZAZA (RUSTLE)

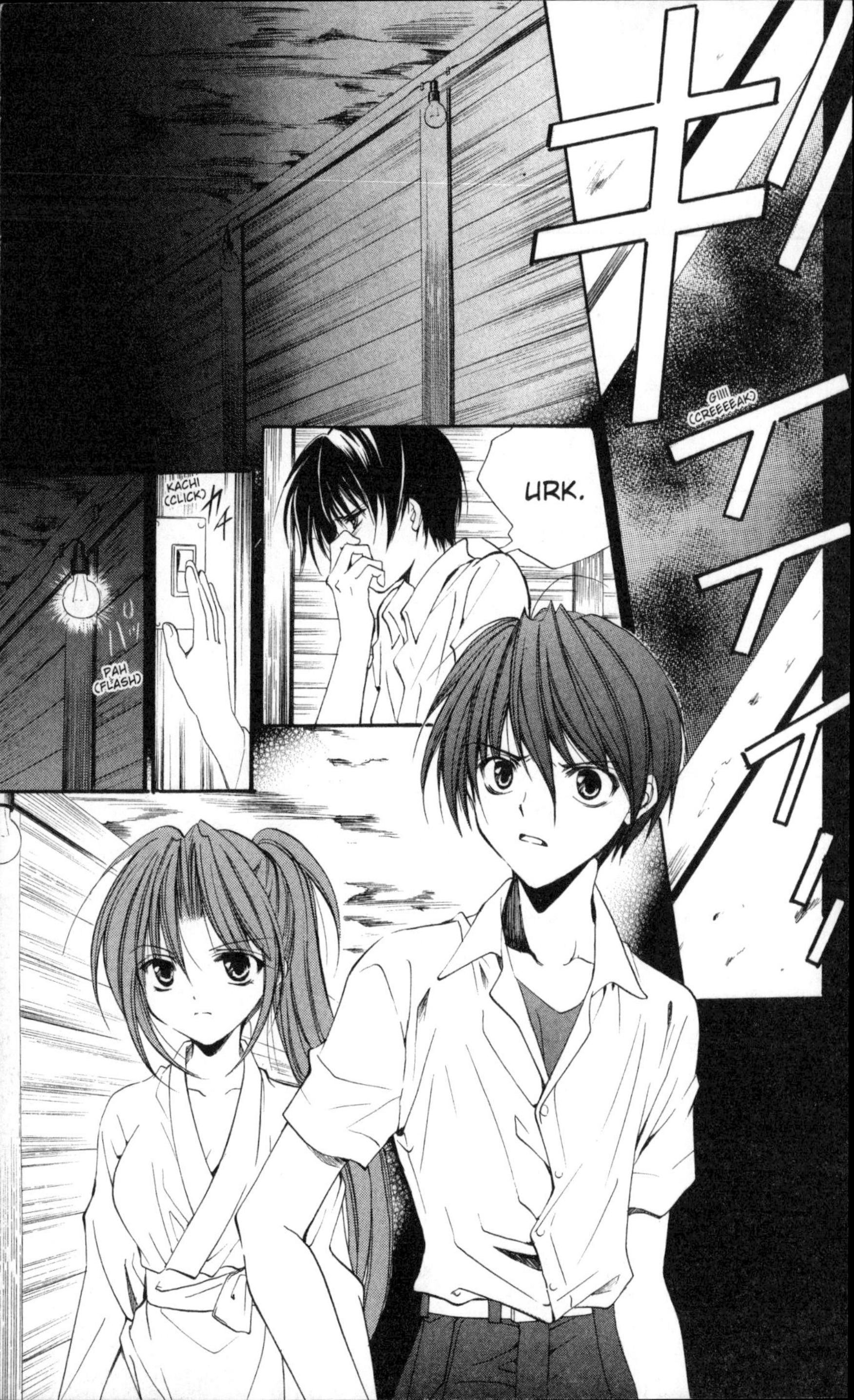
GIIII (CREEEEAK)
URK.
KACHI (CLICK)
PAH (FLASH)

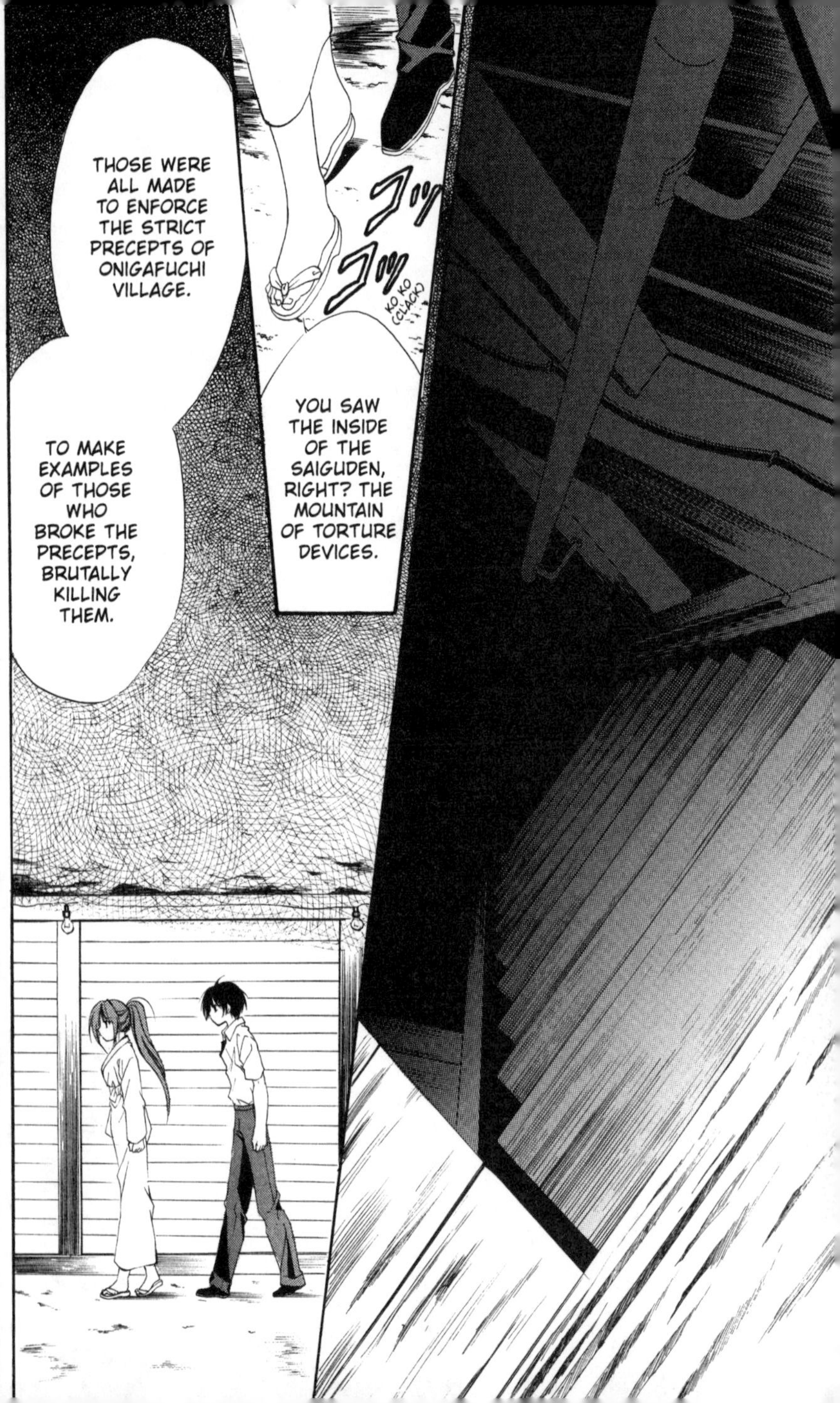
KO KO (CLACK)
YOU SAW THE INSIDE OF THE SAIGUDEN, RIGHT? THE MOUNTAIN OF TORTURE DEVICES.
THOSE WERE ALL MADE TO ENFORCE THE STRICT PRECEPTS OF ONIGAFUCHI VILLAGE.
TO MAKE EXAMPLES OF THOSE WHO BROKE THE PRECEPTS, BRUTALLY KILLING THEM.

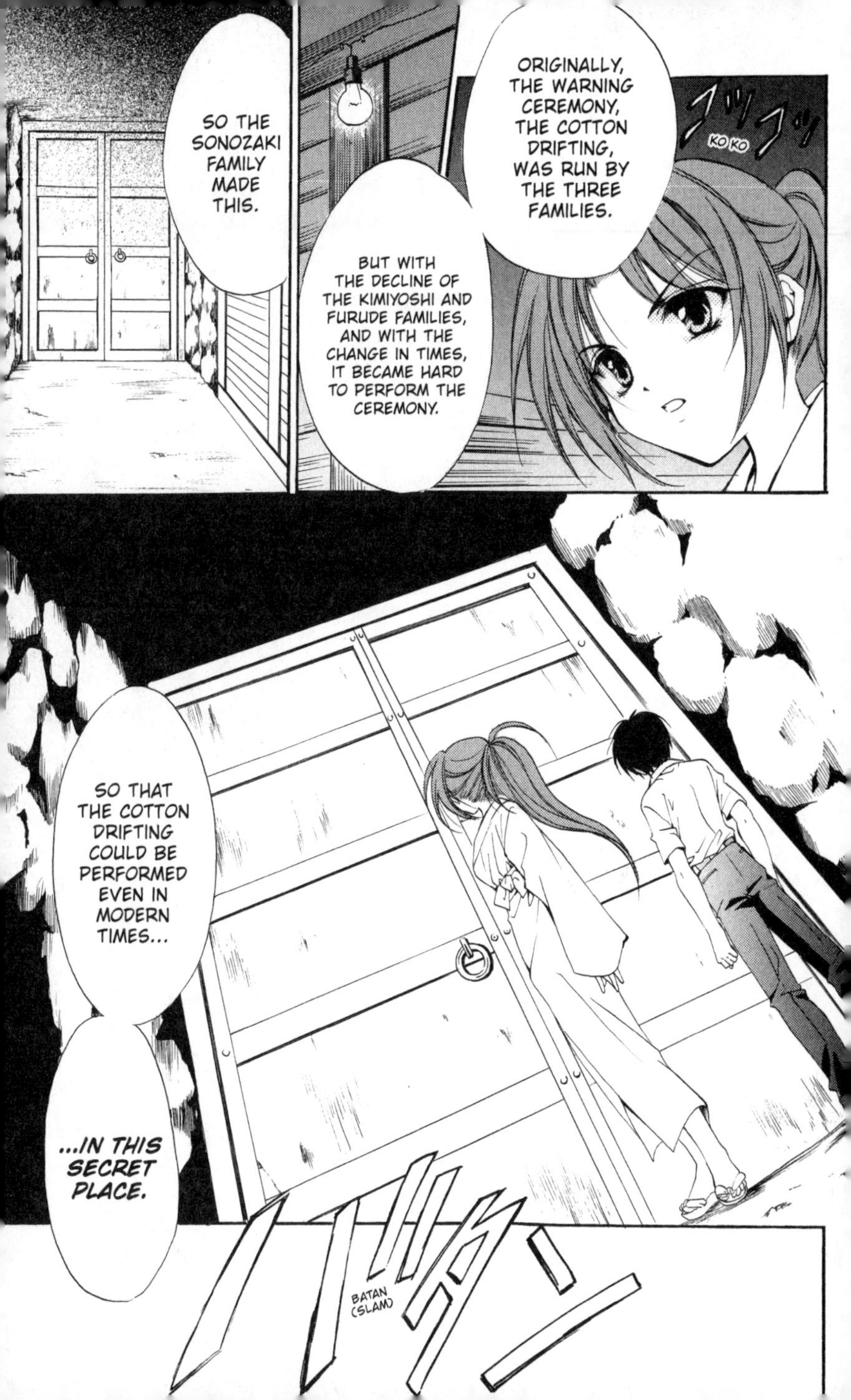
KO KO
ORIGINALLY, THE WARNING CEREMONY, THE COTTON DRIFTING, WAS RUN BY THE THREE FAMILIES.
BUT WITH THE DECLINE OF THE KIMIYOSHI AND FURUDE FAMILIES, AND WITH THE CHANGE IN TIMES, IT BECAME HARD TO PERFORM THE CEREMONY.
SO THE SONOZAKI FAMILY MADE THIS.
SO THAT THE COTTON DRIFTING COULD BE PERFORMED EVEN IN MODERN TIMES...
...IN THIS SECRET PLACE.
BATAN (SLAM)

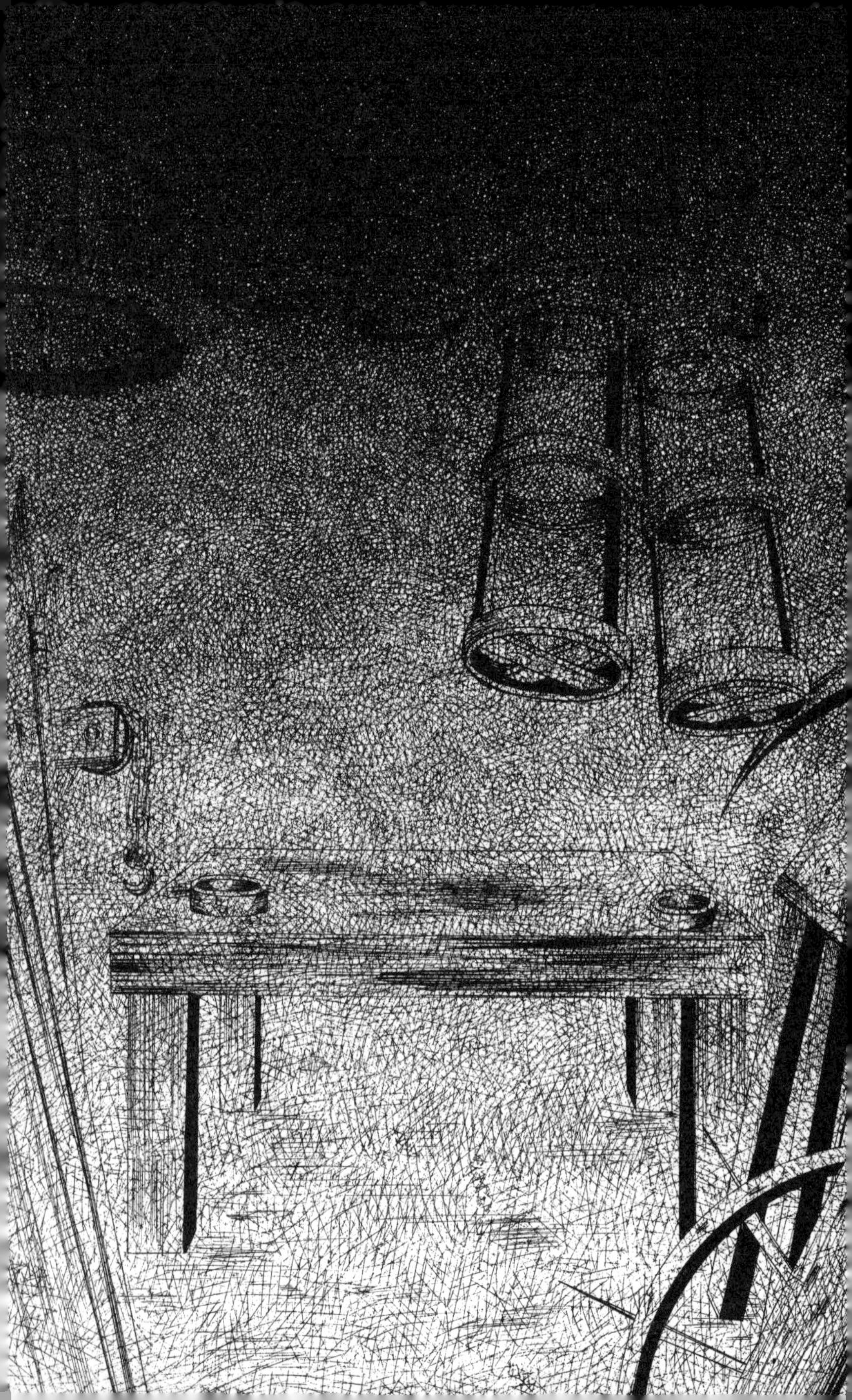

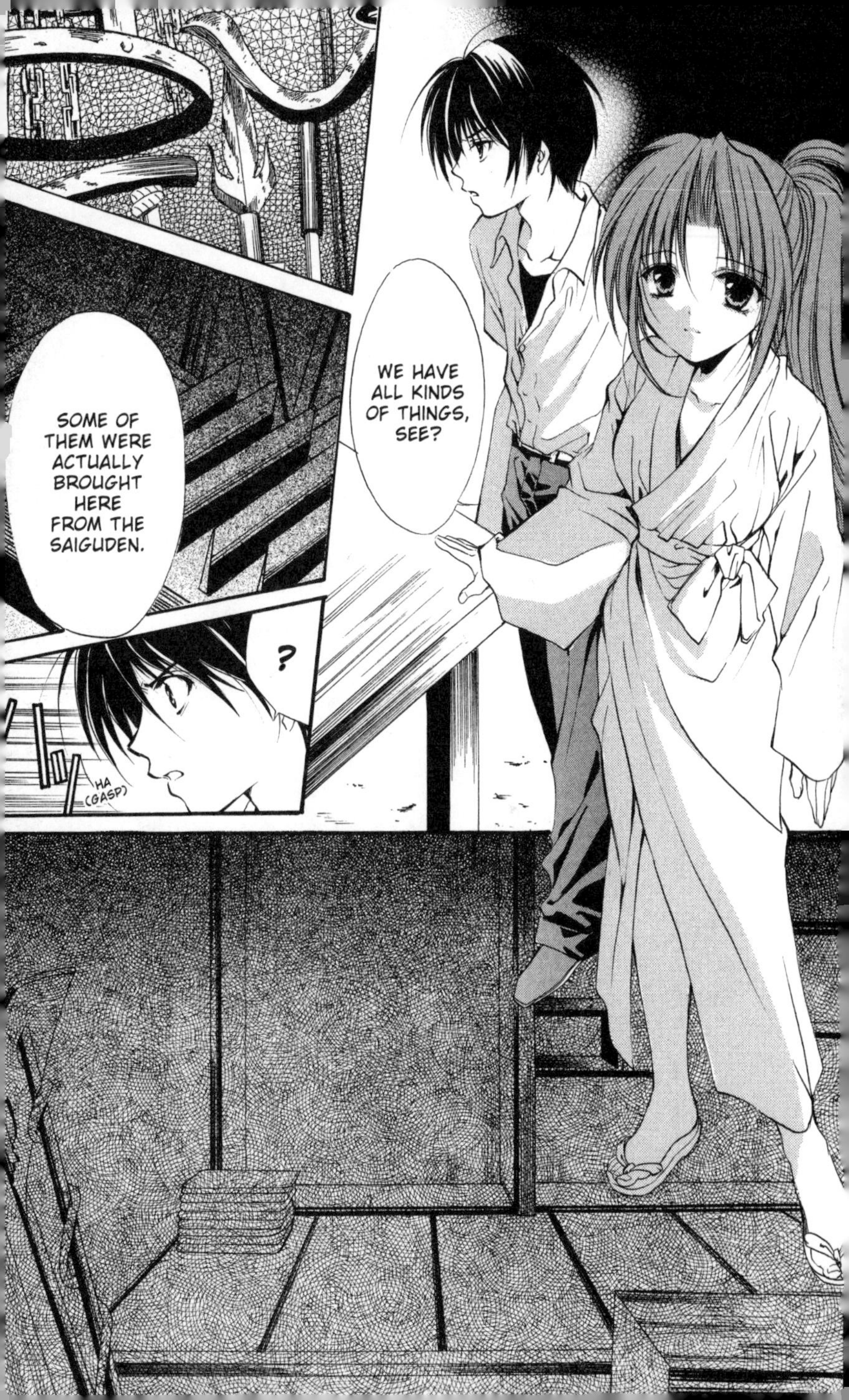
WE HAVE ALL KINDS OF THINGS, SEE?
SOME OF THEM WERE ACTUALLY BROUGHT HERE FROM THE SAIGUDEN.
?
HA (GASP)

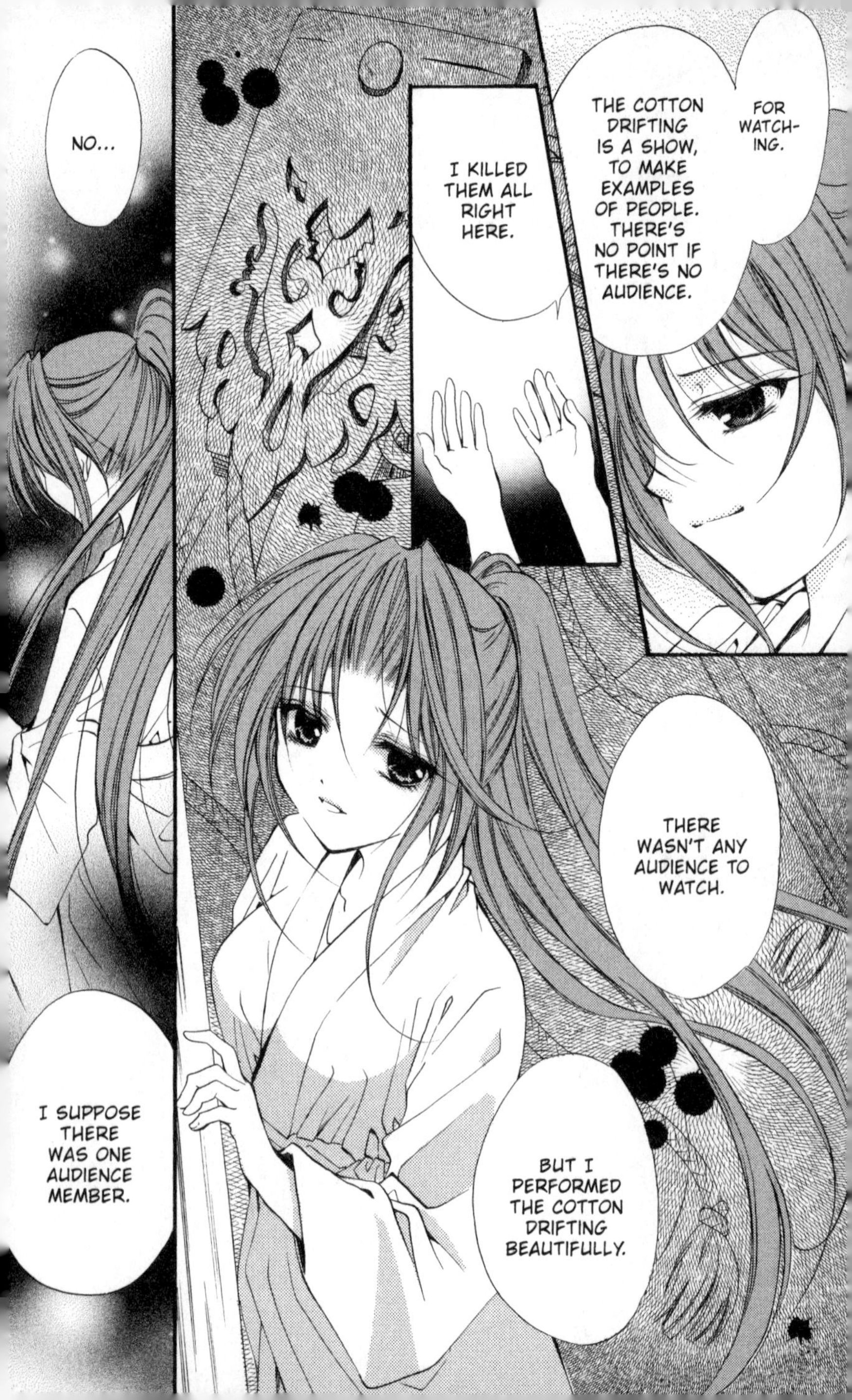
FOR WATCHING.
THE COTTON DRIFTING IS A SHOW, TO MAKE EXAMPLES OF PEOPLE. THERE'S NO POINT IF THERE'S NO AUDIENCE.
I KILLED THEM ALL RIGHT HERE.
THERE WASN'T ANY AUDIENCE TO WATCH.
BUT I PERFORMED THE COTTON DRIFTING BEAUTIFULLY.
NO...
I SUPPOSE THERE WAS ONE AUDIENCE MEMBER.

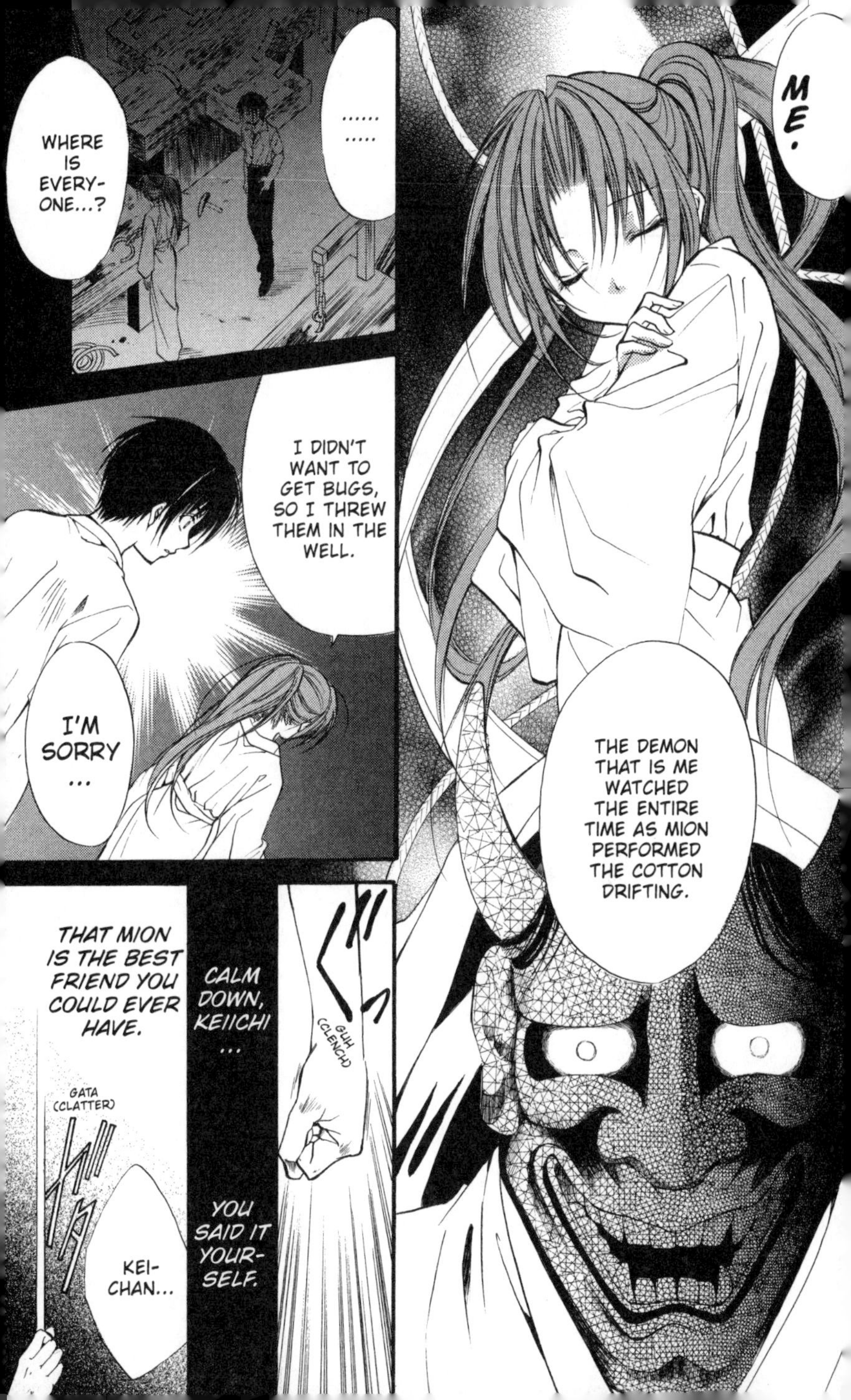
ME.
THE DEMON THAT IS ME WATCHED THE ENTIRE TIME AS MION PERFORMED THE COTTON DRIFTING.
....
WHERE IS EVERYONE...?
I DIDN'T WANT TO GET BUGS, SO I THREW THEM IN THE WELL.
I'M SORRY ...
GUH (CLENCH)
CALM DOWN, KEIICHI ...
YOU SAID IT YOURSELF.
THAT MION IS THE BEST FRIEND YOU COULD EVER HAVE.
GATA (CLATTER)
KEI-CHAN...

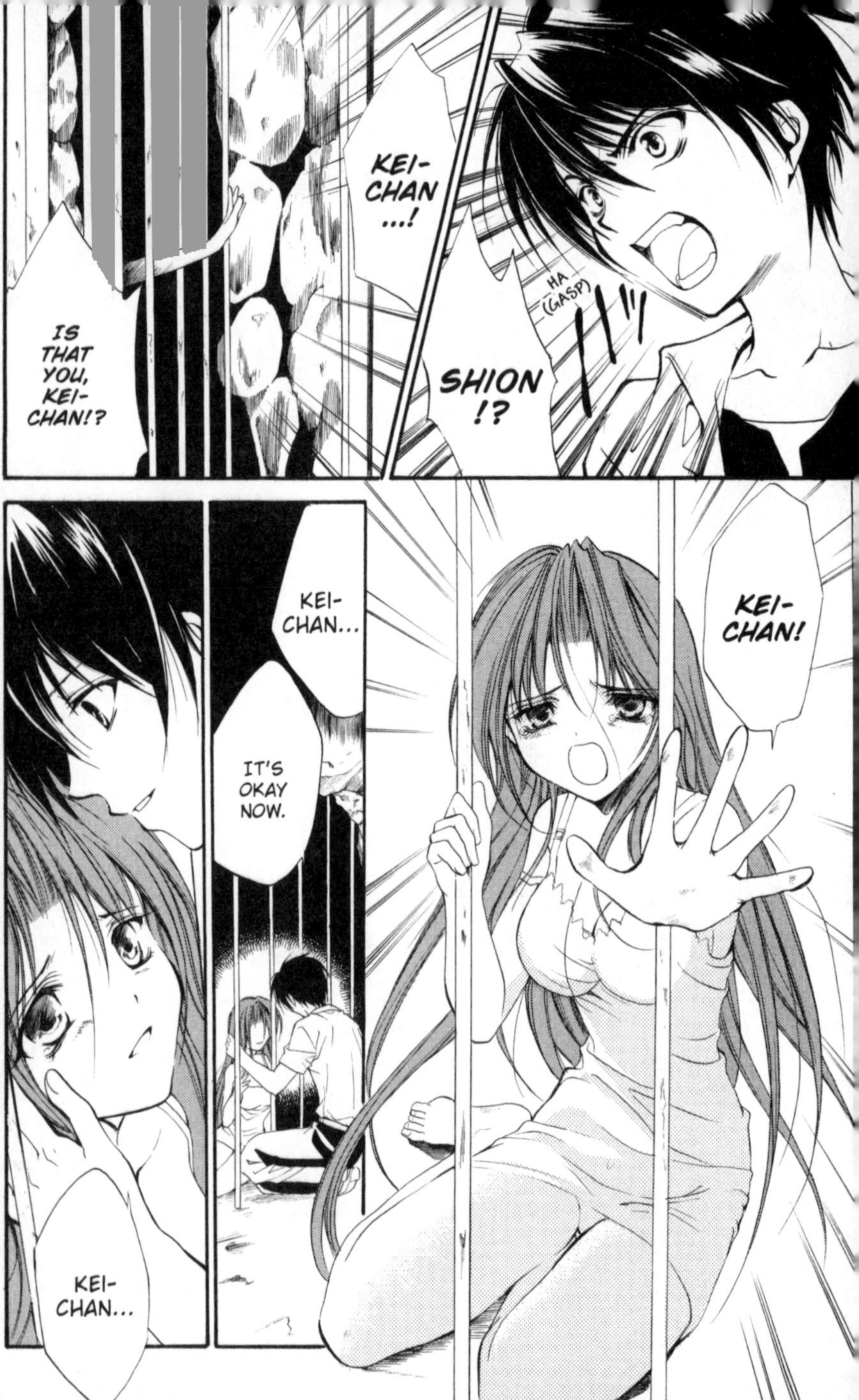
HA (GASP)
SHION !?
KEI-CHAN ...!
IS THAT YOU, KEI-CHAN!?
KEI-CHAN!
KEI-CHAN...
IT'S OKAY NOW.
KEI-CHAN...

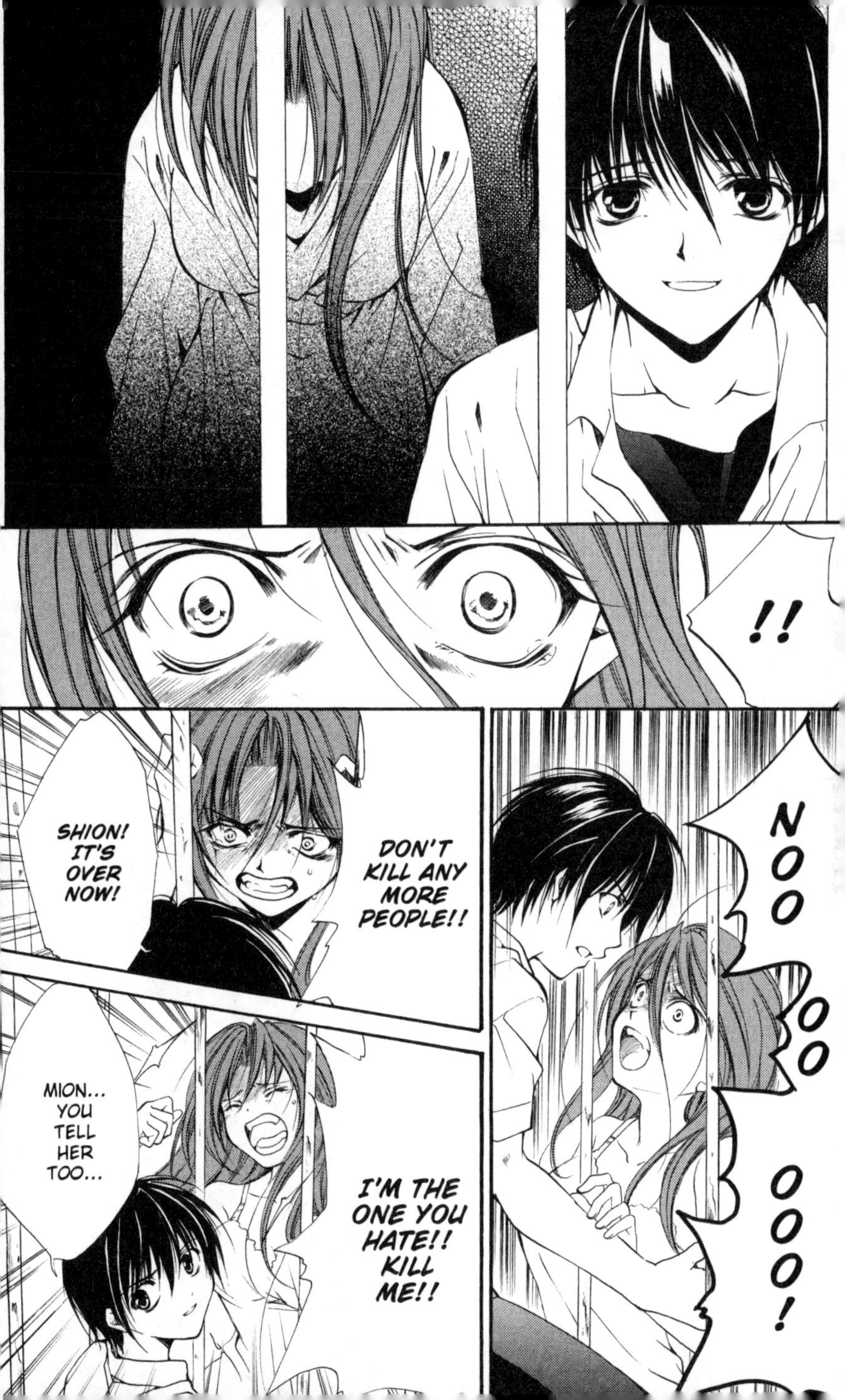
!!
NOOOOOOO!
DON'T KILL ANY MORE PEOPLE!!
SHION! IT'S OVER NOW!
I'M THE ONE YOU HATE!! KILL ME!!
MION... YOU TELL HER TOO...

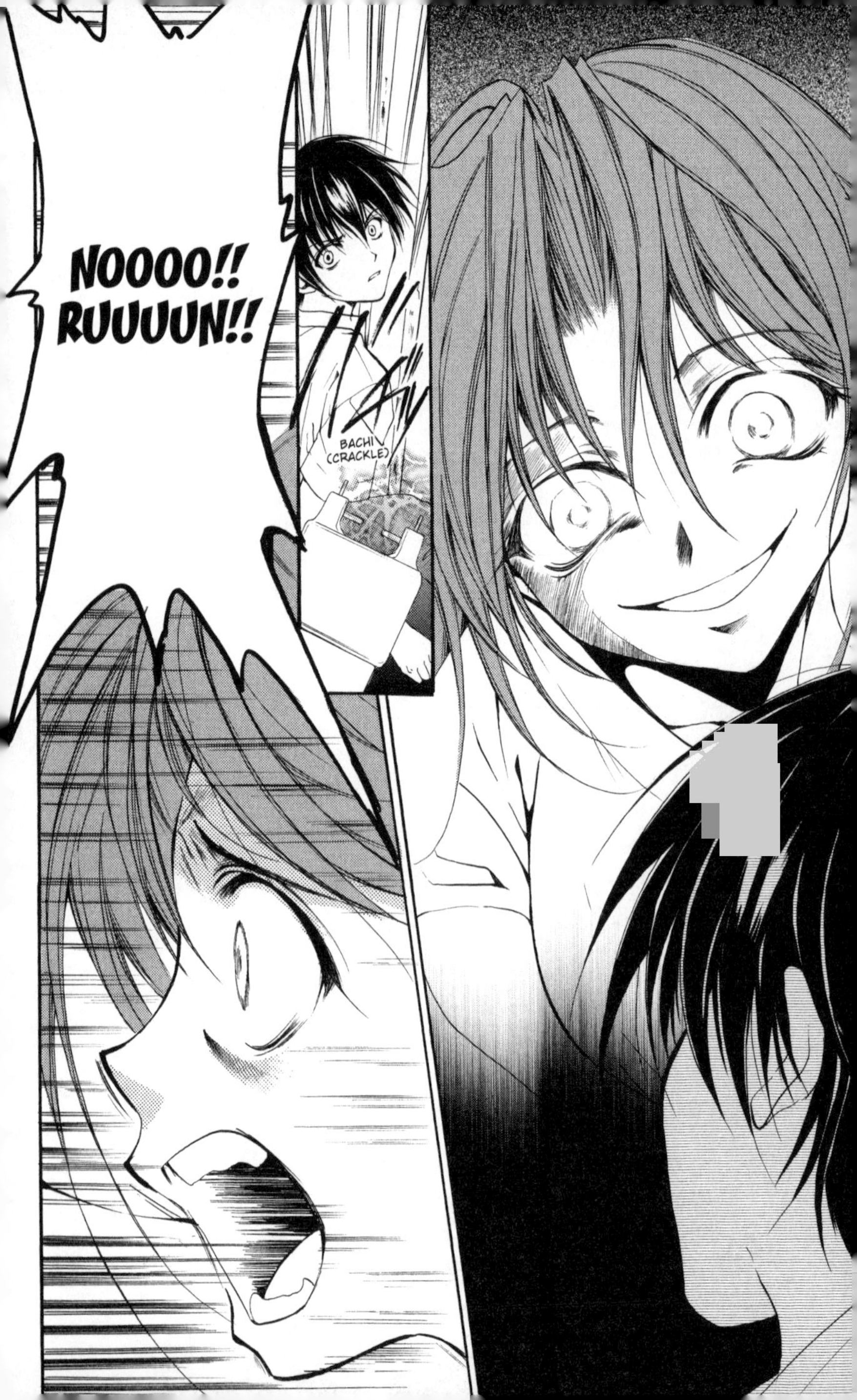
BACHI (CRACKLE)
NOOOO!! RUUUUN!!

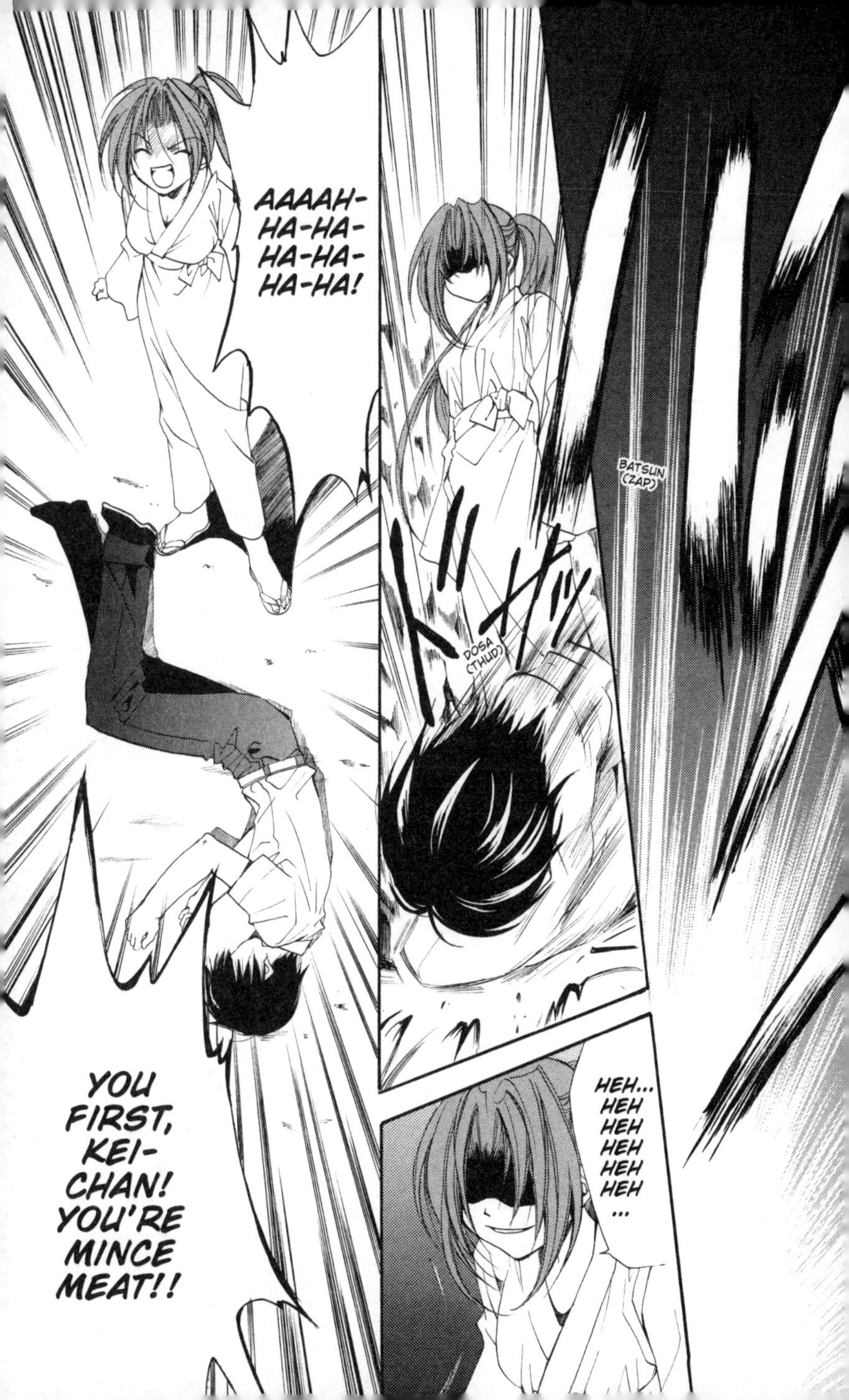
BATSUN (ZAP)
DOSA (THUD)
HEH... HEH HEH HEH HEH HEH ...
AAAAH-HA-HA-HA-HA-HA-HA!
YOU FIRST, KEI-CHAN! YOU'RE MINCE MEAT!!

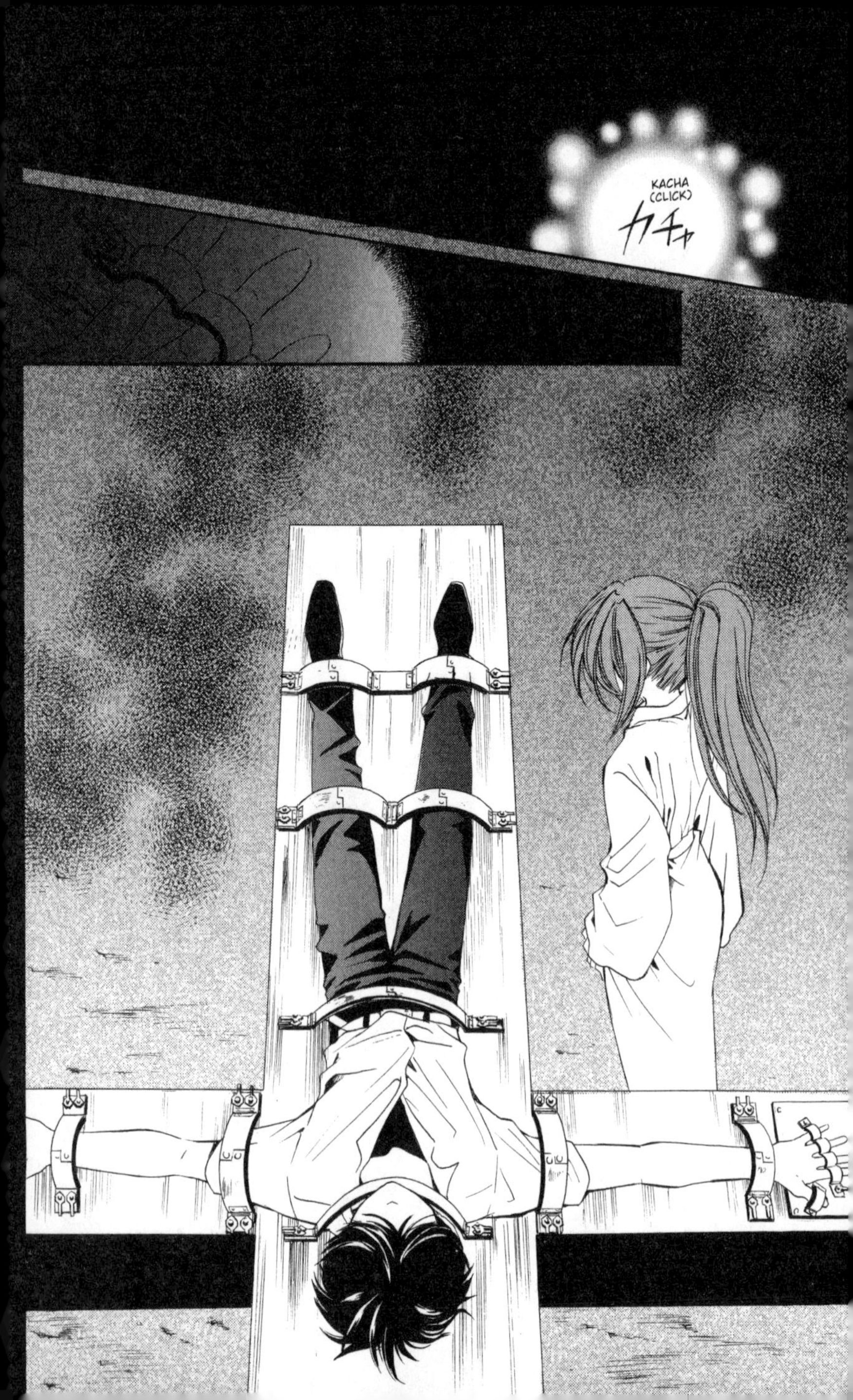
KACHA
(CLICK)
カチャ

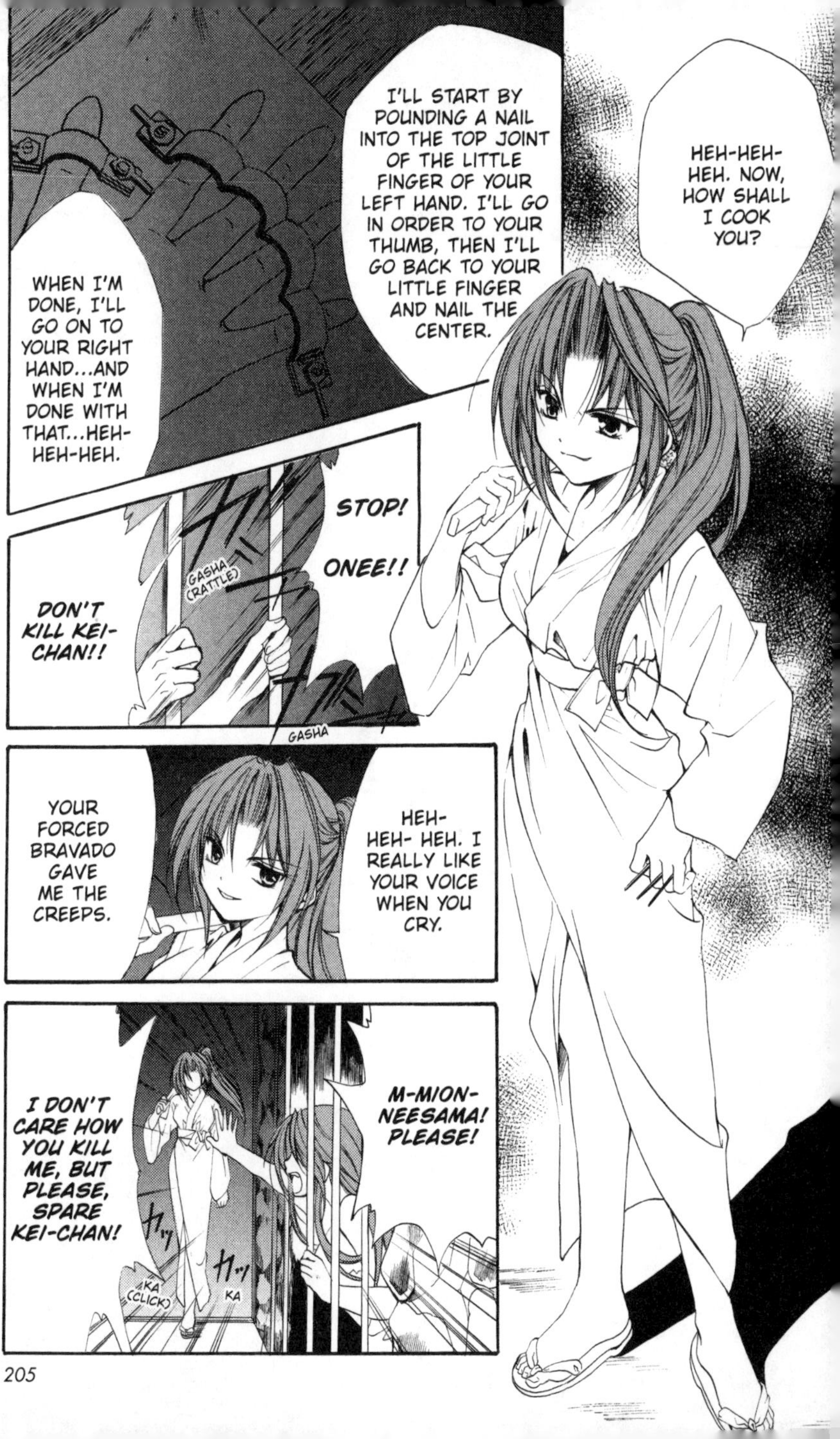
HEH-HEH-HEH. NOW, HOW SHALL I COOK YOU?
I'LL START BY POUNDING A NAIL INTO THE TOP JOINT OF THE LITTLE FINGER OF YOUR LEFT HAND. I'LL GO IN ORDER TO YOUR THUMB, THEN I'LL GO BACK TO YOUR LITTLE FINGER AND NAIL THE CENTER.
WHEN I'M DONE, I'LL GO ON TO YOUR RIGHT HAND...AND WHEN I'M DONE WITH THAT...HEH-HEH-HEH.
STOP!
ONEE!!
GASHA (RATTLE)
DON'T KILL KEI-CHAN!!
GASHA
HEH-HEH- HEH. I REALLY LIKE YOUR VOICE WHEN YOU CRY.
YOUR FORCED BRAVADO GAVE ME THE CREEPS.
M-MION-NEESAMA! PLEASE!
I DON'T CARE HOW YOU KILL ME, BUT PLEASE, SPARE KEI-CHAN!
KA
KA (CLICK)

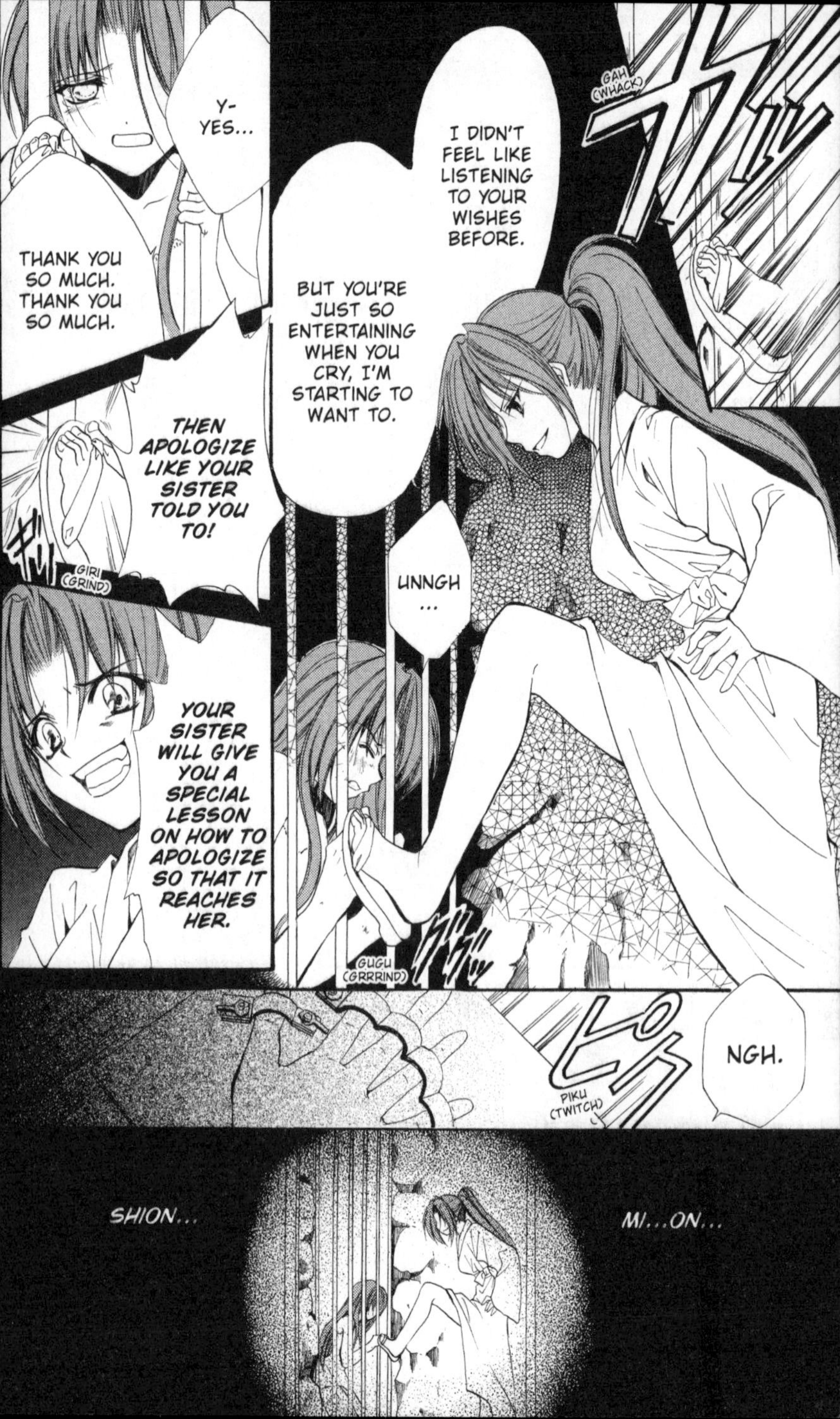
GAH (WHACK)
I DIDN'T FEEL LIKE LISTENING TO YOUR WISHES BEFORE.
BUT YOU'RE JUST SO ENTERTAINING WHEN YOU CRY, I'M STARTING TO WANT TO.
UNNGH...
GUGU (GRRRIND)
Y-YES...
THANK YOU SO MUCH. THANK YOU SO MUCH.
THEN APOLOGIZE LIKE YOUR SISTER TOLD YOU TO!
GIRI (GRIND)
YOUR SISTER WILL GIVE YOU A SPECIAL LESSON ON HOW TO APOLOGIZE SO THAT IT REACHES HER.
NGH.
PIKU (TWITCH)
MI...ON...
SHION...

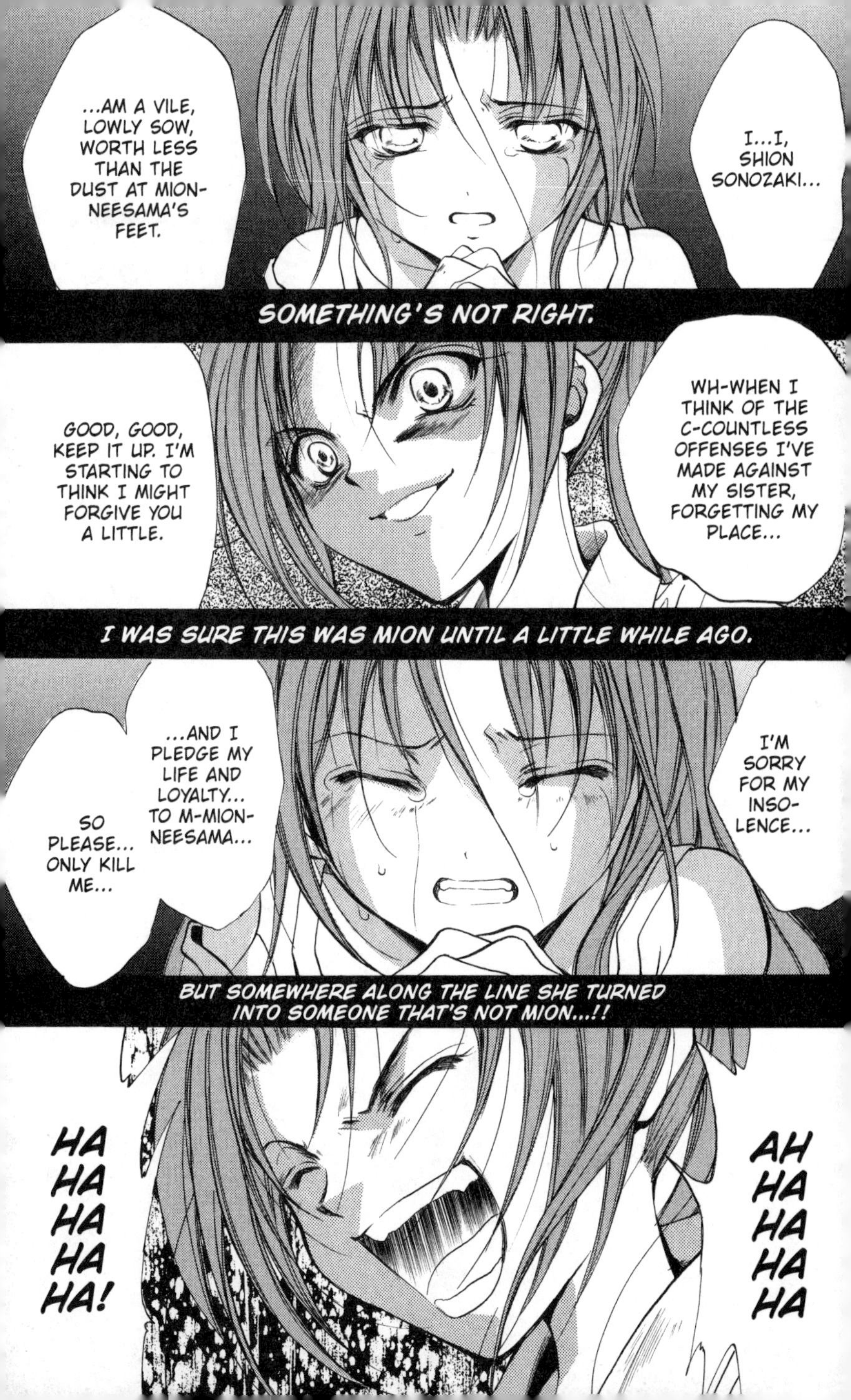
I...I, SHION SONOZAKI...
...AM A VILE, LOWLY SOW, WORTH LESS THAN THE DUST AT MION-NEESAMA'S FEET.
SOMETHING'S NOT RIGHT.
WH-WHEN I THINK OF THE C-COUNTLESS OFFENSES I'VE MADE AGAINST MY SISTER, FORGETTING MY PLACE...
GOOD, GOOD, KEEP IT UP. I'M STARTING TO THINK I MIGHT FORGIVE YOU A LITTLE.
I WAS SURE THIS WAS MION UNTIL A LITTLE WHILE AGO.
I'M SORRY FOR MY INSO-LENCE...
...AND I PLEDGE MY LIFE AND LOYALTY... TO M-MION-NEESAMA...
SO PLEASE... ONLY KILL ME...
BUT SOMEWHERE ALONG THE LINE SHE TURNED INTO SOMEONE THAT'S NOT MION...!!
AH HA HA HA HA HA
HA HA HA HA HA HA!

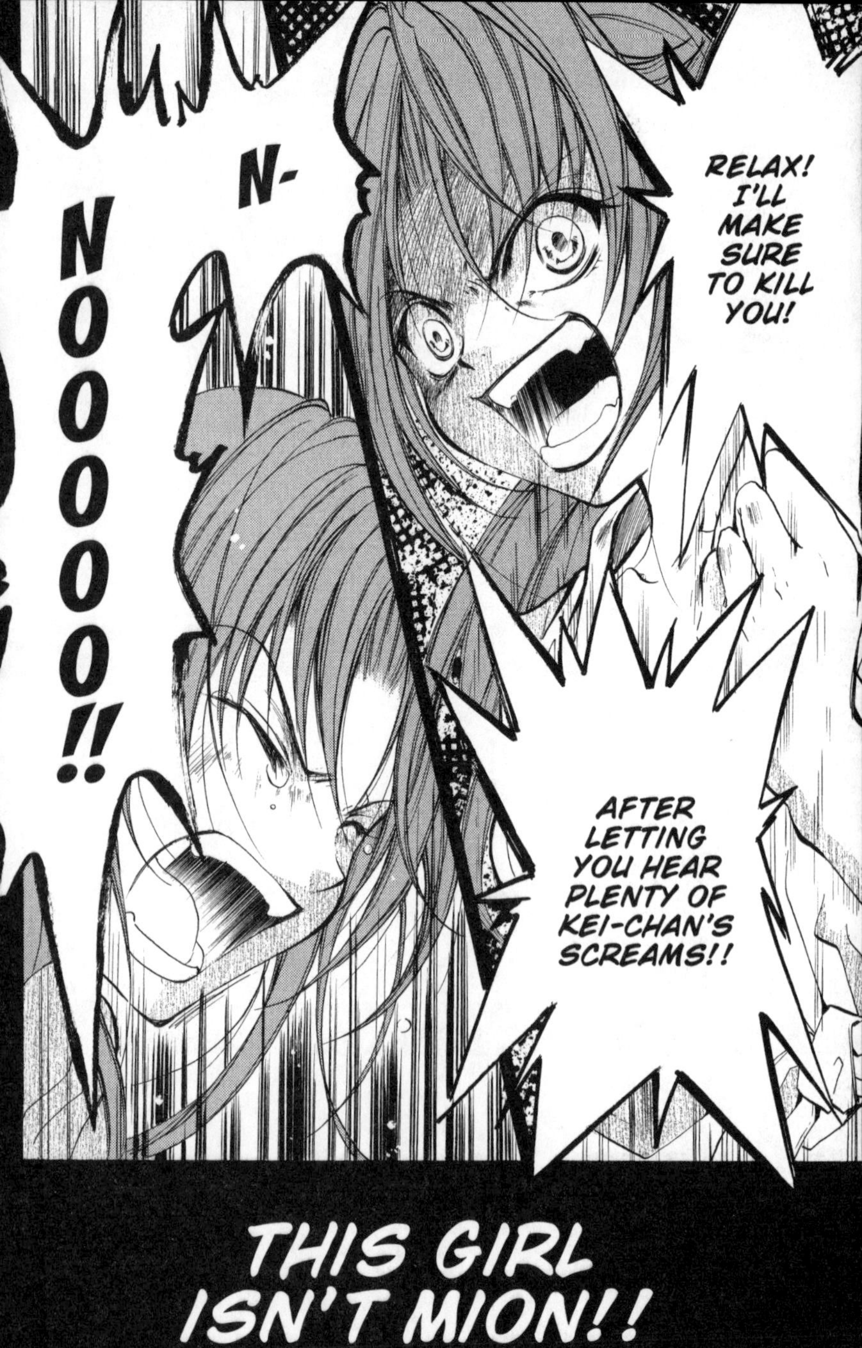
RELAX! I'LL MAKE SURE TO KILL YOU!
AFTER LETTING YOU HEAR PLENTY OF KEI-CHAN'S SCREAMS!!
N-
NOOOOOO!!
THIS GIRL ISN'T MION!!

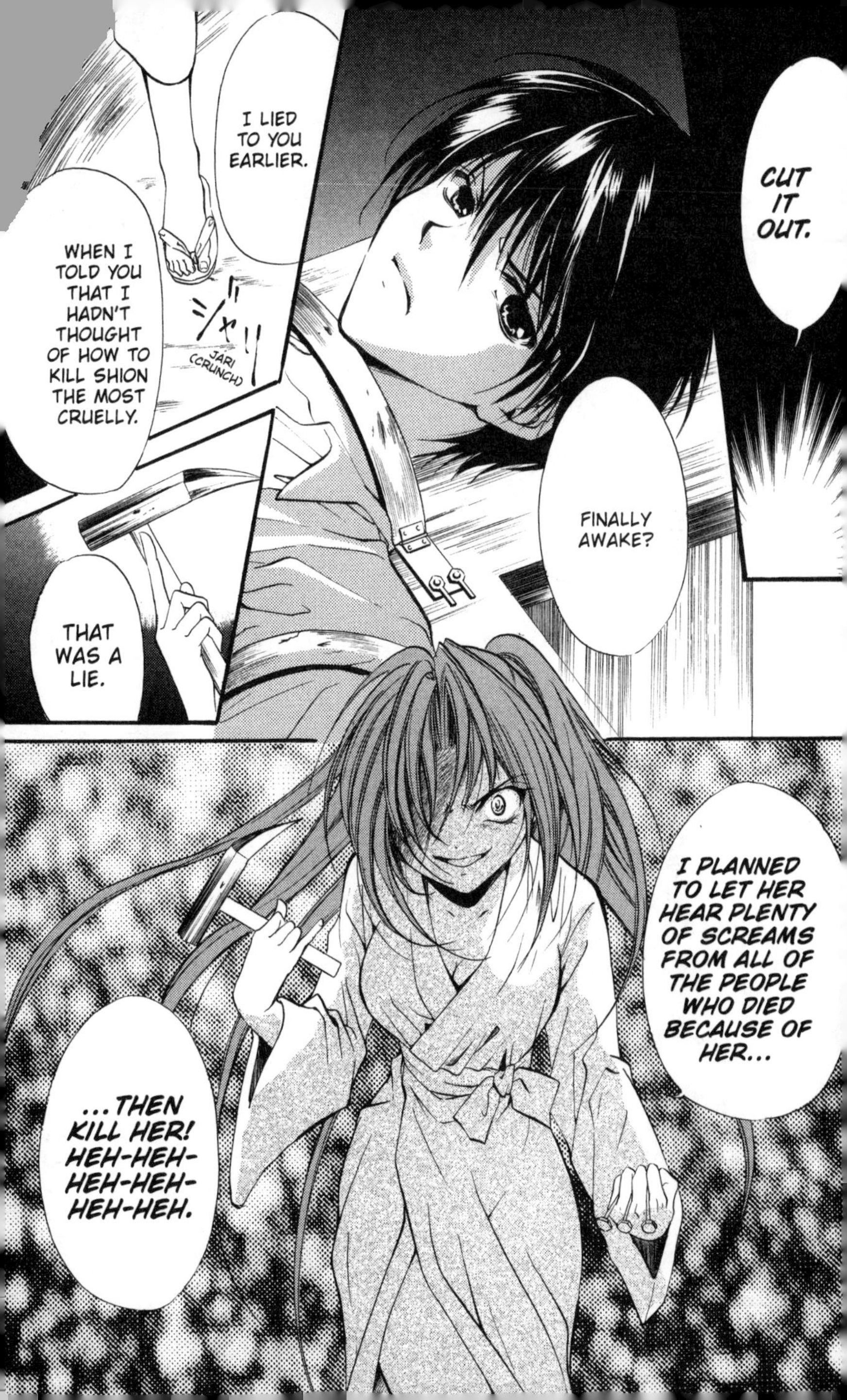
CUT IT OUT.
FINALLY AWAKE?
I LIED TO YOU EARLIER.
WHEN I TOLD YOU THAT I HADN'T THOUGHT OF HOW TO KILL SHION THE MOST CRUELLY.
ジャリ!!
JARI (CRUNCH)
THAT WAS A LIE.
I PLANNED TO LET HER HEAR PLENTY OF SCREAMS FROM ALL OF THE PEOPLE WHO DIED BECAUSE OF HER...
...THEN KILL HER! HEH-HEH-HEH-HEH-HEH-HEH.

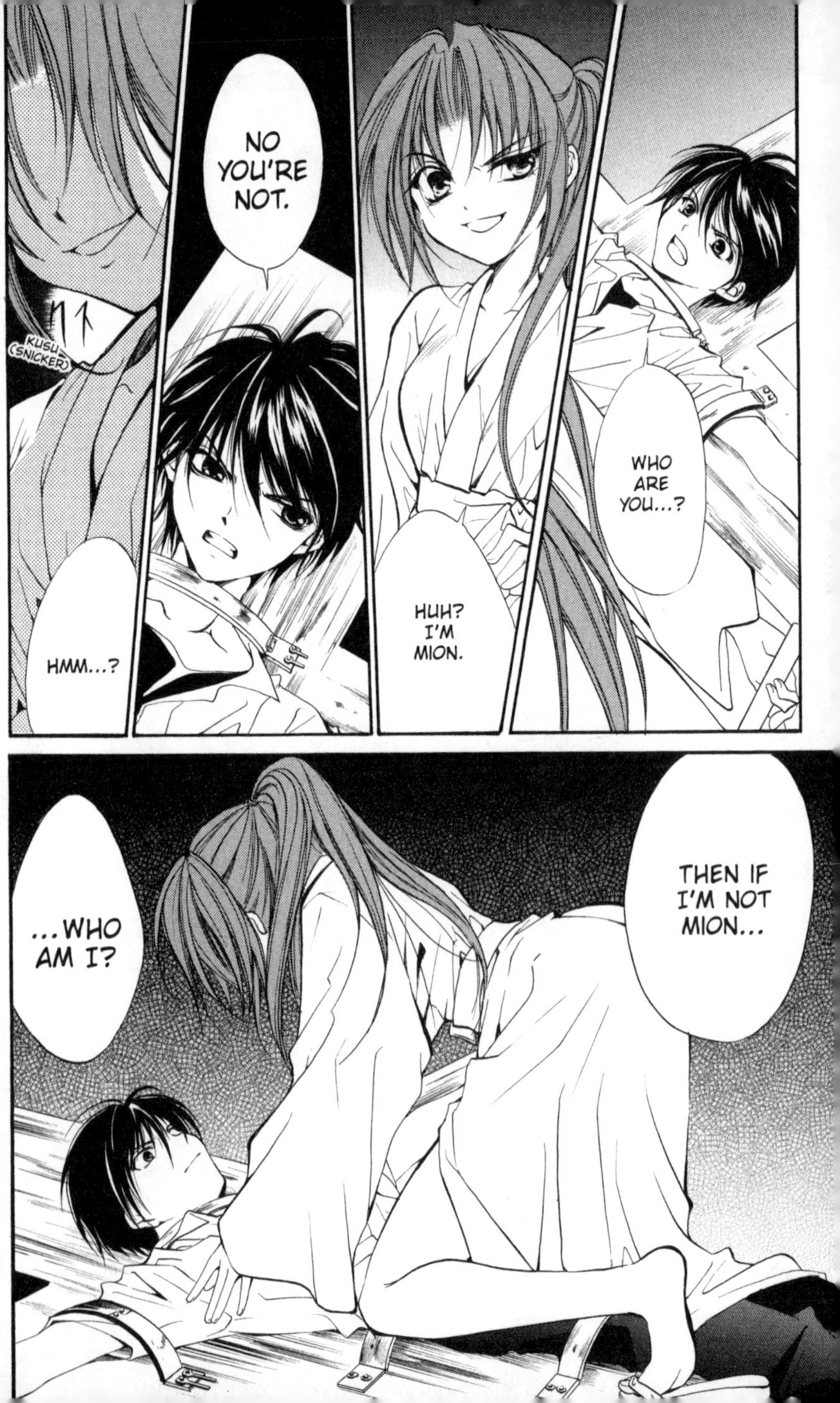
WHO ARE YOU...?
HUH? I'M MION.
NO YOU'RE NOT.
KUSU (SNICKER)
HMM...?
THEN IF I'M NOT MION...
...WHO AM I?

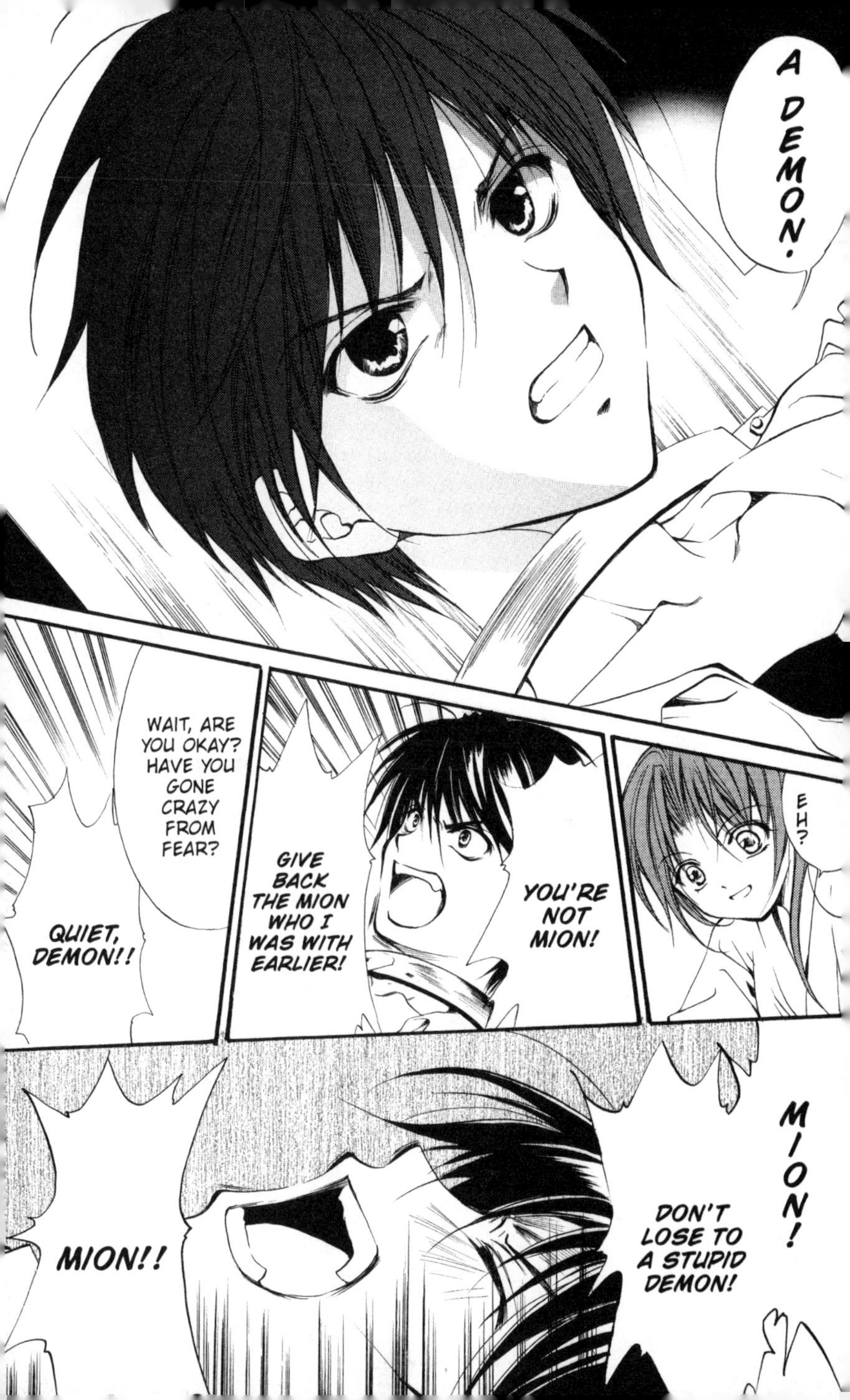
A DEMON!
EH?
YOU'RE NOT MION!
GIVE BACK THE MION WHO I WAS WITH EARLIER!
WAIT, ARE YOU OKAY? HAVE YOU GONE CRAZY FROM FEAR?
QUIET, DEMON!!
MION!
DON'T LOSE TO A STUPID DEMON!
MION!!

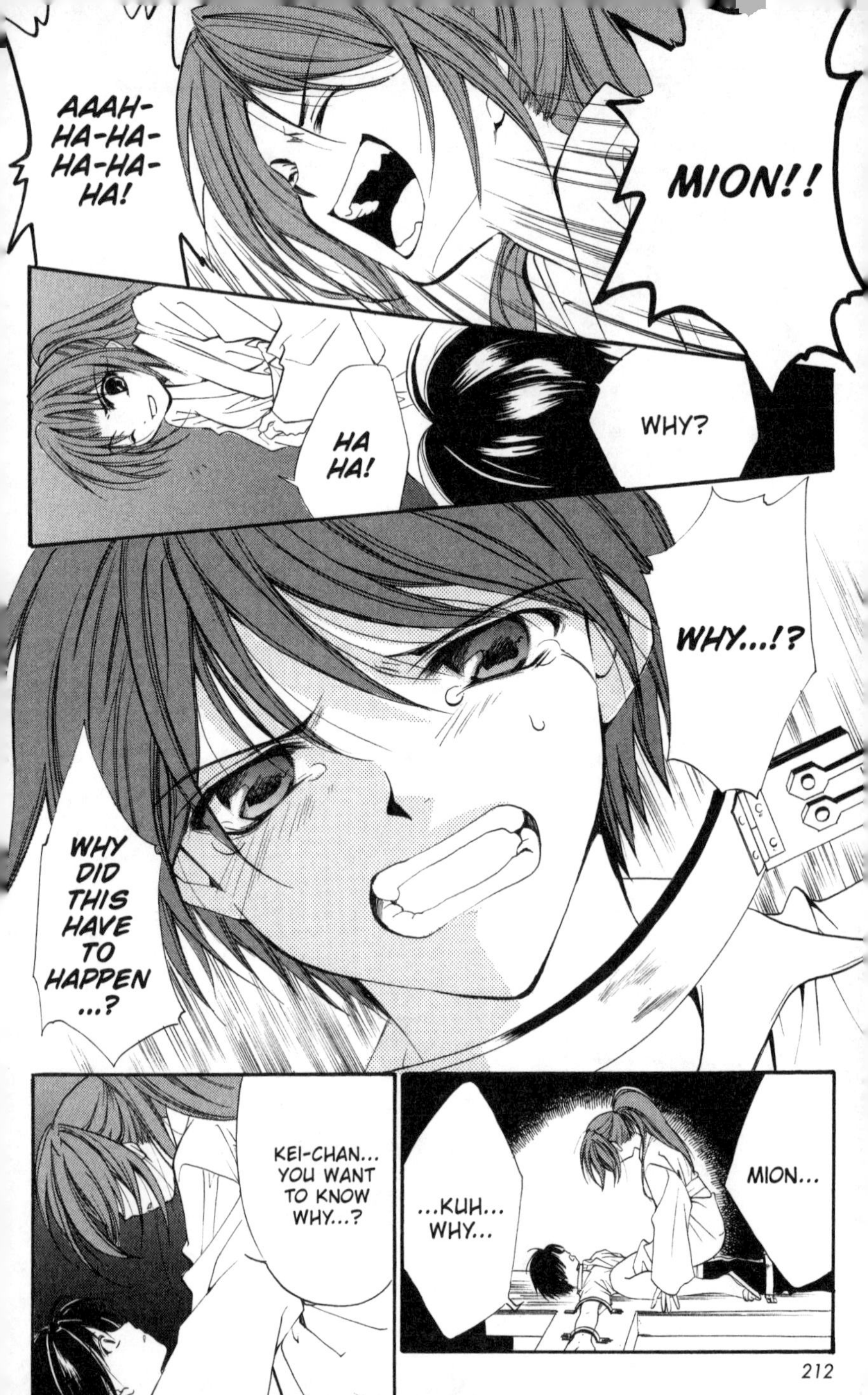
MION!!
AAAH-HA-HA-HA-HA-HA!
WHY?
HA HA!
WHY...!?
WHY DID THIS HAVE TO HAPPEN...?
MION...
...KUH... WHY...
KEI-CHAN... YOU WANT TO KNOW WHY...?

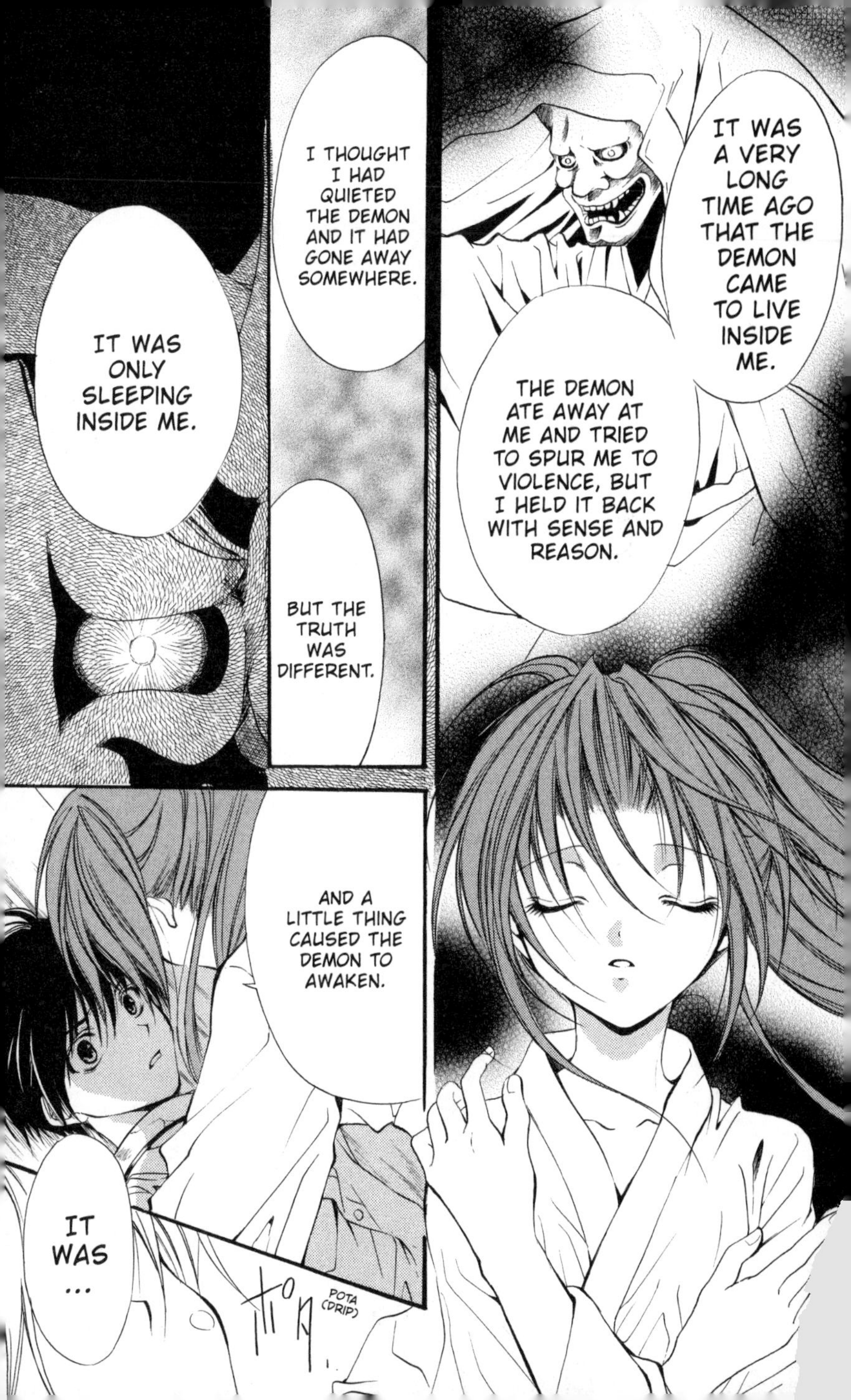
IT WAS A VERY LONG TIME AGO THAT THE DEMON CAME TO LIVE INSIDE ME.
THE DEMON ATE AWAY AT ME AND TRIED TO SPUR ME TO VIOLENCE, BUT I HELD IT BACK WITH SENSE AND REASON.
I THOUGHT I HAD QUIETED THE DEMON AND IT HAD GONE AWAY SOMEWHERE.
BUT THE TRUTH WAS DIFFERENT.
IT WAS ONLY SLEEPING INSIDE ME.
AND A LITTLE THING CAUSED THE DEMON TO AWAKEN.
IT WAS ...
POTA (DRIP)

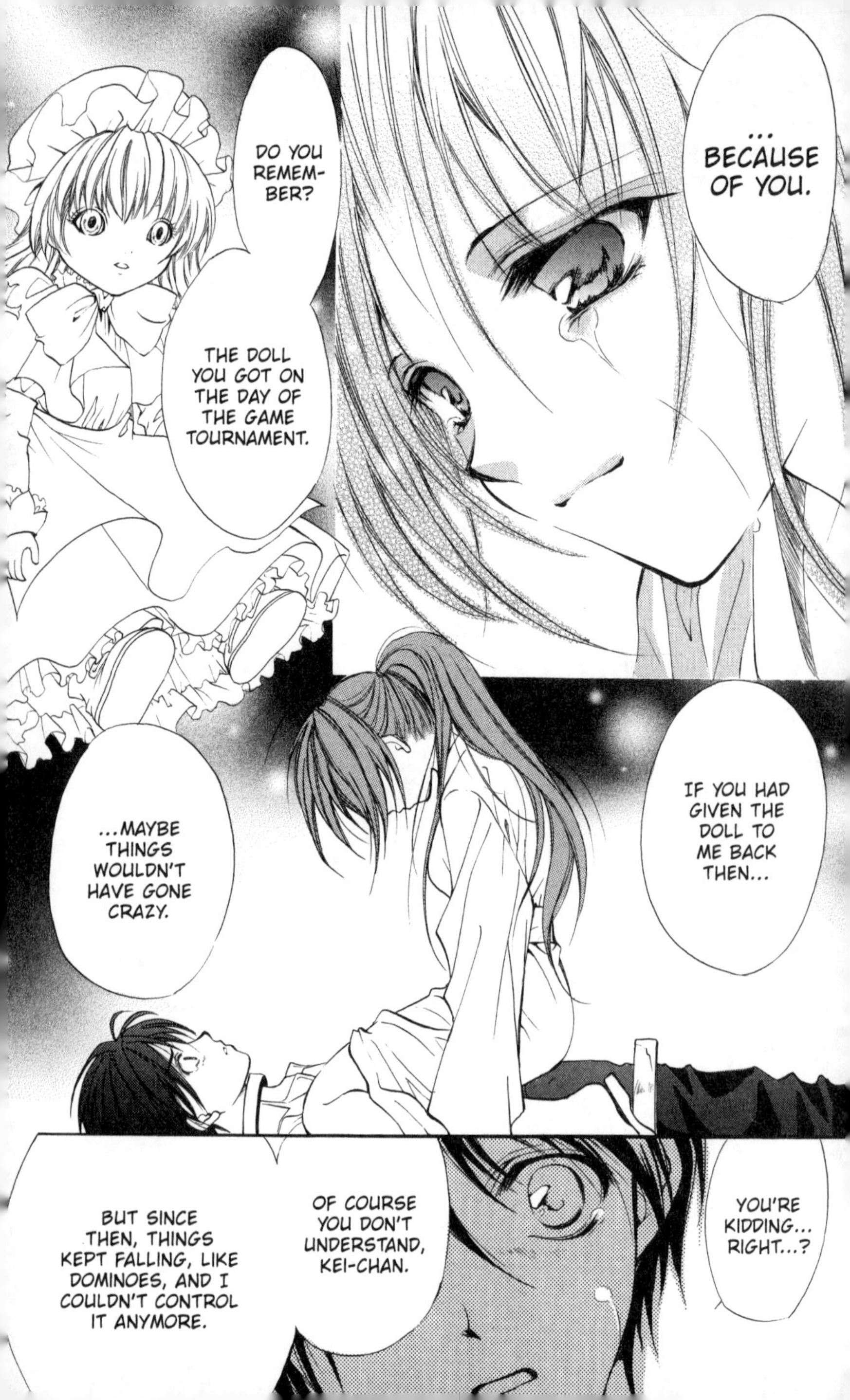
...BECAUSE OF YOU.
DO YOU REMEM-BER?
THE DOLL YOU GOT ON THE DAY OF THE GAME TOURNAMENT.
IF YOU HAD GIVEN THE DOLL TO ME BACK THEN...
...MAYBE THINGS WOULDN'T HAVE GONE CRAZY.
YOU'RE KIDDING... RIGHT...?
OF COURSE YOU DON'T UNDERSTAND, KEI-CHAN.
BUT SINCE THEN, THINGS KEPT FALLING, LIKE DOMINOES, AND I COULDN'T CONTROL IT ANYMORE.

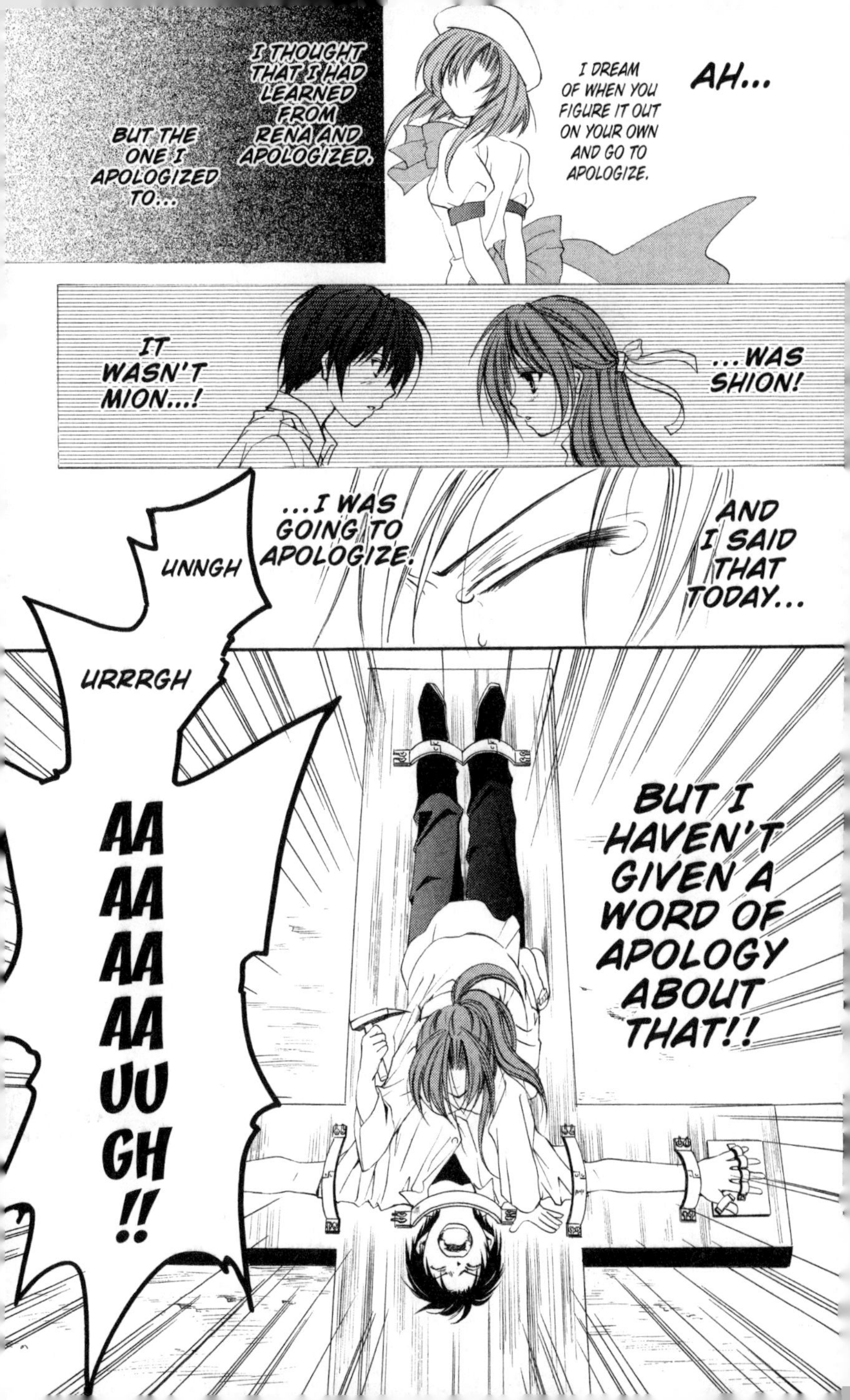
AH...
I DREAM OF WHEN YOU FIGURE IT OUT ON YOUR OWN AND GO TO APOLOGIZE.
I THOUGHT THAT I HAD LEARNED FROM RENA AND APOLOGIZED.
BUT THE ONE I APOLOGIZED TO...
...WAS SHION!
IT WASN'T MION...!
AND I SAID THAT TODAY...
...I WAS GOING TO APOLOGIZE.
UNNGH
BUT I HAVEN'T GIVEN A WORD OF APOLOGY ABOUT THAT!!
URRRGH
AAAAAAAAUUGH!!

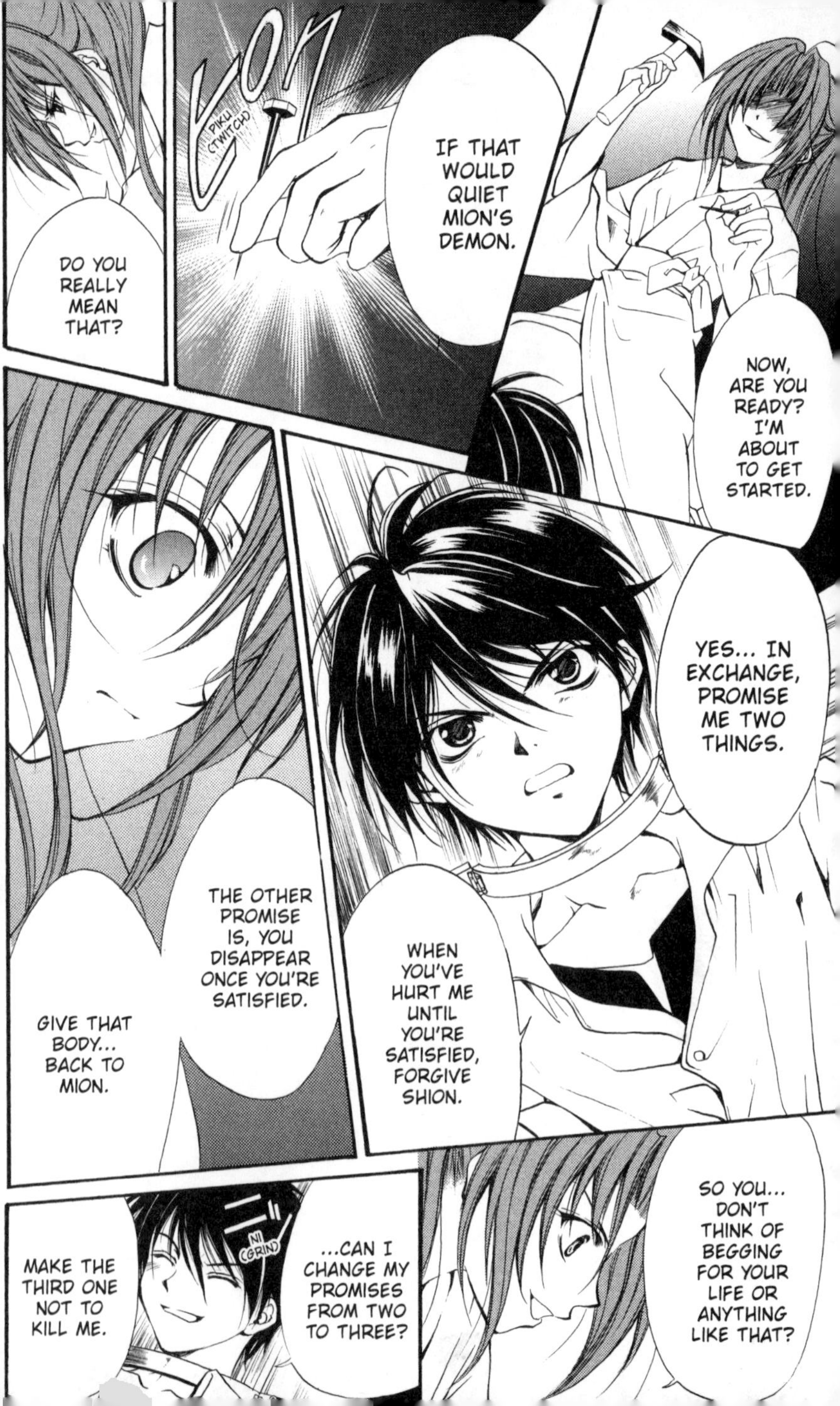
NOW, ARE YOU READY? I'M ABOUT TO GET STARTED.
IF THAT WOULD QUIET MION'S DEMON.
PIKU (TWITCH)
DO YOU REALLY MEAN THAT?
YES... IN EXCHANGE, PROMISE ME TWO THINGS.
WHEN YOU'VE HURT ME UNTIL YOU'RE SATISFIED, FORGIVE SHION.
THE OTHER PROMISE IS, YOU DISAPPEAR ONCE YOU'RE SATISFIED.
GIVE THAT BODY... BACK TO MION.
SO YOU... DON'T THINK OF BEGGING FOR YOUR LIFE OR ANYTHING LIKE THAT?
...CAN I CHANGE MY PROMISES FROM TWO TO THREE?
NI (GRIN)
MAKE THE THIRD ONE NOT TO KILL ME.

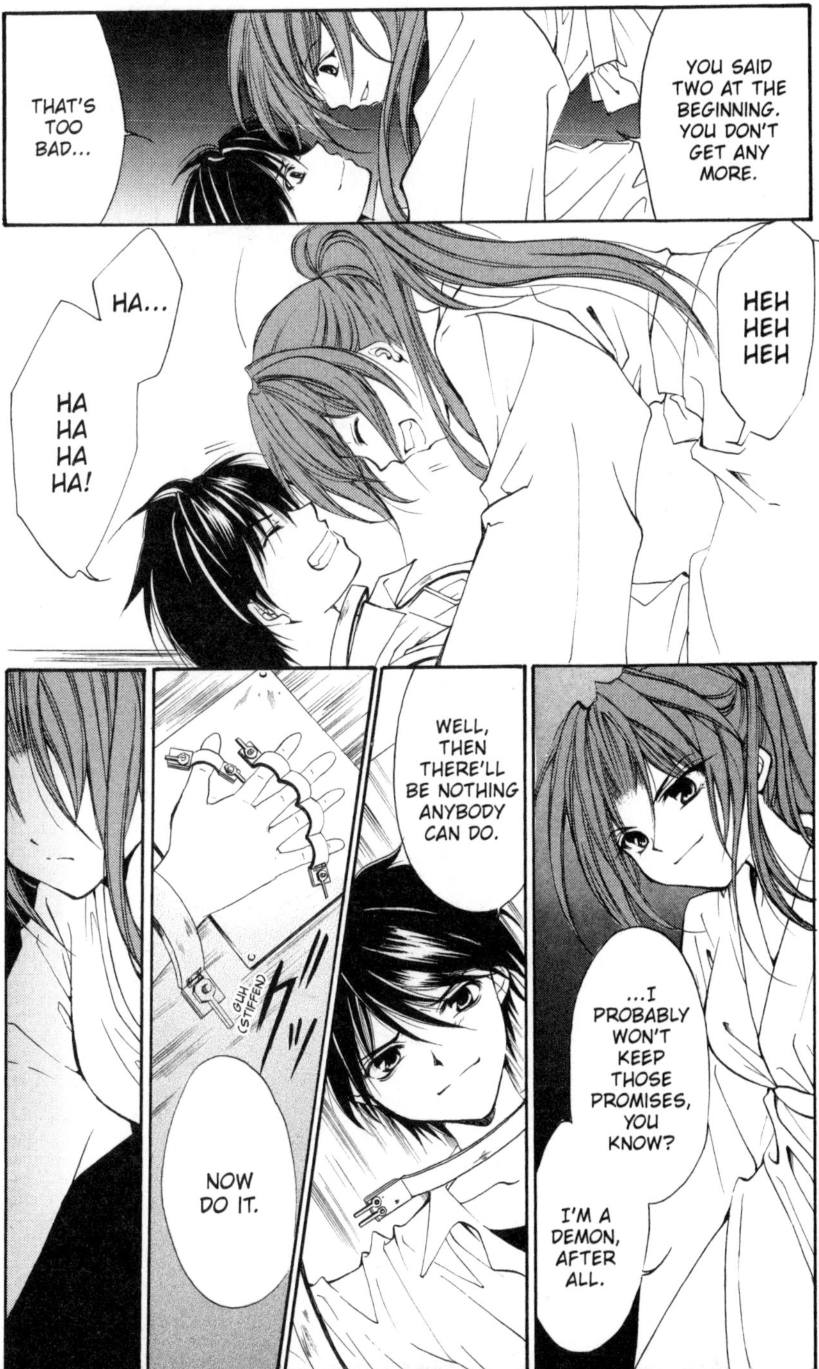
YOU SAID TWO AT THE BEGINNING. YOU DON'T GET ANY MORE.
THAT'S TOO BAD...
HEH HEH HEH
HA...
HA HA HA HA!
...I PROBABLY WON'T KEEP THOSE PROMISES, YOU KNOW?
I'M A DEMON, AFTER ALL.
WELL, THEN THERE'LL BE NOTHING ANYBODY CAN DO.
GUH (STIFFEN)
NOW DO IT.

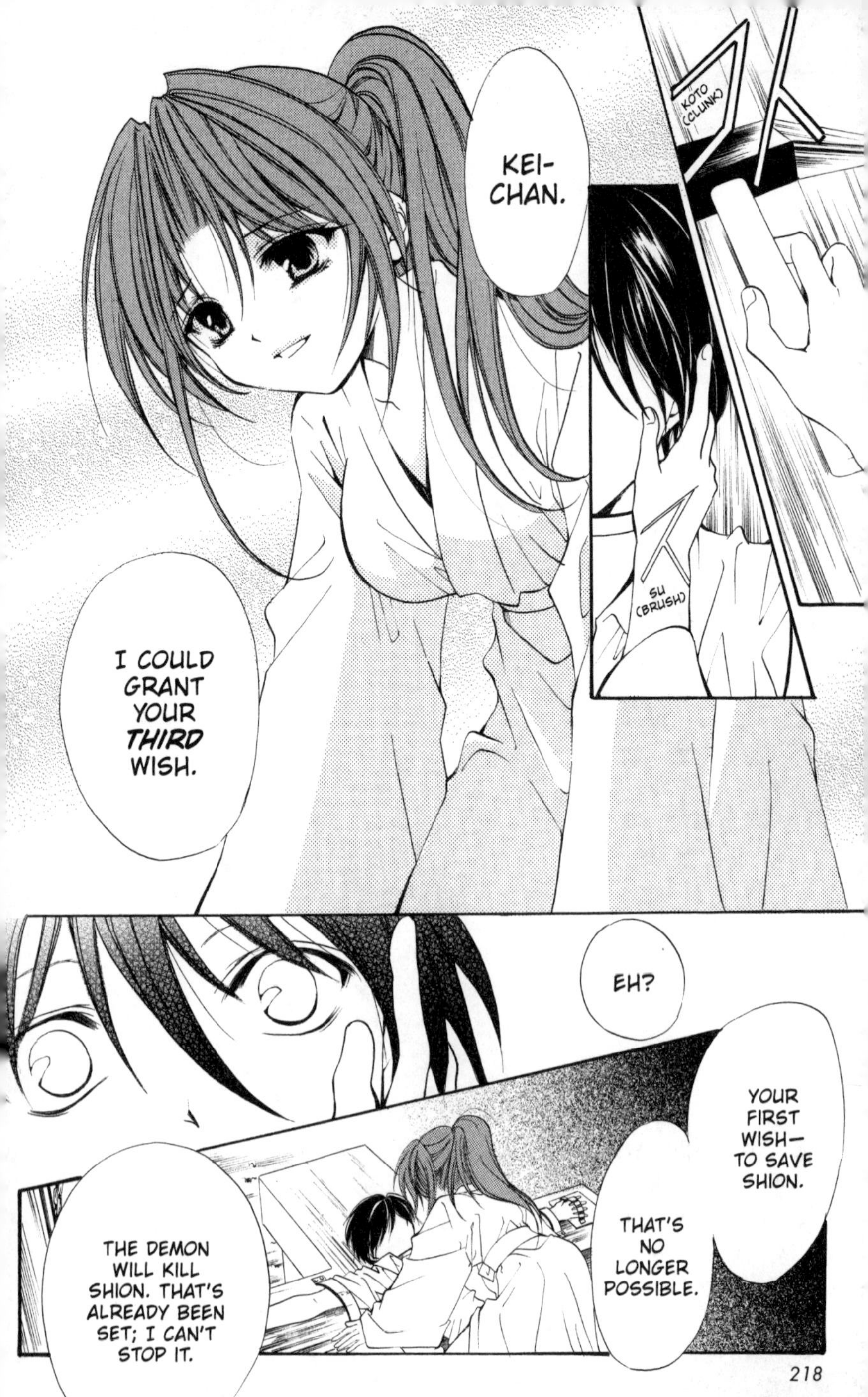
KOTO (CLUNK)
SU (BRUSH)
KEI-CHAN.
I COULD GRANT YOUR *THIRD* WISH.
EH?
YOUR FIRST WISH— TO SAVE SHION.
THAT'S NO LONGER POSSIBLE.
THE DEMON WILL KILL SHION. THAT'S ALREADY BEEN SET; I CAN'T STOP IT.

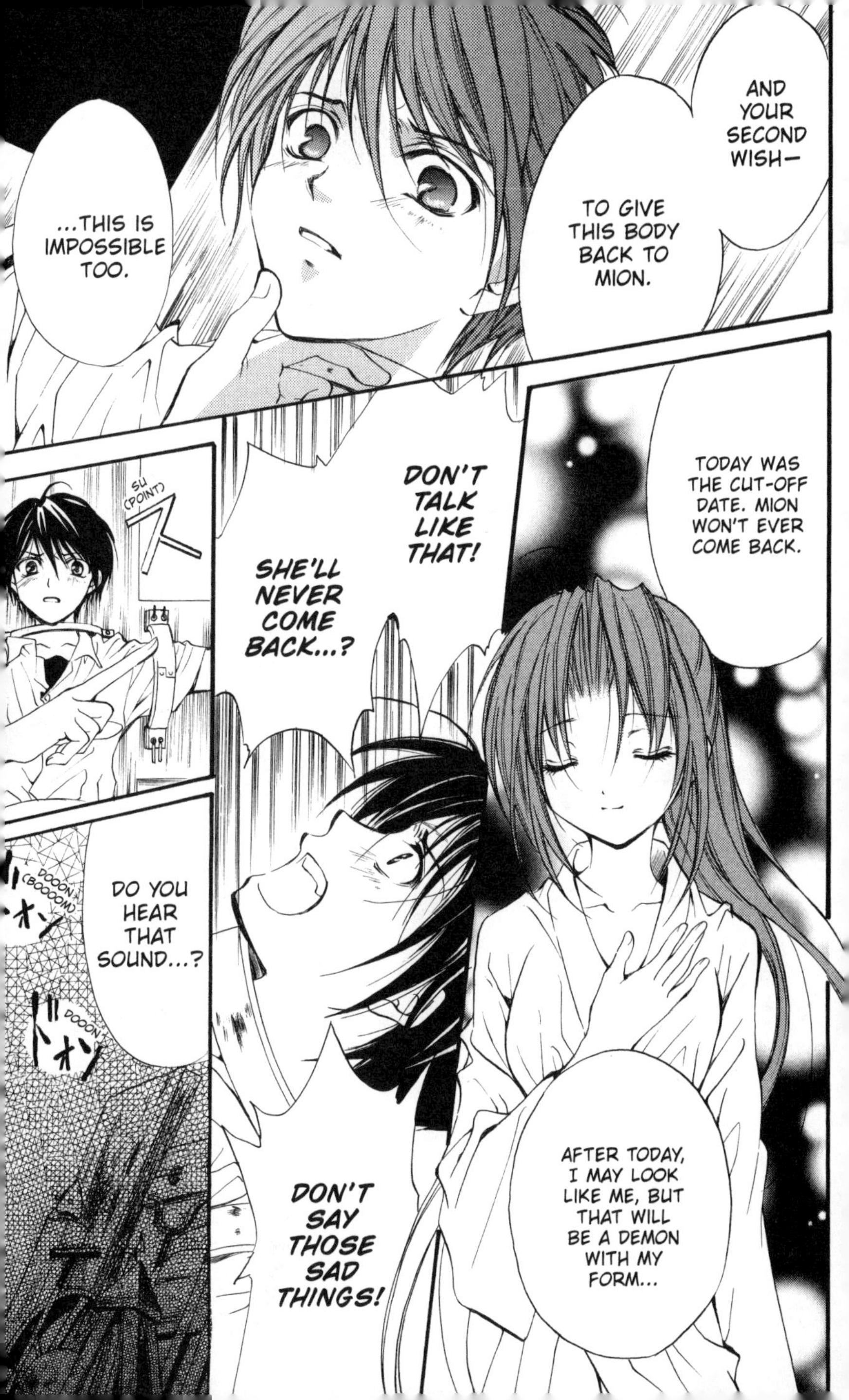
AND YOUR SECOND WISH—
TO GIVE THIS BODY BACK TO MION.
...THIS IS IMPOSSIBLE TOO.
TODAY WAS THE CUT-OFF DATE. MION WON'T EVER COME BACK.
DON'T TALK LIKE THAT!
SHE'LL NEVER COME BACK...?
AFTER TODAY, I MAY LOOK LIKE ME, BUT THAT WILL BE A DEMON WITH MY FORM...
DON'T SAY THOSE SAD THINGS!
SU (POINT)
DOOON (BOOOOM)
DO YOU HEAR THAT SOUND...?
DOOON

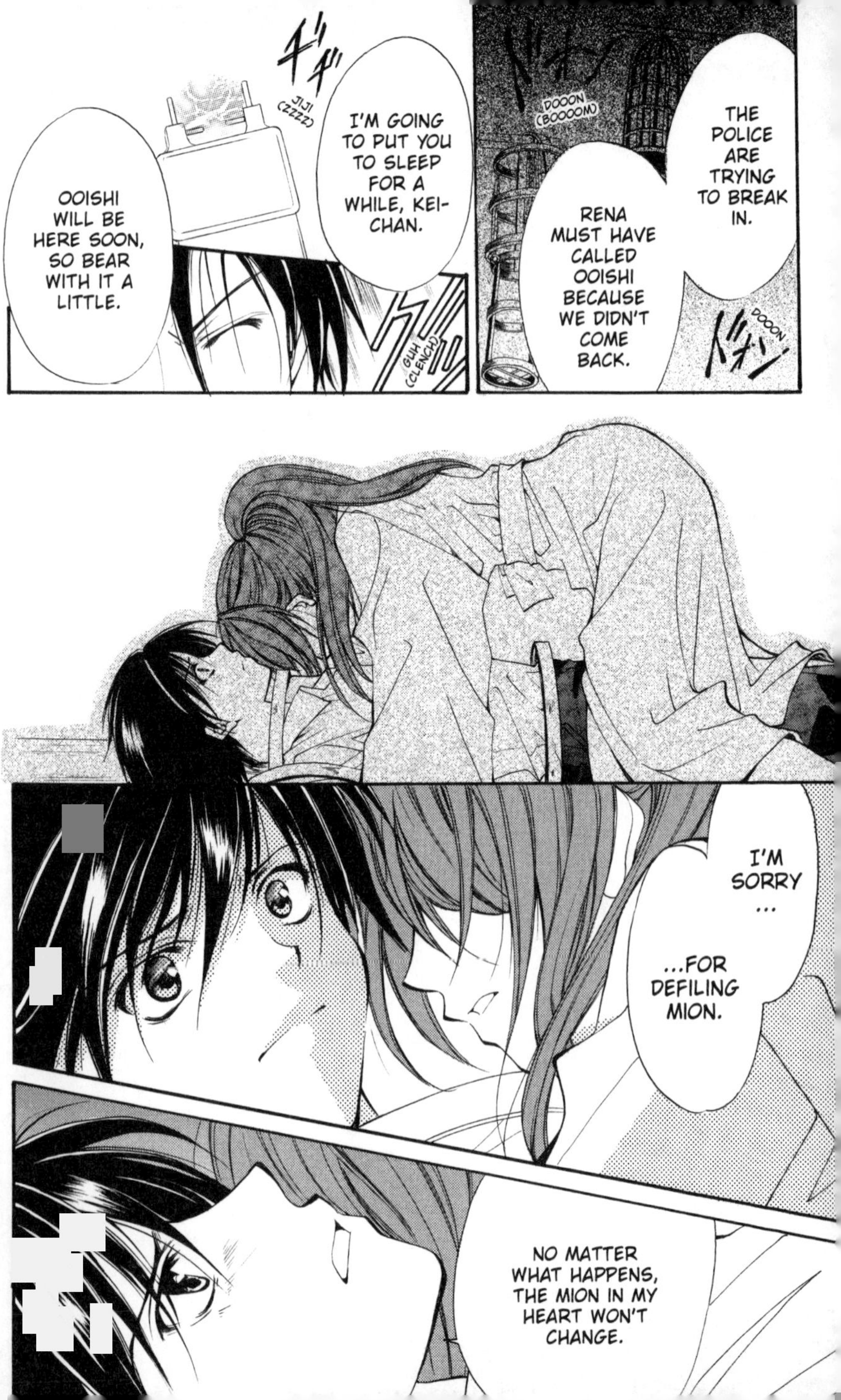
THE POLICE ARE TRYING TO BREAK IN.
DOOON (BOOOOM)
RENA MUST HAVE CALLED OOISHI BECAUSE WE DIDN'T COME BACK.
DOOON
JIJI (ZZZZ)
I'M GOING TO PUT YOU TO SLEEP FOR A WHILE, KEI-CHAN.
OOISHI WILL BE HERE SOON, SO BEAR WITH IT A LITTLE.
GUH (CLENCH)
I'M SORRY ...
...FOR DEFILING MION.
NO MATTER WHAT HAPPENS, THE MION IN MY HEART WON'T CHANGE.

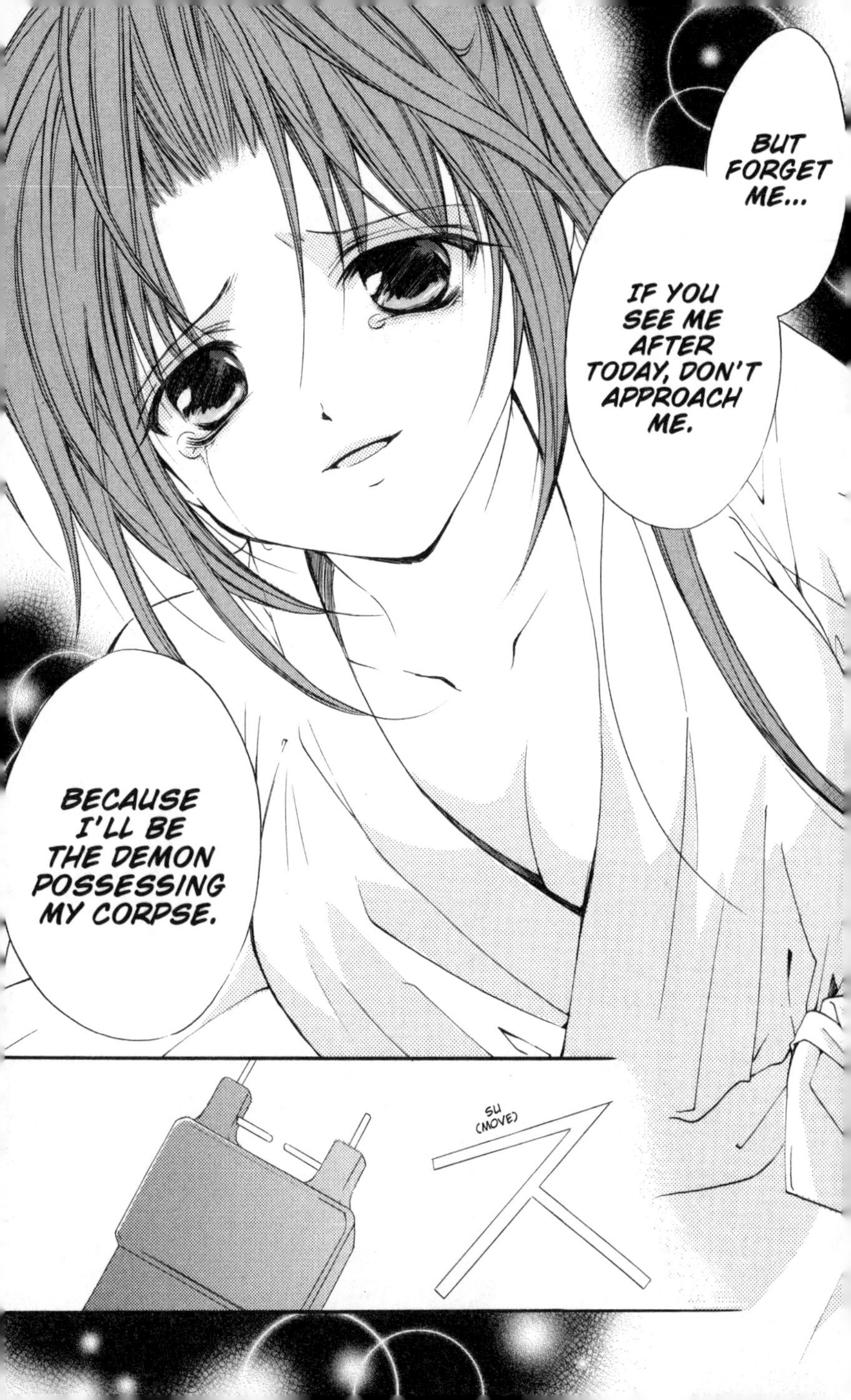
BUT FORGET ME...
IF YOU SEE ME AFTER TODAY, DON'T APPROACH ME.
BECAUSE I'LL BE THE DEMON POSSESSING MY CORPSE.
SU (MOVE)

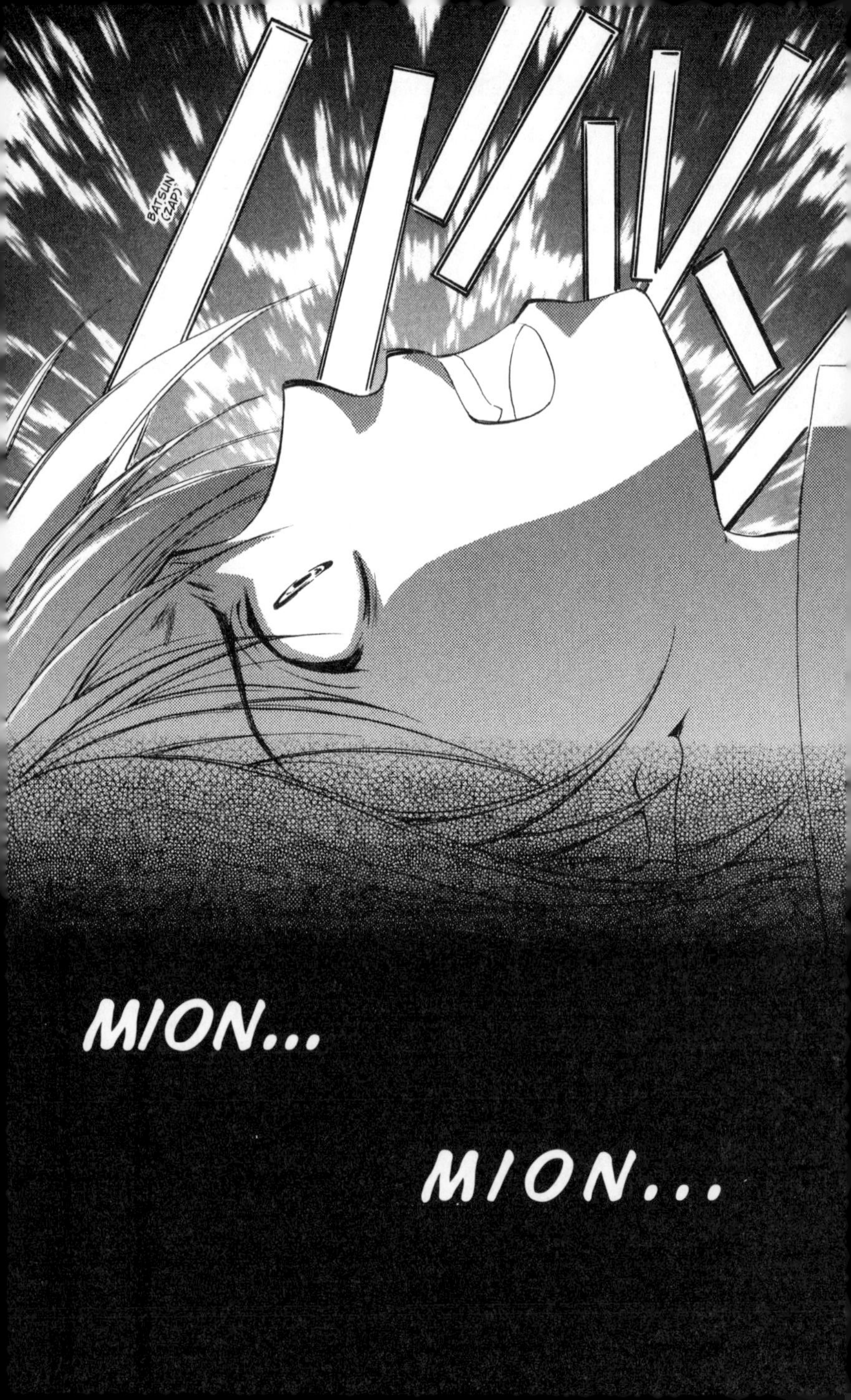
BATSLIN (ZAP)
MION...
MION...

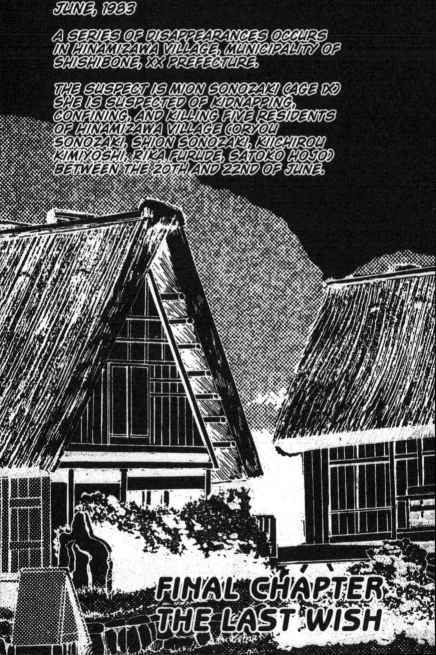

JUNE, 1983

A SERIES OF DISAPPEARANCES OCCURS IN HINAMIZAWA VILLAGE, MUNICIPALITY OF SHISHIBONE, XX PREFECTURE.

THE SUSPECT IS MION SONOZAKI (AGE 1X) SHE IS SUSPECTED OF KIDNAPPING, CONFINING, AND KILLING FIVE RESIDENTS OF HINAMIZAWA VILLAGE (ORYOU SONOZAKI, SHION SONOZAKI, KIICHIROU KIMIYOSHI, RIKA FURUDE, SATOKO HOJO) BETWEEN THE 20TH AND 22ND OF JUNE.

FINAL CHAPTER
THE LAST WISH

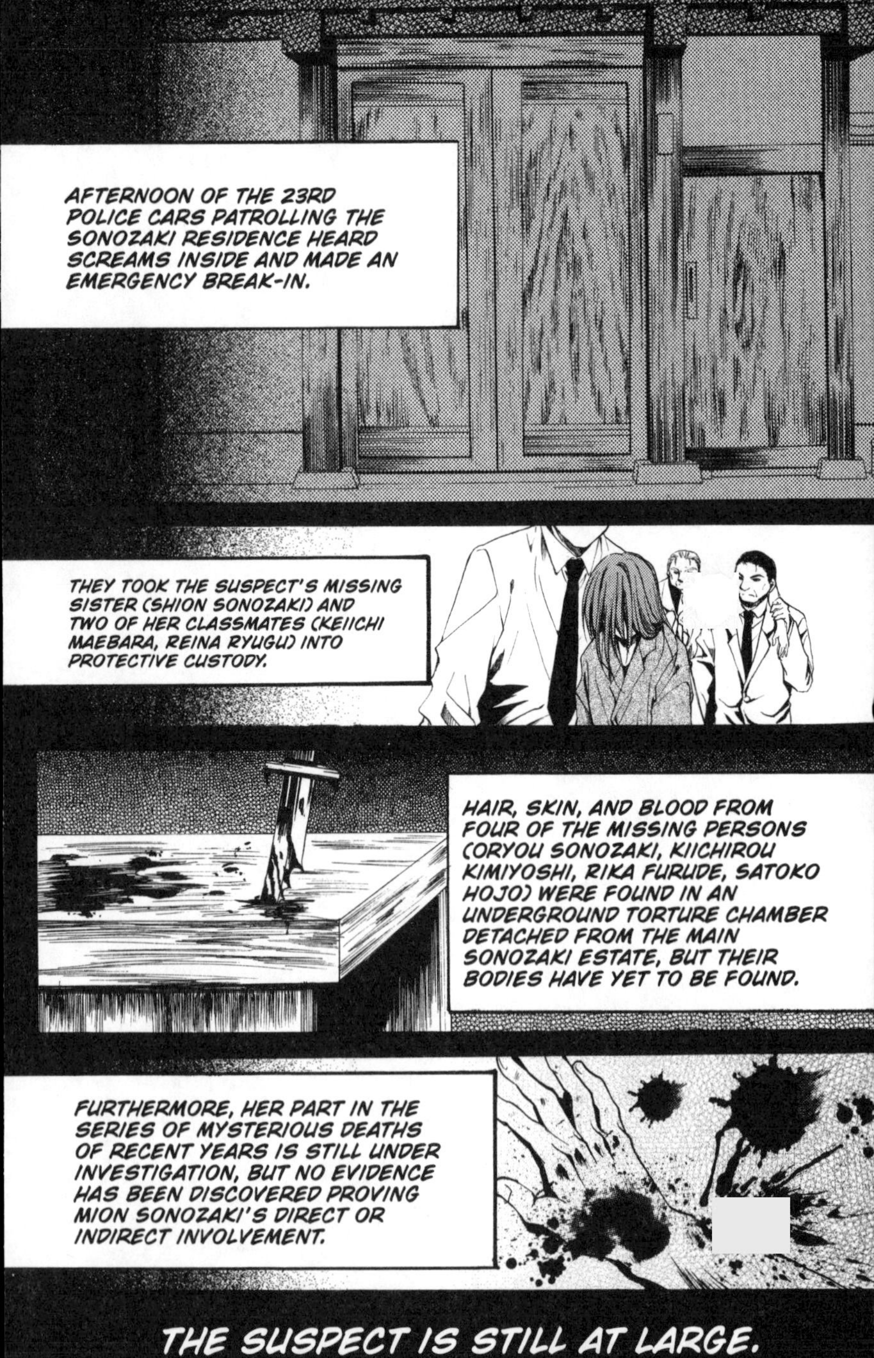
AFTERNOON OF THE 23RD POLICE CARS PATROLLING THE SONOZAKI RESIDENCE HEARD SCREAMS INSIDE AND MADE AN EMERGENCY BREAK-IN.
THEY TOOK THE SUSPECT'S MISSING SISTER (SHION SONOZAKI) AND TWO OF HER CLASSMATES (KEIICHI MAEBARA, REINA RYUGU) INTO PROTECTIVE CUSTODY.
HAIR, SKIN, AND BLOOD FROM FOUR OF THE MISSING PERSONS (ORYOU SONOZAKI, KIICHIROU KIMIYOSHI, RIKA FURUDE, SATOKO HOJO) WERE FOUND IN AN UNDERGROUND TORTURE CHAMBER DETACHED FROM THE MAIN SONOZAKI ESTATE, BUT THEIR BODIES HAVE YET TO BE FOUND.
FURTHERMORE, HER PART IN THE SERIES OF MYSTERIOUS DEATHS OF RECENT YEARS IS STILL UNDER INVESTIGATION, BUT NO EVIDENCE HAS BEEN DISCOVERED PROVING MION SONOZAKI'S DIRECT OR INDIRECT INVOLVEMENT.
THE SUSPECT IS STILL AT LARGE.

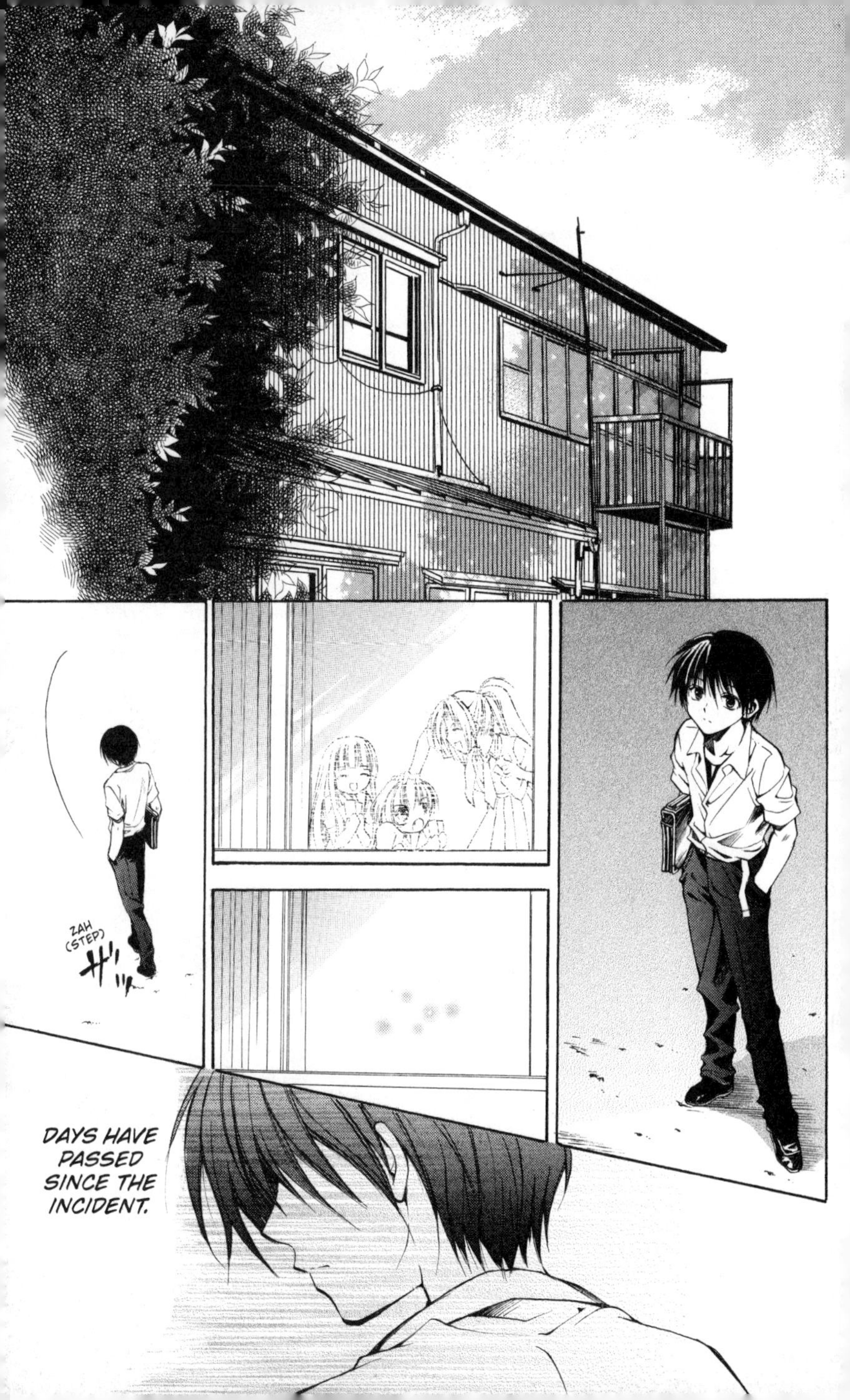
ZAH (STEP)
ザッ
DAYS HAVE PASSED SINCE THE INCIDENT.

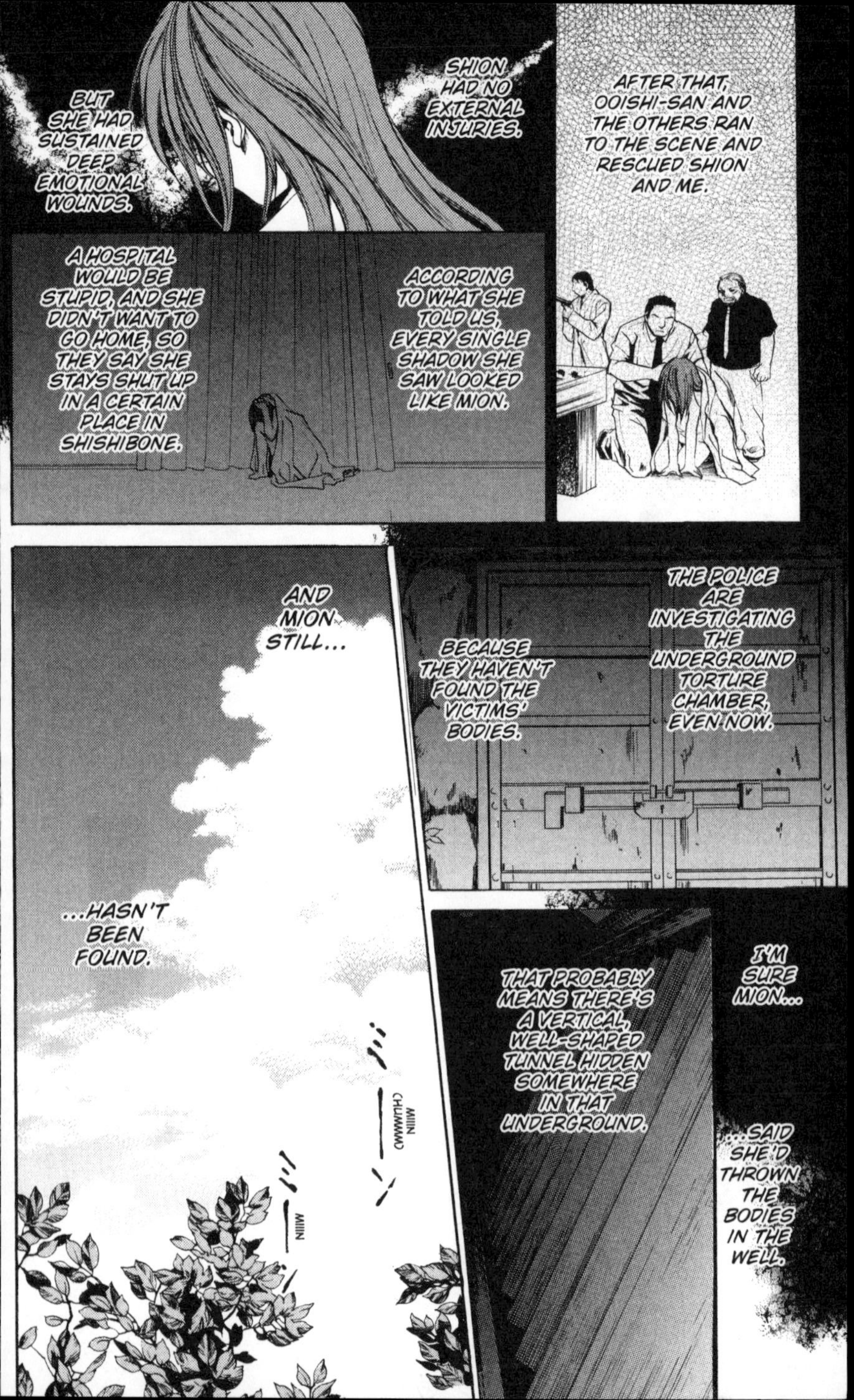
AFTER THAT, OOISHI-SAN AND THE OTHERS RAN TO THE SCENE AND RESCUED SHION AND ME.
SHION HAD NO EXTERNAL INJURIES.
BUT SHE HAD SUSTAINED DEEP EMOTIONAL WOUNDS.
ACCORDING TO WHAT SHE TOLD US, EVERY SINGLE SHADOW SHE SAW LOOKED LIKE MION.
A HOSPITAL WOULD BE STUPID, AND SHE DIDN'T WANT TO GO HOME, SO THEY SAY SHE STAYS SHUT UP IN A CERTAIN PLACE IN SHISHIBONE.
THE POLICE ARE INVESTIGATING THE UNDERGROUND TORTURE CHAMBER, EVEN NOW.
BECAUSE THEY HAVEN'T FOUND THE VICTIMS' BODIES.
I'M SURE MION...
...SAID SHE'D THROWN THE BODIES IN THE WELL.
THAT PROBABLY MEANS THERE'S A VERTICAL, WELL-SHAPED TUNNEL HIDDEN SOMEWHERE IN THAT UNDERGROUND.
AND MION STILL...
...HASN'T BEEN FOUND.
MIIN CHUMMM
MIIN

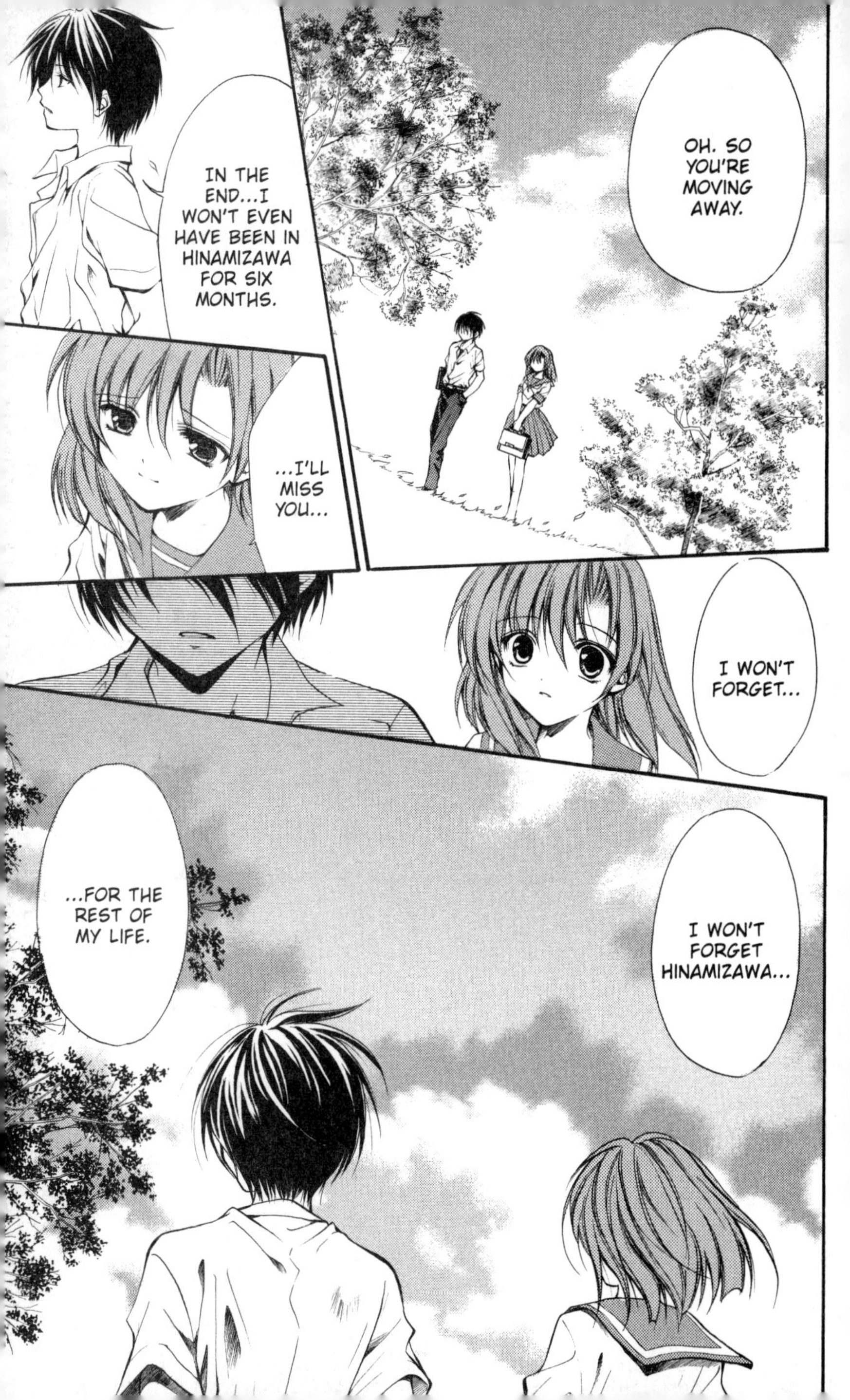
OH. SO YOU'RE MOVING AWAY.
IN THE END...I WON'T EVEN HAVE BEEN IN HINAMIZAWA FOR SIX MONTHS.
...I'LL MISS YOU...
I WON'T FORGET...
I WON'T FORGET HINAMIZAWA...
...FOR THE REST OF MY LIFE.

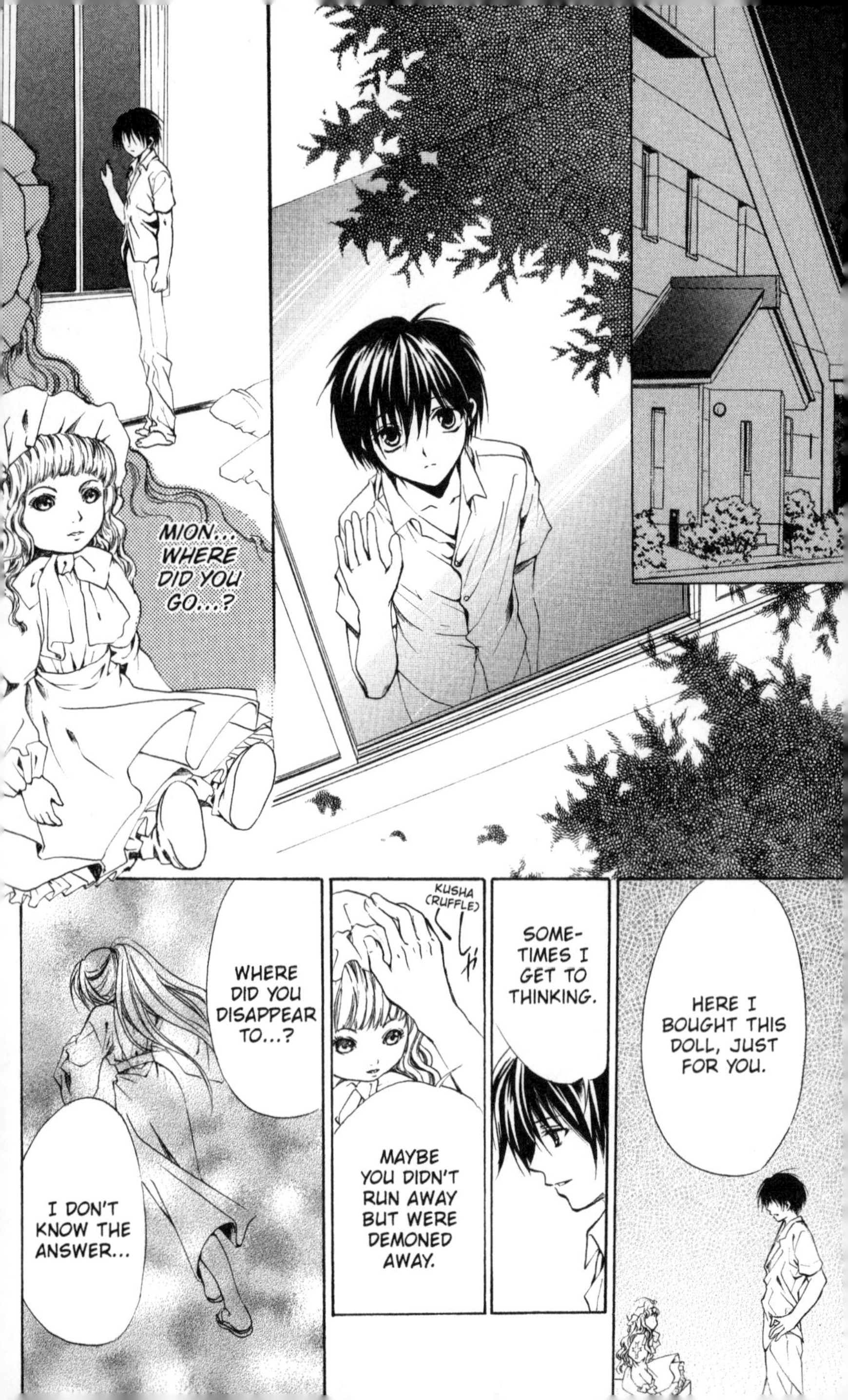
MION... WHERE DID YOU GO...?
HERE I BOUGHT THIS DOLL, JUST FOR YOU.
SOME-TIMES I GET TO THINKING.
KUSHA (RUFFLE)
MAYBE YOU DIDN'T RUN AWAY BUT WERE DEMONED AWAY.
WHERE DID YOU DISAPPEAR TO...?
I DON'T KNOW THE ANSWER...

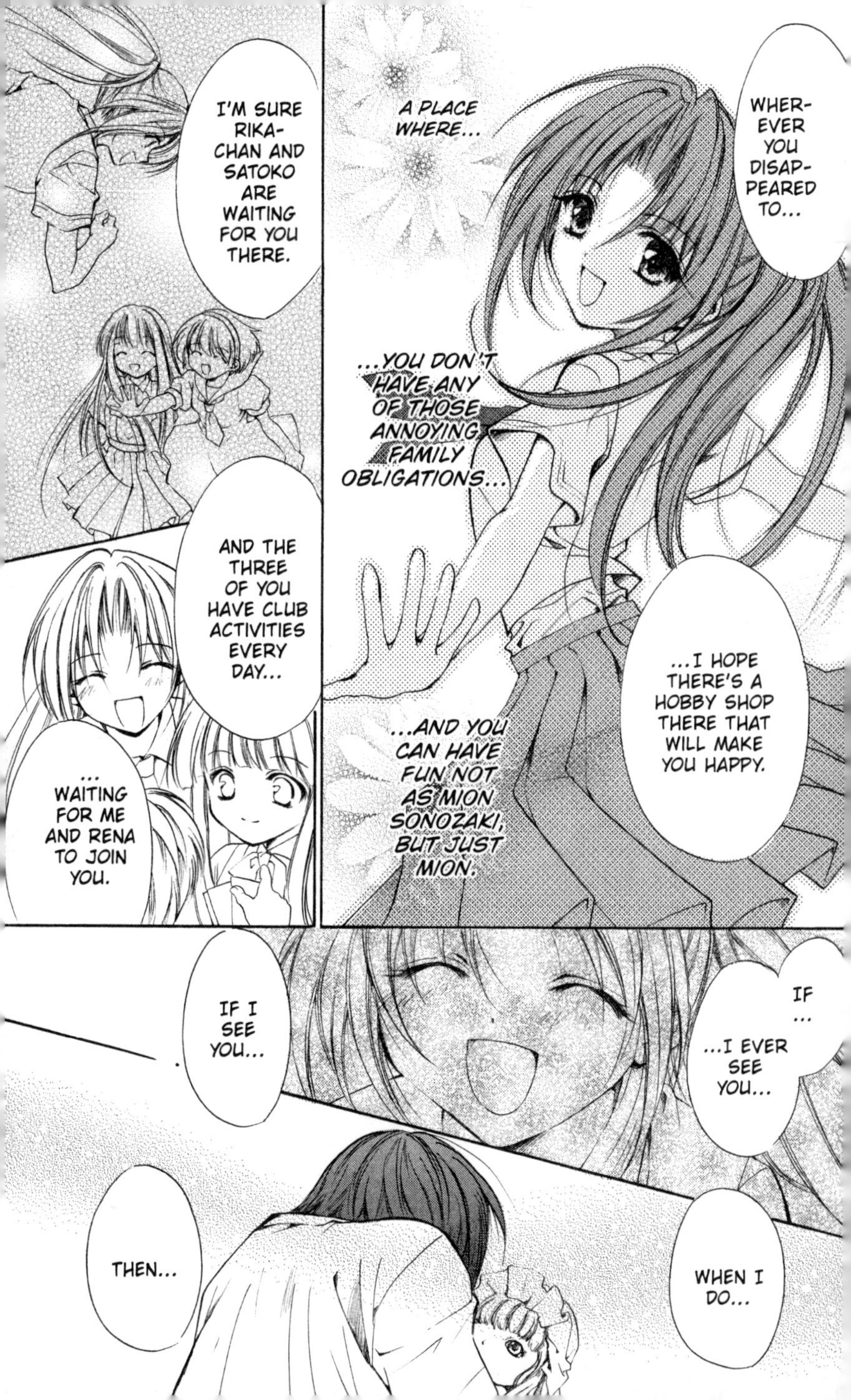
WHER-EVER YOU DISAP-PEARED TO...
A PLACE WHERE...
...YOU DON'T HAVE ANY OF THOSE ANNOYING FAMILY OBLIGATIONS...
...I HOPE THERE'S A HOBBY SHOP THERE THAT WILL MAKE YOU HAPPY.
...AND YOU CAN HAVE FUN NOT AS MION SONOZAKI, BUT JUST MION.
I'M SURE RIKA-CHAN AND SATOKO ARE WAITING FOR YOU THERE.
AND THE THREE OF YOU HAVE CLUB ACTIVITIES EVERY DAY...
...WAITING FOR ME AND RENA TO JOIN YOU.
IF...
...I EVER SEE YOU...
IF I SEE YOU...
WHEN I DO...
THEN...

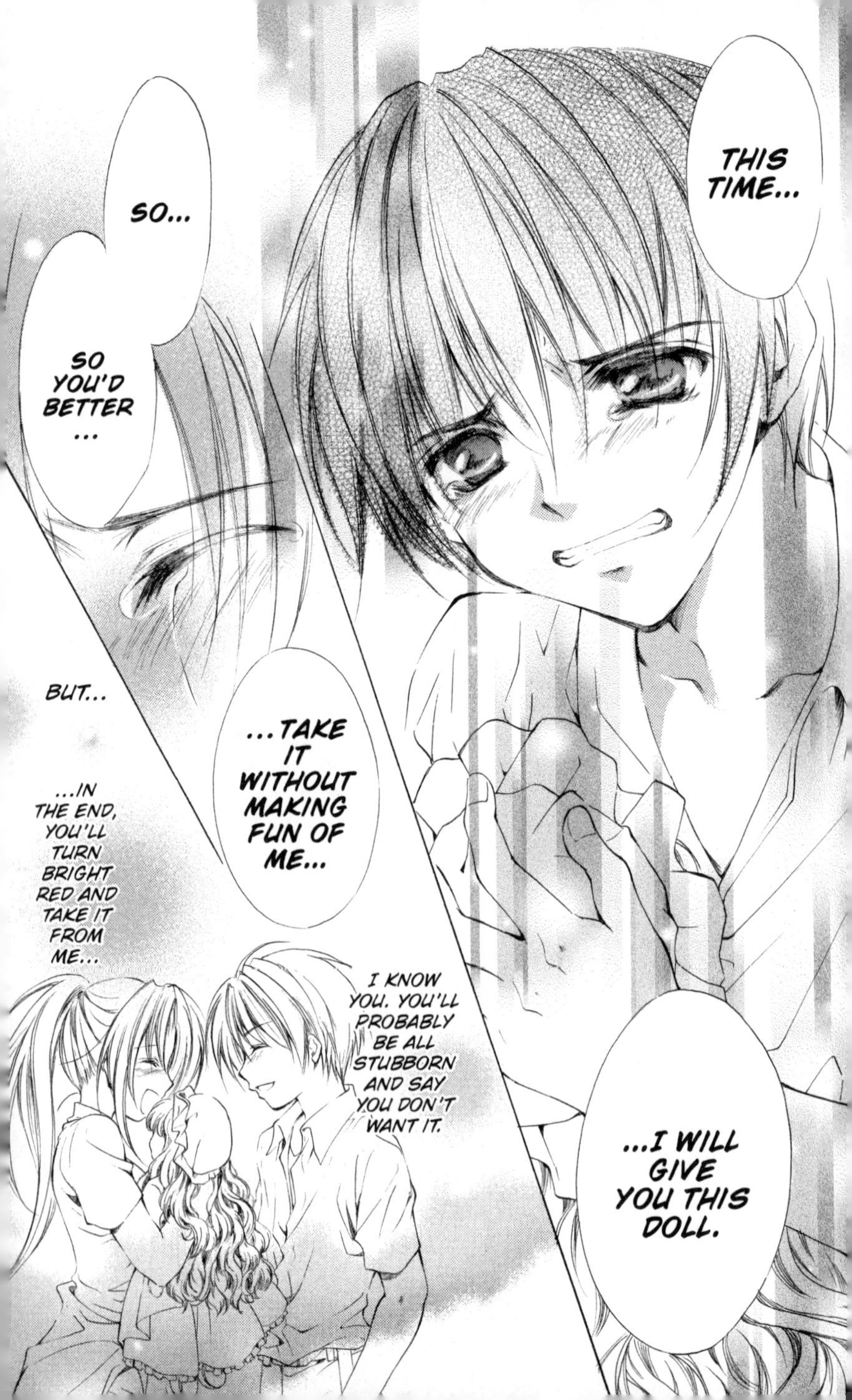
THIS TIME...
...I WILL GIVE YOU THIS DOLL.
SO...
SO YOU'D BETTER ...
...TAKE IT WITHOUT MAKING FUN OF ME...
I KNOW YOU. YOU'LL PROBABLY BE ALL STUBBORN AND SAY YOU DON'T WANT IT.
BUT...
...IN THE END, YOU'LL TURN BRIGHT RED AND TAKE IT FROM ME...

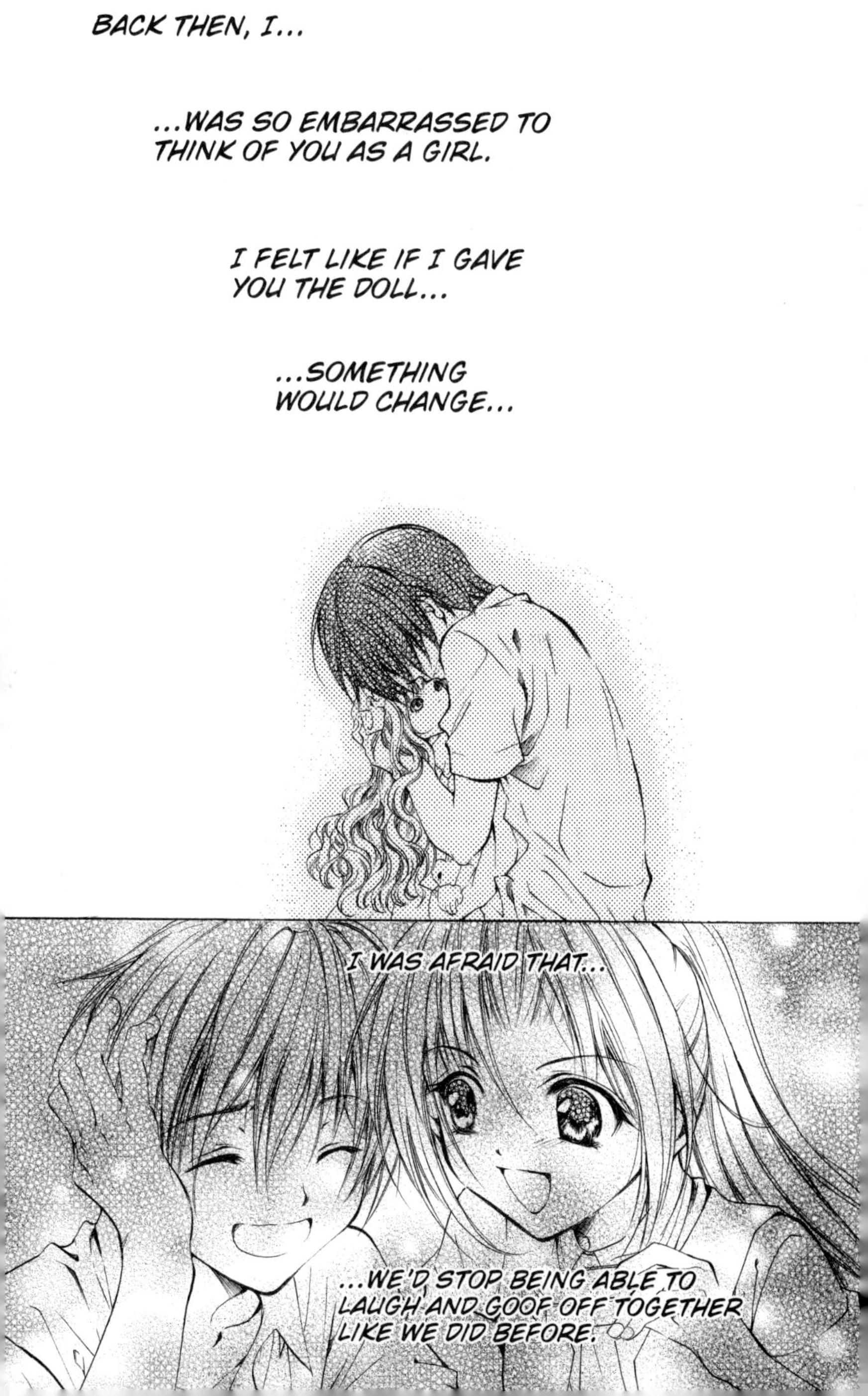
BACK THEN, I...
...WAS SO EMBARRASSED TO THINK OF YOU AS A GIRL.
I FELT LIKE IF I GAVE YOU THE DOLL...
...SOMETHING WOULD CHANGE...
I WAS AFRAID THAT...
...WE'D STOP BEING ABLE TO LAUGH AND GOOF OFF TOGETHER LIKE WE DID BEFORE.

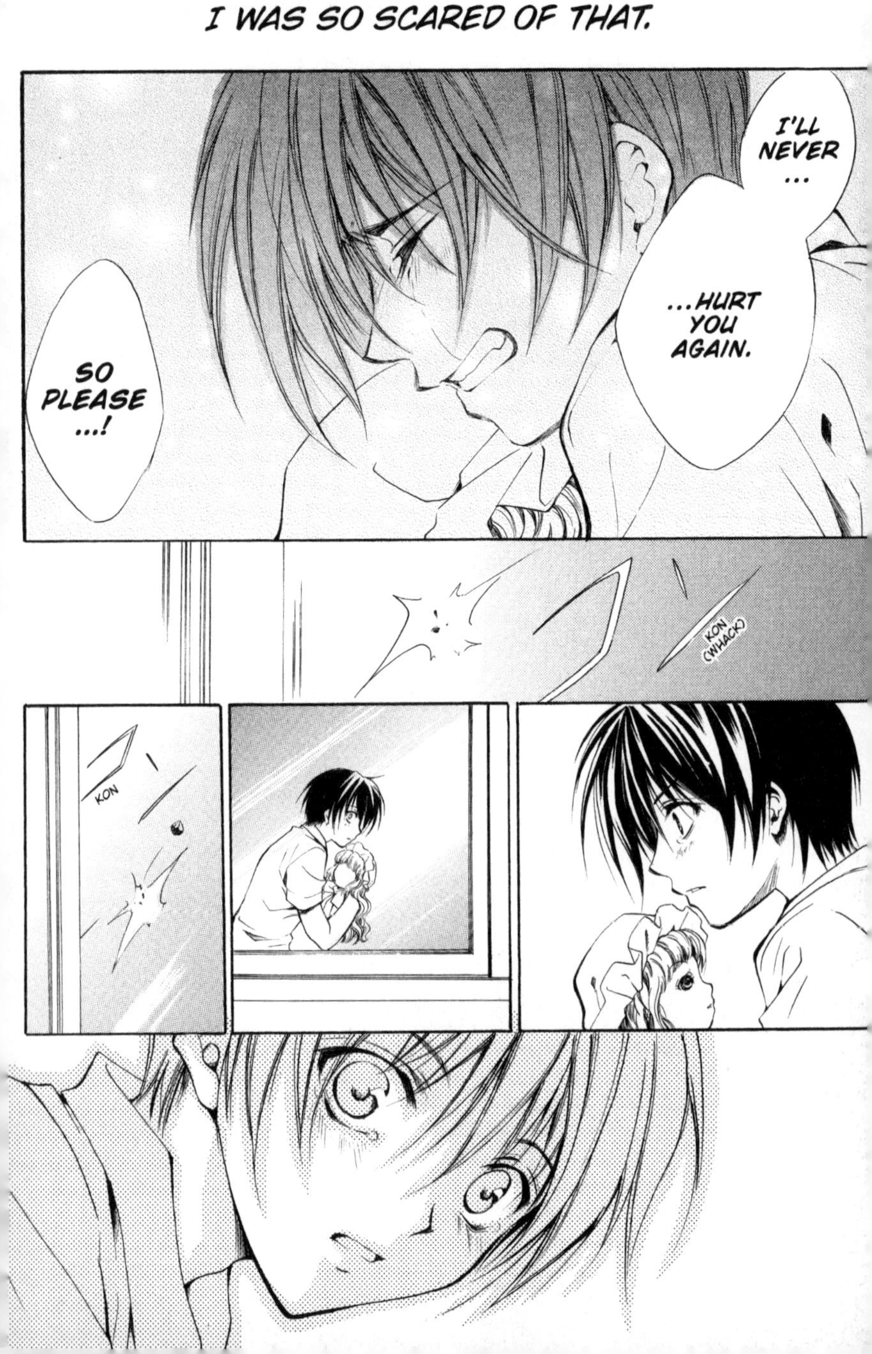
I WAS SO SCARED OF THAT.
I'LL NEVER ...
...HURT YOU AGAIN.
SO PLEASE ...!
KON (WHACK)
KON

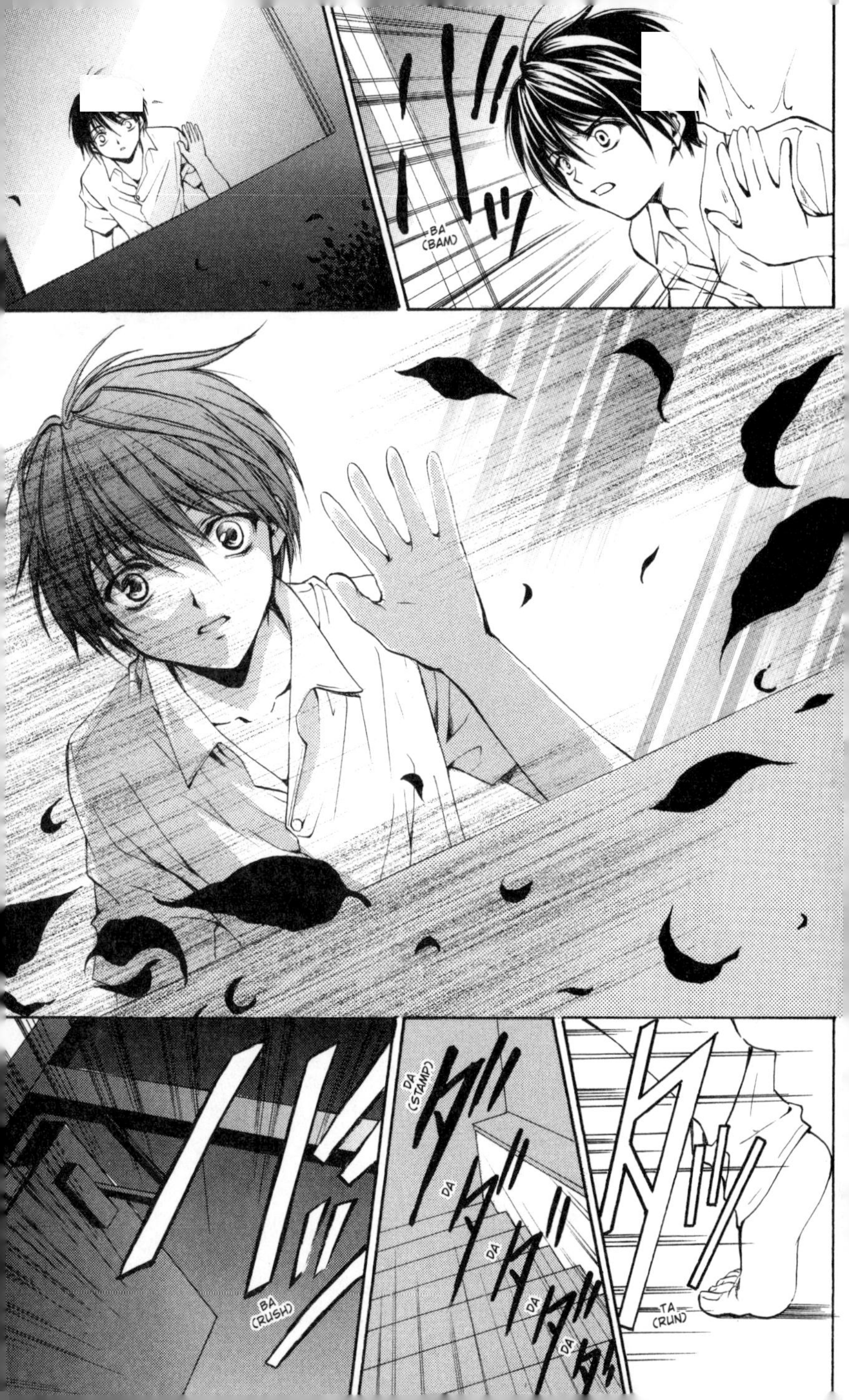
BA
(BAM)
TA
(RUN)
DA
(STAMP)
DA
DA
DA
DA
BA
(RUSH)

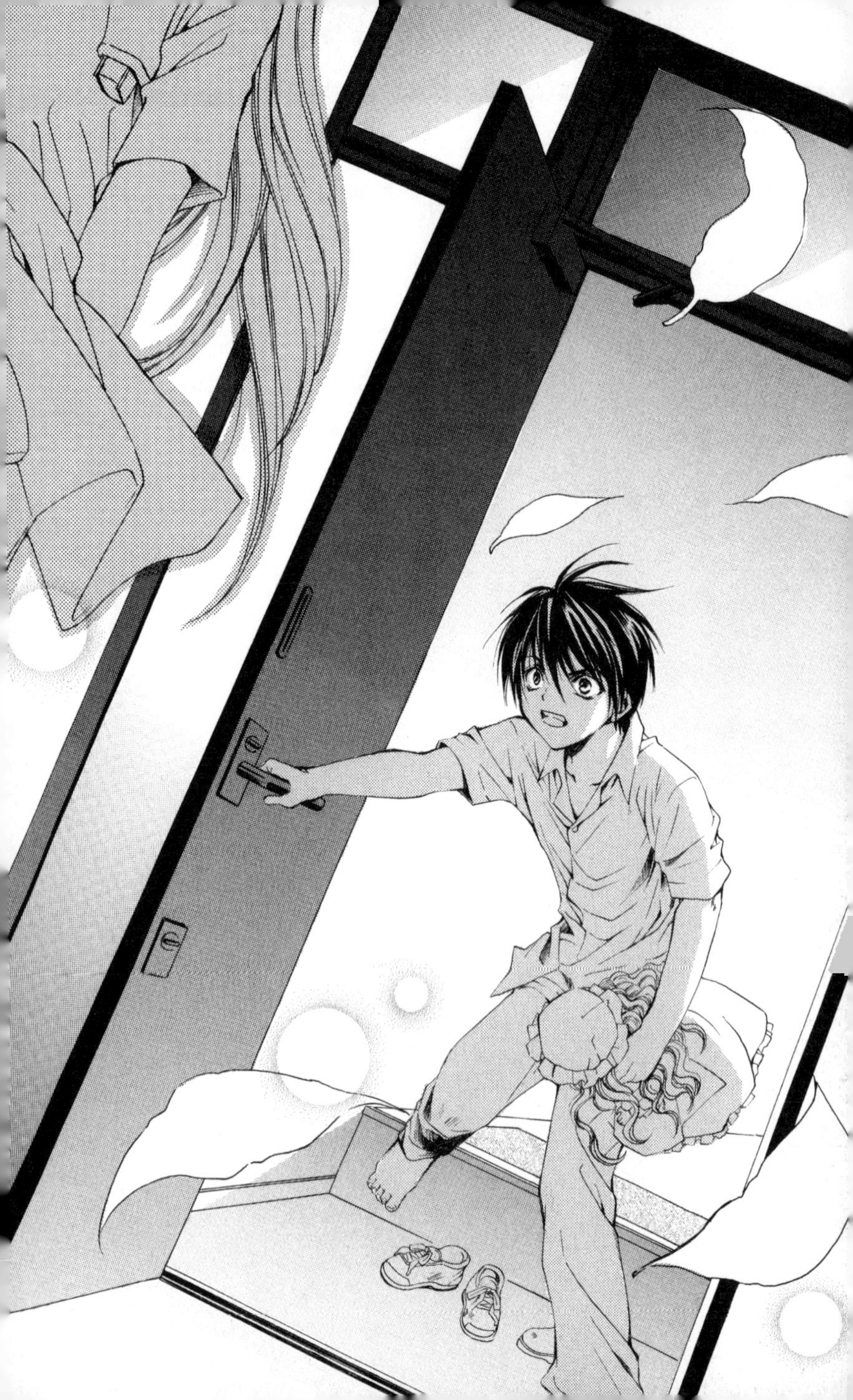

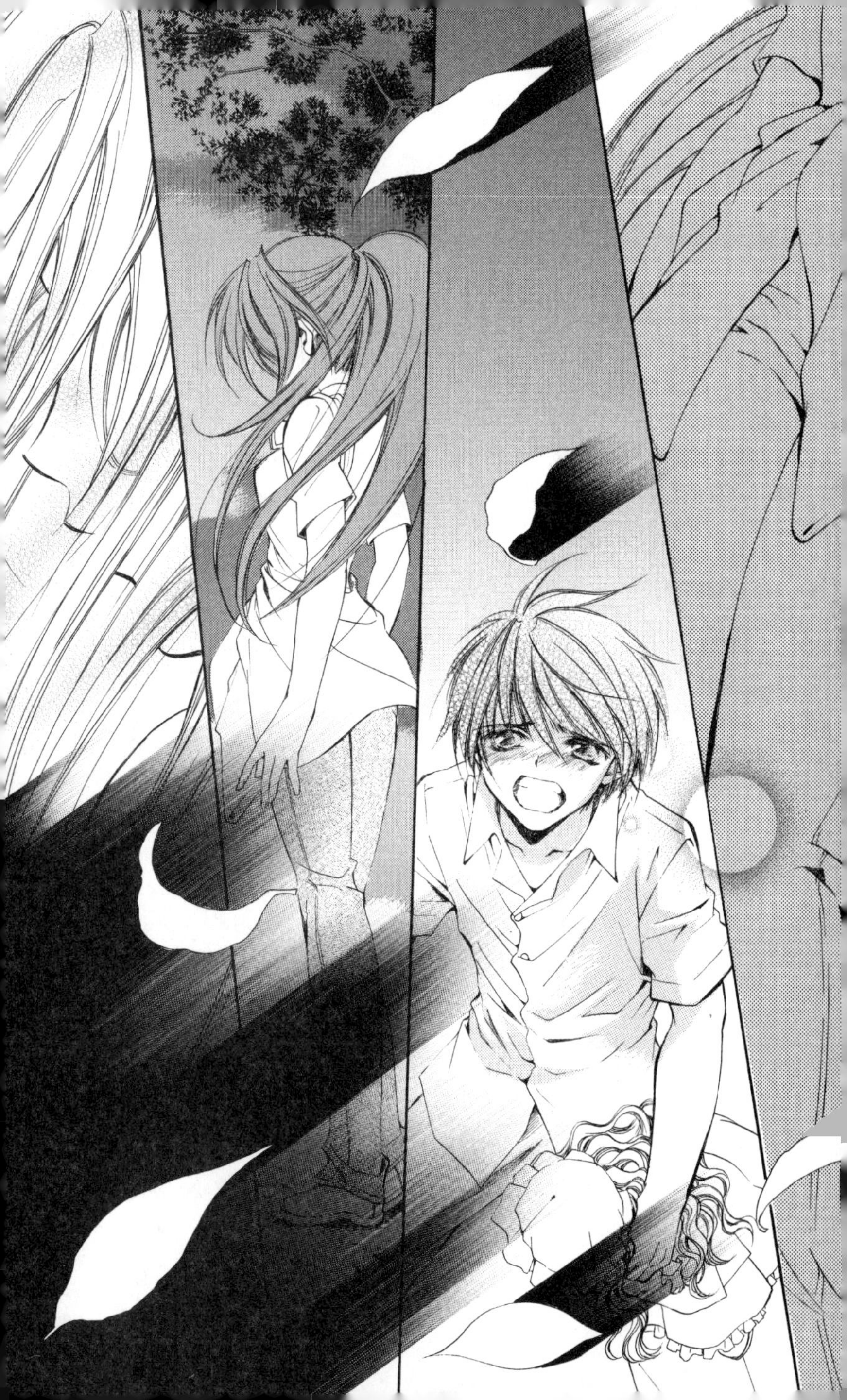

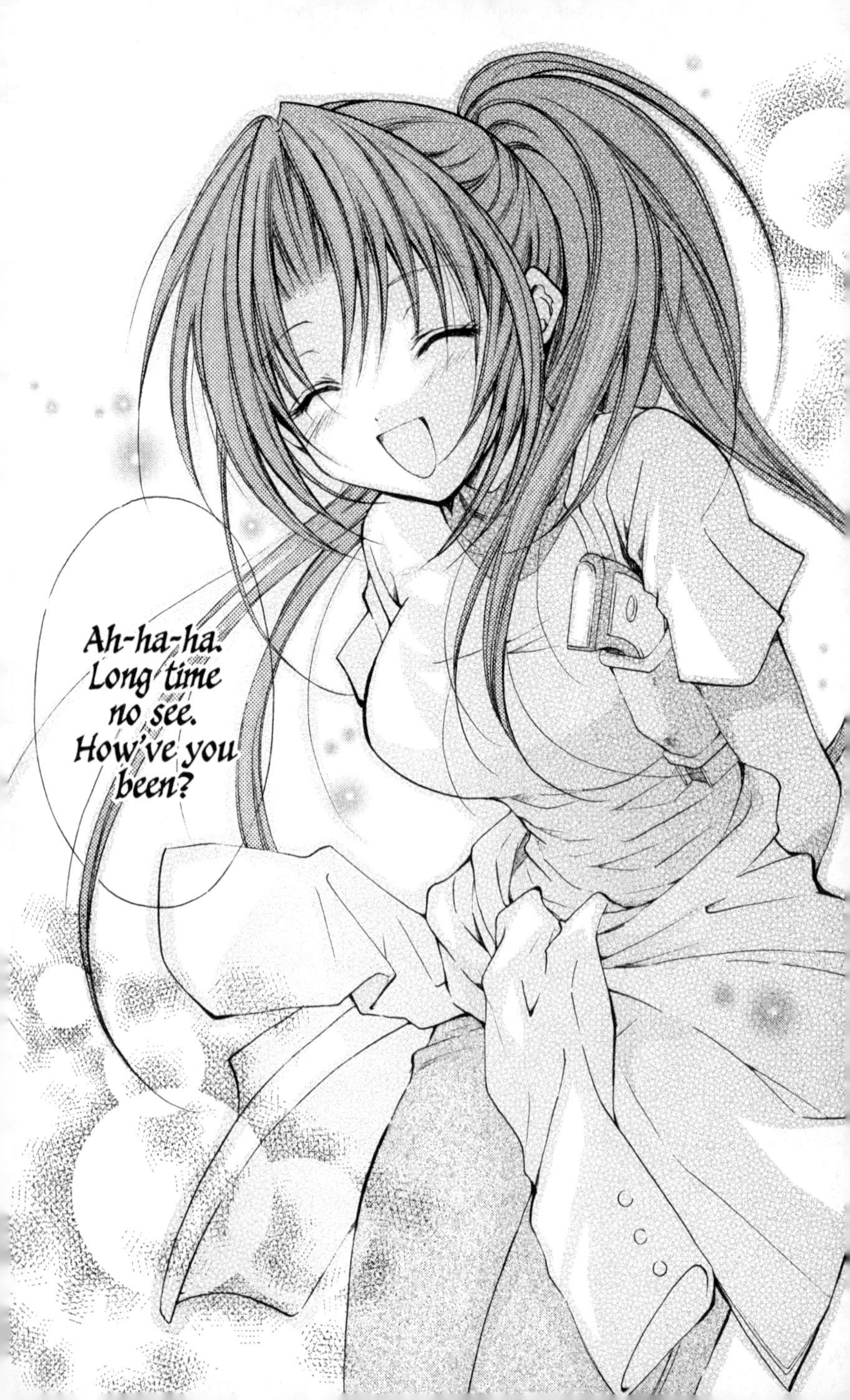
Ah-ha-ha. Long time no see. How've you been?

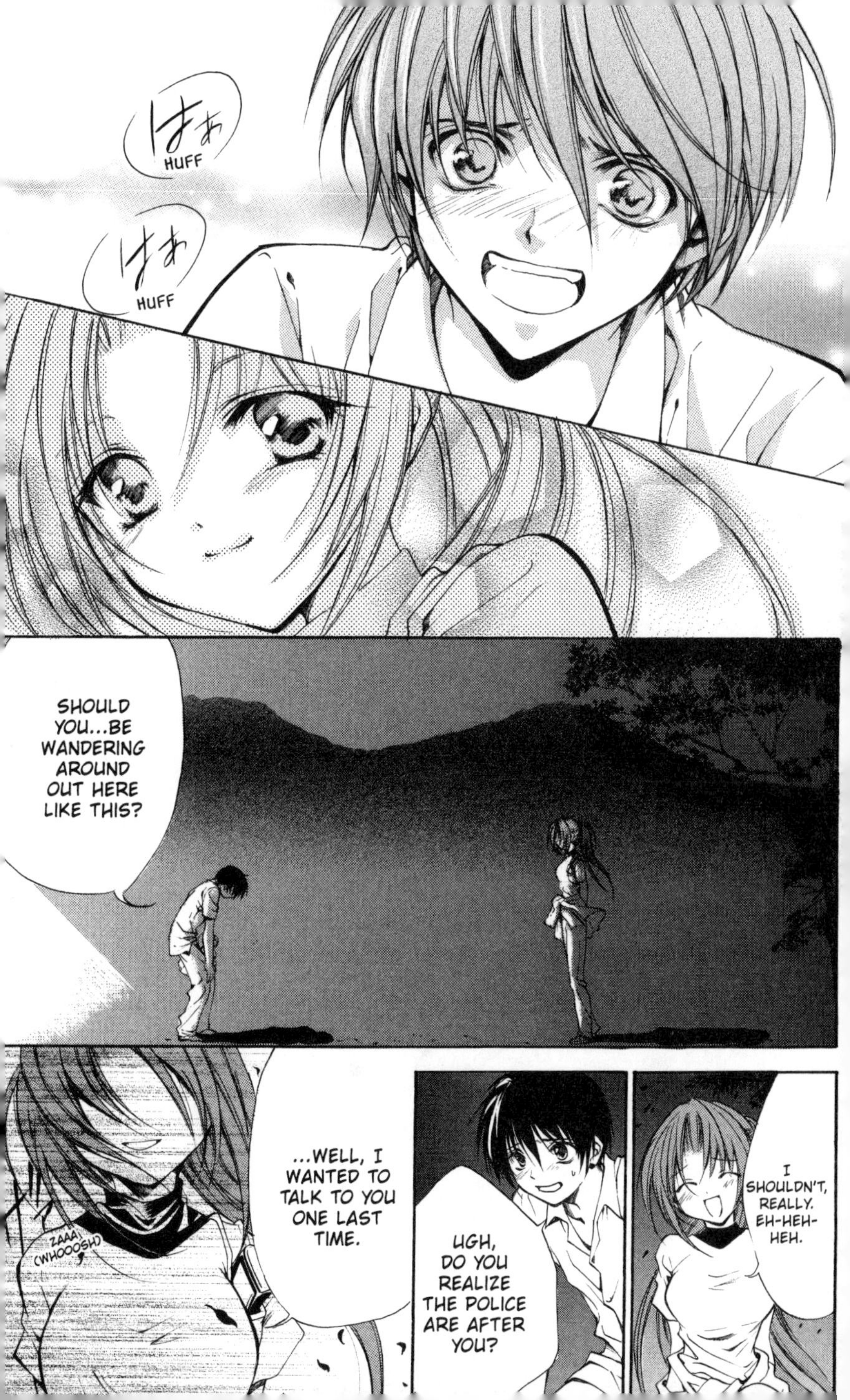
はぁ
HUFF
はぁ
HUFF
SHOULD YOU...BE WANDERING AROUND OUT HERE LIKE THIS?
I SHOULDN'T, REALLY. EH-HEH-HEH.
UGH, DO YOU REALIZE THE POLICE ARE AFTER YOU?
...WELL, I WANTED TO TALK TO YOU ONE LAST TIME.
ZAAA (WHOOOSH)

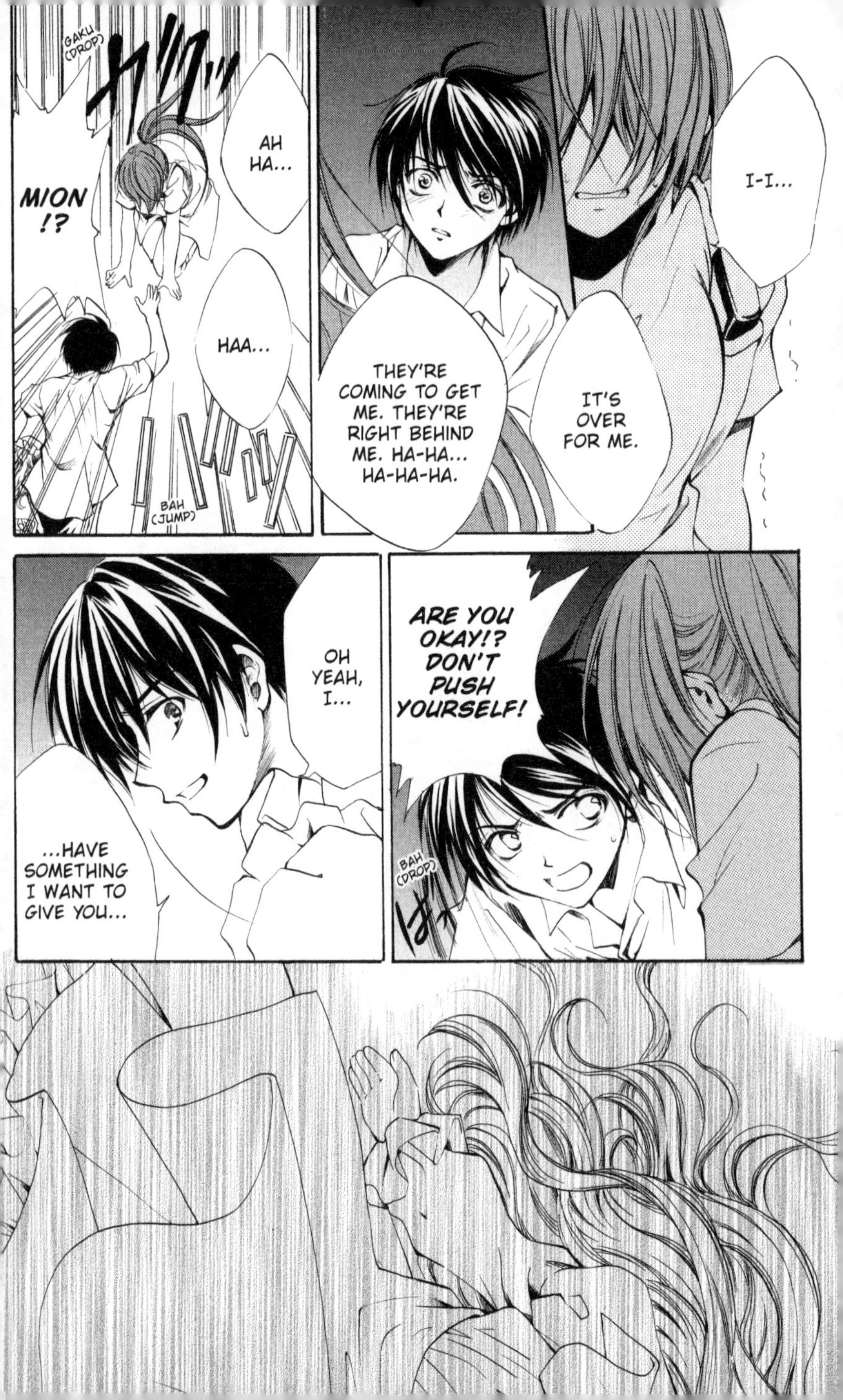
I-I...
IT'S OVER FOR ME.
THEY'RE COMING TO GET ME. THEY'RE RIGHT BEHIND ME. HA-HA... HA-HA-HA.
GAKU (DROP)
AH HA...
MION !?
HAA...
BAH (JUMP)
ARE YOU OKAY!? DON'T PUSH YOURSELF!
BAH (DROP)
OH YEAH, I...
...HAVE SOMETHING I WANT TO GIVE YOU...

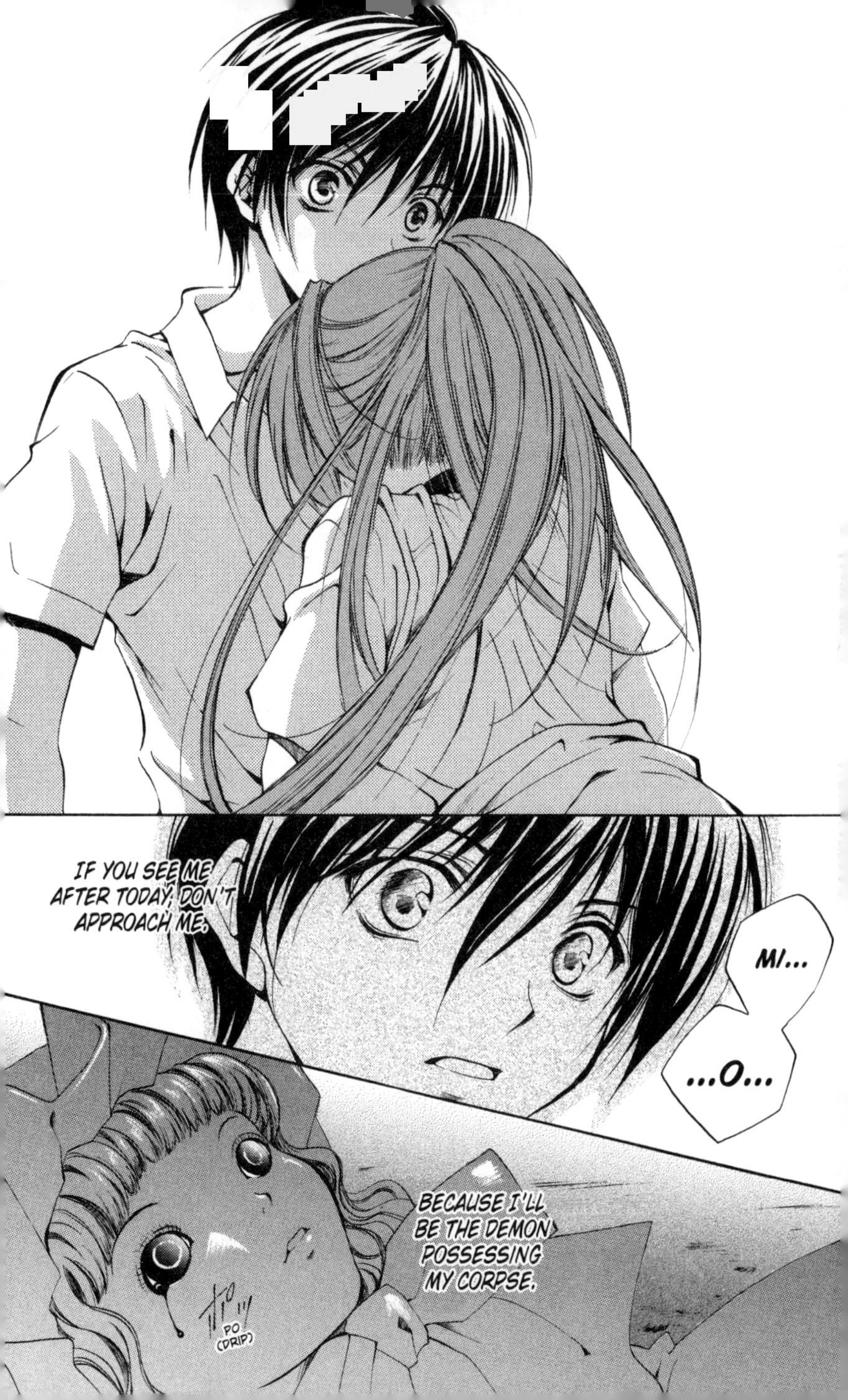
MI...
...O...
IF YOU SEE ME AFTER TODAY, DON'T APPROACH ME.
BECAUSE I'LL BE THE DEMON POSSESSING MY CORPSE.
PO (DRIP)

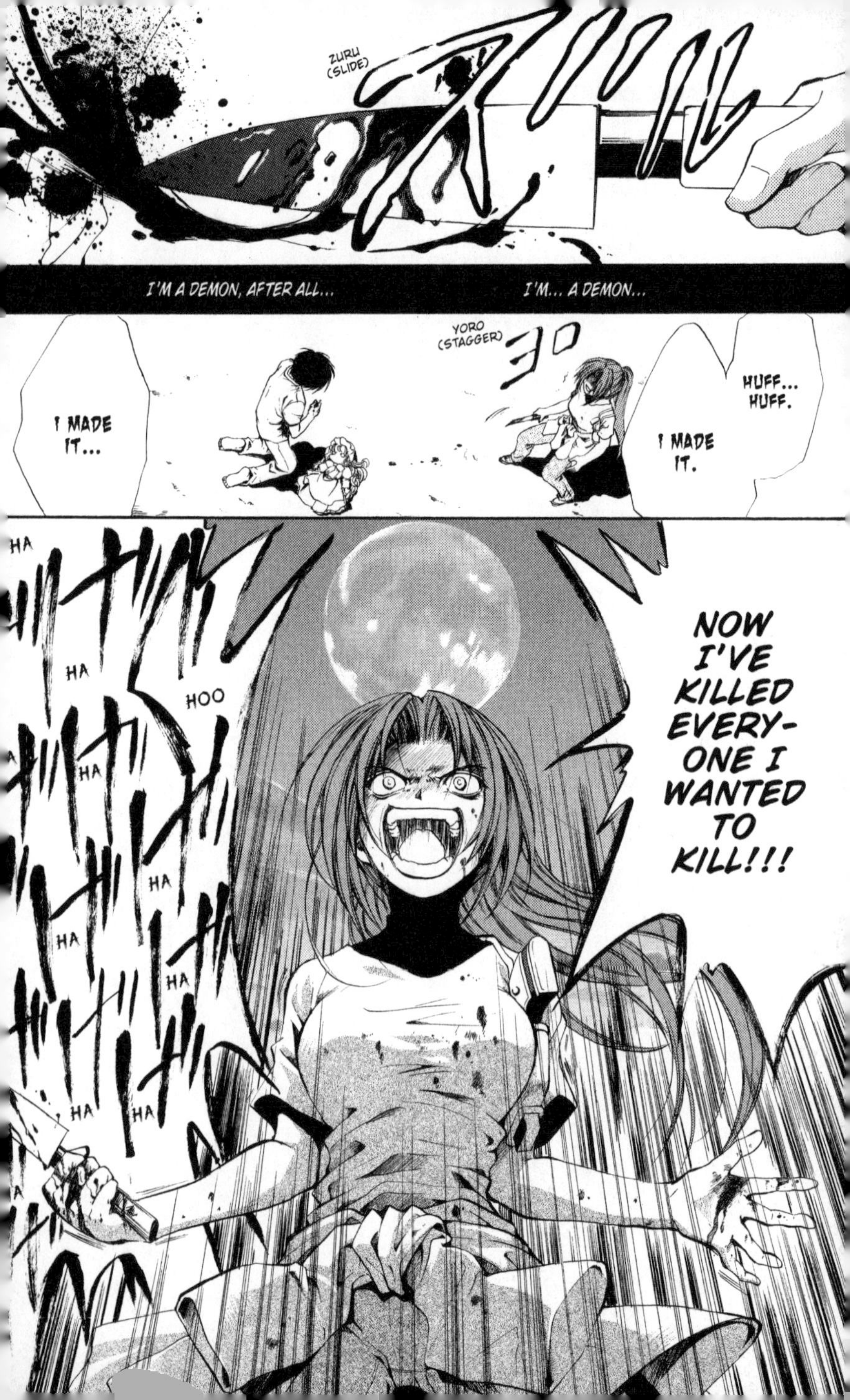
ZURU (SLIDE)
I'M... A DEMON...
I'M A DEMON, AFTER ALL...
HUFF... HUFF.
I MADE IT.
YORO (STAGGER)
I MADE IT...
NOW I'VE KILLED EVERY-ONE I WANTED TO KILL!!!
HA
HA
HOO
HA
HA
HA
HA
HA
HA

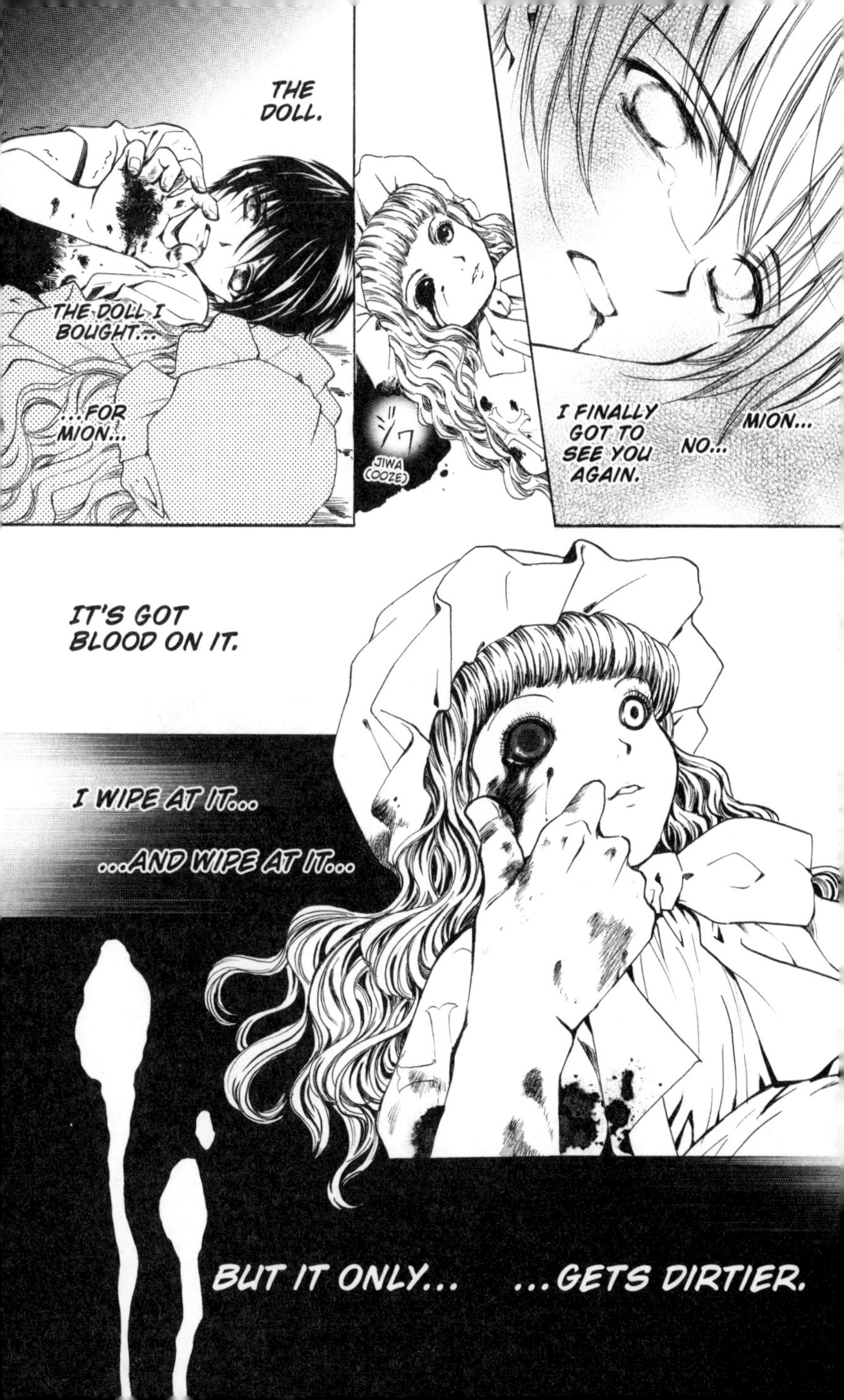
MION...
NO...
I FINALLY GOT TO SEE YOU AGAIN.
ジワ
JIWA (OOZE)
THE DOLL.
THE DOLL I BOUGHT...
...FOR MION...
IT'S GOT BLOOD ON IT.
I WIPE AT IT...
...AND WIPE AT IT...
BUT IT ONLY...
...GETS DIRTIER.

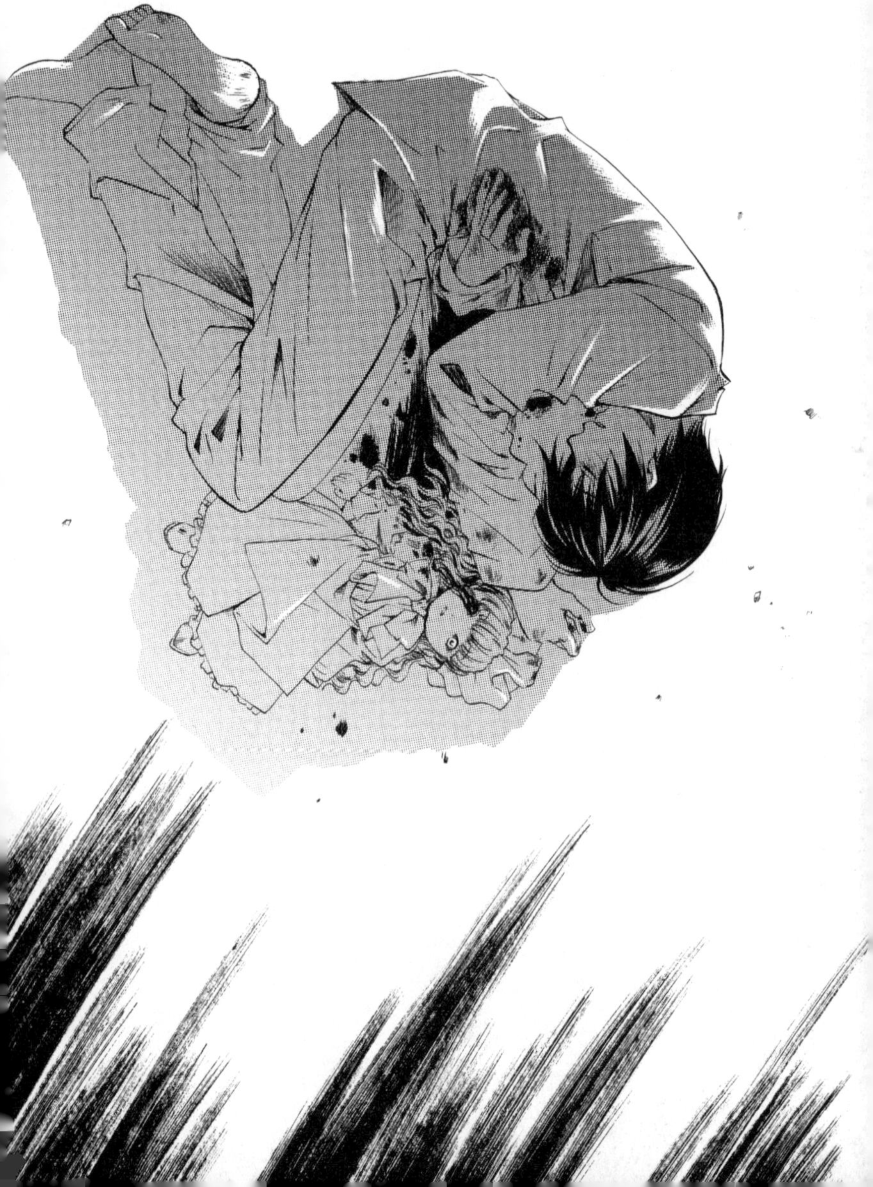

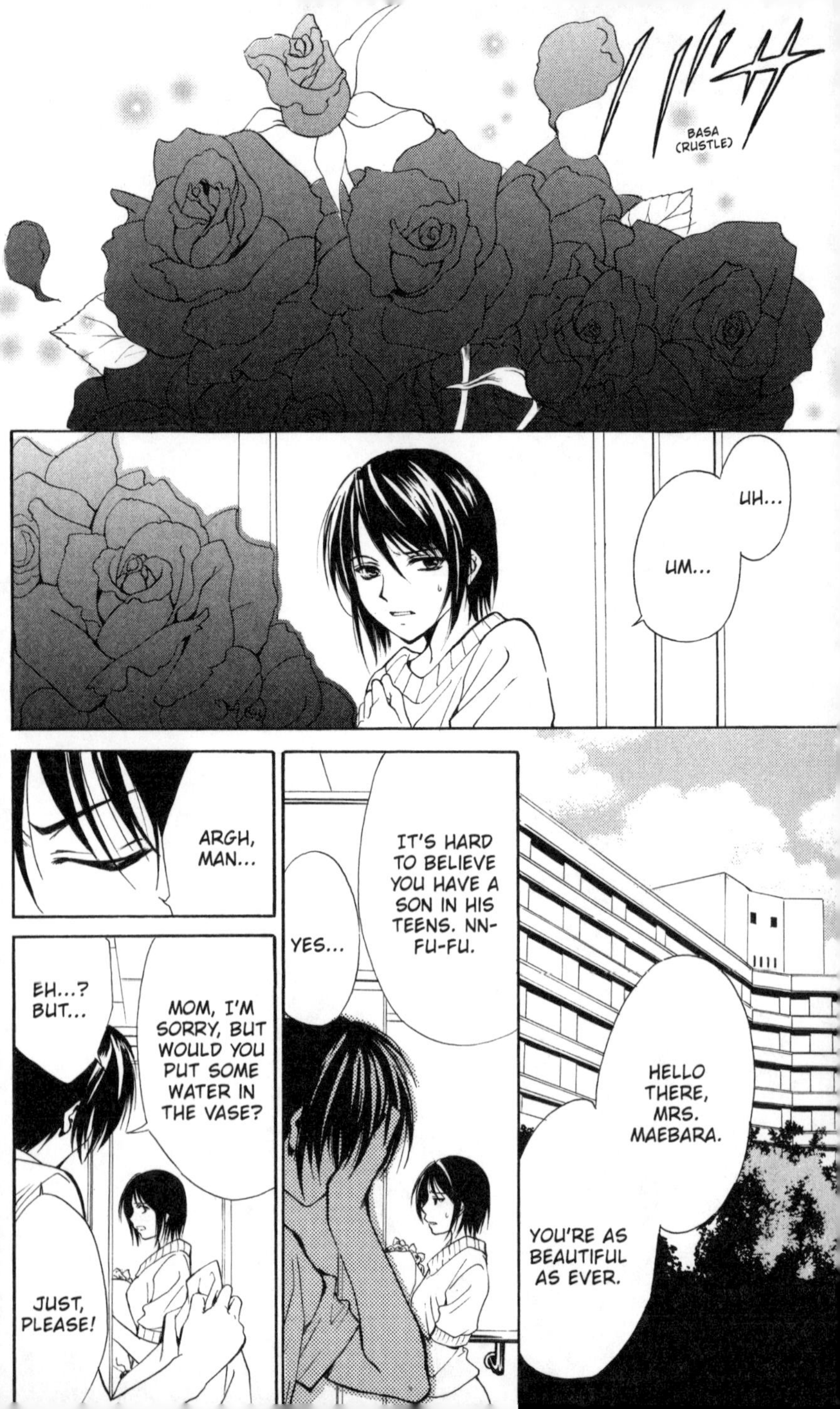
BASA (RUSTLE)
UH...
UM...
HELLO THERE, MRS. MAEBARA.
YOU'RE AS BEAUTIFUL AS EVER.
IT'S HARD TO BELIEVE YOU HAVE A SON IN HIS TEENS. NN-FU-FU.
YES...
ARGH, MAN...
MOM, I'M SORRY, BUT WOULD YOU PUT SOME WATER IN THE VASE?
EH...? BUT...
JUST, PLEASE!

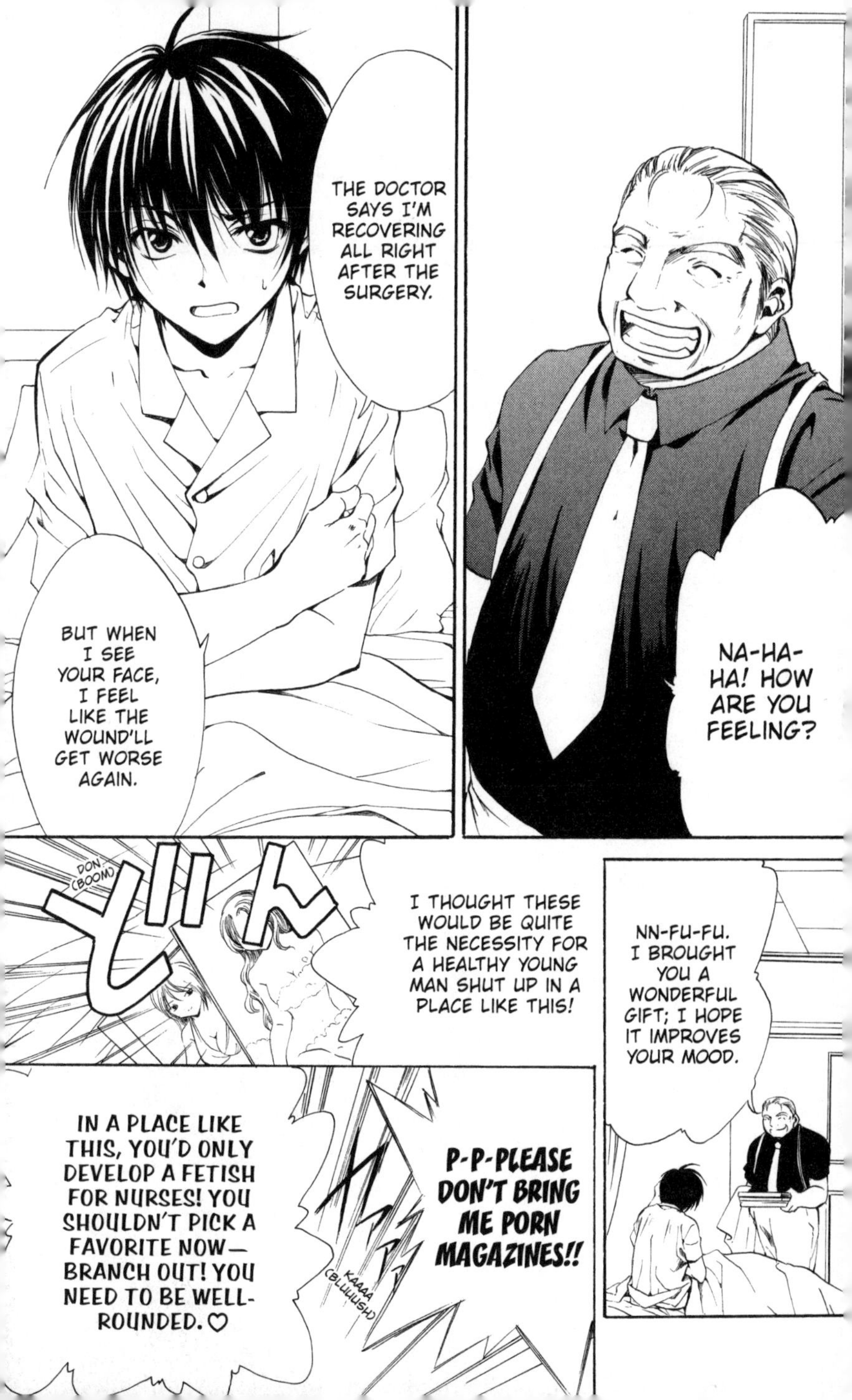
NA-HA-HA! HOW ARE YOU FEELING?
THE DOCTOR SAYS I'M RECOVERING ALL RIGHT AFTER THE SURGERY.
BUT WHEN I SEE YOUR FACE, I FEEL LIKE THE WOUND'LL GET WORSE AGAIN.
NN-FU-FU. I BROUGHT YOU A WONDERFUL GIFT; I HOPE IT IMPROVES YOUR MOOD.
I THOUGHT THESE WOULD BE QUITE THE NECESSITY FOR A HEALTHY YOUNG MAN SHUT UP IN A PLACE LIKE THIS!
DON (BOOM)
P-P-PLEASE DON'T BRING ME PORN MAGAZINES!!
KAAAA (BLUUUSH)
IN A PLACE LIKE THIS, YOU'D ONLY DEVELOP A FETISH FOR NURSES! YOU SHOULDN'T PICK A FAVORITE NOW—BRANCH OUT! YOU NEED TO BE WELL-ROUNDED. ♡

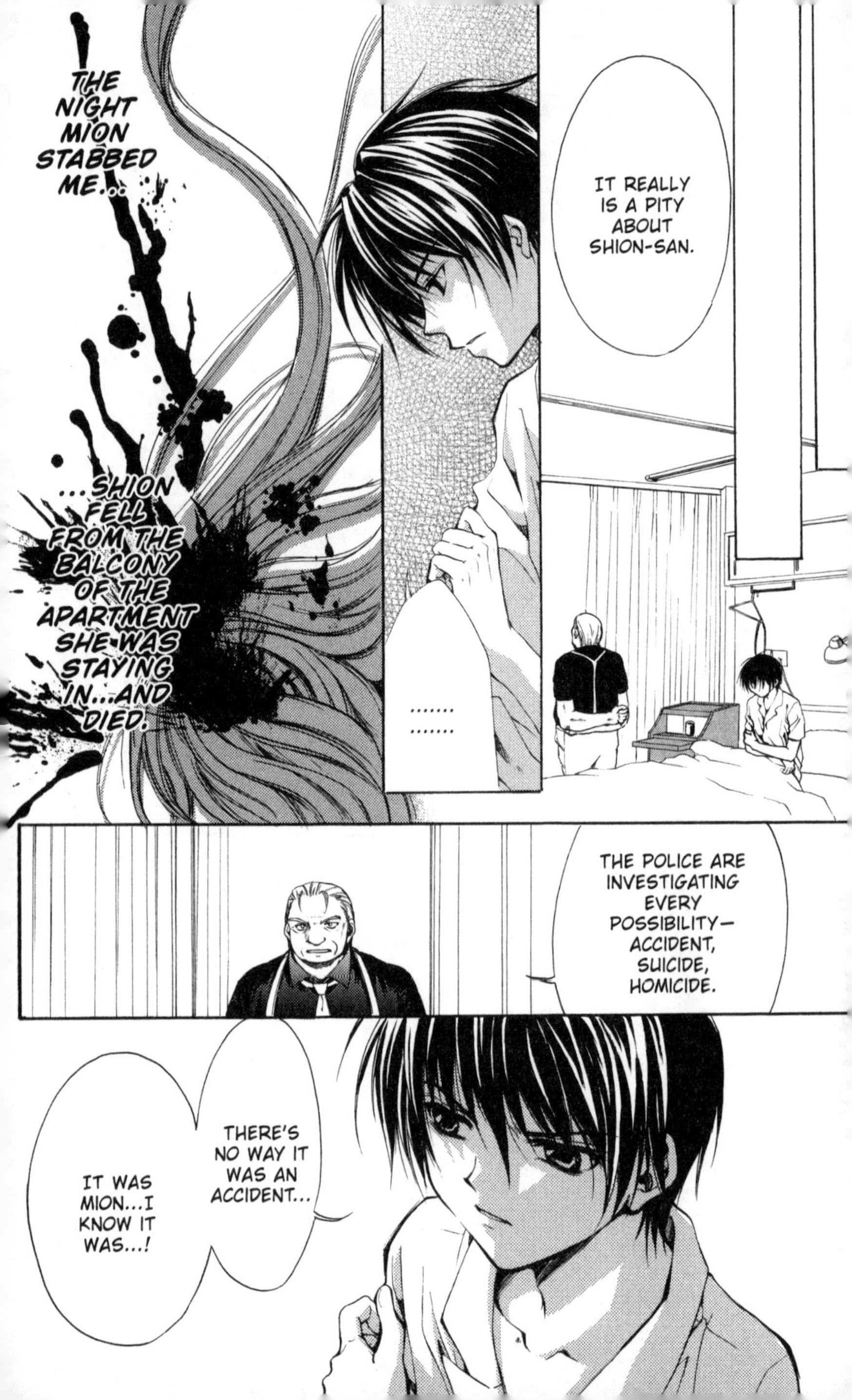
IT REALLY IS A PITY ABOUT SHION-SAN.
....
....
THE NIGHT MION STABBED ME...
...SHION FELL FROM THE BALCONY OF THE APARTMENT SHE WAS STAYING IN...AND DIED.
THE POLICE ARE INVESTIGATING EVERY POSSIBILITY—ACCIDENT, SUICIDE, HOMICIDE.
THERE'S NO WAY IT WAS AN ACCIDENT...
IT WAS MION...I KNOW IT WAS...!

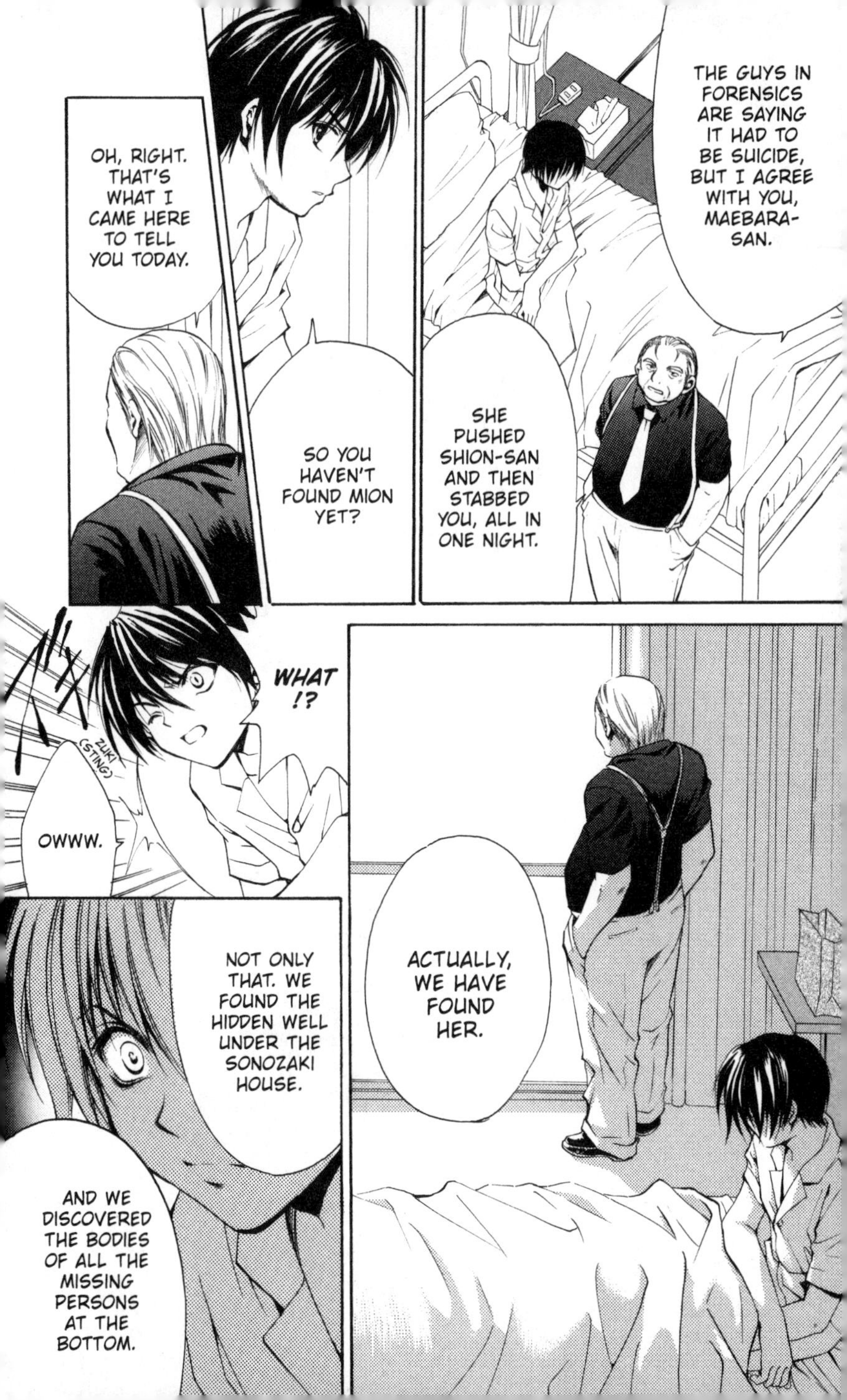
THE GUYS IN FORENSICS ARE SAYING IT HAD TO BE SUICIDE, BUT I AGREE WITH YOU, MAEBARA-SAN.
SHE PUSHED SHION-SAN AND THEN STABBED YOU, ALL IN ONE NIGHT.
SO YOU HAVEN'T FOUND MION YET?
OH, RIGHT. THAT'S WHAT I CAME HERE TO TELL YOU TODAY.
ACTUALLY, WE HAVE FOUND HER.
WHAT !?
ZUKI (STING)
OWWW.
NOT ONLY THAT. WE FOUND THE HIDDEN WELL UNDER THE SONOZAKI HOUSE.
AND WE DISCOVERED THE BODIES OF ALL THE MISSING PERSONS AT THE BOTTOM.

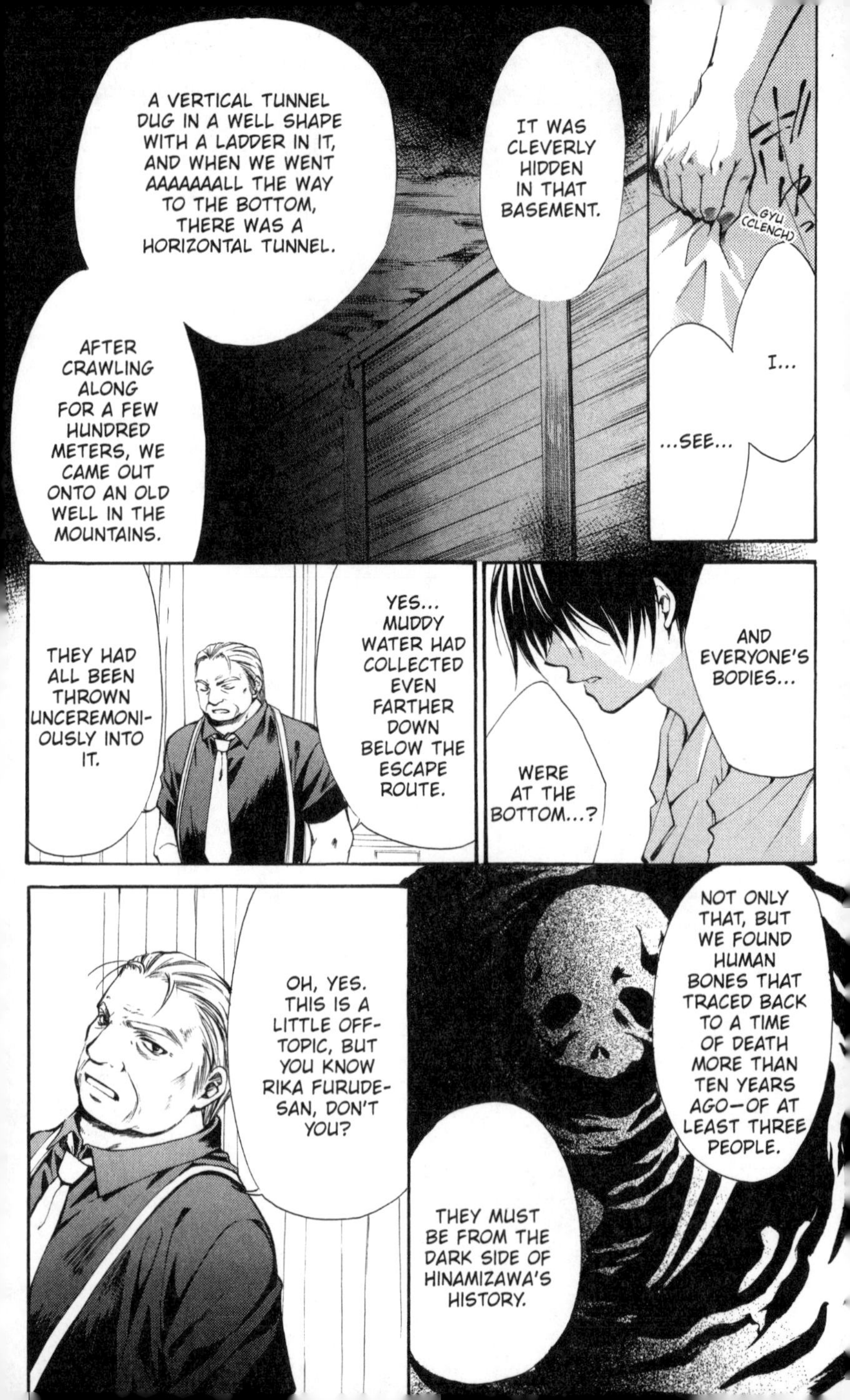
GYU (CLENCH)
I...
...SEE...
IT WAS CLEVERLY HIDDEN IN THAT BASEMENT.
A VERTICAL TUNNEL DUG IN A WELL SHAPE WITH A LADDER IN IT, AND WHEN WE WENT AAAAAAALL THE WAY TO THE BOTTOM, THERE WAS A HORIZONTAL TUNNEL.
AFTER CRAWLING ALONG FOR A FEW HUNDRED METERS, WE CAME OUT ONTO AN OLD WELL IN THE MOUNTAINS.
AND EVERYONE'S BODIES...
WERE AT THE BOTTOM...?
YES... MUDDY WATER HAD COLLECTED EVEN FARTHER DOWN BELOW THE ESCAPE ROUTE.
THEY HAD ALL BEEN THROWN UNCEREMONIOUSLY INTO IT.
NOT ONLY THAT, BUT WE FOUND HUMAN BONES THAT TRACED BACK TO A TIME OF DEATH MORE THAN TEN YEARS AGO—OF AT LEAST THREE PEOPLE.
THEY MUST BE FROM THE DARK SIDE OF HINAMIZAWA'S HISTORY.
OH, YES. THIS IS A LITTLE OFF-TOPIC, BUT YOU KNOW RIKA FURUDE-SAN, DON'T YOU?

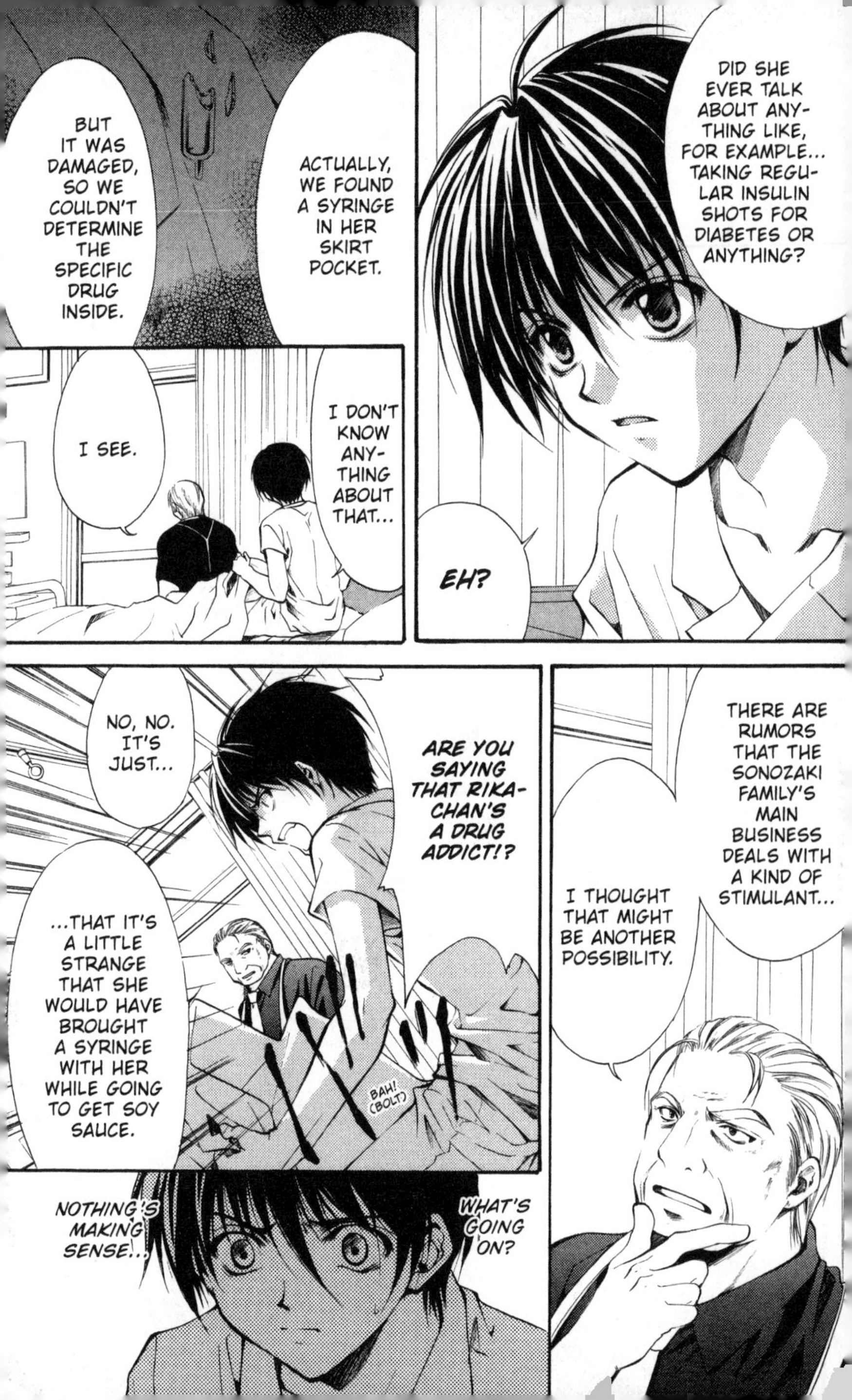
DID SHE EVER TALK ABOUT ANY-THING LIKE, FOR EXAMPLE... TAKING REGU-LAR INSULIN SHOTS FOR DIABETES OR ANYTHING?
EH?
ACTUALLY, WE FOUND A SYRINGE IN HER SKIRT POCKET.
BUT IT WAS DAMAGED, SO WE COULDN'T DETERMINE THE SPECIFIC DRUG INSIDE.
I DON'T KNOW ANY-THING ABOUT THAT...
I SEE.
THERE ARE RUMORS THAT THE SONOZAKI FAMILY'S MAIN BUSINESS DEALS WITH A KIND OF STIMULANT...
I THOUGHT THAT MIGHT BE ANOTHER POSSIBILITY.
ARE YOU SAYING THAT RIKA-CHAN'S A DRUG ADDICT!?
BAH! (BOLT)
NO, NO. IT'S JUST...
...THAT IT'S A LITTLE STRANGE THAT SHE WOULD HAVE BROUGHT A SYRINGE WITH HER WHILE GOING TO GET SOY SAUCE.
WHAT'S GOING ON?
NOTHING'S MAKING SENSE...

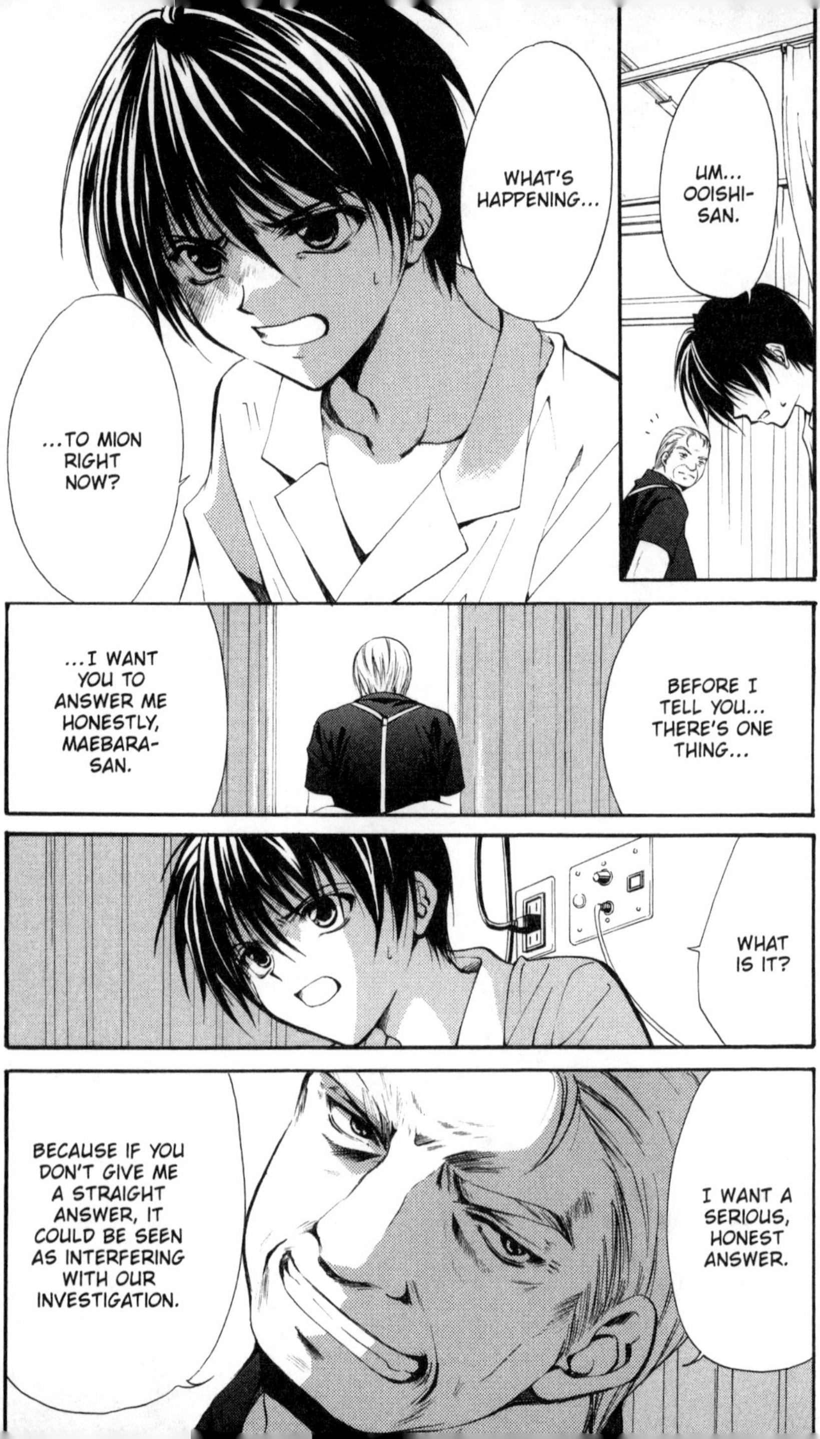
UM... OOISHI-SAN.
WHAT'S HAPPENING...
...TO MION RIGHT NOW?
BEFORE I TELL YOU... THERE'S ONE THING...
...I WANT YOU TO ANSWER ME HONESTLY, MAEBARA-SAN.
WHAT IS IT?
I WANT A SERIOUS, HONEST ANSWER.
BECAUSE IF YOU DON'T GIVE ME A STRAIGHT ANSWER, IT COULD BE SEEN AS INTERFERING WITH OUR INVESTIGATION.

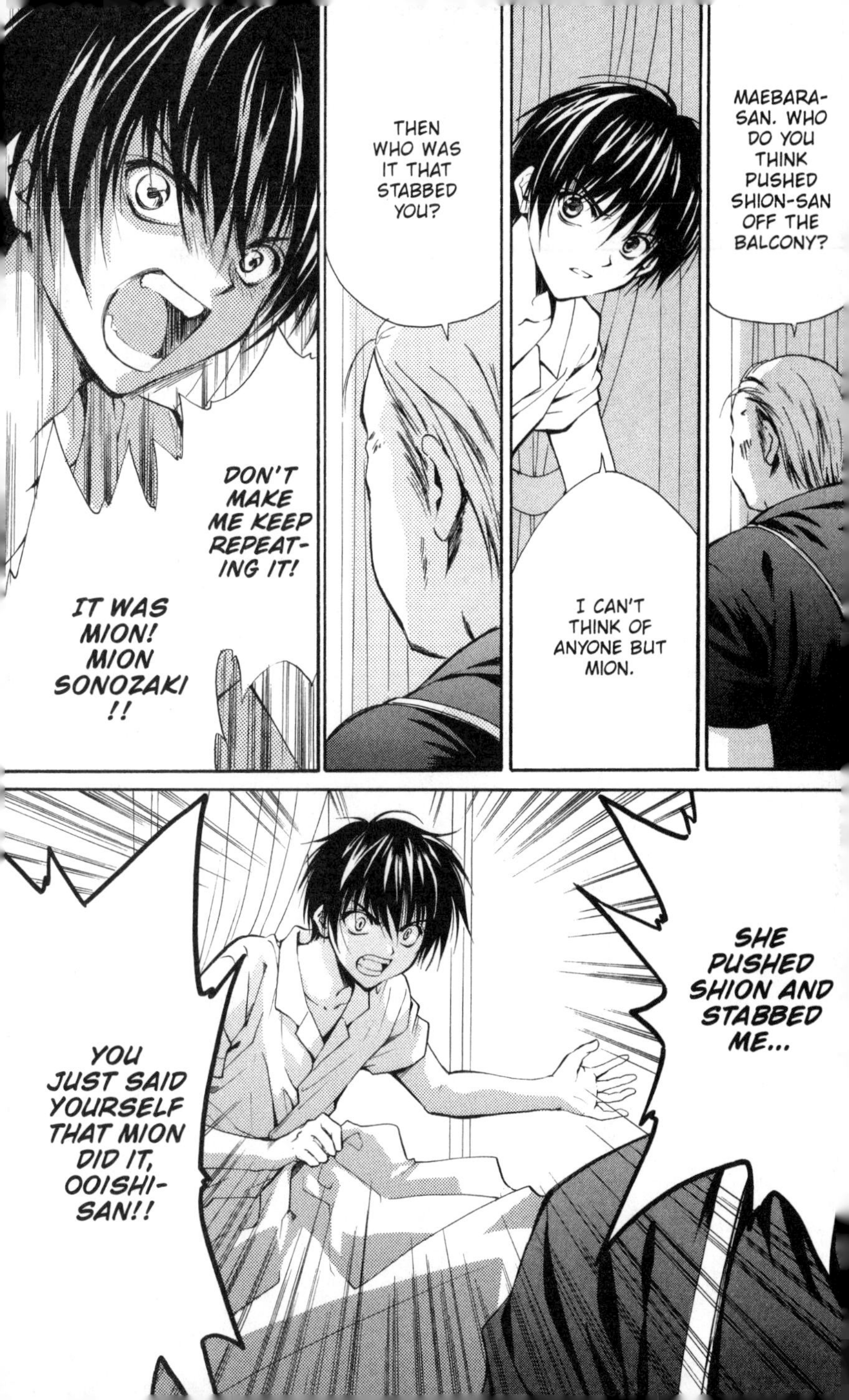
MAEBARA-SAN. WHO DO YOU THINK PUSHED SHION-SAN OFF THE BALCONY?
I CAN'T THINK OF ANYONE BUT MION.
THEN WHO WAS IT THAT STABBED YOU?
DON'T MAKE ME KEEP REPEATING IT!
IT WAS MION! MION SONOZAKI!!
SHE PUSHED SHION AND STABBED ME...
YOU JUST SAID YOURSELF THAT MION DID IT, OOISHI-SAN!!

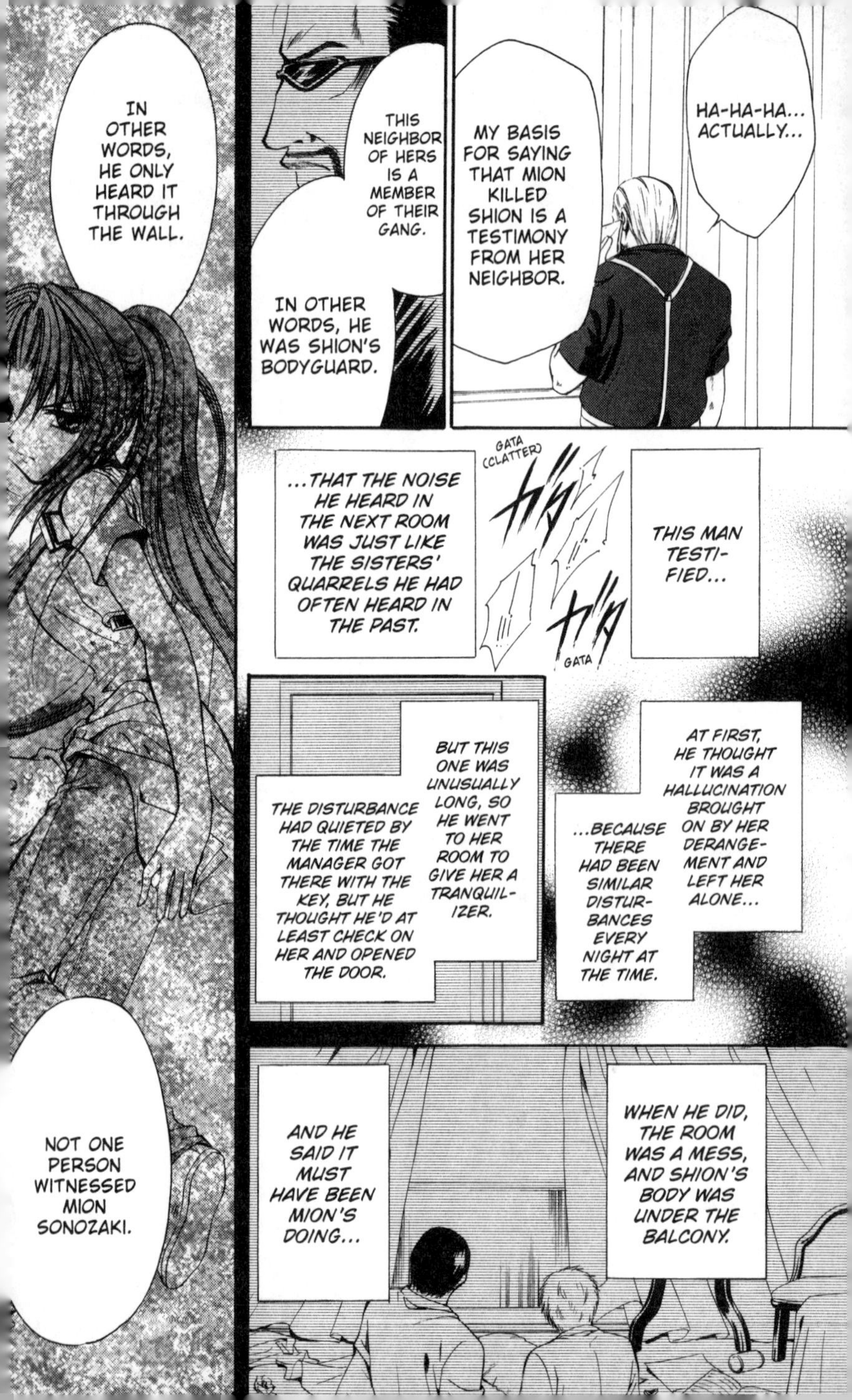
HA-HA-HA... ACTUALLY...
MY BASIS FOR SAYING THAT MION KILLED SHION IS A TESTIMONY FROM HER NEIGHBOR.
THIS NEIGHBOR OF HERS IS A MEMBER OF THEIR GANG.
IN OTHER WORDS, HE WAS SHION'S BODYGUARD.
THIS MAN TESTIFIED...
GATA (CLATTER)
GATA
...THAT THE NOISE HE HEARD IN THE NEXT ROOM WAS JUST LIKE THE SISTERS' QUARRELS HE HAD OFTEN HEARD IN THE PAST.
AT FIRST, HE THOUGHT IT WAS A HALLUCINATION BROUGHT ON BY HER DERANGE-MENT AND LEFT HER ALONE...
...BECAUSE THERE HAD BEEN SIMILAR DISTUR-BANCES EVERY NIGHT AT THE TIME.
BUT THIS ONE WAS UNUSUALLY LONG, SO HE WENT TO HER ROOM TO GIVE HER A TRANQUIL-IZER.
THE DISTURBANCE HAD QUIETED BY THE TIME THE MANAGER GOT THERE WITH THE KEY, BUT HE THOUGHT HE'D AT LEAST CHECK ON HER AND OPENED THE DOOR.
WHEN HE DID, THE ROOM WAS A MESS, AND SHION'S BODY WAS UNDER THE BALCONY.
AND HE SAID IT MUST HAVE BEEN MION'S DOING...
IN OTHER WORDS, HE ONLY HEARD IT THROUGH THE WALL.
NOT ONE PERSON WITNESSED MION SONOZAKI.

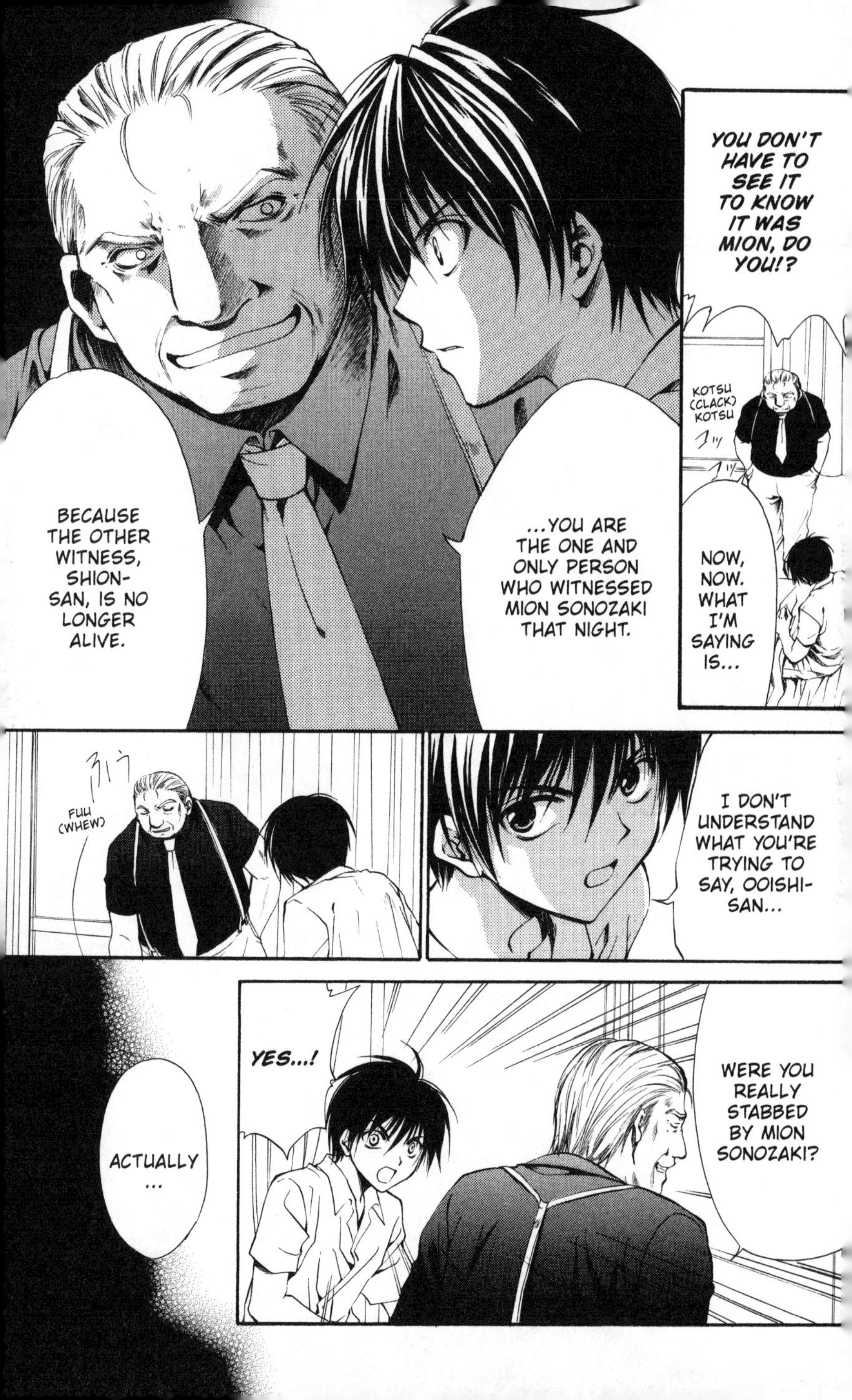
YOU DON'T HAVE TO SEE IT TO KNOW IT WAS MION, DO YOU!?
KOTSU (CLACK) KOTSU
NOW, NOW. WHAT I'M SAYING IS...
...YOU ARE THE ONE AND ONLY PERSON WHO WITNESSED MION SONOZAKI THAT NIGHT.
BECAUSE THE OTHER WITNESS, SHION-SAN, IS NO LONGER ALIVE.
I DON'T UNDERSTAND WHAT YOU'RE TRYING TO SAY, OOISHI-SAN...
FUU (WHEW)
WERE YOU REALLY STABBED BY MION SONOZAKI?
YES...!
ACTUALLY ...

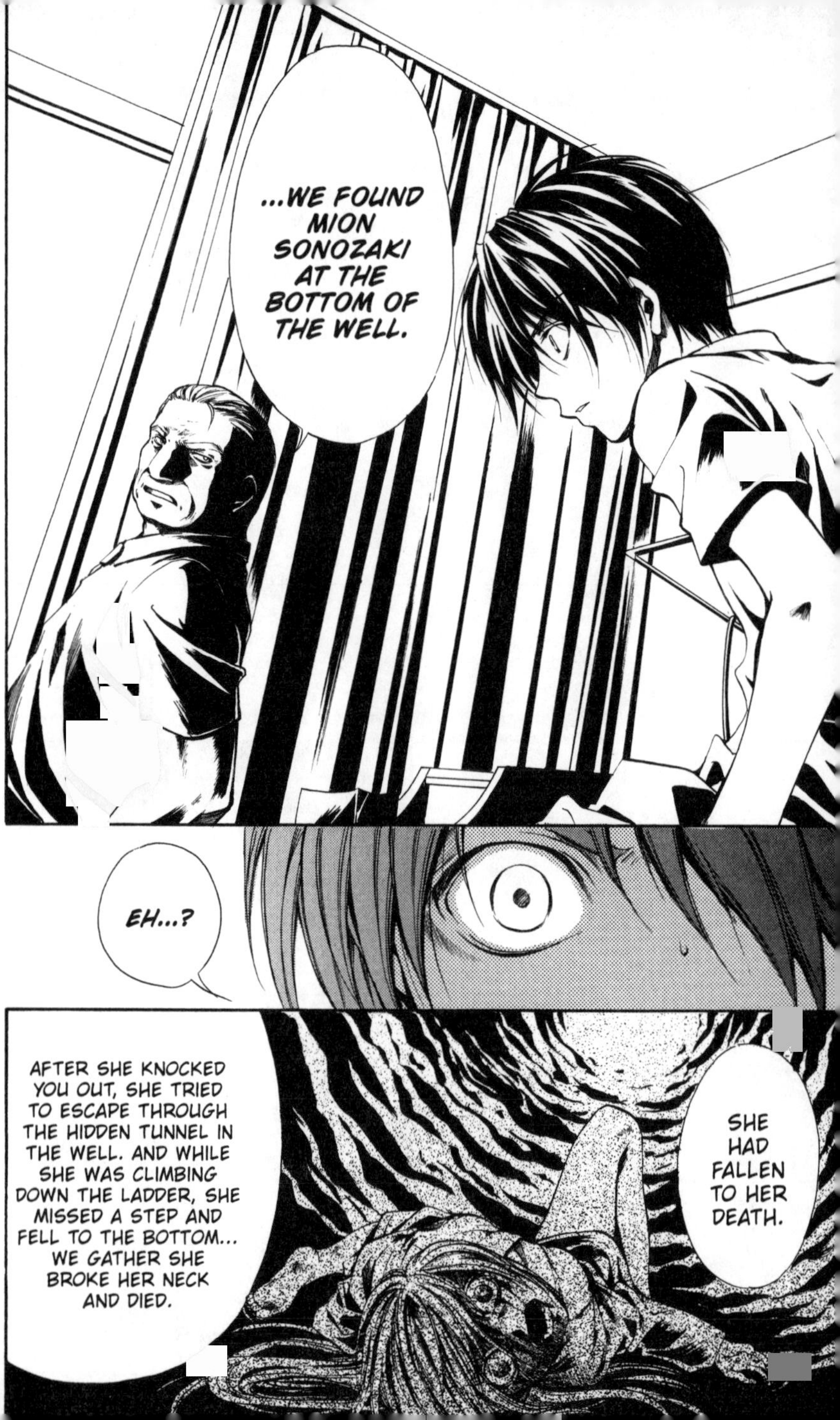
...WE FOUND MION SONOZAKI AT THE BOTTOM OF THE WELL.
EH...?
SHE HAD FALLEN TO HER DEATH.
AFTER SHE KNOCKED YOU OUT, SHE TRIED TO ESCAPE THROUGH THE HIDDEN TUNNEL IN THE WELL. AND WHILE SHE WAS CLIMBING DOWN THE LADDER, SHE MISSED A STEP AND FELL TO THE BOTTOM... WE GATHER SHE BROKE HER NECK AND DIED.

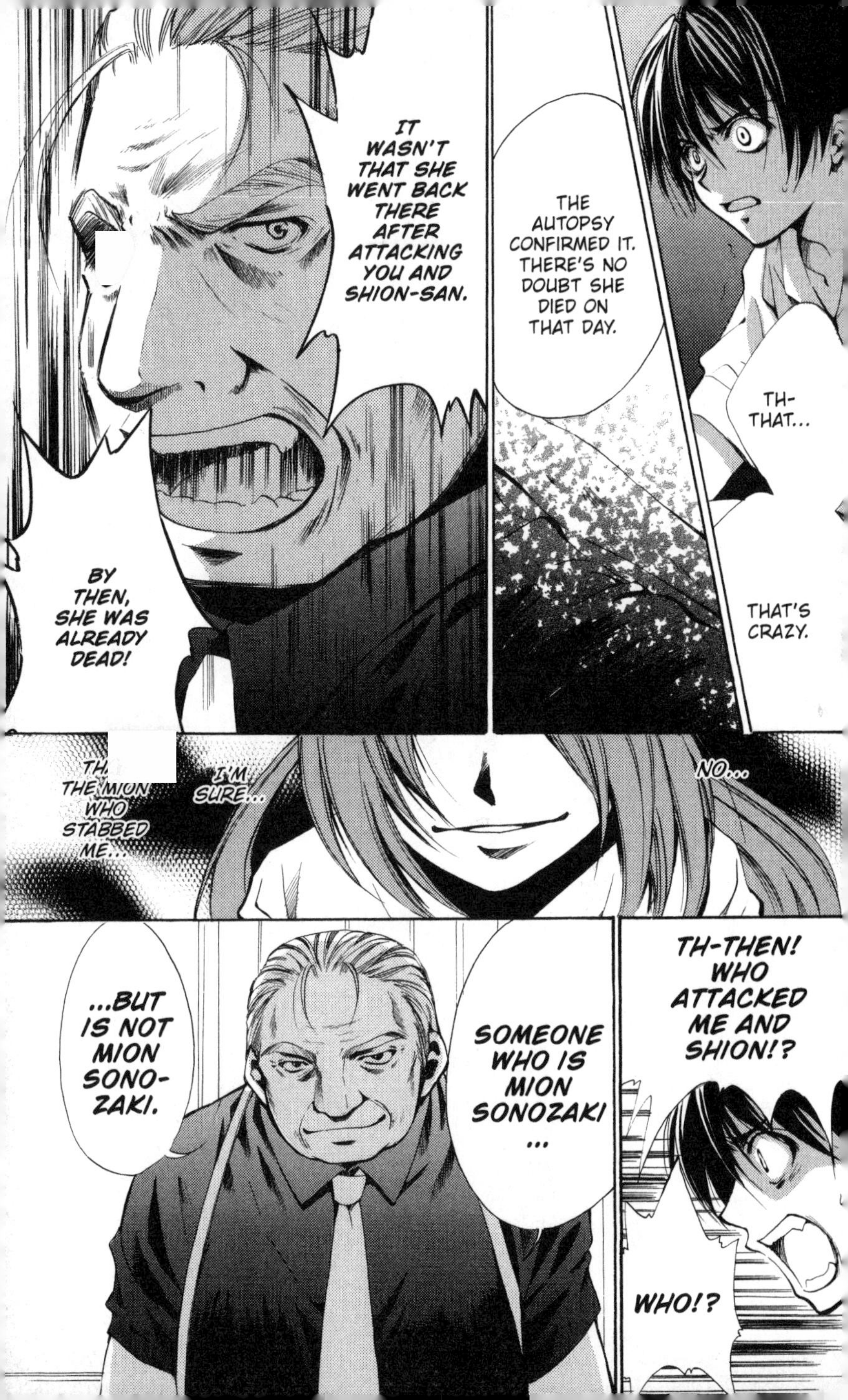
TH- THAT...
THAT'S CRAZY.
THE AUTOPSY CONFIRMED IT. THERE'S NO DOUBT SHE DIED ON THAT DAY.
IT WASN'T THAT SHE WENT BACK THERE AFTER ATTACKING YOU AND SHION-SAN.
BY THEN, SHE WAS ALREADY DEAD!
NO...
I'M SURE...
THA
THE MION WHO STABBED ME...
TH-THEN! WHO ATTACKED ME AND SHION!?
WHO!?
SOMEONE WHO IS MION SONOZAKI ...
...BUT IS NOT MION SONO-ZAKI.

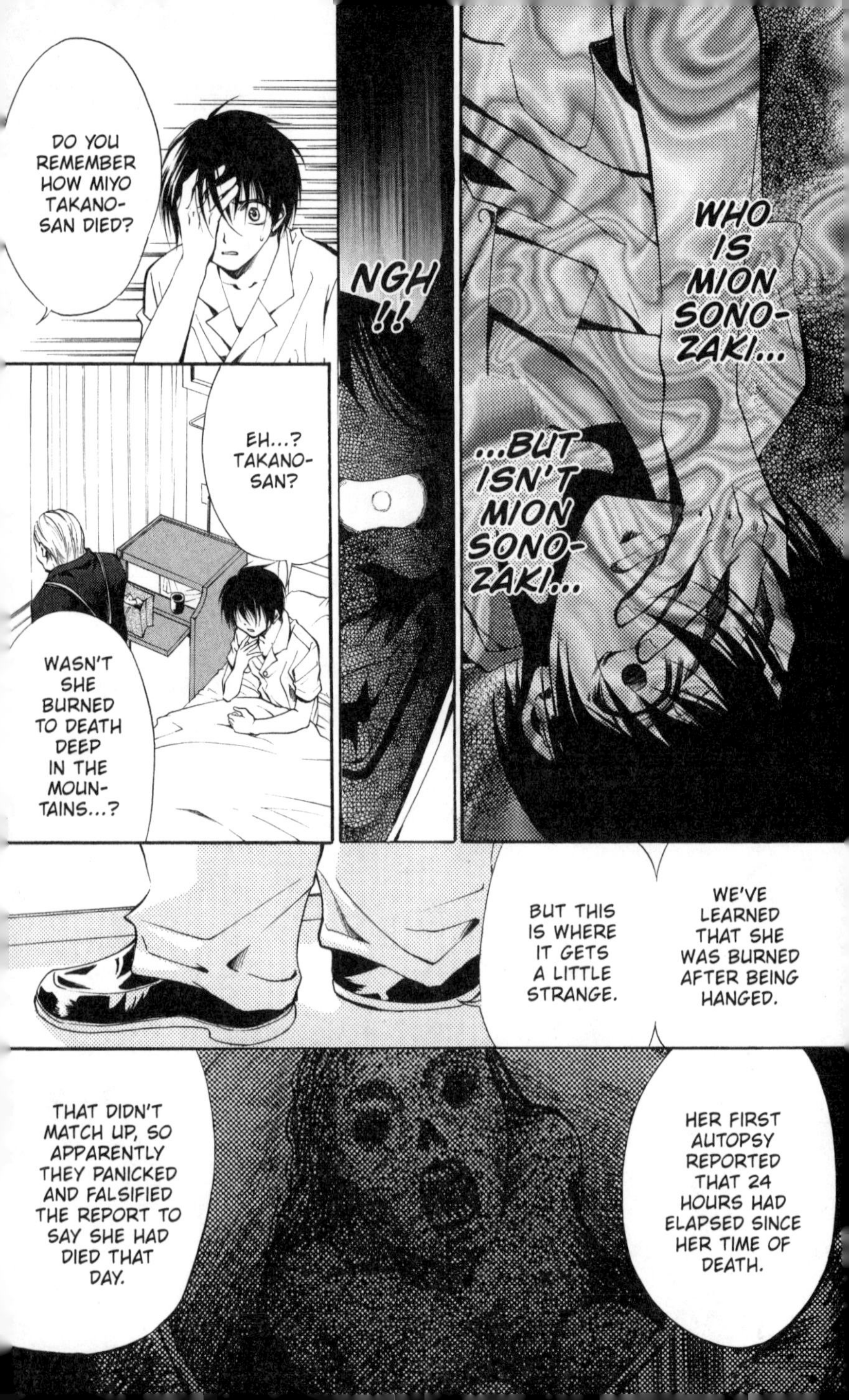
WHO IS MION SONO-ZAKI...
...BUT ISN'T MION SONO-ZAKI...
NGH !!
DO YOU REMEMBER HOW MIYO TAKANO-SAN DIED?
EH...? TAKANO-SAN?
WASN'T SHE BURNED TO DEATH DEEP IN THE MOUN-TAINS...?
WE'VE LEARNED THAT SHE WAS BURNED AFTER BEING HANGED.
BUT THIS IS WHERE IT GETS A LITTLE STRANGE.
HER FIRST AUTOPSY REPORTED THAT 24 HOURS HAD ELAPSED SINCE HER TIME OF DEATH.
THAT DIDN'T MATCH UP, SO APPARENTLY THEY PANICKED AND FALSIFIED THE REPORT TO SAY SHE HAD DIED THAT DAY.

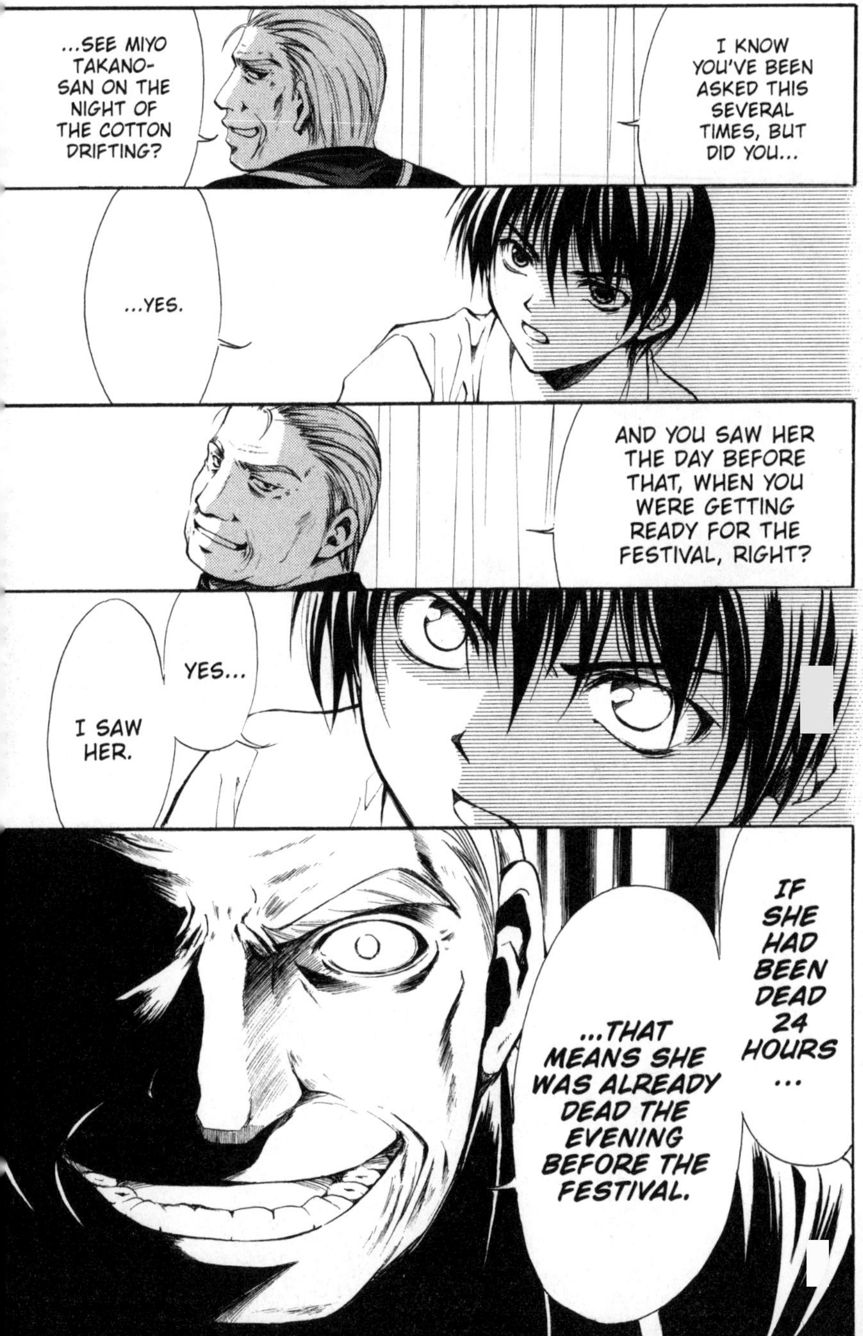
I KNOW YOU'VE BEEN ASKED THIS SEVERAL TIMES, BUT DID YOU...
...SEE MIYO TAKANO-SAN ON THE NIGHT OF THE COTTON DRIFTING?
...YES.
AND YOU SAW HER THE DAY BEFORE THAT, WHEN YOU WERE GETTING READY FOR THE FESTIVAL, RIGHT?
YES...
I SAW HER.
IF SHE HAD BEEN DEAD 24 HOURS...
...THAT MEANS SHE WAS ALREADY DEAD THE EVENING BEFORE THE FESTIVAL.

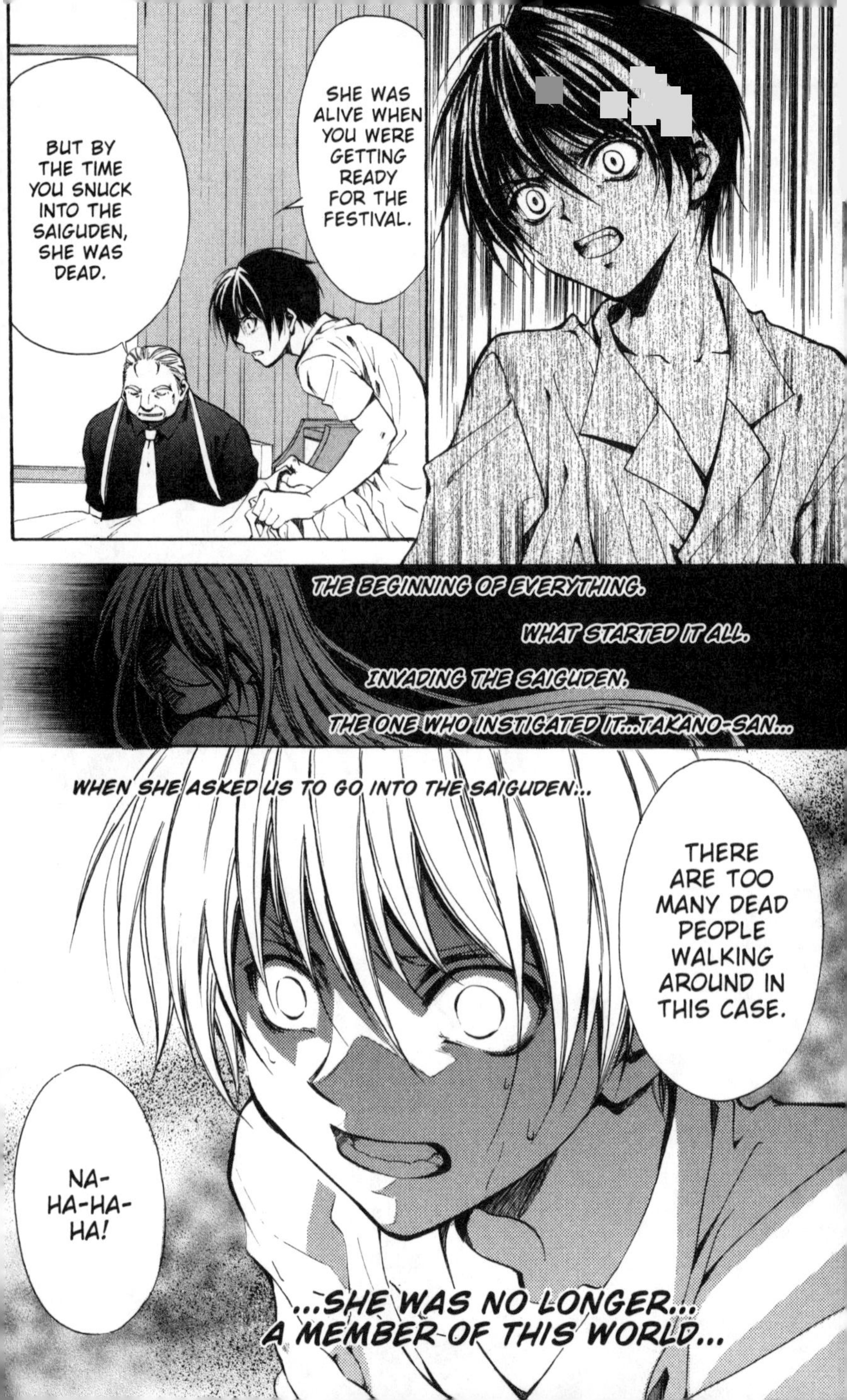
SHE WAS ALIVE WHEN YOU WERE GETTING READY FOR THE FESTIVAL.
BUT BY THE TIME YOU SNUCK INTO THE SAIGUDEN, SHE WAS DEAD.
THE BEGINNING OF EVERYTHING.
WHAT STARTED IT ALL.
INVADING THE SAIGUDEN.
THE ONE WHO INSTIGATED IT...TAKANO-SAN...
WHEN SHE ASKED US TO GO INTO THE SAIGUDEN...
THERE ARE TOO MANY DEAD PEOPLE WALKING AROUND IN THIS CASE.
NA-HA-HA-HA!
...SHE WAS NO LONGER... A MEMBER OF THIS WORLD...

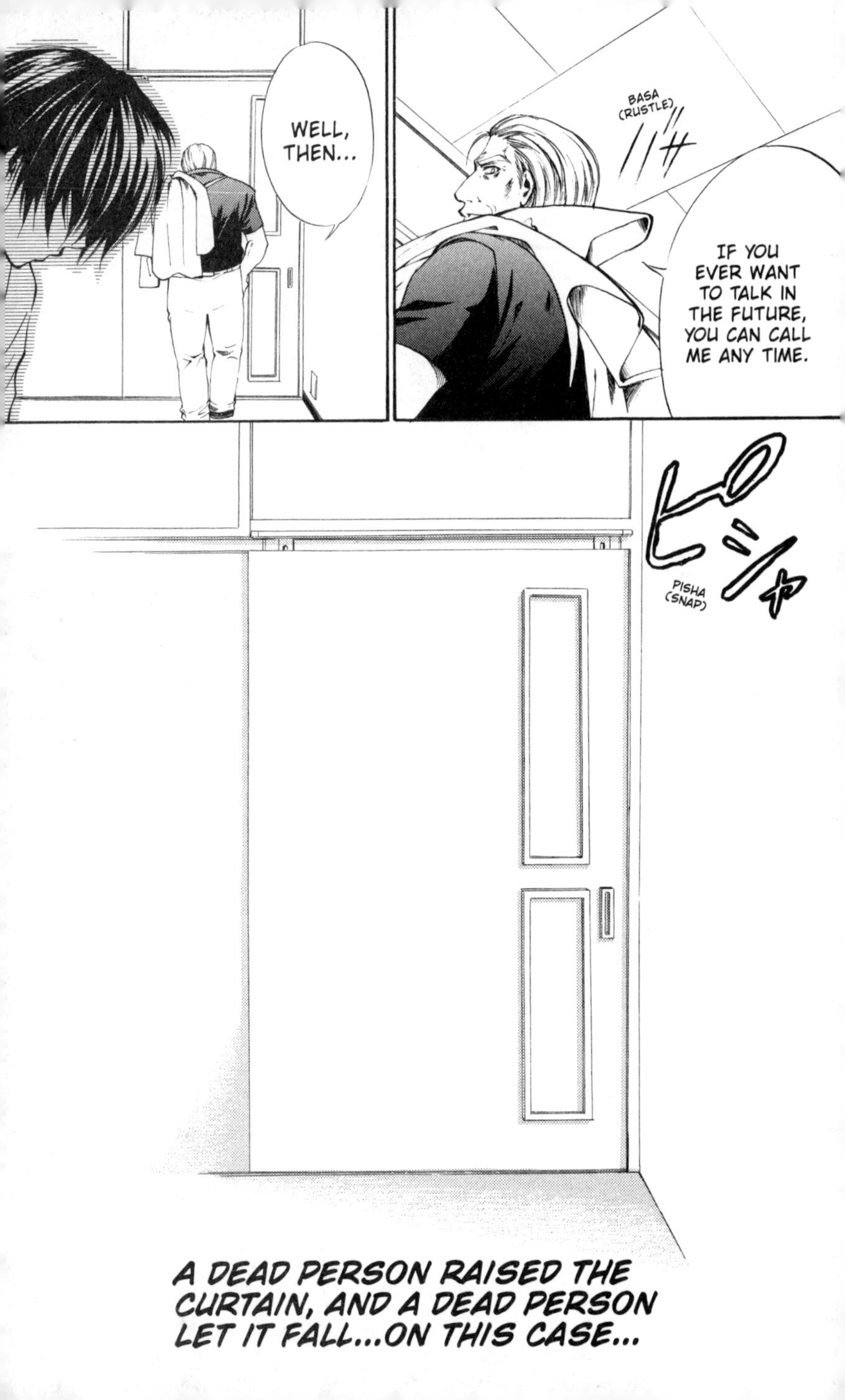
IF YOU EVER WANT TO TALK IN THE FUTURE, YOU CAN CALL ME ANY TIME.
BASA (RUSTLE)
WELL, THEN...
PISHA (SNAP)
A DEAD PERSON RAISED THE CURTAIN, AND A DEAD PERSON LET IT FALL...ON THIS CASE...

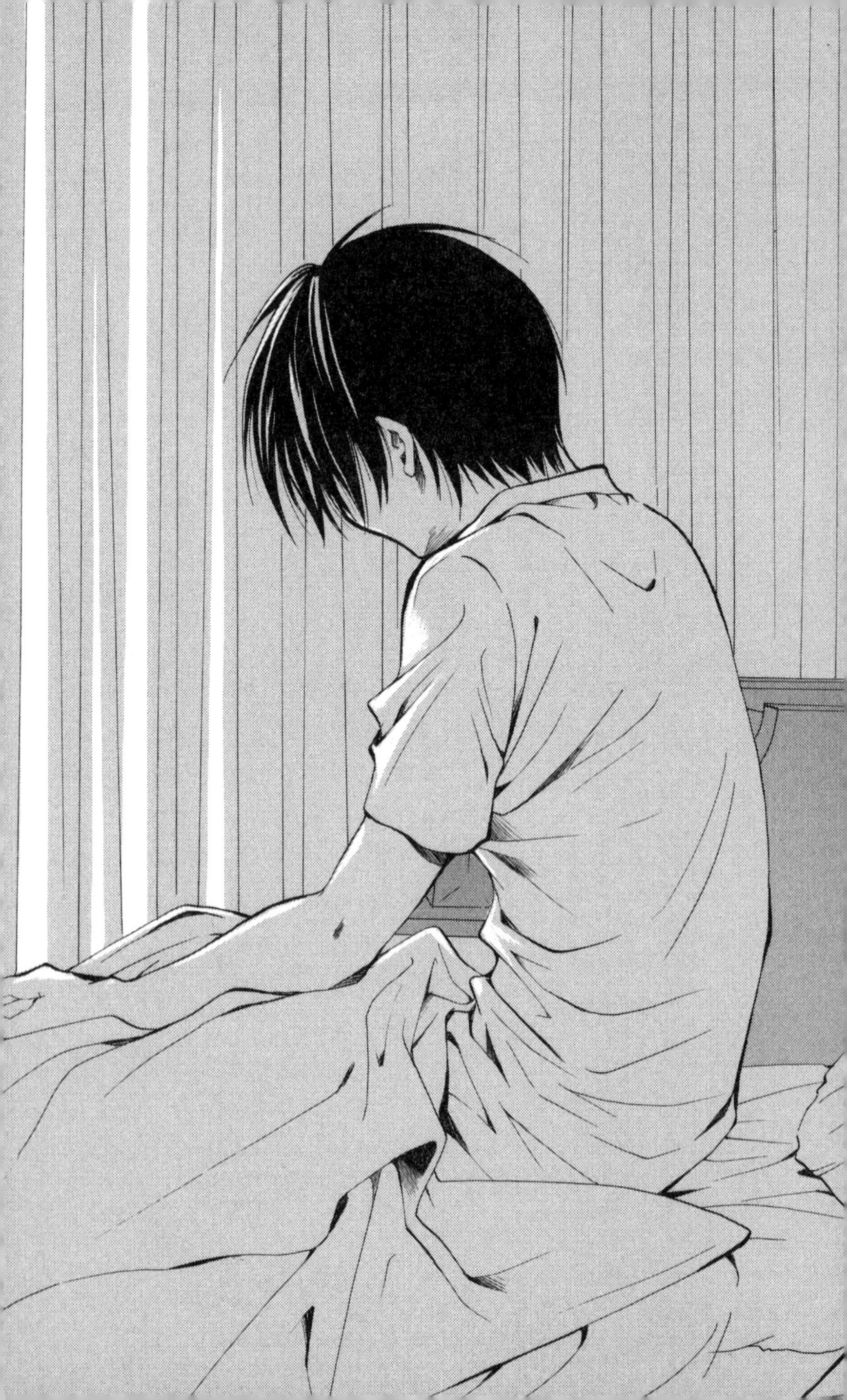

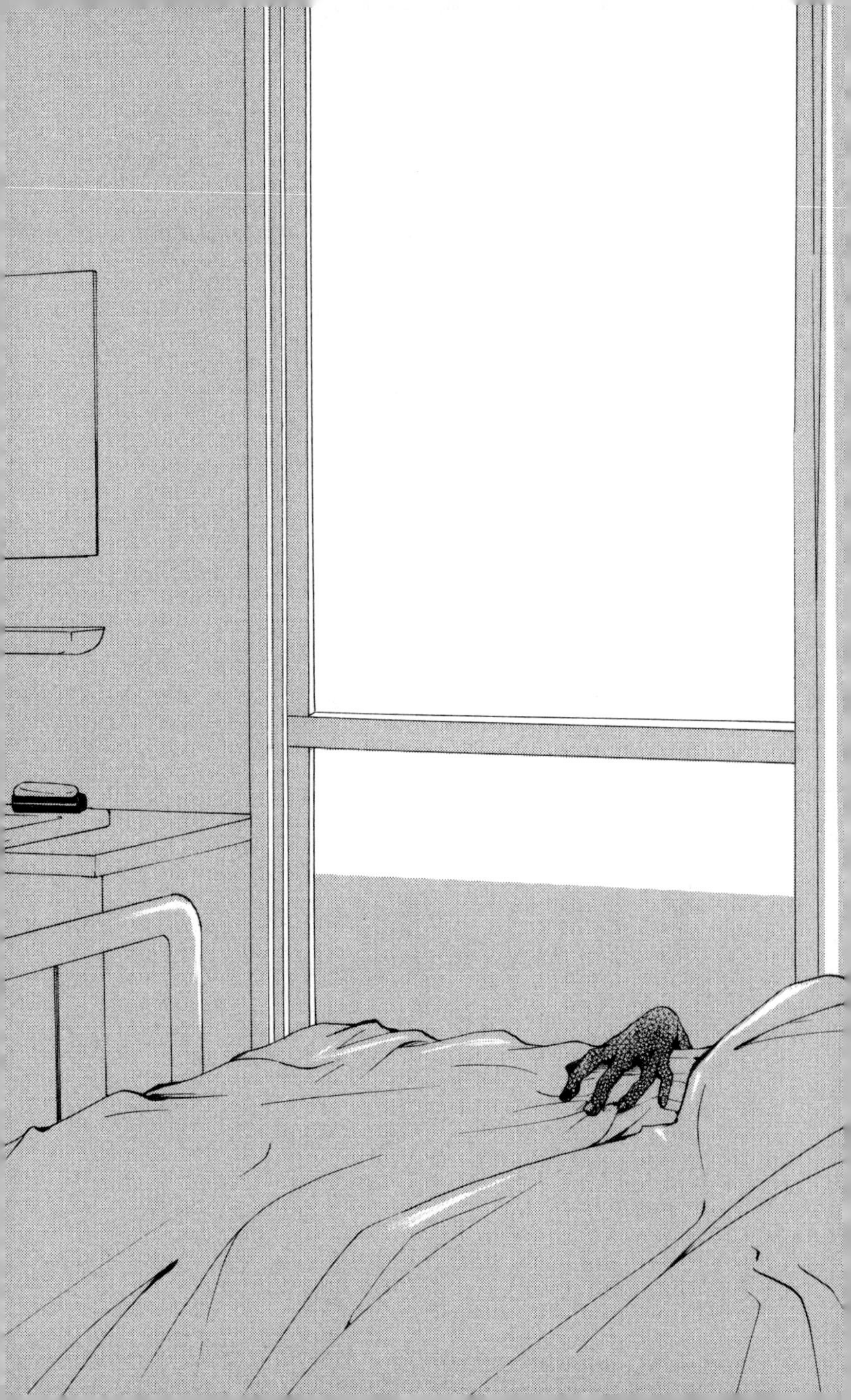

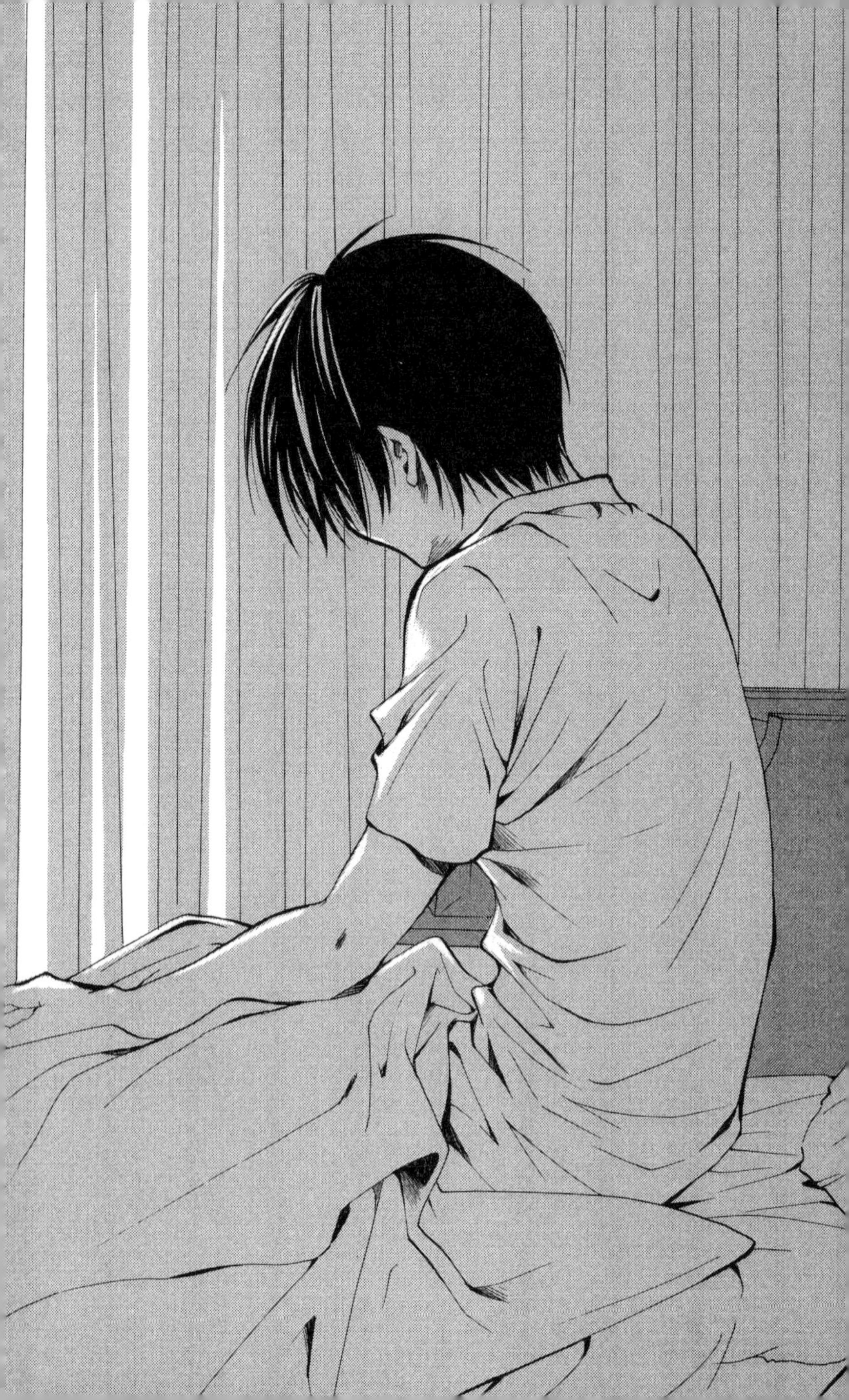

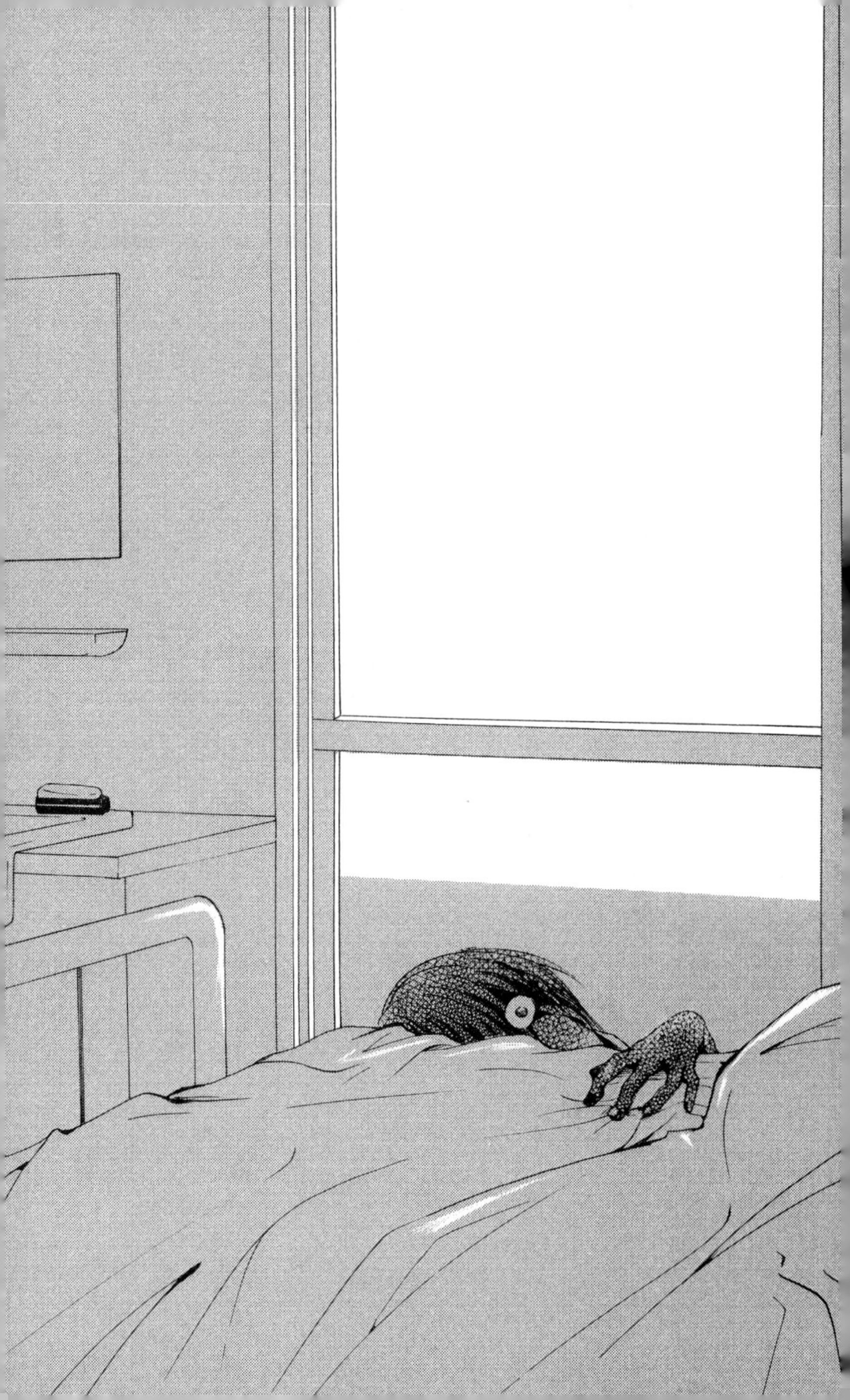

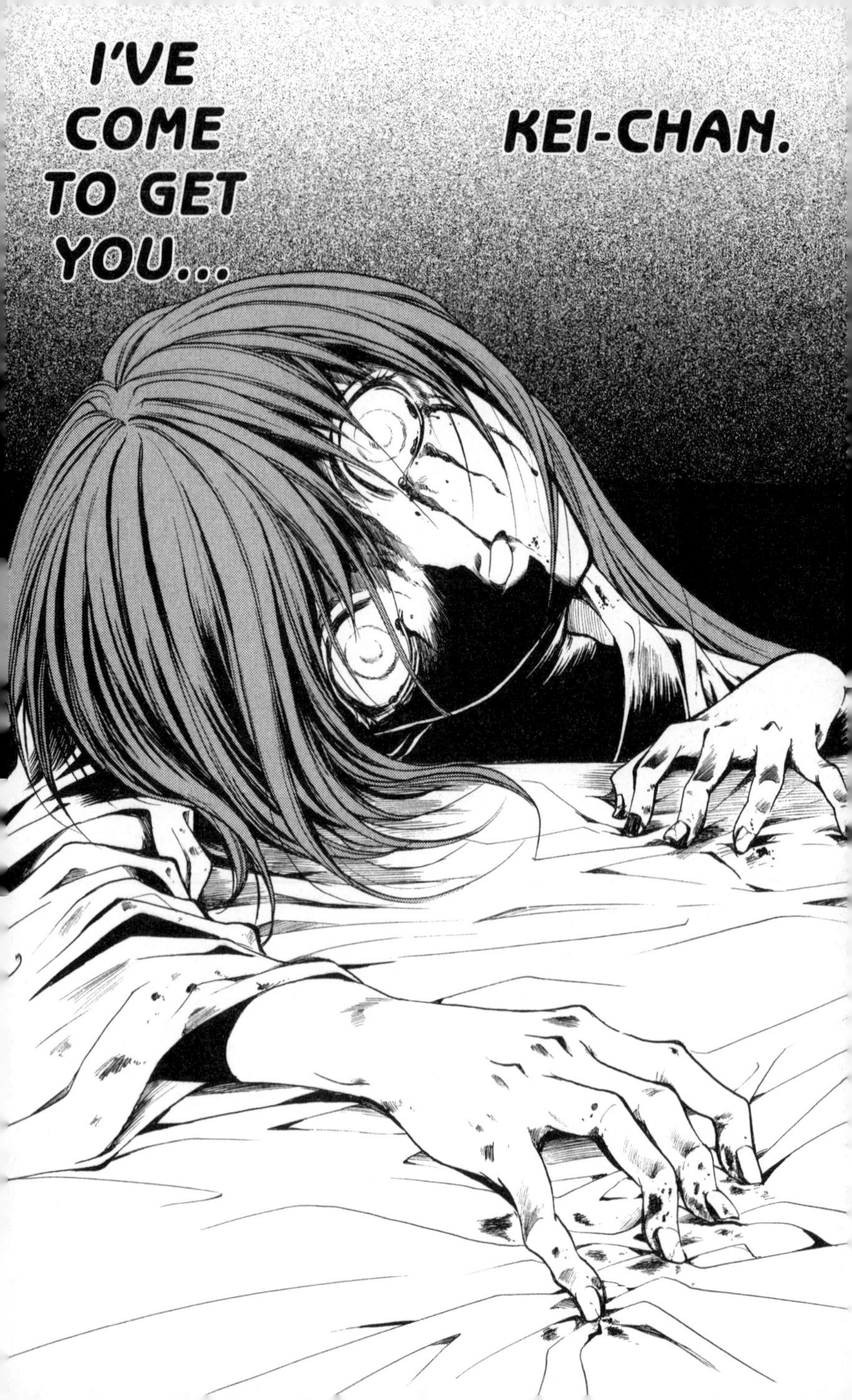
KEI-CHAN.
I'VE COME TO GET YOU...

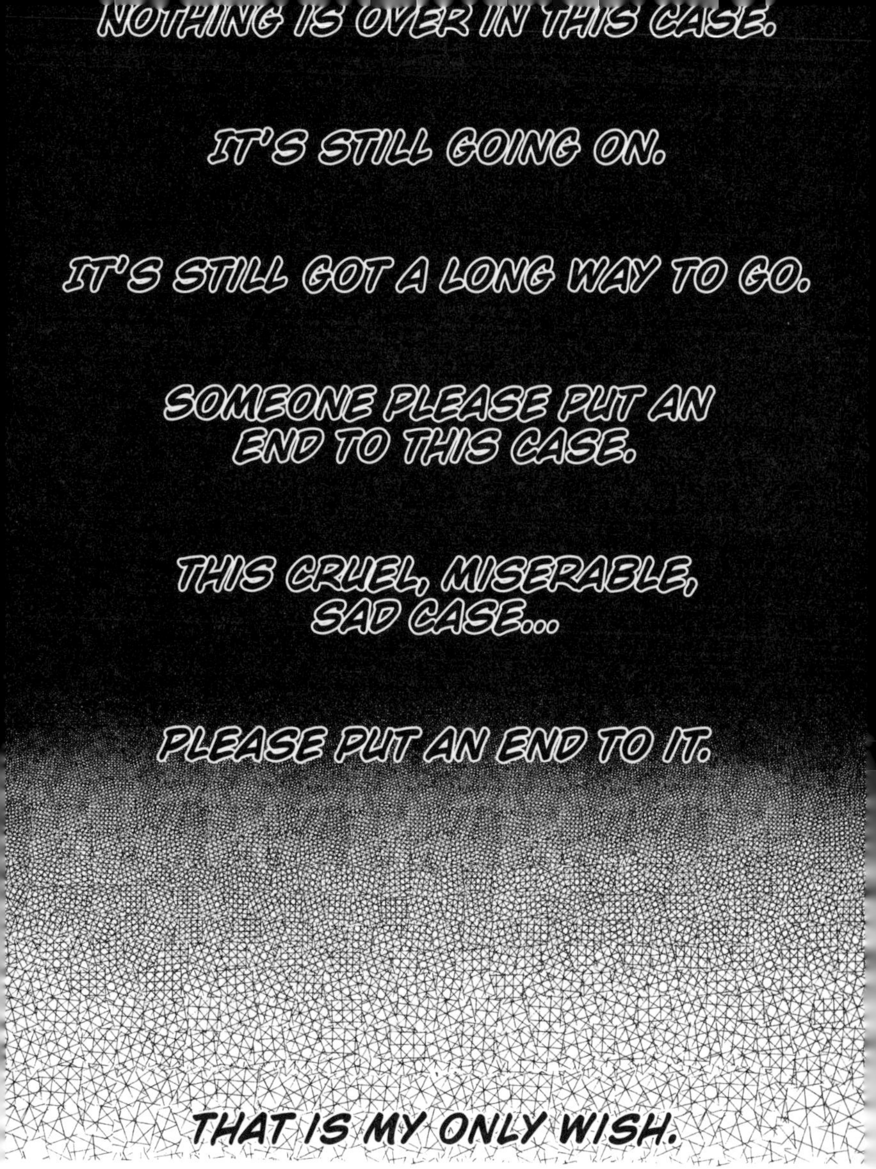
NOTHING IS OVER IN THIS CASE.
IT'S STILL GOING ON.
IT'S STILL GOT A LONG WAY TO GO.
SOMEONE PLEASE PUT AN END TO THIS CASE.
THIS CRUEL, MISERABLE, SAD CASE...
PLEASE PUT AN END TO IT.
THAT IS MY ONLY WISH.

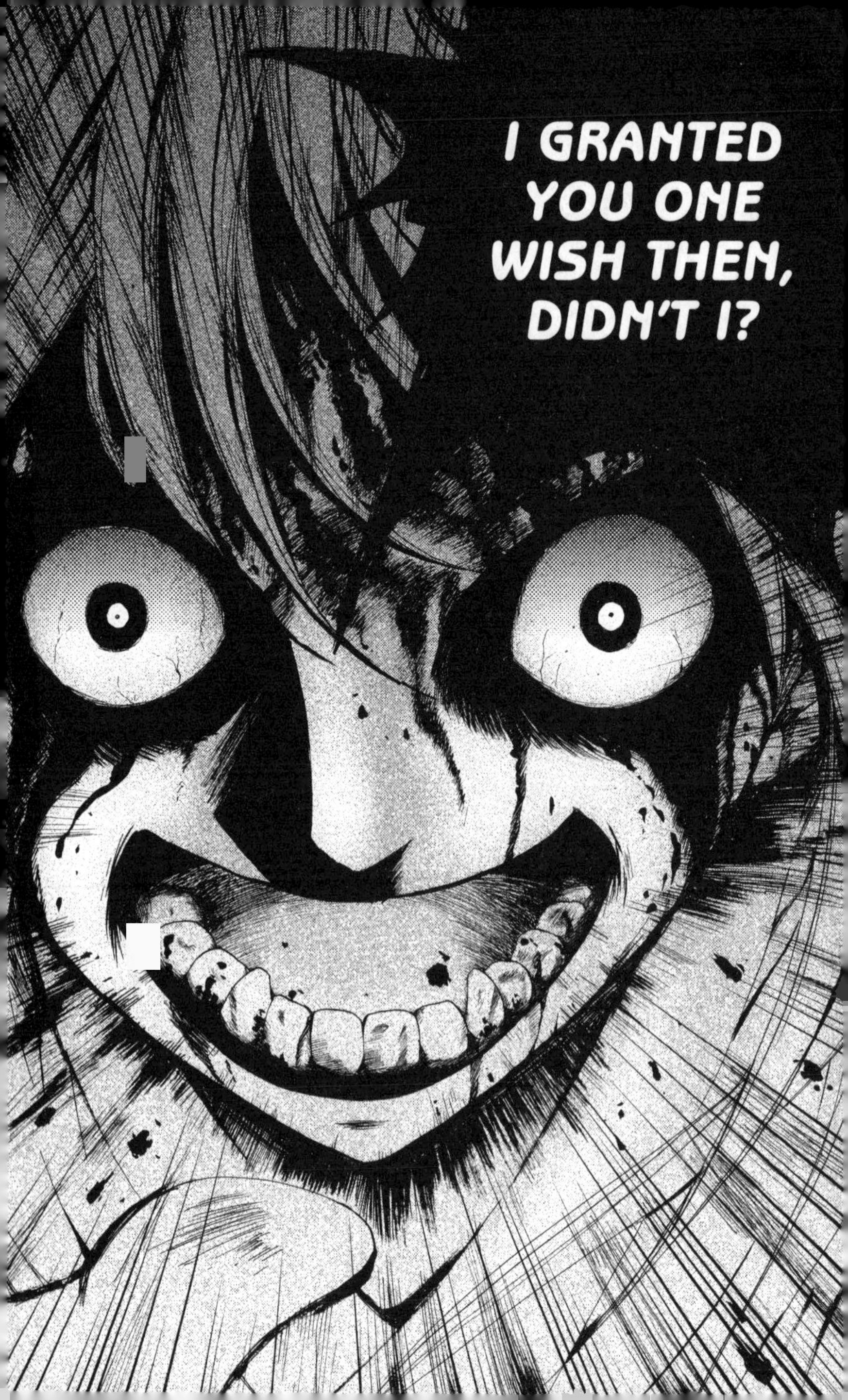
I GRANTED YOU ONE WISH THEN, DIDN'T I?

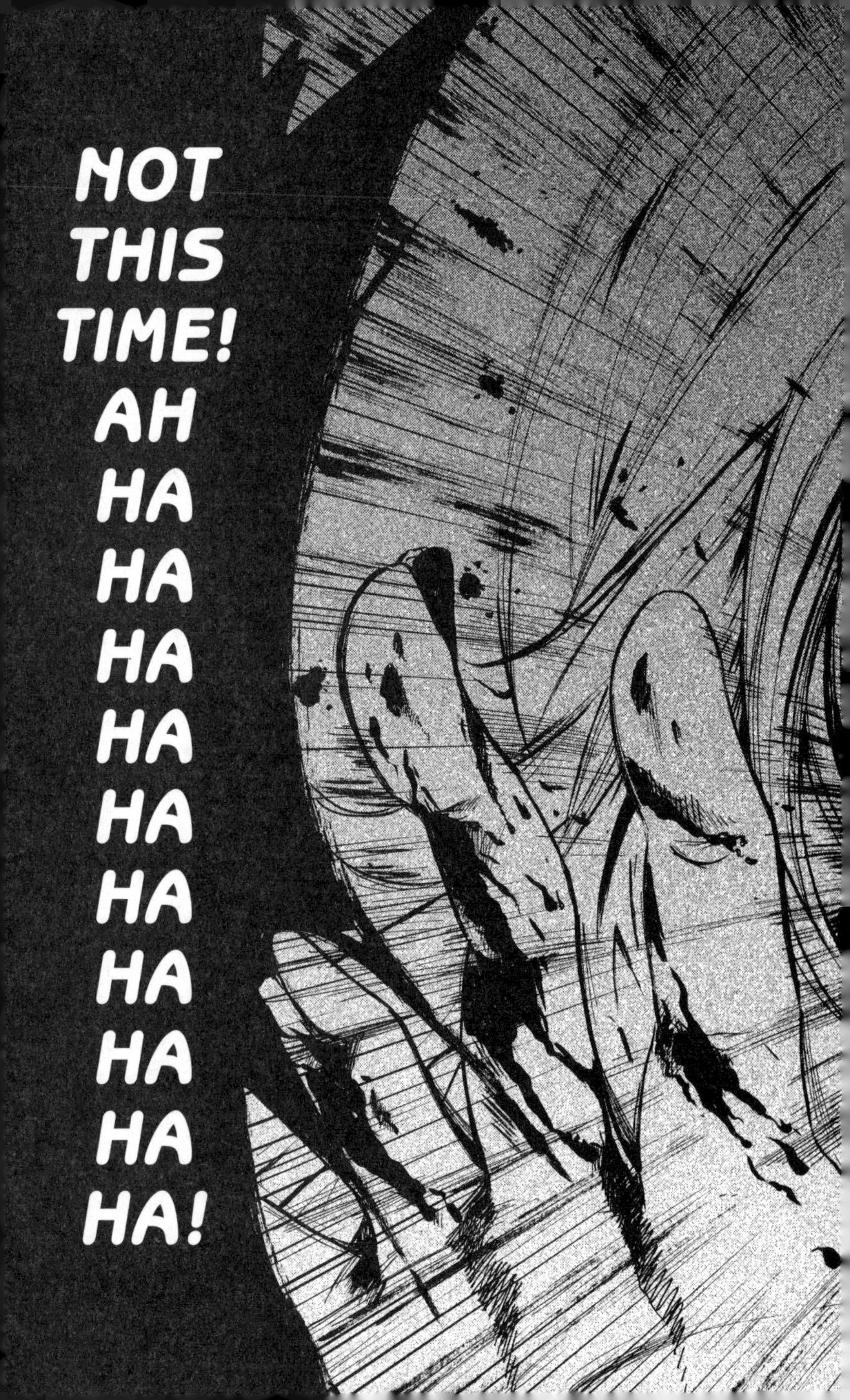
NOT THIS TIME! AH HA HA HA HA HA HA HA HA HA HA!

TRANSLATION NOTES

Page 13
Onigafuchi
Literally means "pit of demons"; a fitting name for a village infested with them.

Page 19
Wata
The Japanese words for "cotton" and "entrails" are both pronounced "*wata*," but are written with different Chinese characters.

Page 26
The Meiji and Shouwa Eras
The Meiji Era lasted from 1868 to 1912 when Emperor Meiji ruled Japan. During the Meiji Restoration, Japan started modernizing to catch up with the Western world in terms of technology, etc. after centuries of isolation. The Shouwa Era refers to Emperor Shouwa's reign in Japan from 1926-1989.

Page 92
Ojiichan
Ojiichan is a friendly way of addressing an elderly man.

Page 183
Inheriting the Demon
As Mion explains, each head of the Sonozaki family has the Chinese character for demon (鬼) in their name, as can be seen with the "mi" in Mion (魅).

Higurashi
WHEN THEY CRY

COTTON
DRIFTING ARC
FIN

HIGURASHI WHEN THEY CRY

07th Expansion presents. Welcome to Hinamizawa.
"WHEN THEY CRY."

ABOUT THE "COTTON DRIFTING ARC"

VICIOUS TRAP

ORIGINAL STORY, SUPERVISOR:
RYUKISHI 07

I WROTE THE "COTTON DRIFTING ARC" AS THE SECOND STORY AFTER THE "ABDUCTED BY DEMONS ARC," AND I WROTE IT WITH THE EMPHASIS ON EXPLAINING THE SETTING OF HINAMIZAWA MORE DEEPLY. IT'S ALSO THE STORY THAT BEST DEPICTS THE MOOD OF DETECTIVE NOVELS FROM THE GOOD OLD DAYS AND, OF THE MANY "HIGURASHI" STORIES, IS ONE OF THE CREATOR'S OWN FAVORITES.

NOW THEN. AS FOR THE DEGREE OF DIFFICULTY OF THE "COTTON DRIFTING ARC," THE CREATOR HAS STATED THAT "IT'S NOT AS DIFFICULT AS THE 'ABDUCTED BY DEMONS ARC,' BUT IT IS EXTREMELY VICIOUS," AND ESSENTIALLY, IT HAS THE LOWEST DEGREE OF DIFFICULTY OF ALL THE "HIGURASHI WHEN THEY CRY" STORIES. BUT, AS ALSO STATED, IT HAS A VICIOUS TRAP, AND IF IT HAPPENS TO GET YOU, YOU'RE IN DANGER OF VICIOUSLY FALLING INTO A PITFALL. AND THE SCARY THING ABOUT THIS TRAP IS THAT THOSE WHO FALL NEATLY INTO IT MAY NOT REALIZE THAT THEY'VE FALLEN INTO A TRAP.

PLEASE CHECK TO SEE IF YOU WERE CAUGHT IN THE "COTTON DRIFTING ARC"'S ANSWER STORY, THE "EYE OPENING ARC."

...IF ON THE OFF-CHANCE YOU HAPPEN TO LEARN THAT YOU WERE NEATLY CAUGHT IN THE TRAP...CONGRATULATIONS, YOU ENJOYED THE "COTTON DRIFTING ARC" MORE THAN ANYONE (LAUGH).

Special Thanks

RYUKISHI07-SAMA
EDITOR-SAMA
KASHI MOCHIZUKI-CHAN
EKO SHIRAYUKI-CHAN
HIROMI ARASE-CHAN
KAMURA-CHAN
MAHIRO TAKANA-CHAN
EVERYONE WHO SUPPORTED ME

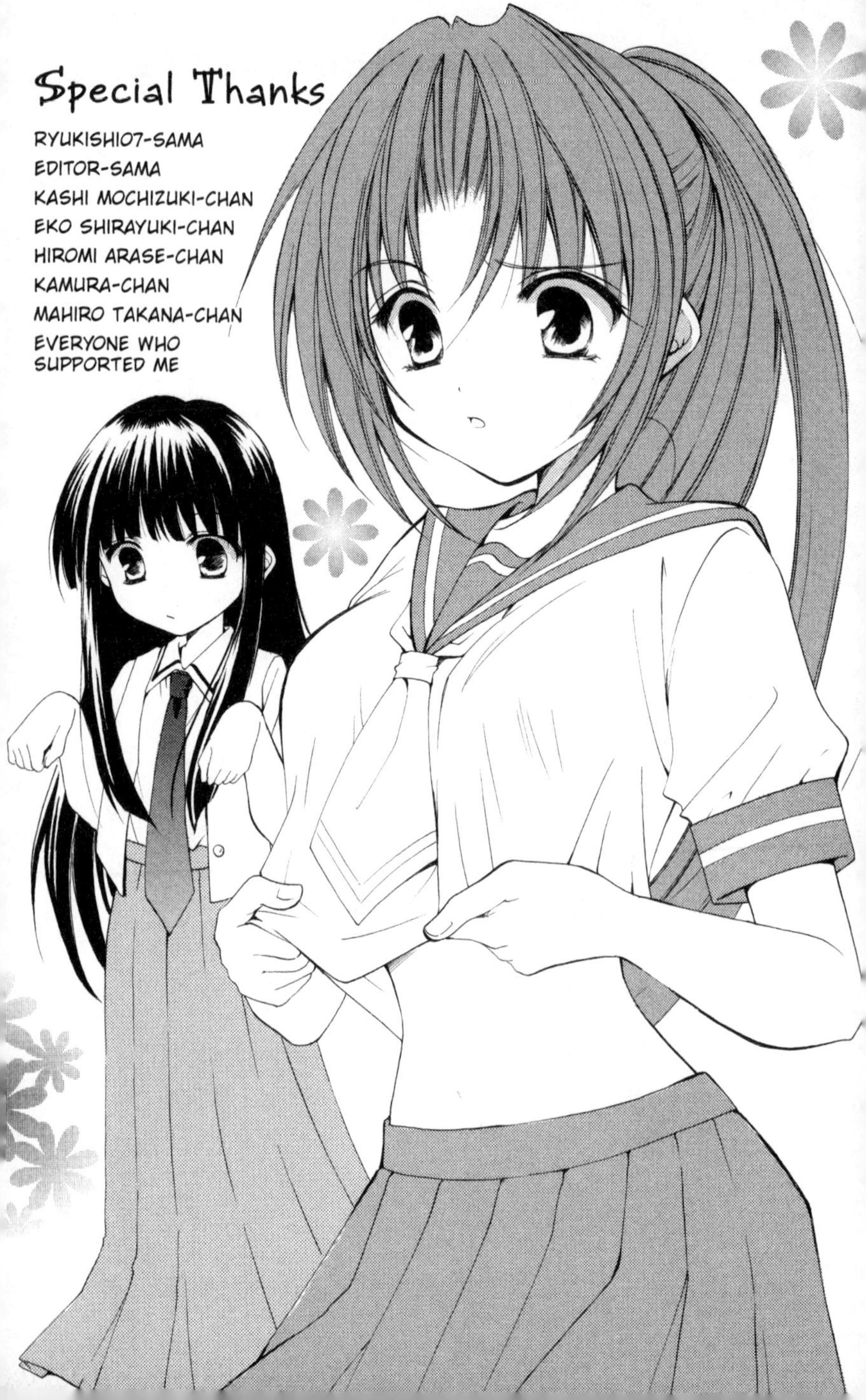

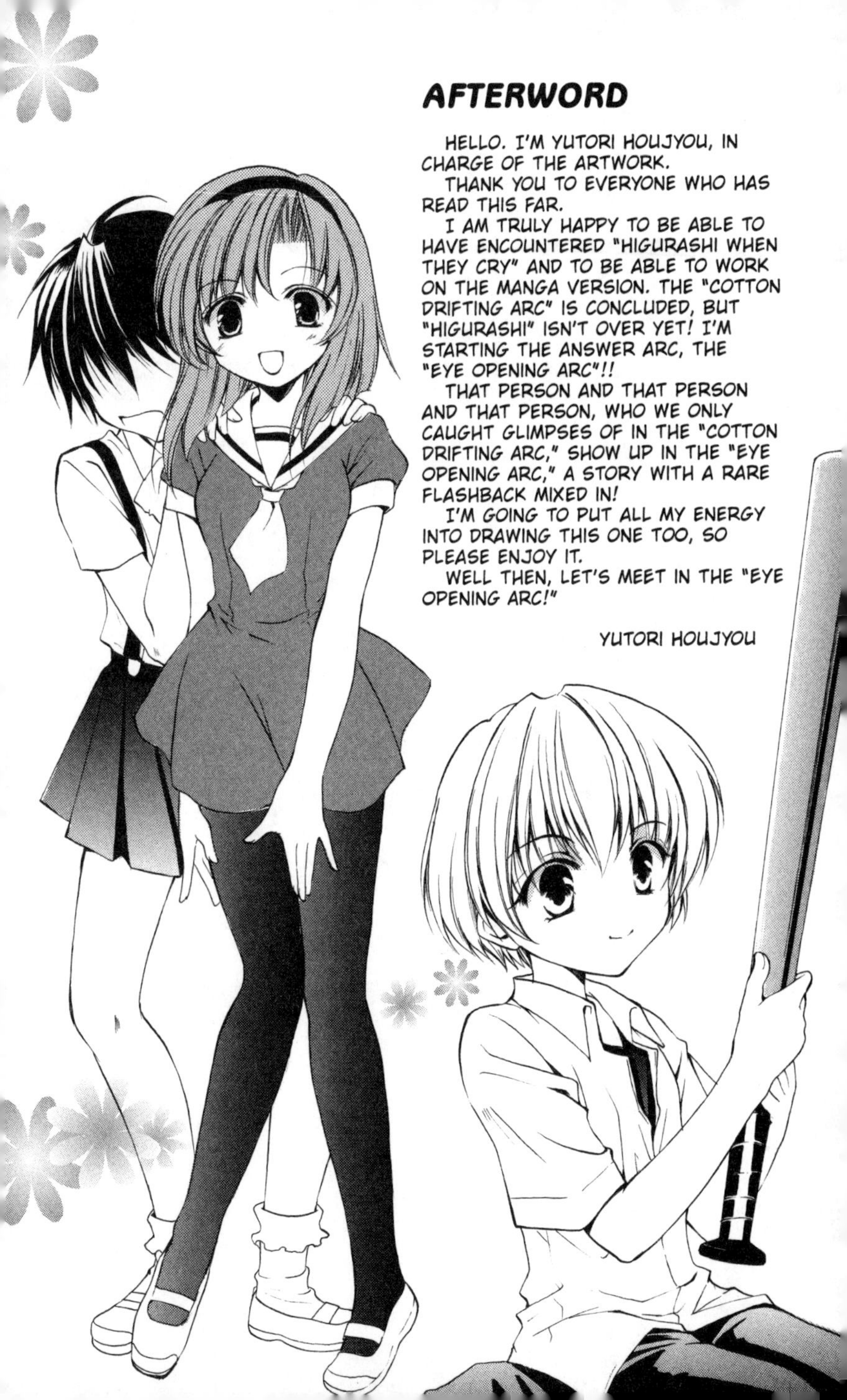

AFTERWORD

HELLO. I'M YUTORI HOUJYOU, IN CHARGE OF THE ARTWORK.

THANK YOU TO EVERYONE WHO HAS READ THIS FAR.

I AM TRULY HAPPY TO BE ABLE TO HAVE ENCOUNTERED "HIGURASHI WHEN THEY CRY" AND TO BE ABLE TO WORK ON THE MANGA VERSION. THE "COTTON DRIFTING ARC" IS CONCLUDED, BUT "HIGURASHI" ISN'T OVER YET! I'M STARTING THE ANSWER ARC, THE "EYE OPENING ARC"!!

THAT PERSON AND THAT PERSON AND THAT PERSON, WHO WE ONLY CAUGHT GLIMPSES OF IN THE "COTTON DRIFTING ARC," SHOW UP IN THE "EYE OPENING ARC," A STORY WITH A RARE FLASHBACK MIXED IN!

I'M GOING TO PUT ALL MY ENERGY INTO DRAWING THIS ONE TOO, SO PLEASE ENJOY IT.

WELL THEN, LET'S MEET IN THE "EYE OPENING ARC!"

YUTORI HOUJYOU

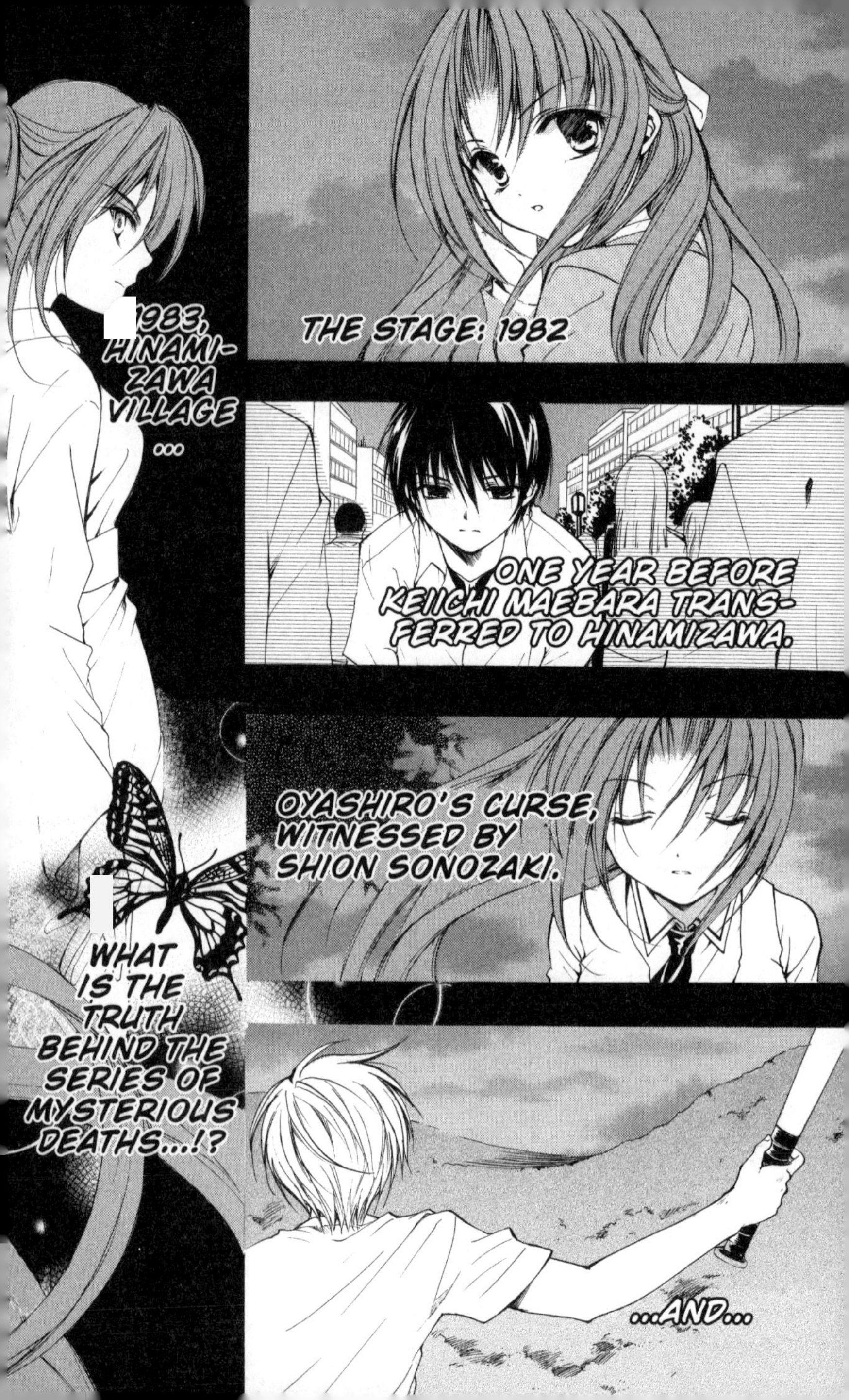
THE STAGE: 1982
ONE YEAR BEFORE KEIICHI MAEBARA TRANS-FERRED TO HINAMIZAWA.
OYASHIRO'S CURSE, WITNESSED BY SHION SONOZAKI.
...AND...
1983, HINAMI-ZAWA VILLAGE ...
WHAT IS THE TRUTH BEHIND THE SERIES OF MYSTERIOUS DEATHS...!?

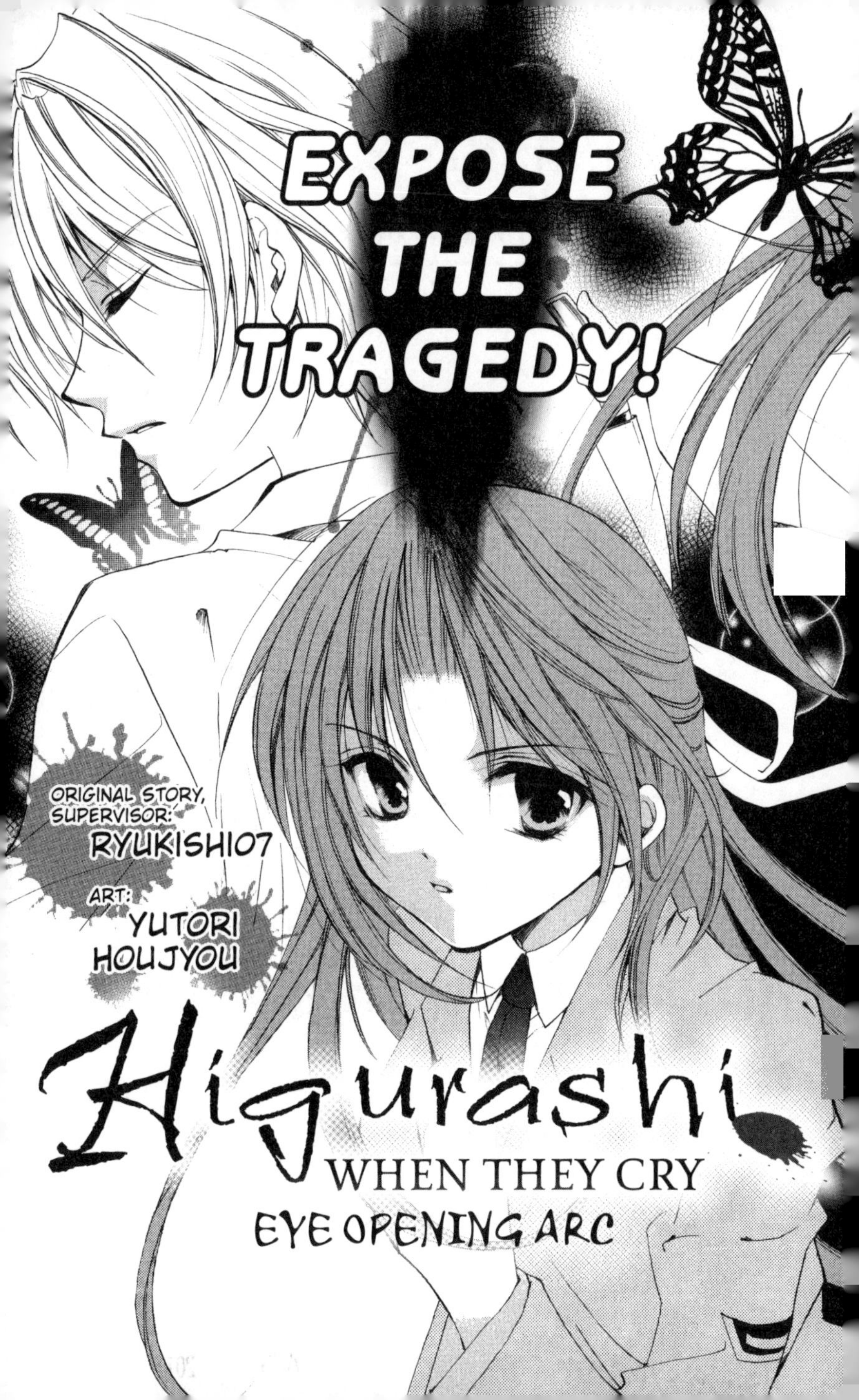
EXPOSE THE TRAGEDY!
ORIGINAL STORY, SUPERVISOR:
RYUKISHI07
ART:
YUTORI HOUJYOU
Higurashi
WHEN THEY CRY
EYE OPENING ARC

HIGURASHI
WHEN THEY CRY
COTTON DRIFTING ARC ②

RYUKISHI07
YUTORI HOUJYOU

Translation: Alethea Nibley and Athena Nibley

Lettering: Shelby Peak

Higurashi WHEN THEY CRY Cotton Drifting Arc, Vol. 2 © 2006 RYUKISHI07,
07th Expansion © Yutori Houjyou / SQUARE ENIX CO., LTD. All rights reserved.
First published in Japan in 2006 by SQUARE ENIX CO., LTD. English translation
rights arranged with SQUARE ENIX CO., LTD. and Hachette Book Group through
Tuttle-Mori Agency, Inc. Translation © 2009 by SQUARE ENIX CO., LTD.

Yen Press
Hachette Book Group
237 Park Avenue, New York, NY 10017

Visit our Web sites at www.HachetteBookGroup.com and
www.YenPress.com.

Yen Press is an imprint of Hachette Book Group, Inc. The Yen Press name and
logo are trademarks of Hachette Book Group, Inc.

First Yen Press Edition: September 2009

ISBN: 978-0-7595-2986-1

10 9 8 7 6 5 4 3 2 1

BVG

Printed in the United States of America

MG   AUG   2017